KU-185-823

INTERNATIONAL FINANCIAL MANAGEMENT

SECOND EDITION

Rita M. Rodriguez
E. Eugene Carter

University of Illinois at Chicago Circle

Prentice-Hall, Inc., Englewood Cliffs, New Jersey 07632

Library of Congress Cataloging in Publication Data

Rodriguez, Rita M. (date)
International financial management.

Bibliography: p.
Includes index.
1. International finance. 2. International business enterprises—Finance. I. Carter, E. Eugene, joint author. II. Title.
HG3881.R584 1979 658.1′5 78-23324
ISBN 0-13-472977-3

To Our Spouses and the Offspring

Editorial/production supervision and interior design: Marian Hartstein
Cover design: A Good Thing, Inc.
Manufacturing buyer: Trudy Pisciotti

Printed in the United States of America

10 9 8 7 6 5 4 3 2 1

Prentice-Hall International, Inc., *London*
Prentice-Hall of Australia Pty. Limited, *Sydney*
Prentice-Hall of Canada, Ltd., *Toronto*
Prentice-Hall of India Private Limited, *New Delhi*
Prentice-Hall of Japan, Inc., *Tokyo*
Prentice-Hall of Southeast Asia Pte. Ltd., *Singapore*
Whitehall Books Limited, *Wellington, New Zealand*

Contents

PART TWO

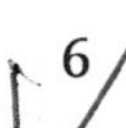

Preface

The tool kit of a financial officer operating in the international area is formed by contributions from several traditional disciplines. International monetary economics, usually referred to as international finance, provides the framework for understanding the environment where international business takes place. Corporate finance contributes the analytical concepts to manage the funds of an enterprise. Financial market theory furnishes the basis to appraise the institutions where funds are traded. The objective of this book is to scan these fields, to select those tools which individuals working in the area of applied international finance will find useful, and to illustrate their application in practice.

In Part One we focus on the assessment of the external position of countries. In this endeavor we center the analysis around the accounts presented in the balance of payments for the given country. Part Two deals with the problems that firms encounter as a result of dealing in a diversity of currencies. The financial problems associated with international trade are discussed in some detail. Also studied are the financial opportunities and risks involved in foreign operations other than trade.

Part Three approaches the issue of international capital budgeting. The first two chapters in the section deal with the problems attendant to the determination of the relevant cash flows and discount rate. The last two chapters of Part Three consider other theories of the motivation for foreign direct investment and the analysis of portfolio capital budgeting in the international setting. Finally, Part Four deals with financial markets on two levels. The international capital markets that operate independently of national boundary lines, the so-called Euro-dollar markets, are analyzed first. Then, a framework for studying specific capital markets is presented while showing some of the major characteristics of the most important capital markets in Europe. Appendices dealing with comparative accounting practices, discounting, project risk evaluation, and the Euro-dollar multiplier follow the appropriate chapters. We also include appendices at the end of the book containing a glossary, present value tables, and material on international taxation. Bibliographies accompany each chapter to aid those who are particularly interested in specific subject areas.

In the second edition our major concern has been to update various institutional figures and improve the basic presentation. The balance among the major portions of the book is relatively unchanged. We have included more material on purchasing power parity and interest rate parity in Chapter 4, 5, and 6 with a new appendix to Chapter 5. Major text changes are in the tax appendix. Other changes are seen in Part One, which deals with the new method of presenting the U.S. balance of payments and with a discussion of monetarism and the balance of payments; Part Two's approach to foreign exchange exposure; Chapter 7's analysis of exposure management; Chapter 12's discussion of legal and historical analyses of foreign direct investment; and Chapter 14's discussion of the Euro-dollar market. Although many instructors preferred cases of the length in the first edition, many others preferred more cases and/or shorter cases. To that end, we have added several cases, deleted one, and condensed many others. The especially long cases of the first edition (i.e., Cummins Engine and FNCB Finance) have been cut in half, but we have hopefully retained most of the key elements that we used for our teaching, as discussed in the Instructor's Manual. On balance, we hope that the content changes and the editorial improvement will make the book more useable to a wide audience while continuing to serve well the basic group reached with the first edition. Our thanks to the many professors and financial executives (many of whom are listed below) whose ideas helped us complete this new edition. Naturally, there is always a conflict of views, with a solution in the null set. However, we hope that the balance we have chosen here, together with what we have said about particular topics, will be welcomed.

The text is ideally designed for upper-level undergraduates or MBA/MS students who have completed introductory courses in finance and economics. There are exercises, questions, and cases at the end of most chapters, which can be used by the instructor to emphasize different points. Some instructors will want to include all the cases in their courses, perhaps using the chapters only for casual or background reading. Given the detail with which some of these cases may be handled (computer output and other materials are included in the Instructor's Manual), these cases and exercises can require at least 20 class sessions. Additional cases could be used in the remaining classes in a typical 30-class, one-semester course. Other instructors will prefer to emphasize the text and exercises supplemented by articles. The detail of these chapters and exercises easily can support 20 or more classes. The supplementary articles and notes on various capital markets and other items (which are available through us) could complete the one-semester course.

Instructors with a one-quarter course also could use this text, assuming they have only 20 or 25 classes. If all the topics are to be covered, we suggest having students read Chapters 2 and 3 and the summary to Chapter 4, with the instructor lecturing on various proposals regarding the balance of payments once the students understand the background materials. A single class on the balance of payments for students who are not familiar with the subject might involve reading Chapter 2 and the summaries to Chapters 3 and 4. Chapters 5, 6, and 7 could be read in total, and the more involved framework offered for handling exposure to exchange risk presented in Chapter 9 deleted or left for optional reading. Chapters 10 and 11 outline the basics of international capital budgeting. The additional material from other disciplines and the security/portfolio models in Chapters 12 and 13 could be deleted or reviewed in a lecture. Finally, selected readings from the two chapters on the Euro-markets could complete the text material. Four or five of the simpler cases and the exercises could round out the one-quarter course.

Our approach is to use a simple lecture or case to highlight a problem, then have a chapter and a lecture to suggest various ways of looking at the problem (the theory), and conclude with the application of the theory to the complex real situation presented by another case. Accordingly, the materials in this book can more than fill a one-semester course of 30 or 35 classes. The selection of materials will be at the judgment of the instructor, consistent with the instructor's background and interests, the previous exposure of the students, and their particular needs in the course.

If students have a strong background in international economics. Chapters 2 through 4 can be skipped. For instructors who particularly want to emphasize this topic, additional readings and texts may be assigned with this material used only as background. Similarly, instructors who are not interested in the particular elements of trade credit financing will have their students skip the latter part of Chapter 6, whereas other instructors will want to supplement this material with one of the bank booklets on international financial instruments. Students who have been exposed to international business courses will not need to read the first half of Chapter 12, which brings in various economic and behavioral theories of foreign investment; other instructors will supplement this chapter with readings from the international business area. In some classes, more time can be spent on the various international security portfolio studies and the capital asset pricing model, with the implications of these topics for corporate diversification. With other groups, Chapter 13 can be deleted if this topic is not of interest or if the small amount of algebra included here is beyond the level of the students. Finally, some instructors will not find the institutional material on the Euro-markets contained in Chapter 14 through 16 (Part Four) of relevance or interest to their students.

The table on the next page summarizes some of our suggestions where instructors have a variety of interests and amounts of time to spend on particular topics. Optional choices for a given day are separated by a slash (/). Within reasonable ranges, these topics are fairly self-contained; the instructor may wish to elaborate on the rudiments of some prior topic if desired. We tend to take a chapter per day as written in total, generally in the order of the book, inserting the taxation appendix prior to Chapter 10. Taxation is deliberately presented as an appendix to the book to emphasize the fact that it may be studied at any time.

Thus, the segmentation of the text in various parts and the inclusion of cases, questions, and exercises provide a range of basic materials. In most classes, this material will provide sufficient coverage for a semester. For those instructors who wish further supplemental materials, the four parts of the text are somewhat self-contained, permitting use of the text as a basic book supplemented by other readings. Our desire has been to present a text that has a sufficient amount

	Number of Classes		
Topic	*1*	*2*	*3–5*
Balance of Payments/ Monetary System	Chapter 2 and Summaries, Chapters 3 and 4	Chapter 2 and Summary, Chapter 3, Chapter 4	Chapter 2 Chapter 3 Chapter 4/Britannic Intl. Shipping
Foreign Exchange (FX)	Chapter 5	Chapter 4 (Purchasing Power) and Chapter 5 Chapter 6 (FX Risks) and Citibank/Ken and Joan Morse Appendix, Chapter 5 optional)	Ken and Joan Morse Chapter 4 (PPP) and Chapter 5 Chapter 6 (FX Risks) and Exercises, Chapter 5 Citibank (Appendix, Chapter 5 optional)
Trade Instruments	Chapter 6 (Trade Instruments)	Chapter 6 (Trade Instruments) AP&M/Chapter 6. Question 6	Chapter 6 (Trade Instruments) Question 6 AP&M
Exposure Management	Chapter 7	Chapter 7 Chapter 8/Continental Group	Chapter 7 Marwick/Continental Group/ Chapter 8 Chapter 9/Green Valley/ Farmatel
International Accounting and Control	Chapter 7 and Appendix, Chapter 8	Chapter 7 Chapter 8	Chapter 7 Chapter 8/Marwick/Farmatel Continental Group/Green Valley
Capital Budgeting	Chapter 10 and Summary, Chapter 11	Chapter 10 Chapter 11/Chaolandia	Chaolandia Chapter 10 Chapter 11
Capital Budgeting and Financial Strategy (Assumes at least one day from Capital Budgeting section above)	Chapter 12/International Tire	Chapter 12 Chapter 13/International Tire/ Cummins Engine/Freeport	International Tire Chapter 12/Cummins Engine Chapter 13 Freeport
Eurocurrency Markets	Chapter 14	Chapter 14 and Appendix, Chapter 14 Exercises on Euro-$/Citicorp Leasing	Chapter 14 Appendix, Chapter 14 and Exercises Citicorp Leasing/ Green Valley
International Capital Markets	Chapters 15 and 16	Chapter 15 Chapter 16/Altos Hornos/FNCB Finance	Chapter 15 Chapter 16 Altos Hornos/FNCB Finance
International Taxation	Appendix 1	Appendix 1 Sola Chemical/Questions 1–4 and 5 (optional)	Sola Chemical Appendix 1 Questions 1–5

of basic material from which many instructors can select topics for their international corporate finance course.

This textbook reflects our biases and prejudices toward the blending of various disciplines under the umbrella of an international corporate finance framework, and toward the mix of theory, practice, and institutional description. We have benefited from the suggestions on portions of the text from many individuals. Gunter Dufey (University of Michigan), Hai Hong (University of Singapore), and Warren Law (Harvard Business School) commented on the entire first edition manuscript in detail with many useful and insightful suggestions. We thank them of behalf of the readers.

Our appreciation also to Tamir Agmon (Tel Aviv University); Mark Eaker (Duke University); Ian Giddy (Columbia University); Edward M. Graham (Department of the Treasury); Charles Kindleberger, Stephen J. Kobrin, Donald Lessard, Franco Modigliani, James Paddock, and Richard Robinson (Massachusetts Institute of Technology); John Ingersoll (University of Chicago); Michael McIntyre (Wayne State University); David A. Ricks (The Ohio State University); Roslislov Romanoff (Northern Trust); Henry Schloss (University of Southern California); N. Jackendoff (Temple University); Oscar Holzmann (University of South Carolina; Lemma Senbet (University of Wisconsin-Madison); Dennis Logue (Dartmouth); D. M. Pattille (Northeastern University); L. William Murray (University of San Francisco); and Christine Hekman, Robert Stobaugh, Raymond Vernon, and William White (Harvard Business School) for reacting to various ideas and chapters. Our appreciation is offered to Professors Raymond Vernon and Robert Stobaugh for permission to use the Sola Chemical case. With the exception of *Citibank's Foreign Exchange Problems* (a collection of news articles), all of the other cases were authored by Rita M. Rodriguez, and we gratefully acknowledge the assistance or co-authorship of Marc Buxton, Henri de Bodinat, Cesar Duque, Kenneth Morse, Jules Pogrow, L. E. Simmons, Endre Toth and Mark Wallerstein. Dev Purkayastha helped in the preparation of Chapter 8, and Manu Parpia helped in the revision of Part Four. We are also grateful for the outstanding contribution of our first edition editor, Paul McKenney, who endured the convoluted prose emerging from an immigrant's and a technocrat's collaboration. His efforts sharply improved the text.

Completion of the second edition was considerably helped by the careful editorial work of Barbara Satz, and we thank her for her patience. Our thanks also to Marian Hartstein, production editor of the second edition, who managed tardy authors at multiple mailing addresses with patience and effectiveness.

Any deficiencies in style or substance are the responsibility of the authors.

Rita M. Rodriguez
E. Eugene Carter

CHAPTER 1

Introduction

During recent years, the corporate financial manager has become increasingly concerned with the changing international scene. Fluctuating foreign exchange rates, the power of multinational corporations, balance of payments deficits, and the growth of "petrodollars," have come to be important issues for all U.S. and foreign corporations with international operations. To confront these problems with some hope for resolution requires a knowledge of both the macro-economic environment in which the firm operates (balance of payments, government policies, credit availability) and the micro-economic environment which relates to the specific decisions that the manager will face (how the firm manages its exposure to foreign exchange risk, how it analyzes its capital budgeting problem, how it accommodates the demands for funds from subsidiaries in different countries). Before we embark on the discussion of specific financial problems, however, it may be useful to briefly introduce the business institution that houses the international decision makers: the multinational company.

THE MULTINATIONAL FIRM

For many critics, the multinational firm is a global octopus, which at best is spreading knowledge and technological pollution around the world while swallowing assets everywhere and evading all national attempts to control it.

Multinationals have been charged with subverting governments (with or without another government's help), adding to the instability of the international money markets by switching funds between currencies, avoiding taxes everywhere by the use of tax havens, and encouraging apartheid in South Africa and the continuation of low-wage unskilled labor forces in Colombia, among other sins.

In their own defense, the multinationals emphasize their rationalization of resources and the spread of technology. Deemphasizing the impact of their economic power, they also argue that in seeking profits they are doing good in the societies in which they operate by contributing much-needed capital and other resources of the industrialized world to less developed areas. Thus, they are the chronological reverse of many Hawaiian missionaries, whose families today have major fortunes based on pineapple and other commodities. As has often been observed, the missionaries came to do good and did right well.

While there are many definitions of the multinational firm, for the purposes of this text the term will mean a company with substantial operations (usually 30% or more of its total activity) carried on outside its own national borders. These activities may be trading or manufacturing. There may be many separate corporations outside the national borders, with the parent functioning as an operating/holding company. Whatever the particular corporate form, the important fact is that the firm must make decisions about project returns which have a sizable impact on the company and are in more than one currency. A $500,000,000 business which occasionally sells a few million dollars worth of goods to a Dutch manufacturer will probably not care much about currency rates. The sale is infrequent; its size is relatively small; and the guilder is a known, freely traded currency. On the other hand, a $10,000,000 firm which has three plants in three different nations and whose business represents sales from all over the globe (such as a small specialty goods manufacturer) will be very interested in currency rates, barriers to trade, and fund repatriation.

The philosophy of business of international firms is a separate study, often called international business policy, and is not the purpose of this text. Similarly, the reform of the international monetary system and the analysis of why nations trade belong in a course in international economics. However, the impact of judgments in these two areas will affect the field of international corporate finance. Multinationals are often entangled in the web of doing nothing (which supports the status quo) and acting for good or ill (which supports charges of interference in the domestic affairs of one or more nations). Multinationals usually have legal and financial talent beyond the level of the department of inland revenue in a small nation of limited resources. On the other hand, the small nation often has what the multinational wants (a market or a natural resource) and is in a position to demand a suitable price for access to that desired feature. Some of these relationships, and the behavior of various parties involved in these international financial decisions, are explored in this text.

In making public pronouncements, many economists forget that the firm operates within society and not just within an industrial sector. As a noted economist, Arthur Okun, observed, economists are the only people who have to be reminded that not everything should have a price. Societies set the ground rules for firm behavior. An important issue is whether the markets in which a firm operates are sufficiently competitive for the benefits of firm rivalry to create an efficient allocation of resources, the key benefit of the market economy.

A second issue is whether the resulting allocation of resources is desired. The firm may allocate assets efficiently, but is the final distribution equitable? There is nothing sacrosanct about free enterprise per se, nor is it enshrined in the U.S. Constitution, as some social critics frequently remind business executives.

However, one should also bear in mind that the various proposals to reform corporations on the international scene often come from social critics who ignore the benefits of resource allocation. The evils of pollution and materialism may seem less threatening when a booming economy slides into recession; unlimited personal freedom can appear less important if one is out of a job. The median per capita income on Earth is less than $50 per year. Even allowing for comparability of purchasing power and standards, government security systems (political and social), a rural economy for many people, and the like, a conservative doubling of the figure does not give one room for comfort. Many Americans are amazed to learn that *only* 20% of U.S. families have an after-tax income of more than $20,000. Most governments cannot be so oblivious to statistics such as these.

An even narrower view than that of the economists and the social critics comes in the self-serving nonsense sometimes presented by the multinationals themselves. Anxious to assuage public opinion in a particular nation so as to move ahead with the task of making XYZ International more powerful and more profitable, rhetoric is put forth which frequently is based on little knowledge of the actions of various subsidiaries. Limits on information from the field and the whole problem of decentralization mean that headquarters officials rarely know details of activities in other lands and often are only vaguely aware of their lack of knowledge. Further, this ignorance may be deliberate, thus creating the possibility of deniability, which has counterparts in political and military leadership. By design, the top managers can deny they knew anything about the nasty activities of underlings, while they continue to make subordinates aware that it is their job to see that "things are taken care of." This supervisory problem is merely an international extension of the common issues of accounting and managerial control, with the difficulties compounded by distance, culture, and language-related complexities.

This text is primarily concerned with international corporate finance; therefore, many of the above issues will be left to the reader's appraisal of contemporary socioeconomic and political trends and to his or her particular value system. Although most of our examples deal with the position of the U.S. multinational, the issues and problems that we address apply to all multinationals.

AN OVERVIEW OF THE TEXT

The following chapters are divided into four major parts. Part One provides a basic understanding of the forces that affect the relative values of currencies in international markets. This section of the text largely corresponds to the information traditionally related in a course on international monetary economics. We will approach this important material from the point of view of the participants in the international markets who have to take the world system as given. Chapter 2 begins with the mechanics of the foremost reporting tool used to assess the international situation of a country: the balance of payments. Chapter 3 confronts the economic forces that lie behind the figures reported in the balance of payments and that affect the international purchasing power of a currency. In Chapter 4, the situation of a given country and the insights derived from the previous two chapters are placed within the context of the international monetary system and domestic economic priorities. The objective of these three chapters is not to demonstrate how to forecast foreign exchange rates, but to build a framework for analyzing the forces that produce changes in foreign exchange rates. Chapter 5 focuses directly on the foreign exchange market. It analyzes how price relationships are established in this market and discusses in detail the behavior of the major actor in the foreign exchange market—the foreign exchange trader.

Part Two discusses the major problems encountered by the firm in financing large international operations. The money market and the forward exchange market, as well as their mutual relationships, are emphasized in studying the financing alternatives open to the merchandise trader and the manager with business operations in foreign countries. Chapter 6 looks at the problems of financing international trade. How does an importer obtain credit? How does a merchandise trader approach exchange risk? Chapter 7 studies the cost of financing foreign operations and the management of the foreign exchange position of the company. Should the manager of a British firm hold a net asset position in liras? If not, what can be done about it? Chapter 8 analyzes the impact of inflation and exchange fluctuations on operations and discusses how to measure these effects for management control purposes. An appendix to this chapter reviews accounting practices for different countries and methods to report the impact of inflation. Chapter 9 consolidates the elements developed in the previous three chapters with traditional financial theory on costs of funds and presents an integrated approach to the decision of how to finance the operations of a firm that functions across several national boundaries.

Part Three covers the issues associated with capital budgeting. Chapter 10 discusses the analysis of a single project and discusses the types of international project risk. Chapter 11 introduces the problems of selecting the relevant acceptance criteria for projects. It provides an extended computer simulation model of a mining project in Australia. Appendices to these chapters, respectively, review discounting procedures and some of the approaches to project risk evaluation. Chapter 12 highlights the various economic and behavioral reasons for international investment, including an historical analysis of U.S. foreign direct investment and a discussion of anti-trust issues. Chapter 13 reviews some of the evidence from international security portfolio studies, outlining how a corporation can employ these concepts in selecting its portfolio of capital budgeting projects.

Part Four returns the discussion to the macro-economic area. Throughout the previous chapters the business firm was presented as a rate taker, which makes decisions on the basis of prices given to it. Part Four aims to create an understanding of the forces that shape rates in the international markets as well as in some specific national markets. Chapter 14 and 15 discuss the international capital markets, with Chapter 14 emphasizing the Euro-currency market and Chapter 15 concentrating on international bonds. The appendix to Chapter 14 analyzes the Euro-dollar multiplier and problems raised by the use of Euro-dollars. Chapter 16 completes the tour of international finance with a study of comparative capital markets. In this chapter the problems of raising funds in domestic markets other than the United States, and the issues associated with understanding their functioning, are presented. An appendix to the text outlines the basic characteristics of international corporate taxation, with exercises of various degrees of complexity to illustrate taxation issues.

Bibliography

Aharoni, Yair, "On the Definition of a Multinational Corporation." *Quarterly Review of Economics and Business,* Autumn 1971, pp. 27-37.

Behrman, Jack N., *National Interests and the Multinational Enterprise.* Englewood Cliffs, N.J.: Prentice-Hall, Inc., 1970.

Eiteman, David K., and Arthur I. Stonehill, *Multinational Business Finance.* Reading, Mass.: Addison-Wesley Publishing Co., 1973, Ch. 1.

Ewing, David W., *Freedom Inside the Organization: Bringing Civil Liberties to the Workplace.* New York: E. P. Dutton, 1977.

Naumann-Etienne, Ruediger, "A Framework for Financial Decisions in Multinational Corporations–Summary of Recent Research." *Journal of Financial and Quantitative Analysis,* 1974 Proceedings, November, 1974, pp. 859-874.

Phatak, Arvind V., *Managing Multinational Corporations.* New York: Praeger Publishers, 1974, Ch. 5.

Robinson, Richard D., *International Business Management.* New York: Holt, Rinehart and Winston, 1973.

Stobaugh, Robert B., "The Multinational Corporation: Measuring the Consequences." *Columbia Journal of World Business,* Jan.-Feb. 1971, pp. 59-64.

Tarleton, Jesse S., "Recommended Courses in International Business for Graduate Business Students." *Journal of Business,* Oct. 1977, pp. 438-447.

Vernon, Raymond, *Sovereignty at Bay: The Multinational Spread of U.S. Enterprises.* New York: Basic Books, 1971.

——, *Storm over the Multinationals: The Real Issues.* Cambridge, Mass.: Harvard University Press, 1977.

——, and Louis T. Wells, Jr., *Manager in the International Economy,* 3rd ed. Englewood Cliffs, N.J.: Prentice-Hall, Inc., 1976.

Weston, J. Fred, and Bart W. Sorge, *International Managerial Finance.* Homewood, Ill.: Richard D. Irwin, Inc., 1972, Ch. 1.

PART ONE

One of the major problems that the financial officer encounters in the international markets is the fact that different nations have different currencies and that the relative value of these currencies is not always maintained constant through time. Accordingly, this section attempts to provide an introduction to the major macro-economic considerations that shape the foreign exchange markets.

Chapter 2 covers the mechanics of the balance of payments. This is the information most often used in evaluating the changes in the external position of a given country, and therefore the possible changes in the value of its currency. Once the technicalities of the balance of payments are understood, Chapter 3 proceeds to explain the major economic forces that contribute to the performance of the accounts in the balance of payments. The objective in this chapter is to develop an understanding of economic relationships that can be used not only to explain the past, but also to forecast the future behavior of the various accounts and the exchange rate. The understanding cannot be complete unless one also includes an analysis of the alternatives available to settle imbalances in the external position of a country. This is done in Chapter 4, which presents some of the automatic mechanisms that tend to solve a situation of imbalances in the external accounts and which also discusses the international monetary agreements that have governed these adjustments. Appendices to this chapter provide a chronology of the major events in the international monetary system during the post-World War II period and the major organizations that helped shape the international system during this period.

Chapter 5 examines the characteristics of the market in which currencies are actually traded and their foreign exchange rates determined. An appendix presents the algebra associated with the concepts of interest rate parity, purchasing power parity, and the international Fisher effect. In addition to introducing some of the technical aspects of these markets, this chapter concentrates on the behavior of the financial institutions that "make" the foreign exchange market. The behavior of nonfinancial businesses in the foreign exchange market is discussed in Part Two.

CHAPTER 2

Financial Accounting Among Countries

One of the central problems in international finance is the need to deal in a multiplicity of currencies that do not keep their relative values constant. A financial officer based in the United States who contracts to pay £2,000 every year for the following 20 years is bound by that obligation independent of changes in the exchange rate between the U.S. dollar and the pound sterling. Therefore, one of the most important pieces of information in international finance is an assessment of the future foreign exchange value of a country's currency. Such an assessment is not an easy task. However, it can be aided enormously by an understanding of the international economic transactions of the given country. These transactions for historic periods are summarized in financial statements that each country prepares in relation to the rest of the world. The statement most used to accomplish the financial reporting among countries is the so-called *balance of payments.*

Like any system of record keeping, the reporting of the balance of payments figures is subject to preestablished rules. These include defintions of terminology as well as rules of procedure. Some of the most important rules used in the construction of balance of payments figures are summarized in this chapter.

THE CONCEPT OF BALANCE OF PAYMENTS

The balance of payments catalogs the *flow* of economic transactions between the *residents* of a given country and the residents of other countries during a certain *period of time.*

The balance of payments measures flows rather than stocks.[1] These flows represent payments and receipts. That is, only *changes* in asset holdings and liabilities are presented in this statement, not the *levels* of these items. In this sense, the balance of payments for a country is very similar to a statement of sources and uses of funds for a firm. For a country as a whole, sources of funds represent an acquisition of external purchasing power, the right a country has to claim goods and services or to invest in another country. Uses of funds for a country mean a decrease in its external purchasing power. When a country sells its goods and services to foreigners (a decrease in its asset holdings) or when it borrows from foreigners (an increase in liabilities), the country acquires external purchasing power. Conversely, when the country buys goods and services from foreigners (an increase in asset holdings) or redeems its obligations (a decrease in liabilities), the country uses some of its external purchasing power. These changes are measured in terms of a monetary unit, e.g., U.S. dollars or French francs.

In the context of the balance of payments, a resident is any individual, business firm, government agency, or other institution legally domiciled (not necessarily a citizen) in the given country. Therefore, the subsidiary (but not a branch) of a German company legally established in the United States would be treated like any other U.S. enterprise for balance of payments purposes.

The balance of payments measures transactions among countries. Transactions that only affect the local residents and that only involve the national currency—in contrast to foreign exchange—are not recorded in the balance of payments. However, these domestic transactions can lead to conditions that are reflected in the balance of payments. For example, if the monetary authorities of the United States decide to sell part of their portfolio of securities to U.S. residents, this transaction will not enter the U.S. balance of payments accounts. However, as a result of the selling of the securities, an increase in U.S. interest rates is likely to occur which could induce the British to purchase U.S. securities. This latter transaction, in contrast to the first one, will be between the residents of two different countries, the United States and England, and it will be registered in the balance of payments accounts.

Finally, the balance of payments can be prepared for any specific period of time. Typically, it is prepared quarterly and annually. To facilitate comparisons, the quarterly figures are often multiplied by four and presented on an annual rate basis. When analyzing quarterly figures one must be careful to consider whether these figures have been adjusted for *seasonal* fluctuations. The presence of such fluctuations, if not identified, might lead one to confuse a recurrent seasonal pattern with a change in trends in the balance of payments accounts.

[1] The statement measuring the levels of foreign assets and liabilities among countries is the *balance of indebtedness.* This statement will be discussed at the end of Chapter 3.

THE BALANCE OF PAYMENTS ACCOUNTS

The balance of payments may be divided into three major types of accounts: (1) the current account, (2) the capital account, and (3) the official reserves. Exhibit 2.1 presents a simplified balance of payments for a country called Lilliput in the year 1900.

EXHIBIT 2.1. Balance of Payments for Lilliput for the Year 1900

(Sources of Funds +; Uses of Funds –)

CURRENT ACCOUNT:			
Trade account			
Exports	$5,000		
Imports	-4,000		
Balance of trade			$ 1,000
Service account			
Receipts for interest and dividends, travel, and financial charges	2,500		
Payments for interest and dividends, travel, and financial charges	-1,200		
Balance in invisibles (services)			1,300
Unilateral transfers			
Gifts received from abroad	500		
Grants to foreign countries	-1,000		
Balance in unilateral transfers			-500
Current account balance			$ 1,800
CAPITAL ACCOUNT:			
Long-term capital flows			
Direct investment			
Sale of financial assets	2,000		
Purchase of financial assets	-4,500	$-2,500	
Portfolio investment			
Sale of financial assets	5,000		
Purchase of financial assets	-3,000	2,000	
Balance on long-term capital			-500
Basic balance			1,300
Private short-term capital flows			
Sale of financial assets	8,000		
Purchase of financial assets	-2,000		
Balance on short-term private capital			6,000
Overall balance			$ 7,300
OFFICIAL RESERVES ACCOUNT:			
Gold exports less imports (–)			$-5,000
Decrease or increase (–) in foreign exchange			-2,300
			$-7,300

Current Account

The current account records the *trade in goods and services and the exchange of gifts among countries.*

The trade in *goods* is composed of exports and imports. A country increases its exports when it sells merchandise to foreigners. This is a source of funds, a decrease in real assets. It increases its imports when it buys merchandise from foreigners. This is a use of funds, an acquisition of real assets. The balance between exports and imports is called the *trade balance.* Exhibit 2.1 shows that for the year 1900 Lilliput had a positive trade balance of $1,000. The *sources* of external purchasing power exceeded the *uses* on the trade balance by $1,000.

The balance on *service* accounts is often called the *balance in invisibles.* Service accounts include interest and dividends, travel expenses, and financial and shipping charges. Interest and dividends received measure the services that the country's capital has rendered abroad. Payments received from tourists measure the services that the country's hotels and shops provided to visitors from other countries. Financial and shipping charges to foreigners measure the fees that the financial community and shipowners charged to foreigners because of the special services they rendered. In these cases the nation gave the service of assets it possessed (e.g., hotel) to foreigners. Thus, these transactions are a source of external purchasing power. When, in contrast to the above cases, the country's residents are the recipients of the services from foreign-owned assets, then the given country loses purchasing power to the rest of the world. Lilliput provided more services to foreigners (a source of funds) than it received from them (a use of funds). Therefore, Lilliput had a positive balance in invisibles of $1,300. That is, its sources of external purchasing power exceeded its uses on the invisibles account by $1,300.

Finally, gifts are recorded in the *unilateral transfers account.* This account is also labeled *remittances* or *unrequited transfers.* A typical entry in this account is the money that emigrants send home. Another example is a gift that one country makes to another. In these cases when the country makes a gift it can be said that it is acquiring an asset which we may call goodwill. Like any other asset acquisition, the gift represents a use of external purchasing power. Lilliput had a negative balance in unilateral transfers of $500; uses of funds exceeded sources by this amount.

The total current account of Lilliput shows a positive balance of $1,800, which is composed of the positive balances in trade and invisibles and the negative balance in unilateral transfers.

Capital Account

The capital account records the international movement of funds reflected in changes in financial assets and liabilities. The various classifications within the capital account are based on the original term to maturity of the assets and on the extent of the involvement of the owner of the financial asset in the activities of the security's issuer. Accordingly, the capital account is subdivided into *direct investment, portfolio investment,* and private *short-term capital flows. Direct investment* and *portfolio investment* involve financial assets which had a maturity of more than a year when issued initially. *Short-term capital movements* consist of financial paper with an original maturity of less than one year. The distinction between direct investment and portfolio investment is made on the basis of the degree of management involvement. Considerable management involvement is presumed to exist in the case of *direct investment* (usually a minimum of 10% ownership in a firm), but not of *portfolio investment.*

Lilliput had a deficit in direct investments. While foreigners invested $2,000 in Lilliput (Lilliput increased its liabilities to foreigners—a source of funds for Lilliput), Lilliput made direct investments in foreign countries in the amount of $4,500 (Lilliput acquired foreign financial assets—a use of funds for Lilliput). Many of these investments involved acquiring whole ventures in other countries. Although in some cases the ownership had to be shared with others, the direct investor retained a substantial share (at least 10%) of the total ownership (and therefore of the management). The deficit in direct investment accounts of Lilliput was somewhat compensated for by the surplus in the portfolio account. Foreigners bought $2,000 more of long-term financial assets in Lilliput than Lilliput bought in other countries. When the negative balance of $500 in the long-term capital account is added to the current account balance, this produces the *basic balance.* Lilliput's basic balance was $1,300.

In the private short-term capital account foreigners bought $8,000 worth of short-term securities issued by Lilliput, while Lilliput invested only $2,000 in short-term foreign securities. The sum of the private capital accounts and the basic balance produces another subtotal. This subtotal is often refered to as *overall balance.* In Lilliput the overall balance produces a surplus of $7,300. This surplus is a net source of external purchasing power for Lilliput.

Official Reserve Accounts

This account is composed of the immediate means of international payment that the monetary authorities in the country acquired or lost during the given period. These are composed mainly of gold and convertible foreign exchange (i.e., foreign exchange like U.S. dollars which are freely convertible into other currencies, but not currencies like the Indian rupee where the Indian government does not guarantee the free conversion of its currency into others). An increase in any of these financial assets, like an increase in any other asset, constitutes a use of funds. A decrease in reserve assets, like a decrease in any other asset, implies a source of funds. At times this fact seems to run against intuitive interpretations. This is the case when we say that an increase in gold holdings is a use of funds (signified by a minus sign in Lilliput's balance of payments). Well, it is! An increase in gold holdings is a use of funds in the sense that Lilliput might have chosen to purchase an alternative asset such as a bond issued by a foreign government.

Note that the country's own currency cannot be considered as part of its reserve *assets.* When foreigners hold the country's currency, it is a *liability* of the country. When the currency's ownership returns to its country of origin, a reduction in the *liabilities* of that country to foreigners occurs. However, to the extent that other countries are willing to hold the currency of the country in question, let's say U.S. dollars, the United States can use the changes in its liabilities to foreigners as an alternative to changes in the level of its reserve assets.

An increase in official reserves (or decrease in official liabilities) will occur as a result of a surplus in the current accounts and the capital accounts. The increase in reserves measures the excess of sales of goods, services, and financial assets of the given country over the purchases of such items by the given country from foreigners. Lilliput had a surplus in the current and capital accounts of $7,300; therefore, the official reserves increased by this amount.

THE ACCOUNTING SYSTEM

In the preceding section we discussed separately each major account in the balance of payments. However, the balance of payments accounting is a double-entry system in which the part of a transaction that gives rise to an *increase in the external purchasing power* of the country is called a *source* of funds and the part of a transaction that gives rise to a *decrease in the external purchasing power* of the country is called a *use* of funds. It is impossible to talk about any transaction in the balance of payments accounts without discussing both sources and uses of funds. Like any other double-entry accounting system, the balance of payments is kept in terms of debits and credits. In this accounting terminology uses of funds are debits (dr.) and sources of funds are credits (cr.).

A country *increases* its external purchasing power whenever it *decreases* (sells) its tangible or intangible assets (exports goods and services), when it *decreases* its foreign financial assets (through their sale), or when it *increases* its liabilities to foreigners (by, for example, a domestic corporation taking out a loan from a foreign source, or a domestic bank accepting a deposit from a foreigner). All of these transactions represent *sources* of external purchasing power—credit entries.

A country *decreases* its external purchasing power whenever it *increases* (buys) tangible or intangible assets (imports goods or services), when it *increases* (buys) holdings of foreign financial assets, or when it *decreases* its previous liabilities to foreigners. All of these transactions represent *uses* of external purchasing power—debit entries.

Let us try to use these definitions in a series of examples for the United States:

EXAMPLE 1. A manufacturer in the United States exports $1,000 in goods to a customer in Greece. According to the sales terms, this account will be paid in 90 days. In this case two things happen: the merchandise exports, a reduction in real assets, provide the United States with an increase in claims on external purchasing power—a credit entry; but the exporter has simultaneously bought a financial document. She has made a short-term investment abroad (i.e., the exporter's accounts receivable has increased by $1,000). This acquisition represents a use of the country's external purchasing power—a debit entry. Therefore, in the U.S. balance of payments accounts this transaction will appear as follows:

	Debit	Credit
Increase in short-term claims on foreigners (the account receivable)	$1,000	
Exports		$1,000

EXAMPLE 2. A Japanese resident visits the United States. Upon his arrival he converts his $2,000 worth of yen into dollars at the airport bank. By the time the visitor departs he has no dollars left. In this case the United States provided services to foreigners in the amount of $2,000. In exchange for these services U.S. banks now have $2,000 worth of yen. The services that the United States provided to the Japanese are clearly a source of purchasing power, and therefore a credit entry. However, the accumulation of yen in U.S. banks is an increase in the U.S. holdings of foreign financial obligations, a use of purchasing power, and therefore a debit entry. In the U.S. balance of payments this transaction will appear as follows:

	Debit	Credit
Increase in short-term claims on foreigners (the yen holdings)	$2,000	
Travel services to foreigners		$2,000

EXAMPLE 3. A U.S. resident who left his family in Hungary sends a $1,000 check to his wife in Hungary. The gift that the U.S. resident sent is a unilateral transfer. For accounting purposes it can be treated as a purchase of goodwill (wife's devotion?), which reduces the U.S. purchasing power, a debit entry. However, this gift was made possible by the credit that the Hungarians extended to the United States when they accepted a financial obligation, a check, in U.S. dollars from a U.S. resident. This latter part of the transaction, an increase in U.S. liabilities to foreigners, is a source of external purchasing power, and therefore a credit entry. The entry of this transaction in the U.S. balance of payments would be as follows:

	Debit	Credit
Remittances	$1,000	
Increase in short-term liabilities to foreigners (the check)		$1,000

EXAMPLE 4. A Swiss bank buys $3,000 worth of U.S. treasury bills. It pays by drawing on its dollar account with a U.S. bank. The sale of treasury bills to a foreigner is equivalent to the United States borrowing external purchasing power from foreigners, an increase in liabilities to foreigners, a credit

entry. However, the purchase is paid by reducing another debt that the United States had to foreigners, U.S. dollars in the hands of foreigners. This reduction in U.S. liabilities is a use of funds, a debit entry. In the U.S. balance of payments the transactions would be entered as follows:

	Debit	*Credit*
Decrease in short-term liabilities to foreigners (the dollar account)	$3,000	
Increase in short-term liabilities to foreigners (the treasury bill)		$3,000

EXAMPLE 5. A U.S. resident buys a $1,000 bond newly issued by a German company. The payment is made with a check drawn on a New York bank account. As a result, the U.S. resident now owns a German bond, and the German company owns U.S. dollar deposits. The acquisition of the German bond, a financial asset, implies a decrease in U.S. external purchasing power; therefore, the bond account (investment in foreign securities) must be debited. However, at the same time the dollar balances that the German now owns represent an increase in U.S. liabilities to foreigners; they increase the U.S. foreign purchasing power. Thus, the U.S. short-term liabilities (foreigners' short-term investment) must be credited. In the U.S. balance of payments this transaction will appear as follows:

	Debit	*Credit*
Increase in long-term claims on foreigners (the German bond)	$1,000	
Increase in short-term liabilities to foreigners (the U.S. dollar deposits)		$1,000

An alternative explanation for this set of entries would be the following: a German businessman wishes to maintain dollar balances in the United States for transaction purposes or as part of his investment portfolio strategy. In return for these balances he is willing to issue a long-term claim on his company. The accounting facts of this transaction are the same as in the previous one. From the point of view of the U.S. balance of payments, long-term claims on foreigners (dr.) and foreigners' short-term claim on the United States (cr.) have increased. However, the *motivations* behind this transaction are different from the previous one. In this case the acquisition of a short-term claim on the United States by the German is the primary active force leading to the transaction. In the previous explanation this short-term claim is only accepted passively as a means of payment which can be exchanged later. *It is in this attempt to separate accounts in the balance of payments according to motivation that the concepts of balance of payments surplus and deficit emerge.*

THE CONCEPTS OF SURPLUS AND DEFICIT IN THE BALANCE OF PAYMENTS

The double-entry system of accounting of the balance of payments means that, by definition, *debits equal credits.* In this sense the balance of payments always balances. It is only when one segregates a group of accounts in order to answer the question of what have been the pressures on the international value of the currency that a concept of a balance in the balance of payments emerges. To answer this question it is necessary to separate the accounts in the balance of payments into two groups: (1) those whose changes are induced by economic relationships external to the balance of payments, e.g., relative prices and incomes and (2) those that change mainly as a result of the necessary financing that accompanies the first group. The balance on the first group can be considered a barometer of the pressures on the exchange rate of the home currency.

In the economic literature the first group of accounts, that which is affected by economic reasons regardless of other items in the balance of payments, is called *autonomous.* The second group of accounts, that which changes only in order to finance other items in the balance of payments, is called *compensating* or *accommodating.* Economists often refer to an imaginary line that separates the two groups of accounts. The accounts "above the line" comprise the *autonomous* accounts whose balance determines whether the balance of payments is in surplus or deficit. The accounts "below the line" present the *compensating* accounts that show how the balance of payments surplus or deficit was financed.

The balance of payments is in *surplus,* i.e., the international purchasing power of the country has increased during the period in question, if *autonomous receipts exceed autonomous payments.* In the same way, the balance of payments is in *deficit,* i.e., the international purchasing power of the country has decreased during the period in question, if *autonomous payments exceed autonomous receipts.* A surplus in the autonomous account is accompanied by an increase in foreign reserves or a decrease in official liabilities in the compensating accounts. This puts an upward pressure on the external value of the home currency. A deficit in the autonomous accounts is associated with a decrease in foreign reserves or an increase in liabilities to foreigners. This tends to put a downward pressure on the external value of the home currency. A country cannot endure continuous deficits in its balance of payments without eventually having to devalue its currency.[2]

[2]Throughout this book *devalue* and *upvalue* refer to changes in the parity of a currency vis-à-vis other currencies or gold. *Revalue* is often used interchangeably with upvalue to mean an increase in parity, but technically it means a change in either direction. Accordingly, revalue will be used in this text for any change and upvalue will be used to denote a positive parity change.

Currencies of most countries in the world are pegged to another nation's currency; e.g., most Latin American currencies are pegged to the U.S. dollar, and revaluations take place from time to time. As discussed in the following chapters, most of the heavily traded currencies are now in a system of managed floating vis-à-vis each other. In this system currenices appreciate or depreciate against other currencies. We will tend to use devaluation and depreciation (or upvaluation and appreciation) interchangeably in the text.

Examples of *autonomous* receipts would be all normal commercial exports, gifts, and capital movements which take place because of private enterprise's search for higher profitability. Examples of *accommodating* receipts are the sale of gold or foreign exchange by the central bank in order to finance imports into the country at the current exchange rate or a loan to the government by an international agency for the explicit purpose of bridging the gap between payments and receipts of the country.

In our previous examples we could separate the entries in the following fashion. In the case of the exporter, the exports are an autonomous receipt, the short-term investment abroad is a compensating payment. In the case of the Japanese visitor, the travel services are an autonomous transaction; the yen received in payment are an accommodating transaction. In Example 3 the gift is clearly an autonomous payment; the way in which it was financed is an accommodating receipt. In the case of the Swiss bank buying U.S. treasury bills, the purchase of the security is an autonomous transaction while the reduction in the dollar account is an accommodating payment according to the motivations stated in the example.

The compensating part of each of these transactions involves an accumulation of financial assets by one of the parties to the transactions–the one providing the financing. The exporter has a 90-day account receivable; the airport bank has yen balances; and a Hungarian wife and the seller of the U.S. treasury bill have dollar balances. Will these individuals continue to hold these financial assets as an investment or will they exchange them for financial assets denominated in other currencies? The answer to this question would determine whether this part of the transaction we have called compensating ultimately becomes autonomous or whether it is truly compensating. To the extent that the parties providing initial financing in these examples choose to hold the acquired financial assets as an investment we can say that this part of the transaction is also autonomous. An analysis of relative interest rates, exchange rates, and liquidity conditions would have been the reason for the decision to hold these assets. If this is the case, the net impact on exchange markets of the total transaction (e.g., the Japanese travel and the accumulation of yen balances by the airport bank) will be zero. Autonomous sources of purchasing power would equal autonomous uses for each of the examples.

Alternatively, if the parties financing the transaction in these examples do so only to provide a service and intend to exchange the currency denomination of the financial asset as soon as possible, a net pressure in the exchange markets will be generated. For example, if the U.S. airport bank does not wish to hold yen balances, it will exchange these balances into another currency, let's say U.S. dollars. In the exchange markets yen will be sold and dollars bought. This will tend to decrease the value of the yen relative to the dollar. The earlier sale of U.S. services to foreigners (the Japanese tourist) has generated an upward pressure on the dollar.

The alternative motivations that can be attributed to a financing transaction was clearly illustrated in Example 5. In the case of Example 5, the bond purchase under the first interpretation is an autonomous payment; the foreigner's short-term investment in the United States is a compensating receipt. However, under the alternative interpretation, when the German businessman wishes to acquire dollar balances for transaction purposes, *both* the payment and the receipt are autonomous.

In practice, balance of payments statistics are not compiled on an entry-by-entry basis. In fact, only aggregates of one side of transactions are measured at a time. For example, customs provides the main sources for figures on exports and imports; financial institutions, government agencies, and industry report the changes in foreign financial assets and on liabilities to foreigners. From these figures it is very difficult to establish the motivation behind changes in financial assets and liabilities. This is in addition to the intrinsic difficulty of some cases, such as the example of the U.S. resident purchasing a German bond with dollar-denominated deposits. Countries' response to these difficulties is to offer partial measures of balance in their balance of payments, such as trade balance and balance in the current account, and to report capital flows in terms of maturity, short-term or long-term, and transactors, private or official. This approach circumvents the problem of defining autonomous vs. compensating accounts. The resulting balance of payments are similar in format to the imaginary one presented above in Exhibit 2.1. This is also the approach followed by the International Monetary Fund in its "analytic presentation" of balance of payments which appears in the *Balance of Payments Yearbook.* (A "standard presentation" with more detail, but no balance figures, is also available from this source.)

THE U.S. BALANCE OF PAYMENTS ACCOUNTING

The principles presented above apply equally to the United States and to the other countries in the world. However, in the case of the United States an additional complication must be taken into account: the U.S. dollar is an international reserve currency under the present international payments mechanism.[3] Until August 15, 1971, all the dollars in the hands of foreigners could potentially be presented to the United States for exchange into gold. However, it is also true that the reserve role of the dollar guarantees that not all the dollars in the hands of foreigners will be returned to the United States to be exchanged for other international means of payments. It is when alternative assumptions are made on whether dollar liabilities are of an autonomous or compensating nature that various definitions of U.S. balance of payments surpluses or deficits arise. As noted before, the size of the balance of payments surplus or deficit is a direct function of the balance in autonomous accounts. Therefore, if the definition of an autonomous account changes, then the size of the balance of payments deficit or surplus changes. The problems presented by the availability of alternative definitions are reinforced by the difficulties in obtaining empirical support for any of the definitions. This difficulty is due to the nature of capital flows and the way they are measured, as explained in the previous section.

During the post-war period until June 1976 the United States addressed the problems of inputing a motivation to short-term cash flows by classifying the financial flows according to their liquidity and the nature of the holder. This

[3] The holdings of U.S. dollars by governments other than the United States are considered part of these governments' international reserves.

gave rise to two major balance figures: the *net liquidity balance* and the *official reserve balance.* This was in addition to all the other partial balances, such as trade balance, discussed above.

In the *net liquidity balance* only the *private nonliquid* short-term claims and liabilities were considered of an autonomous nature. These claims include such nonmarketable items as bank loans and corporate accounts receivable. Nonliquid short-term claims and liabilities held by official agencies were classified as compensating. All liquid short-term claims and liabilities, regardless of who held them, were considered of a compensating nature. The rationale behind this definition was that any liquid short-term claim on the United States held by any foreigner could be converted into an immediate claim for redemption into gold (when convertibility existed) or into other foreign exchange.

The *official reserve balance* discriminated among short-term capital movements in terms of whether the assets ended up in the hands of official institutions or in the hands of private residents. If the transaction was made by *private* residents, this definition considered any capital flow as autonomous, whether liquid or nonliquid. If the transaction changed the balances in the hands of official institutions, it was considered to be accommodating.

In both the net liquidity and the official reserve balances, errors and omissions were considered as autonomous transactions.

In June 1976 an advisory committee appointed to study the problems in the presentation of U.S. balance of payments statistics concluded that:

> the presentation should not be predicated upon any judgment about the motives which underlie particular transactions or group of transactors. Since it is not possible to infer from the data themselves whether a transaction is determined by short-run or long-run objectives, or whether an official transaction is "autonomous" or "accommodating," the official statistics should avoid the appearance of revealing more than is known.[4]

Thus, the Committee concluded that no balances be presented in the body of the balance of payments presentation. In particular, the Committee recommended that the net liquidity balance and the official reserve balances were to be eliminated. However, some partial balances such as the balance in goods and services should be presented as memoranda at the foot of the table presenting the U.S. balance of payments.

The Committee's recommendations were adopted with only minor changes. Starting in June 1976, the presentation of the U.S. balance of payments figures is as shown in Exhibit 2.2. To the extent that balance figures are presented, these appear in the memoranda lines 68–71. The most comprehensive of these balances is the balance on current account. None of these balances includes any capital account. Lines 72 and 73 combined coincide with the old

[4]Report of the Advisory Committee on the Presentation of Balance of Payments Statistics, U.S. Department of Commerce, *Survey of Current Business,* Washington, D.C., June 1976, p. 20.

official reserve balance. However, to avoid the temptation of attaching any significance to this number, the Committee recommended that the net balance of these two lines not be presented. The old liquidity balance can no longer be computed because of the level of aggregation in the capital accounts.

The thrust behind this change in presentation was the belief that no single number can adequately describe the position of a country. To emphasize this point, the Committee decided that the federal statistics should not provide any number that could be construed as a summary of the external position of the United States. Although this may be the appropriate position for a government agency, it does not eliminate the need for analysis of the nature of capital flows by parties interested in assessing balance of payments conditions and the future of the U.S. dollar. The government is no longer providing something that could be a substitute for this analysis. Now it is for the analyst to decide whether the outstanding liabilities of the United States to foreigners will be held willingly by foreigners—an autonomous transaction—or whether they will be exchanged for financial assets denominated in other currencies—a financing transaction. In the first case, the value of the dollar would not be affected; in the second case, a downward pressure on its value is certain to occur. Ultimately, one must study the factors underlying the various accounts in more detail before the concept of a deficit or surplus can be specifically determined; Chapter 3 proceeds to analyze the United States accounts.

Questions

1. Examine Exhibit 2.2. Concentrate on the figures for 1977. Taking into consideration that the balance of payments is constructed following the principles of double-entry bookkeeping, what could be the accompanying entries to lines 2, 11, 16, 29, 44, and 47?

2. What happened to U.S. official reserve assets (line 34) during 1977?

3. What was the official reserve balance for the United States for 1977? What does this mean in relation to the other accounts in the balance of payments?

4. What are the most important accounts (the accounts having the largest amounts) in the U.S. balance of payments? What have been the trends in these accounts during the 1960s and 1970s as shown in Exhibit 2.2?

EXHIBIT 2.2. U.S. Balance of Payments, 1965–1977 (millions of dollars)

Line	*(Credits +; debits –)*[a]	*1965*	*1966*	*1967*	*1968*
1	Exports of goods and services[b]	41,090	44,565	47,318	52,373
2	Merchandise, adjusted excluding military[c]	26,461	29,310	30,666	33,626
3	Transfers under U.S. military agency sales contracts	830	829	1,152	1,392
4	Travel	1,380	1,590	1,646	1,775
5	Passenger fares	271	317	371	411
6	Other transportation	2,175	2,333	2,426	2,548
7	Fees and royalties from affiliated foreigners	1,199	1,162	1,354	1,430
8	Fees and royalties from unaffiliated foreigners	335	353	393	437
9	Other private services	714	814	951	1,024
10	U.S. Government miscellaneous services	285	326	336	353
	Receipts of income on U.S. assets abroad:				
11	Direct investments[d,e]	5,505	5,258	5,604	6,591
12	Other private receipts	1,421	1,669	1,781	2,021
13	U.S. Government receipts	515	604	639	765
14	Transfers of goods and services under U.S. military grant programs, net	1,636	1,892	2,039	2,547
15	Imports of goods and services	-32,801	-38,599	-41,606	-48,800
16	Merchandise, adjusted, excluding military[c]	-21,510	-25,493	-26,866	-32,991
17	Direct defense expenditures	-2,952	-3,764	-4,378	-4,535
18	Travel	-2,438	-2,657	-3,207	-3,030
19	Passenger fares	-717	-753	-829	-885
20	Other transportation	-1,951	-2,161	-2,157	-2,367
21	Fees and royalties to affiliated foreigners	-68	-64	-62	-80
22	Fees and royalties to unaffiliated foreigners	-67	-76	-104	-106
23	Private payments for other services	-461	-506	-565	-668
24	U.S. Government payments for miscellaneous services	-550	-644	-691	-760
	Payments of income on foreign assets in the United States:				
25	Direct investments[d,e]	-657	-711	-821	-876
26	Other private payments	-942	-1,221	-1,328	-1,800
27	U.S. Government payments	-489	-549	-598	-702
28	U.S. military grants of goods and services, net	-1,636	-1,892	-2,039	-2,547
29	Unilateral transfers (excluding military grants of goods and services), net	-2,854	-2,932	-3,125	-2,952
30	U.S. Government grants (excluding military grants of goods and services)	-1,808	-1,910	-1,805	-1,709
31	U.S. Government pensions and other transfers	-369	-367	-441	-407
32	Private remittances and other transfers	-677	-655	-879	-836

1969	1970	1971	1972	1973	1974	1975	1976	1977[p]
57,529	65,659	68,790	77,196	109,855	146,080	155,648	171,274	183,214
36,414	42,469	43,319	49,381	71,410	98,306	107,088	114,694	120,585
1,528	1,501	1,926	1,163	2,342	2,952	3,919	5,213	7,079
2,043	2,331	2,534	2,817	3,412	4,032	4,839	5,806	6,164
450	544	615	699	975	1,104	1,039	1,229	1,366
2,652	3,113	3,277	3,555	4,434	5,652	5.785	6,705	6,983
1,533	1,758	1,927	2,115	2,513	3,070	3,543	3,531	3,767
486	573	618	655	712	751	757	822	958
1,160	1,287	1,539	1,764	1,960	2,259	2,868	3,543	3,728
343	332	347	354	399	413	432	488	485
7,649	8,168	9,159	10,949	16,542	19,157	16,615	18,999	19,851
2,338	2,671	2,641	2,949	4,330	7,356	7,644	8,955	10,881
933	912	888	796	826	1,028	1,119	1,290	1,368
2,610	2,713	3,546	4,492	2,809	1,817	2,217	373	194
-54,129	-60,005	-66,496	-79,321	-99,087	-137,208	-132,625	-161,913	-193,727
-35,807	-39,866	-45,579	-55,797	-70,499	-103,673	-98,043	-124,047	-151,644
-4,856	-4,855	-4,819	-4,784	-4,629	-5,035	-4,795	-4,901	-5,745
-3,373	-3,980	-4,373	-5,042	-5,526	-5,980	-6,417	-6,856	-7,451
-1,080	-1,215	-1,290	-1,596	-1,790	-2,095	-2,263	-2,568	-2,843
-2,455	-2,816	-3,078	-3,461	-4,591	-5,818	-5,535	-6,561	-7,263
-101	-111	-118	-155	-209	-160	-287	-293	-253
-120	-114	-123	-139	-176	-186	-193	-189	-194
-751	-810	-935	-1,017	-1,152	-1,211	-1,483	-1,938	-2,383
-717	-725	-746	-783	-862	-966	-1,043	-1,250	-1,359
-848	-875	-1,164	-1,256	-1,610	-1,331	-2,234	-3,110	-2,829
-3,244	-3,617	-2,428	-2,604	-4,209	-6,491	-5,788	-5,681	-6,224
-777	-1,024	-1,844	-2,684	-3,836	-4,262	-4,542	-4,520	-5,540
-2,610	-2,713	-3,546	-4,492	-2,809	-1,817	-2,217	-373	-194
-2,994	-3,294	-3,701	-3,854	-3,887	-7,188	-4,612	-5,022	-4,708
-1,649	-1,736	-2,043	-2,173	-1,933	-5,475	-2,893	-3,145	-2,776
-406	-462	-542	-572	-693	-694	-815	-934	-973
-939	-1,096	-1,117	-1,109	-1,256	-1,020	-904	-944	-959

Continued

EXHIBIT 2.2. Continued

Line	*(Credits +; debits –)*[a]	*1965*	*1966*	*1967*	*1968*
33	U.S. assets abroad, net (increase/capital outflow (–))	-5,718	-7,321	-9,759	-10,987
34	U.S. official reserve assets, net[f]	1,222	568	52	-880
35	Gold	1,665	571	1,170	1,173
36	Special drawing rights				
37	Reserve position in the International Monetary Fund	-94	537	-94	-870
38	Foreign currencies	-349	-540	-1,024	1,183
39	U.S. Government assets, other than official reserve assets, net	-1,605	-1,543	-2,423	-2,274
40	U.S. loans and other long-term assets	-2,463	-2,513	-3,638	-3,722
41	Repayments on U.S. loans[g]	874	1,235	1,005	1,386
42	U.S. foreign currency holdings and U.S. short-term assets, net	-16	-265	209	62
43	U.S. private assets, net	-5,335	-6,345	-7,387	-7,833
44	Direct investments abroad[e]	-5,010	-5,416	-4,806	-5,295
45	Foreign securities	-759	-720	-1,308	-1,569
	U.S. claims on unaffiliated foreigners reported by U.S. nonbanking concerns:				
46	Long-term	-88	-112	-281	-220
47	Short-term	429	-330	-498	-982
	U.S. claims reported by U.S. banks, not included elsewhere:				
48	Long-term	-232	317	235	338
49	Short-term	325	-84	-730	-105
50	Foreign assets in the United States, net (increase/capital inflow (+))	740	3,659	7,378	9,927
51	Foreign official assets in the United States, net	132	-674	3,450	-776
52	U.S. Government securities	-143	-1,529	2,260	-771
53	U.S. Treasury securities[h]	-136	-1,550	2,221	-800
54	Other[i]	-7	21	39	29
55	Other U.S. Government liabilities[j]	65	113	83	-15
56	U.S. liabilities reported by U.S. banks, not included elsewhere	210	742	1,106	10
57	Other foreign official assets[k]				
58	Other foreign assets in the United States, net	607	4,333	3,928	10,703
59	Direct investments in the United States[e]	415	425	698	807
60	U.S. Treasury securities	-131	-356	-135	136
61	U.S. securities other than U.S. Treasury securities	-358	906	1,016	4,414
	U.S. liabilities to unaffiliated foreigners reported by U.S. nonbanking concerns:				
62	Long-term	29	180	85	715
63	Short-term	149	296	499	759
	U.S. liabilities reported by U.S. banks, not included elsewhere:				
64	Long-term	241	188	158	72
65	Short-term	262	2,694	1,607	3,799
66	Allocation of special drawing rights				

1969	1970	1971	1972	1973	1974	1975	1976	1977^{p}
-11,593	-9,340	-12,475	-14,461	-22,824	-34,806	-39,596	-50,608	-34,650
-1,187	2,477	2,348	32	209	-1,434	-607	-2,530	-231
-967	787	866	547					-118
	-851	-249	-703	9	-172	-66	-78	-121
-1,034	389	1,350	153	-33	-1,265	-466	-2,212	-294
814	2,152	381	35	233	3	-75	-240	302
-2,200	-1,589	-1,884	-1,568	-2,645	365	-3,463	-4,213	-3,679
-3,489	-3,293	-4,181	-3,819	-4,639	-5,001	-5,936	-6,943	-6,445
1,200	1,721	2,115	2,086	2,596	4,826	2,476	2,597	2,720
89	-16	182	165	-602	541	-3	133	47
-8,206	-10,228	-12,939	-12,925	-20,388	-33,737	-35,526	-43,865	-30,740
-5,960	-7,589	-7,617	-7,747	-11,353	-9,145	-14,312	-11,614	-12,215
-1,549	-1,076	-1,113	-618	-671	-1,854	-6,235	-8,852	-5,398
-424	-586	-168	-243	-396	-474	-432	5	25
298	-10	-1,061	-811	-1,987	-2,747	-1,015	-2,035	-1,725
297	155	-612	-1,307	-933	-1,183	-2,357	-2,362	-751
-867	-1,122	-2,368	-2,199	-5,047	-18,333	-11,175	-19,006	-10,676
12,701	6,357	22,987	21,696	18,663	34,677	15,525	36,969	50,869
-1,301	6,907	26,895	10,705	6,299	10,981	6,960	18,073	37,124
-2,344	9,437	26,586	8,499	696	4,184	5,313	9,906	32,602
-2,269	9,410	26,594	8,243	114	3,282	4,408	9,333	30,294
-74	28	-8	257	582	902	905	573	2,308
251	-456	-510	383	1,153	724	1,701	4,993	1,644
792	-2,075	819	1,638	4,126	5,818	-2,158	969	773
			185	323	254	2,104	2,205	2,105
14,002	-550	-3,907	10,991	12,364	23,696	8,565	18,897	13,746
1,263	1,464	367	949	2,800	4,760	2,603	4,347	3,338
-68	81	-22	-34	-214	697	2,590	2,783	563
3,130	2,189	2,289	4,507	4,041	378	2,503	1,284	2,869
701	1,112	384	594	298	-90	334	-958	-620
91	902	-15	221	737	1,934	-94	451	877
160	23	-250	149	227	9	-280	231	373
8,726	-6,321	-6,661	4,605	4,475	16,008	908	10,759	6,346
	867	717	710					

Continued

EXHIBIT 2.2 Continued

Lines	*(Credits +; debits –)*[a]	*1965*	*1966*	*1967*	*1968*
67	Statistical discrepancy (sum of above items with sign reversed)	–457	628	–206	439
	Memoranda:				
68	Balance on merchandise trade (lines 2 and 16)	4,951	3,817	3,800	635
69	Balance on goods and services (lines 1 and 15)[l]	8,289	5,966	5,712	3,573
70	Balance on goods, services, and remittances (lines 69, 31, and 32)	7,243	4,944	4,392	2,330
71	Balance on current account (lines 69 and 29)[l]	5,435	3,034	2,587	621
	Transactions in U.S. official reserve assets and in foreign official assets in the United States:				
72	Increase (–) in U.S. official reserve assets, net (line 34)	1,222	568	52	–880
73	Increase (+) in foreign official assets in the United States (line 51 less line 55).	67	–787	3,367	–761

[a]Credits, +: exports of goods and services; unilateral transfers to United States; capital inflows [increase in foreign assets (U.S. liabilities) or decrease in U.S. assets]; decrease in U.S. official reserve assets.

Debits, –: imports of goods and services; unilateral transfers to foreigners; capital outflows [decrease in foreign assets (U.S. liabilities) or increase in U.S. assets]; increase in U.S. official reserve assets.

[b]Excludes transfers of goods and services under U.S. military grant programs (see line 14).

[c]Excludes exports of goods under U.S. military agency sales contracts identified in Census export documents, excludes imports of goods under direct defense expenditures identified in Census import documents, and reflects various other adjustments (for valuation, coverage, and timing) of Census statistics to the balance of payment basis.

[d]Consists of interest, dividends, and branch earnings.

[e]Includes reinvested earnings of foreign incorporated affiliates of U.S. firms or of U.S. incorporated affiliates of foreign firms.

[f]For all areas, amounts outstanding March 31, 1977, were as follows in millions of dollars: line 34, 19, 120; line 35, 11, 658; line 36, 2,389; line 37, 4,812; line 38, 261.

[g]Includes sales of foreign obligations to foreigners.

[h]Consists of bills, certificates, marketable bonds and notes, and nonmarketable convertible and nonconvertible bonds and notes.

[i]Consists of U.S. Treasury and Export-Import Bank obligations, not included elsewhere, and of debt securities of U.S. Government corporations and agencies.

1969	1970	1971	1972	1973	1974	1975	1976	1977[p]
-1,515	-244	-9,822	-1,966	-2,720	-1,555	5,660	9,300	-998
607	2,603	-2,260	-6,416	911	-5,367	9,045	-9,353	-31,059
3,401	5,654	2,294	-2,125	10,766	8,872	23,023	9,361	-10,514
2,055	4,096	635	-3,806	8,823	7,158	21,304	7,483	-12,445
406	2,360	-1,407	-5,979	6,885	1,684	18,411	4,339	-15,221
-1,187	2,477	2,348	32	209	-1,434	-607	-2,530	-231
-1,552	7,362	27,405	10,322	5,145	10,257	5,259	13,080	35,480

[j]Includes, primarily, U.S. Government liabilities associated with military sales contracts and other transactions arranged with or through foreign official agencies.

[k]Consists of investment in U.S. corporate stocks and in debt securities of private corporations and State and local governments.

[l]Conceptually, the sum of lines 71 and 66 (total, all areas) is equal to "net foreign investment" in the national income and product accounts (NIPA's) of the United States. Beginning with 1973-IV, however, the foreign transactions account in NIPA's excludes the shipments and financing of extraordinary military orders placed by Israel. Line 69 (total, all areas) differs from net exports of goods and services in the NIPA's due to the omission in the NIPA net exports of shipments of extraordinary military orders placed by Israel and of U.S. Government interest income payments to foreigners. The latter are classified in a separate category in the foreign transactions account in NIPA's.

[p]Preliminary data.

SOURCE: U.S. Department of Commerce, Bureau of Economic Analysis, SURVEY OF CURRENT BUSINESS, June 1977 and June 1978.

Exercises on Balance of Payments Accounting

Below there is a series of transactions between country A and country B (the rest of the world). Assume the point of view of country A and that A's currency is dollars ($). Do the following:

1. Indicate the accounts to be debited and credited in each transaction.

2. Enter these transactions in the appropriate "T-accounts" provided for that purpose in Exhibit 2.3.

3. Prepare the balance of payments for country A. Assume that all the short-term capital movements are of a compensating nature.

TRANSACTIONS

1. a. A exports goods to B for $1,000. B's importers sign a bill of exchange for the goods they imported from A.

   b. A's exporters discount the bill of exchange with their bank which in turn keeps the bill until maturity. (Assume 10% discount.)

   c. On the bill's maturity A's bank receives payment for the bill in B's currency (as it was originally drawn). A's bank deposits B's currency in B's bank. The interest accrued on the bill is $50.

2. A imports goods from B for $800. A's importers pay B's exporters for the $800 with a loan in B's currency which they get from A's bank.

3. A resident of country A, Mr. X, goes on vacation to country B. He spends all the money he had with him, $5,000, for services received while on his vacation in country B.

4. Mr. X is lucky, however, because on the last day of his vacation he finds in the street a purse with $100 in B's currency. He brings the money home and declares his finding to custom authorities.

5. Another resident of A who has migrated from B a few years ago decides to send $100 to his family. His father uses this money to buy a bond from another citizen of A.

6. A businessman of A, Mr. Y, decides to build a subsidiary plant in B. Therefore, he ships to B all necessary materials for this purpose, which cost $50,000.

7. Mr. Y very soon finds out that he needs another $20,000 for the completion of the plant. Thus, he issues bonds on the parent company for this amount and sells them to the citizens of B.

8. Mr. Y makes $10,000 profit during the first year of operation, which Mr. Y uses to enlarge his business in B. A's citizens are very impressed by

EXHIBIT 2.3. Supporting "T Accounts"

Exports

Imports

Services

Unilateral Transfers

Direct Investment

Long-Term Foreign Financial Assets

Short-Term Foreign Financial Assets

Long-Term Liabilities

Short-Term Liabilities

Gold

the successful operation of Mr. Y's plant in B. Therefore, A's citizens buy from B's citizens half of the bonds issued by Mr. Y.

9. A resident of B, Mr. Z, migrates to A. His only property is $1,000 in B's currency, which he carried with him to A, and his house in B, which he rented to a friend for $100 a month. The house is worth $8,000. No rent payment, however, has been received.

10. Mr. Z, decides to sell his house to his friend for $8,000. Payment is arranged as follows: $4,000 in cash and $4,000 in 5 years. Mr. Z deposits this money with his old bank in B. (Everything here is in terms of B's currency.)

11. Mr. Z, however, thinks he should give back to the church of his village $1,000. Therefore, $1,000 is transferred from Mr. Z's account in B's bank to the account of the church.

12. B is a producer of gold. During the period of time for which the balance of payments is compiled, B produced $1 million. Half of this is consumed at home. However 20% is sold to B's central bank, 20% is sold to A's central bank, and 10% is exported to A for industrial use. For the amount of gold exported to A, B accepts a deposit with the central bank of country A.

13. A citizen of A, Mr. M, who migrated there from B a long time ago, finds out that he has inherited the property of his uncle. The property consists of a farm worth $2,000 and a deposit of $1,000 in B's bank.

14. Mr. M keeps the money with B's bank but he buys a designer's dress for $200 which he sends to his sister in B as a gift. The dress is purchased in A with A's currency.

15. Finally, Mr. M sells the farm for $2,000. He uses the proceeds and his deposit in B's bank to buy bonds issued by B's government.

16. Mr. M makes a gift to his brother in B. This gift consists of a watch which costs $500 and a check for $100. The watch is purchased in country A with A's currency.

Bibliography

The Balance of Payments Statistics of the United States. Report of the Review Committee for Balance of Payments Statistics to the Bureau of the Budget, April 1965, Edward M. Bernstein, Chairman, U.S. Government Printing Office: 1965.

Bame, Jack J, "Analyzing U.S. International Transactions." *Columbia Journal of World Business,* Fall 1976, pp. 72-84.

Meade, J. E., *The Balance of Payments.* London: Oxford University Press, 1952.

Report of the Advisory Committee on the Presentation of Balance of Payments Statistics, U.S. Department of Commerce, *Survey of Current Business,* Washington, D.C., June 1976, pp. 18–27.

Stern, Robert M., *et al.,* "The Presentation of the U.S. Balance of Payments: A Symposium." *Essays in International Finance* No. 123. Princeton: International Finance Section, Princeton University, Aug. 1977.

CHAPTER 3

What Makes the Balance of Payments Accounts Tick?

Because the multinational firm conducts business operations in many currencies, management needs to forecast the performance of various countries and their currencies. Balance of payments forecasting requires an understanding of the forces that trigger changes in the component accounts and, therefore, the country's economy at large; therefore, the exercise of forecasting a country's balance of payments provides an excellent analytical framework to predict the country's economic performance. A simple listing of historical records of the balance of payments is not sufficient; historical figures may show trends, but they provide neither insight into the past nor an analytical foundation to predict the future.

In this chapter we present an introduction to the major factors that affect each balance of payments account. In this presentation we look only at the *immediate* factors that affect the accounts. The whole cycle of events that a change in a given account engenders is not considered at this time. For example, we study the effect on exports of a change in the level of prices, but not the effects of the resulting trade balance on future exports.

The case of the United States will be used to illustrate the principles of analysis presented in the chapter. (The balance of payments of the United States for the period 1965–77 was presented in Exhibit 2.2.) However, the objective of this presentation is to suggest the relationships that a proper analysis would investigate, not to study the U.S. balance of payments in detail. The emphasis is on breadth, not on depth. The appendices to Chapter 4 ("Important Dates in the World Monetary System" and "Some International Associations") may be useful to the reader as a reference at this point.

TRADE FLOWS

Two issues require major consideration when analyzing the trade accounts of a given country. The more general and basic issue is: Why do countries trade? What are the underlying long-term forces that induce countries to trade? The second issue is: Given the basic forces, why do changes in the trade account take place? What are the short-term factors that make trade behavior depart from the expected long-term behavior?

Long-Term Factors

The questions of why countries trade and what items they trade have been the source of a number of theories beginning with David Ricardo in the early 1800s. In a nutshell, all these theories boil down to a relatively simple proposition: Countries export those goods which they know relatively best how to make, or, in other words, for which they have a *comparative advantage*. The source of this competitive edge has been attributed to a number of variables, including labor productivity, the proportion of factors of production available in the country, and the technological lead of the country.

Labor productivity has often been considered one of the major factors determining whether a country will be an exporter or an importer of a given good. Especially in the case of goods that are capable of being produced in several parts of the world, it is easy to see that the countries most efficient in their production will tend to be the producers for the world. This relatively higher efficiency has often been measured in terms of labor productivity (output per man-hour). However, it is clear that labor productivity is affected by the amount of capital with which labor works.

In addition to labor productivity, the relative endowment of resources is also thought to play an important role in the determination of goods traded.[1] Thus, the high capital endowment of the United States was considered to be at the core of the balance of trade surplus the United States enjoyed throughout most of the postwar period. The abundance of capital relative to the amount of labor in the United States was unparalleled by any other country. This factor was thought to explain the large amount of manufactured exports of this country.

However, research presented by Professor Leontief in 1954 suggested that

[1] For a review of this thesis see Harry G. Johnson, "Factor Endowments, International Trade, and Factor Prices," *Manchester School of Economic and Social Studies,* Sept. 1957, pp. 270–83; reprinted in American Economic Association, *Readings in International Economics* (Homewood, Ill.: Richard D. Irwin, 1968), pp. 78–89.

U.S. exports were *less* capital-intensive than its imports.[2] The empirical evidence indicated that the exports of the United States had a higher labor-capital ratio in their manufacture than its imports. In view of the general belief that the United States was richer in capital than in labor, the country was exporting the products that required the most of what it had the least. Initially these surprising findings were explained by referring to the capital imbedded in American labor. If the U.S. labor force were adjusted for its efficiency, it was argued, the United States would appear as a relatively labor-rich country. What made U.S. labor more efficient than the rest of the world's was thought to be the human capital (skills) that this labor possessed. Another factor related to the nature of the U.S. trade was the level of research and development activity in different industries.

Some economists still speak of factor proportions that include human capital. However, a newer trend is to consider labor skills and technology as factors fostering new products and new processes that in turn generate temporary trade advantages. One of the main characteristics of this approach is its dynamism. It considers trade advantages derived from technological gaps to be temporary. This gap narrows continuously as knowledge of the innovation spreads abroad and foreign producers adopt it. Therefore, the entire structure of trade advantages is continually being modified by the simultaneous generation and destruction of technology gaps.[3] Proponents of this theory note that the rate of technology transfer is accelerating. A decrease in the technological lead of the United States has been considered one of the important factors explaining the decline in this country's balance of trade surplus since 1964, and the deficits in the 1970s. Further, the multinational corporation has been thought to be an important element in this transfer process.

Summing up, three major factors have been suggested to explain trade patterns: labor productivity, the relative availability of factors of production, and technological gaps. When analyzing the balance of payments of countries other than the United States, these principles must be accommodated to the specific circumstances. Thus, in a case where exports of a country do not contain any large degree of technological sophistication, the future of its exports would depend on its continued ability to provide raw material at competitive prices and labor at an efficient rate (e.g., keep wage rates low or increase output per man-hour). To the extent that this country can acquire new technologies, its chances to remain competitive in the international market will be enhanced.

Cyclical Factors

Given an understanding of the major forces that induce nations to trade, the next question is: What are the relevant variables that determine the volume of

[2] W. W. Leontief, "Domestic Production and Foreign Trade: The American Capital Position Re-examined," *Economia Internazionale,* Vol. 7, Feb. 1954, pp. 3–22; reprinted in American Economic Association, *Readings in International Economics* (Homewood, Ill.: Richard D. Irwin, 1968), Chapter 30.

[3] Raymond Vernon, "International Investment and International Trade in the Product Cycle," *Quarterly Journal of Economics,* May 1966, pp. 190–207.

trade at a given point in time? These are mainly two: relative prices of traded goods and relative national incomes between trading partners.

Relative Prices. This variable affects trade in two fashions: its impact on production and its effects on demand. Assuming a free trade situation, relative prices will determine whether the country will be an importer or an exporter of a given commodity. As the world prices of a good increase, the chances increase for profitable production of that good in a given country for domestic consumption as well as exportation. For example, Australian gold production, once the world's highest, halved in one decade to 615,000 ounces as a result of its high production costs. However, 1973 production was up 10%. The increase in the price of gold to $90 an ounce from $35 in 1970 made the old Australian gold mines economic again. As gold prices continued to soar, additional gold mines were brought back into production.

Given the cost structure for domestic production of a given good, world prices will determine whether or not the country can produce the good profitably and export it or whether the country would be wiser to import the good from a country with a lower cost structure. If a country finds it advantageous to produce a good and to sell in the export market when world prices increase, the country must then determine how much it wishes to produce at that price. In many cases, costs per unit increase as the quantity produced increases. This will limit the amount that the country exports at world prices. The responsiveness of quantity produced to changes in prices is called *supply price elasticity.*

The price elasticity of supply is limited by available capacity in the short term. If capacity is being used fully, the country would not be able to increase the volume of its exports in response to price increases. If the price increase is perceived as permanent, eventually more productive capacity will be brought on line, but this takes time. Over the short term the price elasticity of supply tends to be low.

The impact of prices on demand depends on the nature of the goods involved. By and large, when prices go down, quantity demanded tends to increase. However, some commodities are indispensable and the quantity demanded of them is relatively independent of the prevalent price. In other cases a decline in price produces a large response in the quantity demanded, which may be proportionally more or less than the decrease in prices. The difference in responsiveness of quantity purchased to changes in the price is called *demand price elasticity.*

An understanding of the price elasticity of the goods traded by a country is essential in determining the impact of forecasted prices. This is particularly so in predicting the effects on trade of a devaluation (or upvaluation) of the country's currency. A change in exchange parity is nothing else than a change in prices. The impact of a change in prices should be analyzed in terms of both local currency and foreign exchange or international purchasing power.

Take the case of the impact of a devaluation on exports. In this example assume that B's currency is used as money internationally; i.e., it is a reserve currency.

INITIAL CONDITIONS:			
Exchange rate:	1A = 1B		
Quantity exported:	100 units		
Price per unit:	5As		
Export revenues:	500As = 500 Bs		
IMPACT OF DEVALUATION:			
New exchange rate:	1.25A = 1B (A devalues by 25% relative to B)		
	Case 1	*Case 2*	*Case 3*
Quantity exported:	130	125	120
Export revenues:	650As = 520Bs	625As = 500Bs	600As = 480Bs

In the three cases described above the quantity demanded increases in response to the decline in prices, and so do the export revenues measured in A's currency. Measured in A's currency, A's devaluation has had an unmistakable beneficial effect on export revenues. However, the export revenues in terms of foreign exchange (B's currency) increases in only one case, Case 1. In terms of B's currency, the decline in price produced by the devaluation of A's currency depresses the revenues received for each unit. In order to compensate for this decline, the number of units sold must increase. If it increases proportionally more than the decrease in prices, there will be an increase in revenues. This is Case 1. However, if the increase in quantity sold is proportionally less than the decrease in prices, there will be a decrease in revenues. This is Case 3. In Case 2 quantity sold increases by a percentage equal to the percentage decline in prices. Therefore, for Case 2, export revenues remain constant and the product has *unitary price elasticity*. The product in Case 1 is considered to be *price elastic;* the product in Case 3, *price inelastic.* In terms of B's currency, the devaluation has reduced the price of one unit from 5Bs to 4Bs. The price decline in terms of B's currency is (5B - 4B)/4B, or 25%, which is the amount of the upvaluation of B vs. A (1B = 1.25A). Hence, unitary price elasticity occurs when demand expands by 25% to 125, as in Case 2. A typical example of a price-inelastic product is a raw material. An example of a price-elastic good is machinery.[4]

Thus, the study of the impact of relative prices on trade must be done along two major dimensions: the magnitude of changes in relative prices and the responsiveness of quantities traded to a given change in prices. Relative

[4]More specifically, import price elasticity is measured by the percentage change in imports associated with a given percentage change in prices.

$$\eta_P = \frac{\Delta Q}{Q} \div \frac{\Delta P}{P} = \frac{\Delta Q}{\Delta P} \times \frac{P}{Q}$$

where

η_p = price elasticity	$\eta_p < 1$ inelastic demand
Q = quantity	$\eta_p = 1$ unitary elasticity of demand
P = price	$\eta_p > 1$ elastic demand

The levels of P and Q, in contrast to changes, are usually measured at the midpoint between the initial and the final levels.

prices may change either because of outright changes in the exchange rate among currencies or because the economic forces that shape domestic prices are altered. When the cost of factors of production such as labor and its productivity change, the prices of products in the local market change, and with constant exchange rates, the foreign price also will be affected. The second dimension, the responsiveness of quantity traded to a given change in price, is largely determined by the nature of the goods.

Let us look at the behavior of the trade accounts of the United States. Exhibit 3.1 presents annual total imports and exports of the United States classified by major types of goods for the period 1967–77. (Further disaggregation by product is available from the same source used in the preparation of the exhibit.)[5] The exhibit shows clearly the strong net export position which the United States holds in the area of equipment (capital goods except automotive) and the large net import position in the field of industrial supplies. The latter position was aggravated since 1974 by the large increase in oil prices. Food products oscillated from a net export to a net import and back to a substantial net export position since 1973 when the increased volume of U.S. exports of grain accompanied by higher world prices of these products made a large positive contribution to the U.S. trade accounts.

The goods for which the United States has a strong position, capital goods except automotive, are also the goods that one would expect both demand and supply to be price elastic; other developed countries, such as Germany, compete for supplying these goods to the rest of the world. Consumption of these goods can be expected to be very sensitive to price changes. In contrast, the largest net dependency of the United States on foreign trade is in goods that one may consider to be price inelastic in both supply and demand. These are industrial supplies: raw materials including oil. In spite of the large increases in the price of oil, Americans continue importing a very large amount of it. On the positive side, the low price elasticity of food consumption allowed the United States to post large export surpluses on food in spite of very high food prices during 1973–77.

Let's look at the behavior of relative prices in more detail. In terms of outright changes in exchange parity, the United States devalued its currency twice in the early 1970s: December 1971 and February 1973. During the subsequent period of generalized floating exchange rates the dollar depreciated through mid-1975 and recovered afterward. Toward the end of 1977, however, the dollar started to decline in value again. (See Exhibit 3.2.)

Exhibit 3.3 shows annual growth rates of relative prices of selected major trading partners of the United States, for the periods 1967–71, 1971 –74, and 1974–77. These countries' exports often compete with the United States. Annual growth rates are also shown for the volume of trade and for some domestic variables thought to affect international prices.

The first panel in Exhibit 3.3 shows the growth rates for export prices expressed in both U.S. dollars and local currency and the growth rates for export volume. The dollar export prices allow one to place all export prices

[5] Note that these trade figures have been computed on the Census Bureau basis in contrast to the balance of payments basis used in Exhibit 2.2. This explains the small discrepancy between the total trade figures in the two exhibits.

EXHIBIT 3.1. United States Merchandise Trade by End-Use, 1967–1977 (millions of dollars)[a]

	1967	1968	1969	1970	1971	1972	1973	1974	1975	1976	1977[p]
Foods, feeds, and beverages											
Exports	4,998	4,813	4,688	5,839	6,054	7,489	15,075	18,459	19,049	19,677	19,611
Imports	4,586	5,271	5,238	6,154	6,366	7,265	9,113	10,570	9,644	11,548	13,981
	412	-458	-550	-315	-312	224	5,962	7,889	9,405	8,129	5,630
Industrial supplies and materials											
Exports	9,971	11,004	11,776	13,782	12,691	13,980	19,766	30,396	30,188	32,005	34,302
Imports	11,856	14,159	14,160	15,106	16,965	20,322	26,713	51,306	48,819	60,904	76,362
	-1,885	-3,155	-2,384	-1,324	-4,274	-6,342	-6,947	-20,910	-18,631	-28,899	-42,060
Capital goods, except automotive											
Exports	9,913	11,072	12,346	14,371	15,119	16,690	21,512	29,921	35,451	38,330	39,304
Imports	2,412	2,819	3,244	3,814	4,127	5,572	7,584	9,302	9,554	10,946	14,002
	7,501	8,253	9,102	10,557	10,992	11,118	13,928	20,169	25,897	27,384	25,302
Automotive vehicles, parts and engines											
Exports	2,784	3,453	3,888	3,652	4,396	5,119	6,343	8,162	10,077	11,243	12,132
Imports	2,604	4,256	5,288	5,894	7,917	9,327	10,886	11,961	11,673	16,155	18,668
	180	-803	-1,400	-2,242	-3,521	-4,208	-4,543	-3,799	-1,596	-4,912	-6,536
Consumer goods (nonfood) except automotive											
Exports	2,111	2,334	2,576	2,719	2,847	3,492	4,705	6,267	6,458	7,901	8,818
Imports	4,213	5,375	6,616	7,553	8,561	11,355	13,185	14,751	13,712	18,410	21,796
	-2,102	-3,041	-4,040	-4,834	-5,714	-7,863	-8,480	-8,484	-7,254	-10,509	-12,978
Other											
Exports (include military-type goods)	1,846	1,961	2,731	2,862	3,023	3,007	3,937	5,302	6,368	5,837	7,074
Imports	1,212	1,346	1,471	1,400	1,627	1,742	1,993	2,362	2,714	2,717	2,862
	634	615	1,260	1,462	1,396	1,265	1,944	2,940	3,654	3,120	4,212
Total											
Exports	31,622	34,636	38,006	43,224	44,130	49,778	71,339	98,507	107,591	114,992	121,243
Imports	26,882	33,225	36,043	39,952	45,563	55,583	69,476	100,252	96,116	120,678	147,671
	4,740	1,411	1,963	3,272	-1,433	-5,805	1,863	-1,745	11,475	-5,686	-26,428

[a]Census basis, including military grant shipments.
[p]Preliminary
SOURCE: U.S. Department of Commerce, Bureau of Economic Analysis, SURVEY OF CURRENT BUSINESS, various issues.

EXHIBIT 3.2. U.S. Dollar: Effective Exchange Rate, 1971-1977[a]

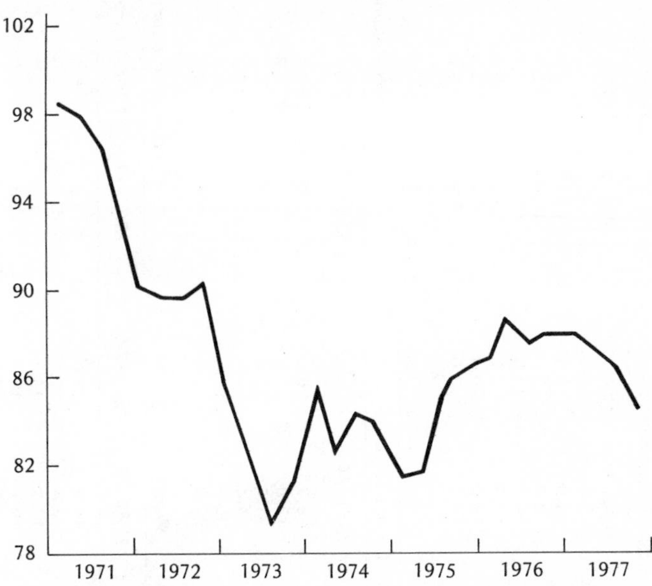

[a]Effective exchange rate changes are an indicator of the extent to which the external value of a country's currency has moved relative to other currencies. Effective exchange rate changes are computed as an index, combining the exchange rates between the currency in question and twenty other major currencies with weights derived from the International Monetary Fund's "Multilateral Exchange Rate Model".* Each weight represents the model's estimate of the effect on the trade balance of the country in question of a change of one percent in the domestic currency price of one of the other currencies. The weights, therefore, take account of the size of trade flows as well as of the relevant price elasticities and the feedback effects of exchange rate changes on domestic costs and prices. The measure is expressed as an index based on the par values in May 1970.

*Jacques R. Artus and Rudolf R. Rhomberg, "A Multilateral Exchange Rate Model," INTERNATIONAL MONETARY FUND STAFF PAPERS (November 1973), pp. 591-611.

SOURCE: Federal Reserve Bank of St. Louis, INTERNATIONAL ECONOMIC CONDITIONS, March 6, 1978, p. 8.

under a common denominator after accounting for changes in exchange rate parities. Export prices expressed in local currency reflect the rate of inflation in the country before adjustments for changes in exchange rates.

The deterioration of the trade account of the United States during 1967-71 can be explained at least partially by the fast growth in the prices of U.S. exports relative to other developed countries. This deterioration in the international competitiveness of U.S. goods was reflected both in a relatively slow growth in export volume and a relatively fast growth in import volume. The factors behind this deterioration in price competitiveness cannot be traced back definitely to the domestic inflation rate relative to other countries or to increases in U.S. wages since the other countries often experienced higher inflation

EXHIBIT 3.3. Trade, Prices, and Costs for Selected Industrialized Countries, 1967–1977 (Compounded Annual Growth Rates, in percentages)

	Export Prices								
	In U.S. Dollars			*In Local Currency*			*Export Volume*		
	1967–71	*1971–74*	*1974–77*	*1967–71*	*1971–74*	*1974–77*	*1967–71*	*1971–74*	*1974–77*
France	2.5	17.3	7.7	5.6	11.9	8.2	12.7	11.3	3.7
Germany	4.4	17.5	7.3	1.1	8.3	3.6	10.6	12.3	2.2
Italy	3.6	17.5	6.3	3.4	19.6	17.8	10.7	7.1	7.3
Japan	2.8	20.6	3.8	2.5	12.3	1.2	19.3	9.5	8.9
United Kingdom	2.5	14.0	9.5	5.8	15.2	20.6	8.7	6.9	5.1
United States	3.4	15.2	7.0	3.4	15.2	7.0	5.2	13.8	0.2
	Import Prices								
	In U.S. Dollars			*In Local Currency*			*Import Volume*		
	1967–71	*1971–74*	*1974–77*	*1967–71*	*1971–74*	*1974–77*	*1967–71*	*1971–74*	*1974–77*
France	1.5	22.3	5.9	4.3	16.7	6.6	12.5	10.6	4.2
Germany	2.8	20.4	5.3	–.8	13.0	1.6	15.2	4.8	7.7
Italy	3.5	28.2	4.4	3.5	31.7	15.8	9.1	5.3	0.4
Japan	2.3	31.2	5.1	1.5	24.4	—[a]	11.6	12.2	—[a]
United Kingdom	2.5	24.5	6.4	6.0	26.1	17.6	5.4	8.5	0.4
United States	3.9	24.0	6.4	3.9	24.0	6.4	9.6	5.2	6.7
	Wholesale Prices			*Wages*			*Industrial Production*		
	1967–71	*1971–74*	*1974–77*	*1967–71*	*1971–74*	*1974–77*	*1967–71*	*1971–74*	*1974–77*
France	4.6	9.0	2.3	10.9	14.8	17.0	7.0	5.1	0.9
Germany	2.5	6.5	3.7	9.6	9.8	7.1	8.1	2.5	1.3
Italy	3.7	19.7	16.1	9.5	17.3	25.4	4.1	6.2	1.0
Japan	1.4	15.3	3.3	14.3	19.7	13.2	11.8	6.3	1.0
United Kingdom	5.8	10.7	20.2	9.6	14.8	17.1	2.4	1.9	—[a]
United States	3.3	12.0	6.7	6.0	7.3	8.5	1.6	5.6	2.0

[a]Negative growth rate.

SOURCE: International Monetary Fund, INTERNATIONAL FINANCIAL STATISTICS, various issues.

rates. Instead, it seems that while the costs of production were not increasing very much relative to other countries, the slow growth in production was not sufficient to hold down export prices. In contrast, 1971-74 shows the United States in a much brighter light. The price competitiveness of the country's goods had improved as its export prices grew relatively less than those in other countries. As a result, the volume of goods exported increased considerably and the growth in volume of goods imported was relatively less than in other developed countries in spite of the oil crisis. During 1967-74 U.S. exports and imports both appear to have a relatively high price elasticity that makes the U.S. trade accounts responsive to changes in the competitiveness of the country's prices. When we examine the price and trade data for 1974-77, however, this relationship appears to break down. U.S. export prices in dollar terms often increased only slightly less than the export prices of other countries, yet on average the U.S. trade account deteriorated drastically over this period. Other factors, such as relative income discussed below, appear to have affected the price-trade relationship.

When the objective of the analysis is a forecast, it becomes necessary to disaggregate export prices between domestic prices and exchange rates and to anticipate the interaction between the two variables. Increases in domestic prices tend to lead to a devaluation of the currency in question. However, the timing of such a devaluation often becomes a political decision in which domestic and balance of payments objectives are weighed one against the other.[6] Even under the current condition of managed floating among the major currencies used in international trade, the acquiescence of any government in a depreciation or appreciation of its currency is sought, and it often depends on domestic economic and political considerations.

Furthermore, the relevant export prices are relative export prices. One must analyze the price behavior for each of the major trading partners and compare each with the country in question. Although a price increase in a given country may be unavoidable because of wage increases and the lack of increases in productivity, the trade account and the exchange rate may remain unchanged. This would be the case if the trading partners of the country experience comparable price increases—relative purchasing power remains constant—and the products traded have similar price elasticities in all the trading countries. The model that links exchange rates or trade performance to the changes in relative prices is the *purchasing power parity theory*. This is discussed in the next chapter.

Relative National Incomes. The impact of national income on trade derives from the impact of this variable on national consumption and investment. When national income goes up, both consumption and investment increase. Some of this consumption and investment is channeled to foreign markets via imports. Therefore, if we want to know the impact of relative national incomes on trade, we must first find out who are the major trading partners and what goods are traded with each partner.

Exhibit 3.4 classifies the merchandise trade balance and the balance on

[6] The relationships between changes in exchange rates and domestic economic variables are explored in detail in the following chapter.

trade in goods and services for the United States by geographic area and selected countries for 1975–1977. The merchandise trade balances show the United States in a large net import position against Japan, Canada, Latin America, and "other countries in Asia and Africa" and as a net exporter to Western and Eastern Europe, and to Australia, New Zealand, and South Africa. Within the European Economic Community the net export position contains sizable imports from Germany. Latin America and "other countries in Asia and Africa," were net importers of goods from the United States until recently. Venezuela in Latin America and the multiple oil-producing countries in Asia and Africa have made the United States a net importer in the trade account with these areas. We saw in Exhibit 3.1 the large increase in the trade deficit of industrial supplies

EXHIBIT 3.4. U.S. Balance of Trade by Selected Areas and Countries 1975–1977 (millions of dollars)[a]

(Surplus +; deficit –)	*1975*	*1976*	*1977*
All areas			
Merchandise trade	9,045	-9,353	-31,059
Goods and services	23,023	9,361	-10,513
European Economic Community (9)[b]			
Merchandise trade	6,341	7,195	4,414
Goods and services	3,700	5,393	2,734
United Kingdom			
Merchandise trade	1,144	947	901
Goods and services	254	23	604
Other Western Europe[c]			
Merchandise trade	2,779	1,689	1,490
Goods and services	2,160	1,521	1,240
Eastern Europe			
Merchandise trade	2,515	3,226	1,786
Goods and services	2,662	3,424	1,998
Canada			
Merchandise trade	1,827	-139	-1,371
Goods and services	6,809	5,931	4,896
Latin American Republics			
Merchandise trade	931	-361	-3,252
Goods and services	5,276	4,788	2,605
Japan			
Merchandise trade	-1,690	-5,335	-7,984
Goods and services	-1,179	-5,359	-8,091
Australia, New Zealand and South Africa			
Merchandise trade	1,266	1,441	988
Goods and services	2,518	3,132	2,543
Other Countries in Asia and Africa			
Merchandise trade	-4,922	-16,760	-26,476
Goods and services	1,442	-8,937	-17,334

[a]Adjusted to balance of payments basis; excludes exports under U.S. military agency sales contracts and imports under direct defense expenditures.

[b]The European Economic Community (9) includes Belgium, France, Germany, Italy, Luxembourg, the Netherlands, the United Kingdom, Denmark and Ireland.

[c]"Other Western Europe" excludes the "EEC (9)".

SOURCE: U.S. Department of Commerce, Bureau of Economic Analysis, SURVEY OF CURRENT BUSINESS, Table 10, various issues.

(including oil) that the United States has experienced, particularly since 1974. In addition, a number of non-oil developing countries such as Brazil, Mexico, Taiwan, and Singapore have stepped up their industrial production at a faster rate than developed countries. They have succeeded in capturing a larger share of both the world market and U.S. imports, besides providing additional competition for U.S. exports.

As Exhibit 3.1 showed, the United States has a strong net export position in capital goods. This is the type of good one would expect to respond to changes in income promptly. Using the concept of elasticity, one may say that the goods for which the United States has a trade advantage tend to be *income elastic.* Similarly, the goods for which the United States has a strong net import position–industrial supplies–tend to be *income inelastic.*[7] However, the decline in the growth of oil imports while the United States was experiencing a slowdown in 1974 reflects a certain degree of income elasticity for these goods.

A complete analysis of the relationship between national income, or aggregate demand, and foreign trade would require a disaggregation of goods traded between the United States and each of its major trading partners. Short of this analysis one can make some inferences from the information in the preceding two paragraphs on the U.S. trade position with major partners and types of goods traded. For example, other things remaining constant, when the trade partners of a country are in an expansionary phase of their business cycle while the country is experiencing a slowdown in its economy, the balance of trade of this country is likely to improve. The country's exports will increase in response to the higher demand from abroad. Its imports will decrease as national income declines.

Different phases in the business cycle are considered to be one of the factors underlying the U.S. balance of trade deficit in 1971 and 1972. During those years the United States was undergoing an expansion while its major trading partners, Western Europe and Japan, experienced a lull in their economies. By 1973 all the major developed economies were in an expansionary stage which reversed itself by 1974 when the rates of change in industrial production became negative.

The protracted recession in the United States through 1975 while other developed countries initiated their recovery contributed to the trade surplus of

[7]More specifically, income elasticity is measured by the percentage change in imports associated with a given percentage change in national income. This is equivalent to the ratio of the marginal propensity to import to the average propensity.

$$\eta_Y = \frac{\Delta M}{M} \div \frac{\Delta Y}{Y} = \frac{\Delta M}{\Delta Y} \times \frac{Y}{M} = \frac{\Delta M}{\Delta Y} \div \frac{M}{Y} = \frac{MPM}{APM}$$

where η_y = income elasticity

Y = national income

M = imports

MPM = marginal propensity to import

APM = average propensity to import

The levels of Y and M, in contrast to changes, are usually measured at the midpoint between the initial and the final levels.

the United States in that year. But by 1976 and 1977 the U.S. expansion was a force behind the large deficit in the trade account. Economic recovery proceeded at a much faster rate in the United States than in the other industrialized countries.

A large amount of U.S. exports are sold to developing countries. In many cases, the income of these countries depends heavily on world prices for the commodities which they produce. As world prices for commodities other than oil skyrocketed in 1974, many of the revenues acquired by these countries found their way into the export account of the United States. Increased international lending to developing countries also has supported the imports of these countries. (See Chapter 14.)

Price or Income Effects. So far we have discussed the effects of changes in prices and income separately. In reality, prices and incomes often change simultaneously. Econometric models in which trade flows are explained in terms of several variables try to capture this reality. Unfortunately, the parameters estimated by these models, although good in explaining historical data, are limited in their forecasting capabilities. The parameters appear to change through time.

Exhibit 3.5 summarizes the types of income and price elasticities that tend to characterize the demand for three major groups of traded goods: food, industrial supplies, and manufactured goods. At one end food can be considered to have both low price and income elasticities. A simplistic picture of the demand for food is that food consumption in the world is relatively fixed, especially as it approaches survival levels. The amount of food the United States will export depends on how successful the world supply is in meeting the demand for food. In cases of bad harvests abroad the United States can expect to have higher demand for its food exports.

The demand for industrial supplies appears to be better explained as being highly dependent on income changes. Once a certain amount of these supplies is determined to be needed, changes in prices do not appear to alter very much the amount of purchases.

The demand for manufactured goods is usually considered to be both price and income elastic. It is here where conflicting results between the analysis of changes in prices and changes in income can easily occur. An increase in domestic prices tends to decrease the demand for exports; however, if foreign countries are expanding at a high rate, this will tend to increase the demand for the given country's exports. The actual result will depend on the relative strength of these two opposing forces. Manufactured goods are also more highly differentiated than commodities. Copper of certain quality has an identifiable world price, but a piece of machinery is not so easily identified and priced. This is especially so

EXHIBIT 3.5. Characteristic Demand Elasticities of Major Types of Goods

	Demand Elasticity	
	Price	*Income*
Food	Low	Low
Industrial supplies (raw materials)	Low	High
Manufactured goods		
Highly specialized	Low	High
Not specialized	High	High

when a high degree of technology is involved. Goods that appear to be substitutes for one another may not be so when the use is highly specialized because of associated technology; e.g., a specific type of radar that operates in conjunction with a specialized family of instruments. In these cases, it would appear that price changes have a very small impact on sales.

Finally, adjustments in purchasing patterns take time. Given a change in prices and income, the longer the time one allows for adjustment, the larger the change in trade patterns. In the very short term, changes in prices can have the opposite effect of the anticipated one. Currency devaluations have often been followed by a deterioration in trade balances.

However, the larger the change in prices or income, the faster the adjustment is likely to occur. This can be so even in commodities that have been considered price inelastic. The large increase in world coffee prices in 1975 succeeded in reducing the total amount of coffee consumption in the United States. Estimates of elasticities relate to price and income changes in the neighborhood of those previously observed. When very large changes in price or income occur, those elasticity estimates are no longer applicable.

Other Factors

In addition to the economic considerations mentioned above, there are other elements that affect trade accounts. Among these, tariffs and nontariff barriers to trade occupy a central position. Though the trend in the postwar period has been toward liberalization of barriers, protectionism is still a strong deterrent to trade. Some of the movements toward liberalization of trade have taken place through the creation of custom unions and free trade areas such as the European Economic Community (EEC) and the European Free Trade Association (EFTA). The entry of the United Kingdom into the EEC in 1973 and the association of other EFTA countries with the EEC promise an eventual total integration of trade policies between EEC and EFTA countries. The recent oil price increases promise either greater integration or a reversion to protectionism, depending on which policies the countries choose in handling the problem. Free trade areas have not achieved much success so far among developing countries.

Another important factor in the trade accounts is provided by the multinational corporation. Companies with a high degree of rationalization in their world production provide continuous trade flows in and out of various countries. These flows accommodate changes in demand throughout the world in general and the production plans of multinational companies in particular.

One more item affecting the trade accounts is "tied" aid. When governmental foreign aid is granted on the condition that funds be used to buy the donor's goods, the export account will benefit unless these exports substitute for exports that would have taken place in any case.

SERVICES

The major categories in this group of accounts are travel, transportation, and income from foreign investment. (See Exhibit 3.6.) The travel figure is composed of the expenditures made by tourists visiting a country. Transportation involves passenger fares as well as shipping freights. The income from

EXHIBIT 3.6. Selected Accounts in the Service Account of the U.S. Balance of Payments, 1971-1977 (millions of dollars)

	1971	*1973*	*1975*	*1977*
Travel (net)	-1,839	-2,114	-1,578	-1,287
Receipts	2,534	3,412	4,839	6,164
Payments	-4,373	-5,526	-6,417	-7,451
Passenger fares (net)	-675	-815	-1,224	-1,477
Receipts	615	975	1,039	1,366
Payments	-1,290	-1,790	-2,263	-2,843
Other transportation (net)	199	-157	250	-280
Receipts	3,277	4,434	5,785	6,983
Payments	-3,078	-4,591	-5,535	-7,263
Income on direct investment (net)	5,362	7,685	7,521	17,022
Receipts	9,159	16,542	16,615	19,851
Payments	-1,164	-1,610	-2,234	-2,829
Income on other private assets (net)	213	121	1,856	4,657
Receipts	2,641	4,330	7,644	10,881
Payments	-2,428	-4,209	-5,788	-6,224
Income associated with U.S. government (net)	-956	-3,010	-3,423	-4,172
Receipts	888	826	1,119	1,368
Payments	-1,844	-3,836	-4,542	-5,540

SOURCE: Exhibit 2.2.

foreign investment is composed of interest, dividends, investment fees, royalties, branch earnings, and earnings reinvested in subsidiaries incorporated abroad.[8]

The determinants of these accounts are easy to identify. Tourists' expenditures are primarily a function of income. Citizens of rich countries tend to travel abroad more than those of poor countries. Transportation figures are related to the amount of travel in which the country's citizens are involved and to the volume and nature of its merchandise trade. This figure also depends on the transportation facilities that the country possesses. Finally, the returns on foreign investment are a function of investments made in the past. Large investments in foreign assets should produce relatively high investment income in the future.

The service account in the U.S. balance of payments shows a large deficit in the travel and transportation balance. However, contrary to statements made to the effect that this account is very insensitive to changes in relative income and prices, 1973 witnessed a reversal in the trend toward larger deficits. The

[8]The definition of income on direct investment in the U.S. balance of payments was modified in June 1978 to include earnings reinvested in subsidiaries incorporated abroad. U.S. balance of payments prepared before that date include the income involved in branch earnings, but not in earnings reinvested in subsidiaries. The figures presented in this text are all in accordance with the new definition. The other account in the balance of payments affected by this change in definition is direct investment.

deterioration in the value of the U.S. dollar relative to the currencies of most developed countries during the early 1970s, together with the recession at home and the increases in the cost of transportation, reduced U.S. travel abroad and encouraged residents of other countries to visit the United States. For example, 1974 witnessed the first year since 1961 when the number of U.S. visitors to Europe failed to increase, with the figure actually declining by 6% from 1973.

The major source of foreign exchange in the service account of the United States is income in investments. Although the bulk of the receipts of investment is concentrated on income from direct investment, the payments are mainly for liabilities of a portfolio nature. This is partially because of the accumulation of U.S. liabilities in foreign hands as a result of protracted past balance of payments deficits.

In terms of the service balances by major areas, Exhibit 3.4 shows that when services are added to the merchandise trade, the balance becomes less positive or more negative in the case of Western European countries. The service account of the United States with these countries is in deficit. With other areas the United States has a surplus in the service account. The travel of U.S. residents to Europe, the income European countries receive from their large holdings of U.S. liabilities, and European receipts for NATO forces make the United States a net importer of services from European countries. For the rest of the world the United States is primarily a net exporter of services.

UNILATERAL TRANSFERS

Traditionally, unilateral transfers are separated between those of the government and those of private citizens. Transfers initiated by the government are of two types: military and others. In the case of the United States, both categories play in important role. (Military grants are not included in the U.S. balance of payments account since the grant account is fully compensated in the export account. See lines 14 and 28 in Exhibit 2.2.) Other government transfers include pensions paid by the U.S. government—Social Security benefits—to individuals who retired to live abroad.

The nature of private unilateral transfers is very much a function of the immigration profile of the country. Countries that are net importers of people, like the United States, have a negative figure in this account. (See line 32 in Exhibit 2.2.) Countries that are net exporters of people (Spain, for example) have a positive figure.

LONG-TERM CAPITAL FLOWS

In the current presentation of the U.S. balance of payments (Exhibit 2.2) capital flows are not grouped by maturity. Instead, there are two major groups: U.S. assets abroad and foreign assets in the United States (lines 33 and 50 in Exhibit 2.2). However, because the analysis is facilitated by separating the flows by maturity and because the balance of payments presentation of the International Monetary Fund (IMF) and of most countries do segregate the flows by maturity, we will follow the conventional classification. This classification was discussed in the first part of Chapter 2.

The major types of long-term capital movements are government flows, direct investment, and portfolio investment.

Government Flows

The motivation behind the changes in long-term loans among governments is similar to that behind government grants. This is in contrast to changes in reserve assets and short-term loans to governments which are discussed later in this chapter. Some of these loans are for development projects, others are associated with defense, and others simply reflect the government's foreign policy. Although all of these loans carry interest, not all have a fixed repayment schedule. The U.S. government is traditionally a net lender to other governments. In 1977 it lent a *net* amount of $3.7 billion to foreign countries. (See lines 40–41 in Exhibit 2.2.)

Direct Investment

Direct investment, broadly speaking, is the purchase of capital goods in one country by residents of another country when substantial ownership and management are involved. Substantial ownership has been arbitrarily defined as 10% or more. Direct investment takes three different forms: intercompany accounts, equity contributions, and retained earnings. Examples of intercompany transactions are shipment of machinery to a foreign subsidiary or a loan from a subsidiary to the parent company. The purchase of equity is any contribution of capital to a foreign subsidiary as long as the owner possesses more than 10% ownership of the foreign company. Finally, the type of foreign direct investment that does not involve a capital outflow is retained earnings in a foreign subsidiary or branch.[9]

The general motivation for international investment is a higher anticipated rate of return in the foreign country than in the home country. A mature country tends to increase its investment abroad as its own stock of capital grows and its rate of return falls relative to other countries. Economists who have found this explanation too general have looked for more specific explanations, such as a cheaper labor or raw material source, or economies of scale in large production units. Some of the factors inducing direct investment are discussed in Part Three.

Direct foreign investment of the United States is considerably larger than that of foreigners in this country. However, starting with 1973 there has been a notable increase in direct investment by foreigners in the United States. The devaluations of the U.S. dollar in 1971 and 1973 appear to have made investment in the United States more attractive to foreigners. (See Exhibit 3.7.)

[9] As noted in the preceding footnote, before June 1978 earnings retained in foreign branches were reported as income (Cr.) and direct investment (Dr.), but earnings retained in subsidiaries were not. The figures presented in this text are in accordance with the new definition.

EXHIBIT 3.7. U.S. Direct Investment, 1970-1977 (millions of dollars)
(+ = decrease in claims or increase in liabilities, a source of funds)
(– = decrease in claims or decrease in liabilities, a use of funds)

	1970	1971	1972	1973	1974	1975	1976	1977
U.S. DIRECT INVESTMENT ABROAD[a]								
Transactions with foreign incorporated affiliates								
Intercompany account								
short-term	-690	-1,132	-216	-1,719	-3,705	-238	-329	-683
long-term	-312	-586	-18	-30	-238	-43	45	330
Capital stock and other equity	-2,311	-1,932	-1,873	-1,771	-1,793	-1,490	-1,128	-1,316
Miscellaneous	-184	-27	-55					
Total transactions with foreign incorporated affiliates	-3,496	-3,677	-2,162	-3,549	-5,736	-1,771	-1,412	-1,669
Reinvested earnings of foreign incorporated affiliates	-3,176	-3,176	-4,532	-8,158	-7,777	-8,048	-7,696	-7,312
Transactions with foreign unincorporated affiliates (branches)	-949	-1,088	-1,242	-1,324	-1,719	-4,425	-2,506	3,235
Total U.S. direct investment abroad	-7,621	-7,941	-7,936	-13,030	-15,232	-14,244	-11,614	-12,216
FOREIGN DIRECT INVESTMENT IN THE U.S.[a]								
Transactions with incorporated U.S. affiliates								
Intercompany accounts	191	-384	-139	818	540	54	1,099	779
Capital stock and other equity	742	232	206	1,487	1,375	1,114	1,249	1,049
Total transactions with incorporated U.S. affiliates	933	-153	66	2,305	1,915	1,168	2,347	1,828
Reinvested earnings of U.S. incorporated affiliates	434	542	569	910	1,065	1,189	1,659	1,572
Transactions with unincorporated U.S. affiliates (branches)	36	86	94	232	308	246	340	-63
Total direct investment in the U.S.	1,403	475	729	3,447	3,289	2,603	4,347	3,338
NET DIRECT INVESTMENT	-6,218	-7,466	-7,207	-9,583	-11,943	-11,641	-7,267	-8,878

[a] These totals differ from those shown in Exhibit 2.2 because the revisions incorporated in Exhibit 2.2 are not available for the disaggregation of this table.

SOURCE: U.S. Department of Commerce, Bureau of Economic Analysis, SURVEY OF CURRENT BUSINESS, Table on Direct Investment, various issues.

Generally, most direct investments are in subsidiaries incorporated in the recipient country rather than branches. The U.S. acquisition of capital stock of companies located abroad has been declining since 1970. However, direct investment in the form of short-term intercompany accounts has increased drastically in some years. The years when U.S. companies extended especially large amounts of credit to their affiliates abroad are 1971, 1973, and 1974. These were years of devaluation and weakness of the U.S. dollar in international markets. Apparently, these companies preferred to leave funds with the subsidiaries instead of remitting them to the parent in the United States. Payments from subsidiaries to the parent were lagged to take advantage of the appreciation of foreign currencies against the U.S. dollar. Intercompany accounts of foreign companies with investments in the United States show a corresponding increase in remittances from the United States in 1971 and 1972. However, 1973 and 1974 saw foreigners increase their investments in the United States both in the form of intercompany accounts and stock acquisitions.

U.S. foreign direct investment tends to be cocyclical. It increases during domestic expansions and decreases during domestic contractions. From 1965 through 1973 these investments were affected by the controls on foreign direct investment imposed by the U.S. government. These controls were imposed initially on a voluntary basis, but they became mandatory from 1968 through 1973; although some reporting requirements remain, the controls were terminated in January 1974.

Portfolio Investment

Portfolio investment involves claims among nations in the form of stocks, bonds, and long-term loans provided the investor does not hold a controlling interest in the foreign company (10% according to U.S. regulations).

The most important factors affecting the behavior of long-term portfolio investments are the levels of interest rates and the expected performances of stock prices in the countries involved. Since the return on foreign securities has to be measured in terms of local currency, the exchange risk of currencies involved also plays an important role. Foreign stocks and bonds are usually exposed to exchange risk. A devaluation in the foreign currency vis-à-vis the local currency will reduce return to the investor. In cases of devaluation-prone currencies, the nominal yield on the investment has to be high enough to compensate for the potential devaluation.

Other factors also affect the relative rate of return on foreign investments. These factors are policies on taxation and regulations that affect foreign investment in particular. The best example is the withholding tax levied by many countries on dividends and interest paid to foreigners. These withholding taxes differ among countries and, in addition, are subject to variations according to special bilateral agreements between particular countries. Other regulations imposed on foreign investments are designed to control them because of balance of payments reasons or nationalistic considerations. Two examples are the former interest equalization tax of the United States and the bardepot tax in Germany during the 1960s and early 1970s. The interest equalization tax was an attempt to deter capital outflows resulting from foreigners borrowing at lower rates in the U.S. market, which caused a drain on U.S. foreign reserves.

Any U.S. holder of a foreign security was subject to a tax on the income from the security. To remain competitive, borrowers would have had to pay a very high interest rate to compensate the security holder for the tax. The bardepot tax was designed to accomplish the opposite, to deter foreigners from investing in German securities; such investment would create a capital inflow, further increasing the level of foreign reserves. In this case the German government imposed special charges on any foreign funds brought into the country.

Exhibit 2.2 (lines 45 and 61) shows the long-term portfolio investment in securities between the United States and the rest of the world. From 1968 to 1973 purchase of U.S. long-term securities by foreigners was considerably larger than the purchase of foreign securities by U.S. residents, a situation that contrasts with the earlier 1960s. In 1974, however, the purchase of U.S. securities by foreigners declined substantially, and U.S. purchases of foreign securities stepped up as controls on investments abroad (the interest equalization tax) were removed. This increase in purchases of foreign securities became very large in 1975-77. The largest share of these purchases is bonds, not stocks.

Foreigners' purchases of securities in the United States are heavily concentrated in stocks. Thus, the changes in foreigners' purchase of U.S. securities have followed the fluctuations in the U.S. stock market. In 1968, when this market peaked, so did foreign purchases of U.S. securities. The decline in foreigners' purchases of U.S. securities between 1968 and 1971 and 1974 was affected by the increased risk of devaluation that foreigners attached to the U.S. dollar. As foreign exchange risk decreased, 1972 and 1973 saw a renewed interest in the U.S. market.

For the whole period, interest rates in the United States have often been among the lowest in the developed countries. The liquidity of the U.S. capital markets is often cited as an advantage which foreign investors appreciate and for which they are willing to accept a lower return in their financial investments.

SHORT-TERM CAPITAL FLOWS

Short-term capital flows represent claims of less than one-year maturity. The classification is on the basis of the instrument rather than on the intentions of the investor. The instruments usually are bank deposits and currency, short-term government securities, commercial paper, export loans, and bankers' acceptances.

Short-term capital flows can be subdivided according to the motivation behind them into two categories: trade capital and speculative flows.

Trade Capital

Most trade transactions are associated with a capital movement, usually of a short-term nature. An exporter who sells merchandise may get paid immediately, in which case demand deposits owned by the country increase. If the sale is invoiced and paid for in local currency, the acquisition of the deposit represents a reduction in liabilities to foreigners. If the payment takes place in a foreign currency, the exporter has acquired a financial claim on foreigners. When credit is extended to the importer either directly by the exporter or through a local commercial bank, the country of the exporter increases its financial claims on foreigners, regardless of the currency in which the sale is denominated.

In the same manner, when merchandise is imported, a capital transaction also takes place. The importing country may pay either with foreign financial assets that it has accumulated earlier or it may receive credit from the exporter. Either a decrease in claims on foreigners or an increase in liabilities to foreigners will take place to finance the imports.

These capital flows, although initially associated with trade transactions, will inevitably be reflected in the financial markets. Take the case of the exporter in the United States. When the export sale is billed in U.S. dollars, the importer must purchase dollars with its own currency before payment is made. When the sale is billed in a foreign currency the U.S. exporter will receive foreign currency in payment. However, since most costs, and certainly most stockholders, are in the United States, the exporter will most likely want to exchange the foreign currency into dollars. Regardless of what currency is used to sell the exports, eventually there will be a sale of foreign currency and a purchase of U.S. dollars. This transaction will usually be done through a commercial bank. Now it is up to the bank to decide whether or not it wishes to maintain the exchange position after selling U.S. dollars to a customer in exchange for foreign currency. The final decision depends on its assessment of relative interest rates and future developments in the exchange markets. This type of decision is discussed below as a speculative flow.

Speculative Flows

Speculative flows are capital movements in search of profits because of interest rate differentials and/or expected exchange rate fluctuations. Speculative flows fall into four major groups:

1. *Flows in the search of higher yield in another currency without foreign exchange coverage.* These flows are undertaken on the assumption that the exchange rate will remain fairly constant so that the higher yield can be converted back into the local currency without much loss in foreign exchange. Governments which increase their discount rate in the hope of attracting short-term capital flows to help their balance of payments position do this in the expectation that individuals are willing to take a speculative position.

2. *Flows in response to temporary fluctuations in a foreign exchange rate which is expected to go back to its normal level.* In this situation capital inflows will take place in a country with a temporary balance of payments deficit. A temporary balance of payments deficit will produce a small downward pressure in the exchange rate. If this is considered to be only temporary, it will attract capital flows to take advantage of the expected increase in the exchange rate. The opposite is true in the case of a temporary balance of payments surplus. Both these movements are stabilizing; they help to correct the balance of payments disequilibrium.

3. *Capital flows in anticipation of a permanent movement in the exchange rate.* In this case capital will flow into the currencies that are expected to

be upvalued and away from currencies expected to be devalued. If a balance of payments surplus is expected to lead to an upvaluation, capital inflows will take place in that country. If a deficit in the balance of payments is expected to lead to the devaluation of the currency, capital outflows will take place. In contrast to the second type of speculative capital flow, this type is destabilizing.

4. *Speculative flows associated with trade, usually known as "leads and lags."* If a currency is expected to appreciate in value, foreigners making payments in that currency will accelerate payment of their obligations in that currency (*a lead*). Similarly, if a currency is under pressure, foreigners making payments in that currency will delay payment as long as possible (*a lag*).

Short-term capital movements are the hardest to measure. Particularly in periods of heavy foreign exchange speculation, many end up in the all-encompassing category "errors and omissions" or "statistical discrepancy." In the sections of the balance of payments discussed earlier, the analysis was simplified as the nature of the flow was properly identified. Once the level of exports, for example, was identified, it was explained in terms of alternative variables. In the case of short-term capital movements, however, the analysis is more difficult. The nature of the capital flow must be derived from the attending circumstances. That is, capital flows in response to trade and capital flows initiated by other considerations are not properly segegated. The problem is not a trivial one since the impact on the future of the country's balance of payments and its foreign exchange rate is completely different depending on the nature of the short-term capital flow.

Exhibit 3.8 shows all the short-term capital accounts for the United States regardless of the definition of deficit. The exhibit presents all the changes in short-term claims on foreigners, including changes in reserve assets, in the upper section. The following section of the exhibit shows the changes in short-term liabilities of the United States to foreigners. Finally, the line for "statistical discrepancy" is included as if it consisted mostly of short-term capital flows. If so interpreted, this account shows a relatively steady increase in holdings of short-term foreign assets until 1973 with a very high increase in 1971. In 1975 and 1976, however, a surprisingly large positive "statistical discrepancy" appeared for the first time in the recent past.

The algebraic sum of the changes in claims plus changes in liabilities plus statistical discrepancy produces the same amount as the balance on current account plus long-term capital.

A major explanation behind the increase in claims of the United States on foreigners since 1964 is the Voluntary Credit Restraint Program initiated in that year to curtail the credit extended from the United States to foreigners. In 1971 a modification in this program exempted loans to foreigners associated with U.S. exports and the loan figure increased significantly for the first time in seven years. In early 1974 the Voluntary Credit Restraint Program was eliminated altogether and the claims of the United States on foreigners soared. A world in dear need for credit to pay for oil imports provided the other element in the substantial lending to the United States to foreigners that year and subsequently.

The changes in liabilities of the United States are more telling of the nature of international capital flows that prevailed during the 1965-77 period.

EXHIBIT 3.8. U.S. Short-Term Capital Flows, 1965, 1967–1977 (millions of dollars)[a]
(+ = decrease in claims or increase in liabilities, a source of funds)
(– = increase in claims or decrease in liabilities, a use of funds)

	1965	*1967*	*1968*	*1969*	*1970*	*1971*	*1972*	*1973*	*1974*	*1975*	*1976*	*1977*
CLAIMS ON FOREIGNERS												
U.S. official reserve assets (line 34)	1,222	52	-880	-1,187	2,477	2,348	32	209	-1,434	-607	-2,530	-231
U.S. foreign currency and short-term assets (line 42)	-16	209	62	89	-16	182	165	-602	541	-3	133	47
Short-term claims reported by:												
U.S. nonbanking concerns (line 47)	429	-498	-982	298	-10	-1,061	-811	-1,987	-2,747	-1,015	-2,035	-1,725
U.S. banks (line 49)	325	-730	-105	-867	-1,122	-2,368	-2,199	-5,047	-18,333	-11,175	-19,006	-10,676
Total changes in short-term claims on foreigners	1,960	-967	-1,905	-1,667	-1,329	-899	-2,813	-7,427	-21,973	-12,800	-23,438	-12,585
LIABILITIES TO FOREIGNERS												
Foreign official assets in the United States (line 51)	132	3,450	-776	-1,301	6,907	26,895	10,705	6,299	10,981	6,960	18,073	37,124
U.S. Treasury securities (line 60)	-131	-135	136	-68	81	-22	-34	-214	697	2,590	2,783	563
Short-term liabilities reported by:												
U.S. nonbanking concerns (line 63)	149	499	759	91	902	-15	221	737	1,934	-94	451	877
U.S. banks (line 65)	262	1,607	3,799	8,726	-6,321	-6,661	4,605	4,475	16,008	908	10,759	6,346
Total changes in short-term liabilities to foreigners	412	5,421	3,918	7,448	1,569	20,197	15,497	11,297	29,620	10,364	32,066	44,910
Net known short-term capital flows	2,372	4,454	2,073	5,781	2,898	19,298	12,684	3,870	7,647	-2,436	8,628	32,325
Statistical discrepancy (line 67)	-457	-206	439	-1,515	-244	-9,822	-1,966	-2,720	-1,555	5,660	9,300	-998
Short-term capital flows plus discrepancy	1,915	4,248	2,512	4,266	2,654	9,476	10,718	1,150	6,092	3,224	17,928	31,327
Balance on current account (line 71)	5,435	2,587	621	406	2,360	-1,407	-5,979	6,885	1,684	18,411	4,339	-15,221
Long-term capital flows	-7,350	-6,835	-3,133	-4,672	-5,881	-8,786	-5,449	-8,035	-7,776	-21,635	-22,267	-16,106
Allocation of SDR's	–	–	–	–	867	717	710	–	–	–	–	–
Basic balance plus SDRs allocation	-1,915	-4,248	-2,512	-4,266	-2,654	-9,476	-10,718	-1,150	-6,092	-3,224	-17,928	-31,327

[a]Line numbers refer to lines in Exhibit 2.2.
[b]Excludes U.S. Treasury securities that are listed as short-term liabilities above.
SOURCE: Exhibit 2.2.

In every year there was an increase in the liabilities of the United States to foreigners. These increases were kept under $3 billion until 1966, but they acquired very large proportions in the subsequent years and reached unparalleled magnitudes in 1971, 1974, and 1976-77. In analyzing the composition of the liabilities to foreigners, the most notable fact is the very large increase in liabilities to official agencies at the expense of the private sector during 1970-71. As the U.S. dollar came under increased attack during those years, the private sector sold its dollar-denominated assets to the public sector. However, during 1974 and 1976-77 when liabilities to official agencies mounted again to record highs, the private sector also shared in the accumulation of dollar-denominated financial assets. Many of these liabilities to foreigners reported by U.S. banks were now owned by OPEC countries in the form of bank deposits.

Two factors can be used to explain the behavior of speculative short-term flows: (1) the strength of the dollar against other currencies and (2) the relative levels of interest rates. As shown in some of the examples above, the relative strength of the dollar finds a one-to-one correspondence with the fluctuations in short-term capital flows. Almost every time the U.S. dollar has weakened in the foreign exchange markets, the liabilities of the United States and the "errors and omissions" (indicating an acquisition of foreign assets by Americans) have increased almost commensurately. Overall the United States has maintained lower interest rates than most of the other developed countries with the exception of Switzerland and Germany. On the basis of relative interest rates alone, there was an incentive for investing in currencies other than the U.S. dollar.

Financing vs. Autonomous Cash Flows

So far we have discussed the various categories of short-term cash flows reported in the U.S. balance of payments and offered some heuristic explanation of the variables that contribute to understanding the behavior of these accounts. However, still to be considered is the distinction between autonomous and compensating transactions.

The impact of the various autonomous transactions on exchange markets can be diagrammed as follows:

MARKET FOR GOODS AND SERVICES

Imports	*Exports*
Supply U.S. dollars Demand foreign currency	Demand U.S. dollars Supply foreign currency

FINANCIAL MARKETS

Sale of Foreign Securities by U.S. *or* *Purchases of U.S. Securities by Foreigners*	*Purchase of Foreign Securities by U.S.* *or* *Sales of U.S. Securities by Foreigners*
Demand U.S. dollars Supply foreign currency	Supply U.S. dollars Demand foreign currency

For the exchange markets to remain in equilibrium and exchange rates constant, the combined effect of transactions in the market for goods and services and the financial markets must produce the following relationship:

$$\left.\begin{array}{c}\text{Supply of U.S. dollars}\\ \text{or}\\ \text{Demand for foreign currency}\end{array}\right\} = \left\{\begin{array}{c}\text{Demand for U.S. dollars}\\ \text{or}\\ \text{Supply of foreign currency}\end{array}\right.$$

The balance of payments figures we have examined report the amount of flows on an historical basis, after the fact. On this basis one can say that all capital flows reported for private parties reflect autonomous transactions. In the absence of controls from the government, the purchases and sales of securities reported in the balance of payments indicate responses to interest rate differentials and anticipations about the exchange markets. In this sense, only the capital flows reported for official authorities can be treated as financing transactions—they filled the gap left by private transactors operating in response to market forces.

Thus, if we want to think of autonomous transactions as a barometer of the pressures in the exchange market, we must look into the future and ask two further questions:

1. How much of future imbalances in the goods and services market will the financial markets want to finance at current interest and exchange rates?

2. How much of the outstanding financial assets will financial markets want to continue holding?

The answer to these questions will provide an estimate of the gap between supply and demand for the various currencies which official agencies will be called to fill if the current rates are to be maintained. If the answers to these two questions indicate that no disequilibrium in the exchange markets will occur and that official agencies can be expected to fill the gap left by financial markets, rates will remain constant. Otherwise, rates will have to change or controls will have to be imposed. To the extent that official agencies are called upon to fill this gap, an assessment must be made of how long these authorities will want, or will be able, to continue in this role.

Assume the basic balance, the balance on current account plus long-term capital flows, is a first approximation to the level of autonomous entries in the U.S. balance of payments. This is presented in the bottom line of Exhibit 3.8. Then we can try to establish whether the short-term capital accounts are of a financing or an autonomous nature. The U.S. basic balance has been in a deficit position consistently, with the minor exception of 1973, throughout the period. This deficit reached astronomical proportions in 1971-72, 1974, and 1976-77.

The accounts of U.S. official reserves and foreign official assets in the United States are basically of a compensating nature and reflect more than any other account the deficits in the U.S. balance of payments. With the exception of 1968 and 1969, the United States decreased the level of its reserve assets in all years between 1960 and 1973. The exceptions for 1968 and 1969 are partly due to the successful efforts to defend the dollar through market intervention in those years. During 1974-77 the United States actually increased its foreign exchange reserves. This is partially because of special international agreements with the International Monetary Fund (IMF). Foreign countries borrowed substantial amounts in U.S. dollars from that institution during 1974-77. This action entitled the United States under the present agreement to increase its unconditional borrowing rights from the IMF. These borrowing rights are considered part of reserves. Finally, the increase in 1975 can be considered caused by the improvement in the current account that year.

Since 1970 the United States has increased its liabilities to foreign official agencies in every single year. The accumulation of dollar-denominated assets in foreign central banks (especially in 1971-72 and 1976-77) reached very large proportions. These were years of record deficits in the U.S. basic balance. Much of this deficit was financed by the willingness of foreign official agencies to extend credit to the United States.

Since 1974 another account that appears to reflect entries of a financing nature is short-term liabilities reported by U.S. banks. Much of this account is represented by deposits owned by oil-producing countries. In effect, these countries also have helped to finance the U.S. deficits by extending credit to the United States in the form of bank deposits. Alternatively, it can be said that these deposits were used to finance the credit needs of the rest of the word as U.S. banks extended loans to these other countries (see short-term claims reported by U.S. banks in Exhibit 3.8). This is what has been called the recycling of petrodollars.

As long as foreign official agencies and oil-producing countries continue to be willing to accept IOUs from the United States, the U.S. deficits on the basic balance and its loans to foreigners could be financed without putting pressure on the exchange rate for the dollar. However, the dollar devaluations in 1971 and 1973 and the dollar's recurrent periods of weakness since then demonstrate that eventually market pressures can be brought to bear on the price of currencies. As the market becomes increasingly reluctant to hold the dollar financial assets generated by the U.S. deficits at existing rates, the dollar rate must depreciate. Nonetheless, the willingness of other countries to hold dollar assets has served as a buffer to the decline in the value of the dollar in the past.

The interest rates in the United States have tended to be among the lowest in the world. It is true that the liquidity offered by the money markets in the United States is unparalleled in any other financial market. This fact was actually used by Professor Kindleberger during the 1960s to argue that the increment in the U.S. liabilities to foreigners was of an autonomous nature.[10] Foreigners were willing to sell long-term financial assets to Americans (foreign direct investment by Americans abroad) in exchange for the short-term securities that the U.S. financial markets had to offer. From this point of view, the U.S. balance of payments was in balance. If short-term capital outflows are considered autonomous, these flows compensate for the deficits in the basic balance. However, the liquidity of the U.S. financial market notwithstanding, as the deficits in the basic balance of the United States mounted, many of the securities issued by the

[10]Charles P. Kindleberger, "Equilibrium in the Balance of Payments," *Journal of Political Economy,* December 1969.

United States must have become less and less desirable to hold as the possibilities of a dollar devaluation increased. The shift in foreign-owned U.S. securities from private to official hands in 1970 and 1971 has to be interpreted as the decision of investors not to hold U.S. dollar denominated securities any longer in contemplation of an imminent devaluation of the U.S. dollar relative to other currencies. Obviously, to the extent that investors anticipated the devaluation and sold their dollar-denominated financial assets or refused to increase their dollar holdings as the dollar deficits continued, they created additional pressures in the foreign exchange market to induce the forecast devaluation. The only way to reduce the possession of dollar-denominated assets is to change the denomination of such assets. For example, exchange U.S. dollar deposits for deutsche mark deposits. In the exchange market, this means an increase both in the supply of dollars and in the demand for deutsche marks. Other things equal, these pressures will tend to decrease the value of the U.S. dollar relative to the deutsche mark.

Thus, we can say that, particularly during the 1970s, speculation on the U.S. dollar's value and relative interest rates reinforced one another to induce autonomous capital flows out of the U.S. dollar and into other currencies. Because of the reserve currency status of the U.S. dollar, the United States was able to finance the deficit in the autonomous accounts by issuing more liabilities on itself.

Notice that this avenue of issuing liabilities to finance balance of payments deficits is open only to reserve-currency countries; only they can issue liabilities (financial assets) that creditors consider to be foreign exchange reserves. Other countries must reduce foreign exchange reserves to finance a deficit in the autonomous accounts of the balance of payments. Even for a country like the United States, one must examine the ability of the country to continue issuing liabilities upon itself before the foreign exchange market decides to penalize the value of the currency. For a developing country, the ability to issue liabilities is much more limited. In these cases an evaluation of the size of the country's reserves relative to its needs is essential to forecasting the future exchange rate of the currency in question.

The above discussion of reserve assets is of great importance in a system of fixed exchange rates where the government is responsible for maintaining the external value of its currency. In such a system, the government exercises its responsibilities by accumulating reserves when it has a surplus in the balance of payments and selling reserves when it has a deficit. In a system of floating rates, market forces determine the external value of the currency; therefore, the government does not have to accumulate reserves to defend the value of the currency when the value is under attack. The international monetary system in operation since 1973 reflects more a system of floating rates than one of fixed rates, at least for the major currencies. These issues are explained in the following chapter.

THE BALANCE OF INDEBTEDNESS

While the *balance of payments* measures the *flows* of economic transactions that take place between the residents of a given country and the rest of the world, the *balance of indebtedness* measures the *levels of assets and liabilities* that the country has vis-à-vis the rest of the world. That is, the changes occurring between two balances of indebtedness drawn at two different points in time are measured by the balance of payments for the period.

The emphasis in the analysis of the international value of a country's currency has been centered around the balance of payments. However, it stands to reason that the two statements, the balance of payments and the balance of indebtedness, should be analyzed in conjunction. Although it is true that a business would go bankrupt for lack of liquidity or inability to pay its current debts, it is also true that continuous deficits in operations can be sustained for a much longer period when the business has a large equity base.

Exhibit 3.9 presents the international investment position of the United States, the balance of indebtedness. The United States has a large surplus of assets over liabilities in its accounts with the rest of the world. However, this surplus had tended to erode throughout the 1960s, although an upturn from this downward trend appeared in 1973. Exhibit 3.9 also shows that although most of the assets the United States has abroad are of a long-term nature, a very large proportion of its liabilities to foreigners have a maturity of less than a year. This fact points to the concern for liquidity in the U.S. balance of payments. However, it should be noted that the net asset position may well be understated since direct investment, the largest U.S. asset abroad, is reported at book value, not market value.

Many of the changes in international exchange arrangements in the last decade will be discussed in the next chapter.

SUMMARY

In this chapter we examined the general economic factors that underlie changes in the balance of payments accounts, with special attention to the U.S. balance of payments.

In *trade*, comparative advantage is the principal factor affecting the *long-term* export/import balance. Whether the advantage comes from comparative labor ratios, capital resources, labor skills as embedded capital, or some other factor is indeterminant. The United States seems to export labor-intensive goods, in spite of relatively high costs per hour of labor. Technological gaps and managerial gaps also have been offered as major explanatory factors for the long-term trade balance. In the *short-term*, changes in relative prices can explain some variability in the trade balance. Relative prices are, in turn, a function of wage rates, productivity, and other costs in a fixed exchange rate world, and they are often measured in a unit cost of production statistic. The price elasticity of demand of each country's imports and exports is important in predicting the ultimate effect of a rise in prices vis-à-vis trading partners for a specific nation. There are different sensitivities in the markets for various goods, and the final trade balance depends on how the elasticities and the volume of each good involved net against each other for the partners. Other major factors in determining the trade balance are shocks (such as the oil crisis), tariff and nontariff barriers, the influence of the multinational corporations in leveling out exports and imports among nations, and the effect of tied aid (military or development aid to a country which must be used to purchase goods from the donating

EXHIBIT 3.9. International Investment Position of the United States at Year-end 1972–1976 (millions of dollars)[a]

Line	*Type of investment*	*1972*	*1973*	*1974*	*1975*	*1976*
1	Net international investment position of the United States	37,130	47,900	58,774	74,597	82,548
2	U.S. assets abroad	198,961	222,809	256,199	295,630	347,369
3	U.S. official reserve assets	13,151	14,378	15,883	16,226	18,747
4	Gold	10,487	11,652	11,652	11,599	11,598
5	Special drawing rights[b,c]	1,958	2,166	2,374	2,335	2,395
6	Reserve position in the International Monetary Fund[b,c]	465	552	1,852	2,212	4,434
7	Foreign currencies	241	8	5	80	320
8	U.S. Government assets, other than official reserve assets	36,134	38,840	38,357	41,814	45,988
9	U.S. loans and other long-term assets	34,136	36,219	36,294	39,819	44,132
10	Repayable in dollars[d]	28,441	30,647	33,053	36,830	41,313
11	Other[e]	5,696	5,571	3,240	2,989	2,819
12	U.S. foreign currency holdings and U.S. short-term assets	1,998	2,621	2,063	1,995	1,856
13	U.S. private assets	149,676	169,591	201,959	237,590	282,634
14	Direct investments abroad	89,878	101,313	110,172	124,212	137,244
15	Foreign securities	27,632	27,792	28,563	35,186	44,581
16	Bonds	17,095	17,766	19,552	25,601	35,128
17	Corporate stocks	10,537	10,026	9,011	9,585	9,453
18	U.S. claims on unaffiliated foreigners reported by U.S. nonbanking concerns	11,427	13,767	16,989	18,425	20,138
19	Long-term	4,658	5,054	5,528	5,960	5,950
20	Short-term	6,769	8,713	11,461	12,465	14,188
21	U.S. claims reported by U.S. banks, not included elsewhere	20,739	26,719	46,235	59,767	80,671
22	Long-term	5,063	5,996	7,179	9,536	11,660
23	Short-term	15,676	20,723	39,056	50,231	69,011
24	Foreign assets in the United States	161,831	174,909	197,425	221,033	264,822
25	Foreign official assets in the United States	63,171	69,639	80,302	87,471	106,337
26	U.S. Government securities	52,906	53,777	57,749	63,292	73,565
27	U.S. Treasury securities	52,607	52,903	56,181	60,846	70,161
28	Other	209	874	1,568	2,446	3,404
29	Other U.S. Government liabilities	1,608	2,761	3,486	5,186	10,125

Line	Item					
30	U.S. liabilities reported by U.S. banks, not included elsewhere	8,469	12,595	18,420	16,262	17,155
31	Other foreign official assets	188	506	647	2,731	5,492
32	Other foreign assets in the United States	98,660	105,270	117,123	133,562	158,485
33	Direct investments in the United States[f]	14,868	20,556	25,144	27,662	30,182
34	U.S. securities other than U.S. Treasury securities	50,693	46,116	34,892	45,338	54,800
35	Corporate and other bonds	11,634	12,600	10,671	10,025	11,934
36	Corporate stocks	39,059	33,516	24,221	35,313	42,866
37	U.S. liabilities to unaffiliated foreigners reported by U.S. nonbanking concerns	10,714	11,712	13,586	13,842	13,018
38	Long term	6,223	6,521	6,431	6,765	5,818
39	Short term	4,491	5,191	7,155	7,077	7,200
40	U.S. long-term liabilities reported by U.S. banks	925	1,152	1,161	881	1,056
41	U.S. Treasury securities and other short-term liabilities reported by U.S. banks	21,460	25,734	42,340	45,839	59,429
42	U.S. Treasury securities	1,159	958	1,655	4,245	7,028
43	Bills and certificates	396	375	1,006	3,214	3,018
44	Bonds and notes	763	583	649	1,031	4,010
45	U.S. short-term liabilities reported by U.S. banks, not included elsewhere	20,301	24,776	40,685	41,594	52,401

[a]Data for 1972–75 are revised; data for 1976 are preliminary.

[b]Total reserve assets include increases from changes in the par value of the dollar, as officially implemented: on May 8, 1972, the increase totaled $1,016 million, consisting of $828 million gold stock, $155 million special drawing rights, and $33 million reserve position in IMF; on October 18, 1973, the increase was $1,436 million, consisting of $1,165 million gold stock, $217 million SDR, and $54 million reserve position in IMF.

[c]Beginning in July 1974, U.S. holdings of special drawing rights and the reserve position include changes in the SDR based on changes in a weighted average of exchange rates for currencies of 16 member countries of the IMF.

[d]Also includes paid-in capital subscription to international financial institutions and outstanding amounts of miscellaneous claims that have been settled through international agreements to be payable to the U.S. Government over periods in excess of one year. Excludes World War I debts that are not being serviced.

[e]Includes indebtedness that the borrower may contractually, or at its option, repay with its currency, with a third country's, currency, or by delivery of materials or transfer of services.

[f]Data for 1973 and subsequent years are based on the results of the 1974 Survey of Foreign Direct Investment in the United States. See the technical note in "Foreign Direct Investment in the United States, 1976," page 30.

SOURCE: U.S. Department of Commerce, Bureau of Economic Analysis, SURVEY OF CURRENT BUSINESS, October 1977, p. 23.

nation). Relative national incomes and different positions in the business cycle also affect the trade balances between nations.

In the area of *services,* which include travel, dividends, and interest, the United States generally exports everywhere except Western Europe. We receive more in these accounts than we give, largely because of past capital exports by the United States. The travel balance for the United States tends to be in deficit and relatively inelastic. However, travel by foreigners to the United States has risen sharply in the last decade. Because of the net imports of immigrants, the United States generally runs a deficit in the *unilateral transfer* account; the immigrant typically sends money home to relatives.

In the *long-term capital account,* government flows are a factor, but the U.S. accounts show particularly large balances in direct investment. Although the U.S. direct investment has been large, increasing fund balances are coming to the United States since 1973. In determining the balance of the third major account in this section, portfolio investment, the major factors are the relative performance of the various stock markets and relative long-term interest rates. Taxation in general and withholding in particular play a part, for many investors in other lands prefer to have no withholding applied to their earnings. Countries that respond to this market demand can have their portfolio investment balance improved.

The most volatile accounts in recent years are the *short-term capital accounts.* These are also the ones most subject to debate over whether they are autonomous or accommodating. As exports increase, the short-term capital account rises with accounts receivable increases, an accommodation. There are often speculative flows of a massive nature, as the pattern of the United States balance of payments during crises in the exchange markets has shown. These flows can be stabilizing or not, depending on whether they accentuate a stampede against a currency or dampen it; most of the managed floating in recent years has sought to ameliorate the effects of these large speculative flows. Finally, although the above comments imply that short-term flows are sometimes accommodating (trade) or autonomous (speculative), they may be autonomous yet derived from a simple desire for access to the U.S. short-term capital markets. Relative interest rates, liquidity, security, and the like many induce foreigners to use the U.S. capital markets for short-term funds. Yet, for balance of payments data collection purposes, we cannot separate funds stimulated by these different motivations.

We also noted the balance sheet for a country, the balance of indebtedness. The United States has a large balance of assets (claims on others) vs. liabilities (claims on the United States). In the short run, long-term capital outflows and travel (for example) both have the same effect on the balance of payments, but the balance of indebtedness treatment of these figures differs. Furthermore, it is hoped that the long-term capital account will furnish economic returns (dividends and interest) in the future. To the extent that past exports of U.S. capital to buy economic interests in the rest of the world have been wise investments, in later years our balance of assets over liabilities, together with our service account in the balance of payments, have benefited. The major source of concern for the U.S. balance of indebtedness is *liquidity*. In recent years about 10% of the assets had a maturity of under one year vs. about 50% or more of the liabilities.

Chapter 4 will discuss many of the issues surrounding changes in the balance of payments adjustment mechanism among countries.

Exercise on Forecasting the Balance of Payments of the United States

Collect the latest data on the U.S. balance of payments. This can be found in *Survey of Current Business* published by the Department of Commerce in March, June, September, and December.

Collect data on the variables relevant to explain the behavior of the various accounts in the balance of payments. Some possible sources are the following:

Department of Commerce, *Survey of Current Business,* special articles on balance of indebtedness (October issue) and international economic indicators.

Morgan Guaranty Trust Company, *World Financial Markets,* monthly issues.

Various Federal Reserve Banks, *Monthly Bulletins,* and special weekly reports.

Board of Governors of the Federal Reserve System, *Monthly Bulletin* and *Weekly Report on Exchange Markets.*

International Monetary Fund, *International Financial Statistics* and *Balance of Payments Yearbook* (pages for major trade partners of the United States).

OECD, *World Trade Statistics.*

The Economist (weekly magazine).

The London Financial Times (daily newspaper).

For each account in the balance of payments, do the following:

1. Describe its behavior:

   a. Performance over the last decade and recently, e.g., fast growth with large fluctuations.

   b. Composition of account, e.g., types of goods traded.

   c. Countries participating in the account, e.g., to whom does the United States export goods?

2. Why did the account behave in that way?

   a. What factors determine the performance of the account? e.g., foreign income.

   b. How did these factors behave during the period analyzed? e.g., foreign income grew less fast than in the U.S.

3. How do you expect these accounts to behave in the future? Why?

Bibliography*

Baldwin, Robert E., "Determinants of the Commodity Structure of U.S. Trade." *American Economic Review,* 1977, pp. 126-146.

Caves, Richard E. and Ronald W. Jones, *World Trade and Payments.* Boston: Little, Brown and Company, 1973.

Denison, Edward F., and William K. Chung, *How Japan's Economy Grew So Fast.* Washington, D.C.: Brookings Institution, 1976.

Deppler, Michael C., and Duncan M. Ripley, "The World Trade Model: Merchandise Trade," *International Monetary Fund Staff Papers,* March 1978, pp. 147-206.

Gray, H. Peter, and Gail E. Makinen, "Balance of Payments Contributions of Multinational Corporations." *Journal of Business,* July 1967, pp. 339-343.

Heller, H. Robert, *International Monetary Economics.* Englewood Cliffs, N.J.: Prentice-Hall, Inc., 1974.

Kindleberger, Charles P., and Peter H. Lindert *International Economics,* 6th ed. Homewood, Ill.: Richard D. Irwin, Inc., 1978.

Kravis, Irving B., and Robert E. Lipsey, "Price Behavior in the Light of Balance of Payments Theories," *Journal of International Economics.* May 1978, pp. 193-246.

Kreinin, Mordechai E., "The Effect of Exchange Rate Changes on the Prices and Volume of Foreign Trade." *International Monetary Fund Staff Papers,* July 1977, pp. 297-329.

Root, Franklin R., *International Trade and Investment,* 4th ed. Cincinnati, Ohio: South-Western Publishing Co., 1978, Part One.

Spitaller, Erich, "A Model of Inflation and Its Performance in the Seven Main Industrial Countries, 1958-76," *International Monetary Fund Staff Papers.* June 1978, pp. 254-277.

Stern, Robert M., *The Balance of Payments: Theory and Economic Policy.* Chicago: Aldine Publishing Company, 1973.

Vernon, Raymond, "A Skeptic Looks at the Balance of Payments." *Foreign Policy,* Winter 1971-1972, pp. 52-65.

—— and Louis T. Wells, Jr., *Manager in the International Economy,* 3rd ed. Englewood Cliffs, N.J.: Prentice-Hall, Inc., 1976.

Walter, Ingo, *International Economics.* New York: The Ronald Press, 1968.

*See also the bibliography to Chapter 4.

Appendix: Checklist for Evaluating the External Position of a Developed Country

A. Environmental and policy factors

   1. Political situation

      a. Goals of ruling party

      b. Permanency of present party. Upcoming elections?

   2. Institutional relationships

      a. Power of central bank to enforce monetary policy

      b. Use of fiscal policy

      c. Relationship between government, financial institutions, and business

   3. Industrial characteristics

      a. Major raw materials

      b. Major outputs

   4. Economic conditions

      a. Unemployment and industrial capacity utilization

      b. Inflation rate

      c. Economic growth: income, industrial production

      d. Currency exchange rate

   5. Government appraisal of economic conditions: to the extent that choices must be made in selecting desired objectives, which ones are likely to be the government preferences? e.g., reduce inflation rate or reduce unemployment?

   6. What tools is government likely to use to achieve goals?

      a. Monetary policy

      b. Fiscal policy

B. Trade account: Exports and imports

   1. Product composition—price and income elasticity

   2. Trade partners

   3. Relative prices

      a. Consumer demand relative to supply

      b. Wages

         (1) Labor organization

         (2) Unemployment rate

         (3) Future labor demands, strikes?

      c. Productivity

         (1) Technological developments

         (2) Labor skills

         (3) Capital investments

- d. Government policy
  - (1) Expansionary vs. contractionary
  - (2) Importance of the export lobby
  - (3) Export subsidies
- 4. Relative incomes
  - a. Growth in national income
    - (1) Consumption
    - (2) Investment
    - (3) Government expenditure
  - b. Distribution of income-consumption patterns
  - c. Government policy
- 5. Trade barriers

C. Service account
- 1. Any important item?
- 2. Why?
- 3. Permanency

D. Unilateral transfers
- 1. Is it important?
- 2. Will it continue?

E. Long-term capital accounts
- 1. Countries involved
- 2. Direct investment
  - a. Need for raw materials
  - b. Product cycle
- 3. Portfolio investment
  - a. Stock market performance
  - b. Long-term interest rates
  - c. Economic outlook for profits
  - d. Demand for funds: private and public
  - e. Monetary policy: money supply and interest rates
  - f. Savings patterns: sectoral financing
  - g. Controls on international capital flows

F. Short-term capital accounts
- 1. Countries involved
- 2. Trade-associated flows
- 3. Monetary policy, money supply, and interest rates
- 4. Needs for funds: private and public
- 5. Flows in speculation of foreign exchange parities
- 6. Savings patterns: sectoral financing
- 7. Controls on international capital flows

G. Reserves
   1. Involuntary changes resulting from changes in previous accounts
   2. Voluntary changes due to government intervention to support foreign exchange values
   3. How long can they continue intervention?
      a. Reserve levels and borrowing power
      b. Economic consequences

Appendix: Checklist for Evaluating the External Position of a Developing Country[11]

Size	Population GNP
Development	GNP/capita Percent GNP from industry Percent population in agriculture
Growth	Real growth per capita Trend Industrial growth
Potential	Investment ratio Minerals
U.S. Involvement	Percent with U.S. (imports, exports) U.S. investment
Political	Stability Relations with U.S.
Ability to Generate Foreign Exchange	Export/import ratio Expected trend of export/import ratio Percent major market(s) Balance of goods, services and transfers Major factors in balance of payments Foreign aid

[11]This list was prepared by Antoine W. van Agtmael, Vice President, Bankers Trust, New York.

External Debt Reserves	Reserves
	Reserves, months of imports
	Net foreign assets
	Total external debt
	Debt servicing ratio
	Debt servicing trend
	Structure of debt
Financial Management	Budget revenues
	Current expenditures
	Investment budget
	Plan

CHAPTER 4

How Do You Repair the Balance of Payments?

As economic pressures start to build imbalances in the external position of a country, an outlet for these forces must be found. Two roads are available: (1) an adjustment in the exchange rate to compensate for the imbalances or (2) a taming of the initial economic pressures through explicit governmental economic policies or through automatic economic mechanisms.

Each strategy or combination of strategies to restore external balance will have a different impact on the exchange market and the domestic economy. Therefore, there will be varying impacts upon individuals operating in various capacities in the international markets. For example, a multinational corporation that borrows funds denominated in Swiss francs but does not have any other business operation in that currency has a very clear preference for how Switzerland should handle any pressure for the Swiss franc to appreciate against other currencies. Since this firm has no other operations in Swiss francs, it cannot generate Swiss francs to pay the debt except by converting another currency, say U.S. dollars, into Swiss francs. If Switzerland chooses to let the exchange rate reflect built-up pressures and if the Swiss franc appreciates relative to other currencies, the multinational company will have to use more U.S. dollars to pay the debt. If, on the other hand, Switzerland chooses to resist the pressures for an appreciation of the Swiss franc and allows domestic prices to increase, the multinational company would not be affected. It would pay back the same amount of U.S. dollars as the Swiss francs were worth when the loan was received.

There is a premium not only in assessing the pressures that will develop in the balance of payments, which is to say in the foreign exchange markets, but also in forecasting how economic authorities will handle the problem. This chapter presents the alternatives available and the trade-offs that government authorities have to make in choosing a course of action when problems emerge in the external balance of the country. The two appendices to this chapter, "Important Dates in the World Monetary System" and "Some International Associations," present a chronology of the major events in the international monetary system during the post-war period and some of the institutions that helped to cope with the problems that developed during this period.

AUTOMATIC MECHANISMS

There are a number of economic relationships that are affected when pressures on the balance of payments develop. Economic forces set in motion as a result of these new conditions often tend to correct the external imbalances created initially. All this happens automatically.

Different schools of economic thought have identified alternative automatic mechanisms as the main conduits by which adjustment in external imbalances takes place. Although acknowledging the existence of other economic relationships, each theoretical camp concentrates its analysis on the relationships they consider to contribute the most to explaining the adjustment process. The differences in emphasis, as will be noted below, can often be traced to the economic conditions which are assumed to be prevalent: full employment or excess capacity and flexibility vs. downward rigidity in wages and prices.

Price Mechanism

This mechanism works through the changes in commodity prices resulting from imbalances in the trade account.

A deficit in the balance of payments caused by an excess of imports over exports implies an increase in demand for the products of the surplus country and a decrease in demand for the products of the deficit country. To the extent that prices are flexible, the increase in demand will cause prices in the surplus country to rise. Meanwhile, the decline in demand in the deficit country will push prices down. This change in relative prices will tend to restore the balance in the balance of payments by stimulating the demand for the products of the deficit country (which has lower prices now) and curbing the demand for the products of the surplus country (where prices have increased).

The specific economic variable assumed to produce the changes in prices is money. In the surplus country the increased foreign sales have produced higher monetary balances in the hands of individuals. It is the expenditure of these additional balances that brings about the price increases in the surplus country—

assuming the economy is working at full employment.[1] Similarly, the loss of money balances in the deficit country will tend to reduce expenditures and decrease domestic prices. This relationship is known as the *price-specie-flow mechanism* and is associated with David Hume, an eighteenth-century philosopher and historian.[2] The gold standard, discussed later in this chapter and prevalent at the time of Hume's writing, relies on this type of relationship to adjust international imbalances.

In a world of downward rigidity in wages and prices and with less than full employment, this automatic mechanism cannot be expected to operate successfully. However, government policy–through a devaluation of the currency–can initiate operation of the mechanism by altering relative prices directly.

The success of a devaluation in correcting the original imbalances depends on the responsiveness of quantity demanded to changes in prices, i.e., the price elasticity of demand for imports. If these elasticities are high, a successful adjustment process is guaranteed. There will be a large increase in the exports of the deficit country and in the imports of the surplus country. If, however, the price elasticities are low, the tendencies would be insufficient to adjust the balance of payments deficit. If the sum of the two countries' respective price elasticities of demand for imports exceeds one, the price adjustment will work. This is known as the *Marshall-Lerner condition.*[3]

Income Mechanism

This adjustment process, which is associated with John Maynard Keynes, concentrates on the relationship between imports and income.[4] When excess capacity exists in the economy, an increase in national expenditures automatically becomes income to the various factors of production–labor, capital, entrepreneurship, and land. When these factors of production spend their increased income, there is a secondary increase in national income and the income-expenditure-income cycle continues. However, each time that the cycle is repeated the increments in income are smaller. This is because there are two major leakages in the system: savings and imports. When consumers have an increase in

[1] This relationship is known as the *quantity theory of money* ($MV = PQ$). Given full employment and a constant velocity of money (V), an increase in money supply (M) produces proportional increases in prices (P).

[2] David Hume, "Political Discourses, 1752." in E. Rotwein, *David Hume, Writings on Economics* (London: Nelson, 1955).

[3] When the supply elasticities in the countries involved are very low (i.e., a given increase in demand can be met only by a very large increase in prices or a given change in price produces a very small change in quantity supplied), the price adjustment process could work even if the sum of the price elasticity of demand for imports were less than one. The Marshall-Lerner condition is sufficient to guarantee the operation of the price adjustment; it is not necessary. A. Marshall, *The Pure Theory of Foreign Trade* (London: The London School of Economics and Political Science, 1930). Abba Lerner, *The Economics of Control* (New York: Macmillan, 1946).

[4] John M. Keynes, *The General Theory of Employment Interest and Income,* (London: Macmillan, 1936).

their income, they do not spend all of it. Part of the income is saved. Of that part of income that is spent, not all of it is spent in the domestic market. Part is spent in foreign markets in the form of imports. This tends to produce a balance of trade deficit, other things remaining equal.

The income changes in the first country affect other countries. An increase in one country's imports is tantamount to an increase in another country's exports. This has an expansionary effect, including secondary income effects, in the exporting country's economy. As a result, there is an increase in imports in the second country. This will affect the initial country which finds its exports increasing, thus compensating its initial tendency to a balance of trade deficit. The final outcome for the two balances of payments depends on the size of the "leakages" (savings and imports) in each country.

Under conditions of full employment the income-adjustment mechanism will be frustrated. When the economy is working at full capacity, increases in expenditure cannot lead to increases in output or real income; they can lead only to inflation. However, inflation can reduce the level of expenditures. At a lower level of expenditures, imports in the deficit country will be reduced and balance will tend to be restored.

The specific conduits by which inflation can reduce the level of expenditures, also referred to as *absorption,* is described by Sidney S. Alexander.[5] In general, the effects depend on the redistribution of wealth created by inflation. With increased inflation, income levels increase in monetary terms but not in real terms. With a progressive system of income tax, higher marginal taxes will increase the proportion of *real* income absorbed by taxation; a decrease in consumption is likely to follow. Inflation also may increase the proportion of income accumulated in the form of profits, instead of wages, and increase the level of savings, instead of consumption. Also, the increase in prices reduces the value of cash and other financial assets held by individuals. This reduction in people's wealth also will tend to decrease consumption. This last effect, the change in value of real money balances, is the core of the monetarists' theory about the adjustment mechanism.

Monetary Adjustments

Given certain levels of income and prices, individuals will decide how much of their income to spend in goods and services and how much to maintain in cash balances (hoarding). If there is full employment, a deficit in the balance of payments implies that the country is spending more than it is producing; i.e., it is spending beyond its current income. In the surplus country the opposite is true: production is larger than domestic expenditures; i.e., the surplus country is accumulating claims on future income of the deficit country.[6]

[5] "The Effects of Devaluation: A Simplified Synthesis of Elasticities and Absorption Approaches," *American Economic Review,* March 1959, pp. 22-41.

[6] A collection of articles on this approach is contained in Jacob A. Frenkel and Harry G. Johnson, eds., *The Monetary Approach to the Balance of Payments* (Toronto: University of Toronto Press, 1976). A good review is presented in Marina *v.* N. Whitman, "Global Monetarism and the Monetary Approach to the Balance of Payments," *Brookings Papers on Economic Activity,* No. 3, 1975, pp. 491-536.

In the absence of an increase in money supply, the deficit country imports are financed by reducing cash balances as individuals pay for the increased purchases. Eventually a minimum of desired cash balances must be reached. At this point foreign purchases will be reduced and the deficit will be eliminated. The process may stop much sooner if the foreign exchange reserves maintained by the country and/or its external borrowing power are not sufficient to meet the increased demand for foreign purchases. On the other hand, the deficit may be prolonged as long as the monetary authorities continue to expand credit in order to replenish the money balances held by individuals. Of course, this credit creation would also be arrested by the decline in exchange reserves and borrowing power.

In the surplus country the increased sales to foreigners translate into increased money balances. If individuals do not want to hold increased cash balances at the current prices, the acquired funds will be channeled into purchases of goods in the domestic market and abroad. The increased level of imports will tend to reduce the initial surplus. Increased domestic purchases will reduce the amount of goods available to foreigners.

The effectiveness of this mechanism rests on the inability of the monetary policy to counteract the changes in money supply produced by a balance of trade surplus or deficit. In the case of a deficit, the level of exchange reserves maintained by the country (plus borrowing power) impose a physical limit to the deficit. In the surplus country the monetary authorities would have to hold increasing levels of foreign exchange in order to absorb the excess liquidity in the economy. The limit to this process is the country's willingness to exchange real resources, exports of goods and services, for financial assets.[7]

Notice that this adjustment mechanism works through changes in expenditures created by changes in real money balances. If prices remain constant, the increased receipts in the surplus country represent real increases in money balances. These increases are then available to become expenditures in goods and services and to bring expenditures in balance with income in each country. Changes in prices are not necessary for the adjustment to take place. Changes in prices are relevant only inasmuch as they affect the value of money balances. Relative prices, the conduit featured in the price mechanism, play a secondary role. However, *general price levels* do affect the real value of money. This latter relationship is also the basic concern of a related adjustment process–purchasing power parity.

[7]The inability of central banks to implement policies to sterilize the impact of the balance of payments on domestic money supply makes domestic money supply an *endogenous* variable in a system of fixed exchange rates. Empirical studies are mixed in their findings about the ability of governments to sterilize the impact of the balance of payments on money supply. In recent history the best success is attributed to Japan where the prolonged trade surplus has not materialized into inflationary growth in money supply. At the other extreme, Germany, confronted with a problem similar to Japan in its balance of payments, appears to have been less successful in controlling the impact of the balance of payments on its economy. See Norman C. Miller and Sherry S. Askin, "Domestic and International Monetary Policy," *Journal of Money, Credit and Banking,* May 1976; pp. 227–238, and Niels Thygesen, "Monetary Policy, Capital Flows and Internal Stability: Some Experiences from Large Industrial Countries," *Swedish Journal of Economics,* March 1973, pp. 83–99. On the other hand, members of OPEC have exhibited a great willingness to exchange real assets, oil, for financial assets, U.S. dollars, in recent years.

The Purchasing Power Parity Theory

A mechanism germane to the one described above under monetary adjustment is the one described by purchasing power parity (PPP). Indeed, PPP is assumed to exist in the monetary approach. In that case the adjustment was realized through changes in money balances, given that a system of fixed exchange rates was assumed to exist. Alternatively, one can see PPP determining the exchange rate.[8]

The value of a currency in one country is determined by the amount of goods and services that can be purchased with a unit of the currency. This is called the *purchasing power of the currency* (the reciprocal of the price level). If there is more than one currency, the exchange rate between two currencies must provide the same purchasing power for each currency. This condition is called *purchasing power parity.* If the exchange rate is such that purchasing power parity does not exist between the two currencies, the exchange rate between the two currencies will adjust until purchasing power parity prevails.[9]

At its simplest level this theory says that commodity prices, after adjustments for transportation and other costs, should be the same in different countries. If this were not the case, there would be incentives to purchase the commodity in the country where its price is the lowest and sell it in the country where its price is the highest. This process of arbitrage will tend to produce the same price for the given commodity in all countries by decreasing its price where arbitrageurs sell it and increasing its price where arbitraguers purchase it. There is ample evidence that for commodities that have world prices (e.g., copper), the price is approximately the same in all countries. As products become more differentiated (e.g., automobiles), it is more difficult to corroborate that this process of arbitrage brings prices in different countries in line.

At the level of saying that prices of specific commodities tend to be the same in different countries, the theory comes close to being a tautology, and it is devoid of much insight into what determines exchange rates. The more interesting interpretation of this theory of determination of exchange rates is based on *general price levels.* It is this general price level that determines the purchasing power of each currency and the real value of money balances discussed above. The exchange rate should bring about purchasing power parity between two currencies whose value is determined by the total amount of goods and services which it can buy, which depends on the general price level.

[8]This theory can be considered to be more or less implicit in the writings of some of the classical economists such as Ricardo and Mill. However, the name of the theory and its applications to practical situations is first associated to Gustav Cassel, "Abnormal Deviations in International Exchanges," *Economic Journal,* Vol. 28, December 1918, pp. 413–15. An excellent review of the theory is contained in Lawrence H. Officer, "The Purchasing-Power-Parity Theory of Exchange Rates: A Review Article," *International Monetary Fund Staff Papers,* March 1976, pp. 1–60.

[9]Whether the line of causation runs from prices to exchange rates, or exchange rates to prices, has been the subject of much debate in the economic literature. The original purchasing power parity doctrine has exchange rates as the variable which adjusts as the result of changes in prices. Keynes, Samuelson, and other economists have pointed to the fact that there are changes in domestic prices which result from changes in exchange rates. Generally, it is accepted that both processes can coexist under the framework of purchasing power parity as long as the effect of prices on exchange rates is stronger than the effect of exchange rates on prices.

The process by which purchasing power parity comes to determine exchange rates is also similar to the one described above as the monetary approach to the balance of payments. If the exchange rate is such that one currency has more general purchasing power in one country than in another, demand for money and expenditures in each country will change, thus affecting the level of imports and exports and eventually the exchange rate. Let's say that the exchange rate of the dollar against the mark shows the dollar to be undervalued relative to the mark when compared with the purchasing power of the two currencies in their respective countries, as in the following example:

Exchange rate: DM/$ = 1.90

$$PP_{DM} = \frac{1}{\text{Price level in Germany}} = \frac{1}{.50} = 2.00$$

$$PP_{\$} = \frac{1}{\text{Price level in U.S.}} = \frac{1}{1.00} = 1.00$$

Then,

$$\text{Purchasing power parity} = \frac{PP_{DM}}{PP_{\$}} = \frac{2.00}{1.00} = 2.00$$

Given that purchasing power parity between the mark and the dollar is 2.00, an exchange rate of DM 1.90/$ is equivalent to increasing mark prices of goods relative to the dollar prices of those goods. Assuming given money supplies in each currency, an increase in mark prices will result in increased demand for liquid funds in marks and decreased expenditures in goods sold by Germany. A decrease in dollar prices results in a decrease in the demand for liquid funds in dollars and an increase in expenditures in goods and services denominated in dollars. This change in expenditure patterns represents an increase in imports from the United States and a decrease in exports from Germany. As a result of this change, in the exchange markets there will be an appreciation of the dollar against the mark, that is, a tendency to correct the initial undervaluation of the dollar and to produce an exchange rate that represents purchasing power parity between the two currencies.

This version of purchasing power parity in which actual price levels are the base for comparisons is known as *absolute purchasing power parity.* An alternative formulation is based on *changes* in price levels: In this version of the theory changes in exchange rates are determined by the relative movements in price levels. This is known as *relative purchasing power parity.*

There are a number of recognized factors that will prevent purchasing power parity in one or both of its presentations from determining exchange rates. These factors include the following:

1. Government intervention either directly in the exchange markets or indirectly through trade restrictions.

2. Speculation in the exchange market.

3. Long-term capital flows that continue in spite of the disequilibrium between purchasing power parity and exchange rates.

4. Structural changes in the economies involved.

However, these departures are considered to prevail only during the short term. Over longer periods of time purchasing power parity will tend to dominate the changes in exchange rates, according to this theory.[10]

The major problem with the applicability of this theory is in the specification of the relevant price level indexes to be used in the computation of the purchasing power parity. Questions pertaining to what is an appropriate sample and the relative weights that should be allocated to each commodity in the sample are the subject of considerable debate. Should the sample represent all goods and services or only those which are traded? Should the weights given to each item be those of the importing country, the exporting country, or a third country? A discussion of the technical problems involved in the calculation of price indices is beyond the scope of this book. Suffice it to say that the problem is complex and that definite answers are not available.

The tendency for exchange rates to compensate for changes in relative prices over long periods of time, such as a decade, is generally accepted.[11] How-

[10] A more serious blow to the theory, because it undermines its basic assumptions, is the challenge that the relationship between traded and nontraded goods varies among countries and through time in a systematic fashion. Although the theory is based on a general value of money, i.e., a general price level, it is assumed that the relationship between prices for traded and nontraded goods is constant through time and varies among countries in a nonsystematic fashion. Balassa has pointed out that poorer countries can be expected to have a ratio of prices of nontraded goods to prices of traded goods lower than richer countries. As countries develop economically, this ratio can be expected to increase. See Bela Balassa, "The Purchasing Power Parity Doctrine: A Reappraisal," *Journal of Political Economy*, December 1964, pp. 584-96.

[11] Some economists consider that exchange rates typically do not depart by more than 20% from purchasing power parity. See Harry G. Johnson, "International Trade: I. Theory," *International Encyclopedia of the Social Sciences*, Vol. 8, New York, 1968, pp. 92-93. Research in support of the validity of purchasing power parity in exchange rates is presented in Henry J. Gaillot, "Purchasing Power Parity as an Explanation of Long-Term Changes in Exchange Rates," *Journal of Money, Credit and Banking*, Vol. 2, August 1970, pp. 348-57. Gaillot bases his study on averages for periods of several years. Prices are measured by wholesale price indices.

Several studies have been made of purchasing power parity and the rapidity by which changes in relative purchasing power have been transmitted into alterations in the exchange rates. In their study of fourteen currencies vs. the U.S. dollar using monthly data from April 1919 through April 1925, Hodgson and Phelps found that over 90% of the variation in exchange rates was explained by their lagged adjustments process for eleven of the fourteen currencies; in all cases the peak impact was primarily realized within the first three months. The *average* lag under one of their test equations was *over* six months for three of the twelve currencies for which sensible results were obtained, including the Japanese yen for which the average lag was over a year. See John S. Hodgson and Patricia Phelps, "The Distributed Impact of Price-Level Variation on Floating Exchange Rates," *Review of Economics and Statistics*, February 1975, pp. 58-64. Again using this period for which currencies were floating freely, Rogalski and Vinso used monthly data for six currencies from 1920-24 and found that the effect of relative prices on exchange rates was realized usually within the month of price change. See Richard J. Rogalski and Joseph D. Vinso, "Price

ever, supporting research has often been based on wholesale price indices, which are heavily weighted by traded goods, instead of an index more representative of the general price level. This becomes a test of the strength of commodity arbitrage instead of the validity of purchasing power parity which is based on the relative value of money expressed in terms of general price levels.[12]

The conditions in which purchasing power parity can be considered to have the heaviest weights in determining exchange rates involve large monetary disturbances such as very high inflation. In these cases, the response of individuals to change in values of real and monetary assets can be expected to be strong and the predictions of purchasing power parity for exchange rate can be realized.[13]

Government Intervention

In spite of these automatic mechanisms to correct problems in the balance of payments, governments have often thought it necessary to intervene in the adjustment process through fiscal and monetary policies. The object of this intervention has ranged from trying to counteract the adjustment process to channeling it and even trying to reinforce it.

The adjustment processes described above all involve a degree of reallocation of resources. A reduction in trade deficit entails not only a reduction in imports, but also a movement of resources from the production of nontraded goods into the production of traded goods. This can involve the mobilization and retraining of large numbers of workers, and it is expensive in terms of social costs. The reduction in income associated with the correction of a balance of payments deficit essentially involves a reduction in economic growth and higher unemployment. In a society in which governments are committed to full employment and economic growth it is easy to understand how policy makers may want to ameliorate the pains produced by these adjustment processes. If, in addition, the balance of payments imbalances are considered to be only temporary, i.e., the causes of the problem are seen as reversible with time, it can be seen how governments will try to protect the economy from the temporary effects of the imbalance.

The automatic adjustment process could also take a very long period of time to work fully. In a world in which disturbances in the economic system are many and continuous, the automatic mechanisms never would have time to operate before a new factor affected the economy.

Level Variations as Predictors of Flexible Exchange Rates," *Journal of International Business Studies,* Spring/Summer 1977, pp. 71-81.

[12]Keynes was the first to point out that tests of purchasing power parity based on wholesale price indices just tested the truism that the price of traded goods must be the same in different countries. Any failure of relative wholesale price indices to support purchasing power parity could be expected to be a result of the few nontraded goods which are included in a wholesale price index and distort the otherwise close relationship between relative wholesale price indices and purchasing power parity. See John M. Keynes, *A Treatise on Money,* Vol. I (New York: Harcourt Brace, 1930, pp. 72-74).

[13]Further elaboration of purchasing power parity and relative interest rates appears in the algebraic formulation of these concepts presented in the Appendix to Chapter 5.

Monetary and fiscal policies, as well as other options open to governments, can work either to reinforce or to delay the impact of the mechanisms discussed above. The choice of policy by any government at one point in time is determined not only by the government's assessment of the nature of the problem, but also by the ranking that external equilibrium has relative to other economic objectives of the government. The observed result will be a combination of the nature of the problem, automatic economic reaction, and government policy.

INTERNATIONAL MONETARY ARRANGEMENTS

The chauvinistic practice of each country having its national currency creates the need for agreements on how to settle payments among nations. By necessity, these agreements incorporate prescriptions on how to correct conditions of surplus and deficit in the balance of payments. These prescriptions can be classified into two groups: (1) those that rely to a large extent on automatic mechanisms–the gold standard and flexible rates and (2) those that rely on government interaction–the fixed rate system.

The Gold Standard

Under this system, international settlements of payments imbalances are made exclusively in gold, and domestic money supply is tied to the amount of gold the country has. Foreign exchange (key currencies such as the U.S. dollar) is excluded from international reserves. The exchange rate for each currency is fixed in terms of the amount of gold into which each currency is fully convertible. In the case of a balance of payments deficit, a gold outflow will take place to finance the external deficit. This would produce a contraction in the domestic money supply and a decrease in prices. As a result, imports will decrease and exports will increase. The opposite forces would be at work in the surplus country. After a while the balance of payments equilibrium would be restored.

In the preceding adjustment of the balance of payments disequilibrium, note that the burden of the adjustment is carried by the domestic economy. It is expected that the domestic economy will inflate and deflate in response to changes in the external balance. In addition, the rules of the game prescribe that monetary policy should not be used to offset gold flows. In cases of downward price rigidity, governments are expected to sit quietly while the economy goes through a period of high unemployment to reduce income and adjust a balance of payments deficit. In the case of a balance of payments surplus, governments are expected to tolerate a period of high inflation.

The gold standard was implemented to some extent before World War I and during the interwar period 1925-31. Its proponents exalt the virtues of leaving the adjustment process to automatic forces instead of in the hands of policy makers. In addition, sole reliance on gold for international payments has the advantage that all currencies are treated in similar fashion. No country has to incur a deficit to provide the world with its currency, and therefore liquidity. This is usually the argument raised in the context of the present situation, in which the U.S. dollar is an international currency. Before 1971, when the role of the U.S. dollar as the world's reserve currency was not even contested by any other currency, countries had to have additional dollars to meet the needs of an expanding world trade. This could be accomplished only by deficits in the U.S. balance of payments. Gold advocates point to this fact as a potential source of inflationary pressures on the world which must see its money supply expanded with the product of its sales to the reserve-currency country.

Opponents of the gold standard, when confronted with the above list of its virtues, mention that the independence from reserve-currency countries' economic policies is gained only at the expense of putting the system at the mercy of natural resources instead. Gold supplies certainly would not be responsive to the world needs for liquidity. In addition, the discipline imposed by this standard on domestic economies is not politically feasible. Today's governments are held responsible for maintaining full employment and reasonable growth in an environment of price stability.

Flexible Exchange Rates

This system, like the gold standard, relies on automatic mechanisms to adjust disequilibria in the balance of payments. Unlike the gold standard, however, flexible exchange rates do not require the domestic economy to carry the immediate burden of the adjustment. Adjustments in the balance of payments are made through changes in the price of foreign exchange.

If a country has a balance of payments deficit, the supply of its currency to foreigners will exceed their demand for it. Alternatively, the country's demand for foreign exchange will exceed the supply of foreign exchange. The result of such tendencies will be to lower the price of the domestic currency in terms of foreign exchange, or, what is the same thing, increase the price of foreign exchange in terms of the local currency. That is, the currency of the deficit country depreciates in value and the currency of the surplus country appreciates.

A reduction of the value of the local currency in terms of foreign exchange means that domestic goods become cheaper to foreigners and foreign goods become more expensive to domestic consumers. It also means that the value of money balances in the deficit country decreases. Such changes in prices together with the overall decline in expenditures in the deficit country will tend to increase the country's exports and decrease its imports. This will help to restore equilibrium to the balance of payments. However, the extent to which changes in relative prices can accomplish this restoration depends on the existence of excess productive capacity in the deficit country and on the responsiveness of imports and exports to price changes. As stated before in the discussion of the price adjustment mechanism, the sum of the price elasticities of demand for imports of the countries involved must exceed one for the price adjustment to be successful.[14]

Before 1973 the system of flexible exchange rates had been implemented only occasionally, when the value of a particular currency was allowed to float. That occurred for the Canadian dollar between 1950 and 1961 and since 1971, and for the British pound since June 1972. However, since 1973 most major

[14] It should also be recalled that if supply price elasticities are low, a sum of import demand elasticities of less than one would be sufficient.

currencies have joined the list of floating currencies. But the currencies have not always been allowed to float completely freely. Governments have frequently intervened to maintain orderly markets and often to support the external value of their currencies—the so-called dirty or managed floating.

The greatest benefit of flexible exchange rates, its proponents argue, is that the adjustment of balance of payments disequilibria can be done with very little sacrifice to the domestic economy. Most of the burden is carried by changes in the exchange rate. Therefore, domestic economic policy can be shielded from the problems of the balance of payments; i.e., domestic policy can be implemented with little regard for its impact on the balance of payments. Under conditions of less than full employment, increased exports, together with decreased imports, produce the adjustments. With full employment, however, a decrease in aggregate expenditures is necessary to eliminate a deficit in the balance of payments. In addition, the danger of making the exchange rate one of the economic targets is always present. This is especially so when the export sector is a substantial part of the economy.

The issue of low elasticities in demand for imports, which will make price adjustments ineffective even when excess productive capacity exists, remains a debatable issue. Empirical data have tended to support the view that import price elasticities are low, but these studies have been full of statistical problems. One of the bases on which they have been contested is that these studies measure short-term responses only; in the long term these elasticities are probably much higher.

There is also a question about whether or not freely floating exchange rates contribute to *inflation.* There may be inflation if each monetary authority takes the reaction of the other into account and responds accordingly, just as in oligopoly theory. Such a conclusion reinforces a need for a controlled international monetary order, for just as companies and money markets have become more international, so must the governments with their central banks.[15]

Critics of the flexible exchange rate system believe that the exchange rates under a pure version of this system would be highly unstable. As a result, the risk of operating in the foreign exchange market would rise and international trade and capital movements would be deterred. Defenders of flexible exchange rates contend that there is no reason to suspect that this would be the case. Fluctuations in the exchange rate would reflect basic economic conditions which, by definition, are not unstable.

Fixed Rates: The Bretton Woods System Until 1973

The monetary system that prevailed in the postwar period through 1971 was initiated in 1944 at Bretton Woods, New Hampshire.[16] It was a system of fixed

[15] An excellent summary of research and a new analysis is presented in Chapter 5 of John Hewson and Eisuke Sakakibara *The Euro-currency Markets and their Implications* (Lexington, Mass.: D.C. Heath, 1975), pp. 101-112.

[16] The appendices to this chapter, "Important Dates in the World Monetary System" and "Some International Associations," present a detailed chronology of the major events in the international monetary system since the Bretton Woods Conference and the names of other international associations that have participated in shaping this system.

exchange rates based on a modified gold standard. In addition to gold, international reserves in this system included foreign currencies and the right to borrow from an institution created by the system. This institution, the International Monetary Fund (IMF), is still alive today.

The resources of the IMF consist of money received from member countries. These resources constitute a pool from which participant countries can draw during short-term balance of payments difficulties. Each country's contribution to IMF resources is determined by its quota. Until 1976 a country's quota had to be deposited in the IMF 25% in gold and 75% in its own currency. Since 1976 the 25% of the quota which used to be contributed in the form of gold is now subscribed to either in currencies acceptable to the IMF or Special Drawing Rights, which are described later in this chapter. Up to the amount of the gold or exchange reserve subscription, countries have an absolute claim on the IMF; i.e., they can draw this amount from the IMF at any time. This is called the *gold or reserve tranche* position and is counted among the countries' reserves. Beyond this point a country can draw upon its *credit tranche*—the additional credit the IMF can grant.[17] Approval from the IMF is necessary for a country to draw on its credit tranche. This approval is usually accompanied by restrictions that become increasingly tight as the drawings on this credit rise. Approval from the IMF used to be required in order to alter the par value of a currency; this has not been the case since 1973 when major currencies joined in the present system of managed floats.

In this monetary system the foreign exchange rate for each currency was initially fixed in terms of its par value vis-à-vis the U.S. dollar or gold. The value of the U.S. dollar, however, was defined in terms of gold only. Under the IMF rules, the market exchange rate for each currency was allowed to fluctuate only within a narrow margin of 1% around the par value of the currency. When the exchange rate of a currency approached the limits of the band within which it was allowed to fluctuate, the country was expected to intervene in the foreign exchange market by buying or selling the given currency. When the market stepped up the volume of the given currency offered for sale, thus putting downward pressure on the foreign exchange rate of that currency, the monetary authorities of that country were expected to buy the currency by offering other foreign exchange in return. Similarly, when market forces indicated upward pressure on the value of the currency, the monetary authorities were expected to offer more currency for sale in return for other foreign exchange. That is, fixed rates in this system were maintained by monetary authorities using the official reserves of a country as a buffer against market fluctuations.

The role of gold and the behavior of the United States following Bretton Woods present a mixed picture. People at the conference, including John Maynard Keynes, thought of gold as a means to link the parities of 100 national currencies. Using the dollar as a reserve currency with gold as the link meant that the whole system rested on uncertainty. As the president of the Netherlands Bank remarked at a 1961 IMF meeting, if gold were to be upvalued, firms and nations would not want dollars. Yet, if this upvaluation were never going to occur, no one would want gold; the earning asset, dollars, would be preferred.

[17]The credit tranche is the amount of drawings beyond the gold tranche that would bring the fund's total holdings of that currency to 200% of quota.

Right after World War II the U.S. gold stock was $20 billion, 60% of the official world holdings. Even by 1957 the gold reserve of the U.S. exceeded by three to one the dollar holdings of foreign central banks.

In this system of adjusting short-term imbalances in the external accounts, a country with a deficit in its balance of payments lost foreign reserves; a country with a surplus in its international accounts accumulated foreign reserves. If, however, the imbalance in payments persisted over a longer period of time, this short-term method of adjustment became ineffective. It was certainly not available to the deficit country (which might run out of reserves), and it was very undesirable to the surplus country (which accumulated an excessive amount of low-return assets). At this point the system offered two avenues to correct a disequilibrium in the balance of payments. In the case of a deficit, a country could choose either to deflate the domestic economy or devalue its currency. In the case of a balance of payments surplus, a country could choose either to inflate the domestic economy or to upvalue its currency. Theoretically, countries would resort to changing the parity value of their currencies whenever a "fundamental disequilibrium" existed. In any case, the corrective mechanism was operated at the discretion of the countries having the imbalance.

If a country having a deficit in its balance of payments chose to correct its imbalance through adjustments in the domestic economy, it would apply measures similar to the ones that would occur automatically under the gold standard. The difference here is that the changes would take place according to an explicit government policy instead of an automatic mechanism. The government could use either monetary policy or fiscal policy, or both, in order to accomplish its objectives.

The problems with using special policies to correct a balance of payments disequilibrium arose when the measures required to improve the balance of payments ran counter to measures that domestic objectives indicated. For example, it is easier to conceive of a deliberate deflation of the economy when the balance of payments deficit is accompanied by an overheated economy than when the economy is in a recession. The other avenue open to a government to correct a continuous imbalance of payments in this system was to change the foreign exchange rate of its currency: devaluation for a country with continuous deficits in the balance of payments and upvaluation for a country with continuous surpluses. The adjustment mechanism here was similar to that under flexible exchange rates. It worked through a change in price and it avoided adjusting the domestic economy directly. In this case, however, the mechanism did not work automatically but was manipulated by the government like any other policy instrument. Its success, however, depended on the same conditions as the success of the flexible exchange rate system: availability of excess productive capacity and a certain degree of price elasticity in the demand for imports in the countries involved.

Historically, the difficulty with relying on governmental decisions to change the foreign exchange parity of currencies has been the reluctance of governments to take such steps. For surplus countries, an upvaluation of their currencies has exposed their governments to the wrath of the export industry and of labor in general. For deficit countries, a devaluation has been considered a loss of international economic power. In addition, the Bretton Woods system appeared to impose the burdens of adjustment in a biased fashion. Surplus countries were under less pressure to correct their imbalances than were deficit countries. The accumulation of reserves in the surplus countries failed to induce any sense of urgency in the need to correct the imbalance, for excessive reserves only have an opportunity cost. And, while deficit countries had to ask for the collaboration of the IMF to continue borrowing from it, little pressure was applied by the IMF on a surplus country which chose neither to adjust its domestic economy nor to upvalue its currency. When the surplus countries refused to carry their part of the adjustment burden, the total adjustment process had to be carried by the deficit country alone, making the required deflation or devaluation in that country larger than if the adjustment process had been shared by the surplus country.

In general, the 1960s were a period of attempted stabilization. One stabilization tool created in this period was the *swap line of credit* arranged on a bilateral basis between central banks. The objective was to support existing exchange rates.[18] In these swap lines, two countries agree to borrow one another's currency for a specified period of time with offsetting interest payments and protection against revaluations. The proceeds from these swap loans are then used for central bank intervention in the foreign exchange market. Let's say that the United States and France agree to a swap line of credit in the amount of $100 equal FF500. The United States receives FF500 and France receives $100 when the swap line of credit is used. This provides the U.S. central bank operating through the New York Federal Reserve with francs to stabilize the franc/dollar exchange rate. Upon maturity of the swap, the United States repays FF500 to France and receives $100 in exchange.

Another stabilization tool devised during this period was the London gold pool. The gold pool was created in November 1961 to stabilize the gold price after the first serious wave of speculation against the value of the U.S. dollar since the Bretton Woods Agreement. With a stock of gold contributed by the central banks of the major countries, the Bank of England was empowered to trade with the objective of stabilizing the gold price. The pool had just about run its course in 1967 and 1968 with massive purchases of gold and sales of the U.S. dollar from the world market. As a result, in March 1968 a two-tier price system was created in which the central banks would no longer attempt to peg the

[18] The Bank for International Settlements (BIS), in addition to the IMF, provided the forum for the negotiation of many of these policies. The BIS was created after World War I to facilitate the transfer of funds among countries whose currencies were not then convertible into one another in Europe. Since free convertibility was established for most of these currencies in the late 1950s, the major function of the BIS was to provide a forum for the monetary authorities of various countries to meet and to exchange ideas. Charles Coombs described the BIS in graphic terms, noting that some people considered Basel, where the BIS is located, a Swiss Philadelphia. The BIS is a converted hotel with rooms made into small offices. It is located near the Bahnhofplatz, with a small doorway between a pastry shop and a jeweler. No agreements were ever signed and no memoranda of understanding were ever initialed at the BIS. However, the press learned to seek out bankers coming from BIS meetings where new agreements were discussed. As a U.K. banker told reporters outside the offices (after being asked whether he thought a new 1968 agreement would stop the gold rush), "Yes, I think this will do the trick; I am sure it will." Later he remarked that the major duty of every central banker was to "learn how to exude confidence without positively lying." Charles Coombs, *The Arena of International Finance* (New York: Wiley Interscience, 1976), p. 166.

world price, but would trade among themselves at the official price, $35 per ounce of gold.[19]

Thus, during the first 25 years of the Bretton Woods system the tendency was for countries to try to defend their exchange rates through market interventions and adjustments in the domestic economy and to use changes in the exchange rate only as a last resort. England was a classical example in the 1960s, for its "stop-go" policies delayed the devaluation of the pound for four years at a very high cost to domestic objectives. Since 1971, however, there appears to have been a change in the participants' attitudes. Countries, including the United States, appear to be more willing to use the change in exchange parity route than to sacrifice their domestic economies. The British pound, which was allowed to float in the exchange market in June 1972 while its foreign reserves were at record heights, provides an example of the new tendencies in the system.

TOWARD MORE FLEXIBILITY: THE CURRENT MONETARY SYSTEM

The Bretton Woods system proved to present three major problems: (1) it had difficulties in achieving adjustment of persistent imbalances in the payments positions of individual countries; (2) it required continuous deficits in the U.S. balance of payments to meet demands for liquidity for an increasing volume of international transactions; and (3) it was accompanied by severe periods of crises that resulted in a lack of confidence in reserve media. Obviously, these problems were interrelated. The slower the adjustment mechanism, the higher the volume of liquidity required, and vice versa. The higher the amount of liquidity available to a country, the easier it is for the adjustment mechanism to operate without creating problems of confidence.

The difficulties presented by the Bretton Woods system produced some solutions through changes and innovations in the system. These include the introduction of Special Drawing Rights (SDRs), the Smithsonian Agreement on December 18, 1971, the establishment of the European monetary union, and the abandonment of fixed rates of European currencies vis-à-vis the U.S. dollar on March 1973. Finally, in April 1976 the Board of Governors of the IMF approved a number of amendments to the Articles of Agreement of the Fund which legitimized the changes that had taken place in the system in recent years and provided a new degree of flexibility for settling imbalances in the international monetary system.

[19]The London pool losses in late 1967 prior to its suspension were:

January-June, 1967	$113 million
November 1–17	$145 million
November 22	$106 million
November 23	$142 million
November 24	$256 million

Total $576 million (November 20–24)

See Charles Coombs, *op, cit.,* p. 161.

Special Drawing Rights

The machinery of SDRs creation was activated on August 6, 1969, when the required majority of IMF members became participants in the SDR system. SDRs are international paper money created and distributed by the IMF in the quantities and at the times dictated by special agreements among member countries. This paper money is used only in transactions among governments and between the IMF and these governments. The first allocation was made in January 1970, with the creation of $3.5 billion for that year. Another $3 billion was allocated at the beginning of each of the two following years. No allocations were made for 1973–78.

Allocations of SDRs are made for *basic periods,* usually five years in duration, and they are allocated to IMF members on the basis of IMF quotas at a uniform rate throughout the basic period. The amount of SDRs must be approved by a majority of the IMF participating countries with 85% of the weighted voting power of the Fund.

When a participating member receives an allocation of SDRs, it is not required to deposit an equivalent amount of its own currency, as it must when drawing on its IMF borrowing rights. SDRs are a permanent addition to the stock of international liquidity.

SDRs were initially expressed in terms of a fixed amount of gold that was equivalent to the gold content of the U.S. dollar. After the value of the dollar was severed from gold and allowed to float in exchange markets (see following section), the value of the SDR had to be redefined. Thus, since June 1974 the value of the SDR in terms of the U.S. dollar is determined by the sum of the dollar value of sixteen currencies, based on market exchange rates. The weight given to each of these currencies is based on the country's participation in world trade, subject to some modifications.[20] This new approach to the valuation of SDRs created a relatively stable measure of value in a time when the values of independent currencies were fluctuating widely in the foreign exchange market. As a result, many participants in the international financial markets who were looking for some stability in the value of international financial transactions began to use the SDR as a unit of account. In 1975 the first Euro-bond denominated in SDRs was issued. In addition, the ministers of the Organization of Petroleum Exporting Countries (OPEC) agreed to price oil in SDRs effective October 1, 1975. Also in 1975 Saudi Arabia, Iran, and Burma decided to state the value of their

[20]Effective July 1, 1978, the value of the SDR is the sum of the dollar value of the following number of units of each of the sixteen currencies:

U.S. dollar	0.40	Belgian franc	1.60
German mark	0.32	Saudi Arabian riyal	0.13
Japanese yen	21.00	Swedish krona	0.11
French franc	0.42	Iranian rial	1.70
Pound sterling	0.05	Australian dollar	0.017
Italian lira	52.00	Spanish peseta	1.50
Netherlands guilder	0.14	Norwegian krone	0.10
Canadian dollar	0.07	Austrian schilling	0.28

SOURCE: IMF *Survey,* July 3, 1978, p. 203.

currencies in terms of SDRs. The intellectual or economic purity of some of these changes might be suspect, however, for when the dollar strengthened in late 1975, some decisions were reversed. For example, OPEC never implemented the SDR basis for oil, although the idea reappeared with the dollar's weakness in 1978.

The Smithsonian Agreement

On December 18, 1971 the Group of Ten nations agreed on a new set of parity rates (called *central rates* because they lacked the approval of the IMF at the time).[21] The U.S. dollar was still defined in terms of gold (although not convertible into gold) and the other currencies were defined in terms of either the U.S. dollar or gold. This followed a period after August 15 of the same year when all major currencies had been allowed to float in the exchange markets and the U.S. dollar's convertibility into gold was suspended.

In addition to the new set of central rates, currencies were allowed to fluctuate over a band wider than in the past, 2.25% on either side of the central rate, without requiring government intervention. Previously, a currency had been allowed to fluctuate only within a margin of 1% (¾% in practice) on either side of par value. Under the new band, a currency could fluctuate 4.5% from floor to ceiling with reference to the U.S. dollar. This implied that a currency could fluctuate by as much as 9% against a currency other than the U.S. dollar. That would be the case if before the change occurred one of the currencies was at the lower limit against the U.S. dollar and the other currency was at the upper limit. If the currencies reversed positions completely, each currency would have changed by 4.5% against the dollar and by 9% against one another. This was expected to make speculation more expensive and to reduce the amount of control that a government would have to exert on the foreign exchange.

The other major feature of the Smithsonian Agreement was the end of convertibility of the U.S. dollar into gold. Contrary to the previous 25 years, the United States refused to return to the convertibility into gold suspended the previous August 15. The need for a reform in the system was apparent and a committee of 20 nations was created to draft a proposal for a new system.

The European Monetary Union and the Events of March 1973

The members of the European Economic Community (EEC or Common Market) agreed in early 1972 to keep their currencies fluctuating against one another within a band narrower than the one allowed under the Smithsonian Agreement.[22] When the agreement was reached in 1972, the EEC countries, the United Kingdom, and Denmark (who were scheduled to join the EEC in 1973) agreed to allow their currencies to fluctuate only a maximum of 2.25% among

[21] For the country composition of the Group of Ten, see the appendix to this chapter. "Some International Associations."

[22] The initial European Common Market included France, West Germany, Italy, Belgium, Luxembourg, and the Netherlands. See the appendix to this chapter, "Some International Associations."

themselves. However, the group as a whole could fluctuate against other currencies within the larger band provided by the Smithsonian Agreement. This created what has been called a *snake within a tunnel.* The snake was the narrower band allowed among the EEC currencies; the tunnel was the wider band allowed by the Smithsonian Agreement.[23] Soon the snake was to be allowed to move freely outside the tunnel in 1973.

The year 1973 opened with the enlargement of the European Common Market to include the United Kingdom, Ireland, and Denmark. This was followed by a series of international monetary crises during the first quarter that led to a devaluation of the U.S. dollar in February, the floating of several other currency rates, and the elimination of the tunnel binding the snake created by the European monetary union.

In mid-March, after a couple of weeks when the values of all the major currencies were allowed to fluctuate according to market forces, the foreign exchange market opened again with a new set of rules. The European currencies participating in the narrow margins of the European monteary union were to continue maintaining the parities with small fluctuations among themselves. The snake was to be kept alive. However, the currencies in the monetary union, as a group, were to be allowed to fluctuate in value with regard to the U.S. dollar according to market forces. The tunnel had been eliminated and a measure of floating exchange rates was accepted officially. But the floating was expected to be kept within certain, not specified, limits through the intervention of the monetary authorities in the foreign exchange market. These limits were to prove very flexible.

The European monetary union has tried to provide a measure of stability for exchange rates of participating currencies. In a world where major currencies have moved toward greater flexibility in exchange rates, the objectives of the monetary union have met with only limited success. As domestic economic pressures in the participating countries have mounted, many of the initial members have had to abandon, at least temporarily, attempts to fix the parity of their exchange rate. Some of these episodes have been short-lived and a change in parity has been enough for the given currency to reenter the snake. Thus, effective August 29, 1977, the Danish krone was devalued by 5% against the U.S. dollar and new intervention rates for the krone against the other currencies in the snake were established. Under the revised parity the Danish krone can fluctuate against the German mark between DK277.555 and DK265.345 per 100 marks; i.e., 2.25% around the new parity rate of DK271.450 per 100 marks.

In many other cases of conflict between domestic economic goals and exchange stability, the intensity of domestic pressures has been such that countries have abandoned all attempts to maintain any exchange parity of their currency and have left the snake arrangement. This is the case of France, which, since March 1976, has abandoned its participation in the snake.

As of June 1978 only six currencies were participating in the snake: the Belgian franc, the Danish krone, the German mark, the Luxembourg franc, the Netherlands guilder, and the Norwegian krone. Three of the main initial partici-

[23]The original snake within the tunnel agreement forbade using dollars to maintain internal EEC parity, giving speculators, who knew that the peak country had to use a weaker currency to push its own currency down, a two-way play. This provision was subsequently ended.

pants had abandoned the snake some years earlier: the United Kingdom, France, and Italy.

Many experienced officials in the field reject the floating that began in late 1971. Thus, Charles Coombs notes that 85% of the 1965-71 deterioration in the U.S. foreign trade position was associated with three trading partners: Canada, Japan, and Germany. He argues that the United States should have negotiated changes in rates with these nations and should have continued to use the swap system. For example, from 1962-67, of the $7.7 billion in central bank swaps, 90% paid back within six months and all repaid within a year.[24] Thus, renegotiation of rates and/or an end to a particular speculative flow permitted this system to stabilize exchange rates.

Floating rates have witnessed a volatility that bothers many executives, whatever the joy of market discipline for economists. First, for example, from 1973 through 1974 the dollar dropped against the mark by 31%, rose by 30%, dropped by 17%, rose by 12%, and finally fell by 10%. Others, however, have noted that swaps do have an inherent problem, namely, that they must be repaid. Second, it was notoriously difficult to get nations to agree to revalue their currencies in this period, and it is not clear how Germany and Japan especially could have been convinced to upvalue their currencies. Third, the goal of the United States to move away from gold convertibility was not so much to remove gold from international finance as it was to stem the United States gold losses.

Exchange Rate Systems During 1973-78

Although proposals for a change in the Bretton Woods Agreement were not approved officially by the IMF until 1976, the floating of major European currencies against the U.S. dollar in 1973 initiated a *de facto* system of much greater flexibility than the regime that dominated the postwar period until then.

Exchange rate practices during this period ranged from countries with a relatively free floating of their currency value, with very little government intervention, to countries that pegged the value of their currency to a single major currency and intervened in the market to maintain this value. Canada, the United States, and the snake as a group are among the countries with floating currencies with limited government intervention. Of course, among the currencies participating in the snake a system of fixed rates exist, except when individual countries temporarily abandon the agreement.

However, most countries still pursue a policy of fixed exchange rates. Floating on a continued basis has been practiced only by some of the most developed economies. Among the countries with fixed rates the pegging technique is not as homogeneous as it was before. In April 1978 some 42 countries retained a peg to the U.S. dollar, 14 were pegged to the French franc, and 9 were pegged to other single currencies. A growing number of countries (32 in April 1978) chose to peg the value of their currencies to a basket of other currencies specially selected or to the SDR. Finally, 6 countries with relatively high infla-

[24] Coombs, *op, cit.,* pp. 220-25.

tion rates followed a system of crawling pegs—a hybrid between fixed and floating rates where exchange rates are adjusted according to a set of economic indicators.[25] However, even for countries pegging the value of their currencies, there has been a greater willingness to reassess the exchange rate policy and to change the parity value if necessary. Exchange rates for the period 1974-77 are presented in Exhibit 4.1.

Amendment of Articles of Agreement of the IMF

The system of managed floating rates among major currencies accepted in practice since 1973 terminated the exchange rate system as envisaged by the Bretton Woods Conference in 1944. However, it was not until April 1976, that the Board of Governors of the IMF officially approved a series of changes to the system. The changes were agreed to during protracted negotiations among important member countries during 1973-76. These changes came into effect two years later in April 1978 after the official approval of the necessary number of participating countries was obtained. The amendments have two major features;

1. Legalization of the existing regime of floating exchange rates and freedom for each country to peg or to let float the value of its currency.

2. Termination of the system of par values based on gold. The 25% of quota contribution that used to be made in gold is now made in the form of currencies acceptable to the IMF or SDRs—whose value was severed from gold since 1974. One third of the IMF's gold is to be sold in the market over a period of four years starting in early 1976. The profits on gold sales over the official price of SDR 35 per ounce would be placed in a Trust Fund available for loans to developing countries. The Fund is required to avoid the management of the price of gold.

The Fund has the responsibility of surveillance over the exchange rate arrangement that each country chooses and it provides guidance to countries on their exchange rate policy.

The major powers of the IMF continue to be in the area of providing temporary financing for countries with balance of payments difficulties. By 1978 the IMF's lending facilities had increased considerably. In addition to the gold tranche, now called reserve tranche, and the four credit tranches established by the Bretton Woods Conference, the IMF has three permanent credit facilities: (1) the compensating financing facility (established in 1963 and liberalized in 1975); (2) the buffer stock financing facility (established in 1969); and (3) the extended facility (established in 1974). Exhibit 4.2 shows a summary of the major facilities and the conditions under which member countries can draw on them.

In addition to the permanent facilities, the IMF has other temporary credit facilities. These include the Trust Fund mentioned above which is to be administered independently from the size of the countries' quota. Earlier, in June 1974, a special $3 billion IMF fund was created to help countries whose balances

[25] IMF *Survey,* May 22, 1978, pp. 156-57.

EXHIBIT 4.1. Spot Exchange Rates, 1974–1977 Dollar Prices of Foreign Currencies (Averages for Week Ending Wednesday)

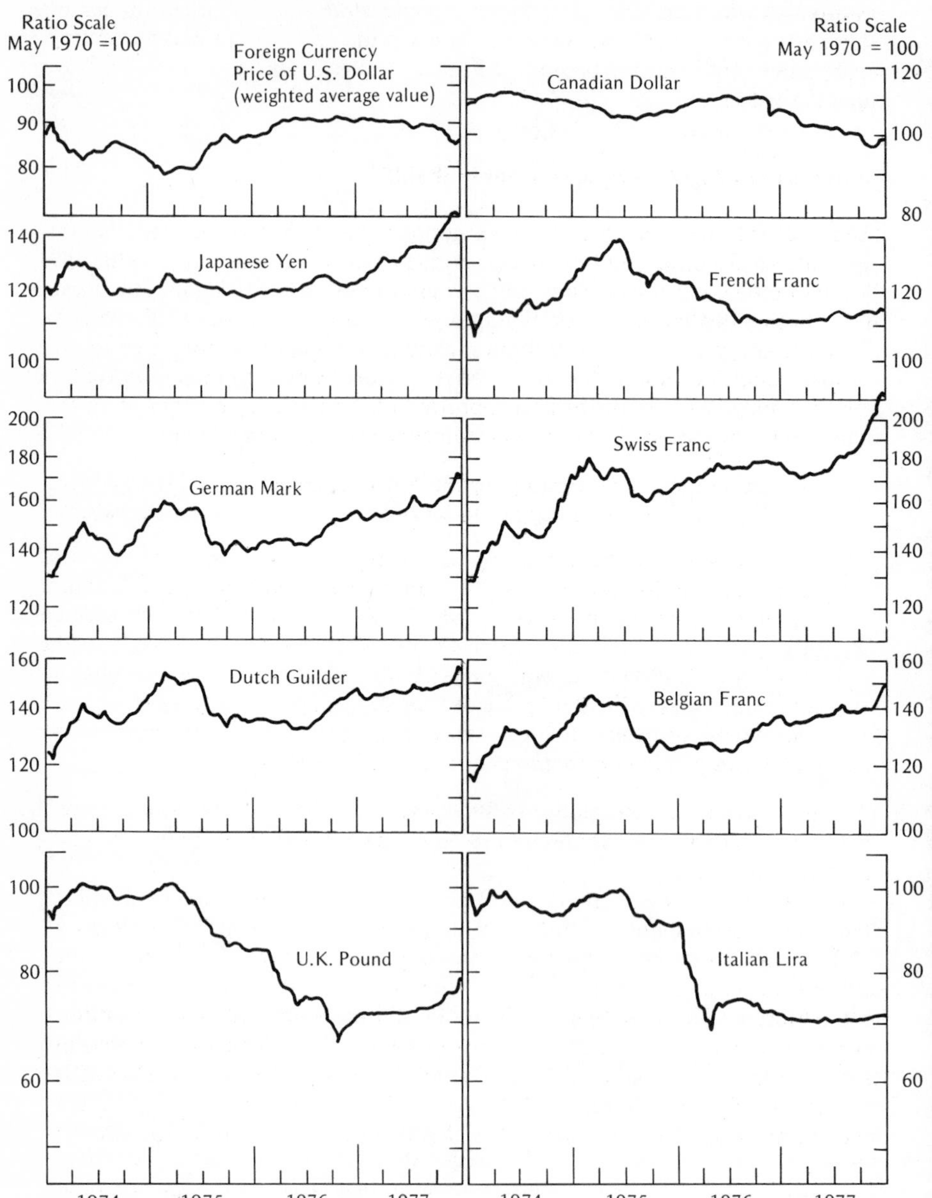

SOURCE: Board of Governors of the Federal Reserve System, SELECTED INTEREST & EXCHANGE RATES, Chart 1, January 3, 1978.

EXHIBIT 4.2. Permanent Financial Facilities of the International Monetary Fund and Their Conditionality[a]

Type of Facility	Per Cent of Quota Available	Cumulative Per Cent of Quota Available
Gold tranche	25	25
Condition—balance of payments need.		
First credit tranche	25	50
Program representing reasonable efforts to overcome balance of payments difficulties; performance criteria and installments not used.		
Higher credit tranches	75	125
Program giving substantial justification of member's efforts to overcome balance of payments difficulties; resources normally provided in the form of stand-by arrangements which include performance criteria and drawings in installments.		
Extended facility	140	190[b]
Medium-term program for up to three years to overcome structural balance of payments maladjustments; detailed statement of policies and measures for first and subsequent 12-month periods; resources provided in the form of extended arrangements which include performance criteria and drawings in installments.		
Compensatory financing facility	75[c]	265
Existence of temporary export shortfall for reasons beyond the member's control; member cooperates with Fund in an effort to find appropriate solutions for any balance of payments difficulties.		
Buffer stock financing facility	50	315
Existence of an international buffer stock accepted as suitable by Fund; member expected to cooperate with Fund as in the case of compensatory financing.		

[a]Members are not expected, and may not qualify, to use all of the available facilities at the same time. In addition, use of the maximum available resources under a particular facility, namely, tranche policies, is usually made in a period of years, not in one year.

[b]The combined use of the extended facility and the regular credit tranches may not be above 165 per cent of quota. Adding the use of the gold tranche raises the maximum to 190 per cent of quota.

[c]Normally, not more than 50 per cent of quota in any 12-month period.

SOURCE: IMF SURVEY, SUPPLEMENT ON THE FUND, Fall 1976, p. 3.

of payments were especially disrupted by the increase in oil prices. An additional $6 billion was added in 1975. This was based on funds from the Arab nations but with the IMF guaranteeing payment of principal and interest, thus easing the recycling problem of the oil producers. Final drawings on this facility were made in May, 1976. As a special assistance to Fund members most seriously affected by the higher oil prices, the Fund established a Subsidy Account from contributions by member countries. Recipient countries receive subsidies in the amount of the 1975 oil facility still outstanding. Finally, decisions to establish a supplementary financing facility were taken on August 1977. This facility will enter into effect when agreements for loans to the Fund of more than SDR7.75 billion are reached. The facility will be available to countries with serious balance of payments difficulties that are large in relation to the country's quota with the IMF.

The cost of the credit extended by the IMF from the permanent credit facilities in 1978 depended on the maturity of the loan. For less than one year, loans could be obtained for 4.375%. Additional years of maturity increased the cost of funds by 0.5%. The maximum rate was 6.875% for eight-year loans. (Loans over five-year maturity are available only from the extended facility.)

Rumbles for More Stability: A European Monetary Fund?

In contrast to the movements toward more flexible exchange rates discussed above, European countries appeared to be eager to return to a measure of fixed rates in 1978. The sharp fall in the exchange rate of the dollar during the second half of 1978 further bolstered the desire for exchange stability among European currencies. As a result, a European Monetary System (EMS) was expected to start functioning in early 1979. The major features of this system, as envisioned by November 1978 were: (1) a system of bilateral exchange rates defining central rates and allowing fluctuations only within a 2 1/4% band around the central rates, as in the snake; (2) establishment of the European Currency Unit (ECU), a cocktail of European currencies with weights to be defined, as the unit of account of the system; (3) establishment of a European Monetary Fund with contributions of domestic currencies and international reserves in the amount of $35 billion to be made available to participating countries in the form of credit facilities; and (4) commitment to increased transfers of funds to participating countries with weaker economies.

SUMMARY

To the observer who is not an economist, much of economics seems odd, for the economist deals with issues that "everyone" knows how to consider. Economic theory, however, ought to help us predict and *understand* how major forces in the economy create certain outcomes. Such insights may come from careful expository writing as well as from mathematical and econometric analysis. The last, econometrics, has been used in the last two decades to provide empirical support or refutation to a variety of issues in economics, but most of the original framework within which the econometrician worked was pure economic theory.

All insights come from simplification, for a model as complicated as the world brings little useful analytical innovation. Thus, the economists are concerned with the *key* factors useful in explaining some phenomenon. They recognize that other issues may be important, but they presume that these other factors are constant during the period studied. All economists regret that the laboratory possibilities for experimentation available in physical science are usually not possible in social science. Even psychologists sometimes have trouble explaining why rat behavior has relevance to human interaction. Human studies, even under laboratory conditions, are artificial by nature because the laboratory can never be as complex as the world is.

In Chapter 3 we summarized the traditional explanations of why nations trade, why there are imbalances in a nation's balance of payments, and how these balances change over time. This was done within a framework which could be called post-Keynesian economics. Those economists who are commonly called monetarists also have explanations for these international economic trends. Just as the monetarist/fiscalist (or neoclassicist) views of domestic employment/inflation/growth issues often agree on a number of factors that affect the outcome of a particular government monetary or fiscal action, so too, do these people of different persuasions agree on certain variables when they view the international scene. Again, however, the monetarists and the fiscalists part company on which are the *major* factors affecting the outcome. Furthermore, they often disagree on what *equilibrating process* causes prices, trade balances, output, interest rates, and monetary balances to change.

The *nature* of the equilibrating process in the international economic world becomes very important because of major philosophical disagreements about the *competitiveness* of factor input markets (such as labor and raw materials) and final good/service output markets. Monetarists (by which we mean a synthesis of classical economists and monetary economists) generally have greater faith than neoclassicists do in a competitive world that will bring prices and output into equilibrium by the nature of the market process. Fiscalists, viewing international trade barriers and costs of information, oligopolist and monopolist producers, and the like, do not see competitiveness in the world economy. Most economists would not view money and real money balances as the obvious stimulus to a new equilibrium level of output and prices as monetarists would argue. In this chapter we have tried to review the implications of these two philosophical approaches for international finance.

There are various automatic mechanisms that operate to correct payment imbalances. Demand for goods in the surplus country tends to drive up *prices,* dampening demand for its goods abroad. Thus the effect on the price of goods tends to restore the balance. There are also *income* effects; returns to capital, labor, land, and entrepreneurship from balance of payments surpluses induce greater spending, some of it on imports. Such spending counteracts the surplus. Reverse effects for both prices and income occur in deficit countries. The effectiveness of these factors is related to the level of employment, the rigidity of prices and wages, and the elasticities of demand for goods.

By focusing on the money balances of individuals, one can also visualize an equilibrating process. Deficit countries are spending more abroad than they earn from production; therefore money balances must decline. When the foreign reserves are exhausted and/or the central bank frustrates the desire of consumers to rebuild their money balances, imports will decline. In the surplus country, excess money balances will go to import more goods and to purchase more domestic goods. With constant prices, both of these reactions tend to reduce the surplus.

Purchasing power parity operates to balance the real prices of goods among countries over the long run. Through the trading of goods and the exchange of currencies, exchange rates tend to move toward those rates that will restore the relative prices of goods; higher differential inflation in one country will be balanced by deterioration in the country's currency in a floating rate world or by pressure toward a devaluation in a fixed rate environment.

The effectiveness of any of the above factors is debatable. Often, no technique or mechanism is allowed to operate fully because a government intervenes. A government intervenes because public officials are unwilling to sacrifice the domestic economy in terms of inflation or full employment for the sake of international balance of payments equilibrium.

There are various international monetary arrangements that act to offset balance of payments surpluses and deficits. With a domestic money supply tied to *gold,* which is the only means of settling international accounts, a deficit country faces a reduction in its money supply after settlement. This reduction leads to an increase in interest rates, lower investment, lower income, and lower prices. Then, capital inflows occur in order to take advantage of the higher relative interest rates; imports decrease and exports increase because of the change in relative prices. This effect tends to restore balance. The gold system lets the domestic economy carry the burden in employment and inflation for restoring international equilibrium. A *reserve currency* (such as the U.S. dollar) is added to gold as eligible for counting in a country's reserves in order to provide for world liquidity beyond the levels generated by gold production. This action leaves the world to react to the domestic monetary policies of the reserve country as well as to absorb the required deficits of the reserve country in its balance of payments.

Under *flexible exchange rates,* alteration of a country's exchange rate by market forces helps to restore equilibrium; deficit countries find their currencies depreciating because there are excess amounts of their currency abroad. This depreciation raises the price of their imports and decreases the price of exports, tending to restore balance.

Under a *fixed rate* system, such as generally prevailed until 1971 following the 1944 Bretton Woods conference, a central source such as the International Monetary Fund permits a buffer stock of currency, gold, and credit to be used to offset short-run national deficits. Currency swaps and gold pools may be used by central bankers to stabilize currency parities. In the long run, central bankers and other officials could exert pressure upon the deficit country's officials to put the economic house in order or to devalue the currency. In theory, they also encourage surplus countries to inflate or to upvalue their currencies.

To meet the demand for international liquidity, *Special Drawing Rights* were created by the IMF and distributed among various countries. These SDR's were to serve as an additional reserve asset for nations to use in settling accounts. They were required in part because the supply of gold did not expand at the same rate as international trade. By the *Smithsonian Agreement of 1971* wider bands of ±2.25% around revised exchange parities of most international currencies were agreed upon. Currencies could fluctuate in this range vis-à-vis each other without the central banks being required to intervene by buying or selling currencies. In addition, the commitment of the United States to convert dollars to gold upon demand by international sources was ended. This convertibility had enabled the dollar to serve in large part as the means of international liquidity in the post-World War II environment. Countries in the European monetary union agreed to a tighter parity among their own currencies of ±1.125%, but subsequent international floating of many currencies has made the 1971 parities somewhat obsolete.

Since 1973 countries have been more inclined to change the parities of their currencies, although many nations continue to peg their currencies to the dollar or some other currency. Under the International Monetary Fund, central bankers of many nations attempt to manage the short-run exchange rates in line with long-run trends. The *de facto* system was ratified by the IMF in 1976, and the IMF will gradually sell its gold reserves.

Questions

1. At the end of Chapter 3 you were asked to analyze the current U.S. balance of payments. In light of recent events in the international financial markets, what is your forecast for the future value of the U.S. dollar relative to other major currencies within a year? In five years? Why?

2. In late 1977 and early 1978 the value of the U.S. dollar declined sharply against the yen, the mark, and some other currencies. Many critics maintained that this depreciation was not supported by the basic economic conditions in the United States and other countries. Instead, they argued, it was due to unstable speculation in the exchange markets. Do you agree? Why or why not?

3. Assume that you have been called upon by Mr. William Miller, the new Chairman of the Federal Reserve System, to advise him on a policy course to follow in relation to the value of the dollar. He wishes to know what alternative schools of economic thought you would advise. Also, he wants your opinion on which one you consider most applicable in this situation.

4. What changes would you make in the present international monetary system? Why?

5. What changes in the present international monetary system do you consider *likely* to occur in the near future? Why?

6. What role will the U.S. dollar play in international financial markets in the future? Why?

Bibliography

Aliber, Robert Z., "The Interest Rate Parity Theorem: A Reinterpretation." *Journal of Political Economy,* Dec. 1973, pp. 1451-1459.

Ando, Albert, Richard Herring, and Richard Marston, eds., *International Aspects of Stabilization Policies.* Proceedings of a Conference at Williamstown, Massachusetts, June 1974, sponsored by the Federal Reserve Bank of Boston and the International Seminar in Public Economics. Boston: The Federal Reserve Bank of Boston, 1974.

Balassa, Bela, "The Purchasing-Power Parity Doctrine: A Re-appraisal." *Journal of Political Economy,* Vol. 72, 1964, pp. 584-96.

——, "European Monetary Arrangements: Problem Areas and Policy Options." *European Economic Review,* August 1977, pp. 265-81.

Bergsten, C. Fred, *The Dilemmas of the Dollar.* New York: New York University Press for the Council on Foreign Relations, 1975.

Bhagwati, J., and A. Krueger, "Exchange Control, Liberalization, and Economic Development." *American Economic Review,* May 1973, pp. 419-27.

Bilson, John F. O., "The Monetary Approach to the Exchange Rate: Some Empirical Evidence." *International Monetary Fund Staff Papers,* March 1978, pp. 48-75.

Blackman, Courtney N., "Making Reserves for Development." *Columbia Journal of World Business,* Fall 1976, pp. 34-40.

Bodner, David E., "Official Intervention in the Foreign Exchange Markets: The System in Transition." *Columbia Journal of World Business,* Fall 1976, pp. 16-22.

Brittain, Bruce, "Tests of Theories of Exchange Rate Determination." *Journal of Finance,* May 1977, pp. 519-29.

Burns, Arthur F., "The Need for Order in International Finance." *Columbia Journal of World Business,* Spring 1977, pp. 5-12.

Cline, William R., *International Monetary Reform and the Developing Countries.* Washington, D.C.: The Brookings Institution, 1976.

Coombs, Charles A., *The Arena of International Finance.* New York: Wiley Interscience, 1976.

Corden, W. M., *Inflation, Exchange Rates, and the World Economy: Lectures on International Monetary Economics.* Chicago: University of Chicago Press, 1977.

Day, William H. D., "Flexible Exchange Rates: A Case for Official Intervention." *International Monetary Fund Staff Papers,* July 1977, pp. 330-43.

DeGrauwe, Paul, "The Interaction of Monetary Policies in a Group of European Countries." *Journal of International Economics,* August 1975, pp. 207-28.

de Vries, Tom, *An Agenda for Monetary Reform.* Princeton, N.J.: International Finance Section, Department of Economics, Princeton University, *Essays in International Finance,* No. 95, Sept. 1972.

Frenkel, Jacob A., and Harry G. Johnson, eds., *The Monetary Approach to the Balance of Payments.* Toronto: University of Toronto Press, 1976.

Frenkel, Jacob A., "The Purchasing Power Parity: Doctrinal Perspective and Evidence from the 1920's." *Journal of International Economics,* May 1978 pp. 169-92.

Friedman, Milton, and Robert V. Roosa, "Free Versus Fixed Exchange Rates: A Debate." *Journal of Portfolio Management,* Spring 1977, pp. 68-73.

Gailliot, Henry J., "Purchasing Power Parity as an Explanation of Long-Term Changes in Exchange Rates." *Journal of Money, Credit and Banking,* Aug. 1970, pp. 348-57.

Hahn, F. H., "The Monetary Approach to the Balance of Payments." *Journal of International Economics,* August 1977, pp. 231-49.

Harland-Thunberg, Penelope, "Oil, Petrodollars and the LDC's." *Financial Analysts Journal,* July-Aug. 1977, pp. 55-58.

Hodgson, John S., and Patricia Phelps, "The Distributed Impact of Price-Level Variation on Floating Exchange Rates." *Review of Economics and Statistics,* Feb. 1975, pp. 58-64.

International Monetary Fund, *The Monetary Approach to the Balance of Payments: A Collection of Research Papers by Members of the Staff of the In-*

ternational Monetary Fund. Washington, D.C.: International Monetary Fund, 1977.

Johnson, Harry G., *The Problem of International Monetary Reform.* London: Athlone Press, 1974.

——, "The Monetary Approach to the Balance of Payments Theory and Policy: Explanation and Policy Implications." *Economica,* August 1977, pp. 217-29.

——, "The Monetary Approach to the Balance of Payments: A Nontechnical Guide." *Journal of International Economics,* August 1977, pp. 251-68.

Kindleberger, Charles P., *Europe and the Dollar.* Cambridge, Mass.: M.I.T. Press, 1966.

——, "Measuring Equilibrium in the Balance of Payments." *Journal of Political Economy,* Nov.-Dec. 1969, pp. 873-91.

——, and Peter H. Lindert *International Economics,* 6th ed. Homewood, Ill.: Richard D. Irwin, Inc., 1978.

Meier, Gerald M., *Problems of a World Monetary Order.* New York: Oxford University Press, 1974.

Monroe, Wilbur F., *International Monetary Reconstruction.* Lexington, Mass.: D.C. Heath and Company, 1974.

Mussa, Michael, "Our Recent Experience with Fixed and Flexible Exchange Rates: A Comment," *in* Karl Brunner and Allan Meltzer, eds., *Institutional Arrangements and the Inflation Problem.* Carnegie-Rochester Series on Public Policy. Vol. 3. Amsterdam: North Holland, 1976, pp. 123-39.

Officer, Lawrence H., "The Purchasing Power Parity Theory of Exchange Rates: A Review Article." Washington, D.C.: *International Monetary Fund Staff Papers,* March, 1976, pp. 1-60.

Parkin, Michael, "A 'Monetarist' Analysis of the Generation and Transmission of World Inflation: 1958-1971." *American Economic Review,* Feb. 1977, pp. 164-71.

Root, Franklin R., *International Trade and Investment.* 4th ed. Cincinnati, Ohio: South-Western Publishing Co., 1978, Parts Two and Three.

Salant, Walter S., "International Transmission of Inflation," in Lawrence B. Krause and Walter S. Salant, eds., *Worldwide Inflation.* Washington, D.C.: Brookings Institution, 1977, pp. 167-243.

——, "A Supranational Approach to the Analysis of Worldwide Inflation," in Lawrence B. Krause and Walter S. Salant, eds., *Worldwide Inflation.* Washington, D.C.: Brookings Institution, 1977, pp. 633-56.

Schadler, S., "Sources of Exchange Rate Variability: Theory and Empirical Evidence," *International Monetary Fund Staff Papers,* July 1977, pp. 253-96.

Solomon, Robert, *The International Monetary System, 1945-1976.* New York: Harper & Row, 1977.

——, "On the Past and Future of the International Monetary System." *Columbia Journal of World Business,* Fall 1976, pp. 23-27.

Swoboda, Alexander K., "Monetary Approaches to Worldwide Inflation," in Lawrence B. Krause and Walter S. Salant, eds., *Worldwide Inflation.* Washington, D.C.: Brookings Institution, 1977, pp. 633-56.

Triffin, Robert, *Our International Monetary System: Yesterday, Today, and Tomorrow.* New York: Random House, Inc., 1968.

Whitman, Marina v N., "Global Monetarism and the Monetary Approach to the Balance of Payments." *Brookings Papers on Economic Activity,* No. 3, 1975, pp. 491-536.

Whitman, Marina v N., "Global Monetarism: Theory, Policy and Critique," *Journal of Portfolio Management,* Spring 1977, pp. 7-18.

Appendix: Important Dates in the World Monetary System[1]

1944 Conference at Bretton Woods, New Hampshire, establishes a fixed exchange rate based on the U.S. dollar. The International Monetary Fund (IMF) and the International Bank for Reconstruction and Development (IBRD), the World Bank, are created.

1948 The U.S. President signs bill appropriating funds for the European Recovery Plan—the Marshall Plan.

1949 Exchange rates of major European countries and many non-European countries devalue. U.S. gold stock peaks at $24.6 billion.

1950 U.S. balance of payments on a liquidity basis swings into deficit and stays in deficit for a protracted period with only a few exceptions. European Payments Union (EPU) is created by recipients of the European Recovery Plan—the Marshall Plan.

1958 The European Economic Community (EEC) is established. Most European countries restore convertibility of their currencies for nonresidents. EPU is eliminated.

1960 Run on gold pushes price to $40 an ounce and forces central banks to intervene in London market to hold down price. London gold pool is established by central banks of major countries to support price of gold.

1961 German mark and guilder upvalue. Organization for Economic Cooperation and Development (OECD) comes into existence.

1962 French begin turning in dollars for U.S. gold. Policy continues through 1966 and costs United States $3 billion in gold.

1963 United States levies interest equalization tax on foreign borrowing in this country.

1965 United States imposes "voluntary" controls on the export of dollars.

[1] For a very detailed chronology of the monetary events during this period, see Robert Solomon, *The International Monetary System, 1945-1976.* (New York: Harper & Row, Publishers), 1976.

1967 British pound devalues touching off world money crisis that lasts into 1968.

1968 United States adopts mandatory controls on direct investment.

Run on gold in March brings central banks to Washington and leads to elimination of the London gold pool and the creation of a two-price gold market.

1969 French franc devalues in August.

German mark upvalues in October after floating in exchange markets for a very brief period.

1970 Special Drawing Rights (SDRs) are used as supplement to gold and dollars in reserves of nations. The value of one SDR equals one U.S. dollar.

U.S. balance of payments deficit reaches record $10 billion.

1971 Massive inflows of money in early May enforce Germany to float the mark and Switzerland to upvalue the franc.

U.S. gold stock falls below $10 billion for first time since World War II.

United States runs international trade deficit in first half for first time in twentieth century.

U.S. payments deficit in first half is at a $23 billion annual rate.

On August 15 the U.S. dollar is floated, convertibility of the U.S. dollar into gold is eliminated, and an import surcharge is imposed in the United States.

On December 17, in the Smithsonian Agreement, central rates are fixed and the U.S. dollar is devalued. Also, a wider margin of 2 1/4% on either side of the central rate is established. The United States agrees to eliminate the import surcharge but the convertibility of U.S. dollars into gold is not reinstated.

1972 In May the original Common Market countries, the United Kingdom, and Denmark jointly agree to a narrow range of exchange rate flexibility of 1 1/8% among themselves while maintaining the currencies within the 2 1/4% band on either side of the par value vis-à-vis the U.S. dollar.

On June 23 the pound is floated after a brief speculative period when British international reserves are at record highs. The United Kingdom is joined by Denmark in withdrawing from the monetary agreement with the European countries. Denmark rejoins the agreement later in the year.

1973 In order to protect the domestic economy from international monetary problems, the Swiss franc is floated on January 23.

On February 12, renewed speculation on the dollar leads the United States to devalue the U.S. dollar again. The lira and the yen are floated. Italy leaves the European monetary union.

In March renewed attacks on the U.S. dollar lead governments to close their exchange markets for two weeks. Finally, it is decided to keep the currencies participating in the European monetary agreement, the snake, within 2 1/4% fluctuation from one another, but to float against the U.S. dollar. Sweden becomes an associate member of the snake.

During the summer, attacks on the dollar are renewed. Prices of major currencies move up relative to the U.S. dollar. However, no official parity changes are made and during the last quarter of the year the pressures on the dollar recede. When the oil-producing nations establish an embargo on oil exports to developed countries, the United States is perceived to be in a more self-reliant position than the other developed countries. After the embargo is suspended, oil prices more than quadruple within a short period of time.

1974 In January the three programs controlling capital outflows from the United States are eliminated. This leads to massive U.S. lending to foreigners.

The French franc withdraws from the European joint-float program.

The oil-producing countries maintain a large portion of their increased reserves in the form of deposits with banks. Recycling these petrodollars to countries with deficits in their balance of payments appears as a new problem for the international monetary system.

In the first half of the year several bank failures with large losses in foreign exchange bring fears to international financial markets. Credit worthiness of institutions is questioned.

On June 28 the IMF redefines the value of SDRs. The new value is based on the weighted value of 16 major currencies instead of reflecting only the value of the U.S. dollar.

1975 Negotiations toward an agreement on a new international monetary system continue unsuccessfully. In practice, major currencies operate on a managed-float basis and the IMF votes to abolish the "official price" of gold.

In July the French franc rejoins the European joint-float program.

The balance of payments surpluses of the oil-producing countries are reduced to almost half of the surplus amount of the preceding year as these countries step up imports from developed countries. The current accounts of developed countries improve considerably as a result.

The balance of trade of the United States becomes a large surplus; the balance on current account is in a surplus of more than $11 billion for the year.

In November, at Ramboillet, France, heads of six major countries acknowledge the need for a compromise system which allows for currencies to float while pursuing economic goals of growth and price stability.

1976 In Jamaica the decisions to accept a system in which currencies are allowed to float and to stop pegging the price of gold are ratified. A Trust Fund is established to manage the proceeds from sales of IMF gold to be distributed to developing countries.

In March the French franc abandons the European joint-float agreement and its value is allowed to float in the exchange markets.

On April the Board of Governors of the IMF officially accepts the proposals for ammendments to the Fund's articles of agreement.

The U.S. balance on merchandise trade reaches a record deficit of $9.3 billion this year.

1977 In August Sweden leaves the European monetary union.

The U.S. deficit on its balance on merchandise trade reaches a new high, $31.0 billion.

1978 On April 1 the ammendments to the IMF's articles of agreement come into force as the acceptance from the necessary number of participating countries is obtained.

On July 7 the heads of state of the nine countries in the European Common Market agree to work toward closer monetary cooperation. A monetary union where parities are maintained within narrow margins ("at least as strict as the snake") is proposed. Also, plans for an European monetary fund financed with a portion of the reserves of the participating countries is envisaged.

In spite of improvements in the balance of trade and current accounts of the United States, the dollar falls sharply throughout the year, particularly against the German mark, the Swiss franc, and the yen.

On November 1 the United States announces measures to defend the dollar. The package includes increased swap lines, drawings from the IMF, sales of SDRs and gold, and bond issues in the Euro-markets. The dollar recovers.

Appendix: Some International Associations

International Monetary Fund (IMF). Institution created in 1944 to supervise the monetary system established at Bretton Woods. The Fund also provides credit to finance balance of payments problems of member countries. Membership at the end of 1977 included 131 countries. Communist countries are not represented at the IMF.

International Bank for Reconstruction and Development (IBRD or World Bank). Institution created together with the IMF. Its purpose is to provide credit to governments for development purposes. Membership is similar to the IMF's.

European Economic Community (EEC or Common Market)–The Original Six. France, Germany, Italy, Netherlands, Belgium, and Luxembourg.

Enlarged Common Market–The Nine. The original six plus the United Kingdom, Ireland, and Denmark.

Group of Ten. The ten major industrial countries (the six less Luxembourg plus the United Kingdom, the United States, Sweden, Canada, and Japan) which agreed in October 1962 to stand ready to lend their currencies to the IMF under the General Agreements to Borrow (GAB). Switzerland has also joined the GAB making the Group of Ten actually eleven. Meetings of the Group of Ten finance ministers and central governors (and those of their deputies) have engineered the main changes in the world's monetary system in the 1960s and 1970s. Central bank governors of these countries hold regular monthly meetings at the Bank for International Settlements (BIS) in Basel. Representatives from the IMF, the Organization for Economic Cooperation and Development (OECD), BIS, and the European Economic Community (EEC) may also attend these meetings.

Bank for International Settlements (BIS). Organization which operates as the central bank for the central bankers of the Group of Ten.

Interim Committee or Group of Twenty. Group of finance ministers within the IMF. The United States, Japan, Germany, France, and the United Kingdom plus 15 members elected by the remaining members of the IMF. These same 20 countries from the joint World Bank/IMF Development Committee.

OPEC. Organization of Petroleum Exporting Countries. Group formed by major oil-producing countries. Its major function has been to provide a forum where a common oil pricing policy can be established and enforced through a cartel.

Group of Fourteen. A group of seven OPEC countries and seven industrial countries considered to be major creditors among countries. The seven IMF industrial countries are the United States, Japan, West Germany, Canada, the Netherlands, Belgium, and Switzerland.

OECD. Organization for Economic Cooperation and Development. Established in 1961 as successor to the Organization for European Economic Cooperation. Group of 23 developed nations: the Group of Ten plus Austria, Denmark, Luxembourg, Norway, Switzerland, Finland, Greece, Iceland, Ireland, Portugal, Spain, Turkey, and Australia. (Yugoslavia is an associate.)

Group of Seventy-Seven. The club of the developing countries, originally with a membership of 27. In 1978 it included 115 developing countries. Formed by Paul Prebisch of the United Nations Commission on Trade and Development (UNCTAD).

Group of Twenty-Four. Eight countries each of Latin America, Africa, and Asia, deputed by the Group of Seventy-Seven to consider monetary matters.

BRITANNIC INTERNATIONAL SHIPPING, LIMITED [C][1]

On March 26, 1969, the Board of Directors of Britannic International Shipping, Limited (BIS) decided to increase their shipping business in crude oil cargo and to acquire a VLCC (Very Large Crude Carrier), popularly called a supertanker. BIS was considering purchasing a Swedish tanker for £8.5 million in kronor to avoid the risk of exchange losses. However, fears that the Swedish shipyard would go bankrupt before the tanker could be built had made the Board concentrate its analysis on two other alternatives: a German vessel for £7 million or a Japanese vessel for £7.5 million. (See Exhibit 1.)[2] Both proposals involved exchange risks associated with possible revaluation of these currencies. This risk was an extremely important consideration since 80% of the cost of the ship was financed in the country—and therefore the currency—of the shipyard.

It was common understanding at the time that the deutsche mark and perhaps the yen were likely to be upvalued vis-à-vis the pound. If this happened, both vessels would carry a much higher price because of the higher exchange rate of the yen and the deutsche mark that would prevail when payments for the loan were made.

EXHIBIT 1. Ship Specifications and Financing Proposals (thousands of dollars)

	German	Japanese
Total cost	£7,000	£7,500
Delivery date	April 1973	December 1972
Cost per DWT	£33.2	£32.6
Percentage of cost financed by shipyard	80%	80%
Interest rate	6%	6%
Currency	Deutsche mark	Yen
Loan Covenants		
Standby guarantee	£1,500	£2,000
Minimum cash balance	£300	£300
Capital base of firm	£1,500	£2,000

Payment Schedule

German	10% on order, 5% on keel laying, balance on delivery. Loan to be repaid over ten years, payments semiannually beginning six months after delivery.
Japanese	5% on order, 10% when propulsion system in place, balance on delivery. Loan to be repaid over eight years, payments semiannually beginning six months after delivery.

[1] A summary of the (A) and (B) cases of Britannic International Shipping Limited is contained in the appendix to this case.

[2] The problems of the Swedish shipyard originated for the most part from inflation in construction costs. These costs had soared in the last couple of years, and companies which had contracted many years in advance of ship construction on a firm-price basis had been subject to severe pressures. In addition, in contrast to the situation in other countries, Swedish shipyards did not receive much direct support from their government. One Swedish shipyard had fallen into bankruptcy, and others were near it. In 1977 most of the major shipyards were merged into one firm under government aegis.

The members of the Board acknowledged that they were not experts in the foreign exchange market. Indeed, they wondered if such a person existed. The BIS executive who seemed most competent in these matters was Mr. Hugh F. E. Cooper; therefore, he received the task of analyzing in detail the foreign exchange risks involved in the Japanese and German proposals. His report was due at the next Board meeting on April 3. A summary description of the background to the March 25 decision is contained in the appendix to the case.

Mr. Cooper knew he should first focus on forecasting the future developments in exchange rates for the yen and the deutsche mark vis-à-vis the pound. Then, he had to show clearly how each of the two proposals would be affected if his forecasts were accurate and what hedging policy, if any, he should recommend to the Board. He also had to consider how the financial reporting would be affected under different combinations of financing and currency parities. (see Exhibit 2).

Forecasting Exchange Rates

Mr. Cooper wanted to analyze economic data for Japan, Germany, and the United Kingdom (Exhibits 3 through 12) in the context of comments he had heard in the City[3] or read in the papers about the present international monetary situation. These comments are summarized below.

Germany. A year before, in May 1968, the Germans had indicated that by letting their economy grow faster than initially planned, they would solve their huge balance of payments surplus that originated primarily in the trade sector (Exhibit 3). The speculation on a deutsche mark upvaluation that intensified during the gold crisis of the previous March was expected to recede. However, by September the president of the Bundesbank was admitting that an upvaluation might be necessary in the future.

German trade surpluses continued. In November speculation on a mark upvaluation again mounted, with $1 1/2 billion flowing into Germany in a single week. Foreign exchange markets closed and the Group of Ten finance ministers met in Bonn to discuss the crisis. Germany refused to upvalue and instead imposed a 4% border tax on exports and an equal subsidy on imports.

For a few months, trading and fluctuations remained reasonably quiet, but it became clearer that eventually this currency would have to be upvalued. Germany's Finance Minister, Herr Strauss, recently had talked of a possible 8% to 10% upvaluation in the deutsche mark as part of a package in which Switzerland, the Netherlands, and Italy would upvalue their currencies as well, and the French franc would be devalued by 10% or 15%. This statement combined with the recent de Gaulle resignation placed considerable pressure on the currencies involved, since de Gaulle was a strong opponent of French devaluation. The franc and the pound were both near their floors. Yet, the situation was not hectic as at the time of the gold rush in March 1968, or during the November crisis. One reason the situation was not worse was that the usual movers of large amounts of funds across the exchanges had already taken their positions in

[3]The financial district of London is referred to as "the City."

EXHIBIT 2. Taxation and Financial Reporting of Selected Items

	Upvaluation Does Not Take Place		*Upvaluation Takes Place*	
	Before Ship Delivery	*After Ship Delivery*	*Before Ship Delivery*	*After Ship Delivery*
Asset and loan	—	—	Written up	Remain fixed
Depreciation	—	—	Increases	Unchanged
Interest expense	—	—	Increases	Unchanged
Exchange losses	—	—	None	Realized as loan is repaid if hedged
Hedging costs	Reduce cash and equity—not tax deductible	A business expense	Reduce cash and equity—not tax deductible	A business expense
Gain from upvaluation if hedged	—	—	Netted against cash and equity. If greater than hedging costs, it is taxed	Create reserve and net it against exchange losses as loan is repaid

EXHIBIT 3. Germany: Balance of Payments (millions of dollars)

	1966	1967	1968	1968 First Quarter	1968 Second Quarter	1968 Third Quarter	1968 Fourth Quarter	1969 First Quarter
A. Goods, Services, and Unrequited Transfers								
Exports f.o.b.[a]	20,138	21,741	24,851	5,826	5,701	6,159	7,165	6,397
Imports c.i.f.	-18,024	-17,352	-20,150	-4,695	-4,819	-5,110	-5,526	-5,677
Other merchandise	-236	-223	-211	-60	-39	-58	-54	-5
Trade balance	1,878	4,166	4,490	1,071	843	991	1,585	715
Paid services to foreign troops	1,224	1,310	1,337	322	330	344	341	313
Other services (net)	1,419	-1,436	-1,193	-205	-279	-496	-213	-341
Total goods and services	1,683	4,010	4,634	1,188	894	839	1,713	687
Unrequited transfers (net)	-1,564	-1,576	-1,796	-410	-119	-391	-576	-381
Total	119	2,464	2,838	778	475	443	1,137	306
B. Long-Term Capital								
Private liabilities	1,096	414	434	62	55	93	224	52
Private assets (increase -)	-654	-830	-2,961	-459	-684	-1,024	-794	-1,454
Advance debt redemption	-235	—	—	—	—	—	—	—
Other government long-term capital	-409	-385	-386	-65	-63	-117	-141	-72
Total	-202	-801	-2,913	-462	-692	-1,048	-711	-1,474
C. Total (A plus B)	-83	1,663	-75	316	-217	-600	426	-1,168
D. Short-Term Capital, n.i.e. (including net errors and omissions)								
Government short-term capital	-42	49	329	64	38	212	15	-36
Other short-term capital	470	-409	134	16	-32	127	23	125
Net errors and omissions	149	—	733	378	217	326	-188	444
Total	577	-360	1,196	458	223	665	-150	533
E. Commercial Bank Short-Term Capital								
Liabilities	-102	297	1,493	-27	180	590	750	-741
Assets[a]	-41	-1,503	-879	-365	151	-346	-319	-438
Total	-143	-1,206	614	-392	331	244	431	-1,179
F. Total (C through E)	351	97	1,735	392	337	309	707	-1,814
G. Official Monetary Movements								
Net IMF accounts	-181	205	-163	-82	-466	44	41	161
Bundesbank investment in U.S. and U.K. Treasury paper (increase -)	—	-250	-675	-125	-175	-125	-250	—
Freely usable assets (increase -)	-537	-143	-345	-435	637	-81	-466	1,584
Miscellaneous claims (net)	249	27	60	5	7	-3	51	71
Monetary gold (increase -)	118	64	-312	255	-340	-144	-83	-2
Total	-351	-97	-1,735	-382	-337	-309	-707	1,814

[a]U.S. dollars put at the disposal of the commercial banks by the Bundesbank through swap arrangements are included in the commercial banks' assets in Group E and excluded from Bundesbank assets in Group G.

EXHIBIT 4. Japan: Balance of Payments (millions of dollars)

				1968				1969
	1966	1967	1968	First Quarter	Second Quarter	Third Quarter	Fourth Quarter	First Quarter
A. Current and Long-Term Capital Transactions								
Exports f.o.b.	9,641	10,231	12,751	2,569	3,112	3,327	3,743	3,283
Imports f.o.b.	-7,366	-9,071	-10,222	-2,451	-2,566	-2,482	-2,723	-2,676
Receipts for services								
Transportation	816	908	1,110	238	268	291	303	277
Investment income	244	284	324	86	79	83	76	115
Military	474	523	589	130	147	144	168	145
Other	397	467	594	134	139	157	164	172
Payments for services								
Transportation	-1,422	-1,724	-1,969	-471	-485	-486	-527	-509
Investment income	-432	-462	-578	-145	-126	-151	-156	-181
Other	-963	-1,168	-1,366	-326	-332	-355	-353	-396
Private unrequited transfers (net)	-6	-23	-26	-25	-2	-2	-1	-28
Central government unrequited transfers (net)	-129	-155	-149	-34	-43	-26	-46	-25
Long-term capital								
Direct investment	-77	-78	-144	-21	-14	-8	-101	-12
Trade credits and loans extended	-550	-702	-823	-192	-215	-198	-218	-232
Other	-181	-32	728	103	211	213	201	291
Total	446	-1,002	809	-405	173	511	530	224
Trade balance	2,275	1,160	2,529	118	546	845	1,030	607
Services and unrequited transfers	-1,021	-1,350	-1,481	-413	-355	-341	-372	-430
Long-term capital	-808	-812	-239	-110	-18	7	-118	47
B. Net Errors and Omissions	-45	-75	84	44	68	-1	-27	61
C. Short-Term Capital, n.i.e.								
Nonmonetary sectors								
Trade credits (net)	-29	486	140	75	-19	-5	89	9
Other (net)	-35	20	69	39	-1	36	-5	-16
Commercial banks								
Liabilities	-276	989	486	170	7	1	308	-63
Assets (increase –)	-113	-487	-724	37	-219	-166	-376	104
Total	-453	1,017	-29	321	--232	-134	16	34
D. Official Monetary Movements								
Net IMF accounts	-66	82	-50	14	-46	-7	-11	3
Other reserves (increase –)								
Foreign exchange	100	16	-809	31	47	-372	-515	-314
Gold	-1	-9	-17	-3	-14	—	—	-1
Other (net)	19	-29	12	-2	4	3	7	-7
Total	52	60	-864	40	-9	-376	-519	-319

SOURCE: Same as Exhibit 3.

EXHIBIT 5. United Kingdom: Balance of Payments (millions of dollars)

				1968				1969
	1966	*1967*	*1968*	*First Quarter*	*Second Quarter*	*Third Quarter*	*Fourth Quarter*	*First Quarter*
A. Goods, Services (net), and Unrequited Transfers (net)								
Exports f.o.b.	14,302	13,882	14,647	3,595	3,564	3,574	3,914	3,789
Net adjustment for recording of exports	168	229	312	77	74	79	82	84
Imports f.o.b. (excluding U.S. military aircraft)	-14,590	-15,326	-16,322	-4,140	-4,013	-4,010	-4,159	-4,255
Payments for U.S. military aircraft	-115	-270	-262	-55	-75	-84	-48	-79
Trade balance	-235	-1,485	-1,625	-523	-450	-441	-211	-461
Transportation	85	130	204	17	70	79	38	22
Travel	-219	-112	27	14	-2	-24	39	29
Investment income	1,164	1,156	1,005	288	319	283	115	456
Government services, n.i.e.	-812	-759	-681	-166	-174	-173	-168	-165
Other goods and services	837	1,048	1,048	264	256	259	269	269
Private transfers	-137	-173	-187	-60	-43	-38	-46	-48
Government transfers	-504	-517	-427	-139	-106	-91	-91	-129
Total	179	-712	-636	-305	-130	-146	-55	-27
B. Long-Term Capital, n.i.e.								
Private investment (net)								
In United Kingdom	762	1,031	1,375	199	264	610	302	324
Abroad	-851	-1,253	-1,766	-481	-410	-325	-550	-444
Official long-term capital								
U.S. Export-Import Bank loans received (net)	143	207	177	53	67	55	2	41
Other	-367	-354	-127	-89	31	-38	-31	-108
Total	-313	-369	-341	-318	-48	302	-277	-187
C. Total (A plus B)	-134	-1,081	-977	-623	-178	156	-332	-214
D. Net Errors and Omissions	-225	442	-311	-309	-62	38	22	432

E. Exchange Equalization Account Losses on Forward Commitments	—	-252	-602	-287	-199	-55	-61	—
F. Short-Term Capital, n.i.e.								
Miscellaneous capital	-260	-186	-58	36	77	-55	-116	245
U.K. banks' net liabilities in overseas sterling area currencies	-126	68	-110	2	84	-143	-53	14
U.K. banks' net liabilities in non-sterling area currencies								
Euro-dollar financing of new private investment abroad	34	135	372	71	53	84	164	84
Other	-482	-17	-288	8	-12	-10	-274	-118
Sterling liabilities (net) other than to central monetary institutions								
Sterling area countries	143	-27	-149	41	-211	211	-190	-24
Other countries	-546	-320	-878	-321	-274	-41	-242	-242
International institutions	36	-43	29	-12	9	10	22	29
Total	-1,201	-390	-1,082	-175	-274	56	-689	-12
G. Total (C through F)	-1,560	-1,281	-2,972	-1,394	-713	195	-1,060	206
H. Official Monetary Movements								
Net IMF accounts	-42	-851	1,262	10	1,413	-75	-86	-304
Gold deposit liabilities to IMF	35	1	-3	—	-3	—	—	—
Sterling liabilities (net) to central monetary institutions								
Sterling area countries	-129	-299	-192	204	-533	-209	346	490
Other countries	867	1,111	1,589	902	-400	413	674	-212
Official liabilities in foreign currencies	39	424	43	305	197	-290	-169	-132
Transfer of securities from dollar portfolio to reserves	885	490	—	—	—	—	—	—
Convertible currency reserves (increase –)	-420	-245	456	175	20	-22	283	-46
Gold reserves (increase –)	325	650	-183	-202	19	-12	12	-2
Total	1,560	1,281	2,972	1,394	713	-195	1,060	-206

SOURCE: Same as Exhibit 3.

EXHIBIT 6. Gross National Product

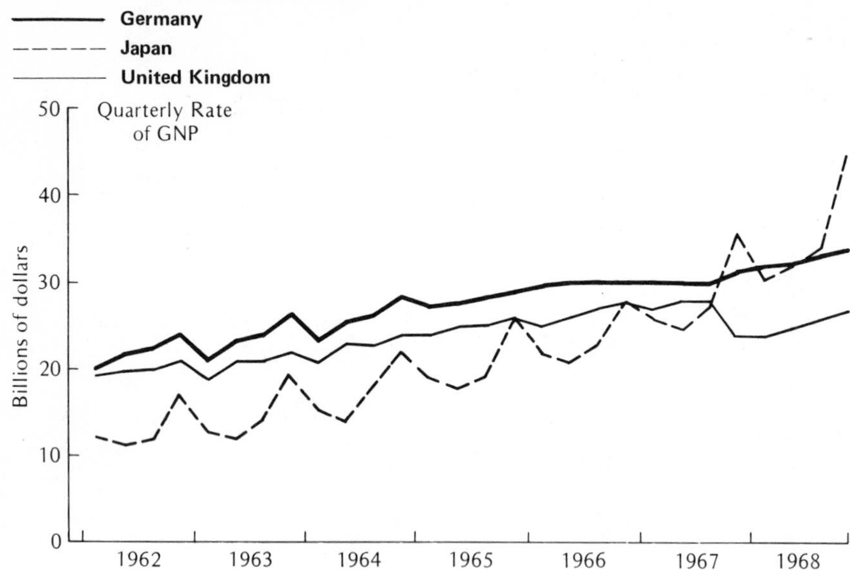

EXHIBIT 7. Earnings Per Employee in Manufacturing

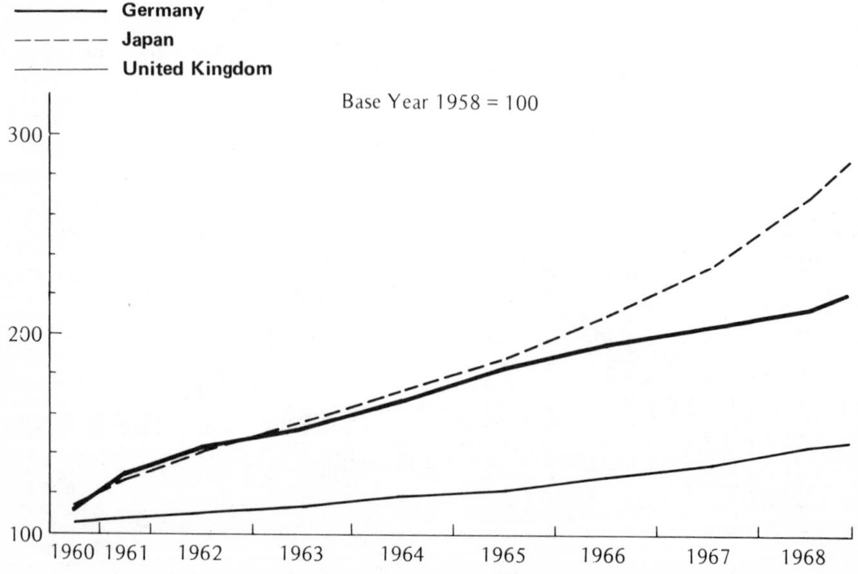

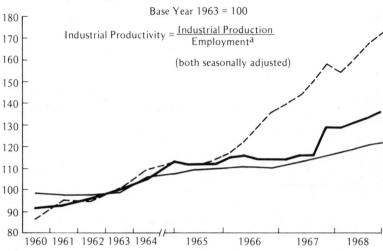

EXHIBIT 8. Industrial Productivity

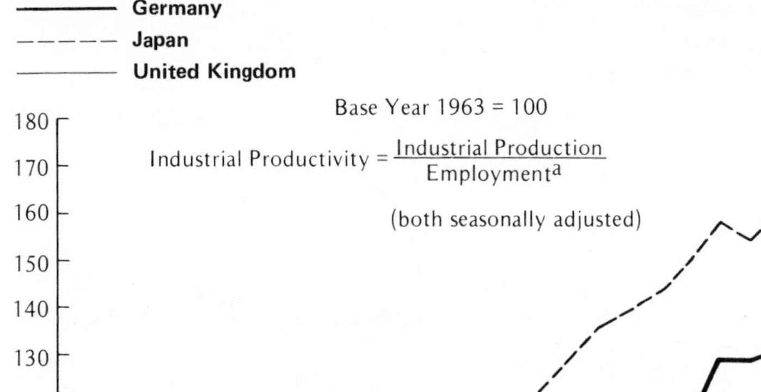

EXHIBIT 9. Consumer Prices

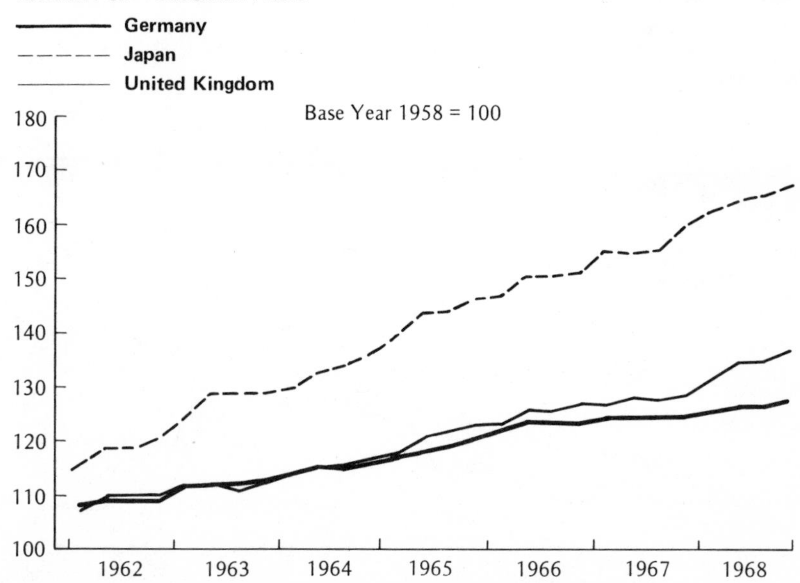

EXHIBIT 10. Net Barter Terms of Trade

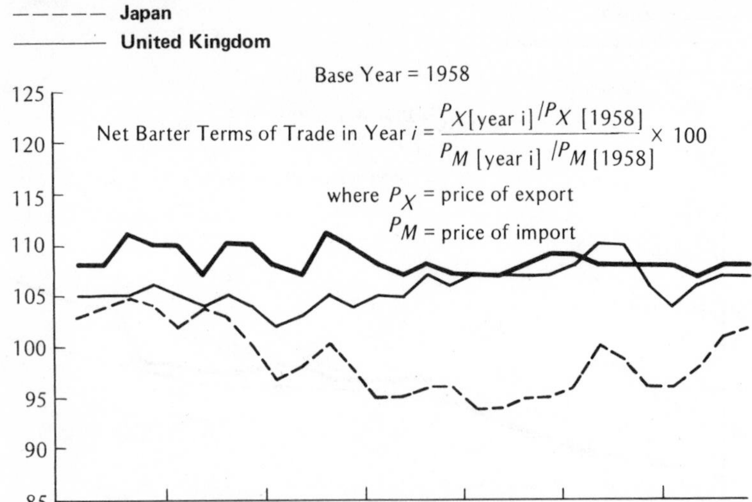

EXHIBIT 11. Short-Term Interest Rates

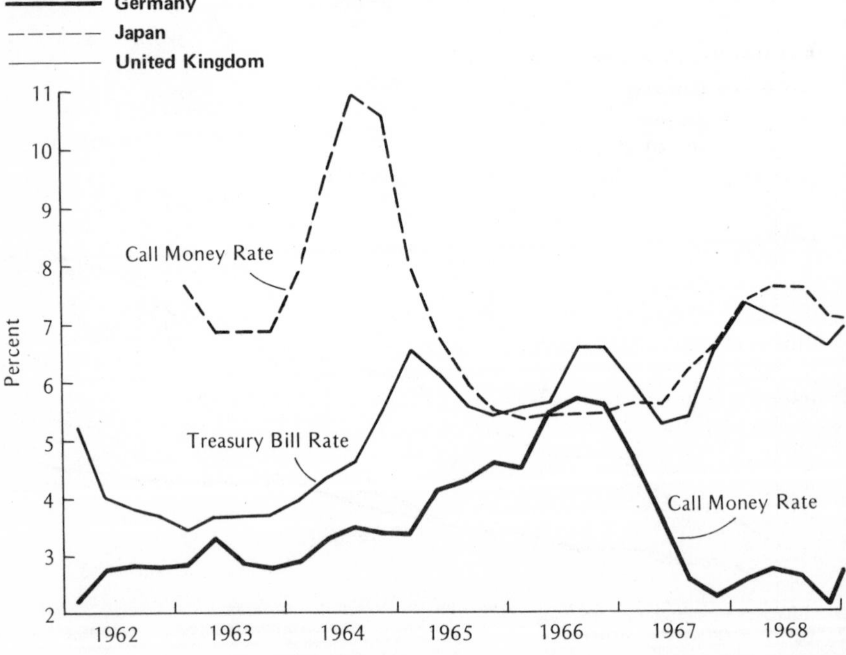

EXHIBIT 12. **Long-Term Interest Rates**

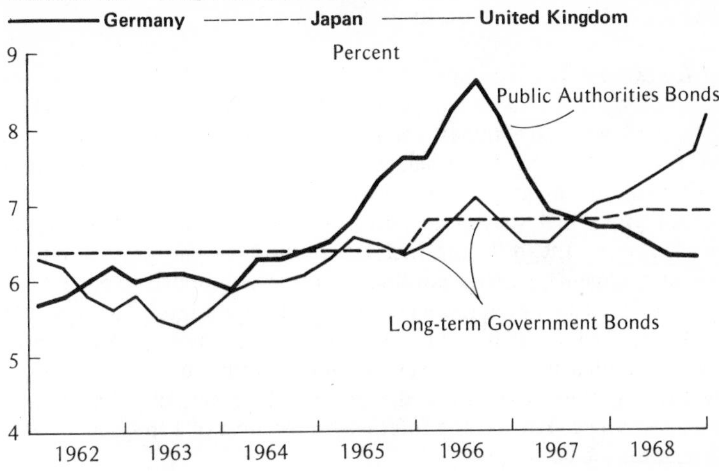

November. Another reason was a rumor that Herr Kiesinger, the German Chancellor, opposed an upvaluation of the deutsche mark. Herr Kiesinger's position was supported by a public poll that showed 87% of the Germans against upvaluation. In the upcoming election on September 28, 1969, the Finance Minister, Herr Strauss, in spite of his personal views, was likely to support any decision that the Chancellor took on these matters. However, the Economics Minister, Herr Schiller (a Social Democrat), was outspokenly for upvaluation. The consensus appeared to be that the mark would be upvalued by the end of the year, particularly if the Social Democrats won the September elections.

Japan. This country was in its longest postwar boom, and Mr. Cooper viewed its economy and currency as being very strong indeed. He even felt that with the furor over the mark, the increasing balance of payments surplus of Japan had not been given appropriate attention. After a slow period in 1967 and the first four months of 1968 when Japan's balance of trade surplus had been relatively small, Japan had been increasing its reserves by about $100 million a month (Exhibit 4). Even the most pessimistic sources were forecasting well over a $1 billion surplus in Japan's balance of payments for fiscal 1968 (April 1968-March 1969), in sharp contrast to the $535 million deficit for the year ended March 1968. The year just ending had experienced a 24% increase in exports and better than 10% increase in real GNP (Exhibit 6). The influential Japan Economic Research Center (JERC) was forecasting a further increase in foreign reserves. These increases in reserves were caused by a buoyant export trade, a moderate recovery of imports from the previous recession, and an enormous injection of foreign capital. The increase in reserves was in agreement with a recent announcement from the Tokyo government that it had raised its reserve target level from $3 billion to $4 billion.

Even though the consensus in the market was that the yen was a strong currency, there had been no wild speculative currency movements into the yen induced by expectation of an imminent upvaluation. One reason for this may have been that the Bank of Japan exercised very stringent controls over the yen and over the inflow and outflow of foreign currencies.

United Kingdom. The November 1967 devaluation of the pound had been followed by a wage-price control measure called the Price and Income Bill in May 1968. Its goals were to eliminate the balance of payments deficits by the second half of 1968 and to achieve a balance of payments surplus of $1.2 billion for 1969. Control on foreign exchange was exercised by granting it only to people who could prove that they were performing a bona fide business transaction abroad. However, the outcome had fallen short of the desired targets: The balance of payments deficits continued, for even though exports performed well, imports increased even more (Exhibit 5). Expectations of an upvaluation in the mark attracted speculative money away from the pound. A continued high interest differential in favor of New York produced a large flow of short-term money to New York away from the pound. Moreover, large long-term capital outflows continued. Finally, the forecasts for the rest of 1969 did not anticipate any change for the better.

In addition to the intrinsic problems of the British situation, there was fear that even if currency realignments took place in an otherwise neutral fashion vis-à-vis the pound, the international nature of the pound would attract problems to this currency. It was particularly feared that if another speculative flow into the deutsche mark took place, it would be out of either French francs or British pounds, whichever was weaker at the time.

On the other hand, there were political pressures to maintain the pound at the $2.40 level. A devaluation of the pound would increase the pressure on the U.S. dollar which was considered to be overvalued. The position of the British government also appeared to be one of holding to a $2.40 rate. Their attitude seemed to be that they had done their part by devaluing in 1967; it was now up to the other currencies to make the remaining adjustments.

Hedging Policies

There were two policies Mr. Cooper was contemplating to protect BIS against an upvaluation of the currencies involved. One possibility was to borrow pounds in England at 9 1/2%, convert them to deutsche marks or yen, and invest them in Germany or Japan at the prevailing low market rates in those countries. However, it was highly doubtful that the Bank of England would agree to withdrawal of currency for this purpose.

The other alternative was to sell pounds for deutsche marks or yen in the forward market. Mr. Cooper thought that it would be very hard to buy a single forward contract to cover the life of the loan from the shipyard. Instead, it would be necessary to buy a 90-day or perhaps a six-month contract and to renew it at the end of that time period if a hedging policy was still considered appropriate. He estimated that the cost of the forward contract would be approximately 3% per annum if no currency crisis took place; however, in the event that a crisis did occur, the cost could run to infinity if the market dried up. As a working hypothesis, Mr. Cooper decided to use 15% as the cost of forward contracts in times of monetary turmoil.

In any case the amount hedged at each point in time would be the cost of the ship still to be paid (both equity and loan) plus the full amount of future interest payments, less the 20% of cost covered by the Investment Grant from the British government (see the appendix).

Taxation and Financial Reporting

The treatment of hedging costs and valuation of assets for taxation and financial reporting purposes depended heavily on whether a currency revaluation actually took place and whether it took place before or after the ship had been delivered.

If *upvaluation occurred before the ship was delivered and began operation,* British Inland Revenue regulations and accounting practices provided both for increasing the asset cost for depreciation purposes and also for increasing the loan payable. Interest charges would be higher based on the increased size of the loan outstanding. In addition, since ships involved progress payments made from the cash/equity accounts as construction proceeded, these accounts would be adjusted. The British Investment Grant also was adjusted to correspond to any upvaluation of currencies.

If *upvaluation occurred after the ship was delivered and began operations,* there would be no write-up in assets (ship) or liabilities (loan payable). Instead, the differential in loan repayment required because of the upvaluation was added to the interest accrued for the year, and the total amount of revised interest would be expensed annually for tax purposes. For reporting purposes, exchange losses would be shown as a separate line entry annually.

If *hedging* took place, the hedging costs would *not* be deductible for tax purposes nor could they be capitalized for amortization at a later date *before the delivery of the ship.* Hence, these hedging costs would be deducted from the cash and equity accounts each year prior to the commencement of ship operations. Should upvaluation occur when the firm's position was hedged, there were taxes payable equal to 42 1/2% of any proceeds of the hedge which exceeded the cost of the hedge in that year. Proceeds were then credited directly to cash and equity accounts. *After delivery of the ship,* then both hedging costs and the proceeds (if any) from a successful hedge were considered as an expense or income item, respectively, for both Inland Revenue and reporting purposes. They would net to a reserve against which the annual exchange loss would be charged.

A summary of the effects of these rules is contained in Exhibit 2.

Appendix: Summary of Brittanic International Shipping, Limited [A] and [B][1]

A publicly traded British Corporation, Britannic International Shipping, Limited (BIS), started operations in 1948. By 1969 the company had expanded to a twenty-three vessel fleet exceeding 500,000 tons, made up of eleven tankers, five dry cargo ships, and seven bulk carriers.

[1] This appendix is essentially a summary of the (A) and (B) cases of Britannic International Shipping Limited available from Intercollegiate Clearing House, case numbers 9-272-023 and 9-272-024, prepared by E. Eugene Carter.

Expected Operating Profits

BIS's estimates of cash flows associated with a supertanker of the type the company was considering are presented in Exhibit 13. One critical assumption in these estimates was the shipping rate. The estimates were based on a rate of Worldscale 45.[2] This was one of the figures hardest to forecast given the instability of prices that plagued the industry. Recently these rates had fluctuated between a peak of approximately Worldscale 200 with the closing of the Suez Canal and a low of Worldscale 17.5 in periods of excess supply of tankers. The average rate during the early 1960s had been around Worldscale 40–50. Current crude voyage rates for 100,000 DWT tankers were Worldscale 60 (a $2.74 time-charter equivalent). Longer-term time-charters for 250,000 DWT tankers were currently averaging $1.10 for a three-year charter, corresponding to Worldscale 34. The spread between these two rates was explained on two accounts. First, present voyage rates were still somewhat abnormally high as a result of the undercapacity that developed in 1967 with the closing of the Suez Canal during the Arab-Israeli war. Second, the shipping industry had a large amount of capacity ordered which was expected to depress rates when it came on stream. The company contracted shipping rates in sterling to avoid exchange risks on this account.

Another source of concern in the estimates in Exhibit A.1 was the operating cost figures. Inflation in the past had produced fast rates of growth in these expenditures. This was particularly critical in the face of the forecast for excess capacity and depressed rates. Still another source of uncertainty was the cost of returning the ship to classification standards after each Special Survey every four years.[3]

Financing Provided Through the British Government

The British Investment Grant effective at the time entitled the shipping industry to a 20% refund on the cost of a new ship. This grant was payable 12 months after each payment by the firm on the ship. In addition, the firm could take

[2]Two rate systems existed in the industry. The chartering of a vessel *for a particular voyage* (voyage charter) was usually based on Worldscale rates. The chartering of a vessel *for an agreed period of time* in operating conditions with crew and operating expenses included but excluding fuel and port costs (time charter) was based on rates expressed in dollars (US$) per deadweight ton (DWT) per month. The Worldscale rate was an attempt to provide the owner of one sample tanker the same net per diem income for a voyage between any pair of ports allowing for a nonrevenue earning voyage in ballast on the return leg. Therefore, the operating margin for the basic tanker was identical regardless of the ports between which the ship operated. Worldscale rates could be converted to a dollar per DWT rate by multiplying the Worldscale rate for the voyage times the deadweight tonnage, subtracting the fuel and port costs, and dividing this figure by the tonnage and time period involved.

[3]Classification of ship standards was done continually by any one of the eight major classification services, with major reviews every four years. The Classification Report required the owner to remedy such defects as were cited in order to maintain classification. Two main rating services were the American Bureau of Shipping (ABS) and Lloyds. Employment conditions, acceptance in ports, insurance rates, and chartering were dependent on the vessel being fully classified.

EXHIBIT A.1. Cash Flow of Swedish 252,000 DWT Very Large Crude Carrier (thousands of pounds sterling)

	1969	*1970*	*1971*	*1972*	*1973*	*1974*	*1975*	*1976*	*1977*	*1978*	*1979*	*1980*	*1981*	*1982*	*1983*	*1984*	*1985*	*1986*	*1987*
Payment for Ship	(415)	(830)	(7,255)																
Investment Grant		83	166	1,451															
Loan Receipt (Repayment)			6,640	(830)	(830)	(830)	(830)	(830)	(830)	(830)	(830)								
Operating Revenues[a]				1,810	1,810	1,810	1,653	1,810	1,810	1,810	1,653	1,810	1,810	1,810	1,653	1,810	1,810	1,810	1,810
Operating Expenses[b]				(456)	(456)	(456)	(456)	(456)	(456)	(456)	(456)	(456)	(456)	(456)	(456)	(456)	(456)	(456)	(456)
Interest on Loan[c]				(405)	(351)	(297)	(243)	(189)	(135)	(81)	(27)								
Special Survey							(200)				(200)				(200)				
Net Income Before Depreciation				949	1,002	1,057	754	1,165	1,219	1,273	972	1,354	1,354	1,354	997	1,354	1,354	1,354	1,354
Depreciation (Inland Revenue)[d]				(949)	(1,002)	(1,057)	(754)	(1,165)	(1,219)	(654)	0	0	0	0	0	0	0	0	0
Taxable Income				0	0	0	0	0	0	619	972	1,354	1,354	1,354	997	1,354	1,354	1,354	1,354
Tax Payments[e]				0	0	0	0	0	0	(263)	(413)	(575)	(575)	(575)	(424)	(575)	(575)	(575)	(575)
Depreciation (Book)[f]				(404)	(404)	(404)	(404)	(404)	(404)	(404)	(404)	(404)	(404)	(404)	(404)	(404)	(404)	(404)	(404)
Net Income Before Tax (Book)				545	598	653	350	761	815	869	568	950	950	950	593	950	950	950	950
Net Income After Tax (Book)[e]				313	345	376	201	438	469	500	327	546	546	546	341	546	546	546	546
Salvage (Net of Tax)																			196
Equity	2,250	2,250	2,250	1,500	1,500	1,500	1,500	1,500	1,500	1,755	2,352	2,120	1,888	1,656	1,424	1,192	960	728	0
To (From) Shareholders[g]	(2,250)			1,213	345	376	201	438	469	245	(272)	779	779	779	573	779	779	779	1,275
Ending Cash Balance[h]	1,908	1,205	786	1,144	973	825	548	446	367	300	300	300	300	300	300	300	300	300	0

[a] Based on \$1.50 DWT per month (Worldscale 45) for 11 1/2 months. An extra four weeks of revenue is lost every fourth year during the Special Survey.

[b] Based on £1250 per day for 365 days.

[c] At 6 1/2% per annum on balance.

[d] The free depreciation option is used on a cost basis of 80% of ship (£8,500,000 × .8 = £6,800,000). Depreciation to the extent of all income is taken each year until the ship is fully depreciated. A small part of the ship's cost is not covered by the 80% financing arrangement.

[e] Inland Revenue tax rate of 42 1/2%.

[f] Straight line on balance of ship after Grant for 16 years, 5% residual ((£6,800,000 − £340,000)/16) = £404,000 yearly depreciation charge for book purposes.

[g] Cash payments to shareholders are maximum permitted. Equity must not decline below £1,500,000 and cash balance must not fall below £300,000 prior to full loan repayment. After loan repayment, equity may decline to £500,000.

[h] For 1969–1971, cash balances are invested in short-term securities to net 4% after tax, and the proceeds are added to the ending cash balance figure. Accumulated interest of £149,000 is paid out with return of capital in part in 1972 after the first year's trading and the receipt of the final Investment Grant.

advantage of United Kingdom Inland Revenue regulations permitting free depreciation for ships owned by British corporations. The option allowed the firm to charge annually whatever yearly tax depreciation it wished, subject to the restriction that, if the Investment Grant were received, only the balance (i.e., 80%) of the ship could be depreciated. Once the cost of the ship had been set off against profits, normal tax would have to be paid on profits. The current rate of taxation was 42 1/2%.

Financing Provided Through the Shipyard

Each of the shipyards with which BIS was dealing was willing to arrange for 80% of the cost of the ship to be financed. This was facilitated by the existence in each of these countries of an institution that provided a guarantee for the loans and/or provided part of the loan at subsidized rates on a first mortgage on the ship.

In every case the loan covenants contained various restrictions. These covenants referred to a minimum cash balance and capital base of the firm. In addition, the lender required the shipowner to provide a standby guarantee. The Japanese proposal required a bank guarantee in contrast to the company's guarantee in the other proposals. This guarantee entitled the lender to have recourse to shareholders' funds or bank funds in case of bankruptcy. The other loan terms (interest rate, installment payments, and so on) were somewhat different for each proposal. But in every case the 20% equity contribution had to be made during the period of construction, and the loan repayment would begin six months after the ship's delivery.

CHAPTER 5

An Introduction to the Foreign Exchange Market

Every international financial officer must deal in a variety of currencies that often fluctuate in value. The earlier chapters analyze the forces that make currency values change; this chapter will look at the markets where these changes take place: the money market and the foreign exchange market. We will show the relationships that regulate these financial markets and the behavior of the participants who "make the market."

The relationships discussed here prevail in the absence of interferences with the market, such as governmental control. This is the situation existing in the markets where currencies are traded outside national regulations, such as the market for Euro-currencies. Discussing the free-market situation will establish the nature of the interrelationships among the money markets and the foreign exchange markets. Deviations from the prescribed behavior can then be identified as opportunities for profit.

NATURE OF THE FOREIGN EXCHANGE MARKET

Background

The foreign exchange market is where buyers and sellers of currencies meet. This market is somewhat similar to the over-the-counter market in securities. There is no centralized meeting place (except for a few places in Europe and the International Monetary Market of the Chicago Mercantile Exchange) and no fixed opening and closing time. The trading in foreign exchange is done over the telephone or through the telex. The currencies and the extent of participation of each currency in this market depend on local regulations which vary from country to country. Of the more than one hundred member countries of the International Monetary Fund, only a few have established full convertibility of their currencies for all transactions. The currencies with restricted convertibility play a very small role in the foreign exchange market.

Foreign exchange markets may be *spot* or *forward.* In the spot market currencies are bought or sold for immediate delivery, although in practice delivery and payment occur two days following the conclusion of the deal. In the forward market currencies are bought or sold now for future delivery. In this market payment is made upon delivery, but the exchange rate is agreed upon at the time of the contract. The date of the delivery is called the *value date.*

The major participants in the foreign exchange market are large commercial banks that actually "make the market." In the United States about a dozen banks in New York and another dozen banks located in other U.S. cities maintain a position in twelve or fifteen major currencies and to a lesser extent in other currencies. These banks operate in the foreign exchange market at two levels. At the retail level they deal with their customers—corporations, exporters, etc. At the wholesale level banks maintain an interbank market. Contact in this market in the United States is usually made through a foreign exchange broker who receives a small commission. In this country there are about six of these brokers. By preserving the anonymity of the parties until the deal is concluded, the broker's function is to provide a fuller market than if the banks were to contact other banks directly. However, when dealing with institutions in other countries, banks usually deal directly with each other without the intermediation of brokers.

The other important participants in the foreign exchange market are the various countries' central banks. These institutions frequently intervene in the market to maintain the spot rates of their currencies within a desired range and to smooth fluctuations within that range. For countries which generally maintain a fixed exchange rate between their currency and other currencies a band of permissible fluctuations is established. When the market rate of the currency reaches the upper limit ("upper intervention point") of the band, the central bank of that currency must increase sales of its currency in exchange for other currencies. Similarly, the central bank must sell foreign exchange and buy its own currency when the market rate reaches the "lower intervention point." Under a system of flexible exchange rates, central banks are not supposed to intervene in the foreign exchange market. However, historically, every time that a country has floated its currency, the central bank has continued to intervene in the foreign exchange market. This behavior of the central banks has led to the creation of what is called managed floating as noted in Chapter 4.

The other participants in the foreign exchange market are nonfinancial businesses and individuals who deal in the market through commercial banks. Their behavior will be discussed in later chapters.

Using Foreign Exchange Quotations

A foreign exchange quotation is the price of a currency expressed in terms of another currency. Quotations in the foreign exchange market are generally made in terms of the amount of local currency required to buy a unit of foreign currency. Thus, in the United States, exchange rates are quoted in terms of dollars required to purchase one foreign monetary unit, e.g., $0.20/FF, and in France the quotations are made in terms of French francs per unit of foreign exchange, e.g., FF5.00/$. The major exception to this practice is the United Kingdom, where foreign exchange prices are quoted in terms of foreign monetary units required to purchase one pound sterling.

Foreign exchange quotations are usually difficult to understand for those who do not exchange currencies frequently. The difficulty arises from the fact that a quote involves statements about two currencies simultaneously. However, the formal quote is given in terms of a single number without explicitly establishing the role that each currency plays in the quote.

In a foreign exchange quote one currency plays the role of unit of account in terms of which the price is given; the other currency is the unit for which the price is being quoted. Actually, these two roles are always present in the quote of price for any article. When we say that "the price is $3.00 per pound of beef," the quote for beef is $3.00. In this quote the unit of account is the dollar and the unit for which the price is offered is a pound of beef. Similarly, when the price for one German mark is given as $0.50, the dollar is the unit of account and one mark is the unit for which the price is offered. To make explicit the role of each currency in an exchange quote, it is helpful to write down the names of the two currencies in their appropriate positions. The currency used as a unit account is placed in front of the quote. The unit of the currency being priced follows the quote. Thus, in the above quote for marks the complete quote should be:

$0.50/DM

where the *unit of account* is the U.S. dollar, and the *unit of currency being priced* is one mark.

One usually expects to hear a higher number when the price of an item increases. This may or may not appear to be true in a foreign exchange quotation. An appreciation of a currency is shown by an increase in the numbers quoted only when the currency in whose price we are interested is in the role of unit being priced by the specific quote. For example, if we are interested in the price of the mark relative to the dollar and the price moves from $0.50/DM to $0.53/DM, we can say that the mark has appreciated relative to the dollar by $0.03. This is the same as saying that the dollar has depreciated relative to the mark. Had we been interested in the performance of the dollar, its depreciation would have been associated with a higher number! When the quoted number increases, this implies an appreciation in the value of the currency used as the item purchased or sold (German mark), but a depreciation for the currency used as the unit of account (dollar).

Given that we are used to associating appreciation with larger numbers and depreciation with smaller numbers, it is useful initially to express the quote in a fashion where the currency whose price we want is used as the unit of the item priced. If the original quote is not given in these terms, a conversion can be achieved by simply taking the reciprocal of the given quotation. For example:

$$\$0.50/\text{DM}^{1} \text{ is the same as } \$1.00 = \frac{\text{DM}1}{0.50}$$

$$= \text{DM } 2.00/\$$$

Having understood how the roles of the two currencies involved in an exchange quote can be inverted through simple arithmetic, we can now see how the relationships among three or more currencies are reflected in exchange quotes. Thus, the exchange rate between two currencies can be obtained from the rates of these two currencies in terms of a third currency. This is called the *cross rate.* For example, suppose an American trader gave the following quotations in New York:

$$\$0.50/\text{DM}$$

$$\$1.80/\pounds$$

To find the price of one mark in terms of sterling in New York:

First. Convert both quotations to a common denominator, i.e., use as the unit priced the currency present in both quotes, the U.S. dollar:

$$\$0.50/\text{DM} = \text{DM } \frac{1}{0.50}/\$ = \text{DM } 2.0000/\$$$

$$\$1.80/\pounds = \pounds\ \frac{1}{1.80}/\$ = \pounds\ 0.5556/\$$$

Second. Given that $1.00 equals $1.00, then:

$$\text{DM}/\pounds = \frac{2.0000/\$}{0.5556/\$} = \text{DM } 3.5997/\pounds$$ (i.e., the price of one pound in terms of DMs)

Similarly,

$$\pounds/\text{DM} = \frac{0.5556/\$}{2.0000/\$} = \pounds\ 0.2778/\text{DM}$$ (i.e., the price of one DM in terms of pounds)

[1] Algebraically, this is equivalent to stating:

$$0.50 \text{ US\$} = 1 \text{ DM}$$

and then solving for US$.

A foreign exchange trader will usually quote two numbers: the price at which (s)he is buying and the price at which (s)he is selling a given currency. The first price is the *bid* price; the second price is the *offer* or *ask* price. In either case, the currency for which the bid or offer price is given is the unit of the item priced. In the *bid* quote $0.50/DM the trader is willing to *buy marks* at the price of $0.50 per mark. However, this is tantamount to being willing to *sell dollars* at the price of $0.50 per mark. Implicitly, the quote also establishes the offer price for the currency used as unit of account. Similarly, the trader's *offer* price per *mark* implicitly quotes the rate at which *dollars* would be *bought* per mark.

Usually in transactions among traders only the last digits of the bid and offer rates are quoted; the rest is understood. These last digits are called *points.* For example, the quotation of the spot dollar-lira rate might be 1250/1260. Given that most lira quotes are usually given with six decimal places, this means:

willing to buy liras at $0.001250 per lira and
sell liras at $0.001260 per lira

which is the same as

willing to sell U.S. dollars at $0.001250 per lira and
buy U.S. dollars at $0.001260 per lira

A foreign exchange dealer receiving a call asking for a quote is under a general moral obligation to quote and to deal at the rate quoted. (S)he need not deal for unlimited amounts, but if the dealer is asked the price at which (s)he will buy a given currency and then offers to transact only a small amount, it is clear that the dealer prefers to be at the other end of the transaction–in this case, to sell that currency. A good dealer will provide a prompt response (to avoid giving the caller the opportunity to shop around) and narrow spreads. Otherwise, it is obvious what side of the transaction (s)he wishes to be. Quotations are stated both to buy and to sell. Given the narrow spreads, a dealer will very often sell when a buy is preferred, and vice versa.[2]

The quotations for forward rates can be made in two ways. They can be made in terms of the amount of local currency at which the quoter will buy and sell a unit of foreign currency, as it was described above. This is called the *outright rate* and is used by traders in quoting to customers. The forward rates also can be quoted in terms of points of discount and/or premium from spot, called the *swap rate,* and used in interbank quotations. The outright rate is the spot rate adjusted by the swap rate.

A foreign currency is at a *forward discount* against a given currency when the forward price of the foreign currency is lower than its spot price. The opposite is true in the case of a forward premium. For example, if the spot rate of the French franc is $0.20 per French franc, then the quote of U.S. $0.19 for three-month French francs shows a discount in the forward rate of the French franc against the U.S. dollar. That is, a unit of French francs buys fewer dollars for delivery in three months than for immediate delivery. This quote also shows

[2]For a detailed explanation of how traders establish their quotes, see Heinz Riehl and Rita M. Rodriguez, *Foreign Exchange Markets.* (New York: McGraw-Hill, 1977), Chapter 7.

that the U.S. dollar is at a forward premium against the French franc. One U.S. dollar buys more French francs for delivery in three months than for immediate delivery.

The percentage of per annum discount (-) or premium (+) in a forward quote in relation to the spot rate is computed by the following formula:

$$\text{Forward premium (discount)} = \frac{(\text{Forward rate–Spot rate})}{\text{Spot rate}} \times \frac{12}{\text{No. months forward}}$$

Let's say the following rates prevail in the market for sterling:

Spot rate:	\$1.80/£
Three-month forward:	\$1.79/£

Then the discount on sterling is determined as follows:

$$\frac{1.79 - 1.80}{1.80} \times \frac{12}{3} = -0.022 = -2.2\% \text{ p.a.}$$

Notice that the forward rate has to be adjusted by the actual fraction of the year to which the discount refers to convert it to an annual basis.

To find the outright forward rates when the premiums or discounts in quotes of forward rates are given in terms of *points* (swap rate), the points are *added* to the spot price if the foreign currency is trading at a forward *premium;* if trading at a forward *discount,* the forward quotations are *subtracted* from the spot price. The resulting number is the outright forward rate.

It is usually well known to traders whether the quotes in points represent a premium or a discount from the spot rate, and it is not customary to specifically refer to the quote as a premium or discount. However, this can be readily determined in a mechanical fashion. If the first forward quote (the bid or buying figure) is smaller than the second forward quote (the offer or selling figure), there is a premium, i.e., the swap rates are added to the spot rate. Conversely, if the first quote is larger than the second it is a discount.[3] This procedure assures that the buy price is lower than the sell price, and the trader profits from the spread between the two prices. Example: When asked for spot, one-, three-, and six-month quotes on the French franc, a U.S.-based trader might quote the following:

.2186/9 2/3 6/5 11/10

In outright terms these quotes would be expressed as follows:

Maturity	*Bid*	*Offer*
Spot	.2186	.2189
1-month	.2188	.2192
3-month	.2180	.2184
6-month	.2175	.2179

[3] A 5/5 quote would require further specification as to whether it is a premium or a discount.

Notice that the one-month forward is at a premium whereas the three- and six-month forwards are at discounts.

The remaining sections of this chapter and most parts of the book will ignore the existence of bid and ask prices. Instead, there will be only one rate, which can be treated as the *mid-rate* between bid and ask prices.

Economic Forces in Exchange Markets

Geographical Arbitrage. In principle, the rate quoted for a given currency should be the same in any market dealing in that currency. However, temporary discrepancies among various markets may occur. These discrepancies provide an opportunity to profit by buying the currency in the market where it is selling at a lower price and selling the currency in the market where a higher price prevails. The nature of these transactions is called *arbitrage.* The individual who performs them is the *arbitrageur.*

For example, assume that the quotes of the pound sterling against the U.S. dollar in New York and London are as follows:

New York	*London*
$1.8000	$1.8001

The pound commands a higher price against the dollar in London than in New York. As a result, one can benefit by buying pounds with dollars (selling dollars in exchange for pounds) in New York and selling the pounds in exchange for dollars (buying the dollars with pounds) in London. This arbitrage tends to eliminate the incentive that initially triggered it. The purchase of pounds in New York will tend to increase the price of the pound against the dollar in that market. In London opposite pressures will occur, for the continuous sale of pound sterling in London will tend to reduce the price of the pound against the dollar. This process will tend to continue until the price of the two currencies is the same in both locations.

The arbitrage transaction of buying and selling currencies in two different locations follows the basic finance principle of "buy low–sell high." However, confusion can arise when this principle is applied to foreign exchange. The role of each currency in the quotes must be the same before prices can be compared, and their role must be established. The following process simplifies this:

1. Establish the currency whose unit is being priced. Assume currency A.
2. Establish the currency to be used as the unit of account. Assume currency B.
3. Then ask what the B currency prices per unit of A currency are in each geographic location.

Then compare the price of A in the two locations and act accordingly.

Consider these questions in a slightly more complex example. Take the following data:

New York	*Frankfurt*
$0.51/DM	DM2.00/$

1. Establish the currency whose unit is being priced.
   The dollar.
2. Establish the currency to be used as the unit of account.
   The mark.
3. What are the quotes in each market in terms of DM/$?

New York	*Frankfurt*
DM 1.96/$ (= 1 ÷ 0.51)	DM2.00/$ (as originally given)

It is clear that the dollar commands a higher price in terms of marks in Frankfurt than in New York. Therefore, do the following in each location:

In New York	*In Frankfurt*
Buy $s Sell DMs	Sell $s Buy DMs

The steps presented above serve just to organize one's thoughts. If step 1 were answered with marks and step 2 with dollars, then the quotes would be expressed in terms of $/DM:

New York	*Frankfurt*
$0.51/DM (as originally given)	$0.50/DM (= 1 ÷ 2.00)

So, buy DMs against dollars in Frankfurt and sell DMs against dollars in New York. This is the same conclusion as in the previous paragraph when the quotes were expressed in terms of DM/$.

The principle of establishing mental discipline becomes particularly necessary when more than two currencies are involved. For example:

New York	*Zurich*
$0.51/DM $0.60/SF	SF 0.87/DM SF 1.67/$

In this case there are three relationships to be analyzed: \$/DM, \$/SF, and SF/DM. One could add three more relationships by also considering the reciprocals of the previous relationships, i.e., DM/\$, SF/\$, and DM/SF. The three relationships in the two markets produce the following quotes:

	New York	*Zurich*
\$/SF	\$0.60/SF	\$0.60/SF[4]
\$/DM	\$0.51/DM	\$0.52/DM[5]
SF/DM	SF0.85/DM[6]	SF0.87/DM

Reading down the list of quotes, notice that:

1. There is no arbitrage incentive between the Swiss franc and the dollar;
2. The DM against the dollar is higher in Zurich than in New York;
3. The DM commands a higher price in terms of SF in Zurich than in New York.

Therefore, there are two arbitrage opportunities:

1. Buy DMs against dollars in New York; sell DMs against dollars in Zurich;
2. Buy DMs against SFs in New York; sell DMs against SFs in Zurich.

Covered Interest Arbitrage. In a free market a good such as money should have the same price wherever it is traded. Thus, interest rates should be equal throughout the world. Yet, if interest rates in a given currency are higher than

[4] In Zurich SF1.67/\$

then,
$$\$/SF = \frac{1}{1.67} = \$0.60/SF$$

[5] In Zurich

$$\$/SF = \$0.60/SF \text{ (from footnote 4)}$$

we know

$$SF/DM = SF0.87/DM$$

then
$$DM/SF = \frac{1}{0.87} = DM1.15/SF$$

and
$$\$/DM = \frac{\$/SF}{DM/SF} = \frac{0.60}{1.15} = \$0.52/DM$$

[6] In New York

$$\$0.51/DM = DM1.96/\$$$

$$\$0.60/SF = SF1.67/\$$$

then
$$SF/DM = \frac{SF/\$}{DM/\$} = \frac{1.67}{1.96} = SF0.85/DM$$

for another currency, the arbitrage process will ensure that people will invest money in the high-interest currency. To protect their purchasing power in their own currency, they will arrange to return to their home currency at the end of the loan period, and such covering (discussed in Part II) will change the forward exchange rates between the two currencies. Thus, if the rate for one-year dollars is 7% and for sterling is 10%, the international arbitrage process would tend to move the one-year *forward* rate for sterling to a discount of about 3% vis-à-vis dollars. The investor has two items that affect the return on investment: the interest rate and the exchange rate. Similar analysis and results hold for the borrower. Thus, in a completely free market the relationship between the spot and the forward rates of a currency will be determined by the relationship between interest rates in the given country and in the rest of the world. This is called *interest rate parity.*

In a free market, the currency with the higher interest rate will sell at a discount in the forward market; the currency with the lower interest will sell at a premium in the forward market. This outcome will be brought about by the individuals who engage in *covered interest arbitrage,* the interest arbitrageurs. For example, if interest rates on one-year interbank deposits in dollars are 4% while in DMs they are 6%, the investors in search of a higher yield will tend to move funds from dollars into DMs. In order to avoid the foreign exchange risks of converting the marks back into dollars, the investors will cover the transaction by selling marks, buying dollars for one-year delivery. The only way in which the 2% interest differential in favor of DMs would not induce an international flow of funds would be if the mark for one-year delivery were selling at a 2% discount.

Consider the sequence of events when the interest differential and the premium or discount in the forward market are not the same. Assume the following data for DMs and U.S. dollars:

Spot rate	\$0.4000/DM
1-year forward rate	\$0.3960/DM
Interest rates:	
DM	6%
US\$	4%

Then compute the percentage discount on the one-year DM by using the formula presented before:

$$\text{Forward premium (discount)} = \frac{\text{Forward rate} - \text{Spot rate}}{\text{Spot rate}} \times \frac{12}{\text{No. months forward}}$$

$$= \frac{0.3960 - 0.4000}{0.4000} \times \frac{12}{12} = -1\%$$

That is, the discount of the forward DM against the dollar is only 1% as compared to the interest differential in favor of DMs of 2%.

The alternatives for covered interest arbitrage are the following:

A.	Borrow DMs @	-6%	B. Borrow $s @	-4%
	Convert DMs into $s spot		Convert $s into DMs spot	
	Invest $s @	+4%	Invest DMs @	+6%
	Sell $s forward against DMs at a premium for $s	+1	Sell DMs forward against $s at a discount for DMs	-1
	Net loss	-1%	Net profit	+1%

Obviously, alternative B is the profitable one.

To benefit from this situation the following transactions would take place:

Spot Market		*Forward Market*	
	Today		
1. Buy 100,000 DM at $0.4000	$40,000	3. Sell 106,000 DM one-year delivery at $0.3960	$41,976
2. Buy 100,000 DM worth of one-year DM deposits paying 6% per annum. Expected interest is 6,000 DM			
	One Year Later		
4. Collect principal, 100,000 DM, and interest, 6,000 DM, on DM deposit for a total of 106,000 DM		5. Deliver the 106,000 DM against the forward position	
	Profit in the transaction		
	Dollars Received		$41,976
	Dollars Paid		40,000
	Profit		$ 1,976

Alternative investment: $40,000 is invested in U.S. deposits at 4% rate of return:

Investment	$40,000
Rate of Return	X.04
	$ 1,600

In this case there is an advantage in investing in DMs (1,976–1,600 = $376 or 1%).

As more investors are attracted by the higher net yields in DMs the following pressures will develop:

In exchange markets:

1. The *spot* rate of the DM against the dollar will tend to *appreciate* as DMs are bought against dollars.

2. The *forward* rate of the DM against the dollar will tend to *depreciate* as DMs are sold against dollars.

This will tend to *increase the initial forward discount* of the DM against the dollar.

In money markets:

1. The interest rate for the dollar will tend to increase as dollars are borrowed.

2. The interest rate for the DM will tend to decrease as more funds are available to invest in DMs.

These will tend to *decrease the initial interest differential* between the DM and the dollar. As these tendencies continue over time, the returns on the two alternative investments move toward each other. At that point the discount on the forward mark against the dollar will equal the difference in interest in favor of DMs.

In general, under covered interest arbitrage there is an incentive to invest in the higher-interest currency to the point where the discount of that currency in the forward market is less than the interest differential. If the discount on the forward market of the currency with the higher interest rate becomes larger than the interest differential, then it pays to invest in the lower-interest currency and take advantage of the excessive forward premium on this currency.

A word of warning before leaving this subject. In calculating the opportunities for covered interest arbitrage or in estimating rates from other available information, mistakes are frequently made. To avoid them, it is well to keep in mind the following concepts:

1. A covered transaction must begin and end with the same currency.

2. Only rates applicable to the same period of time (e.g., quarters) and credit risk can be compared.

It is essential to note that *except* for cases such as the Euro-currency market, financial markets are usually *not* completely free and strict interest rate parity does not hold. In these cases the forward discounts and premiums reflect other factors in addition to interest differentials. This is particularly so in periods of heavy speculation about a future change in the spot rate. The theory presented above applies only to *net accessible interest rates.*

The existence of opportunities to profit from covered interest arbitrage between the dollar and two other currencies is shown in Exhibit 5.1. For sterling and the mark, the exhibit compares the interest rate obtained on those currencies on a covered basis (nominal rate plus forward premium or discount against the dollar), with the rate on Euro-dollars. The difference between these two rates is plotted by the line labeled "differential." The differential line hovers around zero for the mark. However, according to this chart, in the case of sterling there were clear opportunities to profit from covered interest arbitrage. Specifically, a positive return could have been made by borrowing sterling on a covered basis and investing the proceeds in dollars. Why did arbitrageurs not take advantage of this opportunity? Simply because the sterling rate was not *accessible* to them. Foreign exchange controls in England made these rates available only to domestic users and forbade the use of the funds to invest in foreign currency. In the case of Germany during 1975-77 there were no exchange controls; therefore, the observed rates were also accessible to arbitrageurs. Before 1975, however, Germany had exchange controls to hinder the movement of foreign funds into marks. The negative differential line during the first portion of that year is the result of these controls.

Empirical research has shown that once the *net accessible* rates are considered, the market has eliminated the opportunities to profit from covered interest arbitrage.[7]

Relationship Between Goods Market and Exchange Markets. The economic forces of geographical arbitrage and covered interest arbitrage are generally recognized to operate effectively in the exchange markets. These forces achieve balance within financial markets. In addition, monetary economists consider that there are other very strong economic forces that link the prices of real goods with the price of money in the financial markets–interest rates and exchange rates.

One link between the goods market and the financial markets is provided by the theory of purchasing power parity, which was discussed in Chapter 4. According to this theory, exchange rates are determined by the relative value of the two currencies involved. The value of a currency, in turn, depends on the price level within each country. With inflation, an increase in the domestic price level, the exchange rate will adjust to reflect the change in relative purchasing power among currencies. The currency with the higher price level will have its value depreciate in the exchange markets relative to other currencies.

While today's price level and purchasing power parity theoretically determine the real value of money today, the *expected* rate of inflation and forward exchange rates establish the value of money in the future. A measure of expected inflation is embedded in the nominal rate of interest. The observed interest rate can be considered to be the sum of some basic "real" interest rate and the expected inflation rate.[8] Lenders who anticipate inflation will charge an interest

[7]See Jacob A. Frenkel and Richard M. Levich, "Transaction Costs and Interest Arbitrage: Tranquil versus Turbulent Periods," *Journal of Political Economy,* Dec. 1977, pp. 1209-26.

[8]This is known as the *Fisher effect* in honor of Irving Fisher who first presented this relationship. See Irving Fisher, *The Theory of Interest.* (New York: Macmillan, 1930).

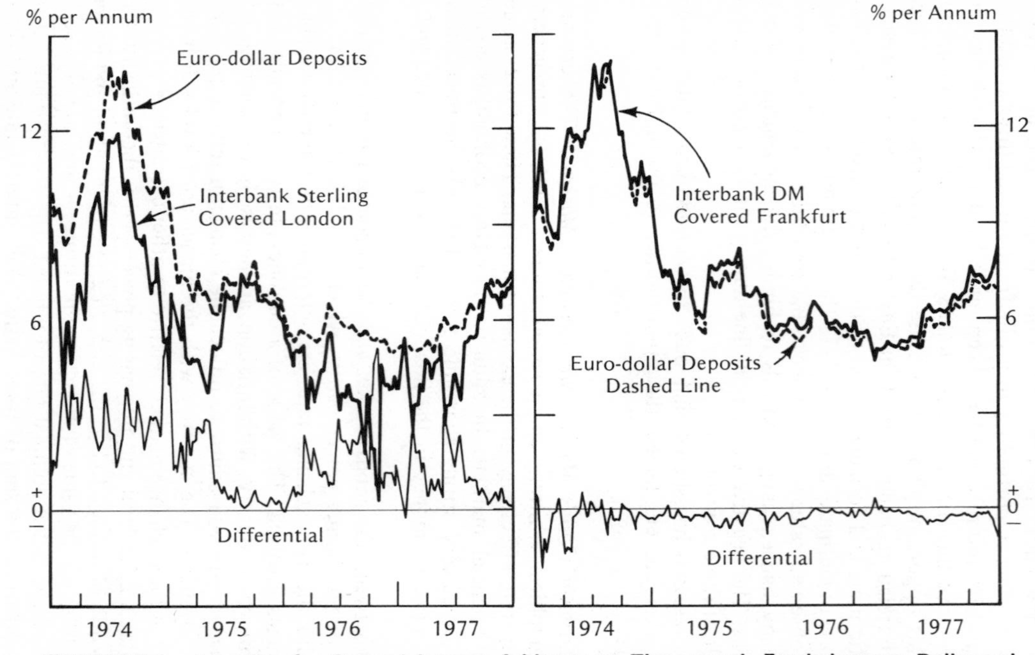

EXHIBIT 5.1. Incentive for Covered Interest Arbitrage on Three-month Funds between Dollar and Sterling and Between Dollar and Mark, 1974–1977 (Averages for Week Ending Wednesday)

Differential: (+) favors borrowing sterling or DMs and investing in $s
(–) favors borrowing $s and investing in sterling or DMs

SOURCE: U.S. Board of Governors, Federal Reserve System, SELECTED INTEREST AND EXCHANGE RATES, Chart 8, January 3, 1978.

rate high enough to compensate for the loss of purchasing power of the money during the loan period. To the extent that the forward exchange rate equals today's interest differentials, expected inflation also affects the exchange markets. As the rate of interest increases because of anticipated inflation, the forward rate for that currency will show a higher discount, or lower premium, than before. The change in forward discount or premium will effectively have been dictated by the expected increase in prices.

Putting together the two pieces of economic relationship just described, we have the following:

1. Today's prices affect the spot exchange rate through purchasing power parity.

2. Expected inflation affects the forward exchange rate through its impact on interest differentials.

If we add that financial markets are considered to be efficient markets in the sense that all information available is reflected in the observed prices, we have that the forward rate is an unbiased (not necessarily accurate) predictor of future spot exchange rates. Interest rate differentials, which equal the forward premium/discount, are also unbiased predictors of future spot rates.[9]

Notice that this conclusion hinges on the assumptions that expected inflation rates are measured properly by nominal interest rates and that purchasing power parity prevails. If this is not the case, or if the exchange markets are inefficient, the forward rate does not perform the role of unbiased predictor of the spot rate. This is consistent, however, with successful covered interest arbitrage which does not depend on any assumption about future developments in prices or interest rates.

THE ACTORS IN THE FOREIGN EXCHANGE MARKET

The previous section presented a panoramic view of the mechanics and economics of the foreign exchange markets. The behavior of one of the participant groups in these markets, the arbitrageurs, was described. The motivation of these individuals to realize a profit in the financial markets without incurring foreign exchange risks makes them behave in a way that serves as a lubricant to maintain the relationships in the financial markets.

[9] For an algebraic formulation of the convergence of purchasing power parity theory, interest rate parity theory, and the forward rate theory of exchange expectations, see the appendix to this chapter. Also see Ian H. Giddy, "An Integrated Theory of Exchange Rate Equilibrium," *Journal of Financial and Quantitative Analysis,* Dec. 1976, pp. 883-92. Empirical research supporting this theory is presented in Jacob A. Frenkel, "A Monetary Approach to the Exchange Rate: Doctrinal Aspects and Empirical Evidence," *Scandinavian Journal of Economics,* May 1976, pp. 200-24; and "The Forward Exchange Rate, Expectations, and the Demand for Money: The German Hyperinflation." *American Economic Review,* Sept. 1977. pp. 653-70. Evidence on the efficiency of exchange markets is presented in Ian H. Giddy and Gunter Dufey, "The Random Behavior of Flexible Exchange Rates: Implications for Forecasting," *Journal of International Business Studies,* Spring 1975, pp. 1-32.

If one divides the other participants in the foreign exchange markets according to motivation, one can distinguish four major actors. (Note, though, that a given actor may play more than one role at one point in time or through time.) Two of these actors operate on speculation about financial markets. The other two add the financial considerations to basically nonfinancial business concerns.

The two types guided by speculation on future financial developments are (1) *the outright speculator on spot rates* who expects to profit from a change in the spot rate of a currency or currencies and (2) *the speculator on interest differentials* who expects to profit from anticipated changes in interest rate differentials or premiums and discounts in the forward rates.

The actors with nonfinancial business enterprises approach the foreign exchange market in two different fashions: (1) *The merchandise trader wants to* protect a given cash flow in the future, a payable or a receivable, from fluctuations in the foreign exchange market, and therefore *covers* the transaction. (2) *The corporation with assets and liabilities in foreign countries* (and therefore in foreign currencies) wishes to protect the value of future foreign earnings by *hedging* in the foreign exchange market.

Each of the four actors listed above can achieve his or her goal through either the forward exchange market or the money market. In a perfect market both approaches produce similar results. The relationship between interest rate differentials and forward rates discussed in the previous section guarantees this identity, as long as the accessible interest rates are the same as those determining forward rates, which is not always the case. Therefore, in the following presentation notice the steps that the given actor could follow in either the forward market or the foreign exchange markets. (In this chapter we present the behavior of the speculators. The behavior of the nonfinancial business enterprises will be discussed in the following two chapters.)

Speculation and Cash Flows

Whenever the maturity and the currency of cash inflows and outflows are matched one-to-one (e.g., a planned inflow in pound sterling in one year is matched with a planned outflow in the same currency for the same date), there is a *square* position. In this case the eventual gains or losses can be computed at the beginning because all the relevant rates are *locked in.* However, when a square position as to maturity and/or currency does not exist, the gains or losses in the transactions cannot be determined with certainty in advance. When this matching process does not take place, the final outcome of a gain or a loss depends on the movements in the market in the intervening period. For example, if there is a planned inflow in pound sterling one year hence and a planned sterling outflow fifteen months from now, then for three months a use must be found for the sterling received and not needed. The return of that investment is unknown at the present time. Similarly, if there is a planned inflow in pound sterling one year from now and a planned outflow for the same date in Swiss francs, one does not know with certainty the gain or loss in the transaction at the beginning. To determine the profit or loss in this transaction requires a knowledge not only of the interest rates associated with the known inflows and outflows for the intervening year (assume that the inflow is the product of the maturity of an investment on a British security, and the outflow the result of borrowings in Swiss francs), but also what happens to the value of the pound sterling against the Swiss franc at the end of the year. If the pound sterling depreciates relative to the Swiss franc in the intervening year, a gain that might have been anticipated because of interest differentials could be wiped out by the fluctuations in the exchange market.

In general terms, any time the cash flows of a unit are not square as to maturity and currency, speculation about the future of the money and exchange markets takes place. That is, the final gain and loss of the transaction can be computed initially only by making assumptions about how the markets will behave in the future, which is something no one knows with certainty at the beginning of the period. In this sense, financial institutions such as commercial banks which have liabilities (future outflows) of a much shorter maturity than their assets (future inflows) are in the business of speculating on the future of the money and capital markets. In similar fashion, when an individual or a financial institution has more assets (future inflows) than liabilities (future outflows) in a given currency, performance depends on the ability to anticipate the movements in the foreign exchange markets. This individual or financial institution must speculate as to the future value of the currencies involved at the end of the transaction period to estimate net gains or losses. Obviously, speculation in both the money market and the foreign exchange markets may be carried out simultaneously when neither the maturity nor the currency of the cash inflows and outflows is matched.

Perhaps some of the stigma attached to the word "speculation" has been dispelled in the previous paragraph. In its simplest sense, speculation is nothing more than an educated guess about the future of the financial market. Conceptually, this is not very different from manufacturing a new product based on the existence of an anticipated demand for the product which may or may not materialize. In the financial world the word "speculation" has usually been used in a derogatory manner. In the mind of the individuals who consider speculation an evil thing, speculation is only a financial phenomenom, usually centered around the foreign exchange market and leading to instability. There is no evil intention in the mind of the speculator; like other members of a capitalist society, (s)he is merely trying to make a profit. Whether the actions of the speculator do or do not contribute to the well-functioning of the exchange markets is an empirical question that has not yet been settled.

Speculation in the foreign exchange market takes place when an individual or institution has an amount of assets (a future inflow) different from the amount of liabilities (a future outflow) in a given currency. If there is a change in the par value of the currency in question, the value of the net holdings of the individual in that currency will change. In this case the individual or institution has a *net exchange position* in that currency. This position is *long* if there are more assets (future inflows) than liabilities (future outflows). The net position is *short* if there are more liabilities (future outflows) than assets (future inflows).

The other situation that allows for speculation in the foreign exchange market can occur when the aggregate inflows and outflows for a currency over a period of time are the same; that is, the net exchange position is zero. However, *for given dates,* the inflows and the outflows of the currency may not be the same. In this case the speculation is not based on forecasts about the spot rate.

No matter what happens to the spot rate, overall the speculator will break even; what (s)he gains (loses) on the long positions, (s)he loses (gains) on the short positions since at any time additional transactions will always take place to make the net position square. In this case the speculation is based on forecast changes in the rates in the money market and (therefore) on the premium or discount in the forward markets. In this case the operator has a *swap position.*

Outright Speculation on Spot Rates

What are the steps one must take to benefit from a forecast of a change in the spot value of a currency? The speculation can be in the money market or in the forward exchange market. If a depreciation is expected, speculation suggests borrowing the currency in the money market and investing the proceeds in another currency. In the exchange market the currency would be sold in the futures market. In both cases the operator would move into a short position in the depreciating currency. If the speculation is successful, the borrowed funds will be repaid with a depreciated currency or the forward contract will be closed by purchasing the currency in the spot market at a lower price. If an appreciation is expected, speculation suggests purchasing assets denominated in that currency in the money market, with funds borrowed elsewhere or buying the currency in the futures market, i.e., moving into a long position in that currency.

Speculation in the Forward Market. If the speculator anticipates that the value of the pound will go from a current \$1.80/£ to \$1.70/£ within a year, this individual will try to be short in pound sterling in the forward market. The speculator will sell pounds for delivery in one year against another currency against which the pound is expected to depreciate (assume dollars). At the end of the one year the speculator will purchase pounds with dollars in the spot market to fulfill the forward contract. The extent of the gain (or loss) in this transaction will depend on the eventual value of the pound in terms of dollars in the spot market as well as the price specified in the forward contract for the pound against dollars.

> *Case 1:* Forward pound is sold at \$1.80. One year later the spot rate is \$1.70. The *gain* will be \$0.10 per pound sold in the forward market.
>
> *Case 2:* Forward pound is sold at \$1.80. One year later the spot rate is \$1.90. There will be a *loss* of \$0.10 per pound sold in the forward market.
>
> *Case 3:* Forward pound is sold at \$1.70. One year later the spot rate is \$1.75. In spite of the depreciation, there will be a *loss* of \$0.05 per pound sold in the forward market.

A speculator expecting an appreciation of the currency will want to be long in that currency. The speculator will enter the forward market offering to buy the currency in the future. Thus, if it is expected that the value of the pound will move upward from \$1.80/£ to \$1.90/£, the speculator will offer to buy pounds for future delivery at any price below \$1.90. This will produce a profit between the price at which the pounds are bought in the forward market and the $1.90 expected to prevail in the spot market. As in the previous example, the profits of the speculator depend on the eventual price of the pound in the spot market as well as the price at which the pound is bought in the forward market.

Speculation in the Futures Market. For the individual or institution who wishes to speculate on the future value of a currency, the futures market in the Chicago Mercantile Exchange presents another alternative. The International Monetary Market (IMM) of this Exchange deals in eight currencies: Swiss francs, German marks, French francs, British pounds, Dutch guilders, Canadian dollars, Mexican pesos, and Japanese yen. Of course, the IMM is available for exchange transactions of any type, not only speculative transactions. However, it is speculators in the exchange markets who may find a unique opportunity in the IMM. Most businesses involved in hedging transactions have access to the exchange traders of commercial banks.

In our earlier example of speculation in the forward exchange market, we assumed implicitly that the speculator had access to a bank's foreign exchange trader with whom the transaction was completed in the desired amount. This is a realistic assumption for business corporations and wealthy individuals who have a substantial ongoing business relationship with a bank. For the average individual who just walks into the bank and asks to purchase £10,000 for delivery in three months, having access to the bank's exchange trader is totally unrealistic. The IMM of the Chicago Mercantile Exchange, however, is a possible option.

Conceptually, trading in futures is similar to trading in the forward exchange market. If a currency is expected to depreciate against the dollar, the speculator will want to sell this currency. If the expectation is for an appreciation, the speculator will want to buy the currency. However, the procedure for carrying out these transactions in the forward exchange market and the futures market is different.

From the point of view of a customer, the major characteristic that distinguishes the futures market from the forward exchange market is that a *margin* or security deposit must be maintained with a broker as a guarantee of ability to fulfill a contract in the IMM. This margin is a security designed to cover any initial loss due to adverse price movements. For each currency, the Exchange establishes an *initial margin* and a *maintenance margin* per contract in that currency. The size of a contract for each currency is determined by the Exchange. The original margin is approximately 2 1/2% of the value of the contract. If the initial margin for a sterling contract is $1,500 and the maintenance margin is $1,000, the speculator buying or selling sterling contracts with these margin requirements initially deposits $1,500 per contract with a broker as margin. If the speculator's equity in the contracts declines to below $1,000, the speculator will receive a "margin call" from his or her broker requesting the speculator to add $500 to the margin account. If the contract is liquidated at that point the additional margin becomes a realized loss. Conversely, gains in the price of the contract can become realized gains. These adjustments are done daily. Margin calls must be settled on a daily basis. This is in contrast to the transactions with banks' exchange traders where there are no margin requirements and where the gain or loss in a forward exchange contract is not settled until maturity.

The gains or losses that a speculator in the IMM may suffer in a given day are also limited by the Exchange, which establishes limits on the amount that the price of specific contracts can fluctuate on a daily basis. In case of large changes in prices the Exchange provides a procedure for larger limits for two days and for one day of trading without limits before the normal limits are reinstated. For example, the contract size for the British pound is £25,000. The normal limit of price fluctuation in a given day is $0.05/£; that is, $1,250. After two successive days of the contract losing $1,250 per day, the maximum price loss allowed on the third day is increased to 150% of the normal limit, $1,875. If at the end of the third day the closing price has declined to the allowed limit, the allowed price loss on the fourth day is increased to 200% of the normal limit, $2,500. Finally, on the fifth day of sustained maximum losses, the price of a contract is allowed to float without any limits before normal limits are set again on the sixth day.

As implied in the preceding discussion, the amounts traded in the futures market are multiples of what the Exchange determines to be a contract size in each currency. Fractions of a contract are not traded. The futures market also establishes specific dates of delivery. All contracts are for delivery on the third Wednesday of either March, June, September, or December. Tailor-made contracts of a given amount for specific dates of delivery are not possible in the IMM. As a matter of fact, currencies are treated by the Exchange as any other commodity; e.g., pork bellies, where actual delivery of the contracted merchandise only takes place in a very small percentage of the transactions, less than 3%. Most transactions are settled before maturity.

Transactions in the futures market require payment of a commission to the broker. Since March 1978, the size of the commissions is negotiated between the customer and the broker. Before that date the Exchange imposed minimum commissions. Brokers discourage small transactions by imposing stiff commissions.

Besides the individuals forced to operate through the IMM because of lack of an alternative in commercial banks, businesses have found it advantageous to transact through the IMM on some occasions. These situations arise particularly when the IMM is very active, relative to the banks, and its spreads between bid and offer price become narrower than the banks' market. This was the case on August 1976, with the Mexican peso. The Mexican peso was devalued on September of that year. Generally, there is a considerable amount of arbitrage between the IMM and the banks' market. However, large multinationals still consider the size of their transactions too large for the IMM to handle without destabilizing the market. The IMM is a very active market with more than half of the outstanding contracts often changing hands on a daily basis, but its size is still relatively small.

Speculation through the Money Market. If the speculator anticipates a depreciation in a currency and wishes to speculate through the money market, (s)he will borrow that currency, convert it into some harder currency, and wait until the depreciation takes place. The initial cost of this strategy is the interest differential between the cost of borrowing and whatever return can be obtained in the harder currency, plus transaction costs. The potential return depends on the eventual depreciation of the currency in question.

In the case of an expected appreciation, operations in the money market will reverse the pattern described above. The speculator will increase assets denominated in the currency expected to appreciate by borrowing in softer currencies. The initial cost is the interest differential between the interest on the loan and the return on the asset, plus transaction costs. The potential return depends on the final parity of the currencies in question.

Speculation on Interest Differentials

This situation arises when total "buys" equal total "sells" in the same currency, i.e., there is no net exchange position in that currency; however, the maturity of "buys" and "sells" is not perfectly matched, i.e., speculation. This position is often practiced by traders in commercial banks and is called a *swap position.*

The opportunity for this type of speculation arises when a change in interest rates and (therefore) forward premium or discount is anticipated. For example, take the following situation:

	Money Market	*Foreign Exchange Market*
Initial interest rates:	Dollar—4% Sterling—7%	3% discount per annum on sterling (premium on U.S. dollar)
Forecast rates in one month:	Dollar—4% Sterling—6%	2% discount per annum on sterling (premium on U.S dollar)

Swap through the Money Market. This is the easier transaction to undertake. It can be done without using the foreign exchange markets. If a decline in interest rates is anticipated, the speculation in the money market will take the following form:

Day 1: Invest for 1 year at 7% (to lock in the current high interest). Borrow for 1 month at 7% (to finance the investment temporarily).

Day 31: Refinance borrowings at 6% for 11 months.

Therefore, the investor will enjoy the interest differential of 1% for eleven months.

In this transaction the total volume of outflows and inflows in pounds is the same, i.e., the amounts invested and borrowed are the same at all times. The net exchange position in pounds is zero since the investor is dealing with only one currency and borrowings equal investments.

The risks involved in this transaction arise from the nature of the forecast. What if interest rates do not decline? Worse still, what if interest rates in the United Kingdom go above the 7% return on the investment? In the first case no profit will be made; in the second case there actually will be a loss for the whole transaction.

During the first month the transactions entered on Day 1 produce cash flows which are not matched by maturity. The investor has a swap position as represented by the following schedule of cash flows:

	Maturity Date of Cash Flows	
Transaction Date	*Day 31*	*Day 360*
Day 1	(−): repayment of borrowings @7%	(+): collection of 12-month investment proceeds @7%

If on Day 31 the sterling interest rate has declined as expected, the investor will be able to square the swap position as follows:

	Maturity Date of Cash Flows	
Transaction Date	*Day 31*	*Day 360*
Day 1	(−): repayment of borrowings @7%	(+): collection of 12-month investment proceeds @7%
Day 31	(+): proceeds from new loan (used to repay maturing borrowings)	(−): repayment of 11-month borrowings @6%

The profit can be seen here under Day 360 where the collection of a twelve-month investment carries 7% interest, while the repayment of the eleven-month borrowing carries 6% interest. Remember that the profit is the 1% differential for eleven months, because one month's 7% return on the investment merely pays for the borrowing cost for the first month.

Swap in the Forward Market. To take advantage of an anticipated change in interest rates and the associated forward premium or discount through the foreign exchange market, one must assume that any change in interest differentials will be translated into changes in the forward market. If this is the case, as it should be in an efficient market, then cash flows generated in the exchange markets must be similar to the ones generated through swaps in the money market. The complication in understanding this transaction arises from the basic nature of the foreign exchange market where there are always at least two currencies and two markets, spot and forward.

Assume that the same rates or interest differentials prevail for all maturities within a year. Then we can translate the 3% and 2% interest differentials into forward rates and the corresponding points of discount on the pound. Assuming a spot rate of $1.80/£ we have:

Forward Disc. on 12-Month Pound	*Forward Rate*	*12-Month Point Disc*	*Points Disc./ Month*
3% discount	1.7460	0.0540	0.0045
2% discount	1.7640	0.0360	0.0030

That is, if there is an expected decrease in interest differentials in favor of the pound, there is also an expected decrease for the discount of the pound in the forward market and we can apply the simple rule of buy low and sell high. Buy forward pounds *now,* say for delivery in December, while interest rates in sterling are high and the forward discount is large. Later, after the interest rates decline and the forward price of the pound increases, sell the pounds at a profit for delivery in December.

In the transaction just suggested the investor would have a net exchange position until the pounds are sold. If forward pounds are bought now with the hope of selling them one month later, and if the spot rate of the pound depreciates enough, there will be a loss even if the expected reduction in the forward discount takes place. Even if the change from 3% to 2% discount materializes, the absolute value of the forward pound will be lower than the initial purchase price of $1.7460. (A 2% discount on a small number produces a smaller value than a 3% discount on a large number.)

To avoid the foreign exchange risks introduced by having a net exchange position in the forward pound, this position must be compensated for by a shorter maturity, i.e., a swap position. Since initially it is desired to purchase pounds for delivery in December, in twelve months, we can offset the exchange position by selling pounds for February, in one month, for example. Thus, in January two transactions will be entered:

1. A purchase of pounds against dollars for delivery in December at a 3% discount, in expectation of a reduction in the discount in the future.

2. A sale of pounds against dollars for delivery in January to offset for one month the exchange position created by (1).

	Maturity Date of Cash Flows	
Transaction Date	*February 28*	*December 31*
January 31	Sell £ } @3% p.a. Buy $ } discount on £	Buy £ } @3% p.a. Sell $ } discount on £

Since both transactions are carried out at a 3% p.a. discount on the pound, no profit can be expected from the swap position during February. However, after the forward transaction maturing on February 28 is liquidated that day in the spot market, if interest rates have changed as anticipated, the exchange position for December 31 can be liquidated at a profit.

	Maturity Date of Cash Flows	
Transaction Date	*February 28*	*December 31*
January 31	Sell £ } @3% p.a. Buy $ } discount on £	Buy £ } @3% p.a. Sell $ } discount on £
February 28	Buy £ } Spot Sell $ }	Sell £ } @2% p.a. Buy $ } discount on £

If the interest differential narrowed to 2% p.a., we would enjoy a profit of 1% for eleven months starting February 28.

Using the rates which are known with certainty now, we have the following:

January 31	Sell 1 month £ at (1.8000 − 0.0045)	$1.7955	Buy 1 year £ at	$1.7460
February 28	Buy spot £ at	1.8000	Sell 11-month £ at 1.8000–(11 × 0.0030)	1.7670
	Loss	$0.0045	Gain	$0.0210
	Net Profit: Gain	$0.0210		
	− Loss	0.0045		
		$0.0165		

The profit of $0.0165/£ equals 15 points ($0.0015) for eleven months.

Although at each point in the swap "buy" equals "sell" for each currency, on January 31 the buy is for thirty days while the sell is for one year. This is a situation in which there are mismatched cash flows–a swap position. However, *even if the spot rate had changed during the intervening month, the profit would still be the same.* The profit in this transaction arises from the decline in the discount of the pound, 15 points per month (from 45 to 30 points). Since the trader enjoyed a 45-point discount for the twelve-month buy, at a cost of 45 points for one month and 30 points for eleven months, (s)he netted 15 points for eleven months, or 165 points. Thus, even if the spot pound had changed value, as long as the amount of points discounted forward declined from 45 to 30, the same profit would have materialized. Both the component loss and gain would have been larger, but the net of the two would still have been 165 points.

The risks in this transaction arise from a misassessment of future interest rates. For example, the forecast of the sterling interest rates might have been correct; however, if the dollar interest rates also decline, the discount at the time of closing the transaction might be even larger than at the beginning of the swap, and there will be a loss.[10]

These examples of speculation require forecasting rates, and in this era of managed floating, forecasting which way rates will move is highly speculative. Hence, the speculator making sharp judgments about the natural course of currency in the future does so at his or her own peril!

SUMMARY

Trades in currencies take place in the foreign exchange market for immediate exchange (spot) or future exchange (forward). The market itself is a worldwide network of traders, usually operating from commercial banks, who

[10]For a detailed presentation of the mechanics of swap positions, see Heinz Riehl and Rita M. Rodriguez, *Foreign Exchange Markets* (New York: McGraw-Hill), 1977.

communicate via telephone or telex. Transactions primarily focus on a dozen or so major currencies. Central banks also operate in the foreign exchange market to adjust the value of their nation's currencies.

Spot quotations are usually in terms of the amount of local currency to buy one unit of foreign currency, with the United Kingdom a major exception to this practice. This is the *direct* quotation. The quotient of two foreign currencies in terms of the local currency (cross rate) can be used to find the price of one foreign currency in terms of the other.

The forward quotations can be made at the *outright rate,* which is done in the same terms as the direct price quotation for spot trades. Among dealers, quotes are usually at bid/ask premiums or discounts from spot, called the *swap rate.* The forward premium (discount) of a currency is computed as:

$$\frac{\text{(Forward Rate} - \text{Spot Rate)}}{\text{Spot Rate}} \times \frac{12}{\text{Number of Months Forward}}$$

These exchange rates in the forward market reflect interest rate differentials. *Arbitrageurs* operate to equilibrate the rates for a currency in various parts of the world by buying and selling the same currency for the same maturity at different places. *Covered interest arbitrage* is the process by which the forward exchange rates are brought into equilibrium with differing interest rates in various countries. Through its operation the total return in a period for all currencies from interest plus exchange gain or loss is the same. To the extent that expectations about inflation are reflected in interest rates, these expectations affect forward exchange rates. If purchasing power parity prevails and if exchange markets are efficient, in the sense that all available information is reflected in the observed prices, the forward rate becomes an unbiased (not necessarily accurate) prediction of future spot rates.

There are four major actors in the foreign exchange market. Two actors who speculate on financial markets are the *speculators in changes in spot rates* and the *speculators on changes in interest differentials.* The other two actors have nonfinancial business concerns which create their interest in the market. These are the *merchandise trader,* who wants to protect a future cash flow from exchange rate fluctuations, and the *corporation with net exposed assets in foreign currencies,* which wishes to hedge the value of those assets. The behavior of these two actors is detailed in the next two chapters.

A *square position* occurs when both the *maturity* and *currency* of cash transactions are perfectly matched. Speculation occurs whenever a square position does not exist. The *net exchange position* in a given currency for an individual or institution is *long* if future inflows in a currency exceed outflows and *short* if future outflows exceed inflows. *Outright speculation* refers to a net long or short exchange position. One can speculate in the forward market by using forward contracts or in the money market by borrowing and lending different currencies.

In a *swap* the total net exchange position is zero but it is not zero for specific dates in the future. In the money market a short debt to be rolled over at an expected lower interest rate can be loaned long. Here the speculation on interest rates is clear. The currency can be revalued and there is no effect on the speculation outcome. When the swap involves the foreign exchange market, then the gamble is that the forward premiums or discounts will move in line with the changes in interest rates. Different maturities of forward contracts are used so the net position in a given currency can be zero, yet the expected change in interest rates will result in a gain if the forward discount/premium moves parallel to the interest rates.

Exercises on Foreign Exchange Mechanics

1. Assume the buying rate for deutsche mark spot in New York is $0.40.
   a. What would you expect the price of the U.S. dollar to be in Germany?
   b. If the dollar were quoted in Germany at DM 2.60, how is the market supposed to react?
2. On the same date that the DM spot was quoted $0.40 in New York, the price of the pound sterling was quoted $1.80.
   a. What would you expect the price of the pound to be in Germany?
   b. If the pound were quoted in Frankfurt at DM 4.40/£, what would you do to profit from the situation?
3. On August 2, 1974, the DM was quoted $0.3876/DM, and the French franc was quoted $0.2133/FF in New York. If on this same date Paris was quoting FF1.7500/DM and FF4.6875/$, what are the incentives for arbitrage?
4. You have called your foreign exchange trader and asked for quotations on the Belgian franc spot, one-month, three-month, and six-month. The trader has responded with the following:

   $0.02479/81 3/5 8/7 13/10

   a. What does this mean in terms of dollars per Belgian franc?
   b. If you wished to buy spot Belgian francs, how much would you pay in dollars?
   c. If you wanted to purchase spot U.S. dollars, how much would you have to pay in Belgian francs?
   d. What is the premium or discount in the one-, three-, and six-month forward rates in annual percentages? (Assume you are buying Belgian francs.)
5. The spot Danish krone is selling for $0.15985, and the three-month forward is selling for $0.15900. The three-month treasury bill rate in the United States is 6.25% and in Denmark 7.50%.
   a. Are the forward rates and interest rates in equilibrium? Why?
   b. If not, what would you do to take advantage of the situation?
   c. If a large number of individuals take similar action, what will be the impact in the market? (Assume interest rates remain constant.)

6. Ms. LeRoy is convinced that the Japanese yen is presently undervalued. She wants to profit from her analysis.

Spot rate–day 1	$0.003600
Forecast rate–day 30	0.004000
30-day forward	0.003620
Interest rates–1 month	
Dollar	7.50%
Yen	6.30%

a. What is the premium or discount on the forward yen?

b. What choices does Ms. LeRoy have to profit from her forecast of the future value of the yen?

c. What are the potential costs and gains of each alternative?

	Case A	Case B	Case C
Spot rate–day 30	$0.003600	$0.004000	$0.004200

d. Based on interest rate parity, what should the 30-day yen forward rate be? Why might the actual rate differ? Does it differ?

e. What course of action would you advise Ms. LeRoy to follow?

7. Mr. Morales, a trader at one of the major banks in New York, has received information from the economic research department of his bank that short-term interest rates in the United States are bound to increase by 100 basis points within a month. (100 basis points equal 1%.)

1-year interest rates

United States	6.45%
Canada	4.46%

Spot rate: $0.996800/Canadian dollar

Forward rate:

1 year	$1.016636
1 month	$0.998453

a. What is the premium or discount on the Canadian dollar?

b. What does the new information mean in terms of future rates? If Mr. Morales is bound by the rule "buy equals sell," what opportunities does he have to profit from the information given to him by his economic research department?

c. What are the costs or gains of such alternatives:

i. if the U.S. interest rate increases to 7.45% within a month?

ii. if interest rates remain constant?

iii. if spot Canadian dollars on day 30 were $0.9500?

d. What course of action would you advise the trader to follow?

Appendix: Exchange Markets and Money Market Equilibrium[1]

For readers who prefer a mathematical approach, in this appendix we place the concepts of interest rate parity and purchasing power parity in algebraic form.

For discussion, we will assume a U.S. exporter who will receive pounds in amount £A at time t.[2] For simplicity, it may be useful to assume that t equals one year. All interest rates are also for the period t. The problem for the exporter is how to make a decision among alternatives I (no covering), II (covering in the forward market), and III (covering in the money market).

Definitions

r_0 = spot \$/£ exchange rate *now*

f_0 = forward \$/£ exchange rate *now*

d = discount of £ against \$; if positive, the £ is at a premium against the \$

$\tilde{r}_t$ = spot \$/£ exchange rate at time t, where $\sim$ denotes a random variable which is unknown now

$\tilde{e}$ = depreciation of £ against the \$ from now to time t

$f_0 = r_0(1 + d)$

$\tilde{r}_t = r_0(1 + \tilde{e})$

i_{US} = U.S. interest rate for time t maturity

i_{UK} = U.K. interest rate for time t maturity

Alternative I: Do Not Cover

At time t the firm receives £A and converts this amount to dollars:

$$\$\ \text{Proceeds}_t = \tilde{r}_t A = r_0(1 + \tilde{e})A \tag{1}$$

Since $\tilde{r}_t$ is uncertain, the exporter will examine the costs of covering.

[1] Our thanks to Professor Edward M. Graham for comments and suggestions on this Appendix. A similar analysis is presented in Ian H. Giddy, "An Integrated Theory of Exchange Rate Equilibrium," *Journal of Financial and Quantitative Analysis,* Dec. 1976, pp. 883–892.

[2] The problem of financing foreign trade is discussed in detail in the following chapter. For this appendix, it suffices to assume the existence of a receivable denominated in foreign currency.

Alternative II: Cover in the Forward Market

The exporter will sell sterling for dollars in the amount of £A in the forward market. At maturity, the amount received after delivering £A to purchase the dollars at the agreed upon rate will be:

$$\$\ \text{Proceeds}_t = f_0 A = r_0(1 + d)A \tag{2}$$

Since f_0 is known, there is no uncertainty.

The cost of II vs. I is the difference:

$$\begin{aligned}
\$\ \text{Cost}_{\text{I–II}} &= (\tilde{r}_t A - f_0 A) \\
&= r_0 A\left[(1 + \tilde{e}) - (1 + d)\right] \qquad \text{from (1) and (2)} \\
&= r_0 A(\tilde{e} - d) \qquad (3)
\end{aligned}$$

Alternative III: Cover in the Money Market

The exporter will borrow sterling in the amount of £$A/(1 + i_{\text{UK}})$. At this interest rate, upon maturity the exporter will owe the bank £A, the amount to be received from the customer at time t. The amount borrowed now will be converted to dollars at r_0 and invested in a U.S. bank at i_{US}. Therefore,

$$\$\ \text{Proceeds}_t = r_0\left(\frac{A}{1 + i_{\text{UK}}}\right)(1 + i_{\text{US}}) \tag{4}$$

Since r_0 and both interest rates are known, there is no uncertainty. The cost of III vs. I is the difference:

$$\begin{aligned}
\$\ \text{Cost}_{\text{I–III}} &= \left[\tilde{r}_t A - r_0\left(\frac{A}{1 + i_{\text{UK}}}\right)(1 + i_{\text{US}})\right] \qquad \text{from (1) and (4)} \\
&= \left[r_0(1 + \tilde{e})A - r_0\left(\frac{A}{1 + i_{\text{UK}}}\right)(1 + i_{\text{US}})\right] \qquad \text{from (1)} \\
&= r_0 A\left[1 + \tilde{e} - \frac{1 + i_{\text{US}}}{1 + i_{\text{UK}}}\right] \qquad (5)
\end{aligned}$$

Interest Rate Parity

If the money market and forward market are in equilibrium, then the cost of covering under II and III should be equal. Therefore,

$$r_0 A(\tilde{e} - d) = r_0 A\left[1 + \tilde{e} - \frac{1 + i_{\text{US}}}{1 + i_{\text{UK}}}\right] \qquad \text{from (4) and (5)}$$

Simplifying, we get:

$$d = \frac{1 + i_{\text{US}}}{1 + i_{\text{UK}}} - 1$$

$$= \frac{i_{\text{US}} - i_{\text{UK}}}{1 + i_{\text{UK}}} \tag{6}$$

Notice in (6) that the discount on sterling under interest rate parity is equal to the differences in the U.S./U.K. interest rate discounted to time 0 at the U.K. interest rate. If interest rates are relatively low, interest rate differentials in the numerator are a good approximation of this fraction as the denominator approaches 1.

Purchasing Power Parity (PPP)

Using $\sim$ again for unknown values and Δ for change, then we may compute anticipated price levels and the changes in price levels in the U.S. and the U.K. as:

$$\tilde{\Delta} P_{\text{UK}} = \frac{\tilde{P}_{\text{UK}_t} - P_{\text{UK}_0}}{P_{\text{UK}_0}}$$

$$\tilde{\Delta} P_{\text{US}} = \frac{\tilde{P}_{\text{US}_t} - P_{\text{US}_0}}{P_{\text{US}_0}}$$

and PPP suggests that

$$\tilde{e} = \frac{1 + \tilde{\Delta} P_{\text{US}}}{1 + \tilde{\Delta} P_{\text{UK}}} - 1$$

$$= \frac{\tilde{\Delta} P_{\text{US}} - \tilde{\Delta} P_{\text{UK}}}{1 + \tilde{\Delta} P_{\text{UK}}} \tag{7}$$

"Inflation" is the value (price x quantity) weighted index of goods and services costs between two periods of time. If the weighted general inflation index coincides with the weighted index of internationally traded goods and services, commodity arbitrage will produce this result. Otherwise, according to PPP theory, the general change in value of money produced by inflation and the resulting monetary adjustments are expected to bring about this result.

Fisher Effect

If the Fisher effect holds, a nominal country interest rate consists of a real rate and an expected country inflation rate. Interest rates in various countries reflect differential inflation rates.

$$i_{US} = \text{real rate} + \widetilde{\Delta P}_{US}$$

$$i_{UK} = \text{real rate} + \widetilde{\Delta P}_{UK}$$

Then, a measure of differential anticipated inflation between two countries may be expressed as:

$$\frac{i_{US} - i_{UK}}{1 + i_{UK}} = \frac{(\text{real rate} + \widetilde{\Delta P}_{US}) - (\text{real rate} + \widetilde{\Delta P}_{UK})}{(1 + \text{real rate} + \widetilde{\Delta P}_{UK})}$$

Simplifying, and noting that the real rate is relatively small in the denominator (~ .03), we get:

$$\frac{i_{US} - i_{UK}}{1 + i_{UK}} = \frac{\widetilde{\Delta P}_{US} - \widetilde{\Delta P}_{UK}}{1 + \text{real rate} + \widetilde{\Delta P}_{UK}} \sim \frac{\widetilde{\Delta P}_{US} - \widetilde{\Delta P}_{UK}}{1 + \widetilde{\Delta P}_{UK}} \qquad (8)$$

Conclusion

Therefore, if interest rate parity, the Fisher effect, and purchasing power parity hold as formulated here, then,

$$\tilde{e} = \frac{i_{US} - i_{UK}}{1 + i_{UK}} \qquad \text{from (7) and (8)} \qquad (9)$$

and

$$\tilde{e} = d \qquad \text{from (6) and (9)}$$

So, the expected change in the spot rate of the sterling vs. the dollar equals the discount in the forward market; thus, the forward rate is an unbiased predictor of the future spot rate.

Bibliography

Aliber, Robert Z., "Exchange Risks, Yield Curves, and the Pattern of Capital Flows." *Journal of Finance,* May 1968, pp. 361-70.

——, ed., *The International Market for Foreign Exchange.* New York: Praeger, 1969.

Amihud, Yakov, and Tamir Agmon, "The Forward Rate and the Effective Prediction of the Future Spot Rate," working paper, Tel Aviv University, September, 1978.

Bowers, David A., "A Warning Note on Empirical Research Using Foreign

Exchange Rates." *Journal of Financial and Quantitative Analysis,* June 1977, pp. 315-19.

Burt, John, Fred R. Kaen, and G. Geoffrey Booth, "Foreign Exchange Market Efficiency under Flexible Exchange Rates." *Journal of Finance,* Sept. 1977, pp. 1325-1330.

Burtle, James, "Equilibrating the Foreign Exchange Market." *Columbia Journal of World Business,* Spring 1974, pp. 61-67.

Chicago Mercantile Exchange, *Trading in Tomorrows.* Chicago, Ill.: Chicago Mercantile Exchange, 1977.

Cooper, John, "How Foreign Exchange Operations Can Go Wrong." *Euromoney,* May 1974, pp. 4-7.

Cornell, Bradford, "Spot Rates, Forward Rates, and Exchange Market Efficiency." *Journal of Financial Economics,* Aug. 1977, pp. 55-66.

Einzig, Paul, *A Textbook on Foreign Exchange.* London: Macmillan, 1966.

——, *The Dynamic Theory of Forward Exchange,* 2nd ed. London: Macmillan, 1967.

Fieleke, Norman S., "Exchange-Rate Flexibility and the Efficiency of the Foreign-Exchange Markets." *Journal of Financial and Quantitative Analysis,* Sept. 1975, pp. 409-28.

Folks, William R., Jr., and Stanley R. Stansell, "The Use of Discriminant Analysis in Forecasting Exchange Rate Movement." *Journal of International Business Studies,* Spring 1975, pp. 33-50.

Frenkel, Jacob A., "A Monetary Approach to the Exchange Rate: Doctrinal Aspects and Empirical Evidence." *Scandinavian Journal of Economics,* May 1976, pp. 200-24.

——, "The Forward Exchange Rate, Expectations, and the Demand for Money: The German Hyperinflation." *American Economic Review,* Sept. 1977, pp. 653-70.

——, and Richard M. Levich, "Covered Interest Arbitrage: Unexploited Profits?" *Journal of Political Economy,* March-April 1975, pp. 325-38.

——, "Transaction Costs and Interest Arbitrage: Tranquil versus Turbulent Periods." *Journal of Political Economy,* Dec. 1977, pp. 1209-26.

Giddy, Ian H., "An Integrated Theory of Exchange Rate Equilibrium." *Journal of Financial and Quantitative Analysis,* Dec. 1976, pp. 883-92.

——, and Gunter Dufey, "The Random Behavior of Flexible Exchange Rates: Implications for Forecasting." *Journal of International Business Studies,* Spring, 1975, pp. 1-32.

International Monetary Market of the Chicago Mercantile Exchange, *The Futures Market in Foreign Currencies.* Chicago: The Chicago Mercantile Exchange, undated.

——, *Trading in International Currency Futures.* Chicago: The Chicago Mercantile Exchange, undated.

——, *Understanding Futures in Foreign Exchange.* Chicago: The Chicago Mercantile Exchange, undated.

Kohlhagen, Steven W., "The Performance of the Foreign Exchange Markets: 1971-1974." *Journal of International Business Studies,* Fall 1975, pp. 33-39.

Logue, Dennis E., and Richard James Sweeney, "'White-noise' in Imperfect Markets: The Case of the Franc/Dollar Exchange Rate." *Journal of Finance,* June 1977, pp. 761-68.

Murenbeeld, Martin, "Economic Factors for Forecasting Foreign Exchange Rate Changes." *Columbia Journal of World Business,* Summer 1975, pp. 81-95.

Neukomm, Hans U., "Risk and Error Minimization in Foreign Exchange Trading." *Columbia Journal of World Business,* Winter 1975, pp. 77-85.

Riehl, Heinz, and Rita Rodriguez, *Foreign Exchange Markets,* New York: McGraw-Hill Book Company, 1977.

Rogalski, Richard J., and Joseph D. Vinso, "Price Level Variations as Predictors of Flexible Exchange Rates." *Journal of International Business Studies,* Spring/Summer 1977, pp. 71-81.

Schadler, Susan, "Sources of Exchange Rate Variability: Theory and Empirical Evidence." *International Monetary Fund Staff Papers,* July 1977, pp. 253-96.

Syrett, W. W., *A Manual of Foreign Exchange,* 6th ed. London: Sir Isaac Pitman and Sons, Ltd., 1960.

Westerfield, Janice Moulton, "An Examination of Foreign Exchange Risk Under Fixed and Floating Regimes." *Journal of International Economics,* May 1977, pp. 181-200.

KEN AND JOAN MORSE

On Thursday, June 22, 1972, the ancient city of Florence could be seen clearly from the hillsides surrounding its valley. The lovely view was lost on Ken Morse and his wife, Joan, who were seated rather nervously by a fountain at the Villa le Rondini, waiting for a phone call to get through to their broker at Merrill Lynch in New York.

"If we do nothing," thought Ken, "we'll miss a fantastic opportunity to speculate on sterling. If we are right, we'll double everything that we own. But if we're wrong, we could be in debt for the rest of our lives." "We've run all the numbers," said Joan. "I think we should take the risk and hope like hell that we're right!"

The June crisis in the British pound had not come entirely unexpected to the Morses because they had been following sterling closely during the spring of 1972. Ken, who had just completed the second year of an MBA program, had written on his final exam for International Finance that he expected a devaluation of the pound to be forced upon the United Kingdom before the end of that year. During March, April, and May, 1972, he made several efforts to take a short position on sterling for their personal account. Initially, he contacted some major banks in Boston and proposed to sell £100,000 eighteen months forward at about U.S. $2.6060, the then prevailing rate for that type of contract and a slight discount from the spot rate.

The Response of the Banks

Ken's first telephone call in early March 1972 was to the First National Bank of Boston. The head of the foreign exchange department, Mr. Hartwell, refused even to discuss the possibility of allowing an individual to take a short position on any currency. He stated that it was the strict policy of the bank not to assist individuals to take positions in foreign exchange and that such had been the bank's policy for as long as he could remember.

The same day Ken contacted Arthur Snyder, a senior officer at New England Merchants Bank (NEW). Ken thought his chances would be better because Art had a very good reputation with the New Ventures Department at the school, and Ken had worked with him before. Art said that the bank had no formal policy against allowing individuals to take foreign exchange positions through the bank and that several friends of the bank had done so. This had been allowed in part because the individuals also were treasurers of major corporate clients of the bank who were very familiar with the mechanics and risks of dealing in the foreign exchange market. Mr. Snyder said the he would let Ken take a position provided he backed it with 10% collateral.

Mr. Meehan, the NEM foreign exchange trader, explained that the 10% figure was established in the days when countries had to request permission from the IMF to devalue more than 10% so that the most that could be lost from a surprise change in an exchange rate was 10%. Asking for 10% collateral was tantamount to refusing to help Ken because he did not have $26,000 in ready cash to cover a £100,000 contract, and most of the banks in the Boston area were completely unwilling to loan him more than $1,000 without a guarantee other than his signature. When an officer of one of the local banks heard what Ken wanted to do with the funds, he said, "Can you imagine how the bank examiners would roast us if they found out we loaned you money to do that!"

An Approach to a Brokerage Firm

Leaving NEM on the back burner for the moment because of the collateral constraint, Ken next approached Paine, Webber, Jackson and Curtis, a nationwide brokerage firm where he and his wife kept their small but active account. He asked George Gardner, the local partner, if they would either:

1. Execute a short position in British pounds for him; or
2. Allow him to use his present stocks (mostly over-the-counter or highly speculative securities) as collateral for a transaction at NEM.

Mr. Gardner replied that he was unwilling to help because, first of all, they did not recommend that their clients speculate in the currency market, and secondly, there was no precedent for them to use a person's stock holdings as collateral for another institution. Although the Chicago Mercantile Exchange had announced that it was going to begin dealings in foreign currency futures, Mr. Gardner said that Paine Webber had no intention of participating in that segment of the Exchange. They did, however, allow their customers to take positions in other commodities on the Chicago Exchange, such as wheat, corn, and sugar.[1]

A Return to the Bank

A bit dizzy from the runaround (it was now early April), Ken returned to the New England Merchants Bank and met with their head trader, Mr. Meehan, explaining his desire to short the pound even though he did not have the cash necessary for 10% collateral:

Ken: You and I both know that the 10% collateral figure was arbitrarily chosen. Once it may have been an easy rule of thumb, but now it seems inappropriate for the particular transaction my wife and I have in mind. The spot and forward pounds are trading close to the middle of their bands (parity is $2.6057). Unless the United States devalues again, for all practical purposes the absolute worst case would be if the pound went to the top of its band, exposing me to a risk of about 2¼%.

Meehan: That's absolutely right, Ken, and it makes a lot of sense to me that your collateral should only be about 2½% which means you would need to put up only $6,500 instead of $26,000 for a transaction of £100,000. We could put the collateral in a certificate of deposit

[1] By September 1972 Paine Webber reversed its policy, and clients now take positions in the International Monetary Market of the Chicago Mercantile Exchange.

(CD) at 4% for you until you close your position. I'll talk with Art Snyder and the other powers that be to see what we can do for you. However, because of the weakness in the U.S. dollar, we see sterling as very strong at this time, and we think it will get stronger. You might consider waiting until maybe June or July to take your position.

Ken: Well, the most I could gain by waiting is about 2%, but if I take an eighteen-month forward contract *now*, I eliminate any risk of missing the devaluation in case the British are forced to do it early. Sure, I might miss a few basic points, but I'm betting on a quantum jump. They just have to devalue before entering the Common Market [January 1, 1973], I think.

Meehan: Well, I guess what we're saying is that we really see the pound as very strong and the dollar as relatively weak, and we're not really sure that it's such a good idea to short sterling at this time.

Several weeks later the coalminers' strike in the United Kingdom was settled, and sterling was firm. Ken was convinced that the time was right to take an eighteen-month short position. He called Mr. Meehan at NEM and said that he and his wife had agreed to liquidate all the stocks they owned, if necessary, and get the maximum loan possible on each of their checking accounts so that they could put up the collateral in order to take a short position. It wasn't enough cash to cover a £100,000 contract, but it was certainly every cent they could lay their hands on.

"Well, Ken," said Mr. Meehan, "in the meantime, I've talked with the bank's president, and we've decided that even with 10% collateral, we just can't help you out. Our reasoning is that this may be a risk that you shouldn't take and we've now made it bank policy that we're not going to let any individuals take currency positions even if they're well known to the bank and pay up if the deal goes sour. Besides, you'll probably be glad. With Britain's strong reserve position and another whopping U.S. deficit expected, I'm really not sure that this is a good idea anyway."

The Chicago Mercantile Exchange—His Last Hope

By mid-May Ken was convinced that his only opportunity to go short on pounds would be through the newly established International Monetary Market of the Chicago Mercantile Exchange—called the IMM of the CME. The IMM was founded, in part, because of the exhortations of Milton Friedman, the didactic economist. A few years earlier he had faced frustration similar to Ken's when he had tried to short sterling and no bank in Chicago would assist him to make the short transaction he had wished to make before the 1967 pound devaluation.

Because Paine Webber said they would not participate in the IMM, Ken asked some friends to recommend another broker. They suggested a man at Merrill Lynch in New York who seemed to have a less moralistic attitude toward speculation.

Ken and his wife explained to their new broker what they wanted to do and waited impatiently while he and the IMM tried to get organized. During that time they watched frustratedly as the forward and spot rate of pounds depreciated relative to the dollar. A major factor in this depreciation had been the United Kingdom's announcement of unfavorable trade figures resulting from the coalminers' strike.

After some negotiations, Merrill Lynch allowed Ken and Joan to operate with the *minimum* collateral requirements of the CME–$2,500 per contract. The IMM specifies that a contract equals £50,000[2] and charges a slight fee per contract traded. Ken and Joan scraped together everything they could, bought a $10,000 three-month Treasury bill, and offered four sterling contracts for eighteen months forward at $2.6060, the then prevailing rate among New York banks for that type of contract. They did not buy a longer Treasury bill because they thought rates were going to go up.

The following is a summary of the events that Ken and Joan felt were significant in assessing the future rate of the pound:

December 1971: The Smithsonian Agreement. After four months of floating, the U.S. dollar and other major currencies return to a fixed rate within wider bands (2¼% either side of parity). Sterling parity is set at $2.6057, up from $2.40 in the previous May. Exhibit 1 shows the Smithsonian parities and presents data on the movement of spot rates after September 1971.

January 1972: U.K. balance of trade surplus for 1971 is announced: $750 million (Exhibit 2 presents the U.K. balance of payments for the period 1968-1971). The British government starts pursuing an expansive monetary and fiscal policy. Many experts feel that the United Kingdom's strong reserve position is evidence of a strong pound.

February 1972: Three-month U.S. Treasury bills at all-time low, below 3½% (see Exhibit 3). Low U.S. interest rates lead to massive outflows of "hot" money. Japan and France establish tighter controls on capital flows.

March 1972: Citibank Financial Letter asks, "When will the dollars come home?" All EEC currencies are at the top of their new bands relative to the dollar. (Exhibit 4 shows the spot and forward exchange rates relative to their central rates for various key currencies.)

March 9-12: European central bankers meet in Basel and agree that their present parities with the dollar are appropriate. Arthur Burns assures them that U.S. short-term rates will rise further soon.

Ken and Joan decide that this is a good time to short the pound before the exchange markets react to upcoming changes in interest rates. Ken contacts First National Bank of Boston and New England Merchants Bank for the first time.

[2]One contract also equals 50,000,000 Italian lire, 25,000,000 Japanese yen, 1,000,000 Mexican pesos, 500,000 Swiss francs, 50,000 deutsche marks, or 200,000 Canadian dollars. The size of these contracts was reduced subsequently.

EXHIBIT 1. Spot Exchange Rates, September 1971–February 1972

Left scale: U. S. cents per unit, weekly average of daily rates in New York
Right scale: Percentage change from parities existing as of April 1971
Solid line: Old parity before August
Dotted line: New parity of December

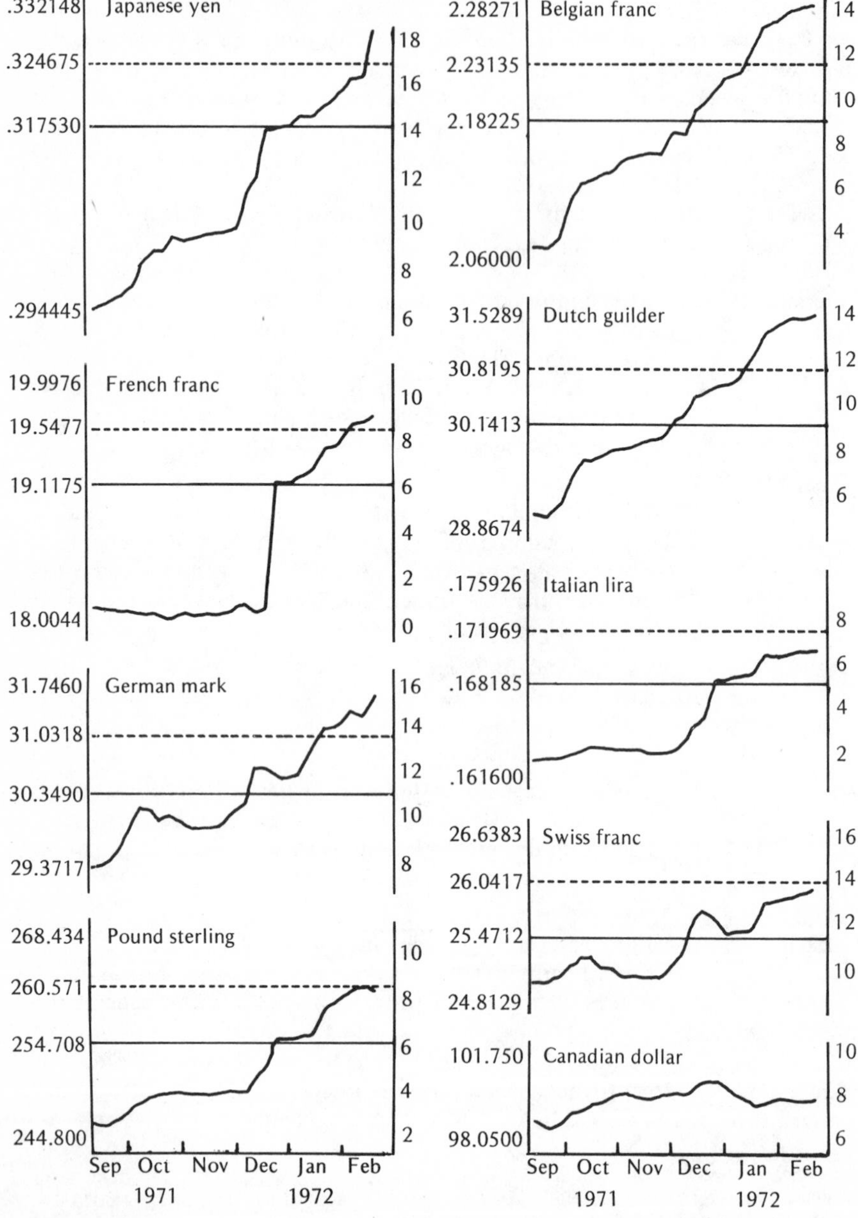

SOURCE: Morgan Guaranty Trust Co., World Financial Markets, January 1972.

EXHIBIT 3. Short-Term Interest Rates, December 1970–June 1972

Treasury Bill Rates

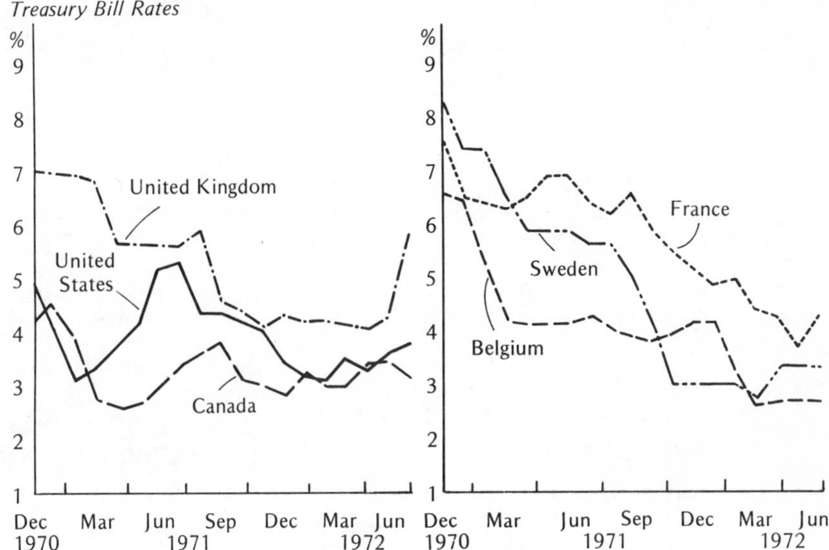

Representative Money Market Rates

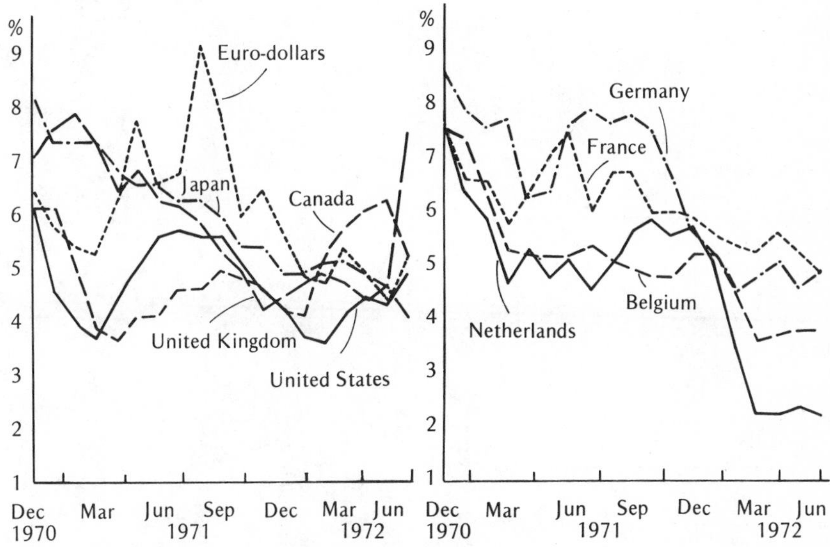

SOURCE: Morgan Guaranty Trust Co., WORLD FINANCIAL MARKETS, July 1972.

EXHIBIT 2. U.K. Balance of Payments 1968–1972 (millions of pounds)

	1968	1969	1970	1971	1971				1972
	Year	Year	Year	Year	1st quarter	2nd quarter	3rd quarter	4th quarter	1st quarter
SEASONALLY ADJUSTED									
Current account									
Exports (f.o.b.)	6,273	7,061	7,886	8,882	1,994	2,286	2,322	2,280	2,218
Imports (f.o.b.)	6,916	7,202	7,879	8,585	2,060	2,173	2,146	2,206	2,336
Visible balance	-643	-141	+7	+297	-66	+113	+176	+74	-118
Interest, profits, and dividends (net)	+341	+502	+490	+506	+117	+134	+140	+115	+124
Services and transfers (net):									
Government	-466	-467	-486	-521	-121	-125	-141	-134	-151
Private	+480	+549	+600	+697	+170	+161	+179	+187	+175
Total invisibles (net)	+355	+584	+604	+682	+166	+170	+178	+168	+148
Current balance	-288	+443	+611	+979	+100	+283	+354	+242	+30
NOT SEASONALLY ADJUSTED									
Currency flow									
Current balance	-288	+443	+611	+979	+51	+338	+331	+259	-50
Investment and other capital flows:									
Official long-term capital	+17	-98	-204	-274	-45	-43	-35	-151	-42
Overseas investment in the United Kingdom	+583	+673	+739	+1,161	+443	+286	+209	+223	+236
U.K. private investment overseas	-727	-667	-761	-762	-223	-211	-185	-143	-359
Foreign currency borrowing (net) by U.K. banks to finance U.K. investment overseas	+155	+72	+189	+255	+35	+120	+50	+50	+175
Other foreign currency borrowing or lending (net) by U.K. banks	-124	-108	+290	+240	+55	+35	-1	+151	-44
Exchange reserves in sterling:									
British government stocks	-22	+237	+63	+55	+57	+36	-40	+2	+64
Banking and money market liabilities	-158	+77	+126	+638	+159	+234	+145	+100	+134
Other external banking and money market liabilities in sterling	-128	-53	+262	+734	+74	+2	+235	+423	+1
Import credit	+83	+156	+25	+76	+29	-5	+29	+23	+71
Export credit	-331	-328	-237	-337	-79	-120	+14	-152	-56
Other capital flows	-102	-58	+86	+72	+121	-28	+53	-74	-126
Total investment and other capital flows	[illegible]	[illegible]	[illegible]	[illegible]	[illegible]	[illegible]	[illegible]	[illegible]	[illegible]

Balancing item	-117	+397	+98	+391	+296	-10	-137	+242	+53
Adjustment for maturing pre-devaluation forwards	-251	—	—	—	—	—	—	—	—
Total currency flow	-1,410	+743	+1,287	+3,228	+973	+634	+668	+953	+57
Allocation of Special Drawing Rights	—	—	+171	+125	+125	—	—	—	+124
Gold subscription of I.M.F.	—	—	-38	—	—	—	—	—	—
Total affecting official financing	-1,410	+743	+1,420	+3,353	+1,098	+634	+668	+953	+181
Official financing									
Net transactions with:									
I.M.F.	+506	-30	-134	-554	-287	-8	-259	—	-10
Other monetary authorities	+790	-669	-1,161	-1,263	-607	-500	+167	-323	+20
Official reserves (drawings on +/ additions to -)	+114	-44	-125	-1,536	-204	-126	-576	-630	-191
Total official financing	+1,410	-743	-1,420	-3,353	-1,098	-634	-668	-953	-181

SOURCE: Bank of England, QUARTERLY BULLETIN, June 1972.

EXHIBIT 4. Spot and Three-Month Forward Exchange Rates, March–June 1972 (percentage deviation from central rates)

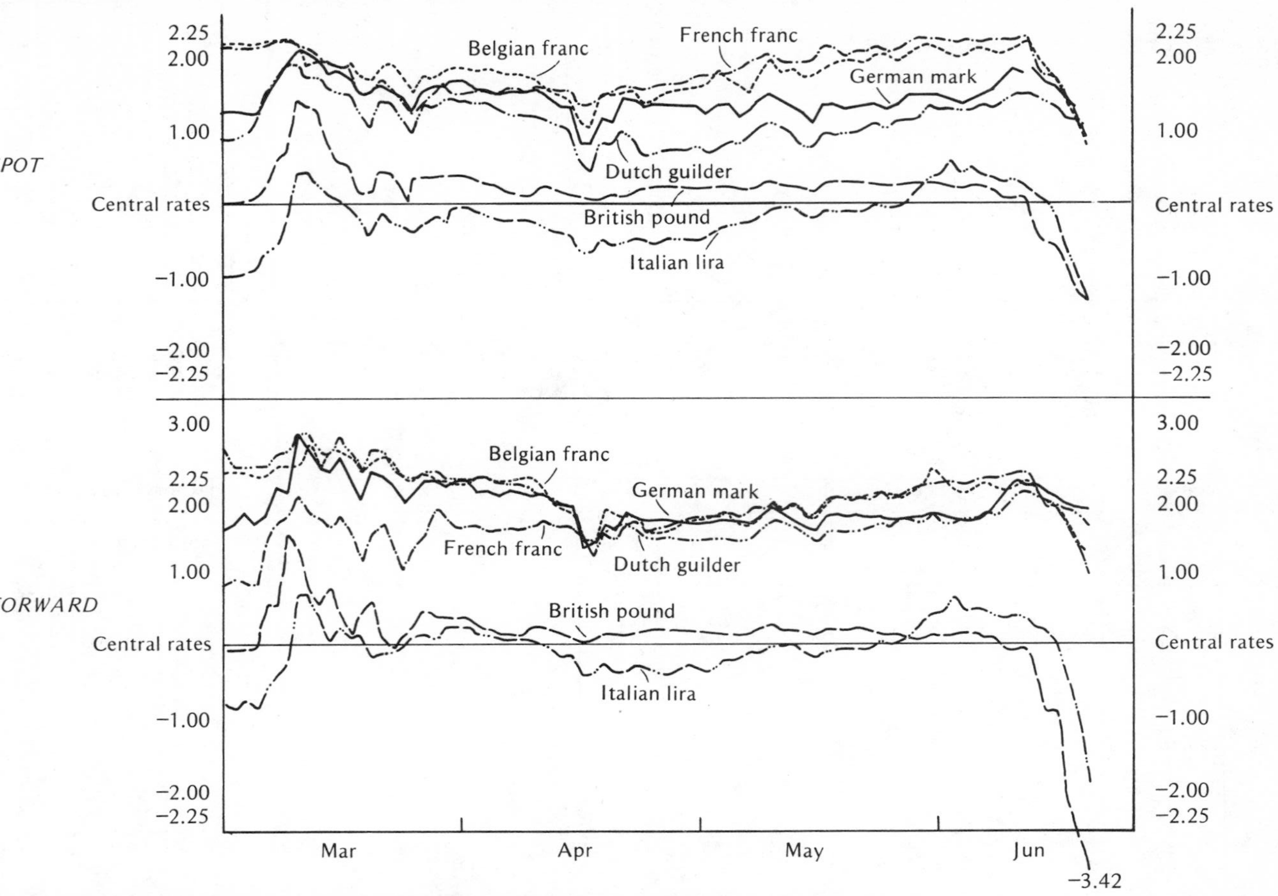

March 15: Three-month U.S. Treasury rates are around 3¾%. Europe adds more controls. United Kingdom forced to import large amounts of coal due to miners' strike. Cuts in electric power force industry to produce below capacity. Exhibit 5 shows the impact of the strike on the United Kingdom's capital utilization, unemployment, and international trade.

March 25: Mr. Barber, Chancellor of the Exchequer, in his budget message states:

> "It is neither necessary nor desirable to distort domestic economies in order to maintain unrealistic exchange rates, whether they are too high or too low. Certainly, in the modern world, I do not believe there is any need for this country, or any other, to be frustrated on this score in its determination to sustain sound economic growth." *The Economist,* March 25, 1972.

March 30: OECD working group states that the U.S. dollar's new parity is sound and that central bankers accept it as such. Furthermore, despite the expectation of further sizable U.S. trade deficits, some hidden reflow of funds is already taking place.

Early April: Cost of apartments in London is seen as considerably higher than New York following spiraling rents in the United Kingdom.

EXHIBIT 5. Capital utilization and unemployment **Balance of U.K. visible trade**

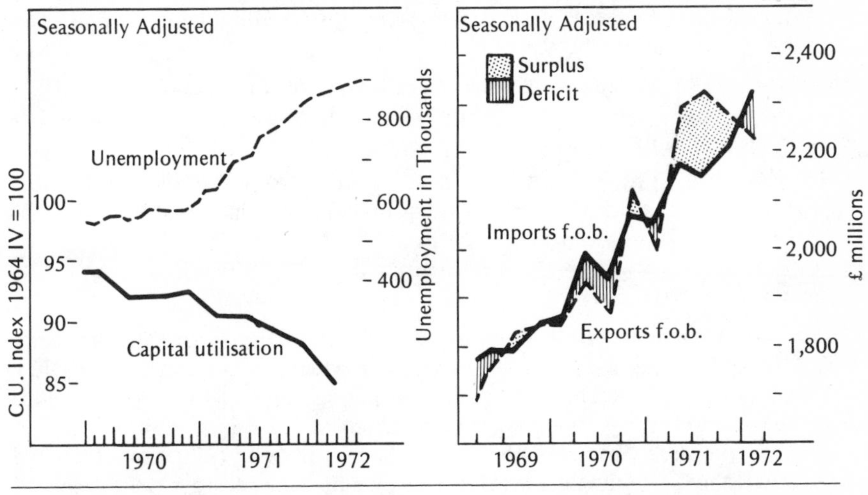

The growth in unemployment showed signs of slackening but capital utilisation fell sharply as a result of the miners' strike.

Capital Utilisation Index

	I	*II*	*III*	*IV*
1969	94-8	95-7	94-9	94-4
1970	94-4	92-3	92-3	92-6
1971	90-8	90-7	89-4	88-1
1972	85-8			

SOURCE: Bank of England, QUARTERLY BULLETIN, June 1972.

Annual consumer price increases in April 1971–March 1972 announced:

United States	3.7%	Germany	6.0%
Japan	5.0%	United Kingdom	9.0%
Italy	5.0%		

U.S. interest rates begin to rise while many European rates remain sluggish (see Exhibits 3, 6, and 7), indicating that business is picking up in the United States before in Europe.

Ken and Joan decide that this is a good time to short the pound before inevitable bad news from miners' strike is announced and before U.S. rates rise further. Ken contacts NEM for the second time.

Mid-April: United Kingdom announces a March trade deficit of $208 million but emphasizes heavy reserve position.

April 24: Europe takes major step toward monetary union. (For details, see Exhibit 8.)

End of April: United Kingdom pays off all loans to the IMF and is now free of short- and medium-term debt for first time since May 1964. During April the price of gold jumps from $48 to $58 per ounce as South Africa announces a reduction in output.

The report to the Club of Rome, *The Limits to Growth,* estimates that if the present increase in the rate of demand for gold continues, the world's total supply will be exhausted in less than four years. (Data on gold price movements are presented in Exhibit 9.)

May: United States announces a massive trade deficit for the first quarter of 1972. Japanese and European central banks are frequently forced to intervene in support of the dollar.

May 5: *The Wall Street Journal* reports, "More workdays were lost through strikes in Britain in 1971 than in any year since 1926 (the year of a general strike)."

The Events of June

After he finished his exams, Ken and Joan left for a trip to Europe on a combination of business and pleasure. In mid-June, when they were in London, they could almost feel a devaluation coming. At parties some of their British friends laughed, "Don't worry about us–Britain will always be Britain." But in the City a banker confided, "We never would try to benefit from a devaluation. But while we were long on sterling earlier this week, we have moved to a more balanced pound position today."

Ken promptly dialed his New York broker and was surprised to hear the following:

Merrill Lynch: We haven't been able to sell your contracts yet. Nobody seems to want to take an eighteen-month position in any currency on the IMM. There just isn't any market that far out.

EXHIBIT 6. Commercial Bank Deposit Rates and Prime Lending Rates, January 1971–June 1972

Commercial Bank Deposit Rates

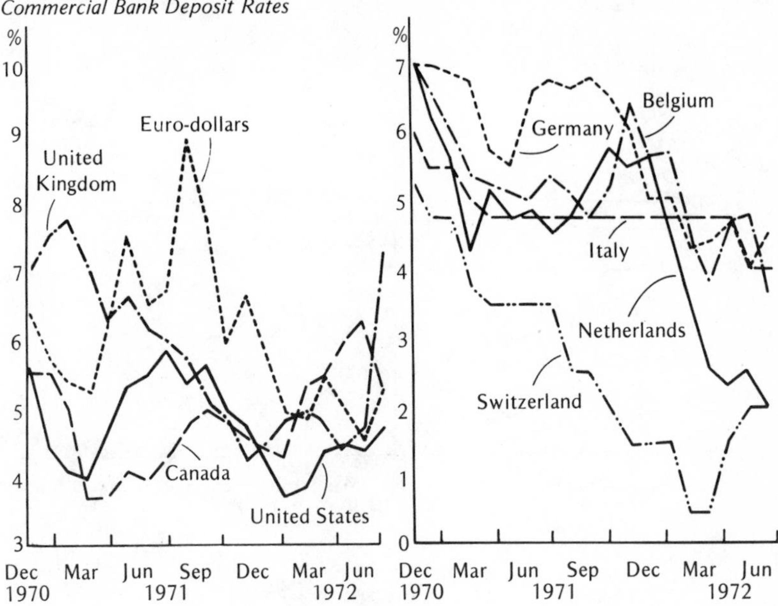

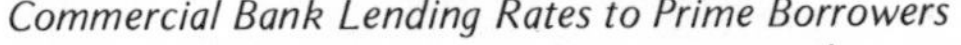

Commercial Bank Lending Rates to Prime Borrowers

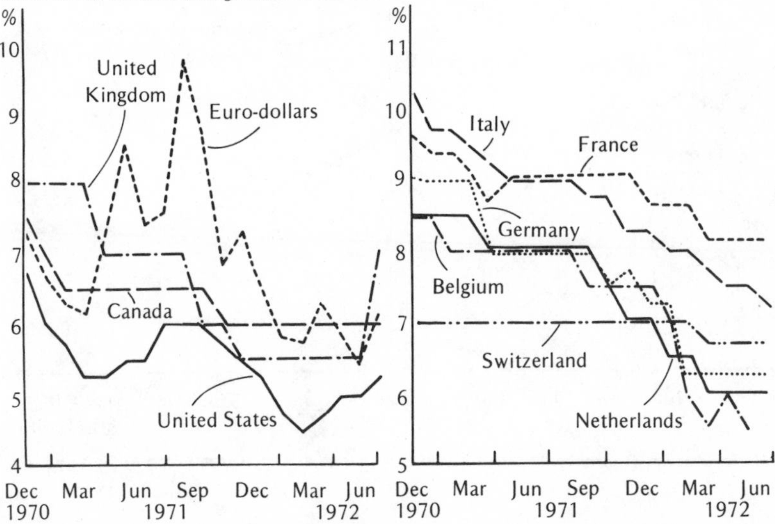

SOURCE: Morgan Guaranty Trust Co., WORLD FINANCIAL MARKETS, July 1972.

EXHIBIT 7. Domestic Government and Corporate Yield Bonds, January 1971–June 1972

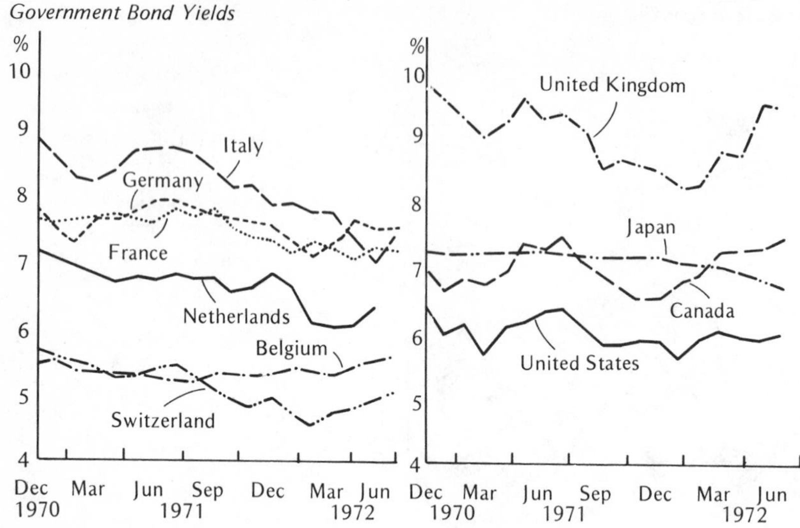

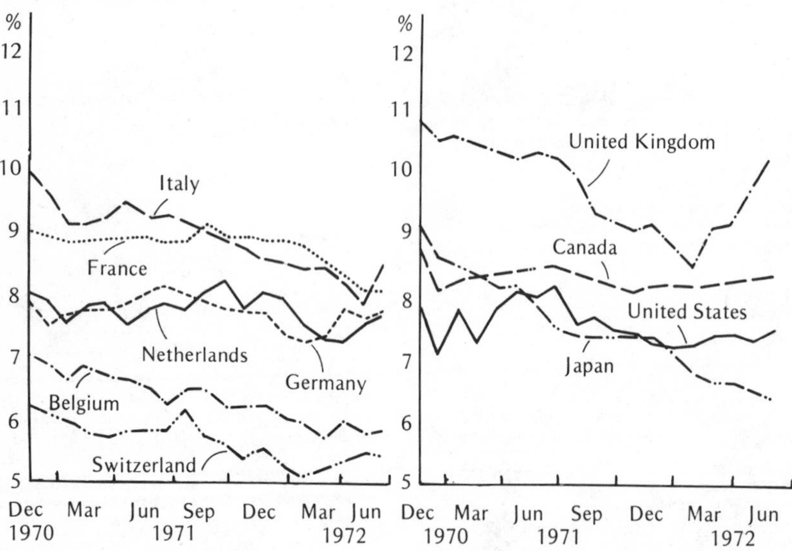

SOURCE: Morgan Guaranty Trust Co., WORLD FINANCIAL MARKETS, July 1972.

EXHIBIT 8. Sterling and the EEC "Snake" in the "Tunnel" (percent premium/discount against US$)

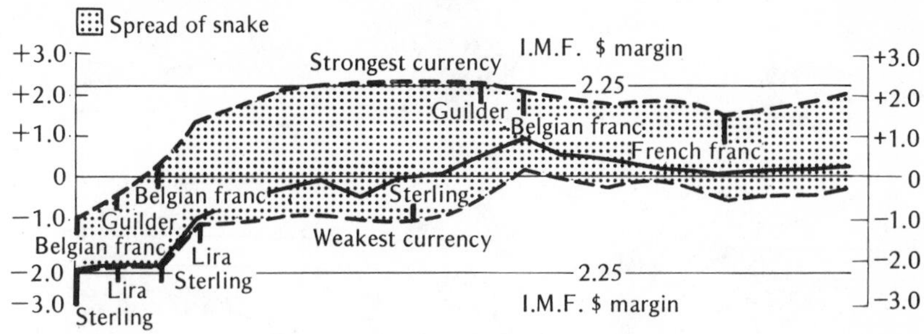

Spread between strongest and weakest currencies in the E.E.C. "snake"

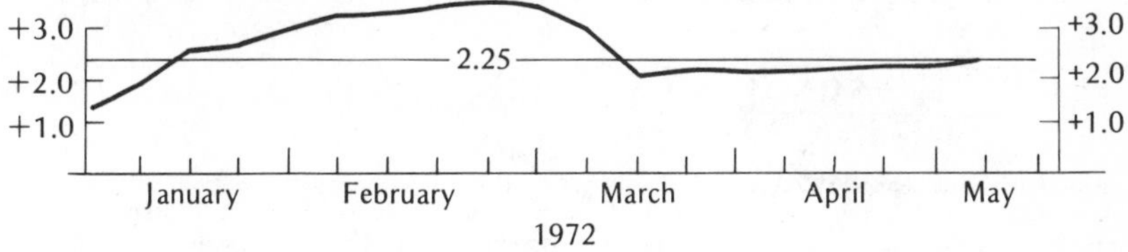

After the E.E.C. currency arrangements took effect on 24th April, most E.E.C. exchange rates and sterling were at a premium against the U.S. dollar.

E.E.C. Currency Arrangements

Under the Washington Agreement of last December which permitted the rates for currencies to fluctuate between margins of 2¼% on either side of their parities or central rates against the U.S. dollar, it was possible for the rate between any two other currencies to vary by 4½% from their cross parity. On 24th April the central banks of the countries of the European Economic Community took steps to halve this possible divergence between any two of their own currencies from 4½% to 2¼%, i.e., to ensure that the rates between any two of their own currencies could not diverge from their cross parities by more than 2¼%. This move was part of a general agreement by these countries to co-ordinate their policies in the foreign exchange markets, and represented an early step towards monetary and economic harmonisation in the enlarged Community. The measures flowed from an E.E.C. Council Resolution of 21st March accepted by the United Kingdom. The central banks were linked by direct telephone lines to allow rapid discussion and concerted action. At the invitation of the founder members, the Bank of England, together with the central bank of Denmark, joined the scheme on 1st May, and the central bank of Norway followed on the 23rd.

The scheme has been put into operation by each participating country quoting buying and selling rates for its currency not only against the U.S. dollar as before but also against the currencies of the other participants at 2¼% on either side of their cross parities. The effect is that, within a total range of fluctuation of 4½% ("the tunnel"), the rates for the participating currencies at any one time are restricted within a community band of 2¼% ("the snake"). When the community band is within the tunnel, intervention at the limits of the community band must take place in community currencies. Intervention may also take place in U.S. dollars when a currency reaches its official U.S. dollar buying or selling rates at the limits of the tunnel. A mechanism for the short-term financing of interventions in community currencies and for subsequent settlement in various reserve assets had been established. Since the scheme came into operation the margin between the strongest and weakest member currencies has ranged between 2% and 2¼%, with sterling in the lower half of the band.

SOURCE: Bank of England, QUARTERLY BULLETIN, June 1972.

EXHIBIT 9. **London Gold Price, January 1969–June 1972**

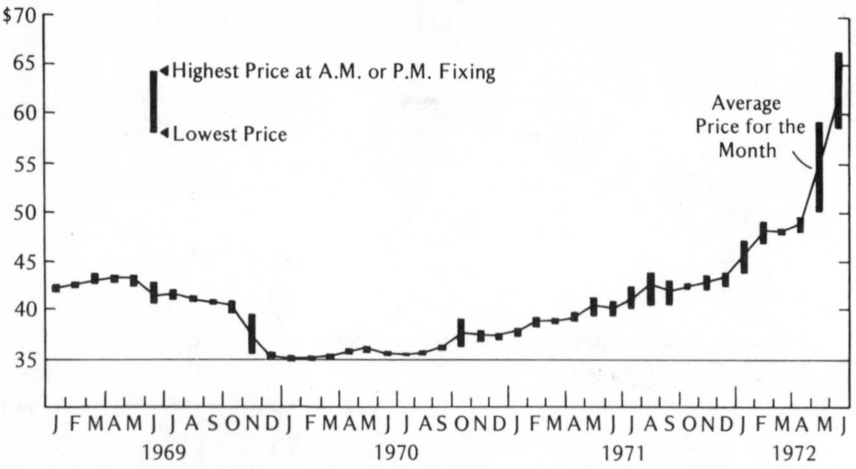

In late 1969 and early 1970, the free market gold price actually averages at or below the official price of $35 per troy ounce. The price began to rise steadily in September 1970, however, and continued upward throughout last year. The tremendous surge in the price this year—to an average of $62.13 in June—appears to be the result not only of strong demand but also of a reduction in supplies. Moreover, the outlook is not very favorable for a change in this situation in the near-term.

SOURCE: First National Bank of Chicago, BUSINESS AND ECONOMIC REVIEW, July 1972.

Ken: Well go ahead and offer at a price below what the New York banks are quoting, and I'll check back with you when we get to Florence.

Merrill Lynch: O.K., Ken. We'll do what we can to generate interest in your offer.

On June 22, 1972, as Ken and Joan waited to talk with Merrill Lynch again, they reflected on recent events which they had been following in the *International Herald Tribune* and local magazines as they traveled by train through Europe:

June 1–21: Bank of England *Quarterly Bulletin* states that United Kingdom cost of inflation is "serious." Bank of England spends $1.5 billion of its reserves to keep the pound inside the EEC tunnel (see Exhibit 8). EEC central banks also are forced to intervene to maintain sterling (see Exhibit 4) with the result that their spot rates weaken against the dollar. In London, students carry signs saying "Devalue Now."

It was 7:15 p.m. local time in Florence, about one hour before the IMM was scheduled to close in Chicago. Ken and Joan had stopped at a local bank after lunch and learned that spot sterling had gone down almost 1% from the Friday before. Presumably the 30-, 90-, and 180-day forward rates were discounted an even greater percentage. The price of the pound sterling had been slipping since early June. However, the decline had accelerated during the most recent week.

Selling Price of Bank Transfers in U.S. for Payment Abroad at 4 P.M.

	Spot	*30-days*	*90-days*
Thursday, June 1	$2.6128	$2.6122	$2.6096
Thursday, June 8	2.6114	2.6113	2.6114
Thursday, June 15	2.5976	2.5964	2.5976
Friday, June 16	2.5940	2.5916	2.5861
Monday, June 19	2.5914	2.5886	2.5822
Tuesday, June 20	2.5875	2.5765	2.5575
Wednesday, June 21	2.5725	2.5575	2.5375

If their eighteen-month contracts had not been sold, should they offer shorter term contracts (30, 90, 180 days) which had a greater probability of being sold? What discount should they sell them at?

"It all depends on the timing and the extent of the devaluation," said Joan, as the owner of the Villa appeared and said, "Telephone for you, Mr. Morse. I believe it's about your call to New York. . . ."

CITIBANK'S FOREIGN EXCHANGE PROBLEMS

In June 1965 the First National City Bank announced a loss of $4 million in foreign exchange operations. It was later revealed that this loss had been incurred by one trader in the bank's Brussels branch who had engaged in forward transactions in the British pound.

As a stimulus for your thinking about the operations of the forward exchange market, you are being given a selection of the published reports on this situation. From these accounts you should develop an explanation of exactly how this loss occurred. This explanation should include timing of transactions and trends in prices and forward market spreads. Useful background information can also be obtained from the articles by Charles A. Coombs on the foreign exchange operations of the U.S. government and a table from the Bank of England's *Quarterly Bulletin* for the period when Citibank sustained the loss.

Newspaper Reports[1]

CITY BANK STOCK SHOWS PRICE DIP[2]

First National Issue Falls After Loss Is Disclosed

The price of First National City Bank stock slipped 3/4 point yesterday to 52 7/8 following the bank's disclosure that its second-quarter net operating earnings would be affected by a $4 million loss of "nonrecurring character."

[1] Reprinted by special permission of *The Wall Street Journal, The New York Times,* and *Business Week.* These articles were originally collected under the supervision of Professor Eli Shapiro.

[2] *The New York Times,* June 16, 1965.

George S. Moore, the bank's president, confirmed reports that the loss had been caused by foreign exchange transactions. . . .

Although the prices in the foreign exchange markets here appeared unaffected by the news, a number of traders reported that customers were hesistant to make commitments until there had been a more complete disclosure of the mechanics of the loss.

Walter B. Wriston, executive vice president of the bank's overseas division, would only say, however, that the loss had been incurred by an overseas branch office that had engaged in "foreign exchange transactions in excess of authorized limits."

Leading bank officials emphasized that as far as could be determined there was no evidence of fraud. . . .

International bankers here and abroad continued to conjure up ideas as to how First National City, with 114 branches in 39 countries, could have lost that much on just foreign exchange transactions. . . .

Foreign exchange experts expressed serious reservations that the loss could have been incurred by one office. One well-informed source noted: "It's hard to lose more than 1% in a convertible currency."

FIRST NATIONAL CITY FOREIGN EXCHANGE LOSS LAID TO $800 MILLION SHORT SALES IN POUND[3]

First National City Bank's recently announced $4 million loss in foreign exchange transactions came as a result of about $800 million in "short sales" of British pounds, it was learned yesterday.

The sales of British pounds, which weren't hedged in the "forward market," were executed for dollars by a trader in the bank's Brussels branch. He apparently was acting in the expectation that the pound would be worth less as a result of possible devaluation when the time came to deliver the sterling to the purchasers. But by delivery time, pounds were selling for a higher dollar exchange rate in the spot market and the trader had to spend more dollars than he anticipated to make good the contracts, it was explained.

The dollar loss to First National City from the transaction was $7.5 million before taxes, resulting in an after-tax loss of the $4 million.

Secrecy Spurs Guesswork

First National City, New York City's largest bank and the second biggest in the United States, first reported the loss in mid-June in a prospectus covering its recent sale of some $266 million of convertible capital notes. The bank at the time said only that the loss resulted from foreign exchange transactions in one of the bank's foreign branches. It wouldn't identify the kind of currency or the branch.

[3] *The Wall Street Journal,* July 20, 1965. Reprinted with the permission of *The Wall Street Journal,* © Dow Jones & Company, Inc., 1965.

The bank's secrecy prompted considerable speculation in banking circles as to the exact nature of the transaction; bank officials refused to comment publicly. One early guess was that the heavy commitment had been made in the foreign exchange of a Latin American country, possibly Colombia or Uruguay, and had involved that nation's foreign central bank. But a number of bankers surmised from the start that the transactions had been in pounds sterling on the ground that the magnitude of the bank's loss suggested the dealings had been in a heavily traded currency. . . .

Two Versions of Trader's Role

. . . Two versions of the Brussels trader's transactions have been circulating in banking circles in the United States and abroad. One holds that he sold the pound short as much as six or seven months in the future late last year. This was at about the time the British government barely staved off devaluation by resorting to an emergency $3 billion line of credit made available by 11 countries. Bankers who subscribe to this view theorize that the trader expected the pound to weaken sharply after a "disappointing" budget message by the Labor government in April 1965. The Labor government, instead, presented a stern "austerity" financial plan aimed at defending the pound.

The other version is that the trader went short initially for only thirty or sixty days in the future. When he had to spend more dollars than he had anticipated in the "spot" market to cover these short positions, he entered into additional futures contracts, again for at least thirty days, "doubling up on his commitments as he went," in the words of one knowledgeable banker.

Bankers noted that if a 10% devaluation had pushed down the dollar value of the pound, he stood to make a profit for the bank of about $50 million. But as it was, the bank absorbed a $4 million after-tax loss, which it was required to divulge in the full glare of publicity surrounding its capital notes issue.

Procedures Being "Tightened"

A First National City official said in answer to a reporter's question that the bank didn't plan to alter its reporting procedures on foreign exchange traders' positions as a result of the Brussels episode. But a spokesman conceded current procedures were "being tightened up" as a consequence. . . .

It was also pointed out that the $800 million in short sales, while sizable in an absolute sense, was relatively small when compared with the total foreign exchange transaction conducted by the bank in a year; this totaled a record $150 billion last year.

The Brussels trader, it was understood, was on salary and didn't receive any commission based on profit he might bring in. One banker observed that he had taken the large short position "for the prestige, perhaps, if everything had worked out all right."

CITY BANK'S LOSS WAS IN STERLING, BY ROBERT FROST[4]

First National's Deficit in Foreign Exchange Area Laid to Brussels Unit

The First National City Bank confirmed yesterday that the $4 million net loss in its foreign exchange operations, which it reported last month, was the result of forward market operations in sterling at its Brussels branch.

At a hastily called press conference at the bank's headquarters here, Edwin A. Reichers, vice president in charge of the bank's foreign exchange operations, explained that the bank's trader in Brussels had persistently overextended his position in forward contracts.

Mr. Reichers said the trader was "operating independently, working on his own initiative and without the authority of the bank."

Contrary to reports the bank had gone short, or sold sterling it did not have in anticipation of covering its sales later at a lower price, Mr. Reichers emphasized the bank had been long on sterling forwards. . . .

First National City's foreign exchange problems began last September at a time when there were doubts about the future value of sterling, Mr. Reichers said. He explained the events that led to the loss as follows:

Confidence in Pound. Despite the gloomy market outlook for sterling, the bank's Brussels trader was still confident in the currency's future.

The apparent reasoning behind his transactions was his expectation that the spot price of the British pound would rise faster than the forward price. Thus, at the time the contract fell due, the bank would have a substantial profit.

As the forward contracts began to fall due, however, the trader found himself short of dollars. To insure that he would have the dollars on the due date, he sold sterling in the near-term market for delivery in 10 to 15 days at discounts considerably below what he had originally paid for the sterling.

Since he still needed the sterling for everyday business, he "rolled over," or renewed, the near-term contracts. Each time, he sold at a price below that which he had originally paid.

He was also forced to sell sterling in the spot markets, often at a price below that which he had originally paid.

In addition, where possible, the trader "rolled over" his forward contracts and continued to add new forward contracts as well.

Apparently, he hoped that in the end the profits from his operations would more than offset the initial spot losses.

At the end of April, the trader's dilemma was discovered by the branch's manager, Arthur Worthington, who directed the trader to reduce his forward position. According to bank sources, Mr. Worthington's directive went unheeded.

The loss itself was discovered at the end of May during a branch examination. It was estimated to be a pre-tax deficit of $8 million and was made public in the bank's June 10 prospectus, which accompanied its $266 million offering of convertible notes. The net loss was $4 million.

[4]*The New York Times,* July 21, 1965.

Because the branch still had a large position in sterling forwards that it was trying to liquidate, Mr. Reichers said, the bank decided not to announce the details publicly for fear the disclosure would scare off potential buyers of forward contracts or create a scarcity of spot sterling.

Although the bank declined yesterday to disclose the amount of the total forward contract commitment at the time the loss was discovered, it has been reported to have been as high as $800 million.

Position Liquidated. The bank's silence over details of the loss reported on June 10 stirred speculation and rumor in financial circles over the site and mechanics of the event.

However, the bank had steadfastly refused to say anything except that the loss involved foreign exchange transactions at an overseas branch until the forward position was liquidated. This was done on Monday.

Since the trader apparently was not buying to meet customer needs, a generally accepted practice in banking, the question was raised at yesterday's press conference whether he was speculating with the bank's money.

Mr. Reichers answered: "Draw your own conclusions."

The bank officer, who is considered to be one of the leading foreign exchange experts in the country, was at a loss to explain what gave the trader confidence in the pound at a time when few were optimistic.

Mr. Reichers asserted that "complete steps have been taken to insure that this situation will not come up again." He would not elaborate.

Accounting Procedures. It was assumed that some of these steps would insure proper accounting practices, which he said had not been enforced at the Brussels branch.

The trader's position at the end of the day was being reported as a "net" balance rather than as a breakdown of forward and spot balances.

A spokesman for the bank confirmed that Mr. Worthington, who has managed the Brussels office since August 1962, was being transferred to Paris. Reportedly there is no tie between the loss and the transfer.

The trader, a Belgian whose name was not disclosed, resigned from the bank, the spokesman said, although under Belgian law, he is still technically employed, but on vacation.

Despite the foreign exchange loss, First National City was able to report record first-half earnings of $1.70 a share, compared with $1.57 for the 1964 period. The foreign exchange loss amounts to about $.15 a share for the year.

A PLAUSIBLE LOSS BY VARTANIG G. VARTAN[5]

Despite lingering skepticism in Belgian banking circles, the monetary authorities and commercial bankers in Brussels have accepted the First National City Bank's $8 million foreign-exchange loss as technically plausible, but hardly believable.

[5] *The New York Times,* Aug. 5, 1965.

During the eight-month period when the bank's branch built up its heavy position in forward sterling, the monetary authorities there were aware of the increase, but since there appeared to be no violations of banking laws they left the bank to its business.

HOW TO LOSE $8-MILLION ON STERLING[6]

New York's First National City Bank Tells How—and Takes Steps So It Won't Happen Again

The Foreign Exchange Market, its devotees like to explain, is like a mirror—a currency transaction in one place is reflected by another currency transaction elsewhere. This week, New York's big First National City Bank explained how it let that mirror crack while losing $8 million.

Citibank's foreign exchange loss was revealed a month ago [B.W. June 1965, p. 134]. But the bank has kept details hidden until it was able to close out a massive position in sterling that a trader in its Brussels branch had taken. That position—reported to be $800 million, though the bank denies the figure is right—was closed this week. Ironically, the trader had bet that sterling would be saved from devaluation, and had not "beared" the pound. It was a good bet, but, given the trickiness of foreign exchange markets, he lost anyway.

Election Effect. Starting last September, the man—a Belgian national, whose name is being kept secret—began selling spot sterling, while buying forward contracts of sterling. A forward contract calls for delivery on a future data at a rate fixed at the time the contract is made. For some time, forward sterling has been selling at a discount to the spot price (now $2.7904), and the Brussels trader was betting that the discount would shrink and bring a profit on the forward sterling when the pound strengthened.

This bet was taken before the British elections, and the maturity of the forward contracts went beyond that time. In the trade, it is regarded as a routine swap deal—you sell sterling for dollars, then use the dollars to buy forward positions. As it turned out, however, the forward purchase commitments had to be closed out at a loss.

As the months rolled on, the trader kept at it, selling spot or near forwards, simultaneously buying forwards of longer maturities, and constantly rolling over his swaps. According to Edwin A. Reichers, vice president in charge of Citibank's foreign exchange operations, the man "exceeded his trading limits on his own initiative."

Hard to Detect. Citibank puts overnight limits on its foreign exchange traders, though they vary from branch to branch. At the beginning, the trader's moves would not have aroused much anxiety: Citibank, along with most other New York banks, was confident sterling could weather an immediate storm, and the trader was bullish on the pound, too. He was on salary, and though he was clearly speculating, the profits would have gone to the bank. The size of his deals, though, soon got out of hand, and controls in the Brussels office broke down.

[6]*Business Week,* July 24, 1965.

The Belgian branch kept track of its foreign exchange transactions only on a net basis–for example, over-all sterling sales and purchases would be toted up and only the balance, plus or minus, would be shown. Each man's trades were not shown and thus a sizable loss could go undetected for some time. Exchange transactions of a branch also appear on its books only, not in New York. Reichers says, too, that "prescribed accounting procedures were not followed by the Brussels office."

According to Reichers, the manager of the Brussels office did not become aware of the size of the trader's position until May. Then, he moved to have the trader close the position, and the losses became apparent. The New York office wasn't notified until early June.

Two-way Loss. The losses came about in two ways: first, in the trading itself, and second, in liquidating the position.

The bulk of the loss, says Reichers, came in trading. The Brussels man was betting that the discount on forward sterling would shrink; but confidence in sterling waned during the British election and after, and even the move to a 7% bank rate didn't help much. At times, the forward discount widened sharply–sometimes it was 3 1/2¢ below the spot price. The trader was whip-sawed by the market's gyrations. He was buying forward contracts at only a tiny discount, and sterling didn't strengthen enough for the forward price to narrow–and thus produce a profit.

The bank also took a loss in closing the position. To do this, Citibank had to buy spot and then sell forward–just the reverse of what the trader had done in building his position. The loss here resulted from the fact that the forward still sells at a discount to the spot price. This week, sterling for delivery in three months could be bought at $2.7776, or a discount of 1.28¢ from the spot price.

The bank insists that it has taken steps to assure that such a mishap does not recur, though it won't spell them out.

Central Bank Reports

STERLING SITUATION: 1964-1965[7]

Late in May [1974] tight conditions in several Continental money markets exerted new pressure on sterling. These pressures became strong toward the end of June because of heavier-than-usual midyear window dressing by Continental banks. To temper the impact of these movements of funds on official reserves, the Bank of England on June 30 drew $15 million against its $500 million swap line with the Federal Reserve; it repaid the drawing on July 13.

As the credit squeeze in the Continental money market centers extended into July, moderate selling of sterling continued, and the spot rate moved downward with a minimum of official support to a low for the month of $2.7874 on

[7]Excerpts from Charles A. Coombs, "Treasury and Federal Reserve Foreign Exchange Operations." Federal Reserve Bank of New York, *Monthly Review,* March 1965, pp. 43-45.

July 20. The decline in the spot rate was taken in stride by the market without any speculative reaction developing. Indeed, market confidence in the sterling parity at that time was such that the discount on forward sterling tended to narrow as the spot rate declined.

In September, sterling came under increased pressure, mainly owing to increasingly widespread recognition of the mounting balance-of-payments deficit of the United Kingdom, which became further aggravated by the usual seasonal weakness during the autumn and early winter months. Uncertainties connected with the general election called for October 15 further unsettled the sterling exchange market, and the problem of maintaining confidence in sterling seemed likely to become increasingly difficult. In anticipation of reserve losses, the Bank of England in mid-September made timely arrangements to supplement the $500 million swap line with the Federal Reserve by another $500 million of short-term credit facilities with other central banks in Europe and with the Bank of Canada. This reinforcement of the British reserve position cushioned the impact of recurrent, and increasingly forceful, waves of selling during September and October. Net drawings by the Bank of England on the Federal Reserve swap line and on short-term facilities provided by other central banks rose to $415 million by the end of October.

The new Labor government elected on October 15 was thus immediately confronted with a grave balance-of-payments situation. The announcement on October 26 of emergency surcharges of 15 per cent on a wide range of imports brought only brief relief as critical reactions appeared among Britain's trading partners worldwide, more particularly the European Free Trade Association (EFTA) group. In a formal budget presented to Parliament on November 11, the government proposed certain new welfare benefits, to be financed by tax increases, and announced that it intended to introduce a capital gains tax and to substitute a new corporation tax for the existing application of the income tax to corporations. These proposals created uncertainty in business circles, in part because the immediate deflationary influence of the increased tax on fuel as well as the import surcharge was to some extent obscured by the other measures. These uncertainties in domestic financial markets were, in turn, communicated to the exchange market. During this period, the exchange market began to anticipate bank rate action on each successive Thursday, and thus a pattern developed of a strengthening of sterling prior to Thursday of each week, followed by a major selling wave on Friday as the bank rate remained unchanged. When the bank rate remained unchanged on Thursday, November 19, reserve losses by the Bank of England on the following day reached such proportions that action could no longer be postponed. On Monday, November 23, the Bank of England raised its discount rate from 5 per cent to 7 per cent.

Perversely enough, market reaction to such forceful use of monetary policy by the Labor Government quickly degenerated into fears that the threat to sterling must have reached a truly crisis stage. Whether these reactions might have been averted by earlier bank rate action, more particularly on the usual Thursday date for bank rate announcements, may be debated for some time to come. In any event, the market seized on rumors that the $1 billion of short-term central bank credits at the disposal of the Bank of England in September had now been exhausted; that the $1 billion standby credit from the IMF secured by the British Government in August had accordingly been fully committed to repayment of such central bank credits; and, hence, that the United

Kingdom would have to fall back in defense of sterling upon its reserves of roughly $2 billion. (The still-substantial unused drawing rights on the IMF would have required longer to mobilize than events at that time allowed.)

This situation assumed increasingly grave significance on the London afternoon—and the New York morning—of November 24 when a virtual avalanche of selling developed. If sterling were to be rescued, it was clear that a major package of international credit assistance would be required. On the afternoon of the 24th, the Federal Open Market Committee—meeting through a telephone conference—committed itself to an increase in the Federal Reserve-Bank of England swap line from $500 million to $750 million if credit assistance on a roughly corresponding scale could be secured from other central banks. That evening the Export-Import Bank gave assurance of a $250 million standby facility. Beginning early on the morning of November 25, the Bank of England, the Federal Reserve Bank of New York, and the central banks of other major countries were in almost continuous telephone communication. At 2 p.m., New York time, it was announced that a $3 billion credit package by eleven countries and the BIS was at the disposal of the Bank of England.

As a result of the heavy reserve losses, the $500 million Federal Reserve swap and the additional $500 million of other central bank credit facilities made available to the Bank of England in September were not only fully exhausted, but immediate drawings of $200 million on the new credit facilities were also required. From the end of October figure of $415 million, recourse by the Bank of England to central bank credit facilities thus rose by $785 million during November to a total of $1.2 billion. Of this total, the Federal Reserve share was $675 million.

In early December the British Government drew the full amount of its $1 billion standby facility with the IMF and so repaid an equivalent amount of the central bank credits outstanding, including $500 million of the Federal Reserve credit. At the same time, Switzerland, which although not a member of the IMF, is associated with the General Agreements to Borrow, provided the United Kingdom with a three-year credit of $80 million; $50 million of the Swiss credit was used to repay an earlier loan from Switzerland outstanding from the sterling crisis of 1961.

With its exchange reserves thus heavily reinforced, the British Government could face with confidence further temporary pressures on sterling during December. Selling was particularly heavy just prior to the long Christmas week end, and during the month the Bank of England increased its use of short-term central bank credit facilities from the $200 million outstanding early in December to $525 million at the year end. Of this $325 million increase, $25 million was secured by an increased use of the Federal Reserve swap line, raising the total outstanding from $175 million to $200 million, while $300 million was drawn from other central banks.

STERLING SITUATION: 1964-1965 (continued)

By mid-January 1965, sterling began to show signs of recovery from the speculative onslaught of late 1964, and this improvement continued through February. In March, however, the market once again became beset by doubts as to whether the British Government's pledge to defend the sterling parity would be matched by truly effective measures to curb excessive domestic demand and to restrain the inflationary trend of wage settlements. New complications arose as the United States Voluntary Foreign Credit Restraint Program led to some withdrawal of funds from London. Large forward commitments previously entered into by the Bank of England also began to mature, but firm defensive operations in both the spot and forward markets facilitated the rolling-over of most of these commitments.

With the announcement of new restraint measures in Chancellor Callaghan's budget message on April 6, sterling moved strongly upward and this trend was reinforced as the Bank of England on April 29 introduced special deposit requirements for the London clearing and Scottish banks and on May 5 requested the London clearing banks to limit the increase in their advances to the private sector to no more than 5 percent during the year ending March 1966. The other banks operating in London and a wide range of other financial institutions were also asked to exercise comparable restraint. However, following the announcement in mid-May of disappointing trade figures for April, the sterling rate once more began to drift downward. The British drawing on May 25 of $1.4 billion equivalent from the IMF and full repayment with the proceeds of $1,097 million of short-term central bank credits did little to bolster market sentiment. On the contrary, publication of figures showing a continuing deterioration in the British trade position during the second quarter further undermined market confidence, and substantial support had to be given to both the spot and forward markets. By late July the market had become convinced that a new crisis was shaping up for the autumn months.[8]

EXHIBIT 1. Foreign Exchange and Money Market Rates

	U.S. dollars		Interest on U.S. $ deposits in London (3 months)	Interest on £ deposits in Paris (3 months)
	Spot 2.80	3 months' forward (cents)	per cent per annum	
Last working days:				
1964 June	2.7917	0.39 pre.	4.31	4.75
July	2.7882	0.47 pre.	4.25	4.88
Aug.	2.7839	0.43 pre.	4.25	4.75
Sept.	2.7833	0.54 pre.	4.44	5.13
Oct.	2.7850	0.59 pre.	4.50	5.19
Nov.	2.7912	2.01 pre.	5.00	7.75
Dec.	2.7901	1.90 pre.	4.50	7.63
1965 Jan.	2.7920	1.87 pre.	4.50	7.00
Feb.	2.7941	1.98 pre.	4.56	7.25
Mar.	2.7905	2.04 pre.	4.81	8.00
Apr.	2.7991	1.65 pre.	4.81	7.06
May	2.7927	1.89 pre.	5.25	7.75
June	2.7917	1.25 pre.	4.81	6.19
July	2.7920	1.47 pre.	4.63	6.56
Aug.	2.7907	1.73 pre.	4.44	6.88
Sept.	2.8018	0.98 pre.	4.94	6.50

SOURCE: Bank of England, QUARTERLY BULLETIN, October 1965.

[8]Excerpts from Charles A. Coombs, "Treasury and Federal Reserve Foreign Exchange Operations." Federal Reserve Bank of New York, *Monthly Review,* Oct. 1965, pp. 202–203.

PART TWO

We can now discuss some of the specific financial problems that a nonfinancial business manager faces when operating in the international markets. Part One created a foundation to aid the international financial officer in evaluating the financial markets and discussed the behavior of some major international financial institutions. Part Two will turn to major problems of the international financial officer of a nonfinancial business. Although the dividing line is not always easy to draw, particularly for large multinational companies with huge financial resources to manage, nonfinancial businesses, in general, come to financial markets more as "market takers" than as "market makers."

One major problem for the nonfinancial business is the financing of international trade. Chapter 6 discusses methods of covering to protect against foreign exchange risks, the institutions and procedures involved in financing international trade, and the risk/return trade-offs in credit and foreign exchange decisions in this area.

Chapter 7 introduces the tools for evaluating some of the major decisions that the financial officer must make. These decisions include raising the necessary funds to finance the business operations, investing any excess funds that the business generates, supervising the flow of intercompany accounts, and protecting the foreign operations against foreign exchange risks. Chapter 8 analyzes the problem of evaluating the performance of foreign operations under conditions of inflation and exchange fluctuations.

The various problems discussed and evaluated in Chapters 7 and 8 are combined in Chapter 9, which presents a framework of specific steps in the analysis of the finance function of a nonfinancial business enterprise in the international markets. Although simplifying assumptions are made to keep the presentation within a manageable size, the issues of risk and the outcomes of alternative strategies under various future states of the world are brought together into a final interacting summary. This summary should serve as a digest of ground rules for management in choosing policies with which it feels comfortable, given attitudes toward risk and the implications of each policy under alternative market outcomes.

CHAPTER 6

Financing International Trade

With the evolution of a greater world marketplace, the trading caravans and ships of many centuries past have been replaced by major air and ship cargo carriers. Similarly, the simple direct exchange of goods for money between buyer and seller has developed into an indirect payments mechanism that often involves several financial institutions.

In earlier periods of international trade, exporters relied on working capital loans and advances against shipment from their own banks to finance their operations prior to receipt of payment from their customer, the importer. In some cases the importer paid cash in advance. The importer, in turn, was usually financed by loans from a local bank. When the importer and exporter were well known to each other, open account arrangements were used just as one may use a charge account at a local department store. Periodically, the importer was billed for goods which had been shipped, and (s)he remitted payment in a form and to a location which had been agreed upon. Consignment shipping was used: The exporter retained title to the goods and was paid as the importer resold them to local customers. All of these patterns are still present in the world marketplace. However, in later years additional financing devices have been used. For example, a bank in the exporter's country may make a direct loan to the importer to finance purchases or the bank may purchase the importer's liability from the exporter. In either case the exporter would receive immediate payment and a large number of documents would be generated.

Although many recent developments in the financial markets have facilitated international trade, two basic factors continue to affect the assessment of trade financing options and the institutions that have evolved in the field: credit risk and foreign exchange risk. Like any other sale which is not paid immediately, international trade has to deal with the problems imposed by credit risk. Credit risk often presents a larger problem in international than in domestic trade because of the greater distance between the trading parties in the international setting. The other problem, which is peculiar to international trade, derives from the potential fluctuations in the relative values of the currencies of the trading parties. In a system of fixed exchange rates such as the gold standard, this aspect of the transaction did not pose any problem. Under such a system foreign exchange problems would arise only if governments chose to impose foreign exchange controls that impeded the flow of trade. However, in a system where the relative values of currencies are subject to change, at least one of the trading parties has to deal in a foreign currency and, therefore, is subject to an uncertain outcome in terms of his or her domestic currency. For example, the importer who promises to pay in foreign currency will not know the exact cost of merchandise in terms of local currency until the payment is effected or insurance measures are taken.

The remainder of this chapter is divided into three major sections. The first section concentrates on the problem peculiar to international trade, foreign exchange risk, while assuming a simple open account credit arrangement. In international trade the party to the transaction who incurs foreign exchange risk may wish to insure against that risk by covering the transaction in either the forward exchange market or the money market. The methods and trade-offs in making this insurance decision are presented in this section.

The second section of the chapter removes the simplifying assumption of open account credit and introduces some of the procedures and accompanying documents that are used to deal with more complex credit arrangements. These procedures also offer alternative ways to handle the problem of foreign exchange risk.

Finally, the third section consolidates the two preceding sections by analyzing the issues of risk and return in international trade from the point of view of both the exporter and the importer.

INTERNATIONAL TRADE AND FOREIGN EXCHANGE RISKS

Whenever foreign exchange is to be received or paid in the future because of a trade transaction on open account, there is a risk that the relative value of the currencies will change in the intervening time. If an Italian exporter sells shoes on credit to a U.S. department store and denominates the account in dollars, there is a risk that three months later when payment is due the value of the dollar may have deteriorated relative to the Italian lira. In that case the exporter will have a loss in foreign exchange that might well erase the trade gains.

Assume that the export transaction takes place on April 23 and that it is payable in U.S. dollars on July 23. The export transaction is in the amount of $10,000. Assume all the exporter's costs are incurred in liras and not paid until the receivable is collected. The exporter's cash flows by currency are as follows:

	Cash Flows in Terms of Dollars July 23	
	Dollars	*Liras*
Collection of receivable	+10,000	
Payment for costs		-10,000

In effect, the exporter has a net exchange position, long in dollars and short in liras. The foreign exchange risk lies in the uncertainty as to the exchange rate at which the dollars will be converted into liras on July 23.

The exporter can eliminate this net exchange position and the associated foreign exchange rate by covering the transaction in the forward exchange market or the money market. The objective of the covering transaction would be to establish cash flows in each currency opposite to the ones created by the export sale and the manufacturing costs at an exchange rate known in advance. In this example the cover transaction must equal in value an outflow of dollars (which will initially be collected from the receivable) and an inflow in liras (which are needed to pay for costs). The exporter's cash flows by currency after the cover are as follows:

	Cash Flows in Terms of Dollars July 23	
	Dollars	*Liras*
Collection of receivable	+10,000	
Payment for costs		-10,000
Cover transaction	-10,000	+10,000

Let's assume that on April 23 the following rates prevail in the market:

Foreign Exchange Market	
Spot rate	$0.001111/lira (lira 900/$)
3-month forward rate	$0.001125/lira (lira 889/$)

That is, the three-month lira is trading at a premium of 5.05% per annum against the U.S. dollar.[1] (The U.S. dollar is trading at a discount against the lira.)

[1] $$\frac{\text{Forward rate} - \text{Spot rate}}{\text{Spot rate}} \times \frac{12}{3} = \frac{0.001125 - 0.001111}{0.001111} \times 4 = 0.0505$$

Money Market	
3-month lira	4%
3-month U.S. dollar	9%

That is, except for 0.05% per annum that can be attributed to transaction costs, the foreign exchange market and the money markets are in equilibrium and there is no incentive for interest arbitrage. Other than 0.05%, interest differentials equal the premium/discount in the forward market–interest rate parity holds.

Covering in the Forward Market

One way to eliminate the uncertainty as to the exchange rate at which the dollars collected on the receivable will be converted into liras (i.e., to eliminate the exchange position) is to cover the transaction in the forward exchange market. On July 23 the exporter will have an inflow of dollars. These dollars are to be converted into liras. If on April 23 the exporter enters into a forward contract to sell dollars against liras for delivery on July 23, an exchange rate to convert the dollars into liras would be locked in from the beginning of the export sale. The sequence of events will be as follows:

April 23: Deliver \$10,000 worth of shoes to a U.S. department store. Payment is due on July 23 in U.S. dollars. At April 23 spot prices of \$0.001111 per lira (lira 900/\$), the export sale is worth 9,000,000 lira.

In order to protect against an adverse change in the value of the dollar against the lira, the exporter sells \$10,000 against liras for delivery on July 23 at \$0.001125 per lira (lira 889/\$), the market price for three-month liras against U.S. dollars. That is, the forward contract will provide 8,890,000 liras.

July 23: Exporter receives check for U.S. \$10,000.

Exporter delivers \$10,000 against forward contract and receives 8,890,000 liras.

From the beginning of the transaction the exporter knows exactly the amount of liras to be received when the payment is finally realized, i.e., 8,890,000 liras. The cost of covering in the forward exchange market relative to the spot rate on April 23 is the 5.05% per annum discount on the three-month dollar against the lira that prevailed at the beginning of the transaction.

In effect, when the dollar receivable is covered in the forward market there are two transactions that take place almost simultaneously on the date of final payment, July 23. One transaction is the delivery of U.S. dollars by the American importer in payment for the goods, regardless of whether or not a forward contract exists. The other transaction, which takes place if a forward contract is outstanding, is the delivery of dollars against liras by the exporter to fulfill the forward exchange contract. The cost of the forward cover is the net exchange gain/loss from these two transactions.

In the absence of a forward cover there will be an exchange gain/loss on the dollars collected and converted into liras on July 23. The foreign exchange gain or loss in the forward contract is the difference between the rate in the contract and the spot rate prevailing on the closing date, July 23. In the absence of the dollar proceeds from the export transaction, the Italian exporter would have to purchase U.S. dollars in the spot market at the rate prevailing on that date, July 23. Since the gain or loss in each component transaction in a covered export sale is calculated by comparing in one case the initial spot rate and in the other case the initial forward rate, with the spot rate at the end of the period, July 23, the net gain or loss from the combined transactions must be the difference between the initial spot and forward rates; i.e., the 5.05% per annum discount on the dollar against the lira. We can illustrate this point further with specific calculations for the case of the Italian exporter:

	Case A	*Case B*	*Case C*
1. Spot rate, July 23	$ 0.001111	$ 0.001222	$ 0.001000
2. Spot rate, April 23	0.001111	0.001111	0.001111
3. Appreciation or depreciation (–) of the U.S. dollar against lira	—	$-0.000111	$+0.000111
4. Forward rate contracted in April	$ 0.001125	$ 0.001125	$ 0.001125
5. Gain or loss (–) on April forward vs. July spot (line 1 less line 4)	$-0.000014	$+0.000097	$-0.000125
6. Gain or loss (–) from converting dollar proceeds into liras: Lit 9,000,000 X (line 3)	—	$ -1,000	$ +1,000
7. Gain or loss (–) on closing forward contract: Lit 9,000,000 X (line 5)[a]	$ -126	$ +874	$ -1,126
8. Total costs	$ -126	$ -126	$ -126

[a]Figures include rounding errors.

In every case the actual cost to the Italian exporter is $126. In every case the gain (loss) in converting the dollar proceeds into liras at the new spot rate when netted against the loss (gain) from the forward contract valued at the final spot rate produces the same net cost of $126. This cost is 1.26% of the total amount of export proceeds, $10,000. Since the cost was sustained over only three months, this is equivalent to 5.05% on a per annum basis—the initial discount of the three-month dollar against the lira.

The coverage transaction represents a purchase of insurance against a weakening of the U.S. dollar relative to the Italian lira between April 23 and July 23. However, if the dollar actually strengthened against the lira by July 23, the Italian exporter would have suffered an *opportunity loss* by having sold the $10,000 against lira in the forward market in April.

More specifically, the price of the lira was locked in by the forward contract at $0.001125/lira (lira 889/$). The spot rate for the lira in April, when the trade took place, was $0.001111/lira (lira 900/$). So, by locking in the forward price, the exporter was accepting a discount of 5.05% on the dollar against the Italian lira (a premium on the forward lira against the dollar). However, this action assured that if the spot rate at the end of the period turned out to be more than $0.001125/lira (less than lira 889/$), i.e., the dollar weakened against the lira below the initial forward price, the exporter would not incur the extra loss. This is the objective of the insurance bought by the forward contract. On the other hand, if on July 23 the dollar had strengthened against the lira and the spot rate was less than $0.001111/lira (more than lira 900/$), the exporter would have an opportunity loss. If (s)he had not bought the insurance of the forward contract the transaction would have been more profitable. As an illustration, compare the three cases below:

	Case A	*Case B*	*Case C*
1. Spot rate on July 23	$ 0.001111	$ 0.001222	$ 0.001000
2. Less contracted forward rate	-0.001125	-0.001125	-0.001125
3. Gain or loss (-) on forward transaction	$-0.000014	$+0.000097	$-0.000125
4. Opportunity foreign exchange gain or loss (-): Lit 9,000,000 X (line 3)[a]	$ -126	$ +874	$ -1,126

[a]Figures include rounding errors.

In Case A the spot exchange rate remains constant between April and July. The exporter could have avoided the discount on the forward dollar and saved $126 by not covering. In Case B the spot dollar has weakened against the Italian lira below the point at which the forward contract was entered. By having the forward contract, the exporter avoided a loss of $874; i.e., an opportunity gain was realized or an opportunity loss avoided.[2] On the other hand, in Case C the exporter would have been better off by not covering in the forward market. In this case the exporter suffered an opportunity loss of $1,126. This loss was

[2]Let's assume that the exporter is not interested in the exchange gains that could be realized from an appreciation of the dollar against the lira (Case C), because the probabilities of such an occurrence are considered to be nil. However, the exchange losses associated with a depreciation of the dollar against the lira (Case B) are very much feared. If the exporter were operating solely on the basis of expected values, when the expected value of such a loss is greater than the cost of the cover, $126, the exporter will cover the receivable. Given that the loss associated with Case B is $874, then the minimum probability of Case B beyond which cover will be advisable is 0.13, Since [(1 - 0.13) X (-$126)] + [(0.13) X $874] = 0. As long as the exporter believes that the probability of the weakening of the exchange rate depicted in Case B is at least as great as 0.13, then the covering transaction will take place. In fact, given a risk averse exporter, the covering transaction will occur even for much lower values of the probability for Case B. The lower expected value for the transaction is offset by eliminating intolerable outcomes associated with receiving a very low exchange rate.

created because the forward contract had the U.S. dollar at a discount against the lira in April when actually the dollar strengthened against the lira by the day of payment in July.

It must be emphasized that the preceding foreign exchange gains and losses are of an *opportunity* nature. These gains and losses can be calculated only after the eventual spot rate prevailing on the date of the final payment is known. Then, with the benefit of hindsight, one can establish the losses that the forward contract avoided or the gains that were foregone because of the covering transaction.

Covering through the Money Market

In the case of the Italian exporter, another way to insure against a large depreciation of the dollar against the Italian lira would be to borrow $10,000 in the United States for three months. The proceeds from this loan would then be converted into liras and invested in the Italian money market at the going rate. Thus, when July 23 arrives, if there is a deterioration of the dollar against the lira, the loss in the receipt from exports will be compensated by the gain in the payment of the loan. The sequence of events in this case will be as follows:

April 23: Deliver the $10,000 worth of shoes to a U.S. department store. Payment is due on July 23 in U.S. dollars. At April 23 spot prices of $0.001111 per lira (lira 900/$) the export sale is worth 9,000,000 liras.

In order to protect against an adverse change in the value of the dollar against the lira, the exporter borrows $10,000 from a New York bank at 9%, discounts the loan, converts the proceeds, $9,775, into liras (8,797,500 liras), and invests in a three-month bill in Italy at 4%. That is, after three months the bill will be worth 8,885,475 liras.

July 23: Exporter receives check for U.S. $10,000.

U.S. dollar proceeds from export sales are used to pay the $10,000 loan from New York bank.

Three-month lira bill is liquidated and it yields the anticipated 8,885,475 liras.

From the beginning of the transaction the exporter knows exactly the amount of liras to be netted from the transaction; i.e., 8,885,475 liras. The net cost of this covering transaction, relative to the initial spot rate, is the interest differential between the cost of the loan in U.S. dollars at 9% and the return on the lira investment, 4%. The net cost is 5%. The initial export sale is 9,000,000 liras. After the sale of the lira bill at the end of the transaction the exporter nets 8,885,475 liras. The covering transaction has cost 114,525 liras. This cost represents 1.27% of the original export sale in liras. Since this cost was incurred over only three months, it represents 5.08% on an annual basis. On an opportunity cost basis, the exporter is insuring against a loss larger than the one implied by the interest differential. However, if the dollar actually appreciates against the lira by the time payment is due, the exporter would have been in a better position by not covering the transaction. Again, these last statements refer to the opportunity gain or loss from covering the export sale in the money market.

The cost of covering in the money market can be dissected in the same fashion as the cost of covering in the forward market. In effect, it is as if two transactions took place on July 23. (1) The export proceeds in dollars are converted into liras; and (2) the proceeds from the lira investment are converted into dollars to pay for the loan in New York. Both of these conversions take place at the spot price prevailing on the day of payment, July 23. The following table presents the gains and losses for the Italian exporter from various parts of the export transaction covered in the money market:

	Case A	*Case B*	*Case C*
1. Spot rate: July 23	$ 0.001111	$ 0.001222	$ 0.001000
2. Spot rate: April 23	0.001111	0.001111	0.001111
3. Appreciation or depreciation (-) of the U.S. dollar against lira	–	$-0.000111	$+0.000111
4. Proceeds from bill in lira:[a] (8,797,500) + (8,797,500 X .04 X 3/12 = Lit 8,885,475			
5. Conversion of proceeds from lira bill into dollars: 8,885,475 X (line 1)[b]	$ 9,873	$ 10,860	$ 8,885
6. Loan due in dollars	10,000	10,000	10,000
7. Gain or loss in money market operation (line 5 less line 6)	$ -127	$ +860	$ -1,115
8. Gain or loss (-) from converting dollar export proceeds into liras: Lit 9,000,000 X (line 3)[b]	–	$ -1,000	$ +1,000
9. Total cost	$ $-127	$ $-140	$ $-115

[a] Assumes that the $10,000 loan was discounted before being converted into lira and invested in the lira money market.

[b] Figures include rounding errors.

The discrepancy in total costs is a function of the conversion of the differential between the interest paid on the loan at the beginning of the period and converted from dollars into liras at the April 23 spot rate, and the interest received in liras and converted into dollars at the end of the period at the spot rate on July 23. If the interest had been paid and received on the same date at the same prevailing spot exchange rate, the cost of covering in the money market would have been the same under every outcome, $127. That is, the cost is about 5% per annum—the interest differential.

If the costs of covering in the money market in the preceding computations are compared with the costs of covering in the forward exchange market computed earlier, the figures are very similar. Besides rounding errors and technical variations based on when the interest rates are converted, the costs differ only by the amount that the interest differential, 5%, differs from the premium on the three-month lira against the dollar at the beginning of the period, 5.05%.

If the markets are in equilibrium under interest rate parity (discounts or premiums in the forward market equal the interest differentials), the two approaches to covering a cash flow in a foreign currency should produce similar results, as was the case in our example.

At a cost of approximately 5% per annum relative to the initial spot rate, both approaches to covering the cash flow generated from the export transaction accomplish the objective of locking in a foreign exchange rate at the beginning of the transaction to eliminate all uncertainty about the total proceeds from the sale. Both approaches also eliminate the possibility of an additional gain of 10% if the dollar strengthens against the lira as indicated in Case C.

Choosing a Cover

The analysis in the preceding two sections showed that when a decision to cover the proceeds from an international transaction is made, it does not make much difference in terms of cost whether the forward exchange market or the money market approach is followed, if the financial markets—money markets and foreign exchange markets—are in equilibrium. However, if the net rates accessible to the exporter are different from the ones available to exchange dealers who establish forward rates, the outcomes from covering in the forward market or the money market will vary. This difference in net rates accessible to exchange dealers and exporters arises on two accounts:

1. The presence of exchange controls producing segmented money markets, domestic and external; and

2. Differences in credit premiums on lending rates charged to different borrowers.

Government controls apply only to transactions within the country boundary, i.e., Italy. However, currencies traded outside the country, e.g., Euro-lira, are not subject to these controls. The subsidiary located in the foreign country has access to its own domestic market. The parent company always has access to the external markets. On the other hand, the credit premiums charged for interbank loans, funds accessible to exchange traders, is much smaller than for industrial companies.

Disequilibrium situations are appealing to the corporate treasurers of firms which are major importers and exporters. The costs of covering in each of these markets may diverge, and when large sums are involved it is worthwhile for the treasurer to have sufficient knowledge of the differentials. Once the basics are mastered, the costs can be computed rapidly under each approach to covering. Then, the comparison of costs under the two alternatives can be made and the best option chosen.

In the previous example with an accessible interest differential of only 3/4%, instead of 5%, the money market alternative would be superior. The forward market approach still costs $126, but the cost in the money market is now only $19; that is, 3/4% × $10,000 × 3/12. Thus, the insurance policy's "cost" would be reduced by approximately 85% ($107 ÷ $126) by choosing the money market route to covering instead of the forward exchange market. If, on the other hand, interest differentials in favor of the United States were much larger than the forward discount on the dollar, the forward market alternative would be the most attractive approach.

One more consideration to be kept in mind when choosing one approach to covering over another is the matter of financial reporting. The money market cover will appear directly on the balance sheet: an investment on the asset side and a liability on the liabilities-plus-equity side. The forward transaction will appear only as a footnote. To the extent that the financial officer is concerned about ratios such as the debt-to-equity ratio, financial reporting considerations introduce a bias against using the money market route to cover international trade and a bias in favor of using the forward exchange market.

One other potential risk which we have avoided in the preceding discussion is that which can result from a mismatch of the maturities of various cash flows involved in a covered trade transaction. The previous calculations assumed that the investment in the Italian money market matured (could be converted into cash) on the same date that the proceeds of the export sale were received. However, in many cases it becomes impossible to find a security with a maturity to match the date of payment for the trade transaction. In these cases there is an additional risk: the value of the security at the time of the receipt from the export sale. If the level of interest rates increases during the investment period, and the security bought has a maturity longer than the trade account, the investor will be able to liquidate the debt security only by offering it at a discount on the closing date—a capital loss. On the other hand, if interest rates decline during the investment period, the exporter will have a capital gain on the investment. A similar risk is incurred if the security bought to cover the foreign exchange risks has a maturity shorter than the length of time until the receipt from the trade transaction is expected. In this case the exporter has to speculate on the interest rate that can be obtained on the security purchased after the initial security matures. If the initial security has only a one-month maturity, at the end of the first month the exporter will have to make another investment for the remaining two months of the trade transaction to continue on a covered basis. In effect, a swap position will exist in these cases.

To Cover or Not To Cover

In the example of the Italian exporter, the cost of covering relative to the initial spot rate was about 5%, regardless of what covering method was used. In some industries 5% may appear to be a small price to pay for insurance against negative fluctuations in exchange rates. However, in other industries 5% may be more than the usual profit margin. In the latter case, covering for foreign exchange risk would make the trade transaction a loss, and international trade will take place only if one of the parties is willing to bear the uncovered foreign exchange risk. This willingness is a function of how likely and how large the people involved in the trade perceive the potential change in spot rates to be. If the expected negative fluctuation in the exchange rate is more than the profit margin, trade will not occur unless the profit margin can be increased accordingly. In a fiercely competitive market, the decision to cover or not to cover may make the difference between whether the company stays in business or not.

The likelihood and possible magnitude of an adverse foreign exchange rate fluctuation, and therefore the willingness of one of the parties to accept the risk, depend to a large extent on whether fixed or floating exchange rates prevail. Under a system of fixed rates, the decision to cover is typically made only when there is a "substantial" probability of loss. Unfortunately, this situation involving a high probability of a devaluation usually coincides with the most severe discounts in the forward market. Even assuming this coincidence, the exporter may rationally cover a loss based on a utility function which accepts a lower return with certainty in exchange for a higher expected return in an uncertain world. This is the typical situation, for the exporter knows that a rational market would prevent a gain on a less risky alternative (the covered position) from exceeding the return on the riskier alternative (the uncovered position).

In a world of fluctuating exchange rates, however, the situation becomes much more complex. In a system of flexible rates, in contrast to a fixed rate system, it is likely that there will be fewer large changes in the relative value of currencies during the typical period involved in trade financing. However, under the flexible rate system there will also be many more changes over all currencies, though of a smaller amount. Given these complexities, major corporations can certainly be expected to consider their covering decisions with much greater care under the present managed floating exchange rate system than in the past. The alternative covering sources and the means of computing gains or losses from covering that we have discussed are essential in this analysis. Various studies of the practices of American multinationals during the 1970s confirm this behavior; however, there have also been changes in the reporting requirements of foreign activities, but it is not clear whether the greater attention to covering comes from managed floating or the greater visibility of foreign operations. This issue is discussed further in Chapter 7.[3]

For the handful of currencies whose value is allowed to float freely from time to time, without much government intervention, the issue to cover or not to cover may be simplified somewhat. In efficient markets the forward rate of these currencies would be an unbiased forecaster of future spot rates. Businesses which through time choose to cover systematically all their future payables and receivables in foreign exchange lock in a series of forward exchange rates. Over the long-term the average of these locked-in forward rates will tend to approximate the average of the spot rates. That is, since the forward rate is assumed to be an unbiased predictor of the spot, the policies of covering or not covering through time produce approximately the same result. At any time the exchange rate applicable to a specific transaction will be either the forward rate, if the

[3]The answer to the question of whether firms or individuals face more or less risk under a floating rate world than under a fixed rate pivots on questions of the utility of small, frequent changes vs. relatively large infrequent changes. Some evidence for evaluating this issue was found by Janice Moulton Westerfield who notes that the non-normality of the distribution of exchange rate changes under both fixed and floating regimes is an important issue, for the changes are more accurately understood in the context of a stable Paretian distribution, with infinite variances (which mean sample estimates of the variance are meaningless). Using several standard statistical indices of risk which may be applied to stable Paretian distributions, she concludes that the floating rate era has produced far more risk to the firm or individual involved with it, even when considering the dirty floating of Canada in the 1950s. See "An Examination of Foreign Exchange Risk Under Fixed and Floating Regimes," *Journal of International Economics,* May 1977, pp. 181-200.

business chooses to cover it, or the spot rate at the time of the collection of payment, if the business chooses *not* to cover the transaction. However, through time the average of exchange rates applicable to the overall business will be the same regardless of the covering policy pursued. In this world the only relevant considerations on whether to cover or not to cover would be of a technical nature: transaction costs involved in the spread between bid and ask prices in the forward market versus the spot market.[4]

INTERNATIONAL TRADE: SPECIAL FINANCING ARRANGEMENTS

There is a whole series of documents that have been developed to facilitate the financing of trade. Among the major instruments involved are the letter of credit, the draft, and the banker's acceptance. Sources of financing for both importers and exporters who use these instruments have been primarily commercial banks and to a lesser extent governments. However, factoring firms and finance companies are involved in this field as well.

Letter of Credit

Suppose Zebracorp, a U.S. manufacturer of widgets, has agreed with Chao-widgets, a distributor of the product in Chaolandia, to sell a certain quantity of widgets to the firm. Although Zebracorp knows that Chao-widgets wants the product, the firm's credit is not well known to Zebracorp, and the firm wonders about the process by which it can assure itself of payment.

In the most typical use of the *letter of credit* (l/c), the buyer, Chao-widgets, will go to its local bank and ask for that bank to issue a letter of credit. In this letter the bank agrees to honor the demand for payment resulting from the import transaction described in the document. In exchange, the importer promises to pay to the bank the required amount plus fees on mutually accepted terms.

Here, Chao-widgets, which applied for the l/c, is the *account party,* and its local bank is the *issuing* bank. Zebracorp is the *beneficiary* of the l/c and receives its money from the *paying* bank, also called the *drawee* bank, whom the issuing bank instructs to make the payment upon presentation of appropriate documents.

It is easiest to see this financing procedure through a few examples of l/c's such as might occur between firms around the world. The bank in the importer's country may well operate through its own affiliate in the exporter's country, but often it will deal through one of its *correspondent* banks. The documents certifying shipment of the goods will be presented to the paying bank—an affiliate of the issuing bank or its correspondent. This situation is shown in Exhibit 6.1. Here, the exporter, Africa Patterns, Ltd., is informed by the issuing bank, Bankers Trust, that Africa Patterns will be paid by the Bank in Manchester when

[4]For some historical evidence on this issue see Ian H. Giddy," "Why It Doesn't Pay To Make a Habit of Forward Hedging." *Euromoney,* Dec. 1976, pp. 96–100.

EXHIBIT 6.1.

THIS BANK MADE OUT THE LETTER OF CREDIT → **BANKERS TRUST COMPANY**
16 WALL STREET · NEW YORK, N. Y., 10015

LONDON E. C. 4
9, QUEEN VICTORIA STREET

April 16, 19--

IRREVOCABLE CREDIT NO. 1234

[X] Forwarded through [ ] Copy sent to

Africa Patterns Ltd.
198 Bunyoro Drive
Entebbe, Uganda

Bank in Uganda
Entebbe, Uganda

Gentlemen:

We hereby authorize you to value on ~~us,~~ Bank in Manchester ← THE BENEFICIARY MUST DRAW HIS DRAFT ON THIS BANK

for account of Mainwaring Frocks Inc., Massachusetts

for a sum or sums in ~~U. S. Dollars~~ pounds sterling not exceeding a total of eight hundred only
£ 800-0-0

by your drafts at sight
accompanied by:

1- Commercial invoice covering 15 bolts of Uganda Pattern #5 cloth, C&F New York.

2- Complete set of clean on board ocean bills of lading to order of Bankers Trust Company, notify Mainwaring Frocks Inc., Massachusetts, marked "freight prepaid."

THE BENEFICIARY MUST PRESENT HIS DOCUMENTS TO THIS BANK

Partial shipments are permitted.
Bills of lading must be dated not later than July 30, 19--

Drafts must be negotiated or presented to the drawee not later than August 7, 19--.
Negotiations are to be made only at the office of Bank in Uganda, Entebbe, Uganda.
Insurance to be effected by buyer
All negotiation charges are for your account.

All drafts must be marked "Drawn under BANKERS TRUST COMPANY Credit No. 1234," and all drawings negotiated under this credit must be endorsed on the reverse hereof by the party so negotiating. If any draft is not negotiated, this credit and all documents as specified must accompany the draft.

This credit is subject to the Uniform Customs and Practice for Documentary Credits (1962 Revision), International Chamber of Commerce Brochure No. 222.

We hereby agree with you and negotiating banks or bankers that drafts drawn under and in compliance with the terms of this credit shall be duly honored on due presentation to the drawee.

SPECIMEN

PER PRO.

F 3332
ABC 6-65
(10-65)

SOURCE: LETTERS OF CREDIT, Book 2. The American Bankers Association. Washington, D.C., 1968, p. 23.

documents certifying shipment of goods are accepted by the Bank in Uganda. The account party is the importer, Mainwaring Frocks, Inc.

Here, once the documents are accepted in good order by the Bank in Uganda and the payment is made through the Bank in Manchester, Bankers Trust reimburses the Bank in Manchester. Bankers Trust then has the problem of collection from Mainwaring Frocks. Thus, the exporter knows that Bankers Trust guarantees that she will be paid upon certification of shipment by various documents as noted in the draft (explained below). She can be relatively unconcerned about the payment eventually made by Mainwaring Frocks to Bankers Trust.

The bank serves as a *guarantor of payment,* and that is the main value of the letter of credit. The date before which drafts must be negotiated, August 7, 19--, in Exhibit 6.1, gives the beneficiary a firm date prior to which (s)he knows the credit is guaranteed. When the buyer and seller are not known to each other, when the credit of the buyer is unknown, or when the seller demands quick payment, the letter of credit can be a useful device.

The security of the bank involved is of concern to the exporter, of course. Hence, there are several varieties of letters of credit depending on the relationships among the account party, the issuing bank, and the paying bank.

Confirmed Irrevocable Letters of Credit. Notice in Exhibit 6.1 the last paragraph in which Bankers Trust has added its *own* confirmation to the letter of credit, meaning that both Bankers Trust and the Bank in Manchester are obligated to pay Africa Patterns once the documents specified in the letter are furnished and accepted by Bankers Trust.

Unconfirmed Irrevocable Letters of Credit. When the local bank rewrites the letter but does not add its name as a confirming bank, it sends an *advice of an irrevocable letter of credit.* In Exhibit 6.2 the Bank in Tokyo is the issuing bank and guarantees the credit. Morgan Guaranty will pay upon presentation of the documents to it by Tewig Spice, the beneficiary. However, should the importer/account party, Lantern Trading Company, not pay the issuing bank, then the Bank in Tokyo must bear the entire loss of the transaction.

Revocable Letters of Credit. In some cases neither bank guarantees payment. Here the advisory statement at the bottom of the letter indicates that there is no guarantee on either of the bank's part. In Exhibit 6.3, once the documents are accepted by Irving Trust showing that Morgan T. Burns, Inc., has shipped the goods as ordered by John Brown Ltd., then payment is made. However, Morgan T. Burns, Inc., the beneficiary, has no guarantee that John Brown Ltd. will not cancel his letter of credit at any time. The only guarantee the exporter/beneficiary has is that, once the documents are accepted by Irving Trust, if the letter of credit has not been canceled, he will be paid.

A summary of the terms and arrangements concerning these three types of letters of credit is shown in Exhibit 6.4. As suggested in the exhibit, l/c's can have their terms altered at the initiation of the account party, subject to approval of certain other involved parties.

EXHIBIT 6.2.

9-66-6M FORM 11-4-946

MORGAN GUARANTY TRUST COMPANY
OF NEW YORK
INTERNATIONAL BANKING DIVISION
23 WALL STREET, NEW YORK, N. Y. 10015

February 10, 19--

Tewig Spice Company
568 Mott Street
New York, New York

On all communications please refer to
OUR REFERENCE NUMBER
K-2000

Dear Sirs:

We are instructed to advise you of the establishment by
• Bank in Tokyo
of their IRREVOCABLE Credit No L3-8120
in your favor, for the account of Lantern Trading Company

for U.S. $1,000.00 (ONE THOUSAND U.S. DOLLARS)

available upon presentation to us of your drafts at sight on us, accompanied by:

Commercial Invoice.

Full set of on board ocean steamer Bills of Lading to order of Bank in Tokyo, marked "Notify Lantern Trading Co.,"

evidencing shipment of PLASTIC CHOP STICKS, C.I.F. Tokyo, From New York to Tokyo.

Except as otherwise expressly stated herein, this advice is subject to the Uniform Customs and Practice for Documentary Credits (1962 Revision), International Chamber of Commerce, Brochure No. 222.

Your drafts must indicate that they are drawn under the aforementioned Advice . . . . , number K-2000 of the Morgan Guaranty Trust Company of New York and must be presented to our Commercial Credits Department, 15 Broad Street, New York, N. Y. 10015 with specified documents, not later than August 3, 19-- on which date this advice expires.

THIS LETTER IS SOLELY AN ADVICE AND CONVEYS NO ENGAGEMENT BY US.

Yours very truly,

SPECIMEN

Authorized Signature

Immediately upon receipt please examine this advice, and if its terms are not clear to you or if you need any assistance in respect to your availment of it, we would welcome your communicating with us. Documents should be presented promptly and not later than 3 P.M.

SOURCE: LETTERS OF CREDIT, Book 2. The American Bankers Association. Washington, D.C., 1968, p. 63.

EXHIBIT 6.3.

Irving Trust Company

ONE WALL STREET
NEW YORK, N.Y. 10015

DATE March 1, 19--
REVOCABLE ADVICE
NO. 123456

Morgan T. Burns, Inc.
1421 Elm Road
New York, New York 10012

GENTLEMEN:

WE ARE INFORMED BY { Bank of Finance London, England }

THAT YOU WILL DRAW ON US AT SIGHT TO THE EXTENT OF

$10,400.00

FOR ACCOUNT OF John Brown Ltd., London, England

YOUR DRAFTS MUST BE ACCOMPANIED BY THE FOLLOWING DOCUMENTS (COMPLETE SETS UNLESS OTHERWISE STATED) EVIDENCING SHIPMENT(S) OF:

Pump Parts, F.O.B. Vessel New York, from New York to Southampton

Commercial Invoice

On board ocean bills of lading issued to order of shipper and endorsed in blank, marked "Notify John Brown Ltd., London, England."

Insurance covered by buyer.

Description of the engagement of the issuing and advising banks to the beneficiary.

DRAFTS MUST CLEARLY SPECIFY THE NUMBER OF THIS ADVICE, AND BE PRESENTED AT THIS COMPANY NOT LATER THAN June 1, 19--

THIS ADVICE IS SUBJECT TO THE UNIFORM CUSTOMS AND PRACTICE FOR DOCUMENTARY CREDITS (1974 REVISION) INTERNATIONAL CHAMBER OF COMMERCE PUBLICATION [illegible]

THIS ADVICE, REVOCABLE AT ANY TIME WITHOUT NOTICE, IS FOR YOUR GUIDANCE ONLY IN PREPARING DRAFTS AND DOCUMENTS AND CONVEYS NO ENGAGEMENT OR OBLIGATION ON OUR PART OR ON THE PART OF OUR ABOVE-MENTIONED CORRESPONDENT.

NOTE

DOCUMENTS MUST CONFORM STRICTLY WITH THE TERMS OF THIS ADVICE. IF YOU ARE UNABLE TO COMPLY WITH ITS TERMS, PLEASE COMMUNICATE WITH US AND/OR YOUR CUSTOMER PROMPTLY WITH A VIEW TO HAVING THE CONDITIONS CHANGED.

YOURS VERY TRULY

SPECIMEN

AUTHORIZED SIGNATURE

150 70 (8-75) Rev. 8-75

SOURCE: Irving Trust Company, One Wall Street, New York, New York 10015.

EXHIBIT 6.4. Summary: Terms of Letters of Credit

	Revocable L/C	*Unconfirmed Irrevocable L/C*	*Confirmed Irrevocable L/C*
Who applies for l/c	account party	account party	account party
Who is obligated to pay	none	issuing bank	issuing bank and confirming bank
Who applies for amendment	account party	account party	account party
Who approves amendment	issuing bank	issuing bank and beneficiary	issuing bank, beneficiary, and confirming bank
Who reimburses paying bank	issuing bank	issuing bank	issuing bank
Who reimburses issuing bank	account party	account party	account party

SOURCE: LETTERS OF CREDIT, Book 2. The American Bankers Association, Washington, D.C., 1968, pp. 23, 137.

Negotiable Letters of Credit. In some cases the beneficiary of the l/c may not find it convenient to present documents to a particular paying bank. In cases when foreign exchange rates quoted by the banks differ, it may be hard for the beneficiary to know before payment date what bank would be most desirable as the paying bank. In these cases the *straight* l/c can be replaced by a *negotiable* l/c which could be used with any bank willing to act as paying bank. The difference in wording specifies which form of l/c is involved, as shown in Exhibit 6.5. Note that Ⓐ requires under a separate paragraph that drafts drawn against that l/c must be endorsed and marked with reference to Credit No. 1234. This is a negotiable l/c. This statement is not necessary in Ⓑ , a straight l/c, since the draft can only be presented to the paying bank designated in the l/c. In addition, Ⓐ , the negotiable l/c, says specifically that the "Drafts must be negotiated or presented to the drawee not later than. . . ." In contrast, Ⓑ , the straight l/c, does not mention the word "negotiated." In the negotiable l/c the expiration date is the last date the letter of credit can be negotiated. Thus, in Ⓐ , the expiration date is August 7.

Time Letters of Credit. In all the examples presented above the issuing bank promises to pay a certain amount "at sight" of a draft (explained in the following section) and certain other documents. However, if the exporter wishes to extend credit to the importer, the exporter would require only a *time l/c.* In a time l/c the issuing bank promises to pay at a specified date *after* the presentation of certain documents. In this way the exporter may provide more lenient credit terms than the bank while retaining the payment guarantee of a major bank.

Transferable Letters of Credit. In many cases a trading house or intermediary may be aware of a possible transaction. In this case the account party (buying

EXHIBIT 6.5.

(A)

Drafts must be negotiated or presented to the drawee not later than August 7, 19--.
Negotiations are to be made only at the office of Bank in Uganda, Entebbe, Uganda.
Insurance to be effected by buyer
All negotiation charges are for your account.

All drafts must be marked "Drawn under BANKERS TRUST COMPANY Credit No. 1234 ," and all drawings negotiated under this credit must be endorsed on the reverse hereof by the party so negotiating. If any draft is not negotiated, this credit and all documents as specified must accompany the draft.

This credit is subject to the Uniform Customs and Practice for Documentary Credits (1962 Revision), International Chamber of Commerce Brochure No. 222.

We hereby agree with you and negotiating banks or bankers that drafts drawn under and in compliance with the terms of this credit shall be duly honored on due presentation to the drawee.

SPECIMEN

PER PRO.

F 3332
ABC 6-65
(10-65)

(B)

THE ABOVE MENTIONED CORRESPONDENT ENGAGES WITH YOU THAT ALL DRAFTS DRAWN UNDER AND IN COMPLIANCE WITH THE TERMS OF THIS CREDIT WILL BE DULY HONORED ON DELIVERY OF DOCUMENTS AS SPECIFIED IF PRESENTED AT THIS OFFICE ON OR BEFORE February 13, 19-- WE CONFIRM THE CREDIT AND THEREBY UNDERTAKE THAT ALL DRAFTS DRAWN AND PRESENTED AS ABOVE SPECIFIED WILL BE DULY HONORED BY US.
THIS CREDIT IS SUBJECT TO THE UNIFORM CUSTOMS AND PRACTICE FOR DOCUMENTARY CREDITS (1962 REVISION), INTERNATIONAL CHAMBER OF COMMERCE BROCHURE NO. 222.

YOURS VERY TRULY,

SPECIMEN

ASST. TREAS./PER PROCURATION

SOURCE: LETTERS OF CREDIT, Book 2. The American Bankers Association, Washington, D.C., 1968, pp. 23, 137.

importer) will open a *transferable letter of credit* between the firm and the trading house. The trading house can then tell prospective sellers that the buyer has a bank that guarantees payment for the purchase. When the trader finds the seller, (s)he instructs the advising bank to transfer the letter of credit to the seller, letting the seller become the new beneficiary. The creation of a transferable letter of credit is noted by simply having a line such as, "This credit is transferable," added to the documentation.

Documents Required by Letters of Credit. The various documents described in letters of credit are usually standard commercial forms. Thus, the *commercial invoice* is simply a bill for the goods which have been shipped. It details the banking arrangements and the product shipped, specifies any charges which are to be paid (such as insurance, freight, handling, and so on), and usually the shipper and ports involved. The *bill of lading* is a control form for the goods. It is issued by the common carrier transporting the goods. It is usually issued to the exporter or to the bank issuing the letter of credit. This document shows that the merchandise has been received by the carrier who agrees to deliver it according to special conditions. Possession of this document often establishes the ownership of the merchandise. Thus, it can be used to insure payment before delivery of goods, and it can also be used as collateral against loans. Various insurance policies, consular/custom forms, or invoices may also be required by terms of the l/c.

When there are irregularities in the documents, the paying bank has the choice of asking to have the l/c amended, asking the beneficiary to complete the documents in a specified manner, or receiving an indemnification from the beneficiary holding the bank not responsible if the account party later refuses to pay. In this situation the beneficiary has lost most of the benefit conveyed by the letter of credit. However, if the documents are in proper order but do not conform to the facts, e.g., description of the color of the merchandise, the paying bank is *not* responsible for this variance. In this case the importer has to refer to the commercial legal code to determine the party responsible for the irregularity.[5]

Import/Export Drafts

The final payment in the trade-financing process is accomplished by a *draft.* When you write a check to someone, that is one form of a draft, drawn against your account with a commercial bank, with payment to another party.

In exporting, when the l/c has specified certain terms as agreed upon by the importer and the exporter, then the exporter/beneficiary will include a draft with the documents. A draft is a written order to pay a specified amount of money at a specified point in time to a given person or to the bearer. A draft is a formal version of the account receivable that the exporter possesses as a result of

[5]The letters of credit shown here all have a standard clause at the bottom which is typical of the U.S.-issued letters of credit. Until recently that phrase was: "This credit [or advice] is subject to the Uniform Customs and Practice for Documentary Credits (1962 Revision), International Chamber of Commerce Brochure No. 222." As you may note on the updated form used for Exhibit 6.3, this phrase now reads: "This advice is subject to the Uniform Customs and Practice for Documentary Credits (1974 Revision), International Chamber of Commerce Publication 290." This clause indicates the regulations under which shipment disputes or any arguments between any of the parties are to be settled. They are available from banks, from chambers of commerce, and from other sources. In addition, the *Revised American Foreign Trade Definitions–1941* specifies common terms for adjudication of disputes arising under most U.S. letters of credit if buyer and seller agree to abide by them. (The definitions were adopted on July 30, 1941 by a Joint Committee representing the Chamber of Commerce of the United States, the National Council of American Importers, Inc., and the National Foreign Trade Council, Inc.)

EXHIBIT 6.6.

Bank in Switzerland Credit ABZ-6033

$ 1,000.00 (U.S.) New York, September 1, 19 --

At sight **Pay to the order of**

Ourselves (A)

One thousand and 00/100 - - - - - - - - - - - - - - **Dollars**

To: Manufacturers Hanover Trust Company New York, N.Y.

G. T. Tyler Company (B)

SPECIMEN

SOURCE: LETTERS OF CREDIT, Book 3. The American Bankers Association. Washington, D.C., 1968, p. 77. By permission of the American Bankers Association and Morgan Guaranty Trust Company of New York.

the sale. The parties involved in a draft are the drawer, the drawee, and the payee. The *drawer* is the exporter who signs the document. The *drawee* is the entity to which the draft is addressed (the importer or his/her bank), who makes the payment on the document. The *payee* is the importer who ultimately pays for the goods. The payee and the drawee may be the same.

For example, from Exhibit 6.6 one may presume that G. T. Tyler, the drawer, Ⓑ , exported goods to (say) XYZ GmbH. XYZ had previously arranged a letter of credit with the Bank in Switzerland, the l/c's issuing bank. Morgan Guaranty may have confirmed the l/c, or it may have been only the agent or the advisor of the l/c. In any case G. T. Tyler completes the documents required under the Bank in Switzerland's l/c and hands them over to Morgan Guaranty, the drawee, with this draft. If all the documents are in order, Morgan Guaranty pays $1,000 to G. T. Tyler. Note that the draft is made payable in this case to the Tyler Company Ⓐ . Unlike a draft on one's personal checking account, an import/export draft is written by the person or company to whom the money is owed. They could have made the draft payable to the bank or to some other entity.

Payment Terms. The draft in Exhibit 6.6 is labeled "At sight." When the documents have been found to be in good order, the draft is honored by Morgan Guaranty and the Tyler Company has its account credited. (Morgan Guaranty, if it is only a paying bank, will examine the documents carefully. Should the issuing bank, the Bank in Switzerland, find them faulty after Morgan Guaranty has paid the Tyler Company, then Morgan Guaranty will not be reimbursed even though it did not confirm or advise on the l/c.)

The *sight* draft is paid on presentation when the documents are in good order. An alternative arrangement which the two parties may have agreed upon and confirmed in the letter of credit is a *time draft.* Time drafts will specify payment typically 30, 60, 90, 120, or 180 days after *date* (after the date the draft is drawn) or after *sight* (after the draft has been presented and accepted by the paying bank). The terms of payment are often called the draft's *tenor.* These terms are agreed upon by the importer and the exporter as part of their business arrangements pursuant to the sale of the product. If a letter of credit is part of the transaction, the paying terms in the l/c must be the same as those in the draft, i.e., a time l/c. A time draft is a way for the exporter to extend credit to the importer.

Often, firms well known to each other will not find the l/c necessary. Instead, the exporter will use a bank as a collection agency, sending a draft drawn according to terms agreed upon by the two parties together with required documents and a letter of instruction to the bank for collection. The exporter's local bank typically will then deal with a bank in the importer's land, arranging for collection of the funds which are due the exporter.[6]

The collecting bank will turn over the documents certifying title to the goods to the importer when the importer pays (when it is a sight draft) or when the importer accepts the draft liability (when it is a time draft). Although the collecting bank can submit the drafts for payment or acceptance at receipt, usually the bank withholds presentation of the drafts until the goods have arrived in the importer's port. As part of the letter of instruction to the local bank, the exporter will specify the fees to be collected (if any), the means and currency for remission of the funds, and so forth.

Documents Required. Drafts are also classified according to the documents that are required to accompany the draft. A *clean draft* does not require any other document. A *documentary draft* requires accompanying documents such as bill of lading, commercial invoices, insurance certificates, and so on.

Lending by Financial Institutions

Trust Receipts. Sometimes goods are shipped under a time letter of credit and a time draft. In this case the importer usually signs a trust receipt for the goods, collateralizing the draft by the goods. Under a trust receipt, the bank retains title to the goods, with the importer operating as a trustee. As the goods are sold, proceeds are to be remitted to the bank in most cases. When the time draft is due, the importer pays the bank which sends the funds to the exporter's account specified in the draft. If the documents are *not* in order when submitted, the exporter can guarantee the paying bank and receive payment according to the terms of the draft.

[6]There is also a documented discount note that is sometimes used. Essentially, it is a corporate note to which is attached a bank's irrevocable letter guaranteeing payment on the note to any purchaser.

Loans to Exporters. When the exporter wants immediate payment and the terms of the sale involve a time draft, there are several means for reimbursement. The bank may lend against a set percentage of the drafts outstanding. This process is similar to receivable financing and is based on the credit history of the exporter's customers. In other cases, the exporter may collateralize a note as needed by the drafts. A third form, and a popular one when a major exporter can convince the bank to agree, is through the bankers' acceptance.

Bankers' Acceptances. Suppose the exporter and the importer have agreed to "ninety-day sight" terms. This arrangement means that the exporter will be paid ninety days after the bank certifies that the documents are in good order. In Exhibit 6.7 the exporter, John Doe and Co., has drawn a ninety-day sight time draft against an l/c from the Bank in Lima, presumably arranged by the importer of goods from Doe and Company. When Morgan Guaranty, the paying bank, acknowledges the forms as being in good order, it then stamps "ACCEPTED" across the face of the check, dates, and signs it. This is a guarantee that Morgan will pay the draft as noted ninety days from the date of acceptance, or December 28.

With this acceptance in hand, the exporter may sell the draft/acceptance (now called a *bankers'* acceptance) to an investor at a discount. The investor knows that the bank will pay the face amount at some future date, and the discount represents the going interest rate for bankers' acceptances. Alternatively, the bank may buy the draft/acceptance from the exporter at a discount, repaying itself when the importer's bank remits funds. Finally, the importer, as the account party to the draft, may have agreed to pay the discount when the beneficiary presents the draft. The beneficiary receives the full face amount and the paying bank receives the discount from the importer. Later, when the bankers' acceptance matures, the bank collects the full amount of the draft (which is what it had paid the beneficiary).

Bankers' acceptances tend to be especially popular in periods of tight money, and have expanded rapidly in total amount in recent years. One reason is that a U.S. bank which sells an export or import acceptance is not required to maintain reserves against it if the original maturity of the acceptance is six months or less. In mid-1945, over $105 million of U.S. bankers' acceptances were outstanding. By the end of 1977, U.S. bankers' acceptances outstanding had climbed to $25.7 billion. Japan's use of dollar bankers' acceptances has contributed substantially to this growth.[7]

Loans to Importers. In many cases the importer will arrange financing through a local bank, notifying the exporter. Usually, the bank will lend against the *import draft* in conjunction with a trust receipt arrangement, so that the loan from the bank supports the import draft which in turn is collateralized by the goods themselves. This instrument is the reverse of the export draft in terms of which party creates it, but the purpose is the same.

[7] See Ralph T. Helfrich, "Trading in Bankers' Acceptances: A View from the Acceptance Desk of the Federal Reserve Bank of New York." *Monthly Review,* Federal Reserve Bank of New York, Feb. 1976, pp. 51-7.

EXHIBIT 6.7.

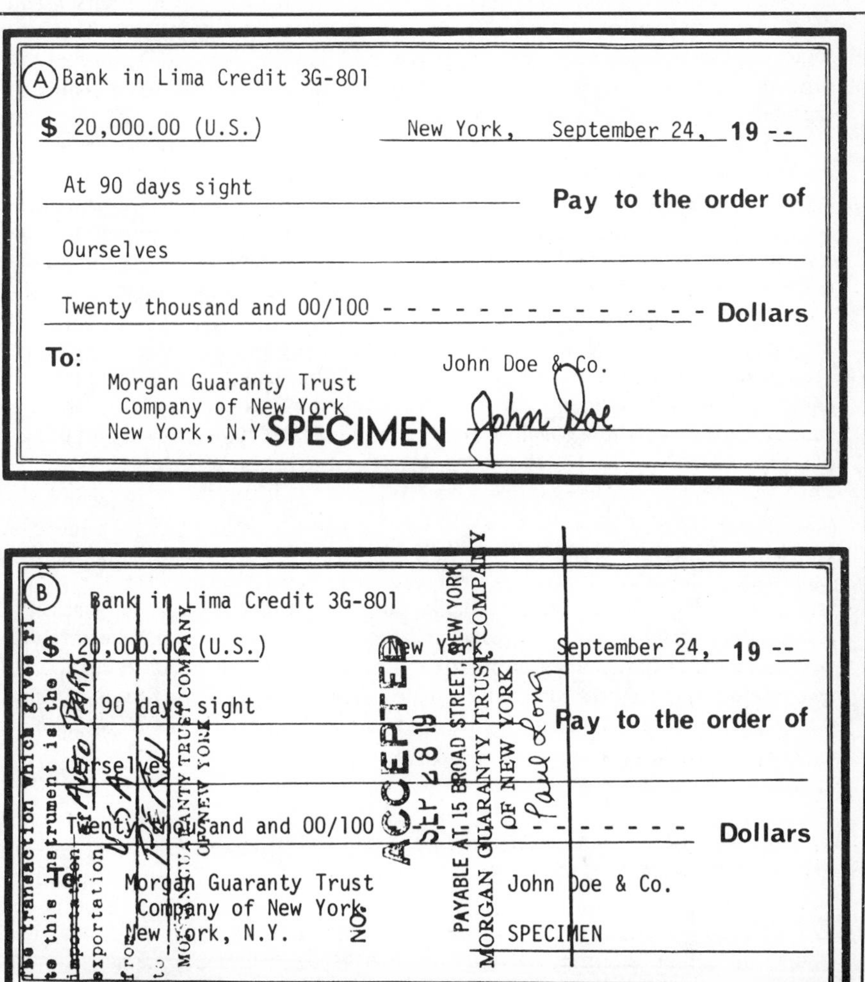

(A) Bank in Lima Credit 3G-801

$ 20,000.00 (U.S.) New York, September 24, 19 --

At 90 days sight Pay to the order of

Ourselves

Twenty thousand and 00/100 - - - - - - - - - - - - - - - - Dollars

To:
Morgan Guaranty Trust
Company of New York
New York, N.Y. SPECIMEN

John Doe & Co.
John Doe

(B) Bank in Lima Credit 3G-801

$ 20,000.00 (U.S.) New York, September 24, 19 --

At 90 days sight Pay to the order of

Ourselves

Twenty thousand and 00/100 - - - - - - - - - - - - - - - - Dollars

To:
Morgan Guaranty Trust
Company of New York
New York, N.Y.

John Doe & Co.
SPECIMEN

The transaction which gives rise to this instrument is the importation of Auto Parts
exportation of
from U.S.A.
to Peru

MORGAN GUARANTY TRUST COMPANY OF NEW YORK

ACCEPTED SEP 28 19
NO.

PAYABLE AT 15 BROAD STREET, NEW YORK
MORGAN GUARANTY TRUST COMPANY OF NEW YORK
Paul Long

SOURCE: LETTERS OF CREDIT, Book 3. The American Bankers Association. Washington, D.C., 1968, p. 35.

Other Aspects of Trade Credit

Commercial attachés of embassies as well as export financing institutions in most countries are well trained to provide interested exporters and importers with information about regulations and restrictions on the movement of various merchandise. For instance, in the United States the Department of Commerce oversees movement of merchandise out of the country. Most goods for export are not controlled, but some strategic goods or items with particular legislation may require special licenses. The Government Printing Office distributes copies of the Department's *Export Control Bulletins* and *Control Regulations* which detail these restrictions. Imports to the United States usually involve duty, and some require licenses from the Department of the Treasury. Information and forms for these imports are available from the Foreign Assets Control Division of the Federal Reserve Bank of New York.[8]

The United States Export-Import Bank (Eximbank), created in 1934, is a major force aiding U.S. exporters. An independent agency of the executive branch, it provides billions of dollars of credit to help foreigners import U.S. goods. The credits often are in the form of insurance or a guarantee. For instance, for a fee the Eximbank will guarantee the payment of a receivable which the exporter has sold to a local bank if the receivable is from a foreign customer. The guarantee covers all political risk and portions of normal business risk. The Eximbank will also guarantee the direct loan by a U.S. bank to a foreign purchaser of a U.S. good, often capital equipment. In many cases the foreign purchaser will be a government. In these financial guarantees to the bank, there is usually a 100% guarantee against political and business risks including all principal and interest up to 1% above the U.S. Treasury rate on comparable debt. Through the Foreign Credit Insurance Association, involving more than sixty firms in various insurance fields, a variety of policies are available to exporters to protect them against nonpayment by their overseas customers. In many cases Eximbank will participate with commercial banks and/or the exporter in a direct loan to a foreign customer. Eximbank will take the loans of longer maturity, leaving the shorter ones to the banks and the exporter. For a comprehensive discussion of various financing alternatives, the exporter will want to consult financial sources, such as banks and finance companies, in the involved nations. Other countries have financial institutions similar to those for the United States discussed above to encourage the export of their goods.

FOREIGN EXCHANGE RISKS AND CREDIT RISKS: SOME TRADE-OFFS

The first section of this chapter concentrated on analyzing the foreign exchange risk that international trade involves and offering a framework for evaluating the price of buying insurance against these risks. The second section introduced a series of documents and financing procedures and focused on the terms of these documents as well as the protection they afford to various parties. However, these documents also indicate the foreign exchange risks for each party through the currency in which the l/c and drafts are drawn and the time

[8]Based on estimates for one recent trade year, documents for U.S. imports and exports were complex in number and detail. The average shipment required 46 documents and a total of 360 copies, at an average shipment cost of about $350. By 1972, this total amounted to over 8% of the cost of imports and exports. Fortunately, efforts have been made to streamline this process by a reduction in the number of forms and simplification of the remaining forms. See Arthur E. Bayalis, "The Documentation Dilemma in International Trade." *Columbia Journal of World Business,* Spring 1976, pp. 15-22.

period involved in the payment. For example, for the Italian manufacturer who exported shoes to the United States, there was an assumption that this transaction was made on open account and that the payment was to be made by the U.S. buyer in U.S. dollars three months after delivery. Modifications to these assumptions involve two major issues: (1) How much foreign exchange risk does each party bear? (2) How much credit risk does each party bear?

Abstracting from the complications of the special commercial documents, one can answer the two questions for the Italian exporter in the following manner:

1. The foreign exchange risk is at a maximum to the exporter if he sells in terms of U.S. dollars for payment in the future and does nothing else but wait. The foreign exchange risk is eliminated if the billing is made in Italian liras or if a U.S. dollar billing is covered in the financial markets.

2. The credit risk is at a maximum to the exporter when selling on time or on open account. The credit risk is at a minimum if an irrevocable confirmed letter of credit is required from the importer against a sight draft.

Obviously, the exporter would like to keep these risks at a minimum. But so would the importer. In this example the Italian exporter would prefer to be paid in liras at presentation of a sight draft drawn against an irrevocable confirmed letter of credit. On the other hand, the U.S. importer would rather have the transaction as initially presented–denominated in U.S. dollars to be paid later and on open account. How are these conflicting interests reconciled?

When we discussed the foreign exchange risks in international trade and how to insure against them, the focus was on the explicit costs associated with covering a cash flow as well as the opportunity gains and losses of the two alternatives of covering or not covering. To the extent that time elapses between the entering of the transaction and the receipt or payment of a foreign currency, there is a foreign exchange risk. If this risk is considered high enough to require insurance, somebody is going to have to pay for the price of that insurance. The first section showed how to calculate the cost of covering a cash flow. Whether the exporter bears this cost or whether it is passed on in terms of higher prices or explicit extra charges depends on the bargaining power of each party. An apparent alternative is to bring in a financial intermediary to pay the Italian exporter in liras and extend a loan to the U.S. importer in dollars. Now the risk is shifted to a financial institution. However, this action has not necessarily shifted the cost of buying insurance. The financial intermediary has had its foreign exchange position altered as a result of this transaction. So it is not difficult to imagine that the costs of changing its foreign exchange position back to the original one will be passed along to the trading parties. If the market is working efficiently, the situation is virtually the same as that of trading under open account, except that now the necessary fees for the financial intermediary are added!

The amount of credit risk incurred by the exporter also has a cost attached to it. Such credit risk can be minimized by bringing in the largest possible number of financial institutions to share the responsibility for payment of the merchandise. However, each of these institutions will testify that payment will be forthcoming only because it receives a fee from the importer as a charge for the letter of credit. This fee effectively increases the price of the merchandise to the importer, therefore minimizing the competitiveness of the exporter's prices.

The solution to the problem of how much credit the exporter will provide to the importer is similar to the evaluation of how much foreign exchange risk each party assumes. To the exporter, the extension of trade credit is similar to the acquisition of a financial asset. The account receivable has an explicit return to the extent that it is a substitute for lower prices or higher quality goods. However, the account receivable has an opportunity cost that can be measured by the net return that the exporter could make were those funds not used in financing the importer. Notice that this is a *net* return. In order for the exporter to extend this credit a source of funds must be found, and these funds have a cost attached to them. So the other consideration in extending credit to the importer is the cost of money to the exporter, who in this regard is operating as a financial intermediary. Obviously, if the exporter refuses to extend this credit, the problem is only shifted to the importer who must find a source of funds to finance inventories until sold. This loan also has an interest rate attached to it that can be translated into higher cost of goods purchased.

In not every case are the interests of the exporter and the importer diametrically opposed. On occasions the alternatives appear to be somewhat biased. This bias comes from the fact that most business enterprises consider their local currency as the unit of account. An Italian considers the Italian lira as the unit of account; an American considers the U.S. dollar as the unit of account. So there is some tendency to ignore the opportunity gains from dealing in a currency other than the local one. Thus, the Italian exporter might be very happy to be paid in lira. If the American importer, and even the market, actually thinks that the Italian lira is likely to depreciate by the time that payment is due, the importer will be glad to have the import liability denominated in Italian liras, and might even be willing to pay the interest charges for term credit. In these cases of different appraisals of the market or different assessment of the opportunities, a compromise is easy to achieve. Given the market facts, the final word will be determined by the bargaining power of each party.

SUMMARY

Credit risks occur for the international trader as well as for the domestic trader, but they are accompanied by foreign exchange risks when the payment for the goods at a future date will be in a currency different from the currency the trader desires. The seller may specify the home currency, in which case the buyer faces the foreign exchange risk.

To resolve this risk, the buyer or the seller may use the forward markets. The initial cost depends on the price of the forward contract relative to the spot price. The opportunity gain or loss depends on what happens to the spot rate in the future vs. the forward rate on the date the forward contract was entered.

The parties may also use the money market. An exporter may borrow the foreign currency, convert to the local currency, and invest the funds. When the receivable from the customer is paid, the gain or loss in the exchange rate of the foreign currency applied to the receivable is balanced by the loss or gain in repayment of the loan. The initial cost is simply the interest differential between the currencies, plus or minus the small impact that any foreign exchange rate change may make on the interest payment.

If the markets are in equilibrium under interest rate parity, then covering in either market produces similar results. However, the rates accessible to importers/exporters may be different from those available to the interbank market.

An importer, as the account party, may arrange with a bank to issue a letter of credit in which the bank guarantees payment subject to successful production and certification of shipment of goods. This letter of credit assures the exporter that there will be reimbursement for goods shipped to the importer. The local bank of the exporter may advise of the l/c or may confirm it, in which case the local bank becomes a co-guarantor of the payment. When not confirmed by either the issuing bank or the local bank, l/c's are revocable at the discretion of the account party. However, once the documents and the draft going with them are accepted by the paying bank, they cannot be canceled. Letters of credit may be transferable (which facilitates the use of a trading intermediary who has found a buyer with credit but is still seeing a supplier) and may be negotiable (which permits the exporter to seek the best rate of foreign exchange or simply to select the bank for collection at a later point).

The actual payment is completed by means of a draft. It is simply a demand for payment by the drawer (the exporter, or benficiary of the l/c) sent to the collecting bank against the l/c of the issuing bank. The draft may be on sight, in which case there is immediate payment once the paying bank has acknowledged receipt of the draft and certifying documents. It may be a time draft, in which case payment will be so many days beyond the date of the draft or from sight when the draft is accepted by the bank. When a time draft is accepted by the bank, it becomes a bankers' acceptance and may be negotiated. Hence, the holder of the draft may sell it to the bank or to an investor at a discount, receiving payment immediately. Upon the maturity of the acceptance, the account party pays the holder of the draft the full face amount. In some cases the beneficiary/drawer of the draft will receive the full amount immediately with the account party paying the discount plus the full face amount to the bank at a later date.

In many cases the drafts are used by the exporter and the importer on terms which they have agreed upon without the l/c of an issuing bank. In these cases the banks usually act as collecting parties, remitting funds to the exporter subject to completion of certain requirements as specified by the importer.

Most countries have various regulations governing imports and exports of certain products. In the United States the restrictions on exports are noted in the Department of Commerce's *Control Regulations* and *Export Control Bulletins.* Restrictions on imports, in addition to duty collected by the Department of the Treasury, are noted in publications of the Foreign Assets Control Division of the New York Federal Reserve Bank.

The U.S. Export-Import Bank is a major force for helping U.S. exporters sell their goods to foreign importers. This independent government agency encourages the growth of U.S. exports through a program of guaranteed loans; direct loans to foreign buyers who may be individuals, firms, or governments; loans to exporters; insurance programs and other items. Other countries have similar institutions to facilitate the financing of exports of their goods.

The nature of the foreign exchange risk and the financing arrangements between importer and exporter fundamentally depend on the relative bargaining power of the parties when their interests conflict. When financial intermediaries are involved to absolve the participants of some risks, the fees for these intermediaries must be added to the cost of the transaction.

Questions

1. An English exporter scheduled to receive payment in Italian liras sells the liras on a forward contract, so that she knows the sterling value of the receivable. How will she know the cost of this cover? When will she know the cost?

2. "As long as the forward rate for the currency is below the spot rate, I should cover my transactions if I have receivables in that currency; the forward discount shows that the currency is likely to devalue." Do you agree with this statement? Why?

3. A U.S. distributor purchases perfume from France in the amount of French francs 22,850 (approximately $5,000). Payment is due in three months in French francs.

		Day 90		
	Day 1	*Case A*	*Case B*	*Case C*
Exchange rates:				
Spot	$0.218850	$0.218550	$0.240735	$0.196965
3-month forward	$0.218140			
Interest rates:				
United States	6.00%	6.00%	6.00%	6.00%
France	7.30%	7.30%	6.80%	7.80%

a. On day 1 what is the premium or discount on the forward French franc? What is the interest differential between the U.S. and France? Is there an incentive for interest arbitrage?

b. If the importer wants to cover its transaction against foreign exchange risks, what alternatives are open?

c. What is the cost of each alternative? (i) if a three-month treasury bill is bought; (ii) if a one-year bill is bought (do not make specific calculation in the latter case).

d. Would you advise the importer to cover the foreign exchange transaction? Why or why not?

4. The U.S. distributor which imports perfumes from France is notified by the French exporter that in the future the exporter does not wish to sell on open account any longer. You are a bank officer who considers the distributor's account a valuable account. What financing arrangements would you offer to the U.S. distributor?

5. A small U.S. manufacturer of specialized heavy equipment has found an export market for his products in Argentina. He now approaches you, an officer in the bank with whom he usually works, to inquire about alternative financial arrangements available. What would you tell him?

6. If there is no change in the spot rate of a currency in a given period, does it make any difference whether one covers a transaction in the forward market or the money market? Give an example to support your answer.

7. What is the purpose of a letter of credit? What are the major types of l/c's?

8. How may an exporter use a letter of credit to extend credit to an importer?

9. Who are the parties involved in a draft? Why is a check you write to your department store a draft? Who are the parties in that "draft"?

10. What is meant by a draft's tenor? What are examples of different tenors? Why do these differences exist?

11. Can a banker's acceptance be sold to another party? Since it does not pay interest, why would a person buy it? Who guarantees payment?

12. Edward M. Graham, a United States wholesaler of specialty clothes for men and women, hopes to expand his operations considerably by emphasizing a new line of leisure wear to be marketed through various clothing boutiques. As part of this plan, he has contacted three exporters with a view toward supplying his needs. He considers the products and offerings of each comparable in terms of his business, although each reflects certain national styles and trends.

Assume the three potential suppliers have offered him various terms. Mary Freed Ltd. of London has suggested that an appropriate financial arrangement would involve a revocable letter of credit since she knows his general reputation. They agree that if Mr. Graham can arrange the letter of credit through a bank, Ms. Freed will draw a time draft payable sixty days after sight in sterling.

Thomas Rodriguez of Spain has an interest in supplying Mr. Graham, but he indicates that he would expect a confirmed irrevocable negotiable letter of credit, with drafts drawn under the l/c payable at sight. Credit would be available, he suggests, at a rate of 2% per month, but should not exceed ninety days after shipment.

Finally, Heinz Riehl of Geneva manufactures an Austrian style of après-ski lounging clothes and has indicated that he has long wished to have an American distributor. He suggests that an appropriate method of operation would be for Mr. Graham to deposit funds to the Riehl account in Basel thirty days prior to a shipment, with the deposit equal to 50% of the invoiced value of the goods. After shipment, the balance would be due within ten days of receipt by Mr. Graham. Mr. Riehl noted that his general impressions of Mr. Graham's business were sufficient to commend the Graham firm as a customer, and he has no need for a letter of credit arrangement.

If you were to help Mr. Graham with this decision, what data would you need? How would you analyze the decision. In addition to any factors you believe are particularly important, consider the following elements and how they would alter the decision. Give an example of how Mr. Graham might favor one supplier over the others depending on the facts surrounding each item noted below:

a. The currency prospects of each of the exporters vis-à-vis Mr. Graham's currency, the U.S. dollar.

b. The cost of funds for payable financing by Mr. Graham.

c. The option to accept or to reject the Spanish credit terms as each order is due.

d. The cost of different letters of credit from the banks involved.

Bibliography

Bayalis, Arthur E., "The Documentation Dilemma in International Trade," *Columbia Journal of World Business,* Spring 1976, pp. 15-22.

Bloch, Henry Simon, "Export Financing Emerging as a Major Policy Problem," *Columbia Journal of World Business,* Fall 1976, pp. 85-95.

Eiteman, David K. and Arthur I. Stonehill, *Multinational Business Finance.* Reading, Mass.: Addison-Wesley Publishing Co., 1973, Ch. 6.

The Financing of Exports and Imports. New York: Morgan Guaranty Trust Company, 1973.

Greene, James, *Organizing for Exporting.* New York: National Industrial Conference Board Business Policy Study Number 26, 1968.

Harrington, J. A., *Specifics on Commercial Letters of Credit and Bankers Acceptances.* Jersey City, N.J.: Scott Printing Corporation, 1974.

Hollis, Stanley E., *Guide to Export Credit Insurance.* New York: Foreign Credit Insurance Association, 1971.

Letters of Credit, Books 2 and 3. Washington, D.C.: The American Bankers Association, 1968.

Overseas Private Investment Corporation, *An Introduction to OPIC.* Washington, D.C., 1973.

Riehl, Heinz, and Rita M. Rodriguez, *Foreign Exchange Markets.* New York: McGraw-Hill Book Company, 1977.

U.S. Government, Department of Commerce, *Control Regulations.* Washington, D.C.: Government Printing Office.

——, *Export Control Bulletins.* Washington, D.C.: Government Printing Office.

Weston, J. Fred, and Bart W. Sorge, *International Managerial Finance.* Homewood, Ill.: Richard D. Irwin, Inc., 1972, Chs., 4, 8, and 9.

THE AP&M TRADING COMPANY

In preparation for his upcoming trip to Japan in early October 1972, Mr. H. Hinson, President of the AP&M Trading Company, was reviewing his company's position in the Japanese import business.

Mainly importers of synthetic fabrics from Japan, the AP&M group had 1971 sales of $14 million. Their success was based on the service they performed and the low cost and excellent quality of the Japanese goods. Since the 1971 monetary crisis, however, the yen upvaluation, the quotas on Far Eastern textile imports, and the increasing European aggressiveness in exports of certain fabrics to the United States had caused severe problems for the smaller U.S. import businesses dealing in Japanese textile products. The likelihood of another yen upvaluation and the cost of hedging were only two of several key issues Mr. Hinson had to deal with in formulating his tentative strategies prior to his meeting with the Japanese in October.

The AP&M Trading Company was incorporated in New York in 1948 by Mr. H. Hinson and Mr. R. Kroner, two Polish refugees who arrived in the United States in 1945. From 1948 to 1951 the firm imported $6 to $8 million annually of surplus Japanese silk fabrics left from before the war. These unfinished dyed fabrics (grey goods) were sold to converters for the ladies' garment industry. AP&M commissioned Far Eastern Exporters (Japan) Ltd., a branch of a large U.S. trading and shipping concern owned by Mr. Hinson's relatives, as AP&M's export agents in Japan. Far Eastern's functions were to handle all dealings with suppliers, shippers, foreign exchange dealers, Japanese banks, and the several official Japanese agencies involved.[1] Mr. K. Yokoma was put in charge of handling the AP&M account. For its services, Far Eastern Exporters charged AP&M 2% of the f.o.b. value of the goods shipped.

Financial data for the company are contained in Exhibit 1.

Customer Relationships

Because of the fluctuations in the dollar price of the yen and the high obsolescence factor in fabrics, AP&M's policy was to minimize ordering for inventory. As a result, only the more standard items were stocked in anticipation of customers' orders. All other items were purchased on the basis of confirmed orders received from customers.

For goods bought through Mr. Yokoma and paid for in yen, prices to AP&M's customers were quoted in dollars based on the f.o.b. yen price converted at the spot rate on the day of the customer's order. However, the contracts with the customers stipulated that all fluctuations in the yen's parity from the date of order were to be absorbed by the customers. (Many contracts were renegotiated, however, especially during the period from August 15 to December 18, 1971, when the 10% U.S. import surcharge was also being passed on to the buyers.)

Shipment of these goods ordered from Far Eastern generally took place

[1] Japanese regulations required that all exports be routed to the foreign buyer through a licensed Japanese exporting agent.

EXHIBIT 1. AP&M Trading Company: Financial Data

Sales, Expenses, and Net Income, 1964–1971 (thousands of dollars)

	1964	1966	1968	1969	1970	1971
Sales	$9,338	$8,098	$9,446	$8,598	$9,782	$14,124
Cost of goods	8,376	7,068	8,366	7,572	8,564	12,544
Other expenses	840	912	924	920	1,114	1,394
Taxes	32	36	64	46	32	72
Net Income	$ 90	$ 82	$ 92	$ 60	$ 72	$ 114

Balance Sheet, December 31, 1971 (thousands of dollars)

Assets		*Liabilities & Equity*	
Cash	$ 224	Accounts payable	$1,382
Accounts receivable	4,264	Acceptance and loans payable	3,662
Inventory	2,254	Accrued taxes	62
Notes receivable	306	Accrued expenses	132
Total current assets	$7,048	Total current liabilities	$5,238
Long-term investments	51	Notes payable	310
Net fixed assets	39	Capital stock	546
		Retained earnings	1,044
Total assets	$7,138	Total liabilities and capital	$7,138

within 120 to 150 days of the order date. The ocean voyage, clearing through customs and distribution to the customers, required another 45 days. Receivables were due 90 days following the customer's receipt of the goods.

Import Financing

Of the approximately $12.5 million of AP&M purchases in 1971, $5.5 million were from the New York representatives of several major Japanese trading companies. The other $7 million were ordered from Mr. Yokoma of Far Eastern Exporters. On goods ordered from Mr. Yokoma, the f.o.b. price to AP&M was always fixed in yen. Payment in yen was due upon Mr. Yokoma's presenting of a sight draft, the bill of lading, and other stipulated documents to AP&M's paying agent in Japan.

The means of financing the orders from Mr. Yokoma were limited by several factors. The Japanese Ministry of Finance required that all foreign exchange payments for export orders be remitted to Japan immediately upon transfer of the ownership documents from the exporter to the buyer's agent. Also, in order to be licensed as "receipts for exports" (one of the processes required before the exporter could obtain the necessary export permits) all such foreign exchange remissions had to be linked to a specific commercial transaction. As a result, AP&M made use of only two modes of financing its purchases from Far Eastern Exporters. One method of financing employed was the direct transfer of dollars to the special "export receipts" account of Far Eastern Exporters held in a Tokyo bank. Dollars cabled to this account were immediately validated as export receipts and converted at that day's telegraphic transfer

(TT) rate.[2] Mr. Yokoma had indicated several times that no interest was paid on this special account due to its revolving short-term nature. Mr. Hinson obtained these dollar advances from his New York banks at a cost of 1.5% above prime rate.

The second means of financing employed by Mr. Hinson was the opening of letters of credit (l/c's) in favor of Far Eastern Exporters. The l/c's were "negotiated" through a Japanese bank designated by Yokoma.

The banks indicated that, on a normal basis, AP&M's need for continual short-term funds secured by fabric inventories alone could be met only under an l/c arrangement. The conventional loan advances mentioned above were made available only for specific emergencies. Mr. Hinson understood that banks enjoyed several advantages in l/c financing as opposed to regular short-term loans. The banks, however, had never elaborated on this point with Hinson.

Since mid-1971 AP&M had had lines of credit of $2 million with each of two New York banks. The lines represented contingent liabilities of the banks and were utilized in two parts: letters of credit (l/c's) and trust receipts.

The dollar l/c's were opened with AP&M's New York banks who then advised the "negotiating" banks in Japan of the dollar credits in favor of the exporter (Far Eastern Exporters). To receive payment in yen, Mr. Yokoma presented a sight draft (bill of exchange), a bill of lading, a commercial invoice, and a consular invoice (for customs purposes) to the negotiating bank. This bank paid Yokoma in yen the face amount of the draft and forwarded the documents to AP&M's bank. In times of currency fluctuations, AP&M could request that the Japanese bank cable New York immediately, advising of the negotiation of the draft and the equivalent amount in dollars at that day's spot rate. The New York bank credited the dollars to the Japanese bank's account that same day, even prior to the arrival of the documents in New York. Mr. Hinson could opt to instruct his banks to await receipt of the documents. In that case, however, the negotiating bank in Japan converted the dollar l/c's at a rate based on the quotation for contracts five days forward. The increase in the dollar cost was borne entirely by AP&M.

Upon receipt of the documents by airmail at the New York bank, some three days later, the second phase of the credit was initiated. AP&M was issued a trust receipt under which the New York bank retained title to the imported goods while AP&M was commissioned as the selling agent. Receipts were due in 120 days. The costs to AP&M were 0.25% of the l/c plus cabling charges (approximately $8) for opening the l/c, and 1.25% above prime rate for the 120-day trust receipt loan. The bank could then guarantee the trust receipt loan and discount it in the money market. Exhibit 2 summarizes the steps of the l/c process.

An alternative to the above system was the "time l/c" and "bankers' acceptance." The time l/c instructed the negotiating bank to pay the exporter 120 days (or other specified period of time) following his presentation of a "time draft." The interest was borne by the exporter, who could simply raise the f.o.b. cost of the goods. AP&M could obtain the bank l/c for 1.25% while Yokoma could have his time draft "accepted" by the Japanese bank and discounted at a rate slightly above the Japanese discount rate. All exchange rate risk, however, was clearly borne by the buyer who might choose to cover in the forward market.

[2] Slightly more favorable than that day's spot rate at the time.

EXHIBIT 2. AP&M Trading Company: Letter of Credit Process

Description				Accounting							
AP&M	*U.S. Bank*	*Japanese Bank*	*Far Eastern*	*AP&M*		*U.S. Bank*		*Japanese Bank*		*Far Eastern*	
				Dr.	*Cr.*	*Dr.*	*Cr.*	*Dr.*	*Cr.*	*Dr.*	*Cr.*
1.			Advises Hinson of particulars of shipment								
2. Requests l/c from U.S. bank	Issues l/c against Far Eastern on the basis of AP&M's line					Contingent claims on AP&M↑	Contingent l/c payable↑ (Far Eastern)				
3.	Sends l/c to Japanese bank	Notifies Far Eastern									
4.		Pays Far Eastern. Notifies U.S. bank. Sends documents to and debits U.S. bank	Presents sight drafts and other documents to Japanese bank. Receives payment					Deposits in N.Y.↑	Demand deposits↑ (Far E.)	Inventory↓ Cash↑	
5.	Credits account of Japanese bank and cancels l/c						Demand deposits ↑ (Jap. bank) Contingent l/c payable ↓ (Far Eastern)				
6. Accepts promissory note. Receives merchandise on consignment	Issues trust receipt and promissory note to AP&M			Merchandise on consignment ↑	Notes Payable ↑	Contingent claim on AP&M ↓ Advances ↑ (trust receipt to AP&M)					

A variation of the time l/c and the bankers' acceptance described above was an instrument instructing the negotiating bank to pay Mr. Yokoma the face value of his "time draft" immediately. Upon receipt of the documents, the New York bank immediately credited the Japanese bank's account. A 120-day fixed dollar loan was then automatically credited to AP&M's account. Thus, AP&M avoided the exchange risk during the credit period. The New York bank could then "accept" the time draft by countersigning it and discount it in the money market. The cost to AP&M for the loan was the bankers' acceptance rate plus a 1.5% per annum commission for the bank's accepting the draft. If the time draft had been issued in yen, the U.S. bank would have a yen liability against a dollar asset (the loan to AP&M). In this case the bank would make a charge to AP&M for the additional risk involved.

Mr. Hinson had not investigated the possibility of borrowing yen in Japan to finance the purchases. AP&M had no direct credit relations with banks in Japan, and Mr. Hinson could not be sure that the payments to the exporter under such an arrangement would qualify as "export receipts."

Factoring of accounts receivable provided another reliable source of short-term liquidity when needed. Factors guaranteed payment of receivables for 1.25% and discounted them, if cash was needed before the due date, for 2% to 3% above the "bankers' acceptance" rate.

Selected U.S. and Japanese financial market rates are presented in Exhibit 3.

The 1971 Monetary Crisis

Following President Nixon's August 15, 1971, announcement that the U.S. dollar's value against gold would not be supported and that the U.S. dollar would not be convertible into gold any longer, the Japanese attempted to support the yen at 360 units per dollar. By August 28 the billions of dollars pouring in forced the Japanese into a managed floating of the yen. The yen floated upward to 320.5 on December 18, 1971. The Smithsonian Agreement that weekend reset the yen/US$ parity at 308 within a 301-315 band. The rate continued to float upward from 314.8 on December 20 to 310 in late January 1972 and to almost 300 by early August 1972.

The December 1971 monetary agreements had terminated the U.S. dollar float and the 10% surcharge, but they had raised the dollar cost of Japanese goods 17% and had forced the main Far Eastern textile exporters to levy quotas on their exports to the United States. Many less resourceful importers were forced out of business. Mr. Hinson, by a combination of pressures on the mills to reduce their yen prices and several shrewd financial maneuvers, was able to carry AP&M through the entire crisis period until August 1972 with all its customers and suppliers intact.

AP&M's Financial Tactics During the Monetary Crisis

In order to take into account the floating exchange rates during the period from late August until mid-December 1971, AP&M contracts with the mills and customers had called for renegotiation in the event of unacceptable adjustments in

EXHIBIT 3. Selected Financial Market Rates, 1968–1972

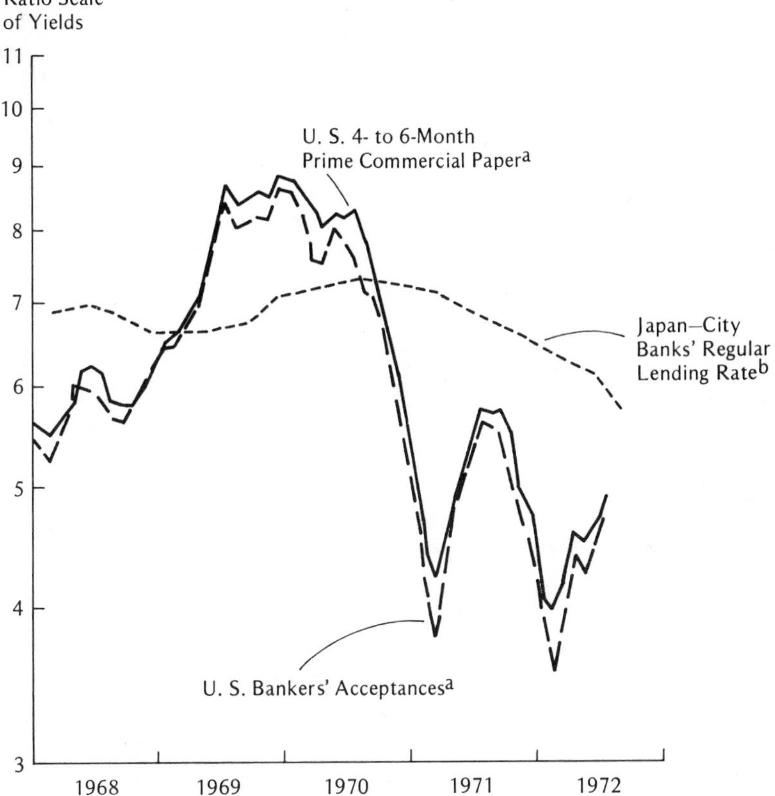

[a]Monthly averages of daily figures.
[b]End of the quarter figures.
SOURCES: Federal Reserve Bank of St. Louis and Bank of Japan

costs to either party due to the floating of the yen. Rather than tolerate the serious disruptions that would ensue under such arrangements. Mr. Hinson engineered a triangular agreement with the mills and customers. In this agreement the first 6% increase in the yen's parity above 360 would be immediately absorbed by the mills who would lower their yen prices proportionately. Any further increase in the yen's value would be shared between AP&M and its customers—the latter having already accepted the burden of the 10% surcharge.

In addition to the previous arrangements to absorb the actual increase in Japanese prices, AP&M was able to execute several specific financial transactions. This was done in spite of the increasingly tighter Japanese controls on dollar transfers of all types. The transactions described below were possible only as a result of the close daily telegraphic contacts Mr. Hinson maintained with Mr. Yokoma in Japan.

1. A total of $2 million was transferred by cable to Far Eastern's special export account in Japan in late August and early September to cover shipments in the first quarter of 1972. This money was transferred to the account at the telegraphic transfer (TT) rate, slightly more favorable than the day's spot rate. $1.3 million of the funds was received from AP&M's two banks as an advance against future l/c's. The banks insisted, however, that all these advances be converted into l/c's by the end of the first quarter of 1972. The rate on the loan was the same as for the trust receipt loans–1.25% above prime. Of particular importance in these transactions was the fact that the transferred funds were then licensed by the Bank of Japan as "export receipts," applicable, however, only to exports routed from Far Eastern to AP&M. The remaining $700,000 were "borrowed" in yen from surplus funds in Far Eastern's noninterest bearing yen account in Japan in a special arrangement with the Bank of Japan. Title to the yen was retained in Far Eastern's hands, but forms were issued stating that the funds had been earmarked for payment of future AP&M shipments. AP&M issued promissory notes to Far Eastern for an equivalent amount of dollars calculated at that day's TT rate at 6% per annum.

2. To cover shipments from August 1971 through January 1972, several l/c's were opened in favor of Far Eastern within thirty days prior to shipments during that period. The rates on these contracts varied, but they were always less than 5 yen per dollar lower than the spot rate prevailing on the day of the contract. Approximately $2 million in credits were transferred under these forward contracts during the period.

3. In late December 1971 the Japanese government became concerned over the plight of the smaller manufacturers whose export sales were being severely curtailed by the effects of the revaluation, quotas, etc. By special proclamation, the Bank of Japan authorized negotiating banks to accept pro forma invoices submitted by exporters on behalf of importers. The Bank of Japan guaranteed conversion of the future l/c's at the TT rates prevailing on the day the pro forma invoices were submitted. The contracts were to be valid for shipments through June 15, 1972, only. Mr. Yokoma drew up pro forma documents for $3 million in orders through June 1972 and submitted them along with guarantees from the New York banks stating that they would open l/c's in that amount to cover the shipments. In this manner, Yokoma guaranteed the conversion of the $3 million at rates of 319 to 315. For each thirty days forward, the rate was reduced by 1 yen per US$. As with other transactions, the yen obtained subsequently were for use only in payment for goods shipped from Far Eastern to AP&M.

By the end of March 1972 these forward contracts were still unused due to the existence of the TT yen which the banks were still demanding be converted into l/c's. By June 15, 1972, the date of the contract's deadline, $1.4 million of the forward contracts still remained unutilized. The Bank of Japan agreed to extend their guarantees but discounted the guaranteed rates by 1 yen per dollar for each thirty days beyond the original contract date. Thus, an unused February contract for 318 could be sold in September 1972 for 311.

The Situation in August 1972

With only $0.5 million left out of the $3 million pro forma invoices negotiated by Mr. Yokoma, and with requirements for the remaining part of the year in the neighborhood of $3 to $4 million, Mr. Hinson worried about the increasing number of rumors about an impending second yen upvaluation by year-end, 1972. The only avenue open to protect himself against a further upvaluation of the yen appeared to be the purchase of forward yen against dollar l/c's. In addition, Mr. Hinson had to negotiate with Japanese trading companies to use some of their export quota, since Far Eastern's quota appeared to be already at its limit.

The Forward Contracts. Mr. Hinson had received a letter from Mr. Yokoma on July 15, 1972 indicating that two large banks in Japan were quoting rates on dollar l/c's sold forward. On l/c's to be negotiated in sixty days, one bank guaranteed conversion at 287 yen per dollar. The second bank quoted 281 yen for the same contract.

A phone call to his own New York bank the first week of August had yielded Mr. Hinson the following quotations for such l/c's sold forward:

Forward Yen Rates per Dollar l/c

Term	*30 days*	*90 days*	*120 days*
Rate	285.5	272.1	272.7

The Export Quotas. The quotas imposed by Japan on her textile exports in late December of 1971 limited annual growth in exports of many major synthetic fabrics to 5%. By March 1972 Far Eastern had used up its allocation for polyester tie fabric exports. The large Japanese traders, on the other hand, had been allotted permissible volumes well in excess of their needs. Mr. Hinson instructed Far Eastern to implement the following procedures:

1. Polyester fabrics were invoiced out to AP&M by Far Eastern under the description "polyester-rayon blends." This exempted Mr. Yokoma from the quota limitations for polyesters.

2. A bargain was struck with two large Japanese traders that specified polyester shipments would be invoiced out to AP&M on the traders' forms, relieving Far Eastern of accountability for those shipments. For their service, the traders charged 6 cents per yard shipped under these arrangements. (The average price per yard was $1.50.)

To aid him in his analyses of future financial strategies, Mr. Hinson had compiled data on the Japanese balance of payments (Exhibit 4). Reflecting on the general status of Japanese textile exports, Mr. Hinson posited that the Japanese would maintain their competitiveness in textiles by controlling raw material prices, developing new fabrics, introducing subsidies at various levels in the textile industry, and continuing to maintain the technical and design superiority they now enjoyed in several synthetic fabric classes.

EXHIBIT 4. Japan Balance of Payments, 1962–1972 (millions of dollars)

Year	or Month	Current Balance	Trade			Services			Transfers			Long-Term Capital[a]			Short-Term Capital[a,b]	Errors & Omissions	Overall Balance	Gold & Foreign Exchange Reserves	Others
			Balance	Exports	Imports	Balance	Credits	Debits	Balance	Credits	Debits	Balance[a]	Assets	Liabilities					
Calendar Year	1962	Δ48	401	4,861	4,460	Δ420	1,088	1,508	Δ29	68	97	172	Δ309	481	107	6	237	355	Δ118
	1963	Δ780	Δ166	5,391	5,557	Δ569	1,134	1,703	Δ45	68	113	467	Δ298	765	107	45	Δ161	37	Δ198
	1964	Δ480	377	6,704	6,327	Δ784	1,323	2,107	Δ73	72	145	107	Δ451	558	234	10	Δ129	121[c]	Δ70
	1965	932	1,901	8,332	6,431	Δ884	1,563	2,447	Δ85	63	148	Δ415	Δ446	31	Δ61	Δ51	405	108	297
	1966	1,254	2,275	9,641	7,366	Δ886	1,931	2,817	Δ135	69	204	Δ808	Δ706	Δ102	Δ64	Δ45	337	Δ33	370
	1967	Δ190	1,160	10,231	9,071	Δ1,172	2,182	3,354	Δ178	74	252	Δ812	Δ875	63	506	Δ75	Δ571	Δ69	Δ502
	1968	1,048	2,529	12,751	10,222	Δ1,306	2,607	3,913	Δ175	83	258	Δ239	Δ1,096	857	209	84	1,102	886	216
	1969	2,119	3,699	15,679	11,980	Δ1,399	3,261	4,660	Δ181	85	266	Δ155	Δ1,508	1,353	178	141	2,283	605	1,678
	1970	1,970	3,963	18,969	15,006	Δ1,785	4,009	5,794	Δ208	98	306	Δ1,591	Δ2,031	440	724	271	1,374	903[d]	593
	1971	5,898	7,900	23,650	15,750	Δ1,748	4,842	6,590	Δ254	124	378	Δ1,161	Δ2,317	1,156	2,993	Δ53	7,677	10,836[e]	Δ3,031
1968	1–3	Δ295	118	2,569	2,451	Δ354	588	942	Δ59	23	82	Δ110	Δ237	127	114	44	Δ247	Δ42	Δ205
	4–6	191	546	3,112	2,566	Δ310	633	943	Δ45	20	65	Δ18	Δ243	225	Δ20	68	221	13	208
	7–9	504	845	3,327	2,482	Δ317	675	992	Δ24	21	45	7	Δ252	259	31	Δ1	541	384	157
	10–12	648	1,020	3,743	2,723	Δ325	711	1,036	Δ47	19	66	Δ118	Δ364	246	84	Δ27	587	531	56
1969	1–3	130	560	3,236	2,676	Δ377	709	1,086	Δ53	20	73	49	Δ286	335	Δ7	106	278	322	Δ44
	4–6	551	913	3,794	2,881	Δ309	779	1,088	Δ53	22	75	80	Δ323	403	Δ17	23	637	Δ124	761
	7–9	672	1,067	4,155	3,088	Δ357	873	1,230	Δ38	19	57	Δ106	Δ320	214	61	31	658	137	521
	10–12	766	1,159	4,494	3,335	Δ356	900	1,256	Δ37	24	61	Δ178	Δ579	401	141	Δ19	710	270	440
1970	1–3	55	579	4,036	3,457	Δ465	896	1,361	Δ59	23	82	Δ438	Δ670	232	185	182	Δ16	372[d]	Δ266
	4–6	373	845	4,586	3,741	Δ422	974	1,396	Δ50	24	74	Δ463	Δ435	Δ28	149	Δ36	23	Δ99	122
	7–9	599	1,105	4,939	3,834	Δ458	1,072	1,530	Δ48	23	71	Δ315	Δ392	77	244	122	650	Δ213	863
	10–12	943	1,434	5,408	3,974	Δ440	1,067	1,507	Δ51	28	79	Δ375	Δ534	159	146	3	717	843	Δ126
1971	1–3	450	1,071	4,932	3,861	Δ541	1,079	1,620	Δ80	26	106	Δ194	Δ649	455	131	222	609	1,059[e]	Δ322
	4–6	1,292	1,778	5,765	3,987	Δ433	1,123	1,556	Δ53	32	85	177	Δ445	622	660	159	2,288	2,141	147
	7–9	2,127	2,516	6,261	3,745	Δ354	1,300	1,654	Δ35	39	74	Δ304	Δ507	203	1,991	246	4,060	5,785	Δ1,725
	10–12	2,029	2,535	6,692	4,157	Δ420	1,340	1,760	Δ86	27	113	Δ840	Δ716	Δ124	211	Δ680	720	1,851	Δ1,131
1972	J	Δ18	180	1,539	1,359	Δ186	388	574	Δ12	8	20	Δ275	Δ175	Δ100	465	24			
	F	390	623	2,004	1,381	Δ198	471	669	Δ35	8	43	Δ118	Δ174	56	469	Δ100			
	M	588	887	2,474	1,587	Δ197	537	734	Δ102	10	112	Δ366	Δ487	121	Δ127	23			
	A	510	722	2,219	1,497	Δ159	449	608	Δ53	10	63	Δ261	Δ310	49	Δ68	Δ24			
	M	183	515	2,085	1,570	Δ191	486	677	Δ141	12	153	Δ250	Δ300	50	Δ23	112			
	J	531	759	2,169	1,410	Δ206	438	644	Δ22	11	33	Δ227	Δ325	98	Δ113	49			
	J[p]	750	971	2,390	1,419	Δ202	477	679	Δ19	10	29	Δ483	Δ545	62	198	Δ63			
	A[p]	626	729	2,374	1,645	Δ95	594	689	Δ8	10	18	Δ346	Δ397	51	325	Δ48			
	S[p]	719	918	2,583	1,665	Δ164	594	758	Δ35	10	45	Δ315	Δ462	147	159	16			

[a] Δshows outflow of capital (an increase in assets or a decrease in liabilities).
[b] Excluding transactions which belong to monetary movements.
[c] Gold tranche of 180 million dollars at the end of March 1964 is included.
[d] Including the allocation of Special Drawing Rights, 122 million dollars.
[e] Including the allocation of Special Drawing Rights, 128 million dollars.
[p] Preliminary

SOURCE: Bank of Japan, MONTHLY ECONOMIC REVIEW, various issues.

CHAPTER 7

Financing the Multinational Enterprise

When a firm carries on activities overseas, it immediately makes itself vulnerable to possible gains and losses on the value of its monetary holdings denominated in various currencies. A British firm that decides to sell a product to customers in Italy who insist on being invoiced in liras will be concerned about the value of the lira vis-à-vis the pound until the receivable is paid. This is the type of problem discussed in Chapter 6.

When the firm expands its operations abroad to include direct investment in a foreign subsidiary (or branch), the problems created by foreign exchange risk become more complicated. Financing for the foreign operations must be found and a decision on the exposure of the firm to foreign exchange risks must be made. In the short term, the financial officer is endowed with a set of investment and operating decisions made in the past that result in the firm's having a diversity of assets in various countries. This situation generates three major problems for the financial officer:

1. Some assets *require financing;* funds must be raised.

2. Some investments become *cash generators;* a proper use for these excess funds must be found.

3. The location of the assets, as well as the decision taken under (1) and (2) above, generates *foreign exchange positions* which must be evaluated and altered if necessary.

The problem of financing foreign assets was partially discussed in the preceding chapter on financing foreign trade. In this chapter, this discussion is carried further by providing a methodology to evaluate financing costs under alternative schemes. This methodology can easily be extended to evaluate the returns on different financial investments, the second problem listed above. Then the chapter deals with the problems of foreign exchange risk generated by foreign direct investment.

THE VALUE OF MONEY IN INTERNATIONAL FINANCE

For the financial officer of a multinational company, the value of money represents specific costs and returns to the firm. These financial costs and returns traditionally have been measured in terms of interest rates and percentage discounts or premiums. In international finance one can use the same units, as has been done in preceding chapters. When the finance function is evaluated within the scope of solely domestic operations, only one currency in one financial market is involved. However, when the scope of the finance function is expanded to the international arena, there is a variety of currencies and financial markets. In order to compare these options it is necessary to compute effective interest rates in terms of one base currency, usually the currency of the parent company.

Effective Interest Rate

Definition. Assume the following quotes for one-year deposits:

Pound sterling	18%
U.S. dollar	13%
Swiss franc	11%
Italian lira	22%

Where should funds be invested? Based on the figures for interest rates alone, the answer is to invest funds in Italian liras. However, what would happen if the Italian lira depreciated 15% against each of the other three alternatives? In terms of liras, there would have been a larger percentage return than any alternative. But converting the proceedings of such an investment into any of the other three currencies would create a loss of 15% on both the principal and the interest.

As a rough approximation, in terms of the other three currencies the

Italian lira's *effective interest rate or yield* would be only 7%, (22% - 15%),[1] that is, *the nominal interest rate less the percentage change in the value of the currency.* (Notice that since the analysis is for one year, adjustments for fractions of a year or compounding after one year are not necessary.)

The previous example assumed that the exchange rates for the other currencies remained constant throughout the period with the exception of their value against the Italian lira. If at the same time that the lira depreciated, the Swiss franc appreciated 4% against the U.S. dollar and the pound sterling, and 19% against the Italian lira (15% depreciation of the lira plus 4% appreciation of the Swiss franc against every other currency), what would be the effective interest rates? In order to answer this question, we must choose a currency in terms of which to measure the effective yield.

In the following table the numbers in the four columns to the right state the *net effective yield* in terms of each of the currencies involved. For example, in terms of francs, investing funds in sterling would produce a net effective yield of 14%. This is composed of the nominal 18% return on sterling investment less the 4% lost when converting the pound proceeds into Swiss francs which have appreciated 4% against the pound. If the funds were invested in dollars the net effective yield would be 9%. The nominal yield for the dollar is 13% and there is a 4% exchange loss when converting into francs.

		Effective Rates in Terms of			
Currency	*Nominal Rates*	*£*	*US$*	*SF*	*Lit*
Pound sterling	18%	18%	18%	14% (18 - 4)	33% (18 + 15)
U.S. dollar	13%	13%	13%	9% (13 - 4)	28% (13 + 15)
Swiss franc	11%	15% (11 + 4)	15% (11 + 4)	11%	30% (11 + 19)
Italian lira	22%	7% (22 - 15)	7% (22 - 15)	3% (22 - 19)	22%

The columns for the net effective rates in terms of pounds and U.S. dollars produce the same results because there has not been any change in the value of the pound against the U.S. dollar. The diagonal of the table shows that effective rates are the same as nominal rates when funds are invested in the currency used as unit of account. Dealing with only one currency, foreign exchange considerations do not enter the analysis. Finally, ranking of the investments yields the same list of priorities regardless of the currency used as unit of account or base currency. The lowest return belongs to the lira and the highest one to the pound. In between are the U.S. dollar and the Swiss franc investments, in that order.

The computations of future effective rates involve an element of speculation, and, consequently, risk. The speculation is on the future exchange rates of the currencies being considered. The previous example took this as a given; however, in real life one would have to make forecasts that are subject to risks. To

[1]This formula provides a good approximation for the effective interest rates as long as the interest differentials are not large. If interest rates differ by large amounts, then the impact of variations in exchange rate on interest received or paid will alter the results obtained by this simple formula. An elaboration of this formula is presented later in the chapter.

act on the basis of these forecasts (e.g., in the previous example, to invest the funds in pound sterling) and not cover the flow means to accept foreign exchange risks. If the forecasts turn out to be wrong, then, with the benefit of hindsight, we may see that the approach chosen—which we thought was optimal—was actually suboptimal.

Time and the Effective Interest Rate. The remarks above have dealt with investments and borrowings of a one-year maturity. Once longer maturities are introduced, explicit assumptions must be made for repayment of principal in the case of borrowings, or for intended changes in the amount of financial investment. (Actually one would have to make the same refinements within a year, but the results will not alter the decision very much.)

The question of what happens to the size of the borrowings or investments is relevant when the transaction is made on an open basis without coverage in the foreign exchange market. Without foreign exchange cover, when one borrows in a currency that appreciates against the base currency, the appreciation loss will be the most damaging the sooner the appreciation happens. Similarly, when one invests in a currency that depreciates against the base currency, the depreciation loss will hurt the most the earlier the depreciation takes place.

Specifically, look at the net present value (NPV) of the cost of borrowing. In this stream of cash flows, first there are the inflows for the proceeds from the borrowings, and subsequently there are cash outflows for the payment of interest and repayment of principal:

$$\text{NPV} = \text{Borrowings} - \frac{\begin{array}{c}\text{Interest}_1 + \\ \text{Principal} \\ \text{Repayment}_1\end{array}}{(1+r)} - \frac{\begin{array}{c}\text{Interest}_2 + \\ \text{Principal} \\ \text{Repayment}_2\end{array}}{(1+r)^2} \cdots - \frac{\begin{array}{c}\text{Interest}_n + \\ \text{Principal} \\ \text{Repayment}_n\end{array}}{(1+r)^n}$$

where r is the interest rate on the loan and only one currency is considered. The timing of principal repayment will have no effect on the NPV to the extent that interest is charged only on the loan balance outstanding. NPV will be zero.

To compute the cost of borrowing in a foreign currency in terms of the unit of account, the home currency, another factor is included in the calculations: the change in relative value between the two currencies. In this case r is unknown and finding its value, while holding NPV = 0, will produce the net effective interest cost.

The denominator in the above equation, regardless of the size of r, becomes larger with time because every year the exponent in the denominator increases by one. The value of whatever happens in later years when discounted by the appropriate factor expressed in the denominator tends to be small. Therefore, the sooner the appreciation takes place in a borrowed currency, the greater the impact on the effective interest rate, r.

Whether the loan is a level principal payment loan or a balloon note also affects the impact of the appreciation or depreciation. Throughout the life of a loan, the amount of the loan outstanding is higher with a balloon payment than with a level payment loan. Appreciation of the currency in which the loan must be paid hurts a balloon payment loan more than a level principal payment loan if the appreciation takes place in later years.

As an example, the table below shows the different effective interest costs for a 10% loan and a 5% appreciation under the two different types of borrowings. For a five-year, $1,000 loan, a one-time appreciation in the last year affects the effective interest cost more on the balloon payment loan than on the level payment loan. A relatively large part of the loan, $600, is still outstanding in the balloon payment loan while only $200 of principal remains on the level payment loan. The 5% appreciation "surcharge" is applied to a larger amount in the balloon payment loan than the level payment loan when the appreciation occurs in the last year. If the one-time appreciation occurs in the first year, a major part of the effect is not realized until later years in the balloon payment loan. The effect of the exponential discounting in the effective interest cost *relative to the level payment* denominator of the present value formula reduces the impact of the appreciation on the cash flows for later years. So, when the appreciation takes place in the first year, the effective interest cost of the loan is lower for the balloon payment loan than for the level payment loan. Note, however, that in *both* loans, the effective interest cost is higher the earlier the appreciation occurs in the life of the loan.

	Effective Interest Cost	
	Level Principal Payment	*Level Principal and 50% Balloon Payment*
Year of Appreciation		
1	12.0%	11.6%
2	11.5	11.3
3	11.0	11.0
4	10.6	10.8
5	10.3	10.7

Inflation and the Effective Interest Rate. This topic will be explained in more detail in Chapters 9 and 10, but a couple of issues should be clarified here. The first point is the effect of inflation on interest rates in the domestic market. It is well accepted that the interest rates in a given currency have two elements: One is the "real return" that the investor expects; the other is the expected rate of inflation that will erode the value of money received in the future. To the extent that the borrower has reason to believe that his or her forecast of the rate of inflation is higher than the forecast that the market is making, the borrower in effect is anticipating payment of a real rate below what the market expects. Given that the repayment of the debt and interest are contracted in advance, to the extent that inflation proceeds at a rate faster than what the market anticipated, the lender will be hurt; however, the borrower will benefit. It is this thinking that gives rise to the prescription: "Borrow as much as possible in inflationary situations."[2]

[2]Brazil, Finland, France, and Israel, among other countries, have offered a number of bond issues that have provisions for adjustment of principal and interest payments by some cost level. Usually these indexed bonds are linked to a general level of prices, although sometimes the adjustment is made to particular cost indices. For example, Finland (1952–67) and France in the late 1950s issued several series of government bonds that were linked to national wholesale price indices. Other debt issues of various governmental bodies can be linked to particular indices. For example, the Austrian Electric Authority issued bonds in

The second point to make regarding inflation has to do with the relationship between inflation and the foreign exchange rate. It is true that there is a general tendency for relatively high inflation rates to be followed eventually by a devaluation of the currency in question against other currencies. However, in this general tendency, notice that there are two factors that must be evaluated carefully before translating the effect of the rate of inflation into a net effective rate. One is the phrase, *relative inflation.* To the extent that all the countries are experiencing a similarly large rate of inflation, there is no cause for one particular currency to devalue relative to the other, other things remaining constant. The other factor is derived from the word *eventually.* This eventuality might take a long time to materialize, and it might not even materialize if the government can smooth the external implications of the domestic inflation until a turnaround situation arises; e.g., other countries catch up with the country's rate of inflation.

If purchasing power parity held all the time, i.e., exchange rates were determined by relative inflation rates only at each time, higher interest rates would be compensated by devaluation of these currencies. This is the assumption behind the usual recommendation that lending in a foreign currency with a high interest rate does not pay if the inflation rate is also high. However, if purchasing power parity holds only over the long term, if at all, and one removes the investment from the country before the devaluation actually takes place (if it takes place at all), one will realize a high rate of return regardless of the rate of inflation in the local markets.

Financial Transactions on a Covered Basis

Covered Transactions in Perfect Markets. If the markets are in equilibrium and interest rate parity holds, one would expect in our earlier example the following premiums and discounts to prevail for one-year forward currencies:

		Currencies Against Which Premium or Discount Is Maintained			
Currency with Premium or Discount (-)	*Nominal Rate*	£	*US$*	*SF*	*Lit*
Pound sterling	18%	—	-5% (13 - 18)	-7% (11 - 18)	+4% (22 - 18)
U.S. dollar	13%	+5% (18 - 13)	—	-2% (11 - 13)	+9% (22 - 13)
Swiss franc	11%	+7% (18 - 11)	+2% (13 - 11)	—	+11% (22 - 11)
Italian lira	22%	-4% (18 - 22)	-9% (13 - 22)	-11% (11 - 22)	—

1953 that were indexed to the cost per kilowatt hour of electricity. France's railroad authority (SNCF) issued bonds in the 1950s that were indexed to the price of third-class railway tickets. Argentina issued a 1972 bond that was indexed to the price changes in nonagricultural goods. In 1977, a major Swedish bank, Svenska Handelsbanken, issued $23 million of preferred shares whose dividend was linked to Sweden's cost of living, but with no adjustment in the redemption price of the shares.

Indexed bonds are not unknown in the United States. The only issue after World War II was in 1959 by the municipality of Carlsbad, New Mexico. It offered a $3 million conventional issue with a 7% coupon and a twenty-year maturity. At the same time, it offered a $4 million issue with a 6% coupon and a thirty-year maturity, but with an increase in the coupon as well as the redemption value by the annual percentage rise in the cost of living.

Notice that in the earlier table where effective rates were computed, we referred to *future spot rates* for the various currencies; this table refers to the *forward rates* for the currencies. Interest rate parity, which might be assumed to hold in the external markets for major currencies, suggests the equilibrium premium/discount shown in this later table, except for small differentials that transaction costs preclude eliminating. Generally, in a free and efficient market the interest rates, forward rates, and spot rates would adjust until interest rate parity occurs.

If interest rate parity holds, this table shows that the pound sterling must be at a discount of 5% against the U.S. dollar (the U.S. dollar must be at a premium of 5% against the pound). The discount on the pound, or the premium on the U.S. dollar, is measured here by the interest differentials for one-year money. The interest rate on the pound is 18%; the interest rate on the U.S. dollar is 13%. Therefore, there must be a 5% discount on the pound against the dollar. In this table each side of the diagonal is a mirror image of the other except for the sign. This only means that the premium of currency A against currency B is the same as the discount of currency B against currency A.[3]

For the few currencies where the forward rate may be considered an unbiased predictor of future spot rates (purchasing power parity and Fisher effects hold), the cost of funds, whether covered or uncovered, is approximately the same over the long term. The cost of uncovered funds in the interest rate plus the changes in spot rate. The cost of covered funds is the interest rate plus the premium/discount on the forward rate. If the forward rate is a good predictor of the spot rate the two alternatives cost the same, when exercised over a longer period of time.[4]

Covered Transaction in Imperfect Markets. Imperfect markets arise when the arbitrageurs who keep the interest differential equal to the premiums or discounts in the forward markets are not allowed to operate. In these cases the markets for a given currency are segmented between the domestic market regulated by the country's governmental authorities and the external markets traded outside the reach of government control. In these situations the equilibrium in the markets will exist only in the external markets. The domestic money market will present a situation of disequilibrium when compared with the foreign exchange market. When this situation arises, opportunities to profit appear for those individuals who have access to both markets. This is typically true for the multinational company with a subsidiary within the country's boundaries but with access to international markets.

[3]The mirror image of the premiums and discounts of the currencies in the table is only approximately correct. For large interest differentials and forward discounts and premiums, the results are different in percentage terms given different reference currencies. Assume 1A = 6Bs, and the premiums and discounts in the forward markets imply that 1A will equal 9Bs in the future. In the forward market, A would have a premium of [(9B – 6B) ÷ 6B], or 50%. In the same market B would have a discount of [(.11A – .17A) ÷ .17A], or 35%. This occurs because of the difference in the currency used as the base. For smaller changes, however, in the context of the interest rate examples of this table, the mirror image analogy is reasonably accurate.

[4]A more detailed discussion of these issues was presented in the sections on covered interest arbitrage and relationship between goods market and exchange markets in Chapter 5 of this book and in the Appendix to Chapter 5.

An example of the situation described will occur when the domestic markets are restricted to domestic users in one way or the other. For example, only domestic entities can borrow in the domestic market; outsiders are not allowed to borrow in that market. At the same time if that currency is important enough (such as the pound sterling), there will be an external market in both the money and foreign exchange markets. These external markets will be in equilibrium. Assume the following with the U.S. dollar as the alternative borrowing source:

Domestic borrowing rate for pound sterling	18%
External borrowing rate for pound sterling	20%
External borrowing rate for U.S. dollar	12%
External discount on the pound against the U.S. dollar	8%

Consider the dollar as the base currency. Thus, the alternatives which do not involve exchange risks are: (1) to borrow dollars or (2) to borrow pounds on a covered basis.

Because of segmented markets, the domestic sterling rate is 2% below the external rate. If the multinational company has a subsidiary in the United Kingdom which meets the lending requirements of that country, it has access to the domestic rate, 18%. To avoid the exchange risk of the pound appreciating against the dollar, the multinational will want to lock-in an exchange rate in advance, i.e., to cover the transaction. This can be accomplished by purchasing sterling forward at an 8% discount against the dollar, and could be done by the parent company in the external market.

The effect is to keep the value of the sterling borrowings stable in terms of dollars. This is accomplished at a net cost of funds of 10%:

Cost of borrowing domestic sterling at today's spot rate (booked by subsidiary)	18%
Less today's discount on sterling bought forward (booked by parent)	(8%)
Net cost of borrowing sterling on a covered basis	10%

This compares favorably with the alternative of borrowing dollars at 12%.

Technically, the steps followed here are the same as those followed to benefit from covered interest arbitrage. The only difference is that here we have not specified that the proceeds from borrowing sterling at 18% be converted into dollars and invested at 12%. The company borrowing the funds presumably needs them to finance its operations. Whether the sterling proceeds are converted into dollars or any other currency depends on where the needs for funds are located. The purchase of sterling forward stabilized the cost of sterling in terms of dollars. However, the value of the foreign investment where the funds are finally utilized remains unprotected in terms of dollars. This is a separate problem and it is discussed later in this chapter.

An opportunity for investment by the domestic subsidiary while the parent company does the covering in the external market will occur when interest rates in the domestic market are higher than in the external market. (Remember the two markets are segmented by regulations.) Example:

Domestic investment rate for deutsche marks	12%
External investment rate for deutsche marks	10%
External investment rate for U.S. dollars	12%
External discount of the U.S. dollar against the deutsche mark	2%

In this case the domestic subsidiary will invest its funds in the domestic DM market at 12%. If the dollar is used as the unit of account, the covering transaction to be made by the parent company will involve selling marks against U.S. dollars at a premium of 2%. The net effect of the transaction covered in this fashion is a yield of 14% (12% realized by the subsidiary, 2% by the parent). This alternative dominates the opportunity of investing in the base currency, U.S. dollars at 12%, and the foreign exchange risks are the same in terms of U.S. dollars—zero.

DIRECT INVESTMENT AND FOREIGN EXCHANGE EXPOSURE

As soon as a firm chooses to maintain a physical presence in a foreign country, an exposure to foreign exchange risk develops. In the future the value of the assets located abroad will depend on the behavior of foreign currencies. In similar fashion, when the firm chooses to finance its operations in foreign currencies, an exposure to exchange risk also arises. Both of these exchange risks are usually analyzed in the context of the initial investing and financing decisions. Thus, when the financial officer worries about the impact on the value of the firm of a previously unforeseen depreciation of the French franc against the dollar, (s)he is worrying about the wisdom of investment and financing decisions taken in the past. In this sense, exposure management is a continuous reassessment of previous decisions as more information on exchange risks becomes available. Decisions to cover an exposure can then be seen as reversals of earlier financial decisions.

Before the manager establishes the impact of an exchange fluctuation on business, it is necessary to define *what* can be affected by exchange fluctuations, i.e., the exposure to exchange risk. Is it future exchange *transactions*? Or is it the future *net value* of the firm?

Transaction Exposure

The exposure problems discussed in the text so far have two characteristics in common:

1. The maturity of the cash flow could be established with certainty; for example, the exporter in Chapter 6 knew that the account receivable would be collected ninety days after the date of the sale.

2. The cash flow required a foreign exchange transaction on the maturity date; for example, the Italian exporter invoicing in dollars intended to convert the dollars into liras upon collection.

This type of exposure to foreign exchange risk is usually referred to as *transaction* or *conversion exposure.*

The transactions we have discussed involved trade payables and receivables, notes payable, and short-term investment. There are many other cases in business where transaction exposure occurs. Examples are intercompany trade accounts between two subsidiaries located in different countries, dividend remittances from subsidiaries to the parent, payments for services contracted from third parties in a different country, etc. In all of these situations, there is an identifiable cash flow which requires an exchange transaction at maturity. Notice that these cash flows may involve known future commitments that are not shown on the year-end balance sheet; e.g., an agreement to pay a supplier within thirty days after a delivery of raw materials six months from now.

A foreign subsidiary which is financed in the local currency and which operates only in its domestic markets has a potential transaction exposure in only one instance: the remittance of dividends to the parent. It is only in this case that a foreign exchange transaction is required. Although the subsidiary has many cash flows in its daily operations, none of these other cash flows involve foreign exchange transactions.

Many business people argue that transaction exposure is the only relevant type of exposure. In this view self-contained foreign subsidiaries which do not intend to pay dividends in the forseeable future are not exposed to foreign exchange risk until the time when dividends start to be declared. Many private companies in the United States and most companies outside the United States agree with this conclusion. These companies are usually not concerned with the stock market's valuation of their earnings.

A reporting system to monitor conversion exposure requires information on the exchange transactions scheduled for different points of time by each subsidiary. As an example, a form suited for this purpose is presented in Exhibit 7.1. To obtain the consolidated transaction or conversion exposure for the company as a whole, the reports from each of the subsidiaries are aggregated by currency and maturity of the cash flows.

Translation Exposure

When recession afflicts the economy, stock prices usually decline even for those companies which maintain a stable dividend. Although no change in cash flow between a company and its stockholders may take place, the market penalizes the price of the stock. The market, in fact, is saying that under the new economic conditions the *value* of the company is less than before. By analogy, it can be argued that when the currency of a foreign country where a subsidiary is located depreciates, the *value* of the company's assets in that country decreases even if no profits are repatriated.

The decline of stock prices in recessionary conditions occurs in response to the anticipated decline in companies' revenues under depressed economic condi-

EXHIBIT 7.1. Transaction Exposure: Report Form

Foreign Currency Payables and Receivables

Subsidiary: A Home Currency: Sterling

Date: January 1, 2001

	Currency				
	£	FF	Lit	DM	¥
RECEIVABLES:					
1 month		1,000			
2 months		—			
3 months		1,000			
3–6 months		2,000			
6–12 months		4,000			
more than 1 year		—			
Total receivables		8,000			
PAYABLES:					
1 month			—	200	100
2 months			—	200	—
3 months			100	—	—
3–6 months			500	—	—
6–12 months			500	—	—
more than 1 year			—	—	—
Total payables			1,100	400	100
NET EXCHANGE POSITION receivables (+) less payables (–)		+8,000	–1,100	–400	–100

tions. Indeed, financial value is determined by the size and pattern of future streams of cash flows. Proponents of the use of translation exposure maintain that an exposure measure should focus on the potential changes in overall value of the firm; that is, *on all future operating cash flows, and not only those cash flows which involve an exchange transaction.* Translation exposure argues that operating cash flows generated in a depreciating currency are worth less to the parent company even if none of these cash flows involve a remittance to the parent. The value of the company as a whole has diminished as a result of the depreciation.

While the identification of cash flows involved in transaction exposure is relatively uncomplicated, the same cannot be said for the cash flows involved in translation exposure. The one measure of value readily available to the firm or any of its analysts is the one reflected in its reported financial statements. Thus, a series of measures is available to adjust financial statements to reflect changes in exchange parities.

Discrepancy between value measured according to accepted accounting principles and economic value exist. Accountants have a penchant for the use of historical costs as a measure of value, while economists argue that only the future is relevant to a computation of value. Nevertheless, reported financial statements are a reality of life and they provide some measure of value to which the market may be expected to react. Thus, the so-called accounting exposure is one of the most popular measures to exchange risks used by U.S. companies.

Accounting Exposure. Suppose Bongo Corporation, a U.S. company, has a South American subsidiary, Bongo Latino, which carries on manufacturing and distribution activities in Latin America. At the end of one period the balance sheet of Bongo Latino translated into U.S. dollars is as follows:

BONGO LATINO: Balance Sheet for End of Period (thousands of dollars)

Assets		*Liabilities and Net Worth*	
Cash and securities	$ 40	Accounts payable	$ 60
Receivables	80	Taxes payable	20
Inventory	80		
		Total current liabilities	$ 80
Total current assets	$200		
Plant and equipment, Net	100	Long-term debt	120
		Equity	100
Total assets	$300		
		Total liabilities and equity	$300

At the time of this balance sheet the peso is worth $0.14. That is, there are about seven pesos to the dollar.

Suppose the management of Bongo Corporation foresees that a 10% depreciation of the peso is very likely in the coming year. At the end of that year, what would be the loss from translating the now cheaper peso investment of Bongo Corporation in Bongo Latino?

First, this balance sheet is convenient, but to accurately determine Bongo Latino's loss from depreciation of the peso the flow of funds in the future should be merged with this balance sheet. This is a point often overlooked in the analysis. For our purposes, however, assume that Bongo Corporation wants to know what its accounting peso exposure is as of the date of the balance sheet.

If the peso depreciates, then the value of the cash and securities shown on the balance sheet and the receivables collectable from the customers should presumably be valued at the new, current exchange rate. If they were exchanged for dollars, their value would be less by the amount of depreciation. Similarly, the bill from the suppliers would also be less in dollars since the payables would be paid in depreciated pesos.

The basis for most accounting concepts is cost; therefore, the historic cost based on the historic exchange rate for many of the other balance sheet accounts is considered to be relevant. For example, the depreciated book value of the plant may have little relationship to any current market value. Thus, if the value does not match market value, why should one worry about whether the translation rate used for converting its historic book value to dollars is the current one? After all, since the depreciation charges are simply a method to expense the original (historic) cost over a period of time, in this logic there is no point in translating the plant at the current rate.

But what of inventory? If inventory is thought of as historically produced goods not yet sold, or as goods in process, why should the dollar value be adjusted? If they are destined for sale in the Latin economy, then the price may not change with the peso depreciation; so their future value will likely be less in dollar terms. On the other hand, if they are for export, the peso depreciation may make the goods more competitive. Hence, total revenues might actually be higher in the future in pesos so that to translate the inventory at the current value would be too severe a decrease in value. Similarly, if we retain an historic cost basis for goods, then the historic cost in dollars should not be changed simply because of fluctuations in the peso.

A similar conflict develops for long-term debt. Some people would argue that it should not be considered on a current basis. Including the long-term debt, which will only be repaid in the future, lowers the subsidiary's exposure to a foreign exchange loss from a devaluation just as including the current liabilities reduces the exposure. These accountants would argue that the future payment of the liability is many years away, perhaps after other currency revaluations. The value of long-term debt is not adjusted to reflect market changes in interest rates, so why should it reflect changes in exchange rates? Furthermore, long-term liabilities often were incurred to purchase fixed assets; if the plant and equipment valuation is not lowered because of the currency depreciation, then the funds supporting it should not be. Other students of the subject argue that long-term debt should be included; the gain to the parent from financing its subsidiary in a depreciated currency occurs when the currency depreciates, regardless of when the debt is paid.

If the accounts are rearranged to include only those translated on a current basis, and the liabilities are subtracted from the assets to compute a net exposure, then one might complete a table as follows. Three different measures of exposure are calculated depending on what is included or excluded from the definition of exposure. The first method includes current accounts only and is usually called the Current/Non-Current method (also referred to as Net Current Asset or Net Working Capital method). The Monetary/Non-Monetary method excludes inventory but includes the long-term debt. Finally, the Net Financial Asset method includes all current accounts as well as the long-term debt.

		Translation Method		
		Current/ Non-Current	*Monetary/ Non-Monetary*	*Net Financial Asset*
Current assets, except inventory	$120	$120	$120	$120
Inventory	80	80		80
Current liabilities	80	(80)	(80)	(80)
Long-term liabilities	120		(120)	(120)
Net exposure		$120	($ 80)	0

When there is a blank, the account is not included when the determination of net exposure is made. The final exposure is the sum of the positive and negative figures. Under the Current/Non-Current method, the exposure is $120. This means that a 10% devaluation of the peso would result in a $12 translation exchange loss to the parent. Conversely, an appreciation of the peso would result in a $12 exchange gain to the parent. Under the Monetary/Non-Monetary method of calculating exposure, there would be an $8 gain from a 10% peso depreciation, for the firm owes $80 more in the now cheaper currency than it has in cash and other current assets. But there would be an $8 loss if the peso upvalues by 10%. Finally, there is no net exposure under the Net Financial Asset method.

Prior to January 1976, all of the above translation methods, plus variations, were acceptable for U.S. firms. However, since January 1976, Statement No. 8 issued by the Financial Accounting Standards Board requires U.S. companies to use the temporal method of translation, usually referred to as FASB #8.[5]

In general, under FASB #8 accounts measured at cost are translated into dollars using the historical exchange rate on the date when the asset was acquired or the liability incurred. Accounts measured at market prices are translated into dollars using current exchange rates. Thus, we have:

FASB #8—Accounts Translated At:

Current Exchange Rates	*Historical Exchange Rates*
Cash	Inventory at cost
Accounts receivable	Fixed assets
Inventory at market	
Short-term liabilities	
Long-term liabilities	

As in the other methods, the two most controversial accounts are inventory and long-term debt. In the case of inventory, FASB #8 introduces one new element in the translation treatment. Inventory at cost is translated at historical exchange rates, while inventory at market is translated at current exchange rates. However, the choice of whether to report inventory at cost or at market is not only determined by obsolescence, as usual. Now, the choice is made in terms of which figure, cost or market, is lower in *dollar terms.* Thus, we have:

Foreign inventory at *cost* × Historical exchange rate = Dollar inventory at *cost*

Foreign inventory at *market* × Current exchange rate = Dollar inventory at *market*

The reported figure is the lower one of the two dollar inventory figures. Assuming the typical relationship between cost and market values of inventory, cost

[5]The positions of the U.S. accounting profession through time can be seen in the following: *Accounting Research Bulletin No. 43,* American Institute of Certified Public Accountants, 1953; the *National Association of Accountants Research Report No. 36,* 1960; and Statement No. 8 of the Financial Accounting Standards Board. *Accounting for the Translation of Foreign Currency Transactions and Foreign Currency Financial Statements.* Stamford, Connecticut, October, 1975.

lower than market, in the case of an *appreciation* of the foreign currency against the dollar the inventory figure will be translated at *historical* exchange rates. The inventory figure at cost together with an historical exchange rate below the current one will produce a lower inventory measured in dollars than if current rates were used to translate market values of inventory. In the case of a *depreciation* of the foreign currency against the dollar, whether the inventory is translated at historical rates or current rates depends on the size of the depreciation relative to the mark-up of market inventory over cost inventory. With a small mark-up or a large depreciation, market inventory at the current depreciated exchange rate produces the lower dollar inventory figure. However, if the mark-up is large relative to the depreciation, inventory at cost translated at historical exchange rates produces the lower dollar inventory figure. Thus, in cases of appreciation of the foreign currency, inventories are translated at historical exchange rates; in cases of a large depreciation, inventories are often translated at current exchange rates; and in cases of moderate depreciation it depends on the mark-up of market inventory over cost inventory.[6]

In contrast to the controversy on translating various accounts in the balance sheet, there has been agreement on translating the accounts in the income statement. This agreement carried on to FASB #8. Accounts reported at cost are translated at historical exchange rates, and accounts reported at market rates are translated at exchange rates prevailing at the time of the transaction. Thus, we have:

FASB #8—Accounts Translated At:	
Current Exchange Rates	*Historical Exchange Rates*
Revenues	Cost of goods sold
Operating and administrative expenses	Depreciation

where current exchange rates are usually an average of the exchange rates over the period covered by the income statement.

In effect, when inventory is translated at historical exchange rates, the impact of exchange fluctuations on this account is delayed until the merchandise is sold and revenues are reported at the exchange rates then prevailing. For companies with a long turnover period, this treatment may create confusion in the evaluation of reported earnings. Even for companies with a three-month turnover period, this translation method creates additional instability in quarterly earnings. This has been a source of concern to many American companies.

Provided there is an exchange fluctuation, if the amount of assets and liabilities translated at current exchange rates in the balance sheet is not the same, exchange gains or losses arise. Also, the accounts in the income statement translated at current exchange rates produce an exchange gain or loss. The treat-

[6] Assuming appreciations and depreciations occur equally often, FASB #8 has a bias toward translating inventory at historical exchange rates. This is the rationale behind the statement usually heard that under FASB #8 inventory is not exposed because it is translated at historical rates.

ment of these foreign exchange gains and losses has been very controversial. The options are:

1. Charge them against a reserve account in the balance sheet, and do not report them in the income statement.
2. Report them in the income statement as an extraordinary item.
3. Report them in the income statement as part of operating income.

FASB #8 requires the last treatment. Contrary to the theory of clean surplus practiced by the American accounting profession, before 1976 reserve accounts for foreign exchange gains and losses emerged in the balance sheets of many companies. The nature of this reserve varied from company to company, but in general it helped to buffer the income statement from the impact of exchange fluctuations. With these reserves no longer permitted, the instability contributed by the FASB #8 treatment of inventory and long-term debt is fully reflected in current earnings and earnings per share.[7]

In countries other than the United States a common translation practice if foreign subsidiaries are consolidated at all is to translate all assets and liabilities at current exchange rates and to reflect the net change in the equity account. Sometimes the asset and liability accounts are not reduced but the surplus account is. The difference is then a reserve account on the liability side, "Reserve for Foreign Exchange Gains and Losses." In most situations in which this practice is followed, the income statement will reflect the creation of this reserve as well.

Economic Exposure. Economic value is based on future cash flows discounted to a present value. Conceptually, this is very different from the accounting value discussed above. Consider the present value of the subsidiary in the country which has just devalued its currency. That value may be more or less following the devaluation and it is a function of future cash flows. With lower export prices now possible, sales for exports may increase and the expected profits of the firm may have increased for the coming years over and above the percentage of initial devaluation. Similarly, if the devaluation increases domestic income, local sales may increase enough to compensate for the effects of the devaluation on price per unit. On the expense side, if the cost of the goods sold arises largely from within the local country, the cost should not necessarily increase because of the devaluation.

The whole consideration of the issue of price and income elasticity of demand for the products in both the domestic and the export market and the sensitivity of the cost components to the devaluation combine to complete the increase or decrease in the firm's present value. Yet, the result of this increase or decrease in future cash flows is likely to have very little to do with the accounting exposure discussed above.

[7]For a presentation of the impact of FASB #8 on reported earnings of seventy U.S. companies in 1974–75, a period of voluntary compliance, and the reaction of chief international financial officers see Rita M. Rodriguez, "FASB No. 8: What Has It Done For Us?," *Financial Analyst Journal,* March–April 1977, pp. 40–48.

The new conditions created by a change in parity may also call for a change in policies on the part of business. The new economic value of the firm will be the result of the combined interaction of the new economic conditions and management's reactions to these conditions. Therefore, a systematic inquiry covering the following points is necessary:

Revenues 1. How will aggregate demand change at current prices?
2. Are price increases possible? By how much? How fast?

Costs 1. Will inflationary cost increases occur? By how much? When?
2. Will alternative sources of supply be used?
3. Are improvements in production efficiency possible at the new production levels? By how much? When?

Answering these questions is not easy. An evaluation of the competitive environment is necessary in all the markets where the company operates. In any case, the analysis will depend on the information provided by operating management. Financial officers should not be expected to be informed in detail about these matters. But herein lies one of the benefits of analyzing exposure to exchange risks in these terms. It forces operating personnel to plan for fluctuations in exchange rates.

One may think of the answers to these questions as providing information of changes in cash flows per currency for each period. After a while these changes will tend to stabilize to reflect the total adjustment to the new conditions. At that point the level of net cash flows in dollar terms may have reverted to the level before the exchange fluctuation, it may be more, or it may be less.[8]

The exchange gain or loss in economic exposure can be seen as the difference between the dollar net present value of the foreign operation before and after the envisaged exchange fluctuations. Thus, the original dollar net present value for a British subsidiary may be computed using the following formula:

$$\$NPVo = \frac{\begin{pmatrix}\text{Original}\\ \text{Sterling}\\ \text{Cash Flow}\end{pmatrix}_1 \times XRo_1}{(1+r)} + \frac{\begin{pmatrix}\text{Original}\\ \text{Sterling}\\ \text{Cash Flow}\end{pmatrix}_2 \times XRo_2}{(1+r)^2} + \ldots + \frac{\begin{pmatrix}\text{Original}\\ \text{Sterling}\\ \text{Cash Flow}\end{pmatrix}_n \times XRo_n}{(1+r)^n}$$

where XRo denotes the series of exchange rates between sterling and the dollar originally envisaged.

If a depreciation in sterling is foreseen, there will be changes in both the sterling cash flows and the exchange rates used to convert those flows into

[8] For calculation of economic exposure assuming that cash flows are reverted to the pre-devaluation level see Robert Ankrom, "Top-Level Approach to the Foreign Exchange Problem," *Harvard Business Review,* July-August, 1974, pp. 79–90.

dollars. The new dollar net present value can then be computed by adjusting the terms in the preceding formula as follows:

$$\$NPVa = \frac{\begin{pmatrix}\text{Adjusted}\\ \text{Sterling}\\ \text{Cash Flow}\end{pmatrix}_1 \times XRa_1}{(1+r)} + \frac{\begin{pmatrix}\text{Adjusted}\\ \text{Sterling}\\ \text{Cash Flow}\end{pmatrix}_2 \times XRa_2}{(1+r)^2} + \ldots + \frac{\begin{pmatrix}\text{Adjusted}\\ \text{Sterling}\\ \text{Cash Flow}\end{pmatrix}_n \times XRa_n}{(1+r)^n}$$

where XRa denotes the new exchange rates after the sterling depreciation. The gain or loss resulting from the sterling depreciation and the adjustments in operations is then the difference between the original dollar net present value ($NPVo) and the adjusted dollar net present value ($NPVa).[9]

The total change in economic value of the company as a result of an exchange fluctuation can be seen as the change in the dollar net present value of the operating cash flows throughout time.

To monitor economic exposure, a form such as the one presented in Exhibit 7.2 may be used. To obtain the consolidated economic exposure for the company as a whole, the economic exposures of each subsidiary by currency and time period are aggregated.

Whenever an exchange fluctuation is anticipated, these data together with an analysis of the questions listed above provide a combined measure of the value of the company which is exposed to exchange fluctuations and the compensating policies which are available. For example, assume that a depreciation of the foreign currency is expected to occur in March. Operating management estimates that a price increase to compensate for the depreciation is possible within two months, so that the May revenues should reflect the higher prices. No loss in sales is anticipated as a result. On the other hand, local currency costs are expected to remain constant throughout the end of the year when an adjustment in labor rates will be negotiated, probably in the order of 10%. In this case the depreciation will affect the value of the subsidiary as follows:

1. Decrease in value due to revenues for March and April at current prices;

2. Increase in value from May through December after price increase while costs remain fixed.

The net effect of these changes is a loss in revenues for two months; a gain in net profits from May throughout December after selling prices are increased but

[9]Notice, that each component in the net present value formula is translated into dollars separately. The alternative, translating a sterling net present value figure into dollars at the current exchange rate, would require adjusting the discount rate *r* also. Adjustments in discount rates and cash flows to reflect exchange fluctuations are discussed in detail in Part Three of this text.

EXHIBIT 7.2. Economic Exposure: Report Form

Economic Exposure

Subsidiary: A Home Currency: Sterling

Period: Jan.–Dec., 2001

	Month				
	Jan.	*Feb.*	*Mar.*	*Apr.–Dec.*	*Total*
			Currency: Sterling		
Inflows (revenues)	1,000	900	1,200	9,000	12,100
Outlfows (costs)	-800	-800	-800	-7,200	-9,600
Net exposure	+200	+100	+400	+1,800	+2,500
			Currency: French franc		
Inflows (revenues)	–	–	–	–	–
Outflows (costs)	-100	-100	-100	-900	-1,200
Net exposure	-100	-100	-100	-900	-1,200

before costs increase; and reversion to pre-devaluation profits on January, after costs are increased at the end of December. A true measure of changes in economic value would combine these effects after adjusting them for the time value of money; i.e., it would be based on the net present value of the gains and losses discussed above. These adjustments may often include changes in working capital requirements. In this example we assumed that working capital requirements remained constant; however, in practice new monetary conditions may change this assumption. (In Chapter 8 we analyze the impact of exchange fluctuations and inflation on working capital.)

So far this discussion of economic exposure to exchange risk has ignored financing charges. Aren't these costs also subject to changes in value after an exchange fluctuation? The answer is yes, except if the financing involves long-term debt with a fixed interest rate. With short-term debt or long-term debt with a floating rate, it is easy to imagine the dollar cost of debt changing after an exchange fluctuation. For example, after an exchange devaluation the dollar value of interest payments will decrease and domestic interest rates may also be reduced.

Traditionally, the cash flows included in the valuation formula presented above refer to operating cash flows, and the discount rate refers to the overall cost of capital (i.e., the combined cost of equity and debt). The value thus obtained measures the total value of the firm to lenders and stockholders. If we wish to measure the value of the firm to stockholders, we have to take into account the value of financing charges that must be paid to lenders before cash profits are made available to stockholders. To measure the impact of exchange fluctuations on the value of the firm to stockholders, we modify the net present value formulae presented above as follows:

1. Original and adjusted cash flows in foreign currency are reduced by the amount of financing costs.

2. The discount rate, r, is increased to reflect the cost of equity funds alone, instead of the combined cost of all funds available to the firm.

In summary, the value of the firm to stockholders can be seen as a stream of cash profit available to stockholders. If the value of this stream of cash is vulnerable to fluctuations in exchange rates, these cash flows measure the amounts exposed to exchange risk. However, as prices, costs, and interest rates change in response to an exchange fluctuation, the amount of cash flows exposed to exchange risk will also change. Thus, the *economic exposure to exchange risk is the cash profit available to stockholders after operational adjustments are taken into account.* As long as no adjustment is possible in response to an exchange fluctuation, 100% of the cash profit available to stockholders is exposed to the full impact of an exchange fluctuation. If after two months the cash flows in the local currency can be increased so that their dollar value reverts to the pre-devaluation level or higher (as assumed in the previous example), then the economic exposure to the effects of an exchange depreciation is reduced to zero at that point. Of course, this exposure refers only to one exchange move. If after two months another exchange depreciation is envisioned, the economic exposure then would not be zero, but 100% of the cash profit to stockholders for two months.

Exposure Measures Compared

We have discussed three measures of exposure to exchange risk: transaction exposure, accounting exposure, and economic exposure. Let's summarize the similarities and differences among them.

While the accountants' definitions focus on historical figures at one point in time, both transaction and economic exposures concentrate on future cash flows. In the economist's jargon, historical figures are sunk costs! As a going concern, the value of business is measured in terms of the cash flows it can generate in the future. Balance sheet figures are a poor measure of these cash flows.[10]

[10]Fredrikson argues that the relative expected exchange rate at the time of completion of a transaction should be forecast and used in the income statement, rather than the exchange rate in effect at the end of the year for (say) receivables with a foreign exchange loss charged on the financial statement. (See E. Bruce Fredrikson, "On the Measurement of Foreign Income," *Journal of Accounting Research,* Autumn 1968, pp. 208-221.) A related break with accounting convention is in Heckerman, who notes that the value of the firm depends on the discounted value of future cash flows. Changing price levels for the parent and the subsidiary economies and the changing exchange rate affect this discounted value; he compares the adjustments to the balance sheet under this approach with normal accounting standards. (See Donald Heckerman, "The Exchange Risks of Foreign Operations," *Journal of Business,* January 1972, pp. 42–48.)

An illustration of this point can be seen in the treatment of working capital by the various definitions. While accounting exposure considers some measure of net working capital (including or excluding inventory) exposed to exchange fluctuations, the other two definitions ignore this figure. Transaction and economic exposures consider only the changes in net working capital required under the new conditions; e.g., an increase in financing requirements. The only occasion on which these other definitions would consider the level of net working capital exposed to exchange fluctuations would be in the case of liquidation of the foreign operation. Upon liquidation the cash received from the net assets will be remitted to the parent company, and, therefore, be considered a cash flow exposed to fluctuations in the exchange markets. However, notice that the liquidation value of net working capital would, in all likelihood, be different from the balance sheet figure.

The contrast in time horizon between accounting exposure and the other two definitions can be seen in the fashion in which the amount of net exposure is expressed. In the accountants' approach, exposure to foreign exchange risk is summarized in one number that is basically the difference between exposed assets and liabilities at one point in time. Future accounting exposures are basically a combination of this figure and future net income. In contrast, exchange exposure measured in terms of conversion risk or economic risk is defined as a series of exposures throughout time; i.e., specific cash flows at given points in time.

Although both transaction and economic exposures concentrate on measuring the potential impact of exchange fluctuations on the firm's cash flows, there are major differences between the two approaches. While transaction exposure worries only about those cash flows that involve an actual exchange transaction, economic exposure includes all the operational cash flows of the firm, even if they do not involve an exchange transaction. The only occasion when both definitions would produce the same result would be in the case of an all-equity financed subsidiary that remits to the parent company all the cash available every year. If the company maintains intercompany accounts, this introduces one more difference between transaction and economic exposure. Although transaction exposure will include all the cash flows which must cross the exchange markets between sister companies, in economic exposure these cash flows would disappear in consolidation of the cash flows of the two units in the system.

Finally, in our presentation of economic exposure, we have emphasized how the changes in operations triggered by exchange fluctuations should be taken into account in order to compute the amount of operational cash flows exposed to changes in value due to exchange fluctuations. Transaction exposure, as usually defined, considers these operational changes only indirectly as they become identifiable exchange transactions. The thrust of transaction exposure measures, as usually defined, is not in measuring the impact of exchange fluctuations on operations. This factor is central to the concept of economic exposure. However, it must be noted that the use of transaction exposure measures does not need to deter efforts to analyze adjustments in operations. But in current practice this is not done.

Financial theory argues that the objective of the financial officer is to maximize the value of the firm. Economic value is measured in terms of discounted future cash flows. This disqualifies accounting exposure. The question then remaining is what cash flows are relevant, all cash flows, or only those which require an exchange transaction? From the stockholders' standpoint, we can ask whether the value of the foreign operation is determined by all cash flows available to stockholders or only by cash flows repatriated; i.e., dividends.

There are two extreme cases where the answer to the above question is unequivocal. If there are no government controls preventing the repatriation of funds generated in the foreign subsidiary, all generated cash is clearly available to stockholders. If a portion or all of this cash is reinvested in the same affiliate, it is because this is the best use of funds available to the firm. Economic exposure that takes into account all cash flows available to stockholders is the relevant variable in this case. At the other extreme, if repatriation of funds beyond a certain point is forbidden and the company cannot anticipate any profitable investment opportunity in that country in the foreseeable future, then dividends are the only cash of value to the stockholders. Reinvested cash, by definition, is as good as confiscated. In real life situations, companies often find some outlet for excess funds in a country where repatriation is limited. In this case economic exposure, measured to include the return on blocked funds, becomes again the relevant variable.[11]

Obviously, each of the exposure measures discussed here has different objectives. Accounting exposure looks into the impact of exchange fluctuations on financial reports and, therefore, earnings per share. Transaction exposure identifies specific cash flows which can produce realized gains and losses in case of an exchange rate fluctuation. Economic exposure attempts to identify the impact of exchange fluctuations on the overall value of the foreign operations. Financial theory's preferences notwithstanding, the financial manager will want to monitor the three types of exposure.

The Firm's Response to Exchange Risk

When the firm finds that it has an unwanted net exposure to foreign exchange risks, there are a variety of steps it can take. It may try to adjust its operations to change the exposure. Alternatively, it may accept the exposure as given and try to counteract it by operations in the money and foreign exchange markets.

Adjustment in Operations. We discussed some changes in operating policies such as pricing which may be implemented in response to exchange fluctuations. Usually these changes in policy take some time to be carried out and to be accepted. An alternative is to manage the balance sheet; i.e., to alter the amount of net resources exposed to changes in value due to exchange fluctuations. In this task it is useful to distinguish between two types of operating relationships which can be adjusted: operations involving third parties and operations among units of the same multinational company—intercompany accounts.

1. *OPERATIONS WITH THIRD PARTIES.* In the context of the subsidiary's relationship with other firms, a reduction of undesirable exposures would

[11]For an extended discussion of the valuation of blocked funds see the section on terminal rate of return in Chapter 10.

involve the reduction of liabilities in upvaluation-prone currencies and a reduction of financial assets in weak currencies. The net result would be similar to borrowing in weak currencies and investing in hard currencies. In the case of an expected depreciation, local suppliers' terms of credit may be stretched and local customers' receivables reduced if at all possible. Either transaction would reduce the amount exposed to a deteriorating local currency. A conscious effort to reduce sales or size of operations temporarily may be the second line of attack. This can be accomplished by invoicing in a harder currency. However, these measures are bound to encounter very strong opposition from the people in the operating line. No manager ever likes to see his or her operations reduced in size. A tightening in credit terms would be perceived as a direct threat to sales, and lax payments to creditors could result in problems with sourcing materials in the future.

2. INTERCOMPANY ACCOUNTS. When there are several subsidiaries in the same parent's orbit, intercompany accounts can often be used to great advantage. While the subsidiary in the devaluation-prone country might attempt to remit funds to the parent in the form of dividends or royalties (or withhold these payments in the case of an upvaluation-prone currency), usually this route is restricted to some degree by the local authorities. However, intercompany trade offers other opportunities to achieve desired transfers of resources.

The objective of altering intercompany payments practices is simply to reduce the amount of resources exposed in a devaluation-prone currency and increase the resources in an upvaluation-prone currency. The change in the level of the intercompany accounts is only a device to accomplish an exposure objective. Given a level of intercompany accounts receivables and payables, the desired objectives will be accomplished if:

1. Subsidiaries in devaluation-prone countries pay intercompany accounts payable as soon as possible and delay collecting intercompany accounts receivable for as long as possible;

2. Subsidiaries in upvaluation-prone countries delay paying intercompany accounts payable as long as possible and collect intercompany accounts receivable as soon as possible.

In the case of the devaluation-prone subsidiary the company is effectively removing cash from the country through the mechanism of fast payment of intercompany payables, and the company is delaying the entry of additional resources into that currency by extending the collection terms for sister subsidiaries. The opposite is accomplished with the suggestions for the subsidiary in the upvaluation-prone currency.

Although the logic behind these procedures is relatively simple, confusion often arises when the subject is discussed. There are two major sources of puzzlement. One source is the fact that at any point in time consolidated intercompany accounts receivable and accounts payable net to zero. The intercompany account receivable of one subsidiary is the account payable of another. When the two given subsidiaries are consolidated into one reporting unit, the receivable of the first subsidiary cancels the payable of the other. However, this misses the point that the manipulation of the size of these intercompany accounts is nothing else than a tool to move resources from one currency into another. The statement about the impact of consolidation of intercompany accounts at one point in time is correct. However, if one can affect the level of these intercompany accounts *before* the exchange fluctuation takes place, one is effectively redeploying resources. Payables of a subsidiary in a weak currency are reduced only by remitting funds which are then converted to a harder currency.

The other source of confusion in the use of intercompany accounts originates in the role of currency denomination in an intercompany account. Actually, the currency of denomination has an impact only on taxes of foreign exchange gains and losses after the revaluation takes place. Assume two subsidiaries that trade with one another. One subsidiary is in Germany; the other is in France. Further assume that the German subsidiary sells products to the French one. That is, the German subsidiary has an account receivable from the French subsidiary and the French subsidiary has an account payable to the German subsidiary. Now examine the impact from an appreciation of the deutsche mark relative to the French franc when payment is made under alternative billing currencies. If the bill is extended in marks, at the time of payment, the French subsidiary will have a foreign exchange loss; it will have to generate more French francs than anticipated to pay the mark debt. In this case nothing happens to the German subsidiary. If the bill had been invoiced in terms of French francs, when the payment is made there is no foreign exchange effect on the French subsidiary. However, the German subsidiary now receives fewer marks than anticipated at the exchange rates prevailing at the time of the sale. The German subsidiary experiences a foreign exchange loss. Thus, regardless of the currency used in the denomination of intercompany trade, one of the units will have a foreign exchange loss if the payment to the German subsidiary (with the stronger currency) is not made before the appreciation of the mark. If such a loss must be accepted, for example, because of government controls in remittances from France into Germany, the choice of a specific currency for invoicing is immaterial if the tax rate is the same in the two countries. If that is not the case, then one will want to have the foreign exchange loss fall in the country with the higher tax rate so that the highest tax shelter benefit from the loss can be reaped.

As the reader will notice, we have suggested that in the case of an upvaluation-prone currency, debts to third parties in that currency should be decreased while intercompany accounts payable of the subsidiary operating in the country of that currency should be increased. Both are debts of the subsidiary in the upvaluation-prone country. Why decrease one type of debt and increase the other? Both accomplish the desired objective of increasing the net amount of resources in that currency. If asset levels are maintained constant, the reduction of payables to third parties in the upvaluation-prone currency must be accompanied by an increase in financing in a weaker currency. By increasing the intercompany payables, the upvaluation-prone subsidiary is able to keep the resources it has in the relatively harder currency. Both approaches preserve, and might even increase, the resources in that currency.

All the prescriptions we have just mentioned had one goal in mind: reduce exposure to foreign exchange risk. However, each of the actions discussed above has certain costs attached to it. Only if the costs of these measures are less than the impact of the unwanted exposure will they be worthwhile. Otherwise, in economic terms, the firm could be avoiding the appearance of an ugly foreign exchange loss in the financial statements only at an expense higher than the extent of the exchange loss.

As indicated earlier, the reduction in the size of accounts receivable and inventory can have repercussions in the volume of sales. The profits lost on the foregone sales are a clear cost of these approaches. Similarly, denominating export sales in hard currencies might be accomplished only at the expense of a reduction in price—the buyer also has foreign exchange considerations to take into account. This decrease in price might neutralize and even decrease the net effect of billing in a hard currency. On the liability side, extending the terms on which suppliers are paid may be accomplished only by foregoing discounts for prompt payment and by facing higher prices in the future from the supplier to compensate for the larger financing. There is an increase of the funds provided by this source, and that has a price.

The cost of leads and lags in intercompany transactions can be assessed only by making clear who is the final holder of the merchandise (including cash) and who is providing the financing. Once these facts are established, one can proceed to evaluate the interest payments that the financing involves, the net effective cost of the debt, and the returns obtained by the holders of the merchandise. When the merchandise is a financial asset, the return is easy to measure; it is simply the effective interest rate in that market. When the merchandise is goods, then one has to consider inventory carrying costs as well as profit margins.

Finally, in evaluating the cost of these operating adjustments to compensate foreign exchange risk one must consider the factor of time. If these measures are necessary for a very short period because the change in currency values is imminent, then they might be worthwhile even if the net cost is very high in terms of annual interest rates. One would be paying a very high cost for a small period of time, while the devaluation impact would last much longer.

Hedging in the Financial Markets. If a net exposure remains after considering potential adjustments in operations, the financial markets may provide a vehicle to hedge this exposure. The transactions described in Chapter 6 as "covering" are sometimes also called "hedging" operations. Here, however, we attach different meanings to covering and hedging.[12] Covering implies the protection of the value of an identifiable and quantifiable *cash flow* in the exchange markets that could give rise to a foreign exchange loss in the *conversion* from one currency to another, e.g., proceeds from export sales or dividends to be received in a foreign currency. Covering involves a self-liquidating transaction. Hedging, on the other hand, refers to the protection of the value of *assets* located in foreign countries and their financing. That is, hedging attempts to protect the value of future profits generated in foreign currencies although no foreign exchange transaction may be involved.

Assume a U.S. company which has a subsidiary in the United Kingdom. The company expects a *net positive economic exposure* in the amount of £500,000. For simplicity, ignore the distribution of this exposure through time and assume it matures in one year, and that the initial net asset position is zero. No dividends or other exchange transaction is envisaged; i.e., there is no *transaction exposure.* The company faces a potential loss in value in case of a sterling depreciation.

[12]These technical differences in the meaning of hedging and covering were established in Paul Einzig, *A Textbook on Foreign Exchange* (London: Macmillan, 1966).

In order to understand better the mechanics of hedging an economic exposure, express this exposure in terms of explicit cash flows assumed to be available for distribution to stockholders as potential dividends.

	Cash Flows in Terms of Sterling Date: One year later	
	Sterling	*Dollars*
Net exposure	+500,000	
Dividend distribution		-500,000

If sterling depreciates against the dollar, fewer dollars will be available for possible distribution to stockholders one year later. Effectively, the company has a net exchange position, long in sterling and short in dollars.

This formulation of the exposure problem points to the conceptual similarities and differences between exposed *value* and exposed *transactions,* such as financing of foreign trade discussed in Chapter 6. In both there is a net exchange position. However, in value exposure, the case just discussed, the distribution of dollar dividends to stockholders is just an analytical device. The dollar cash outflow is not expected to take place. Only one of the two cash flows, the sterling inflow, will materialize. The books will value the sterling net exposure as if indeed it were to be converted into dollars and made available to stockholders.

To eliminate the uncertainty about the exchange rate at which the sterling exposure will be converted into dollars, we can follow procedures similar to those discussed in Chapter 6 to cover exchange transactions. We have to generate cash flows in each currency to offset the ones producing the exchange position. In this example the hedging transaction must involve an outflow in sterling (to offset the inflow generated by the exposure) and an inflow in dollars (assumed to be needed for distribution to stockholders). The company's exposure by currency after the hedging operation would appear as follows:

	Cash Flows in Terms of Sterling Date: One year later	
	Sterling	*Dollars*
Net exposure	+500,000	
Dividend distribution		-500,000
Hedging transaction	-500,000	+500,000

Assume the following rates prevail in the market:

Foreign Exchange Market	
Spot rate	\$2.50/£
One-year forward rate	\$2.45/£

That is, the one-year pound is trading at a 2% per annum discount against the dollar.

Money Market	
1-year dollar	7%
1-year sterling	9%

That is, interest rate parity holds. There is no incentive for covered interest arbitrage.

In the forward market the covering transaction will be carried out by selling pounds against dollars for one-year delivery, at the forward rates of \$2.45/£. Observe the transactions one year later:

First, assume that the spot sterling actually depreciated to \$2.35/£:

Loss on valuation of net asset position:	
£500,000 X \$0.15/£ depreciation	\$(75,000)
Gain on liquidation of forward contract:	
Buy spot @ \$2.35/£, deliver at contract price of \$2.45/£ = \$0.10/£ gain	
Gain = £500,000 X \$0.10/£	50,000
Net gain (cost)	\$(25,000)

If, instead of depreciating, sterling appreciates to \$2.60/£:

Gain on valuation of net asset position:	
£500,000 X \$0.10/£ appreciation	\$ 50,000
Loss on liquidation of forward contract:	
Buy spot @ \$2.60/£, deliver at contract price of \$2.45/£ = \$0.15/£ loss	
Loss = £500,000 X \$0.15£	(75,000)
Net gain (cost)	\$(25,000)

Regardless of whether the pound appreciates or depreciates, the net of closing the exposure and the forward contract is a loss of \$25,000. This corresponds to the 2% discount on the forward pound relative to the initial spot rate. The forward rate locked-in an exchange rate at which to translate the net exposure. The cost of \$25,000 in terms of today's spot rate insures that if the pound depreciates below \$2.45/£ the company is not hurt. However, should the pound actually appreciate to \$2.60/£, a gain is foregone. These are opportunity gains and losses similar to the ones discussed for covering transactions in Chapter 6.

If the money market is used to hedge the exposure, the steps to be followed are:

1. Borrow £500,000 at 9% for one year;

2. Convert the borrowing proceeds into dollars at the current spot rate, \$2.50/£;

3. Invest the converted dollars at 7% for one year.

Again, a cost of 2% is being locked-in to insure against a potential greater loss if sterling depreciated by more than 2%.[13]

Whether the money market or the forward market is used to hedge net exposure, there will be an exchange transaction involved at the end, a real cash flow. However, the £500,000 net exposure is not available, unlike the exporter's collection of a trade receivable, for settling the hedging transaction. The sterling accounts receivable and payable in the economic exposure are not expected to be liquidated for this purpose. The gain or loss on the valuation of the net exposure is just entered in the books; it does not generate any cash flow. On the other hand, the gain or loss on the forward contract is a real gain or loss in cash. If net exposure does not measure correctly the concept it intends to measure, the company will be trading real cash flow gains or losses for paper ones. Here lies the increasing aversion of many companies to hedges of translation exposure, preferring to hedge only transaction or conversion exposure.

The emphasis in this chapter has been on the similarity in hedging postures which are available under money market and forward exchange market opportunities. Firms may reach a decision on which instrument to use from a variety of factors.

1. There may be sharply different intermediary costs. Banks usually control the forward market whereas the money market is more openly competitive. However, to use the money market requires greater sophistication on the part of the treasurer. The forward market is the simpler alternative, for it merely involves obtaining one or more telephone bids on the forward contract rate and making the decision.

2. There may be different access routes. The foreign subsidiary does not have access to the domestic money markets of the parent or other subsidiaries. However, the parent, acting through subsidiaries, does have access to many markets, and this increases the opportunity for a less costly hedging option but it also increases the analysis required for a decision.

3. Borrowing and lending rates as well as spot rates differ, and often these differentials eliminate some of the benefits of the money market or forward market options. These differentials in part reflect the intermediary fee.

4. In terms of evidence to shareholders, we have noted that the money market activities are usually accomplished between balance sheet periods. If these accounts remain on the firm's balance sheet at the end of the accounting period, then the debt ratio of the firm is increased. This could alter the riskiness of the firm in the minds of the public, even though there

[13]For a more detailed presentation of the procedure and implications of protecting against exchange risks, see the discussion of covering in Chapter 6.

is an offsetting marketable security account. The forward contracts, on the other hand, are rarely revealed, and only appear in footnotes to the financial statements.

5. If there is no differential between forward and money market rates, it is reasonable for the firm to use the simplest and cheapest alternative, often the forward market. However, if differentials do exist (a particularly likely situation for major currencies, which have segmented domestic and external markets), then the firm should evaluate the costs of the alternatives, taking into account both the disequilibrium costs/gains and the intermediation costs.

Multinational treasurers must be aware of these alternatives, and they may use simple computer time-sharing systems and forecasts of future action to calculate which way to hedge. The final decision, of course, is related to the costs to the treasurer for the firm's using the two different markets.

SUMMARY

The corporation with assets and liabilities in more than one currency, together with cash flow surpluses and deficits in various currencies, faces a compound problem in foreign exchange rates. Initially, the effective interest rate may be considered as the nominal yield plus any foreign exchange gain or loss in a given currency. The *net effective yield* in any currency is thus related to the base currency used as a numeraire; two currencies depreciating in concert against all other currencies would create no foreign exchange gain or loss vis-à-vis each other. Under interest rate parity, the forward premium or discount of currencies should bring the *net effective interest differential* on various currencies to zero. In imperfect markets, especially when there are domestic and external markets for given currencies to which the parent or subsidiaries may not have equal access, the net effective yields on various currencies will differ. Standard discounting techniques can compute the yield for longer maturity issues when the currency revaluation takes place at various points in time.

Local interest rates in nominal terms combine a real rate and an anticipated inflation factor. Relative inflation vis-à-vis the rest of the world may result eventually in depreciation of the currency, but there is not a one-to-one mapping of relative inflation and depreciation in each time period.

There are three measures of exposure to exchange risk: transaction exposure, accounting exposure, and economic exposure. *Transaction exposure* involves the cash flows requiring conversion in the exchange markets. *Accounting exposure* is a measure of net assets in the balance sheet translated at current exchange rates. *Economic exposure* measures the impact of exchange fluctuations on *all* operational cash flows regardless of whether or not they require exchange transactions.

In measures of accounting exposure definitions of which accounts are translated at current rates and which are translated at historic or other rates are highly varied. Some of the variations have been the Current–Non-Current method (current assets less current liabilities), the Monetary/Non-Monetary method (current assets except inventory less current and long-term liabilities), and the Net Financial Asset method (current assets less current and long-term liabilities). Accounting rules now require the Temporal method for U.S. firms. In the United States, exchange gains and losses usually are a one-line entry in the income statement. In other nations, exchange gains or losses may be charged directly to the equity account with the assets/liabilities reduced, or gains or losses may be segmented as a reserve liability account with reduction in the equity account but no adjustment in the asset/liability accounts.

The actual *economic* exposure of the firm may be very different from the accounting exposure, depending on whether the present value of the future cash flow is increased or decreased as a result of revaluations.

Firms may reduce exposure by adjusting the exposed accounts through business operations with customers, suppliers, or other members of the same corporate family. The firms also may hedge in the forward or the money markets. When there is an expected foreign exchange loss, a gain may be created by operating in various currencies to offset the anticipated loss. It is particularly important in a hedging situation to correctly predict the relative movements of the currencies in order to have the expected gains and losses cancel each other. In a covering transaction, gains and losses will tend to match closely regardless of revaluation outcomes. Alternatively, the firm may simply lock in a known loss.

Questions

1. MNC Corp. will have a net liability position in Switzerland in the amount of 160 million Swiss francs (approximately $80 million).

Exchange rates	
Spot rate—Day 1	$0.50
Expected future spot rate	0.54
1-year forward	0.52
Interest rates—1 year	
United States	7.50%
Switzerland	2.00%

a. What is the premium or discount in the forward Swiss franc?

b. What would be the consequences of the Swiss net liability position if the forecast changes in the spot rate take place? What are the choices that MNC Corp. has to hedge its liability position in Switzerland?

c. What is the cost of each of these alternatives if the actual spot rate at the end of the period is as follows:

	Case A	*Case B*	*Case C*
Spot rate—Day 360	$0.50	$0.52	$0.55

d. What course of action would you advise MNC Corp. to take?

2. "The rough effective interest rate in a currency is the nominal interest rate for the period adjusted by any change in the value of the currency. This valuation is independent of the other currencies involved in the discussion." Is this true? Explain.

3. What is a quick definition of exposure that applies regardless of the accounting method used by the company? What are some of the different accounting exposure measurements? Which do you think is most realistic? Would your statement hold for all corporations or would it be specific to particular types of business? To particular countries?

4. Why might accounting exposure differ from economic exposure? Do you believe there exists a difference for most corporations? Why or why not?

5. Consolidated Corporation instructed its subsidiary in Devaluland to remit funds to the parent as soon as possible when a new devaluation was likely. This action was completed, and the parent was surprised to see that there was still a large foreign exchange loss on the funds, even though they were owned by the parent. How could this happen? Who should be held accountable?

6. What options are open to reduce exposure in a devaluation-prone subsidiary? How might each of these options affect the business and the management incentives of the subsidiary?

7. How can a firm, which covered itself completely in the forward market based on its expected balance sheet as of the end of the period, still have a foreign exchange loss to report?

8. To hedge an expected $90,000 loss in foreign exchange, a firm intends to borrow $2,000,000 in lira at 12% and invest it in the deutsche mark short-term market at 6%. How much of a depreciation of the lira is the firm expecting in order to cover the anticipated $90,000 loss?

Bibliography

Abdel-Malek, Talaat, "Managing Exchange Risks under Floating Rates: The Canadian Experience," *Columbia Journal of World Business,* Fall 1976, pp. 41-52.

Ankrom, Robert K., "Top-Level Approach to the Foreign Exchange Problem." *Harvard Business Review,* July-Aug. 1974, pp. 79-90.

Barnett, John S., "Corporate Foreign Exposure Strategy Formulations," *Columbia Journal of World Business,* Winter 1976, pp. 87-97.

Eiteman, David K. and Arthur I. Stonehill, *Multinational Business Finance.* Reading, Mass.: Addison-Wesley Publishing Co., 1973, Chs. 11, 12, and 13.

Foreign Exchange Exposure Management. New York: Chemical Bank, 1972.

Foreign Exchange Handbook for the Corporate Executive. New York: Brown Brothers Harriman and Co., 1970.

Fredrikson, E. Bruce, "On the Measurement of Foreign Income." *Journal of Accounting Research,* Autumn 1968, pp. 208-21.

Giddy, Ian H., "Exchange Risk: Whose View?" *Financial Management,* Summer 1977, pp. 23-33.

Heckerman, Donald, "The Exchange Risks of Foreign Operations." *Journal of Business,* Jan. 1972, pp. 42-48.

Liberman, Gail, "Two Ways to Measure Foreign Exchange Risk," *Euromoney,* June 1976, pp. 30-36.

Logue, Dennis E. and George S. Oldfield, "Managing Foreign Assets When Foreign Exchange Markets Are Efficient," *Financial Management,* Summer 1977, pp. 16-22.

Olstein, Robert A., "Devaluation and Multinational Reporting." *Financial Analysts Journal,* Sept.-Oct. 1973, pp. 65*ff.*

Prindl, Andreas R., *Foreign Exchange Risk.* New York: John Wiley and Sons, 1976.

Rodriguez, Rita M., "FASB No. 8: What Has It Done for Us?" *Financial Analysts Journal,"* March-April 1977, pp. 40-48.

Roll, Richard, and Bruno Solnik, "A Pure Foreign Exchange Asset Pricing Model." *Journal of International Economics,* May 1977, pp. 161-79.

Shapiro, Alan C., "Defining Exchange Risk," *Journal of Business,* January 1977, pp. 37-39.

Weston, J. Fred, and Bart W. Sorge, *International Managerial Finance.* Homewood, Ill.: Richard D. Irwin, Inc., 1972, Chs. 6 and 11.

Wheelwright, Steven C., "Applying Decision Theory to Improve Corporate Management of Currency-Exchange Risks." *California Management Review,* Summer 1975, pp. 41-49.

GREEN VALLEY CORPORATION

In the beginning of March 1977, Len Hamberg, Treasurer and Vice President of Green Valley Corporation, was considering how to refinance a recent acquisition done by the company's British subsidiary. Government regulations in the U.K., as well as general unrest in international monetary markets, made the decision particularly complicated. Mr. Hamberg had recently learned about the parallel loan, a new way of financing overseas operations, and he was now in the process of carefully analyzing this alternative.

BACKGROUND

Early in 1977, Green Valley Corporation was a U.S. manufacturer of pharmaceuticals. Founded in 1896, the company had experienced slow but steady growth during its first 50 years of operations, reaching a sales volume of $21 million at the end of the Second World War. The postwar rapid increase in world-wide demand for pharmaceutical products had a dramatic impact on the sales growth of Green Valley and the company increased its sales to $60 million in 1966 and $134 million in 1976. Profits of $21.2 million in 1976 represented an increase in earnings of 15% over 1975 and almost 300% over 1966. At the end of its most recent fiscal year, Green Valley Corporation and its consolidated subsidiaries had total assets of $135 million, of which $93 million was current. Current liabilities were $31 million, long-term debt was $33 million, and shareholder's common equity was $71 million.

Approximately 30% of the company's total sales were made directly to pharmaceutical houses, food processors and other industrial users. Fifty per cent, including prescription chemicals and ethical drugs for medicinal and household use as well as a small part of agricultural and veterinary products, were made directly to wholesale and retail distributors. The remaining 20% were sold overseas through Green Valley's European subsidiaries.

The corporate headquarters of Green Valley were located in Warren, Connecticut, and the production facilities were concentrated on the East Coast. These included both bulk manufacturing plants where the active ingredients in a given pharmaceutical product were produced in bulk form through fermentation or chemical synthesis, and pharmaceutical manufacturing plants where the bulk products were transformed into final dosage forms such as tablets, capsules, ointments, liquids and injectibles.

The Green Valley management team ascribed much of the company's past success to the heavy investments made in research and development programs during the 1960s. A great deal of laboratory R&D work was needed in order to insure a continuing flow of new products. In 1971, the company had several basic new drugs in various stages of clinical evaluation.

GREEN VALLEY U.K., LIMITED

In 1977, Green Valley had sales and manufacturing subsidiaries in five European countries. The oldest and largest of these was Green Valley U.K., Ltd., which was established in 1946 in order to secure the company's participation in the rapidly growing European postwar economy. Green Valley U.K. had originally been constrained in its operations to sales and marketing efforts throughout Western Europe but has subsequently entered into pharmaceutical manufacturing as the European market was deemed large enough to support such local production. The strategy had proven successful and the overseas operations had expanded into four more European countries by 1977, accounting for approximately 20% of total company sales.

THE ACQUISITION OF BEDALES CHEMICALS, LTD.

In December 1976, David Ballard, the Treasurer of Green Valley U.K., Ltd., had been informed by a London merchant banker that a small pharmaceutical company, Bedales Chemicals, Ltd., outside Rhondda in Wales, was for sale. Mr. Ballard decided to visit the company right away and returned two days later full of enthusiasm for the potential acquisition. As there were several other companies interested in acquiring Bedales, he immediately contacted Len Hamberg, the Treasurer and Financial Vice President of Green Valley Corporation in Warren, Connecticut, and after numerous telephone conversations and telegrams, the executive committee of the U.S. parent decided in early January 1977 to give Mr. Ballard authorization to buy Bedales Chemicals, Ltd., for a maximum price of $6 million in cash.

Meanwhile, in England, Mr. Ballard had been in contact with the London branch of the Gotham National Bank, a major New York bank, in order to discuss the financing of the acquisition. Mr. Ballard had realized the hasty nature of the transaction would not permit a permanent financial arrangement to be worked out until after the acquisition had been made. Furthermore, the European monetary scene was quite unstable in early 1977 and Mr. Ballard did not feel inclined to make any long-term financial commitments on the part of Green Valley U.K., Ltd., without full support from the U.S. parent.

It was thus with some kind of bridge financing in mind that Mr. Ballard approached the London representatives of the Gotham National Bank. Green Valley had been a client of Gotham for many years both in the U.S. and in the U.K. and Mr. Ballard knew that the bank would do whatever it could to meet his request. An arrangement was soon worked out whereby Gotham would extend a revolving Euro-dollar credit line to Green Valley U.K., provided that the obligation would be fully guaranteed by the U.S. parent. The maximum amount of the credit would be $5 million and the interest rate adjusted every six months to reflect changes in the Euro-dollar market for short-term money. The initial interest rate in January 1977 was to be 6 3/4%.

As it was a firm policy of Green Valley Corporation to finance all their foreign subsidiaries in local currency as much as possible in order to hedge against any exchange losses, Mr. Ballard had initially requested a credit line denominated in sterling. The bankers had, however, explained that it was virtually impossible for them to extend a sterling credit under the current Bank of England credit ceiling restrictions. Credit ceilings, they said, had been on and off in the U.K. during most of the sixties and the present regulations made it impossible for banks to increase their sterling credits above certain limits set by the

Bank of England. At present, the minimum lending rate (MLR) for short-term sterling was 12%, but such credit was simply not available to Green Valley under the Bank of England restrictions.

When Mr. Ballard received the authorization to buy Bedales Chemicals he activated the credit line from the Gotham National Bank and proceeded to acquire the company as a wholly owned subsidiary of Green Valley U.K., Ltd., for £2.5 million in cash. At the current exchange rate of $1.71/£, the acquisition had a value of $4.275 million. This amount was for plant and net working capital; no long-term debt was acquired as part of the purchase.

THE REFINANCING DECISION

Two weeks after the acquisition, Mr. Ballard was asked to come to the U.S. headquarters of Green Valley in order to discuss the integration of Bedales Chemicals into the company's other U.K. operations. As Mr. Ballard had anticipated, the refinancing question was given high priority.

Len Hamberg, the Corporate Treasurer, did not like having such a substantial dollar liability in a country that appeared so prone to continuous depreciation especially since he did not have any other sterling liability in addition to the U.K. subsidiary's. Also, the short-term character of the obligation ran contrary to his opinion that long-term assets should be financed with long-term capital. Finally, he considered the credit expensive, especially in light of the fact that he paid only 6 1/4% on his bank borrowings for Green Valley in the United States.

As soon as Mr. Ballard arrived in Warren, Mr. Hamberg decided to arrange a meeting in order to discuss the refinancing of the Bedales acquisition. Apart from Mr. Ballard and himself, Mr. Hamberg invited Ed Savage, a vice president from the international department of the Gotham National Bank in New York, and Thomas Rowley, a representative from the New York investment bank Norwich, Stap & Co., whose services Green Valley had used for many years both in the domestic and the international fields.

The following conversation took place during this meeting on February 2, 1977:

Len Hamberg: Well, as you all know, we have gotten together today to discuss the refinancing of the Bedales acquisition in England. Although I don't really like that revolving credit Dave got for us in London, I understand that this was the only solution considering the rush we were in to get the cash on the table to buy that company. I am also sure that your people at Gotham in London did whatever they could to help us out, Ed. In any case, the deal is all done now and today's problem is rather how to get long-term sterling into our U.K. sub instead of all hot dollars we are sitting on right now. What alternatives do we have, Ed?

Ed Savage: Thank you, Len. Well, if you want both sterling *and* long-term money I frankly cannot see any alternatives at all. I have already told you about the credit ceilings in London and although we possibly might give you sterling instead of Euro-dollars towards the end of this year, it can certainly never be of any maturity longer than one year. The market in sterling is just too tight to enable us to make any longer commitments. Also, if you were to get sterling it would be quite expensive. Today, for example, it would cost at least 12% as compared to the 6 3/4% you are currently paying on the dollar revolving credit.

Len Hamberg: Twelve per cent is certainly no alternative! As a matter of fact, I think that even the 6 3/4% we are paying right now is too expensive. Can you explain to me, Ed, why you charge 6 3/4% in London when we only pay 6 1/4% on our bank borrowings here in the U.S.? It's the same bank and the same currency, and don't tell me that the credit risk is any larger in the U.K. as we have given you full parent guarantee for the obligation.

Ed Savage: Same bank and same credit risk, I agree, but not the same currency. You see, the money you get here is what we call domestic dollars but the credit in London is in Euro-dollars, and that's different although the notes may look the same.

David Ballard: But what if Green Valley Corporation here in the U.S. borrows the money from Gotham in New York at the lower rates and then just sends it on to us in the U.K.?

Ed Savage: You can do that, of course. We could also work out a back-to-back loan, in which you deposit funds with us in New York and we lend dollars to your U.K. subsidiary. But that still leaves you with a dollar liability in the U.K. subsidiary.

Len Hamberg: But let's forget about the currency for a moment and look at the maturity instead. As you all know, I don't like to match up fixed assets with short liabilities. In this particular case I would prefer a maturity of six to eight years; this would permit us to keep our minds off this matter for a while without tying us up for too long which could hurt in case the cost of money should go down significantly. Would there be any way of doing this with bonds, Tom?

Thomas Rowley: Sure, Len, you can do anything with bonds! Seriously speaking, you can always get all the money you want with Euro-bonds, but I don't know if that is going to help you because you won't be able to get it in sterling and probably not in the maturity you wanted. The Bank of England would never allow you as a non-resident to sell sterling bonds inside the U.K. and as far as I know there is no Euro-sterling around. Even your U.K. subsidiary, as a non-resident-controlled foreign corporation, would not be allowed to use the domestic sterling market. If there were Euro-sterling available, you would have to obtain it by

Green Valley U.S. As to the maturity, six to eight years is what we would call medium-term money and that is pretty hard to find in the Euro-bond market today. It would cost around 15% or so, I think.

Len Hamberg: Well, that certainly wasn't encouraging! The revolving credit line we already have in London perhaps isn't that bad after all when you consider that. . . .

Thomas Rowley: Excuse me for interrupting you, Len, but I thought I should mention another way we might consider trying to refinance this deal. What I am thinking of is a so-called parallel loan. This seems to be a particularly attractive alternative in your case as I can see that you have a fair amount of excess liquid funds in your balance sheet. In order to arrange one of these transactions we would have to find a U.K. company that has a subsidiary that needs capital here in the U.S. and that would be willing to lend us the sterling we need in the U.K. In exchange for the sterling loan they give us in the U.K., we would lend a similar amount in dollars for the same maturity to their subsidiary over here and both companies would get the money they need without having any funds cross the Atlantic.

Len Hamberg: That sounds interesting–especially considering that we can make use of some of those liquid funds that we accumulated for a California acquisition that recently fell through. You are, however, working under the assumption that the U.K. company would turn to us to get dollars for their sub here in the U.S. What would stop them from just exporting the funds from the U.K. or perhaps getting a regular bank loan in New York from Ed's bank?

Thomas Rowley: Well, you see, the British guys are having a tough time in getting funds abroad. To simply export the funds from the U.K. is possible but very expensive indeed. They have to acquire so-called investment sterling which according to Bank of England regulations is the only currency they can legally bring out of the country. This investment currency is kept in very limited supply by the authorities and is traded in a special market where it currently commands about a 35% premium to buy–so you understand that they are inclined to try to find other solutions before they go ahead and pay 1.35 pounds just to get one pound to bring abroad!

In order for Ed's bank to lend them the money in the U.S., they would like a parent guarantee. The problem is that the U.K. firm needs Bank of England permission to pay on a guarantee, if it becomes necessary. Even then, the U.K. firm has to use that expensive investment sterling, which really makes the guarantee an undesirable aspect of borrowing for the U.K. parent.

Len Hamberg: Tell me, what would the cost be on a loan like this?

Thomas Rowley: As you would have both a payable and receivable in equal amounts, the only thing that really matters is the spread between the interest rates on these two. I could imagine that the U.S. company would have to pay a little more on its payable than it gets on its receivable, say 2 1/2% as the sterling currently is more expensive than the dollar.

Len Hamberg: And what would the Bank of England say about this? Wouldn't the foreign sub still have to have a parent guarantee in order to get a dollar loan?

Thomas Rowley: Not necessarily. You see, included in these loan agreements is always a set-off clause that normally makes parent guarantees superfluous. This clause states that in case of default by either party, principal and interest may be offset against the repayment obligation, or in other words, you can use the payable as security for your receivable. Even if the clause is not written for some regulatory reasons, everyone knows the way the arrangement works.

Len Hamberg: This really seems to add up to a very interesting alternative, Tom, but would you also say that I could get the maturity I want?

Thomas Rowley: That's really a question of negotiations. If you find a U.K. company that wants to go along with your terms, you can put together almost any kind of parallel deal you like.

Len Hamberg: Yes, I realize that what is clearly most important in this kind of a deal is to find the right company in England. I think we know enough about the characteristics of a parallel loan arrangement to realize that it could be a very interesting alternative in refinancing our acquisition of Bedales Chemicals. The next step will have to be to identify the British party in the deal and to negotiate mutually acceptable terms. Do you think that Norwich, Stap & Co. could help us there, Tom?

Thomas Rowley: We would be delighted to, Len. I'll get in touch with our people in London right away and ask them to start looking for a suitable partner for you. I know that you'd like to get this refinancing done the sooner the better, and I'll get back to you with a memorandum outlining the initial negotiations with the U.K. party.

Four weeks after his meeting with Mr. Ballard and the two bankers from New York, Mr. Hamberg received from Norwich, Stap & Co. the memorandum reproduced in the appendix to this case. In the meanwhile, Mr. Hamberg had collected some data on the current state of international financial markets (Exhibit 1).

EXHIBIT 1. Selected Data on International Financial Markets, 1974–1977 (in per cent, end of month)

	1974	1975	1976			1977	
	Dec.	Dec.	Oct.	Nov.	Dec.	Jan.	Feb.
COMMERCIAL BANK DEPOSIT RATES							
United States-3 month	9.25	5.50	5.10	4.70	4.70	4.95	4.85
United Kingdom-3 month	12.25	10.50	15.13	14.50	14.13	11.94	11.13
Euro-dollars-3 month	10.19	5.81	5.31	5.13	5.00	5.25	5.13
Euro-dollars-6 month	10.19	6.63	5.75	5.31	5.38	5.81	5.63
COMMERCIAL BANK LENDING RATES TO PRIME BORROWERS							
United States	10.25	7.25	6.50	6.25	6.00	6.25	6.25
United Kingdom	13.00	12.00	15.00	15.00	15.00	14.00	12.50
Euro-dollars-3 month	11.32	6.69	5.94	5.63	5.50	5.75	5.63
DOMESTIC CORPORATE BOND YIELDS, LONG-TERM ISSUES							
United States	9.25	8.55	8.15	7.90	7.35	8.00	8.10
United Kingdom	19.50	14.90	16.91	16.49	15.76	14.64	14.82
EURO-DOLLAR BOND YIELDS, LONG-TERM ISSUES							
Issued by U.S. Companies	9.35	8.52	7.82	7.76	7.39	7.63	7.72
EXCHANGE RATE ($/£)							
Spot		2.021	1.589	1.654	1.701	1.715	1.714
6 months forward		1.975	1.485	1.572	1.622	1.661	1.653

SOURCE: WORLD FINANCIAL MARKETS, Morgan Guaranty Trust Company of New York; BUSINESS INTERNATIONAL MONEY REPORT, various issues.

Mr. Hamberg had also received a telephone call from Julian DeGray, senior partner of the Warren, Connecticut, accounting firm, DeGray, Erland & Bach. This firm had handled Green Valley's accounting for many years and Mr. Hamberg was often on the phone with Mr. DeGray.

Julian DeGray: Good morning, Len! I'm calling you about this proposed parallel loan with Abbotsholme Assurance Company. We were just thinking about the consolidation of the statements of your foreign subsidiaries and, to put it frankly, I don't think we ever handled one of these parallel deals before. I talked to a friend of mine at Arthur Andersen yesterday and he said that his clients that had done these transactions—including a major drug company by coincidence—usually netted the two transactions so that neither the receivable nor the payable showed up in the balance sheet. It would of course be nice if we could do that too, especially considering that you want to improve your bond rating in time for that issue you are planning this coming fall.

Len Hamberg: Yes, I have been thinking about that myself and it would certainly look much better if we could leave the deal outside the books all together. But I suppose that we will have to mention it in a footnote at least?

Julian DeGray: Look, Len, I think this entire question is important enough to call for an ad hoc meeting. Would it be all right if I bring along one of our whiz-kids and stop by at your office next week?

Len Hamberg: Sure, Julian, I'd be happy to have you come. In the meantime I'll bring some of my material together and do my homework! See you then.

Mr. Hamberg then sat down to carefully review the parallel loan proposal in light of the other alternatives and the market data. He thought it was particuularly important to estimate the actual cost of the parallel financing as compared to the other alternatives discussed during the meeting in early February. Also, monetary markets were still very unstable and he was not quite sure what the impact of a possible parity change between the dollar and the sterling would be on the parallel loan.

These questions would have to be answered one way or another before the next day when Len Hamberg was to give his final recommendation on the refinancing of the British subsidiary to the executive committee on Green Valley Corporation.

Appendix: Memorandum to Green Valley Corporation

MEMORANDUM

To: Mr. Len Hamberg, Treasurer and Financial Vice President, Green Valley Corporation, Warren, Connecticut

From: Thomas Rowley, Partner
Norwich, Stap & Co., New York, New York

Regarding: The partial refinancing of Green Valley U.K., Limited, through a parallel loan transaction.

The London representatives of Norwich, Stap & Co. have been able to identify a U.K. corporation, Abbotsholme Assurance Company Limited, that is willing to participate in a parallel loan transaction with Green Valley Corporation.

Abbotsholme is a U.K. insurance company with total assets of £355 million and total after-tax profits of £9.1 million in 1976. The company established a wholly-owned subsidiary, Abbotsholme U.S. Insurance, Inc., in 1965 in Newark, New Jersey, and their U.S. insurance operations have been growing rapidly since then. The Board of Directors of the Abbotsholme parent organization in the U.K. made a policy decision toward the end of 1976 that their U.S. operations should be expanded into the real estate financing area. A few months later, Abbotsholme Properties, Inc., was founded as a wholly-owned subsidiary to Abbotsholme U.S. Insurance, Inc., in order to coordinate this expansion. The U.S. operations of Abbotsholme are already heavily leveraged and the U.S. parent has found it increasingly difficult to transfer equity funds from the U.K. to finance the expansion of their U.S. subsidiary without running into restrictive Bank of England regulations.

We approached Abbotsholme in the U.K. with our outline for a parallel financing and the corporate treasurer, Alan Weyl, immediately showed a great deal of interest in the proposal. Tentative negotiations have led to the following terms which we feel are very close to the most favorable that Green Valley will be able to obtain:

	Dollar Loan	*Sterling Loan*
BORROWER	Abbotsholme U.S. Insurance, Inc.	Green Valley U.K., Ltd.
LENDER	Green Valley Corporation	Abbotsholme Assurance Company, Ltd.
FORM	Loan Agreement and Promissory Note	Loan Agreement and Promissory Note
PRINCIPAL AMOUNT[a]	U.S. $6 million	£3.5 million
MATURITY[b]	9 years, 360 days	9 years, 360 days

	Dollar Loan	*Sterling Loan*
PRICE AND YIELD[c]	100% to yield 9 1/2% p.a.	100% to yield 12% p.a.
SINKING FUND	None	None
PRE-PAYMENT	None	None
DEFAULT PROVISIONS[d]	Without parent company guarantee but with set-off convenants in case of default.	Without parent company guarantee but with set-off convenants in case of default.
PARITY CHANGE PROVISION[e]	Any time during the life of the agreement when the value of sterling in relation to the dollar decreases by 6% and remains at or below this value for a continuous period of 30 days, the dollar borrower, upon notice, is to reduce the outstanding principal of the dollar loan by paying the dollar lender an amount equal to 6% times the outstanding principal of the dollar loan. (A similar clause existed for the event of dollar depreciation.)	
BANK OF ENGLAND	Abbotsholme Assurance Company, Ltd., has approval for borrowings by Abbotsholme U.S. Insurance, Inc.	Green Valley Corporation will need exchange control approval for sterling borrowings by its U.K. subsidiary.
FEES AND EXPENSES[f]	For the account of Green Valley Corporation.	For the account of Abbotsholme Assurance Company, Ltd.

[a]Abbotsholme is flexible to the amount of the transaction. Green Valley should probably try to borrow as much as Bank of England will allow them. Dollar loan and sterling loan will be of exactly the same amounts at the spot rate of the date of issue.

[b]Abbotsholme insists on minimum maturity of 7 years. Maturity should be kept below 10 years as stamp tax of 1/2 of 1% is levied by Bank of England on all U.K. debt obligations running 10 years or longer. Renewal options can be negotiated.

[c]Abbotsholme will only consider a fixed interest rate over the life of the obligation and argues that market conditions entitle them to a favorable spread of at least 2-1/2%. Twelve per cent on sterling loan equals the minimum lending rate (U.K. equivalent of Prime Rate) and is the minimum interest rate permitted by Bank of England on the sterling part of a parallel transaction.

[d]Green Valley's security for its dollar receivable is its sterling payable. In case Abbotsholme would default on either interest or principal, Green Valley is entitled to withhold interest as well as total oustanding amount of the sterling payable until such default has been recovered.

[e]Assume sterling is at $1.700 and the loan involves $1,000,000, or £588,235. If sterling depreciates by 6% to $1.598, then the U.S. borrower of pounds has a $940,000 loan. The U.K. borrower of dollars has the same $1,000,000 loan. To restore the balance, the U.K. firm with the larger loan will reduce its loan balance by 6%, for a dollar value of the payment of $60,000.

[f]Total legal fees for arranging Green Valley's part of the transaction will be approximately $10,000. Norwich, Stap & Co. expects to retain a fee equivalent to 3/4 of 1% of the principal of the loan.

MARWICK HOME PRODUCTS, INC.

On December 27, 1971, Mr. George Rosenthal, Treasurer of the International Division of Marwick Home Products (MHP), had four days left to reach a decision regarding the company's exposure in pound sterling. Mr. Rosenthal's position was summarized in the following quote.

> For the sixty years that MHP has been operating in the international market, our policy has been to keep our exposure to foreign exchange risks at a minimum. To a large extent, we have accomplished this by financing our subsidiaries with funds raised in the countries where they are located. There are times, however, when borrowing in foreign markets is not sufficient to protect us against currency devaluations. In these cases, other means have to be used—some of which can be very expensive if our judgment proves to be wrong.
>
> In the case of the pound sterling, in spite of our efforts to borrow as much as possible in the United Kingdom, we found the size of our exposure in this currency at the end of 1970 to be too high. In addition, we thought that the possibility of a devaluation in the pound vis-à-vis the dollar during 1971 was significant. So we decided to hedge this risk by buying one-year forward commitments to sell pounds at a discount. Well, a year has now gone by, the pound has not been devalued, but the U.S. dollar has, and we have to go to the market to buy pounds at a high price to fulfill our contract.
>
> The most interesting part of this story, however, is that the present situation is roughly similar to the one we faced last year. The decision to hedge our exposure in pounds at that time has proved to be expensive, but it is not clear to me that we should not take the same course of action now. At the present time, the pound is not in the spotlight of international financial markets, but I do not think England will be able to afford the present exchange rate through the coming year.

If the forward market route to hedging in pound sterling were used again, the options at this point appeared to be: (1) Buy forward contracts to deliver pounds in a year, (2) leave the exposure situation uncovered through next year, and (3) do nothing now, but if the risks of a pound devaluation increase, then sell pounds forward at that time. The previous trading day, the price of bank transfers in sterling had closed at the following prices: $2.5485 for spot transactions, $2.5550 for thirty-day contracts, and $2.5560 for ninety-day contracts.

The International Operations

MHP manufactured a wide variety of household products—deodorants, toothpaste, hair spray, detergents, window cleaners, plastic storage bags, and so on. In 1971 its operations were divided into five major regions: United States, Europe, Africa, Western Hemisphere, and the Far East. The four non-U.S.

regions reported to Mr. Johnson, President of Marwick Home Products International and Corporate Vice President in charge of international operations. Mr. Rosenthal also reported to Mr. Johnson.

By year-end 1970 the firm's total consolidated assets were $650 million, of which $432 million were current, $197 million were fixed, and the balance miscellaneous items. Current liabilities were $190 million, long-term and other liabilities were $83 million, and shareholder's equity was $377 million.

The present organization extended through fifty countries and had developed during the previous fifty years. MHP followed a strategy of cautious penetration of each country. It first exported to a country; then, as the market in the new country expanded, MHP established a distributor in the country. Finally, when the market expanded sufficiently, MHP would start manufacturing in the new country. Once the company decided to undertake manufacturing operations in a country, the whole process was done there. No transfer of goods in process existed among the various subsidiaries because, for the most part, the preparation of the final goods was a one-step production process which was best performed in a single location.

All MHP subsidiaries were 100% owned by the parent company. There were two rationales for this strategy: the zeal in protecting the company's trademark names and the flexibility of sole ownership. The pressures for joint ventures from the host country had been resisted even in the case of Japan where the company preferred to be classified as an "unvalidated company" (unable to repatriate earnings) rather than to share ownership with Japanese interests.

Financial Management

MHP's decision to start operations in a new country was based on the analysis of market potential and production costs in the specific country. The decision of the size and form of the parent's investment was then guided by two general principles: (1) Limit capital investment to the minimum that will be acceptable to the host country and to its financial institutions and (2) use as much local borrowing as possible. From here on, the company gave subsidiaries management freedom, subject to financial controls.

The Budget. The budget was the instrument by which MHP controlled its subsidiaries. Every year around September each subsidiary submitted two detailed budgets for the following year: one for operations and one for capital expenditures. To make the budgets for subsidiaries from different countries comparable, the estimates were converted into U.S. dollars. The exchange rates used in these conversions were the quoted rates (not the official rates) at the end of the month. These quoted rates were adjusted to reflect the parent's evaluation of the strength of the currency in the subsidiary's country, thus anticipating the impact of currency devaluations.

Profits Remittance Policy. The general policy of MHP regarding remittances was to repatriate an average of 65% of annual foreign profits, subject to modifications depending on the subsidiary's ability to pay and on its requirement for funds. The form that these remitted funds took was subject to the negotiations between the company and the host country when the subsidiary was first established. The company tried to have these remittances take the form of royalties to the extent allowed by the host company and to use dividends as a complement to reach the desired 65%. The emphasis on royalties was on two accounts. First, very often royalties were considered business expenses by the host country and were therefore tax deductible. Second, in cases of foreign exchange controls on remittances, it was more likely to get permission from the host country to obtain foreign exchange to pay for royalties than to pay for dividends to the parent company.

A new subsidiary was expected to have an initial period of three to five years when it was not possible to remit funds to the parent company. But once it started remitting profits, it was expected to continue doing so—even if it involved borrowing in the local country—unless it had a heavy program of expenditures.

Parent-Subsidiary Business Relationships. After the headquarter's office approved the subsidiary's budget for the following year, most business transactions between parent and subsidiary were conducted at arm's length. These transactions were largely restricted to the sale of some special raw materials by the parent company to the subsidiary. Such sales were billed in dollars at standard cost plus a surcharge to cover handling costs. The debt was expected to be paid as promptly as possible according to industry terms—usually 30 days.

This arm's length policy also applied to the financing of the subsidiaries. It was the parent's policy not to lend money to a subsidiary for its operations. Moreover, there were virtually no lateral relationships; one subsidiary did not borrow from another. Once the subsidiary was established, the financing of new projects had to be done from retained earnings and local borrowing power. If needs for funds exceeded this limit and the local market was willing to provide the funds, permission had to be obtained from the board to increase the borrowings.

Management of the Foreign Exchange Position

MHP computed the exposure to foreign exchange risk in a given currency by subtracting fixed assets from the subsidiary's net worth. Adjustments for current assets and liabilities denominated in U.S. dollars then were made. In this method, long-term debt, to the extent it did not apply to specific fixed assets, and inventories were valued at current exchange rates. The rationale for treating inventories on a current basis was that, although on some occasions prices of goods in inventory could be increased to take into account the new exchange rates, more often than not price-control measures in the country made this impossible. Long-term liabilities were translated at current rates except when these liabilities had been created to finance the purchase of specific plant and equipment. In the latter case both the asset and the debt were translated at historical rates. In case of devaluations, when exposed assets exceeded exposed liabilities, debt in terms of dollars was overstated for a while until payment in the depreciated currency took place and a gain in exchange was realized. This gain was used to offset the unrealized exchange losses that year. That is, foreign exchange gains were reported only when they were realized. However, foreign exchange losses were reported as soon as they were incurred, and they appeared on the income statement as extraordinary items. (In computing taxes, both losses and gains were recognized when realized.)

Inventory and accounts receivable combined averaged about 20–25% of sales. When the parent company believed a change in the value of the foreign currency was about to occur, it tried to influence the size of these accounts. Another MHP policy was to keep the cash account at a minimum consistent with the size of overdraft facilities available to the subsidiary and the schedule for cash payments in the subsidiary. When sizable amounts of cash were left in the accounts of the subsidiary because of an impending payment, this cash was invested in short-term securities in the local country until payment was due. Under no condition was the subsidiary allowed to invest these funds in another country. To the extent that there was some question about the possibility of devaluation of the subsidiary's local currency, remittances were covered in the forward market. To the extent that an upvaluation of the local currency was possible, an attempt was made to delay the remittance of funds as long as possible.

Control of the operations in foreign exchange was exercised by regular computations for each subsidiary of the cost of borrowing in local markets compared with the alternative of being financed from headquarters. The after-tax interest cost in the subsidiary plus the actual exchange losses incurred were compared with the cost of money after taxes to the parent plus the exchange losses under this second course of action. The performance of the foreign exchange operations as measured by this system had been highly successful. The exchange losses saved in every devaluation had proved more than enough to compensate for the higher interest rates paid in the local borrowing market. As one can see in Exhibit 1, the average loans in local currencies held in the various subsidiaries for particular time periods were computed (column 1) together with the total exchange losses realized in that period (column 2). Had these loans been completed by the parent and submitted to the subsidiary, then the loans would have been in dollars. When the local currencies on the average devalued relative to the dollar, then the foreign exchange losses shown by the parent would have been greater under this policy, because the net exposure in nondollar currencies would have been larger in the absence of local currency loans. Under this policy, the exchange losses can be determined, and the savings in avoiding these losses (versus column 2) are reported in column 3. The local interest cost on the loans is in column 4, and the dollar interest cost had the home loans been used are in column 5. Finally, the firm's computation of the net savings by using foreign loans is shown in column 6 and is the sum of the exchange loss reduction (column 3) and the dollar interest costs which are avoided (column 5) less the local loan interest cost (column 4).

The British Subsidiary

As of late, the company's growth in England was similar to growth in the United States; although not exceptional, it was commensurate with the growth in the economy. Exhibit 2 presents the balance sheet of Marwick's British subsidiary for selected years.

Before taking a final course of action, Mr. Rosenthal decided to review once more the information he had on the British economy and on the stability

EXHIBIT 1. Marwick Home Products, Inc.: Net Reduction in Exchange Loss Due to Loans (thousands of dollars)

Period	*Average Loans (1)*	*Recorded Exchange Losses (2)*	*Exchange Loss Reduction Due to Loans (3)*	*Interest Cost on Loan (Net)[a] (4)*	*Cost of Money to Replace Loans (Net)[a,b] (5)*	*Net Reduction (6) (3) + (5) − (4)*
1/1/48–12/31/52	12,366	4,303	1,582	1,413	927	1,095
1/1/53–12/31/57	27,136	5,581	4,558	4,125	2,036	2,469
1/1/58–12/31/62	41,181	6,408	8,129	7,415	3,089	3,803
1/1/63–12/31/67	44,702	3,155	2,075	8,698	5,301	(1,322)
Total	31,485	19,447	16,344	21,651	11,353	6,045
1/1/68–12/31/68	42,901	57	100	1,853	1,287	(466)
1/1/69–12/31/69	54,084	176	2,016	2,430	1,840	1,426
Total 22 Years	33,543	19,680	18,460	25,934	14,480	7,006

[a] Net after taxes.

[b] 1.5% net for 1948/62   2.7% net for 1966
1.8% net for 1963   3.0% net for 1967
2.1% net for 1964   3.0% net for 1968
2.25% net for 1965   3.4% net for 1969

EXHIBIT 2. Marwick–U.K. Balance Sheets as of December 31, 1965-1971 (thousands of pounds sterling)

	Assets			
	1965	*1967*	*1969*	*1971*
Current assets				
Cash	£ 858	£1,846	£1,615	£ 184
Receivables (trade)	1,362	983	980	1,627
Intercompany accounts	339	170	267	493
Prepayments	none	288	116	126
Inventories	2,760	2,460	2,085	2,210
Total current assets	£5,319	£5,747	£5,063	£4,640
Net fixed assets	3,395	3,440	3,570	3,790
Investment in non-consolidated subsidiaries	102	102	102	102
TOTAL ASSETS	£8,816	£9,289	£8,735	£8,532

	Liabilities and Equity			
	1965	*1967*	*1969*	*1971*
Current liabilities				
Bank overdrafts	£ none	£2,298	£ 23	£1,000
Accounts payable (trade)	1,742	1,595	1,795	2,130
Intercompany accounts	73	132	102	89
Miscellaneous	125	none	none	none
Accrued taxes	1,109	1,101	719	192
Total current liabilities	£3,049	£5,126	£2,639	£3,411
Noncurrent liabilities				
Deferred taxes	819	650	1,090	681
Shareholder's equity				
Issued capital	1,330	1,330	1,330	1,330
Earned surplus	3,618	2,183	3,676	3,110
Total shareholders' equity	£4,948	£3,513	£5,006	£4,440
TOTAL LIABILITIES AND EQUITY	£8,816	£9,289	£8,735	£8,532

of the pound. A few days before, the Group of Ten key industrial nations had put an end to the period of floating rates initiated by President Nixon the previous August 15. In a policy designed to curb U.S. inflation, increase employment, and control the balance of payments, the Nixon administration had cut the U.S. dollar loose from the historic $35-an-ounce gold price. In the four months that world currencies were allowed to float before fixed "central rates" were agreed upon on December 18, the pound had been subject to continuous inflows of speculative funds. These inflows, which brought the British reserves to record levels, continued unabated in spite of the Bank of England's decision to slash its discount rate by a full percentage point to 5%. In the week that the pound had been working under the new fixed rates, its price had remained well within the wider bands now allowed. The feeling in the financial markets appeared to be one of optimism for the pound, at least in the short run. However, some economists did not have such a sanguine view and thought that the pound would not be able to hold its new price for any length of time. These views were reflected in an editorial in *The Economist* (see Exhibit 3). Additional basic economic data for the United Kingdom are contained in Exhibits 4 and 5.

EXHIBIT 3. "The Dirty Fixing"

To help the dollar, sterling is now probably overvalued again, but the DM is almost certainly undervalued. Fortunately, upward pressure on the DM is likely to bring us back to dirty floating once more.

The most important point about the new pattern of world exchange rates is that it will not last for long. That is why all statesmen are having to say the opposite very loudly. President Nixon called it "the most significant monetary agreement in the history of the world." The Group of Ten's communiqué talked about "assuring a new and lasting equilibrium in the international economy," although, unless one makes the odd assumption that all rates of inflation between all countries will always be equal ever after as from midnight last Saturday, "lasting equilibrium" and fixed exchange rates have to be a contradiction in terms. Mr. Barber said that during last weekend's bargaining Britain's competitive position had been preserved. Actually, Britain's exports have been made dearer than they were last week in every important country except Japan and France (which do not buy many of our exports); in such main markets as America, South Africa and, probably, Australia, British exports are being made much dearer.

Since August 15, the Americans have won a bigger depreciation of the dollar than anybody outside America thought possible then, and they have won it mainly at the expense of the Japanese and the "weaker Europeans" (such as Britain, France, and Italy). Incredibly, the DM and Swiss franc have been devalued against us. This is shown by column 3 of the accompanying table. . . . The argument that Britain has maintained its competitive position comes from citing the change since the old May 1 parities, shown in column 2 of the table; but by May those parities were already in total disequilibrium, which is why the DM and guilder floated up (and the Swiss franc was hoisted up). What the ten ministers have managed to do in Europe is to march us back from last August's near equilibrium towards May's disequilibrium, so that all the reequilibrating panics that were necessary in May will slowly become necessary all over again.

		Percentage Upvaluation Against the Dollar		
	(1) New Parity	*(2) Since May 1*	*(3) Since August 13*	*(4) Since December 17*
Yen	308	+16.9	+15.9	+1.9
Sterling	2.6057	+ 8.6	+ 7.8	+3.0
French francs	5.1157	+ 8.6	+ 7.8	+7.8
Liras	581.5	+ 7.5	+ 6.2	+3.3
Swiss francs	3.84	+13.9	+ 5.9	+1.0
Deutsche marks	3.223	+13.6	+ 5.1	+1.1

The main trading consequence is that the German and American balances of payments are likely to do much better in the period ahead than anybody could previously have supposed.

Back to a Dollar Gap?

There may be more reason to worry about the coming improvement in America's external payments. Although the top ten finance ministers and central bank governors hate to

EXHIBIT 3. "The Dirty Fixing" (cont)

recognize this, the equilibrium position for the world economy is that America should be running a balance of payments deficit of a quite easily specifiable amount: namely, the amount of deficit where it is just pumping out into the world the number of dollars that other countries want to hold newly in their reserves. Just before August, America was running a bigger deficit than this. Now it may run a deficit smaller than this world equilibrium level, and a greedy lion's share of the reduced number of dollars that it pumps out is likely to be gobbled up by Germany. The danger is that other countries, feeling indigent in their dollar reserves, may then start to squeeze their internal economies or to impose restrictions on their trade. Contrary to the guff spoken by the top ten finance ministers and central bank governors last weekend, there is obviously a slightly greater risk of this happening under this week's regime of dirtily fixed exchange rates than there was under last week's regime of dirtily floating rates.

Fortunately, there are two reasons why these gloomy possibilities are not really likely to lead to an unnecessary world recession or trade war. First, although the top ten finance ministers and bank governors believed themselves last weekend when they said that they were restoring "stability" by returning to nominally pegged exchange rates, they are now happily likely to unpeg them pretty sharply rather than meet future balance of payments troubles by stopping all economic growth.

The second principal hope of the optimists is that the drain on world liquidity through a new dollar gap could be staunched by a major extension of the use of Special Drawing Rights in the International Monetary Fund. . . . Unfortunately, the recent experience in the Group of Ten does raise doubts about whether intelligent settlements can be made on complicated matters. . . . When all the experts from all the countries were present at these meetings of the Ten, too many experts had too many different points of view for the discussions to proceed sensibly; when, as in the Rome meeting of the Ten, the ministers and governors turned the experts out into the corridors, there was too inexpert a majority among the twenty gentlemen left in the room for sensible discussions to start. After fixing exchange rates at the wrong levels, the Ten's comminuqué last weekend set out this agenda for the coming talks.

. . .

It was agreed that attention should be directed to the appropriate monetary means and divisions of responsibilities for defending stable exchange rates and for ensuring a proper degree of convertibility of the system; to the proper role of gold, of reserve currencies, and of Special Drawing Rights in the operation of the system; to the appropriate volume of liquidity; to reexamination of the permissible margins of fluctuation around established exchange rates, and other means of establishing a suitable degree of flexibility; and to other measures dealing with movements of liquid capital. It is recognized that decisions in each of these areas are closely linked. . . .

Is there any way in which the international monetary system can be rescued from the ministrations of muddled meetings of this kind? Probably only by restoring the ministration to the market. Under the admirable system of dirty floating, into which the so-called currency crisis of last August precipitated us, the value of each currency was set at whatever the market was willing to pay for it—except that nearly all individual governments intervened to cheapen their currencies in dollar terms, by just sufficiently enough to enable the Americans to run the desirable level of deficit where they were pumping out as many dollars as the outside world wanted to hold. It is a pity that the ten countries have spent so many meetings rescuing us from it; luckily they have done the job so very botchedly, chiefly by making the mark too cheap, that their new system is exceedingly unlikely to stand.

. . .

SOURCE: THE ECONOMIST, December 25, 1971.

EXHIBIT 4. United Kingdom: Balance of Payments (not seasonally adjusted, millions-U.S. dollars)

	1965	1966	1967	1968	1969	1970	1971	1971 First Quarter	1971 Second Quarter	1971 Third Quarter	1971 Fourth Quarter
A. Goods, Services (net), and Unrequited Transfers (net)											
Exports f.o.b.	13,558	14,582	14,227	15,122	16,946	18,926	21,654	4,742	5,589	5,445	5,878
Imports f.o.b. (excluding U.S. military aircraft)	-14,140	-14,627	-15,359	-16,368	-17,138	-18,909	-20,921	-5,071	-5,263	-5,064	-5,523
Payments for U.S. military aircraft	-33	-115	-270	-261	-146	—	—	—	—	—	—
Trade balance	-615	-160	-1,402	-1,507	-338	17	733	-329	326	381	355
Transportation	67	85	121	214	50	-139	-60	-91	-5	51	-15
Travel	-272	-218	-109	25	84	115	64	19	17	-32	60
Investment income	1,238	1,064	1,015	760	1,202	1,176	1,263	370	398	342	153
Government services	-549	-594	-532	-465	-696	-753	-818	-166	-197	-225	-230
Other goods and services	501	585	792	866	1,311	1,572	1,691	446	409	408	428
Private transfers	-90	-137	-161	-231	-132	-108	-97	-14	-26	-29	-28
Government transfers	-495	-304	-517	-429	-425	-413	-453	-137	-106	-110	-100
Total	-215	121	-793	-766	1,056	1,467	2,323	98	816	786	623
B. Long-Term Capital, n.i.e.											
Private investment (net)											
In United Kingdom	616	745	979	1,392	1,615	1,774	2,818	1,063	686	511	558
Abroad	-991	-848	-1,267	-1,764	-1,601	-1,826	-1,851	-535	-506	-452	-358
Official long-term capital											
Intergovernmental loans (net)	-185	-172	-97	-15	-115	-428	-461	-94	-91	-78	-198
Other	-53	-53	-48	55	-120	-62	-213	-14	-12	-7	-180
Total	-613	-328	-433	-332	-221	-542	293	420	77	-26	-178
C. Total (A plus B)	-828	-207	-1,226	-1,098	835	925	2,616	518	893	760	445
D. Net Errors and Omissions	87	-72	510	-193	960	274	864	706	-46	-274	478
E. Exchange Equilization Account Losses on Forward Commitments	—	—	-252	-602	—	—	—				

F. Short-Term Capital, n.i.e.											
Nonmonetary sectors' capital—											
Trade credit	202	-320	-92	-62	-413	-509	-672	-103	-288	42	-323
U.K. banks' net liabilities in overseas sterling area currencies	20	-126	68	-110	-5	-17	-34	-14	7	-27	—
U.K. banks' net liabilities in non-sterling area currencies											
Euro-dollar financing of new private investment abroad	25	42	118	422	173	454	583	84	276	98	125
Other	-174	-490		-338	-259	696	628	132	96	22	378
Sterling liabilities other than to central monetary institutions											
Sterling area countries	462	81	7	-256	-115	391	945	163	34	237	511
Other countries	-120	-512	-337	-930	-12	192	873	14	-19	352	526
International institutions	-17	37	-43	38	—	—	—	—	—	—	—
Other	—	—	—	—	-209	175	351	300	-65	191	-75
Total	398	-1,288	-297	-1,236	-840	1,382	2,674	576	41	915	1,142
G. Total (C through F)	-343	-1,567	-1,247	-3,129	955	2,581	6,154	1,800	888	1,401	2,065
H. Allocations of SDRs	—	—	—	—	—	410	300	300	—	—	—
I. Total (G plus H)	—	—	—	—	955	2,991	6,454	2,100	888	1,401	2,065
J. Official Monetary Movements (increase in assets—)											
Gold reserves	-129	325	650	-182	3	122	574	226	319	26	3
SDRs	—	—	—	—	—	-266	-325	-216	-6	-65	-38
Convertible currency reserves	-560	465	245	456	-108	-156	-3,837	-499	-617	-1,355	-1,366
Other claims	—	—	—	—	—	—	-2,109	-500	-1,200	400	-809
Use of fund credit	1,391	-42	-851	1,262	-34	-412	-1,332	-688	-22	-622	—
Gold deposit liabilities to IMF	8	35	1	-3	-2	-9	-4	-1	-2	-1	—
Official liabilities in foreign currency	-202	39	424	43	-146	-360	—	—	—	—	—
Sterling counterpart of official borrowing	510	786	1,291	1,852	-1,458	-2,427	-957	-957	—	—	—
Other sterling liabilities to central monetary institutions											
Sterling area countries	-456	-75	-333	-73	900	507	1,099	509	475	185	-70
Other countries	-219	34	-180	-226	-110	10	437	26	165	31	215
Total	343	1,567	1,247	3,129	-955	-2,991	-6,454	-2,100	-888	-1,401	-2,065

SOURCE: Bank of England, MONTHLY BULLETIN.

EXHIBIT 5. United Kingdom: Basic Financial Data

	1965	1966	1967	1968	1969	1970	1971 I	1971 II	1971 III	1971 IV	1971 Aug.	1971 Sept.	1971 Oct.	1971 Nov.
Exchange Rates				US DOLLARS PER POUND STERLING: END OF A PERIOD										
US Dollar: Spot Rate	2.8025	2.7900	2.4069	2.3844	2.4006	2.3938	2.4169	2.4194	2.4850	2.5525	2.4525	2.4850	2.4912	2.4938
Forward Rate	2.7950	2.7850	2.3900	2.3606	2.3975	2.3881	2.4012	2.4138	2.4969	2.5656	2.4619	2.4969	2.4875	2.5031
London Gold Price (US$ per ounce)	35.11	35.19	35.20	41.90	35.20	37.38	38.88	40.10	42.60	43.62	40.65	42.60	42.34	43.60
Interest, Prices, Production				% OR INDEX NUMBERS (1963 = 100): PERIOD AVERAGES										
Bank Rate (End of Period)	6.00	7.00	8.00	7.00	8.00	7.00	7.00	6.00	5.00	5.00	6.00	5.00	5.00	5.00
Treasury Bill Rate	5.91	6.10	5.82	7.04	7.64	7.01	6.75	5.67	5.39	4.52	5.76	4.84	4.63	4.49
Euro-Dollar London	4.81	6.12	5.45	6.36	9.76	8.52	5.54	6.73	7.71	6.33	8.21	8.46	6.60	6.28
Gov't Bond Yield: Short Term	6.57	6.77	6.66	7.59	8.81	7.89	7.63	7.09	6.66	6.10	6.71	6.55	6.28	6.00
Long-Term	6.56	6.94	6.80	7.55	9.04	9.22	9.30	9.05	8.69	8.12	8.82	8.45	8.23	8.07
Industrial Share Prices	100.4	101.2	108.1	152.8	151.0	133.8	131.6	152.9	172.5	173.4	171.3	176.9	172.6	168.7
Prices: Industrial Output	106.8	109.6	110.9	115.3	119.8	127.7	134.4	137.1	139.2	140.2	139.3	139.5	139.7	140.0
Consumer Prices	108.2	112.5	115.3	120.7	127.2	135.3	142.8	147.9	149.9	151.8	149.9	150.1	151.0	151.8
Wages: Avg. Mo. Earn. All Indust.	107	115	123	127	137	147	178	183						
Industrial Production, Seas. Adj.	112	113	114	120	123	124	124	126	126	125	126	127	125	125
Employment, Seas. Adj.	102.3	102.9	101.9	100.1	99.9	99.0	97.6							

SOURCE: International Monetary Fund, INTERNATIONAL FINANCIAL STATISTICS MONTHLY.

THE CONTINENTAL GROUP, INC.—SLW

January, 1976, marked the beginning of a major concern for the senior management of The Continental Group, Inc. Fiscal years beginning on that date would have to be reported using the Financial Accounting Statement No. 8 approved by the Financial Accounting Standards Board the previous October. This statement was usually referred to as FASB #8, and it specified the procedure to be used to translate the financial statements of foreign operations and to report foreign currency transactions.

By the end of 1977, two years of experience with FASB #8 together with the restatement of two earlier years had confirmed Continental's worst fears about the impact of the Statement on the financial reports. Reported earnings were affected substantially by the appearance of unrealized gains and losses in foreign exchange. For 1976, Continental had to report a foreign exchange loss of 36¢ per share out of $4.01 total earnings per share. The instability of the exchange gains or losses from quarter-to-quarter was even more upsetting.

Impact of FASB #8 on Earnings Per Share, 1974-1976

Quarters	*1976*	*1975*	*1974*
1st	-8¢	-8¢	-22¢
2nd	+9	+4	+5
3rd	-17	+47	+16
4th	-20	-10	-29
Full Year	-36	+33	-30
EPS after adjusting for FASB #8	$4.01	$3.64	$3.77

SOURCE: ANNUAL REPORT, 1976.

Management's dissatisfaction with FASB #8 was intensified because in their view these exchange gains and losses existed only on paper and did not represent true economic gains or losses. This view was summarized by Harley Rankin, Treasurer of Continental, as follows:

> "The economic exposure to foreign exchange risk in our foreign operations is negligible. FASB #8 ignores this economic balance and forces us to report exchange gains and losses without taking this economic exposure into account. This reporting requirement just serves to distort the results of our operations."

A large proportion of the exchange gains and losses reported by Continental originated in the German subsidiary, Schmalbach-Lubeca, GmbH (SLW). SLW contributed $8.8 million of the $11.4 million in exchange losses reported by The Continental Group, Inc., in 1976. In the same year, SLW contributed $467 million to Continental's total sales of $3,470 million.

During the previous two years, Mr. Rankin considered several options available to avoid reporting exchange gains and losses. Since he considered the operations to be covered against exchange fluctuations, incurring the additional costs involved in these alternatives had never appeared to be in the best interest of the company. However, the pressure to find some solution to the problem was increasing.

In December, 1977, Mr. Rankin and other members of senior management decided to review the situation once more. As background for their meeting, Mr. Rankin asked Ms. Bragadir, a financial analyst with the company, to review the problem and to make a recommendation.

OPERATIONS

The Continental Group, Inc., was the name adopted by the earlier Continental Can Company in 1976. The change in name was in recognition of the increasingly diversified nature of Continental's business. In 1977, The Continental Group (CG) comprised the following:

	Percentage of Sales
Continental Can Company	60.5%
Continental Forest Industries	22.3
Continental Diversified Industries	17.2

Continental Can was engaged in the manufacture of cans. Its products included food, beverage, and aerosol cans. Outside the United States, it had European operations in the Netherlands, Belgium, Germany, and Austria. Forest Industries operated four domestic mills and managed a domestic timberland base of 1.5 million acres. Diversified Industries operated specialty packaging and related businesses in six countries.

In the last decade, Continental's management had emphasized diversification from the traditional can operations in the United States into other types of packaging and into foreign operations. The results of these efforts were reflected in a dramatic change in the product and geographic mix:

Net Sales and Operating Revenues

	1976		*1969*	
	$ million	*%*	*$ million*	*%*
Metal	1,308	37.8	959	53.9
Forest products	647	18.7	291	16.4
Diversified products	356	10.2	136	7.6
Discontinued	—	—	106	5.9
Total domestic	2,311	66.7	1,492	83.8
International	1,147	33.3	287	16.2
	3,458	100.0	1,780	100.0

This growth and diversification had been financed largely from internal sources. A summary of financial statistics for The Continental Group is presented in Exhibit 1.

	1976	1975	1974	1973	1972	1971	1970	1969
INCOME STATISTICS (dollars in millions, except per share figures)								
Total sales and operating revenues	$3,469.6	$3,122.4	$3,099.6	$2,547.4	$2,198.7	$2,088.5	$2,048.4	$1,788.5
Cost of goods sold and operating expenses	2,982.2	2,705.5	2,639.3	2,165.0	1,872.5	1,774.7	1,700.0	1,467.2
Selling, administrative and research expenses	232.1	219.6	197.6	178.3	161.5	151.5	146.1	122.5
Foreign exchange loss (gain)	11.4	(12.2)	16.0	3.7	(3.1)	1.3	(2.5)	(.1)
Interest expense	34.7	34.8	38.1	28.8	19.1	22.9	22.5	10.7
Earnings before income taxes and extraordinary charges	209.2	174.4	208.6	171.6	148.7	138.1	182.3	188.2
Percent of sales	6.0%	5.6%	6.8%	6.8%	6.8%	6.6%	9.0%	10.6%
Provision for income taxes	90.9	67.2	97.9	74.6	65.0	65.4	88.9	97.8
Earnings before extraordinary charges*	118.3	107.2	110.7	97.0	83.7	72.7	93.4	90.4
Percent of sales	3.4%	3.5%	3.6%	3.8%	3.8%	3.5%	4.6%	5.1%
Earnings per common share before extraordinary charges*	$ 4.01	$ 3.64	$ 3.77	$ 3.31	$ 2.87	$ 2.50	$ 3.26	$ 3.18
Common dividends paid per share	1.85	1.80	1.65	1.60	1.60	1.60	1.53	1.47
BALANCE SHEET STATISTICS (dollars in millions, except per share figures)								
Working capital	$ 369.7	$ 307.7	$ 295.3	$ 272.9	$ 260.0	$ 259.3	$ 275.8	220.2
Ratio-current assets to current liabilities	1.7–1	1.7–1	1.5–1	1.6–1	1.8–1	1.8–1	1.9–1	2.1–1
Property, plant and equipment-net	1,036.2	1,022.2	974.3	922.6	871.3	894.7	841.4	696.4
Long-term debt	417.3	392.6	390.4	373.6	345.9	311.2	304.9	169.3
Common stockholders' equity	928.2	862.0	806.2	742.7	694.0	776.9	745.3	696.1
Per share	31.47	29.32	27.50	25.43	23.87	26.74	25.98	25.38
After tax return on average equity*	13.2%	12.9%	14.3%	13.5%	11.4%	9.5%	13.0%	13.2%
Ratio-stockholders' equity to long-term debt	2.2–1	2.2–1	2.1–1	2.0–1	2.0–1	2.5–1	2.5–1	4.1–1
Common shares outstanding at year end (millions of shares)	29.5	29.3	29.3	29.2	29.1	29.1	28.7	27.4
OTHER STATISTICS								
Common stock price range	$ 34–3/8 26–3/4	$ 29–5/8 22–5/8	$ 26–1/4 20	$ 30–7/8 19–1/2	$ 34–7/8 27	$ 45–1/4 26–1/8	$ 50–1/4 34–3/4	$ 52–1/8 41–3/8
Capital expenditures (millions of dollars)	155.4	170.1	171.5	149.3	153.8	146.8	165.9	132.4
Depreciation and cost of timber harvested (millions of dollars)	124.9	113.7	109.1	93.8	77.1	72.1	69.2	59.9

*Before extraordinary charges of $120.1 million, equivalent to $4.13 per common share in 1972 and $15.5 million, equivalent to 54 cents per common share in 1970.

NOTE: All common share data adjusted to reflect the 3-for-2 stock distribution in 1970. Effective January 1, 1974, the company expanded its use of the LIFO method of inventory valuation to include all inventories.

SOURCE: ANNUAL REPORT, 1976.

International operations were the fastest growing segment of Continental. In 1977 CG did business in 133 countries through subsidiaries, minority-owned affiliates, licenses and export sales. Equity holdings were maintained in 30 companies operating in 22 countries. International operations also were expected to continue to grow faster than the domestic operations because of the greater potential of foreign markets.

FINANCIAL MANAGEMENT – EUROPE

Continental gave operating autonomy to local managers. Each foreign operation was expected to operate as if it were an independent company.

In spite of the policy of operating autonomy, Continental maintained a relatively high degree of centralization in the finance function. Three levels of responsibility existed for European operations: the local unit officer, the Regional Treasurer in Brussels, and the Head Office Treasury in New York.

Local subsidiaries were responsible for day-to-day management of their financial position in consultation with the Regional Treasurer in Brussels. In principle, a subsidiary would retain cash balances only to assure liquidity for normal business operations. Balances in excess of the amount required for liquidity purposes were managed by the Regional Treasurer. Short-term borrowing also was the responsibility of the operating units which were encouraged to develop local banking relationships. However, borrowing activities were coordinated with the Regional Treasurer who also advised on alternative sources of financing.

In the management of exposure to exchange risk, the local subsidiary was responsible for transaction exposures up to $500,000. Open positions in transactions exceeding that amount were allowed only with the approval of the Regional Treasurer, who monitored the total transactions exposure for each unit. For positions exceeding $2.5 million the consent of the Head Office Treasurer's Department also was required. Translation of balance-sheet exposure was the sole responsibility of the Head Office Treasury.

Corporate policy was not to enter any foreign exchange transaction or exposure unless required for normal business. The management of any exposure was designed to minimize risk. However, in managing cash balances, the Regional Treasurer in Brussels considered relative interest rates in conjunction with the prospects for the currencies involved. The Regional Treasurer maintained a sophisticated reporting system which provided the following for each operating unit: month and weekend cash positions, daily forecasts of cash receipts and disbursements, monthly funds flows and balance sheets, rolling-four quarter forecasts of funds flows and balance sheets, transaction exposure reports with explanation on covered and uncovered positions, liquidity optimization programs which tied in together the best short-term investment opportunities and the cash available for investment.

The relatively small control which subsidiaries had over their own financing was reflected in the method used to evaluate performance of foreign operations. Management of these units was evaluated in terms of dollar profits before taxes, interest expense, and translation exchange gains and losses. To avoid distortions introduced by exchange fluctuations, the initial dollar budget was updated to reflect intervening changes in exchange rates.

THE GERMAN SUBSIDIARY – SLW

The ties between SLW and Continental went back to 1930 when Continental licensed can-making technology to SLW. In 1969, Continental bought additional stock to make SLW a wholly-owned subsidiary.

SLW was a significant factor in the metal can industry in Germany. Most of its sales were in the domestic market. Only 2% of SLW sales were exports. These sales were invoiced in marks (DM).

SLW bought about 80% of its raw materials within Germany. The two important imports are aluminum for easy-opening cans, bought from the United States and Great Britain, and tinplate from France, Holland, and Belgium. These purchases are equally likely to be invoiced in DM or in the suppliers' currency.

Between 1970 and 1976 SLW's sales had grown 9.6% per annum and the DM profit in 1976 was 6.6% of equity. In 1977, Continental's management believed that Western European beverage can expansion should achieve 20% growth over the next five years. Exhibit 2 presents the SLW income statement and balance sheet data.

FINANCIAL ACCOUNTING STATEMENT NO. 8 AND SLW

Prior to the adoption of Accounting Statement No. 8 (FASB #8), Continental followed the Current/Non-Current method of converting foreign currency accounts into dollars. Essentially, all current assets and liabilities were converted at the exchange rate prevailing on the date of the balance sheet (the current rate), while all other assets and liabilities were converted at the rates prevailing at the time of acquisition of the asset or incurrence of the liability (the historical rates).

FASB #8 required that all monetary assets and liabilities be translated at exchange rates prevailing at the end of the reporting period. This meant that long-term debt now had to be translated at current rates. In addition, a large reserve maintained by SLW for the retirement of employees in the future was a non-current liability which was now to be translated at the current rate.

The other major departure of FASB #8 from the Current/Non-Current method was in the treatment of inventory. In the Current/Non-Current method inventories were always translated at current rates; under FASB #8 inventories were usually translated at historical rates. FASB #8 established that inventories reported at cost had to be translated at historical exchange rates; inventories reported at market values had to be translated at current exchange rates. The decision of whether inventories were measured at cost or market values was based on dollar values after translation; i.e., the comparison between market values translated at current exchange rates and cost figures translated at historical exchange rates. Since the accounting rule required that the lower of these two figures be chosen, the market figures translated at current exchange rates would be used mostly in cases of large depreciations of the foreign currency against the dollar.

SLW valued its inventory on a last-in-first-out (LIFO) basis.[1] Thus inven-

[1] Continental adopted the LIFO method of inventory evaluation on a worldwide basis in 1973.

EXHIBIT 2. The Continental Group, INC. – SLW Financial Statements

Balance Sheet as of December 31 [a]

	1976	1975
	(DM millions)	
ASSETS		
Cash and deposits (C)[a]	49.5	22.3
Notes receivable (C)	10.0	3.2
Accounts receivable-net (C)	89.4	97.2
Inventory–LIFO–(H)[a]	165.7	144.1
Fixed Assets–net (H)	318.5	316.4
Others (H)[b]	45.1	43.3
Total	678.2	627.5
LIABILITIES AND EQUITY		
Accounts payable (C)	127.8	143.4
Current portion of long-term debt (C)	4.9	9.7
Other payables (C)	66.9	36.0
Reserves–including pensions (C/H)[c]	191.1	162.0
Long-term debt (C)	45.4	46.0
Inter-company liabilities (C)	1.1	5.9
Equity (H)	241.0	224.5
Total	678.2	627.5

[a]Basis for conversion into U.S. dollars:

C = at current rate
H = at historical rates

[b]In 1976 under FASB #8, DM 27.3 are translated at current rate, DM 17.8 at historical rate. Under the previous method DM 14.7 was translated at current rate, DM 30.3 at historical rates.

[c]In 1975 23% was reported at historical rates, 67% at current rate. In 1976 19% was reported at historical rates, 81% at current rate.

Profit and Loss Statement for the Year Ended[a]

	12/31/76		12/31/75	
	(DM millions)			
Net sales		1175.5		1068.5
Cost of goods sold	1067.9		972.9	
Selling expenses	27.8		27.5	
Research and development	4.2		5.3	
Administrative expense	34.7	1134.6	45.1	1050.8
Operating income		41.0		17.7
Interest on long-term debt		4.3		2.2
Other items		(4.4)		0.8
Profit before income tax		41.1		14.7
Income tax		24.6		8.2
Net income		16.5		6.5

[a]Basis for conversion into U.S. dollars is average exchange rate prevailing during the year, except for depreciation. Depreciation, which represents about 5% of cost of goods sold and selling expenses, is translated at historical rates.

SOURCE: Company records, U.S. accounting basis.

tory was valued at the same rate at the beginning and the end of the year with appropriate adjustment for additions/depletions. Since FASB #8 applied historical exchange rates to inventories in appreciating currencies, the inventory would be translated at the exchange rates prevailing when the inventory was acquired for the purpose of valuation.

Under FASB #8 any material exchange gain or loss derived from translating the financial statements of foreign operations had to be reported as current income or loss. The reserve account which in the past had served to smooth virtually all the effects of exchange gains and losses under the Current/Non-Current method at Continental was not allowed under FASB #8.[2]

The net result of these changes for Continental's SLW at the end of 1976 was to change a prior *net asset* exposure of DM 130 million, under the Current/Non-Current method, into a *net liability* position of DM 225 million, under FASB #8. That is, if the mark appreciated against the dollar, Continental would have reported a credit in its balance sheet under the Current/Non-Current method, but it would have to report an exchange loss in its income statement under FASB #8.

THE PROBLEM AND THE OPTIONS

The weakening of the U.S. dollar in 1977 had continued to have its effects on the financial statements of Continental:

Impact of FASB #8 on Earnings Per Share, 1977

Quarter	*Impact of FASB #8*
1st	+8¢
2nd	-6¢
3rd	-6¢
4th	-37¢
	-41¢ total
1977 Earnings Per Share $4.44	

SOURCE: 10-Q Reports.

It was hard to believe that the financial community would not react to the picture of oscillating exchange gains and losses. Continental appeared to present a *prima facie* case of the negative impact of the risks in international business. The future pointed to a repetition of the past. Forecasts available to Continental predicted a continued appreciation of the mark against the dollar, at least through mid-1978. There would be additional exchange losses to be reported in 1978 unless something could be done to prevent it.

Concern with fluctuations in earnings had already led to the prepayment of DM 25 million in long-term debt and the decision to prepay SF 50 million in

[2]This reserve account had been created from charges to current income or from translation gains. Subsequent exchange losses then could be charged directly to the reserve account without affecting current income for that period. In 1974, Continental's reserve for exchange losses was $31 million and it appeared as a non-current liability in the financial statements.

long-term debt in 1978. The relatively high nominal interest rate on the DM debt, 7%, had made that decision easily justifiable on economic grounds. In the case of the Swiss franc debt, computations of exchange rates under which the advantage of a lower interest rate would have been eroded had showed in early 1977 that it was economically sound to keep the debt denominated in Swiss francs, especially since there was a stiff prepayment penalty. However, since mid-1977 the appreciation of the Swiss franc against the dollar together with the prospect for further appreciation made it highly desirable to prepay this loan.

There were a number of other options available to reduce further levels of exchange gains and losses. So far Continental had either decided against them or not been able to obtain them. These options were:

1. To have an outsider hold the German inventory at his/her risk. The SLW books then would show a receivable in place of inventory and would be converted at the current rate. However, to be a *bona fide* transaction, the third party would have to take over the risk and consequently would have to be compensated. Ms. Bragadir felt it would be appropriate to define the upper bound of such compensation. In addition it was questionable whether this would be acceptable under U.S. reporting standards.

2. To use a forward cover. The 12-month forward rate for DM on December 23 1977 was DM 2.05/$ compared with the spot rate on that day of DM 2.1427/$. However, this was a cumbersome option; Continental would have to purchase over DM 450 million to be fully hedged after taxes because translation gains/losses were not taxed while any gains/losses from transactions would be. Exhibit 3 summarizes spot and forward rates for DM during 1976 and 1977.

3. To reduce the non-current liabilities on the books of SLW. A major part of the reserve account on the SLW balance sheet related to the pen-

EXHIBIT 3. Spot and Forward Rates for German Marks, 1976–1977 (in U.S. dollars per DM)

		Forward Rate		
End of	*Spot Rate*	*3 month*	*6 month*	*12 month*
March, 1976	.3936	.3958	.3986	.4034
June, 1976	.3883	.3900	.3921	.3956
September, 1976	.4098	.4110	.4119	.4136
December, 1976	.4241	.4243	.4251	.4268
March, 1977	.4183	.4189	.4204	.4237
June, 1977	.4269	.4289	.4312	.4352
September, 1977	.4308	.4340	.4374	.4439
December, 1977	.4760	.4815	.4871	.4980

SOURCE: INTERNATIONAL MONETARY MARKET YEARBOOK, 1977 BUSINESS INTERNATIONAL MONEY REPORT, 9/30/77 and 12/30/77

sion liability; at the end of 1976, the pension liability accounted for DM 117 million out of DM 191.1 million in reserve. Ms. Bragadir had been advised that the pension liability could be reduced by increasing the interest rate and return assumptions on the pension reserve; SLW's current rate was too low. This change in assumption would reduce total exposure in DM. However, any such change would have to be acceptable to the auditors.

4. To try to explain the economic significance of the exchange gain/loss to the financial community. Exhibit 4 shows the comments that appeared in Continental's 1976 annual report.

To aid in her analysis Ms. Bragadir also collected the charts in Exhibit 5 showing the stock price of CG and Standards and Poor's 425 industrials.

As Ms. Bragadir sat down to analyze all the options, she remembered her finance professor's favorite dictum: "Doing nothing is always an option."

EXHIBIT 4. The Continental Group, Inc.: Excerpts from the 1976 ANNUAL REPORT

FOREIGN CURRENCY EXCHANGE

Accounting Statement No. 8 of the Financial Accounting Standards Board, issued in October, 1975, covering the translation of foreign currency transactions and financial statements has had a distorting impact on quarterly and annual reported earnings. Gains and losses resulting from foreign currency transactions and the translation of financial statements of foreign subsidiaries must be reflected in income for the quarterly and annual reporting periods. Continental's reported earnings are substantially impacted by valuations of foreign currency positions (principally the U.S. dollar vs. other "hard" currencies such as the deutschemark, the Dutch guilder and the Swiss franc) as of the last business day of our reporting periods. Fluctuating day-to-day currency relationships are influenced by factors unrelated to Continental's operating results for the reported period, and may bear no relationship to obligations maturing many years in the future.

This accounting change has caused fluctuations in reported earnings that mask the real trends in operating results for foreign subsidiaries and for the total company and, therefore, could mislead and may confuse investors. It is interesting to note that, despite the sizeable quarterly and annual gains and losses, the net cumulative per share effect over the last seven years has been to reduce earnings per share by only 12¢. The following table reveals the impact this new translation procedure had on quarterly earnings per share for Continental during the past three years.

Calendar Quarters	*1976*	*1975*	*1974*
1st	−8¢	−8¢	−22¢
2nd	+9¢	+4¢	+5¢
3rd	−17¢	+47¢	+16¢
4th	−20¢	−10¢	−29¢
Full Year	−36¢	+33¢	−30¢
EPS	$4.01	$3.64	$3.77

EXHIBIT 5. Earnings per Share and Stock Prices: S&P 425 Industrials and Continental Group, Inc., 1970-1977

	Earnings		*Stock Price Range*	
	S&P 425 Industrials	*CGI*	*S&P 425 Industrials (1941-43 = 10)*	*CGI*
1970	$5.43	$3.26	75.58-102.87	$34-3/4 -$50-1/4
1971	6.02	2.50	99.36-115.84	26-1/8 - 45-1/4
1972	6.83	2.87	112.19-132.95	27 - 34-7/8
1973	8.86	3.31	103.37-134.54	19-1/2 - 30-7/8
1974	6.69	3.77	69.53-111.65	20 26-1/4
1975	8.55	3.64	77.71-107.40	22-5/8 - 29-5/8
1976.I	2.50	.72	101.64-116.57	26-3/4 - 32
II	2.79	1.25	110.76-117.49	27-1/8 - 33-1/4
III	2.56	1.36	113.23-120.89	30 - 34-3/8
IV	2.83	.68	110.26-119.46	31-1/4 - 33
1977.I	2.65	.94	109.35-118.92	33 - 37-3/8
II	3.11	1.30	105.97-112.17	35-1/2 - 37-1/4
III	2.82	1.48	104.54-111.93	31-1/2 - 36-1/8
IV	3.04	.72	99.88-106.47	30-1/4 - 34-1/2

SOURCE: S&P SECURITY PRICE INDEX RECORD, (1978), S&P, N.Y. and S&P's STOCK RECORD, (1978), S&P, N.Y.

CHAPTER 8

Controlling the Multinational Enterprise

Traditionally, the financial measures of profit and return have provided a yardstick to evaluate the performance of business operations. However, as the multinational enterprise expands throughout the world the yardstick itself is affected by the environment in which it operates. Inflation and exchange fluctuations affect all the traditional financial measures of performance. The problem is particularly acute as the magnitude of these monetary phenomena differ from country to country. Also, within a country inflation and exchange fluctuations affect different businesses in a different fashion. Thus, attempts to compare the results of various affiliates of the multinational which operate under very different rates of inflation and exchange conditions without accounting for these factors is bound to be misleading at best.[1]

In this chapter, we first present the various ways in which inflation and exchange fluctuations affect operations as measured by traditional financial statements. Then, we provide a method to segregate the impact of inflation and exchange conditions from reported operations and to establish comparability

[1] The appendix to this chapter, "Comparative Accounting Practices," includes a section on accounting for inflation.

among the results of different affiliates. The chapter concludes with a section on the organization of the finance function in the multinational company.

THE IMPACT OF INFLATION AND EXCHANGE FLUCTUATIONS ON REPORTED FINANCIAL STATEMENTS

A large portion of any control system is based on establishing standards of performance and comparing actual performance with the standards. Researchers have found that the two most widely used standards are rate of return and performance relative to the budget.[2] Both of these measures are based on the traditional financial statements: income statement, balance sheet, and cash flow statement.

The financial statements used in the evaluation process are usually prepared following the conventions of the so-called "generally accepted accounting principles." These principles can distort the results presented on financial statements when inflation and exchange rate fluctuations prevail. To the extent that a control system relies on these financial statements, it is subject to the same distortions.

To show the impact of monetary phenomena on financial statements we will compare budget figures prepared without any anticipated inflation or exchange fluctuation with actual figures after these phenomena have occurred. For simplicity's sake, assume that the budget is met in volume terms; e.g., number of units sold and produced. Any discrepancy between the budget and the actual figures is due to monetary phenomena–inflation and exchange fluctuations.

The company used in the example manufactures one unit per month. This unit is sold the following month. Thus, in a year it sells twelve units and manufactures twelve units. At the end of the year the company has one unit in inventory which was manufactured during the last month of the year and which will be sold during the first month of the following year. Inflation and exchange fluctuations proceed at an even rate throughout the year.

The Impact of Inflation

Exhibit 8.1 shows the impact of various rates of inflation on the major accounts in the income statement and the balance sheet. Next to the budget column appear three columns showing the result under 10%, 20%, and 30% annual inflation rates.[3]

As an illustration, follow the results of the case with a total annual infla-

[2] See Robert N. Anthony, John Dearden, and Richard F. Vancil, *Management Control Systems,* rev. ed., Richard D. Irwin, Homewood, Illinois, 1972. Similar results were found by Sidney M. Robbins and Robert B. Stobaugh, *Money in the Multinational Enterprise,* Chapter 8, Basic Books, Inc., New York, 1973. They also found that as the size of the company increased, the emphasis on budgets for evaluation purposes also increased.

[3] Since we assume one unit is sold every month and that inflation proceeds at an even rate throughout the year, the average annual inflation rate reflected on sales is 5%, 10%, and 15%, respectively.

EXHIBIT 8.1. Impact of Inflation on Financial Reports

Income Statement
(in foreign currency)

	Budget	Actual with Annual Inflation Rate of: 10%	20%	30%
Sales	1,512	1,594	1,663	1,739
Cost of sales	1,440	1,506	1,560	1,622
Gross margin	72	88	103	117
Depreciation	40	40	40	40
Operating income	32	48	63	77
Interest expense	14	14	14	14
Profits before taxes	18	34	49	63
Taxes	9	17	25	32
Profits after taxes	9	17	24	31

Balance Sheet
(in foreign currency)

	Initial	Budget	Actual with Annual Inflation Rate of: 10%	20%	30%
ASSETS					
Cash	0	58	66	73	80
Accounts receivable	160	160	176	192	207
Inventory	120	120	132	144	156
	280	338	374	409	443
Plant and equipment	220	220	220	220	220
Less depreciation	-	(40)	(40)	(40)	(40)
	500	518	554	589	623
LIABILITIES PLUS EQUITY					
Accounts payable	200	200	220	240	260
7%-notes payable	200	200	200	200	200
Taxes payable	—	9	17	25	32
	400	409	437	465	492
Equity	100	100	100	100	100
Retained earnings	-	9	17	24	31
	100	109	117	124	131
	500	518	554	589	623

tion of 20%, or 1.67% per month. The unit sold the first month is sold at 1.67% over the budgeted price; the unit sold the second month at 3.34% over budgeted price; and so on until the unit sold at the end of the twelth month carries a price of 20% over the budgeted price. Thus, annual sales increase to 1663, a 10% increase over the budget figure of 1512, as the result of price increases to match the inflation rate. However, cost of goods sold increases by only 8%, from a budget of 1440 to the actual 1560. The recorded cost of goods sold is based on historical costs. The unit sold each month is manufactured in the preceding month at costs lower than the ones prevailing during the sale month. For example, the cost of the first unit sold is the cost of inventory before inflation, 120. Because of the discrepancy between the rate at which reported sales and cost of goods sold inflate, reported gross margin increases by much more than 10%. In this example the gross margin increases by 43% from 72 to 103.

Since depreciation charges are based on historical costs, this account is the same in actual outcome as in the budget, 40. Interest expenses remain constant because in the example it is assumed that incremental financing is obtained only from accounts payable, a non-interest bearing debt.

The combination of higher prices in sales and the use of historical costs in other accounts makes reported profits before taxes almost three times as large as the budgeted figure. Unfortunately, the government will tax 50% of the incremental profits. Still, the actual profits after taxes will be more than two-and-a-half times the profits after taxes budgeted in the absence of inflation.

Standard accounting practices used in the preparation of these financial statements make reported profits increase with the rate of inflation. The higher the inflation rate, the more that reported profits will exceed budgeted profits. With budgeted profits of 9, a 10% inflation rate raises these profits to 17, a 20% inflation rate to 24, and a 30% inflation rate to 31.

The figures in the actual balance sheets reflect the effects of inflation depending on the date when assets were acquired or liabilities incurred. Those assets which were acquired before inflation began are reported at cost figures which do not reflect current prices. This is the case for fixed assets. Accounts receivable and payable, on the other hand, reflect the higher prices affecting cost of inputs and products sold. These prices, however, are the ones prevailing at the time of the transactions. They are not current prices which in the example are assumed to be higher. Therefore, the only account in the balance sheet where actual and budget figures are the same is fixed assets.

A quick comparison between the reported performance and the budget will bring happiness when examining the income statement and dismay when looking at the balance sheet. However, according to our assumptions the manager produced and sold the exact number of units expected in the budget. All the changes in these accounts are due solely to the increasing level of prices during the period. Some of these increases were handed to the manager in the form of higher costs. Others occurred at the manager's initiative as selling prices were raised.

The Impact of Exchange Fluctuations

The discussion about the impact of exchange fluctuations can be aided by disaggregating exchange fluctuations into two types:

1. Fluctuations which affect the price of inputs and of the final product in a given business. Examples are: having to purchase foreign raw materials after the local currency devalues or selling final products in a currency which appreciates against the local currency.

2. Fluctuations in the value of the currencies in which the foreign unit operates against the dollar, the parent's currency.

Of course, when one of the currencies in which the foreign unit operates is the parent's currency, then the two types of fluctuations cannot be distinguished.

Export Revenues and Import Costs. When imports and exports are denominated in a foreign currency, exchange rate fluctuations affect the level of operating revenues and costs measured in terms of the domestic currency. In the example an appreciation in the revenue currency or the cost currency relative to the home currency has a very large impact on reported profits, assuming the other accounts remain constant. An appreciation in the revenue currency translates into a comparable increase in revenues. Given constant costs, the resulting profits increase by a substantial multiple. On the other hand, when the appreciating currency affects imports, a substantial loss occurs assuming selling prices are not adjusted to reflect the increase in costs. (See Exhibit 8.2.)

This example serves to point to the similarities between the impact of exchange fluctuations and the effects of inflation on reported profits. If we assume that prices in the local currency are increased by the same percentage as the rise in the cost of imports, the total impact on profits is similar to the effects of a comparable local inflation rate. An increase in import prices in the amount of 10% accompanied by a proportional increase in sales prices produces 17 of profits in our example in Exhibit 8.2. The same profits were obtained when the local inflation rate was 10% in a self-contained unit in the example in Exhibit 8.1. The reported figures for sales and cost of goods sold increase by the same amount over budget in the two cases. Also, regardless of whether the price changes are from inflation or exchange fluctuations, the cost figures measured on a historical basis are not affected by the price changes; e.g., depreciation.

Translated Value of Foreign Operations. If foreign operations are assumed to be self-contained (only dealing in their respective local currencies), the impact

EXHIBIT 8.2. Impact of Exchange Fluctuations on Export Revenues and Import Costs

		Revenue Currency Appreciates		*Cost Currency Appreciates*		*Both Revenue & Cost Currencies Appreciate*	
	Budget	*10%*	*20%*	*10%*	*20%*	*10%*	*20%*
Sales	1,512	1,594	1,663	1,512	1,512	1,594	1,663
Cost of sales	1,440	1,440	1,440	1,506	1,560	1,506	1,560
Gross margin	72	154	223	6	(48)	88	103
Depreciation	40	40	40	40	40	40	40
Operating income	32	114	183	(34)	(88)	48	63
Interest expense	14	14	14	14	14	14	14
Profits before taxes	18	100	169	(48)	(102)	34	49
Taxes	9	50	84	–	–	17	25
Profits after taxes	9	50	85	(48)	(102)	17	24

of exchange fluctuations on these operations can originate only from changes in value of the local currency relative to the parent company's currency. As financial statements expressed in local currency are *translated* into the currency of the parent company, any changes in the relative value of the two currencies will affect the reported figures.

The procedure for translating financial statements is regulated by the accounting profession and was discussed in Chapter 7. In a nutshell, in the U.S., the income statement figures are translated at average exchange rates prevailing during the period, except for expenses based on assets valued on a historical basis such as depreciation. In the balance sheet, financial assets and all liabilities are translated at current rates; the other assets are translated at historical rates. The equity account reflects the net effect of the translation.[4] To illustrate the impact of exchange fluctuations on translation of financial reports, assume that the various examples presented before with different rates of inflation each represent a separate foreign subsidiary. The examples of 10%, 20%, and 30% for domestic inflation rates are now paired with various rates of depreciation and appreciation of the foreign currency against the U.S. dollar (Exhibit 8.3).

When the foreign currency depreciates against the dollar, the translation of sales and cost of goods sold into dollars tends to reduce the impact of local inflation on these figures. Actually, the gross margin figure measured in dollars is the same as the budget figure when the foreign currency devalues against the dollar at the same rate as the local inflation rates. (See Cases A and B in Exhibit 8.3.) However, if the foreign currency *appreciates* against the dollar the discrepancy between budget and actual is increased further by the translation process. (See Case C in Exhibit 8.3.)

In cases where the foreign currency depreciates against the dollar but by a percentage smaller than the rate of local inflation, the distortion created by inflation on the reported gross margin is only partially corrected by the translation process. (See Case D in Exhibit 8.3.)

Depreciation charges are translated at historical exchange rates. Therefore, the figures expressed in dollars and in foreign currency are the same. Financing charges are translated at current exchange rates. Since taxes are translated at current rates, the dollar figure for taxes does not bear much relationship to profits before taxes in dollars—which is a combination of figures translated at current exchange rates and figures translated at historical exchange rates.

In this example the initial exposure in the balance sheet is a net-liability. Thus, when there is a depreciation in the foreign currency there is a foreign exchange gain in translation and when there is an appreciation there is a foreign exchange loss in translation. In Exhibit 8.3 the initial liability position of 240 produces exchange gains in Cases A, B, and D. An appreciation of 10% in case C gives rise to an exchange loss. These gains and losses are slightly reduced by the change in net exposure throughout the year. In the example the changes reduced the net liability position during the year.

[4] Financial Accounting Standards Board, "Statement of Financial Accounting Standards No. 8," (Stamford, Connecticut: October 1975).

EXHIBIT 8.3. Combined Impact on the Income Statement of Local Inflation and Exchange Fluctuations against the U.S. Dollar

		Case A		*Case B*[a]		*Case C*		*Case D*[a]	
		Inflation, 20% Depreciation, 20%		*Inflation, 30% Depreciation, 30%*		*Inflation, 10% Appreciation, 10%*		*Inflation, 30% Depreciation, 10%*	
	Budget	*FC*	*$*	*FC*	*$*	*FC*	*$*	*FC*	*$*
Sales	1,512	1,663	1,512	1,739	1,512	1,594	1,680	1,758	1,679
Cost of sales	1,440	1,560	1,440	1,622	1,440	1,506	1,575	1,638	1,574
Gross margin	72	103	72	117	72	88	105	120	104
Depreciation	40	40	40	40	40	40	40	40	40
Operating income	32	63	32	77	32	48	65	80	64
Interest expense	14	14	13	14	12	14	15	14	13
Profits before taxes	18	49	19	63	20	34	50	66	51
Taxes	9	25	22	32	28	17	18	33	31
Profits after tax and before translation	9	24	(3)	31	(8)	17	32	33	20
Translation gain (loss)									
Initial exposure of 240			40		55		(24)		18
Changes in exposure			(3)		(4)		2		(1)
			37		51		(22)		17
Profits after taxes and exchange translation	9	24	36	31	43	17	10	33	37

[a]The discrepancy between the figures in Cases B and D when measured in foreign currency (both assume a 30% inflation rate) is caused by slightly different assumptions as to the timing of the price increases: the middle of the month vs. the end of the month.

Possible Misleading Conclusions from Management Control Systems

The preceding discussion points to possible consequences of control systems based on financial reports prepared using current accounting practices. These can be summarized as follows:

1. When profits are measured in foreign currency, managers in countries with the highest levels of local inflation show the best performance when compared with budgeted profits.

2. When profits are measured in terms of dollars, the exhibited performance of the foreign operation depends on:

   a. the relationship between the rate of local inflation and the magnitude of exchange fluctuations;

   b. the size of the accounts which are carried at historical costs; and

   c. the relationship between exposed assets and liabilities in the balance sheet.

3. Balance sheet accounts measuring transactions during the inflationary period appear to show lack of control on the part of the manager as inflation increases the level of these accounts measured in local currency.

4. Balance sheet accounts translated at current exchange rates include the discrepancy between inflation and exchange fluctuation rates when measured in dollars.

5. Costs and prices reflected in the financial statements belong to dates when different assets were acquired or liabilities incurred. They *do not* reflect current monetary conditions.

6. Measures of return on assets or return on equity, whether expressed in terms of the foreign currency or dollars, will include all the distortions involved in the component accounts.

A MANAGEMENT CONTROL SYSTEM TO COPE WITH INFLATION AND EXCHANGE FLUCTUATIONS

There are two main approaches to deal with the distortions introduced by inflation and exchange fluctuations:

1. To update the budget figures to include monetary developments; or

2. To segregate the impact of monetary developments from the actual figures.

In both approaches the budget and actual figures are compared on the same basis, with or without the monetary changes. This eliminates some of the possible misleading conclusions discussed above. However, the philosophy behind each approach is very different. Updating the budget figures for inflation and exchange fluctuations assumes that these factors are outside the control of management and, therefore, should be left out of the evaluation process. On the other hand, segregating the impact of these factors from the actual figures allows for a measure of how management has responded to changes in the environment. We advocate the use of the second approach in this chapter.

Objectives of a Management Control System

It is generally well accepted that a good management control system should accomplish the following objectives:

1. Motivate line managers to make decisions which are optimal for the company as a whole; and

2. Provide information which helps to evaluate the quality of management decisions.[5]

Control systems which are based on financial statements prepared according to traditional accounting practices can defeat their purpose. Good decisions require the availability of relevant figures. Historical prices and exchange rates can give the wrong signals for decisions such as pricing, purchase of materials, etc. They can motivate managers to make decisions which will appear to show a good performance in the reports but which are detrimental to the future of the business; e.g., to continue using inefficient equipment because the existing equipment shows a low depreciation charge according to historical costs.

In addition to providing figures which are not always relevant for making decisions, the use of traditional financial statements as the basis of a control system can be faulted with two violations of general managements principles. These principles are:

1. Managers should be held responsible only for variables which they can control; and

2. All managers should be evaluated on the same basis.

It can be argued that inflation and exchange fluctuations are factors over which management has no control and, therefore, should be excluded from evaluation. Also, managers in overseas units can be perceived to be at a disadvantage relative to the domestic units which do not have to deal in foreign exchange.

The consideration of these last two factors raises a conflict between fairness and motivation. The objective of these management principles is equity. On the other hand, the manager should be encouraged to respond to changes in the specific environment. Although the management process may be simpler

[5] Robert N. Anthony, John Dearden, and Richard F. Vancil, *Management Control Systems,* rev. ed., Richard D. Irwin, Homewood, Illinois, 1972.

in a stable situation than under inflationary conditions, a manager operating under the latter conditions should be expected to reflect the increasing prices in the decisions taken. A satisfactory management control system must provide a compromise between the objectives of fairness and motivation.

An Alternative Management Control System

The yardstick which we propose to measure performance is *cash flows available to the parent company after allowing for maintenance of productive capacity in the operating unit.* We can call this *distributable profits.*

We propose that all the figures in the financial statements be analyzed separately and the economic impact of inflation and exchange fluctuations segregated. Some figures, such as sales, already include an inflationary component, so the analysis just requires segregating this last component. Other figures, such as depreciation, are measured in terms of historical costs. In these cases our method requires that a more realistic measure of the impact of inflation be established and then segregated. The adjusted figures are usually referred to as *current values.* (The appendix to this chapter reviews proposals to deal with the impact of inflation on financial statements, including current value accounting.)

Measuring Distributable Profits. The examples discussed in the first part of this chapter suggest that the impacts of inflation and exchange fluctuations on operating cash flows can be divided into three major types:

1. The effects of higher prices and exchange fluctuations on sales;
2. The cash flows, in addition to those measured by historical costs and exchange rates, required to replace inventory and fixed assets; and
3. The additional working capital required under the new monetary conditions.

Reported profits adjusted for the additional charges necessary to maintain productive capacity provide a measure of profits which are available for distribution. However, this measure is expressed in terms of the foreign currency. To establish comparability among all units operating in different currencies, this figure must be expressed in terms of a common currency, say the parent's currency. If the parent repatriated these funds, this is the amount that would be received.

Exhibit 8.4 presents the computation of distributable profits for the examples discussed earlier in this chapter. The adjustments are carried out in terms of foreign currency up to the step before last. Exchange fluctuations are reflected in these computations to the extent that exports and/or imports are denominated in a currency different from the one used to make the cal-

EXHIBIT 8.4. Impact of Inflation and Exchange Fluctuations on Cash Flows

	Annual Inflation Rate		
	10%	*20%*	*30%*
Reported profits	FC17.0	FC24.6	FC31.6
Adjustments to reflect current costs:			
Undercharge in cost of goods sold relative to current cost	FC12.0	FC24.0	FC36.0
Undercharge in depreciation of fixed assets relative to current cost	4.0	8.0	12.0
	FC16.0	FC32.0	FC48.0
Adjustment to reflect changes in working capital requirements. Additional needs for cash plus change in accounts payable	-4.0	-8.0	-12.0
Total adjustments to reported profits	FC12.0	FC24.0	FC36.0
Net cash flow after adjustments to maintain productive capacity	FC 5.0	FC 0.6	FC (4.4)
Funds available to parent in home currency[a]	$ 4.5	$ 0.5	$ (3.1)
Budgeted cash flow[b]	9.0	9.0	9.0
Variance on funds available to parent	$ (4.5)	$ (8.5)	$(12.1)

[a]Assume a depreciation of the foreign currency against the U.S. dollar equal to the inflation rate.

[b]Budgeted profits after taxes. See Exhibit 8.1.

culations. These exchange fluctuations will affect sales as well as cost of goods sold. Also, to the extent that fixed assets must be replaced from sources outside the country, their current cost and depreciation charges would be affected by exchange fluctuations.

Exhibit 8.4 begins with the figures for reported profits. This figure is then adjusted for the current cost of replacing inventory and fixed assets. Inventory must be replaced at the higher costs prevailing at the end of the period. By using historical costs in computing the cost of sales, insufficient allowance for replacement of inventory at current costs was made. The additional cost of replacement not measured in cost of goods sold in these examples is 12, 24, or 36, depending on the annual inflation rate. (The initial unit in the inventory cost 120.)

Additional funds are also necessary to replace plant and equipment at current costs. In the balance sheet this account is measured in terms of historical costs and the annual charge for depreciation is calculated accordingly. Assuming that the replacement cost has increased by the same percentage as the rate of inflation, the initial depreciation charge of 40 must be increased to reflect the additional cash which would be required to replace the fixed assets. The additional amount of cash required to replace fixed assets is 4, 8, or 12 depending on the inflation rate.[6]

To the extent that inflation and exchange fluctuations affect the requirement for working capital, this fact should be taken into account in the computation of distributable profits. If a larger amount of net working capital must be maintained to continue sales at the inflated level, then this increment is not available to be distributed in the form of dividends. This higher level of working capital is necessary to maintain productive capacity. Notice that part of the changes in working capital requirements has already been accounted for in the form of current cost of inventory. The remaining accounts in working capital to be considered are monetary accounts: cash, accounts receivable, and accounts payable. Thus, the additional level of cash which must be kept for transaction purposes as well as the additional funds which are tied up in accounts receivable constitute funds which are not available for distribution. On the other hand, an increase in accounts payable eases the need for funds to be maintained in working capital.

For simplicity's sake, in this example we assume that the need for cash for transaction purposes does not change with inflation. However, accounts receivable and accounts payable are allowed to increase in proportion to the inflation rate. In these examples it is assumed that the number of days' worth of sales and purchases in accounts receivable and payable is maintained. Since accounts payable are larger than accounts receivable initially, an atypical situation, the net impact of inflation in these accounts is to release working capital. Usually a higher level of inflation requires additional working capital. In these examples inflation actually contributes distributable profits in the amount of 4, 8, or 12, depending on the inflation rate. (The initial balance in monetary accounts is 40 in net liabilities.)

We are not recommending any adjustment to distributable profits on account of the notes payable. The capital structure of the subsidiary in terms of the foreign currency is assumed to remain constant. Although the dollar value of debt denominated in a foreign currency decreases when this currency depreciates, this valuation gain is not available to be repatriated if the foreign subsidiary is to be maintained as a going concern. The borrowing power of the subsidiary in the foreign market does not increase because of the change in value of the debt in terms of dollars.

When the additional charges required to maintain productive capacity are subtracted from reported profits in Exhibit 8.4, business operations appear to contribute a much smaller amount than the initial profit figures. In fact, when the inflation rate is 30% the adjusted profits are less than required to maintain the current level of operations.

The use of historical costs in reported profits hides the real economic impact of inflation. The fixed nature of the charges based on historical costs

[6] This treatment is the simplest one, but as the next paragraph on working capital might suggest, one could adjust depreciation in a lump sum for the total change in the fixed asset's value beyond one year's depreciation. This question is related to the inflation accounting issues discussed in the appendix to this chapter.

accounts for the greater negative impact of inflation as the inflation rate increases. To add insult to injury, taxes must be paid on profits generated simply because historical cost figures are used!

If the adjusted profits derived above are repatriated, the parent company would receive the corresponding dollars at exchange rates prevailing at the time. Thus, if a total inflation rate of 10% prevailed, this example shows that distributable profits in terms of foreign currency are FC5.0. However, in terms of dollars, the parent's currency, this is worth only $4.5–if a 10% depreciation of the foreign currency against the dollar took place during the period.

We argue that distributable profits measured in terms of the parent's currency represents the important measure for evaluation purposes. This is the figure which should be involved in setting performance targets and the one which should be compared with the budget afterwards. The comparison with the figure for budgeted profits in these examples–9.0–shows that in all cases the units fell short of achieving the target. Actually, in these examples the deficiency created by inflation becomes more acute as the rate of inflation increases.

Management's Response to Monetary Change. This proposed performance measure makes the manager responsible for managing the impact of inflation and exchange fluctuations on operations. For the manager to deliver the budgeted distributable profits in dollars, gross margins must be controlled, operating costs kept down as much as possible, and prices increased to compensate for all costs on a current basis. In addition, the manager may choose to change credit policy in order to alter the relationship between accounts payable and receivable.

The use of profit figures adjusted for the impact of inflation pinpoints the specific changes triggered by increasing prices and induces the manager to react to them. Since the various impacts can be disaggregated, the manager can then be evaluated on the degree of success with which each factor has been controlled.

Exhibit 8.5 disaggregates the impact of higher prices on operations. The amount of price increase incorporated in reported sales can be estimated by comparing reported sales with a figure for sales estimated at pre-inflation prices. By comparing the costs of operations expressed in terms of current costs with what these cost would have been in the absence of price increases, we can compute the impact of higher prices on costs. The inflationary component in accounts payable and receivable can be determined by comparing the reported net change in these accounts with what these changes would have been in the absence of price increases.

We can think of the decisions on which management is evaluated in terms of the degree of the manager's discretionary power in controlling the impact of monetary conditions. We classify these decisions into three major groups:

GROUP I. Decisions where the manager has the most control:

1. pricing
2. credit policy

EXHIBIT 8.5. Analytic Impact of Inflation and Exchange Rates

	Annual Inflation Rate Equal Currency Depreciation Rate		
	Total 10% Avg. 5%	*Total 20% Avg. 10%*	*Total 30% Avg. 15%*
SALES			
Reported	1594	1663	1739
Revenues at pre-inflation prices	1512	1512	1512
Revenues due to price increases	82	151	227
% increase	5.42%	9.98%	15.01%
COST OF SALES			
Reported	1506	1560	1622
Cost at pre-inflation costs	1440	1440	1440
Costs due to increases in cost of inputs	66	120	182
Additional funds required to maintain inventory	12	24	32
	78	144	214
% increase	5.42%	10.0%	14.86%
DEPRECIATION			
Reported	40	40	40
Additional charge to reflect current costs	4	8	12
	44	48	52
% increase	10%	20%	30%
ADDITIONAL TAXES	8	15	22
CHANGES IN CREDIT POLICY			
Reported increases in accounts payable	20	40	58
Less reported increases in accounts receivable	16	32	47
	4	8	11
Increase in accounts payable had cost of inputs remained constant	—	—	—
Less increase in accounts receivable had selling prices remained constant	—	—	—
Change in credit policy due to price increases	4	8	11

GROUP II. Decisions where the degree of control is only moderate:

1. inventory levels
2. productivity
3. alternative sources of materials

GROUP III. Decisions where the manager has the least control:

1. cost of fixed assets
2. technology

Of course, this ranking only shows relations. These relations may show different degrees of control at different times. Also, the longer the planning horizon, the greater the control which the manager has on these decisions; e.g., using alternative sources of materials.

With this ranking of how much control the manager has over monetary variables we can look again at Exhibit 8.5 where the impact of inflation is measured in terms of different variables. The objective now is to segregate the impact of general conditions from the decisions of the manager.

For sales, we are interested in two variables, pricing policy and quantity sold relative to budget. The amount of revenues from the price increases is shown in Exhibit 8.5 as the difference between reported sales and sales computed at pre-inflation prices. In these examples prices were increased by the same percentage as overall inflation rate. Next, compare the revenue figure at pre-inflation prices with the budget. In this fashion, we have a measure of success in increasing both prices and quantity sold. In these examples it was assumed that the manager met the budget in terms of quantity, so the only difference between budget and reported profits is because of increased prices.

A similar analysis can be performed for the major costs of production. The reported costs measured in terms of current costs can be compared with what these costs would have been in the absence of various increases. This latter figure then can be compared with the budget figures. Thus, the actual increases in the cost of resources and the efficiencies which the manager achieved can be measured. Again, because we assumed that the manager met the budget in volume terms, the differences between budget and current costs is caused only by cost increases.

For both sales and cost of goods sold, the response of management to inflationary conditions can also be measured by comparing the various increases realized in both revenues and costs with the average increases which prevailed in the markets where the manager operates. Success in raising selling prices higher than the prevailing market without affecting the quantity sold is to be praised. A similar success can be attributed to increases in the company's specific costs which are lower than those experienced in the company's input markets in general.

Finally, it seems that the manager should be given credit for whatever improvement can be realized in the amount of net working capital required under the new conditions. The number of days' worth of purchase and sales involved in accounts payable and receivable should be examined. An increase in the former and a decrease in the latter would release working capital, an outcome to be encouraged. In the example, the days' worth of credit on both accounts remains constant. Thus, the release of working capital on these grounds is totally caused by external price/cost changes.

Additional insights into the degree of success with which the manager has met the problems created by inflation can be obtained by comparing the actual increases in gross margin with the increases that would have been required to generate the budgeted profits after allowing for all current costs. Exhibit 8.6 shows, not surprisingly, that the higher the inflation rate, the higher the increase in gross margin which is necessary on an absolute and a relative basis. While a 10% inflation rate requires an increase in gross margin of 16.5%, an inflation rate of 30% requires gross margins to increase by 52.2%. An analysis of current

EXHIBIT 8.6. Realized and Required Increases in Gross Margin

	Annual Inflation Rate In Foreign Currency		
	10%	*20%*	*30%*
Funds available to parent after maintaining operations at current level[a]	$ 4.5	$ 0.5	$ (3.1)
Increase in margin required to meet budget profits of 9	11.9	24.0	37.6
Increase in margin realized	3.9	7.2	10.8
Percentage increase in margin required	16.5%	33-1/3%	52.2%
Percentage increase in margin realized	5.4%	10%	15%

[a]From Exhibit 8.4.

market conditions would show how feasible it was to increase margins by the required amount. This analysis, together with the actual increase realized by the manager, would provide useful information in evaluating the performance of the given operation.

To the extent that allowance was made for inflation in the budget figures, the revised figures need to adjust only for the difference between the inflation rate originally planned and the one actually realized. This can add another dimension to the control system, as management is asked to face the problems created by inflation in advance during the budget procedure. This fact will sharpen management's perception of the impact of the inflationary process.

ORGANIZATION OF THE FINANCE FUNCTION

So far the focus of this chapter has been on control of operations of the multinational enterprise, excluding financing decisions. Although our mesure of distributable profits was based on the bottom line of the income statement, no assessment of the financing decisions was made. In fact, there are two major approaches to the finance function from the point of view of control:

1. The local manager is given the responsibility for all financing decisions and he or she is evaluated in terms of the bottom line of the income statement; or

2. The responsibility for financing decisions is placed at the parent company level and the local manager is evaluated only in terms of operating profits.

A compromise between these two approaches also is found where the parent company or a regional office works in an advisory capacity while the local manager has the full responsibility for the final decision.

The advantages and disadvantages of each of these approaches can be traced to the general pros and cons of centralization vs. decentralization. An analysis of this issue is outside the scope of this book and can be found in most introductory texts on organization theory. However, some insights into this particular decision can be gained by reviewing the dimensions of finance decisions and some of the gains to be realized from centralization, at least for reporting purposes. These decisions have been studied in detail in earlier chapters, so we limit ourselves here to a brief presentation.

Financing

To the extent that some units in the system are net generators of funds while others are net users of funds, a centralized system can channel funds from where they are not needed to where they are needed without having to resort to financial intermediaries who will want to be compensated for the service. Also, when intercompany trade exists, a centralized system can serve as a clearinghouse for intercompany payments without requiring an actual cash transfer through the banking system. Cash transfers take time during which the firm is not compensated for its funds.

Finally, the large size of a parent company may be required to obtain access to some international markets which smaller subsidiaries would be barred from or would not be able to obtain at as favorable terms as the parent company. On the other hand, no centralized office in New York or Zurich may aspire to have an intimate knowledge of all the local financial markets around the world.

Exchange Exposure Management

With affiliates dealing in several currencies the only hope of obtaining an accurate picture of the aggregate exposure of the business to exchange fluctuations is through a centralized reporting system as the one suggested in Chapter 7. Such a report would eliminate the need for many hedging transactions since for any given currency the net receivable position of one unit may compensate the net liability position for another. The alternative of having each unit covering the exposure independently just would serve to generate income for exchange traders.

A compromise between decentralized decision making and centralized exposure management which some corporations exercise is based on having the parent company operate as a bank to the rest of the company. Any manager wishing to cover his or her exchange position can obtain forward contracts from the treasury office of the parent company at current market prices. This guarantees an exchange rate for the financial reporting of the manager. Then, it is up to the parent company to decide whether to actually obtain a forward exchange contract from a commercial bank or not. If the exchange position of the specific manager is compensated by the position of another operating unit, the parent company will see no need to acquire an exchange contract. Indeed, if the two operating positions neutralize one another, the acquisition of a forward contract would actually create an exchange position where none existed before.

Tax Management

There are as many tax authorities as countries in the world. A summary of some of the philosophies of taxation is presented in the appendix to this book. In addition, an understanding of specific laws requires highly specialized skills. Thus, it is impossible to delegate this responsibility totally to operating management which may be conversant with local tax regulations but which could not be expected to be aware of conditions in other countries or of the tax position of the consolidated company. The Sola Chemical Company case at the end of this chapter presents detailed arguments in favor of centralizing tax management.

SUMMARY

Inflation increases nominal profits and exchange rate fluctuations add further to a corporate officer's difficulty in evaluating the performance of company divisions in nations other than the parent's home country. After indicating the variety of distortions created by inflation and exchange rate fluctuations, we suggest a restatement of the traditional income statement to show the specific effect of local country inflation on sales, cost of goods sold (inventory), depreciation (fixed assets), and working capital requirements. The resulting balance is distributable profits, and one can state this figure in the home country currency after evaluating the earlier figures against budget forecasts. Depending on the firm, the local manager may have sharply different abilities to control various aspects of the business, ranging from relatively great control over pricing strategy to relatively small influence over the cost of fixed assets, for example.

Confronting the ultimate philosophical issue of centralized versus decentralized management helps determine the parent company's policy regarding local managers' financing and exposure management responsibilities. One compromise between total local responsibility and total centralized operation is creating a parent bank from which the local manager can borrow or lend idle cash or to cover exposed positions at market rates. The centralized treasury office nets the local positions from the various subsidiaries which it has financed, and then decides whether to offset the resulting cash or foreign exchange position itself in the real marketplace.

This system results in providing useful information in evaluating the local managers and operates to motivate the managers to behave in an optimal way from parent's standpoint. It is offered as a reasonable compromise between the non-intersecting requirements of both complete fairness and effective motivation.

Questions

1. "You characters in New York have all the expensive forecasting services of your big banks to tell you what is going to happen to interest rates and the peso. How am I supposed to know what to do sitting here in Mexico City?" (Mexican local manager). Comment.

2. "I know Latin American countries have relatively high inflation versus Germany, but if you look at the exchange rate, we always seem to receive less, even allowing for the changing parities. Budget is never met. What is wrong?" (Berlin multinational president). Comment.

3. "I am willing to evaluate the Indonesian subsidiary in their local currency, but I do not understand why they keep needing more money. Inflation always seems to drive up profits, but why can they not finance themselves? All we do is ship in more francs every six months. Something is wrong." (French multinational financial vice-president). Comment.

4. "If only I had a British parent instead of a Swiss parent, I would look a lot smarter. That is really absurd." (Brazilian local manager). Comment.

Bibliography*

Berg Kenneth, et al., eds., *Readings in International Accounting.* Boston, Mass.: Houghton Mifflin Company, 1969.

Choi, Frederick D. S. and Gerhard G. Mueller, *An Introduction to International Accounting.* Englewood Cliffs, New Jersey: Prentice-Hall, Inc., 1978.

Lessard, Donald R. and Peter L'Orange, "Currency Changes and Management Control–Resolving the Centralization/Decentralization Dilemma." *Accounting Review,* July 1977, pp. 628-37.

Treuherz, R. M., "Re-evaluating ROI for Foreign Operations." *Financial Executive,* May 1968, pp. 64-71.

Wells, Michael T., "Devaluation and Inflation and their Effect on Foreign Operations." *Accountancy,* Aug. 1965, reprinted in Berg et al. (1969), pp. 262-275.

*See also the bibliography to the appendix to this chapter, "Comparative Accounting Practices."

APPENDIX: COMPARATIVE ACCOUNTING PRACTICES

There are many differences among the accounting conventions used in various lands to prepare financial statements. In addition, the problems of high inflation rates and unstable exchange rates cast doubt on the validity of financial statements prepared according to traditional accounting principles that ignore the impact of these monetary phenomena. This appendix addresses these two issues. In the first section, we review some of the most important areas of discrepancy among accounting principles used in different countries. In the second section, we discuss the proposals advanced to measure the impact of monetary changes.

THE VARIATIONS IN INTERNATIONAL ACCOUNTING STANDARDS

Although this text is not primarily concerned with accounting differences among countries, any financial analyst must assure comparability of reports from firms in different lands. The difficulty is that two firms may both have financial statements which have an auditor's statement that the reports were prepared "in conformity with generally accepted accounting principles applied . . . consistently." Yet the principles may be very different in the two lands. In reviewing and comparing statements from different firms, the reader must confirm that:

1. All the relevant data are present from which one can judge the results of the firm;
2. The standards are consistent across firms and within a given firm over the years; and
3. The principles of accounting are acceptable to the anlyst.

Varying principles which might not be acceptable include practices on consolidation, definition of income, and price level adjustments for inflation.[1] These inconsistencies must be resolved in order to compare firms.

Some of the differences among various nations relate to the function of the auditor. In some cases the auditor is concerned with certifying statements which are in compliance with a body of principles and standards. In other nations the auditor merely agrees to management's statement that the reported figures conform with some governmental rules; the statements may have little to do with economic reality or previous financial statements of the firm. Firms in some nations have only one set of published statements (in contrast to the

[1]See the discussion by Gordon Shillinglaw, "International Comparability of Accounts." *Accounting,* Feb. 1966; or, Edgar Barrett, et al., "Japan: Some Background for Security Analysts," Parts 1 and 2, *Financial Analysts Journal,* Jan./Feb. and March/April 1974, for examples.

sharply different income statements often prepared for taxation purposes in the United States); thus the managers have to resolve a conflict between high earnings for the public (or simply "fair" earnings) and low earnings to reduce taxability. Given a desire to minimize taxes, firms often report just sufficient profits to pay dividends that seem "reasonable," with the remainder of the earnings reduced by various reserves.

Perhaps the largest difference between the U.S. and non-U.S. systems derives from the basic issue of *disclosure*. Secrecy of operations is almost a watchword among many international corporate officers. For example, in 1966 the huge Swiss pharmaceutical house, F. Hoffman-LaRoche, published a statement that showed record profits of 39.7 million Swiss francs. There were no sales figures, no asset figures, and no cost comments. The board of directors noted that the results were an improvement over previous years. "Sales and earnings have increased in approximately equal proportions. . . . The volume of investment was again large and will hardly diminish in the foreseeable future." The report was sent only to shareholders; all other requests were denied.

Such secrecy is related to the reserve of businessmen, the reluctance to alert tax authorities and labor unions, and other causes. One could speculate that the reluctance often is based on a disinclination to alert competitors to the size of the firm's operations. Sometimes management itself does not know what the consolidated profits and losses are, or it knows and does not like to reveal the results. This process of extreme secrecy viewed from the American shareholder's standpoint is diminishing with time and greater demand from shareholders in all lands for information about the corporate holdings. The case presented above is extreme, but discrepancies in disclosure compared to U.S. standards remain very large.

Other critics of non-U.S. financial statements have said that the critical problem is *consolidation.* Many of the foreign statements are not consolidated, or consolidation is optional from subsidiary to subsidiary. The foreign firm may mark up goods sold to unconsolidated sales subsidiaries in order to realize a high reported income for the parent (or at least some income!). The unconsolidated sales subsidiary, inventorying goods at inflated prices, may not be able to sell the goods at all, or at least not be able to sell them to recover cost. The first big Japanese bankruptcy in the economic success of that nation after World War II came in the mid-1960s when the Sanyo Special Steel Company, with capital of only $22 million, went bankrupt after "adjustments" showed the accumulated losses totaled over $222 million. Yet, these losses had been hidden in part by the unconsolidated subsidiary device. Because of a recent standard change, about 600 of the largest Japanese firms must now publish consolidated statements, thus eliminating many of the abuses of past years. However, many of the firms seem to be reducing direct firm ownership in the subsidiary to under 50%, hence avoiding the regulation.

The translation of foreign accounts varies internationally, and the impact can be seen in the U.S. before 1971. Prior to that date U.S. firms could consolidate subsidiaries in which the firm had more than a 50% interest, but ownership of less than 50% could be reported by using the equity method or the cost method. Under the equity approach, the pro rata inclusion of profits and losses of the subsidiary is included in the parent's income statement each year (hence, it is often referred to as "one-line consolidation"). Under the cost method, the initial investment of the firm in the subsidiary is retained as the value of the investment. Dividends as received are the income.

In 1966 the accounting regulations in effect in the United States required that domestic subsidiaries be included on either a consolidated basis or an equity basis, but foreign subsidiaries were excluded from this regulation. As a result, by 1970 the American corporations treated foreign subsidiaries in a wide range of ways. IBM and others consolidated all foreign subsidiaries. Some firms used the equity or the cost method exclusively. Many firms used a mixture of cost and equity, translating subsidiaries in relatively risk-free areas on an equity basis and others on a cost basis.[2] As discussed in Chapter 11, the current requirement is consolidation for more than 50% ownership, equity consolidation for more than 20% ownership, and dividends as received for 20% or less ownership.

A third major problem relates to the creation of *reserves,* secret or not. These reserves are charges against income in a particular year, and they mean that the definition of income is highly variable from year to year within a given firm and across firms in a given year. Generally, the goal is level income over time, with high reserves created in good years and vice versa. The reserves have a variety of purposes. Many of the definitions parallel the previous practice in the United States, where the term denoted any number of different accounts. Thus, reserves may be contra-accounts to reduce the value of a wasting asset, such as a reserve for depreciation. They may represent a contingency payment or future liability, such as a legal settlement or future costs for employee health insurance programs. They may be segmented retained earnings, sometimes earmarked for a particular project by vote of the shareholders or the board of directors ("reserve for future expansion"), or may be general ("free reserves") in the form of the American pattern of retained earnings. Finally, the reserves may be from special government tax programs, such as the British investment program of some years ago in which extremely rapid write-offs of some assets would be permitted when a certain portion of earnings were segmented as reserves for future construction outlays.

Another problem area relates to *depreciation and the revaluation process*. In periods of high inflation, many firms feel forced to revalue assets, as discussed below. Yet this process, which is often most dramatic in its effect on inventory and fixed asset values, can have sharp effects on the income statement through large depreciation charges or through great increases in the net worth of the company. Hence, the application of the depreciation schedule from year to year on a given asset as well as the process of revaluation of assets will often alter the income statement from what a U.S. reader would expect. Furthermore, the nature of the disclosure in footnotes on non-U.S. statements often masks the changes which have been made. The assumptions on which the charges are based are often unstated.

Another major difference is the concept of *retained earnings* or *earned surplus.* To the American shareholder in recent years, *clean* surplus is an accepted fact. It means that adjustments to the retained earnings or surplus account are made only through the income statement: There is no charge directly to the

[2]Exemptions to the rule requiring equity or full consolidation for over 50% ownership occurred when the investor could not have "significant influence" over the policies of the subsidiary and when the subsidiary was operating under particular exchange controls.

retained earnings account. Yet, from a review of many foreign financial statements, charges deemed not to be related to operations or not related to the current period's operations are often charged directly to the earned surplus account without the intermediary appearance in the income statement. Hence, the retained earnings account is sharply different from the American corporation's account under the same name.

Asset valuation is also a major issue. Thus, many U.S. firms use the LIFO method to value inventory; but most other nations forbid that convention. Also, the U.S. tax and financial reporting life for many fixed assets is fairly long compared to the rapid write-offs permitted firms in other lands. Finally, goodwill for some mergers must now be capitalized and amortized over no more than forty years with no tax deductions in the United States. In contrast, other nations following different accounting conventions ignore the goodwill aspects of mergers altogether.

Whether the market of investors perceives the "true" earnings of firms operating under various conventions is a matter of intellectual faith and empirical analysis; the earnings as reported are different, however.

Treatments of tax liabilities, stock dividends, and other accounts also differ from nation to nation, but the preceding comments highlight some of the major difficulties. The form of presentation of financial statements also may differ greatly, since firms may use different conventions in reporting income compared to the U.S. form. However, the reader can often interpret the figures to recast them roughly in the form of the U.S. income statement. The greater difficulty, however, is in the valuation process by which the accounts were determined, as noted above. Accounting firms periodically brief their clients and publish small booklets that outline some of the more pervasive differences in accounting statements.[3]

Some of the variations in international accounting may be removed as a result of the International Accounting Standards Committee formed in 1973. This committee has representatives from twenty-two nations that are pledged to adopt the standards agreed upon. Although most western European nations are included, two significant nonmembers are Switzerland and Italy.

The first standard adopted required disclosure of significant accounting policies, a disclosure of changes in accounting standards in which the change had material effect, and the inclusion of comparable figures for the prior period in all financial statements. Although these standards were not changes for U.S. practitioners, they represented a change for several nations. The next two standards dealt with inventory valuations and the rules for consolidation. Other standards scheduled for adoption deal with depreciation policies, the translation of foreign accounts, inflation accounting, and research and development outlays.

ACCOUNTING FOR INFLATION

The distortions which inflation and exchange fluctuations can cause on traditional financial statements has generated a multiplicity of proposals to mea-

[3]For example, see the *Guide to Foreign Financial Statements,* published annually by Price Waterhouse, New York.

sure the impact of these monetary problems. The major strands of thought in these proposals can be classified into two groups:

1. Proposals in favor of using constant purchasing power values; and
2. Proposals in favor of using current values.[4]

Each of these sets of proposals departs from traditional accounting practices in a different manner. Actually, in the purchasing power proposals all the traditional principles are retained except for a change in the unit of measurement. Instead of using money as the unit of account, these proposals use units of current purchasing power calculated using a general price index such as the GNP deflator. The current-value proposals, on the other hand, depart from one of the basic principles of accounting–the use of historical costs. Current-value methods of accounting measure assets on the basis of their *current value,* not historical costs. However, these methods retain units of money as the unit of account.[5]

The differences between these two systems of accounting for inflation can be seen best by contrasting their treatment of valuation of various assets and liabilities, and their implicit definition of profits.

Valuation of Assets and Liabilities

Monetary Assets and Liabilities. Purchasing-power proposals measure monetary assets in terms of units of current purchasing power. As inflation proceeds the purchasing power of these monetary assets decreases. Thus, monetary assets held at the beginning or acquired during the accounting period are worth less at the end of the period. Purchasing-power accounting identifies this monetary loss as part of operating profits and reports it in the income statement. Likewise, liabilities already outstanding at the beginning of the period or contracted some time between then and the end of the period are worth less. This gives rise to a monetary gain which is considered part of operating profits and is reported in the income statement in purchasing-power accounting.

Current-value systems, on the other hand, use money as the unit of measurement. Therefore, they do not identify any change in the value of monetary assets and liabilities. In terms of current value, $100 of marketable securities or debt are worth exactly $100 today regardless of when they were first acquired and the change in the general level of prices since then. In this system there are

[4]The approach recommended by current-value accounting is the one used in the text to Chapter 8 to estimate the economic impact of inflation on operations.

[5]For a comprehensive examination of these proposals, see *Inflation Accounting,* Report of the Inflation Accounting Committee, Chairman F.E.P. Sandilands, presented to Parliament in September, 1975, London, Great Britain. This report favors the adoption of current value accounting. The accounting profession in the United States has tended to favor the use of purchasing power units. See Financial Accounting Standards Board, *Financial Reporting in Units of General Purchasing Power,* Exposure Draft, December 31, 1974. None of these proposals have been adopted in the corresponding countries.

no monetary gains or losses to be recognized from holding monetary assets or liabilities during an inflationary period. Units of money measure the amount of funds which the monetary assets would fetch if they were redeemed today, or the amount of funds required to liquidate a liability.

Non-Monetary Assets. In the valuation of non-monetary assets such as plant and equipment the use of purchasing power units adjusts cost figures to reflect the change in purchasing power. Inflation increases the cost of equipment. However, the adjustment made for purchasing power reflects only the general increase in price levels, and not the specific increase in the cost of the given piece of equipment. By contrast, current-value accounting abandons the concept of historical cost expressed in whatever unit, and reports instead the *current value* of these assets. Alternatives used to estimate current value include replacement cost, net present value of the asset, and resale price. In practice, replacement cost is the method used most often by the advocates of this sytem of accounting.[6]

Measure of Profits

In the income statement, the thrust of the purchasing-power proposals is to restate all the accounts in terms of units of current purchasing power. However, the traditional valuation basis–e.g., historical costs–is maintained. Basically, all the accounts are inflated to reflect the higher prices prevailing at the end of the period in the overall economy. Thus, the depreciation charge is increased by the overall rate of inflation.

Operating profit in the purchasing-power system is a restatement of sales and various costs of doing business in terms of dollars of the same purchasing power, regardless of when the transaction took place. The problems of mixing sales for, say, March measured in dollars with a purchasing power for that month with cost figures expressed in dollars for, say, December is avoided by expressing all the figures in terms of dollars of the same purchasing power: the purchasing power at the end of the period.

In a current-value system the revenue figure is not altered. But cost of goods sold now reflects the value of the merchandise to the business at the time it was sold instead of historical costs. If a replacement cost system is used, the figure for cost of goods sold is the cost of replacing the inventory involved in the sale. Depreciation is the portion of the current value of the assets estimated to have been consumed during the reporting period. To reflect the higher costs, current-value systems adjust the traditional operating-profit figure by a "cost of sales adjustment." This adjustment measures the difference between historical costs used in the traditional statements and current costs–the cost of replacing

[6]Replacement cost is also the method required by the Security and Exchange Commission in the United States. Replacement cost figures for the balance sheet must be shown in footnotes to statements to shareholders. See Accounting Series Release No. 190, March 23, 1976.

inventory and fixed assets—valued at the time sales took place. This adjustment is a separate entry in the income statement. This treatment is in contrast to the purchasing power systems where the adjustments for changes in purchasing power are mixed with the traditional value for each account.

The implications of using a different unit of account in each system can be seen in what is included in the definition of profits. Current-value systems of valuation consider operating profits, after adjustments for current costs, as the relevant measure of profits for the period. Purchasing-power systems go one step further to compute operating profits. Monetary gains and losses derived from holding monetary assets and liabilities throughout the period are added to operating income to obtain operating profits for the period, all expressed in current purchasing power units.

Profit measures are an attempt to assess the gains or losses accruing to capital. Thus, the different profit concept in each of the two systems can be traced to their definition of capital. In purchasing-power systems the capital invested is measured by the equity account at the beginning of the period, the difference between assets and liabilities at that point. As the purchasing power of initial assets and liabilities changes, so does the purchasing power of capital. So, profits are the contribution to the equity account after the equity investment is updated to reflect its current purchasing power.

In a current-value system of accounting, capital is defined as productive capacity. Profits are the amount of funds which could be distributed after maintaining the productive capacity of assets. Since the monetary gains and losses derived from holding monetary assets and liabilities in an inflationary period are not gains or losses in terms of cash, they are not considered profit. In principle, the profit figure computed under this accounting system is available for distribution withoug impairing the productive capacity of the business. The additional charges over historical costs required to replenish the productive capacity of the business are included in the "cost of sales adjustment."

Under both systems most of the changes in value of non-monetary assets are reflected directly in the equity account. Under purchasing-power proposals, assuming there has not been any change in the physical inventory of non-monetary assets, the change in value in terms of purchasing power units is included in the adjustment of the additional equity for the change in purchasing power. For example, if there was a change in purchasing power of 10% during the period, both the value of plant and equipment and the equity account will be increased by the same amount, 10% of the cost of plant and equipment. However, transactions in these assets during the reporting period, purchases and sales of non-monetary assets, will be reported as part of monetary gains and losses. The value of the receipts and disbursements is adjusted for the change in purchasing power within the period.

In current-value accounting, all the changes in value in non-monetary items are segregated within the equity account. Revaluation reserves measure the gains and losses from changes in the current value of non-monetary assets. Proponents of this accounting system recommend that movements in these reserve accounts be identified separately, not mixed with other portions of the equity account.

A summary of the practices in each system is presented in Exhibit 1.

EXHIBIT 1. Treatment of the Impact of Inflation on Various Accounts under Alternative Accounting Systems

	Purchasing-Power Systems	*Current-Value Systems*
Monetary assets	Gives rise to monetary loss for the decline in purchasing power since initially received. The monetary loss is reported in the income statement.	No change.
Liabilities	Gives rise to monetary gain for the decline in purchasing power since debt was contracted. The monetary gain is reported in the income statement.	No change.
Non-monetary assets	Increases to reflect cost in terms of current purchasing power units. Equity figure increases in the same amount.	Increases to measure "VALUE to the Business." Increase is charged to RESERVE account.
Revenues	Restated in terms of units of current purchasing power.	No change.
Cost of goods sold	Restated in terms of units of current purchasing power.	Increases to measure "VALUE to business" at time of sale. Adjustment is shown as part of OPERATING profits.
Depreciation	Increases to reflect change in units/purchasing power worth of cost consumed during the reporting period.	Increases to measure "VALUE to business" consumed during the reporting period. Adjustment is shown as part of OPERATING profit.
Operating profits	Restated revenues less restated cost of goods sold and depreciation, less monetary gains/losses.	Revenues less current value cost of goods sold and depreciation. NO monetary gains/losses.

Foreign Operations

When the reporting system involves units with operations in other countries, each of these sets of proposals suggests a different treatment. In a system of constant purchasing power units, the relevant price level is the one in the country of the parent company, presumably the stockholders' home. The value of foreign operations is first translated from foreign currency into the parent's currency following the accepted principles of translation in this system. After the accounts are translated, they are adjusted for changes in the purchasing power of the parent's currency following the guidelines discussed above.

For proponents of current-value accounting, the relevant inflation rate is the one affecting the value of the assets to the business, given that the assets are located abroad. For example, what is the replacement cost, given that the asset is to be used in the specific country? Because of its location, the asset may be replaced from sources located in the same country, or it may be imported. Once the value of the assets is determined on this basis, then its equivalent value in terms of the parent's currency can be found by applying current exchange rates.

Bibliography to Appendix*

Barrett, M. Edgar and Jean-Louis Roy, "Financial Reporting Practices in France." *Financial Analysts Journal,* Jan.-Feb. 1976, pp. 39-49.

Benston, George J., "Public (U.S.) Compared to Private (U.K.) Regulation of Corporate Financial Disclosure." *Accounting Review,* July 1976, pp. 483-498.

Cummings, Joseph P. and William L. Rogers, "Developments in International Accounting." *CPA Journal,* May 1978, pp. 15-19.

Davidson, Sidney, Clyde P. Stickney, and Roman L. Weil, *Inflation Accounting, A Guide for the Accountant and Financial Analyst.* New York: McGraw-Hill Book Company, 1976.

Feldman, Stewart A. and LeRoy J. Herbert, "The International Accounting Standards Committee." *CPA Journal,* Jan. 1977, pp. 17-21.

Hole, Roderick C., and Michael A. Alkier, "German Financial Statements." *Management Accounting,* July 1974, pp. 28-34.

International Practice Executive Committee, *Professional Accounting in 30 Countries.* New York: American Institute of Certified Public Accountants, 1975.

Mueller, Gerhard G., "Accounting for Multinational Companies." *Cost and Management,* July-Aug. 1971, pp. 28-34.

Shoven, John B., and Jeremy I. Bulow, "Inflation Accounting and Nonfinancial Corporate Profits: Financial Assets and Liabilities." *Brookings Papers,* No. 1, 1976, pp. 15-66.

Taylor, Natalie Tabb, and M. Edgar Barrett, *Introduction to European Accounting,* ICH 9-174-043. Boston: Harvard Business School, 1974.

Wilkinson, Theodore L., "International Accounting: Harmony or Disharmony." *Columbia Journal of World Business,* March-April 1969, pp. 29-36.

Woo, John C. H., "Accounting for Inflation: Some International Models". *Management Accounting,* Feb. 1978, pp. 37-43.

Wyman, Harold E., "Analysis of Gains or Losses from Foreign Monetary Items: An Application of Purchasing Power Parity Concepts." *The Accounting Review,* July 1976, pp. 545-558.

*See also bibliography to Chapter 8.

SOLA CHEMICAL COMPANY[1]

ORGANIZING THE INTERNATIONAL FINANCE FUNCTION

The year was 1970. The subject before Sola Chemical's board of directors was a set of proposals by Multinational Consultants, Inc., recommending a drastic overhaul in the organization of Sola's overseas business. The board had already agreed, albeit a bit uncertainly, that the International Division would have to be abolished and that its responsibilities for overseas production and overseas marketing be distributed among some new regional divisions. Now the question was: What to do about the finance and control functions for which the International Division had been responsible?

Origins

Ever since World War II Sola had been doing what came naturally in the expansion of its foreign business. In the years just after the war Sola thought of itself as one of five or six companies that made up the leadership in the industrial and agricultural chemicals industry in the United States. At that time, a company with annual sales of $150 million could claim a leadership position. Besides, sales of the company at that time were reasonably well concentrated in only four main product groups. From the perspective of 1970, after nearly twenty-five years of growth and diversification into new products and markets, operations in the immediate postwar period seemed extraordinarily neat and tidy.

In the first years after the war the foreign business of Sola was limited. Historically, it had consisted of the sales that a small export department could drum up in Western Europe and Latin America, relying largely on commission merchants, wholesalers, and industrial buyers in those areas. From time to time Sola would discover that one of its newer products had taken hold in some country, generally at a time five or six years after it had found a market in the United States. After a few years of expansion in any foreign market, however, the attractiveness of the particular line in the area would generally fall away as quietly as it had appeared.

Apart from the seemingly episodic and sporadic lines of business of this sort, Sola's main "foreign" commitment in the years up to World War II was a manufacturing subsidiary in Canada, a subsidiary that Sola had set up in the late 1920s in response to a sharp increase in Canada's industrial tariffs. Except for a few shares nominally held by Canadian directors, this subsidiary was wholly owned by Sola. When the Imperial Preference tariff system was established in 1932, the Sola management had congratulated itself on its foresight in establish-

[1]This case is based on interviews conducted under the direction of R. B. Stobaugh as part of the Harvard multinational enterprise study. The case itself was prepared by Raymond Vernon and edited by Rita M. Rodriguez and E. Eugene Carter for this book.

ing a subsidiary inside the Commonwealth so that it could meet British competitors such as Imperial Chemical Industries on equal terms. From Sola management's viewpoint, however, the Canadian subsidiary could hardly be called "foreign." Situated not far from Windsor, Ontario, it was close enough to Sola's midwest headquarters to be run like any other branch plant. The product policies and marketing policies of Sola seemed to apply about as well to the Canadian plant as any other. True, there were some occasional crises of an unfamiliar sort, as when the Canadians tinkered with the value of their currency in relation to the U.S. dollar, or when they set up unfamiliar provisions in relation to the taxation of profits. But an occasional consultation with the company's bankers and tax attorneys was generally sufficient to deal with crises of this sort.

Very different from Sola's relationship to its Canadian subsidiary in the years immediately after World War II were its ties to a French subsidiary which had been set up at about the same time. Unlike the Canadian subsidiary, only 53% of the equity of this company was owned by Sola, the rest being in the hands of Cie. Chimie Tricolor, a leading French manufacturer whose product lines fell largely within two of Sola's four product groups. Nobody at Sola could recall how this particular liaison had first developed. But there was an impression that Sola had been confronted with an ultimatum by the French chemical industry at one point in the 1920s: Either it must invite a French business interest to join it in the creation of a French manufacturing subsidiary or it must risk losing a lucrative market that was being supplied by exports from the United States. There was some recollection among Sola's oldtimers that the ultimatum had been backed up by hints from the French ministry of industry that the threats might not prove hollow. In any event, whatever the origins of the French partnership might be, the subsidiary had grown away from Sola over the years. By the late 1940s it was thought of as almost an independent entity, operating under the stewardship of the French partner and negotiating with Sola for product information and technology very much on an arm's-length basis.

So much for the situation at the beginning of the postwar era.

Between that time and 1970 the foreign business of Sola had expanded at an astonishing rate, considerably faster than the business in the United States. And as the foreign business grew, not only the policies and strategies but even the very structure of Sola was greatly affected. Step by step, additional locations had been selected for the establishment of new manufacturing subsidiaries: the United Kingdom in 1952; Germany in 1955; Mexico in 1956; Brazil in 1960; Italy in 1962; Australia in 1965; and so on, until Sola's manufacturing facilities covered fifteen different countries. At the same time, operations in Canada had been considerably expanded, covering more of Sola's product lines. In each of these cases, Sola had preferred to go it alone, without local partners. And after a nasty confrontation or two with the French partners over the management of the French facility, a friendly divorce had been arranged, leaving Sola with a wholly-owned manufacturing facility in France in lieu of the old partnership.

Although Sola had not set up more than a portion of the U.S. product line in any one country, the total number of products manufactured overseas was widening every year. In fact, there were even three or four cases in which the U.S. plants had suspended operations on an old staple item, assigning what was left of the business to one of the foreign facilities where the product still seemed to command a market. When that happened, the foreign facility took over Sola's third-country markets as well.

While the manufacturing subsidiaries were spreading over the globe, Sola was setting up other units to facilitate the handling of its foreign business. Sola had discovered very early the tax advantages of a Western Hemisphere trade corporation and had set up a company in Delaware to qualify under the U.S. tax code. A corporation could qualify if it derived practically all its income from trade or business (as distinguished from investment) and confined its business to the Western Hemisphere outside the United States. The profits of such a corporation were taxed at a rate 14 percentage points less than the standard U.S. rate. To exploit this advantage, U.S. Sola billed its exports to Western Hemisphere countries from the United States through its Western Hemisphere trade corporation. As a rule, such exports were billed out by U.S. Sola to the trade corporation at the lowest possible appropriate figure, which Sola calculated in accordance with a formula that included an 8% markup over cost. This formula had the effect of placing most of the profit on such sales in the trade corporation.[2]

Other arrangements to minimize taxes had been made as well. Back in 1958, before the Revenue Act of 1962 had restricted the use of foreign-based holding companies as "tax havens"—that is, as vehicles for postponing the payment of U.S. taxes on foreign income—Sola's treasurer and tax attorney had pushed through the establishment of a Swiss holding company. U.S. Sola owned Sola-Switzerland, which in turn held nominal ownership over Sola's subsidiaries outside the United States. In those days, Sola-Switzerland could perform all kinds of useful services for U.S. Sola. For one thing, like the Western Hemisphere trade corporation, it could act as an intermediary in export sales from the United States. When Sola-Switzerland was used as an intermediary, the tax benefits to U.S. Sola were rather different from those associated with the use of the Western Hemisphere company. Sola-Switzerland's profits were subject to normal tax rates once they got into the U.S. tax jurisdiction. But that did not occur until the profits were declared to U.S. Sola in the form of dividends. Meanwhile, Sola-Switzerland could shuttle the cash generated by export profits to any point in the Sola system that required it.

Sola-Switzerland's cash flow could be built up not only by exports but also by the dividends, royalties, interest, and fees generated in the Sola subsidiaries that Sola-Switzerland nominally owned. As long as Swiss law did not tax the income of the Swiss holding company and as long as U.S. law did not classify the funds as taxable in the United States, Sola-Switzerland was a highly useful mechanism.

That particular arrangement had deferred quite a lot of tax payments for a few years. Subsidiaries could declare dividends and could pay interest, agency fees, administrative charges, and royalties to the holding company without subjecting the income to U.S. taxation; the U.S. tax bite would come only when the income moved upstream as dividends to the U.S. parent. Although the U.S. system of tax credits on foreign-earned income insured that the income would not be taxed twice when it finally appeared on the U.S. parent's books, still there was something to be gained at times from deferring the U.S. tax. The tax advantage was especially important when the subsidiary's payments to its parent had not been taxed locally because they represented expenses to the subsidiary,

[2]The 1976 Tax Reform Act eliminated WHTCs. See the tax appendix to this book for elaboration on some of the tax issues discussed in this case.

or when the subsidiary's income had been taxed at rates well below those in the United States. In those situations, when the payments finally were received as dividends in the United States, some U.S. taxes would be due.

When the Internal Revenue Code was amended in 1962 to restrict the use of tax haven companies, many of the tax advantages involved in the maintenance of such a company disappeared. The provisions that expose the income of such tax haven companies to U.S. taxation are exceedingly complex. But Sola's Swiss holding company clearly fell within its terms. It was controlled by U.S. Sola, and it derived more than 70% of its income from the dividends, interest, royalties, and other fees received from Sola's operating subsidiaries located in third countries. Accordingly, the income of Sola-Switzerland was fully taxable under U.S. law just as if it had been paid directly to U.S. Sola itself.

One tax advantage associated with foreign holding companies still remained, however. Loath to discourage exports from the United States in any way, Congress had exempted from the new provisions such income as the tax haven companies were garnering from their role in the handling of U.S. exports. As long as a spread could exist between the price at which U.S. Sola invoiced its goods for export and the price at which the goods were invoiced for import in the foreign country of destination, there were still tax advantages in assigning the spread to an intermediate company located in a tax-free area.

Despite the fact that Sola-Switzerland had lost much of its original purpose, there was some hesitation about liquidating the Swiss company. It would entail the transfer of the equity of many underlying operating subsidiaries, the transfer of the Swiss company's claims to the long-term and short-term debt of some of the operating subsidiaries, and the shift of the Swiss company's title in patents and trade names abroad that were being licensed to the subsidiaries. Numerous contractual ties between the Swiss company and the subsidiaries also would have to be dissolved, such as the right of the Swiss company to receive payment for administrative and technical services and for sales agency services. All these rearrangements were bound to generate administrative and legal problems in a number of different countries where the increasing curiosity and sophistication of the regulatory authorities could be counted on to stir up difficulties.

Accordingly, Sola decided to leave the Swiss holding company in existence and to create several other intermediate companies besides. One would be a Luxembourg company set up to capture some of the profits on U.S. exports, which still were entitled to tax deferral treatment. Another enterprise would be set up to segregate the income generated by subsidiaries in advanced countries. Under the 1962 law income originating in subsidiaries in the less developed areas, unlike income from the advanced countries, could still be kept beyond the reach of U.S. tax collectors to the extent that it was reinvested in less developed areas.[3] Accordingly, a holding company was set up in Curacao to own Sola's subsidiaries in less developed areas and to receive the income of such subsidiaries for routing to destinations where the income was needed. Curacao's virtue as a holding company headquarters consisted *inter alia* of its willingness to leave such income virtually untaxed as it passed through the holding company on its way to a new destination.

[3] LDC treatment for some foreign income was ended by the 1976 Tax Reform Act.

As if this complex cluster of intermediate companies was not enough, Sola decided in 1966 that another intermediate structure would be useful, namely, a holding company created under the laws of Delaware to act as Sola's alter ego in floating bond issues in the European market.

Well before 1966 it was clear to U.S. Sola that its European subsidiaries' voracious appetite would have to be fed by more borrowing from abroad. Sola itself was under a handicap when raising money in Europe, because U.S. internal revenue requirements obliged it to withhold 30% of interest or dividend payments to nonresident recipients. That provision placed a heavy handicap on the securities of U.S. issuers in Europe. Sola's Swiss holding company had been used two or three times before as the nominal borrower of dollar-denominated funds from European sources. Operating under the umbrella of a guarantee from U.S. Sola, the Swiss holding company had been able to borrow medium-term money at reasonable rates from private European sources. Though the interest costs had run a little higher than they would have in the United States, these flotations had saved the bother of registration with the Securities and Exchange Commission, the problem of qualification under the "blue sky" laws of the state regulatory agencies, and so on; the difference in costs, therefore, was not as great as the interest rates indicated. At the same time, Sola had developed some excellent European banking ties that might help out in the event that the U.S. government really clamped down on the export of capital from the United States. As early as 1958 or 1959 that contingency had become something to worry about, as U.S. officials began to express their misgivings over the condition of the U.S. balance of payments.

By 1965 contingency had turned to reality. "Voluntary" controls had been imposed over the outflow of funds from the United States to subsidiaries in Europe. Although the controls were very loose and left many different ways in which Sola could arrange for the generation of cash flows in its overseas subsidiaries, Sola tried to respond to the spirit of the regulations by raising a larger proportion of its needed funds outside the United States.

One possible step to that end was to continue using the Swiss holding company, as it had been used in the past, to borrow from European sources. But Sola was not eager to expand the use of the Swiss holding company now that it had lost most of its usefulness as a tax haven. True, such a holding company still had some advantages that U.S. Sola did not share, such as the fact that its payments of dividend and interest to non-U.S. recipients were not subject to the reporting and withholding requirements of U.S. tax law. But the use of such a company also had some disadvantages when compared with a Delaware company, such as the fact that losses, if any, could not be consolidated in U.S. Sola's income tax return in the United States.

The upshot was that Sola decided in 1966 to create a second Delaware holding company, with functions carefully designed to retain the advantages of a Swiss holding company as a financing intermediary while avoiding some of its disabilities. The main purpose of the second Delaware holding company was to borrow funds outside the United States with the guarantee of U.S. Sola and to lend those funds to Sola's foreign subsidiaries. As long as the new holding company confined itself to this sort of operation, its only significant income—namely, interest payments from the subsidiaries—was regarded as of foreign origin. Since 80% or more of its income was of foreign origin, the Delaware company, like the Swiss company, was not required to withhold any sums in connection with interest payments to non-U.S. recipients. Such profits as the Delaware company might have were within the reach of the U.S. and Delaware tax jurisdiction. But profits were likely to be trivial, given the purpose of the company. Besides, Delaware tax provisions were traditionally benign in such matters, and U.S. tax provisions, ever since the adoption of the 1962 amendments, made only small distinctions between the profits of domestic holding companies and those of foreign holding companies of U.S. taxpayers.

The creation of the Delaware finance company proved to be a very wise step indeed. On January 1, 1968, the so-called "voluntary" program of capital export controls became mandatory. At the same time, the program was tightened up so that the various alternative means of transferring funds abroad became more restricted. Under the new program, Sola's right to transfer funds abroad was tied to its historical record of investment in the years just prior to 1968. Investment for that base period was defined as capital transfers in cash or in kind made to foreign subsidiaries plus profits retained in the subsidiaries during the period. Once that base figure was calculated, its application was variously defined for different groups of countries. Subsidiaries in the less developed countries, the "Schedule A" countries, were allowed to continue receiving investment from U.S. Sola at their old levels, even a little higher. There was also a "Schedule B" group, which the U.S. regulators thought of as being especially dependent on U.S. capital flows–the oil countries, the United Kingdom, Japan, and a few other areas. Added investments from the United States in these areas were cut down but not eliminated; capital flows to these areas were restricted to 65% of the base period. Canada, originally in this group, was exempted from the regulations altogether.

The real problem for Sola, therefore, was financing the European subsidiaries, that is, the subsidiaries located in "Schedule C" countries. Drastic cuts were made here. At first, added investment from U.S. Sola could only take place through retained earnings. Even the retained earnings could not be used under the rules if this meant a retention rate higher than base period rates or if it meant an investment rate higher than 35% of the base period.

If it had not been for the fact that borrowings outside the United States were exempted from the restrictions, Sola would have been in real trouble at first. That exemption carried the company through 1968. And in 1969 and 1970 the restrictions were eased somewhat.[4] But the experience impressed on the minds of Sola's management more than ever the need to have an intimate knowledge of the world's sources of capital and to have the flexibility in organization to use the sources as needed. This heightened recognition centered attention on just how decisions were taken on such matters inside the organization.

The Financial Organization

As Sola expanded its overseas operations, the legal instrumentalities and national environments that concerned it increased rapidly in number. From World War II

[4]The appendix to this case discusses these controls in more detail. The controls were terminated by President Nixon in 1974.

until 1970, therefore, there was a constant need to restructure the internal organization and procedures that were responsible for formulating and executing financial policies and for controlling financial operations. That restructuring was tied in intimately, of course, with other changes in Sola's organization, including changes in the marketing and production systems associated with a growing overseas operation.

In the early 1960s the foreign business had grown to such proportions that it was thought advisable to create an international division. The first executive in charge of that division, an aggressive and ambitious manager, decided that one of his major needs was to pull together the haphazard structure which up to that time had been formulating financial policy for the foreign areas. With the approval of Sola's top management, therefore, a new structure was created. Some of the essential elements of the organization tying together the financial function at that stage are suggested by the diagram in Exhibit 1. A word or two of elaboration is needed in order to relate this chart of Sola's structure in the early 1960s to financial decisions taken at that time.

Major investment decisions, such as decisions to create a new foreign subsidiary or substantially to increase its capitalization, were generally recommended in the first instance by the international manager to Sola's president; he, in turn, usually sought the advice of his board of directors, as well as the advice of many other sources.

Major policies aimed at reducing taxes on overseas operations were usually initiated by the international treasurer, discussed with U.S. Sola's treasurer and tax attorney, and then cleared with the finance committee.

Policies with regard to borrowing by foreign subsidiaries were no problem. Apart from accounts payable and accrued liabilities and except for a rare local loan initiated by the international treasurer, such transactions did not arise. Subsidiaries were not authorized to borrow; indeed, they were not thought of as managing their own cash flow. Funds were channeled to the subsidiaries by the international treasurer as needed. Before 1965 these funds had come mainly from the parent or the Swiss holding company in the form of short-term dollar debt. Later on, after the Delaware company was formed and had begun to raise dollars through the sale of Euro-bonds, it became the principal creditor for Sola's foreign subsidiaries.

Apart from decisions on whether and how to provide the subsidiaries with their working capital needs, the other major area of financial operating policy was the withdrawal of funds from a subsidiary that held surplus cash. In this case the main problem was viewed as minimizing the tax burden associated with withdrawal, and the main policy variable was the choice between dividends, royalties, interest, and management fees. That choice was made by the tax attorney on the basis of data provided by the international treasurer.

The international controller, as Exhibit 1 suggests, bore a somewhat different relation to the organization than the treasurer. Unlike the treasurer, the controller had representatives in each of the subsidiaries. This difference reflected the fact that the treasurer saw his function as that of managing the money flows of the system, whereas the controller saw his function as that of monitoring the performance of its various parts. The first function, so it seemed, could be performed well enough from the bridge of the enterprise, whereas the second function required getting down into the various holds below.

EXHIBIT 1. Financial Offices in the Structure of Sola Company, 1962

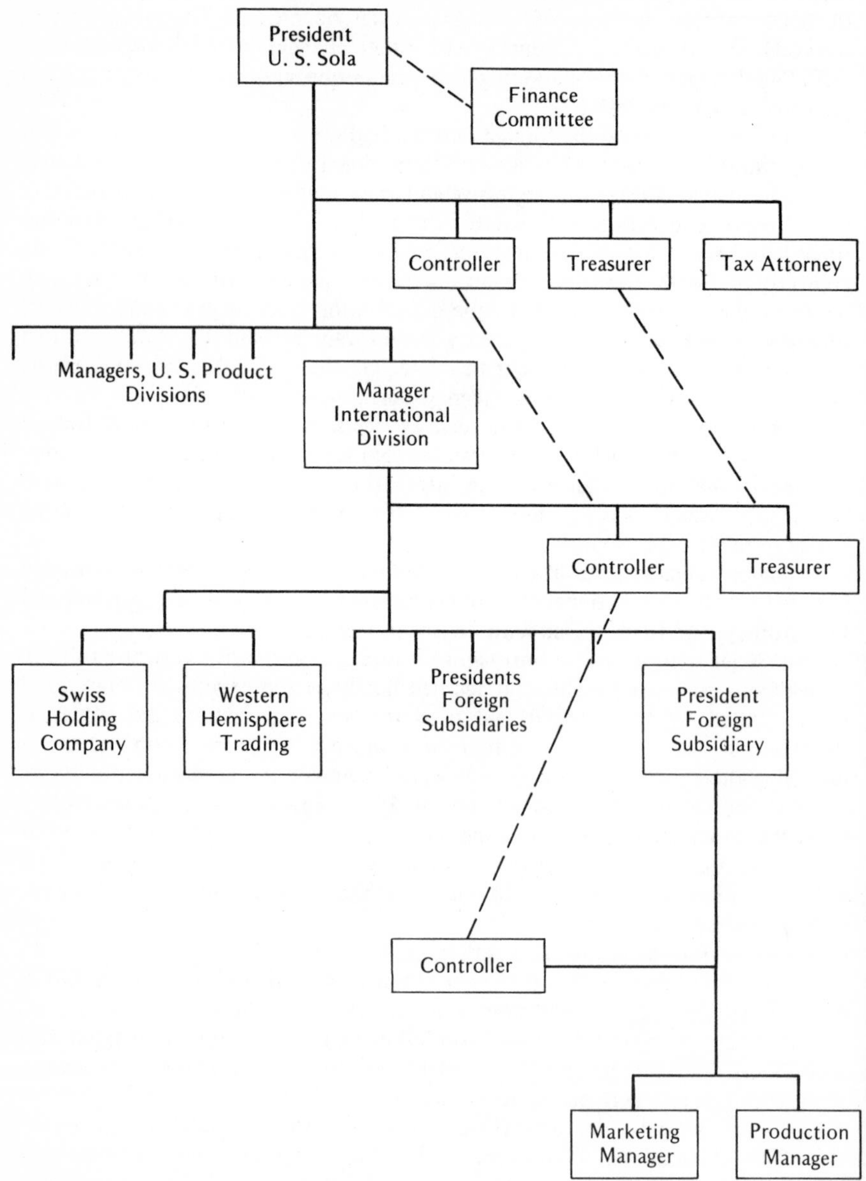

Proposals for Reorganization

As a rule, the international treasurer's problems were not the sort of subject that got discussed very much among Sola's directors. When a major investment abroad was involved, that of course was fairly well explored. But most discussion involved questions of strategy instead of financing and cash flow problems. These were left pretty much for the finance committee and the treasurer's office to worry about. As far as the finance committee was concerned, that group freely admitted that its ability to second-guess the treasurer's office on overseas financing was very limited. The subject was just too specialized, it appeared. And so the international treasurer proved to be performing a vital function.

Fortunately for Sola Chemical, it had filled that post very well indeed. Milray Thaler had been international treasurer ever since 1958 when the post was first created. He had come out of the old export department, seasoned by years of selling in a world of inconvertible currencies. He had learned all about the ways in which blocked currencies could be turned into usable cash and the ways in which avoidable taxes could be avoided. As international treasurer, he ran a tight organization. He kept in close touch with the problems of every subsidiary, especially their problems of cash flow. As far as he could see, the foreign subsidiaries had been well provided for and did not have to worry about money and credit questions for which they were hardly equipped. And as far as taxes were concerned, the foreign side of Sola had done marvelously well in avoiding the avoidable.

Despite that fact, by 1970 the financial organization was showing certain signs of strain. By that time Thaler's unflagging efforts to hold down taxes and to generate money where it was most needed had made a shambles of the periodic profit and loss statements of the subsidiaries. The U.S. system of controls over the export of funds to subsidiaries had increased the complexities of financing. The objective of holding down the total tax bill was now constrained by restrictions on the outflow of capital from the United States. The importance of distinguishing between the treatment of subsidiaries in different countries also was increasing. The differences between less developed countries and advanced countries, and between countries in Schedules A, B, and C, were important. Added wrinkles, such as Canada's special status under the U.S. capital export control program, had to be kept in mind. The difficulties were heightened further by the fact that some countries, especially the United States and Germany, were beginning to take seriously their various fiscal provisions relating to the international pricing of goods and services. Provisions such as Section 482 of the U.S. Internal Revenue Code, authorizing the tax authorities to use arm's-length prices in interaffiliate transactions, were beginning to be applied seriously. Thaler's consultations with the tax people and his demands on Sola's treasurer were constantly rising in number and urgency.

In addition, Thaler's difficulties with the controller's area seemed on the increase. The more strenuous the efforts of the treasurer, the more difficult the problem of the controller. If the reported profit and loss statements of the manufacturing subsidiaries could be taken at face value, most of them were operating at practically no profit; the only exception was the subsidiary in Canada. What actually was happening depended on what the word "actually" meant. Profits were appearing in the Western Hemisphere trading company, in the Swiss holding company, and in the holding companies in Luxembourg and Curacao. Whether these profits were "actual" or not depended on what one thought of the validity of the prices charged for products traded among the affiliates, as well as the royalty charges and administrative fees. Sometimes there was a basis for testing these prices and fees against analogous arm's-length transactions.

But more often, the goods or services involved were sufficiently distinctive so that no independent arm's-length standard could readily be found, assuming an effort were made to find one.

On top of this problem was the fact that Sola's subsidiaries in Europe, facing the elimination of trade barriers in the EEC and EFTA, found themselves competing in one another's territory with similar product lines. Here and there, the problem had been reduced by the timely intervention of the international manager. Once or twice, when specialty items were involved, the subsidiaries had agreed to allocate production tasks between them without bothering to involve the international office. In situations of that sort, the transfer price was fixed according to the bargaining strength of each subsidiary and the transaction was recorded as if it were undertaken with an outside vendor. But as the number of subsidiaries and the number of product lines kept rising, this *ad hoc* approach was beginning to prove inadequate.

For the controllers in the local subsidiaries, all these problems presented growing headaches. The performance reports were beginning to make less and less sense unless they were adjusted in various ways. Adjustments, however, required the refereeing role of the international controller when it involved a decision affecting the relative performance of two foreign subsidiaries, and it required the involvement of U.S. Sola's controller when the decision affected the U.S. company's reported performance. As a result of the accumulation of decision rules arising out of these adjudications, controllers' reports were beginning to bear less and less relation to the financial statements.

With these considerations and others in mind, Multinational Consultants, Inc., a prominent international consulting firm, was called in to advise on the reorganization of Sola's foreign business. After studying the operations of the company for a number of months, Multinational Consultants produced a voluminous report covering the problems of the foreign side of Sola's business. Among other things, it had a number of observations regarding the operation of the financial function, observations that boiled down to three propositions:

1. The treasurer's function had become much too complex and diffuse to be managed effectively from the center. Opportunities were being missed and errors committed. Among the errors cited, for instance, was the failure of the international treasurer to develop a systematic policy toward the threat of currency fluctuations. The opportunities missed as a result of the absence of such a policy were not the sort that were necessarily visible in Sola's financial statements. But once in a while missed opportunities could be detected. One of these was the failure to hedge against a sterling devaluation in 1967, when the likelihood of the devaluation seemed extraordinarily high; this alleged oversight was said to have cost the company \$350,000 in translation losses. Other opportunities overlooked, according to MCI, were those inherent in the possibilities for borrowing in local markets. The tight cash flow controls from headquarters, MCI guessed, reduced the likelihood that such opportunities were being recognized and exploited.

2. The treasurer was much too preoccupied with tax savings and too little concerned with reducing the cost of funds.

3. The financial data essential for the use of the treasurer's office were markedly different from the data needed for the performance of the controller's function, more so than in the case of complex operations within the United States proper. This difference was due to the fact that the units of Sola were in so many different jurisdictions with different rules covering taxation, access to capital, and so on. Essentially, the controller would be obliged to develop a separate score card, gauging the performance of profit centers on the basis of data that were compiled primarily for control purposes.

As a first step toward achieving the needed shifts in direction, Multinational Consultants, Inc., proposed a number of major organizational changes. It was proposed that the international division should be broken up into several foreign area divisions, each of which would have status on a par with a U.S. product division. The international treasurer and the international controller would be moved upstairs into the offices of Sola's treasurer and controller, respectively. A new layer of treasurers, controllers, and tax attorneys would be created at the area division level.

Under the new system, the lowest control center on the foreign side would be a given product line in a given area. When more than one subsidiary in an area was involved in the product, the control center would combine the activities in the product of all such subsidiaries. Presumably, the treasurer could not ignore the performance of the subsidiary, since that performance would affect its tax liability. But for the controller's needs, an area-product approach to performance would be taken. Exhibit 2 indicates how the financial offices would sit in the revised Sola structure after reorganization.

Practically everyone on the foreign side of the Sola organization reacted to the proposals with some degree of hostility or reserve. The international manager saw himself as risking a major demotion: Either he would be moved upstairs into the staff of Sola's president or he would be placed at the head of the "Europe and Africa" area. In either case his status would be a notch lower. Of all the officers reacting to the change, however, it was Milray Thaler, the international treasurer, who felt most threatened.

Thaler was furious at Multinational Consultants' report. A few days after it had been circulated in Sola, Thaler produced a twenty-six page reply, refuting the report point by point. Some of the extracts from his rebuttal were especially provocative.

2. Of course, the international side of the treasurer's function is growing more complicated. Governments get smarter every day. Regulations get more complicated. With Section 482 on one side and the Office of Foreign Direct Investment on the other, it is not easy to do business abroad. But what kind of an answer is MCI offering us? To set up a treasurer in every area, so one area doesn't know what the other is doing? Who will tell German-Sola to stop trying to make a record for itself by gouging Argentine-Sola with its high invoice prices for petrochemicals? And who will stop the subsidiaries from always trying to build up their equity, instead of building up accounts payable? Much better to give me a few

EXHIBIT 2. Financial Offices in Proposed Reorganization of Sola Company, 1970

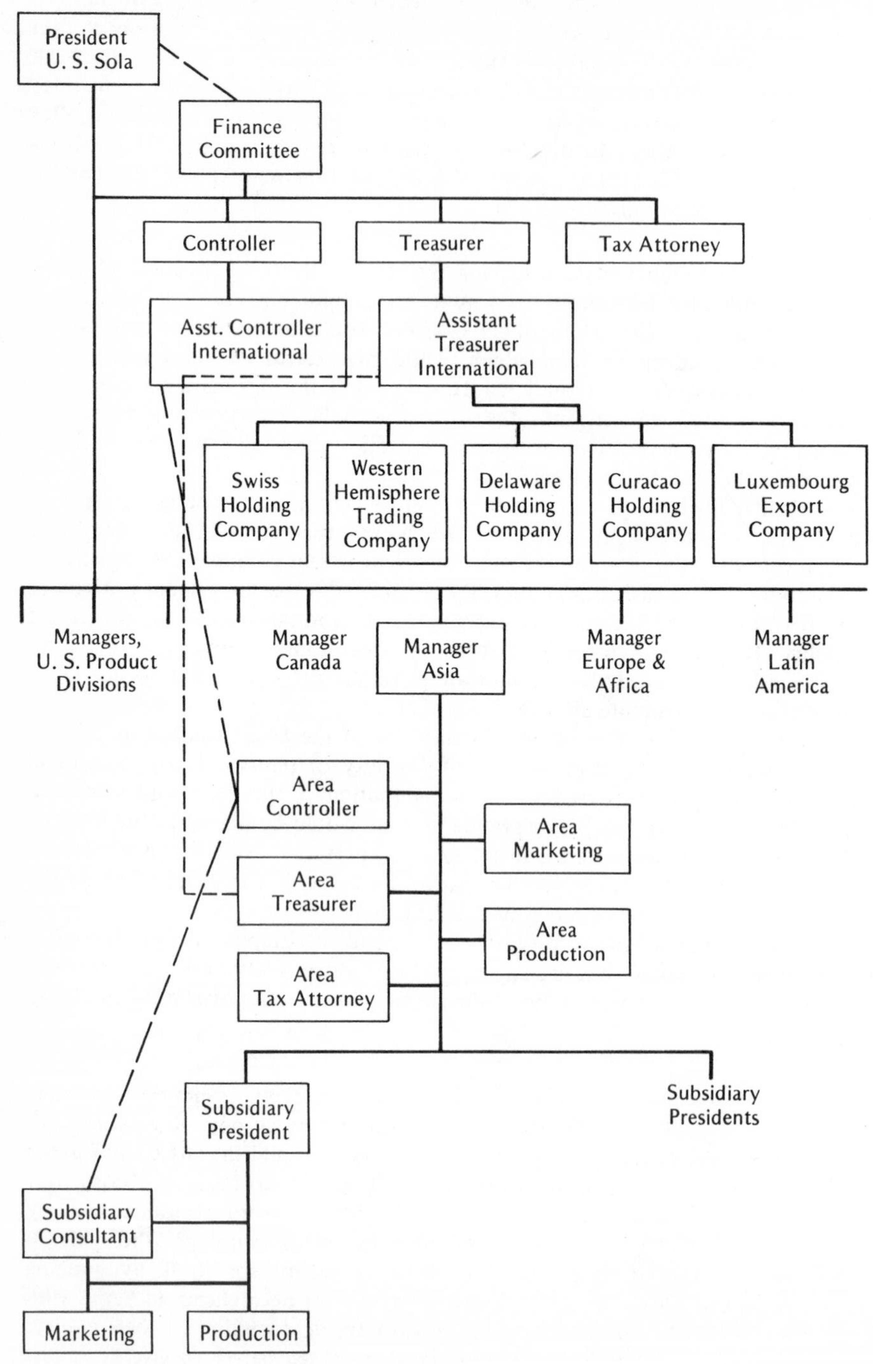

more high-level assistants who have had a little experience with such complicated matters so that we can stay on top of such problems.

3. Maybe production and marketing need some decentralizing at the regional level. After all, the users of industrial chemicals in Nairobi are not exactly the same types you find in Hamburg or Rio. But the management of money is another matter; that should be centralized. Money is money once you get it out of the clutches of a country and make it convertible. A dollar out of Peru is a dollar out of Turkey, and it ought to be managed that way.

5. How would a regional treasurer know how to use the Curacao or Luxembourg companies, or why? Today, if Sola-Switzerland needs to pay a dividend to U.S. Sola, I can easily drum up the money by way of Curacao. I can do it because I know just what to expect in Curacao and I know how to compare it with Berne's cash flow prospects.

14. That famous $350,000 translation loss from the devaluation of sterling is getting a little ridiculous. Translation losses are not money; they are bookkeeping. They mean nothing to Sola's cash flow. Tax payments are a different matter. Real money can be saved there. If I were to worry about every currency that might devalue tomorrow, I would eat up the time of the company and the office chasing paper butterflies.

15. Once the controller starts making up his own score card and the treasurer makes up a separate one, it will be impossible to know where we stand. The controller has everything he needs, without the headaches of a special set of books, if he gets copies of the treasurer's instructions to the subsidiaries. If he wants to adjust his records because of these instructions so that the effect of tax transactions and cash flow transactions are canceled out, it is easy enough for him to do it.

16. Above all, once you start putting the profit centers in the regional offices, you are a dead duck. Europe is not yet a country. Neither is Latin America. The authorities in the central banks and in the national tax administrations are not about to give up their powers and go away. These are the offices you have to keep your eye on if you are going to survive in the international business.

Appendix: The U.S. Office of Foreign Direct Investment (OFDI)

This government agency was created in 1968 to limit the flow of U.S. capital abroad. During its six-year life a series of regulations were issued to explain the restrictions on U.S. corporations' foreign investment. The remainder of this appendix is based on materials contained in the Burroughs case, pages 284-295 of the first edition of this textbook. Although the regulations are no longer in force, continuing concern about the U.S. balance of payments means that their form is of more than historic interest, i.e., that there is life after death in at least some cases.

OFDI Compliance

OFDI regulations were very complex. In short, the regulations and their rationale could be summed up as follows: The United States wished to discourage net export of capital from the States due to the country's balance of payments situation. Thus, the OFDI was established to monitor the flow of capital in the form of direct investment across U.S. borders.[1] OFDI basically monitored two kinds of transfers: (1) purchases of equity or loans to foreign ventures, including increases in intercompany trade accounts receivable and (2) the amount of foreign earnings *reinvested* outside the United States. The regulations stipulated that the total of the two types of transfer (called "direct investment") be restricted to a specific level. For example, a U.S. company that reinvested $1.0 million of its foreign earnings in its foreign subsidiaries and that, in addition, lent another $1.0 million to these subsidiaries from funds obtained in the United States would have accumulated a total direct investment of $2.0 million. If its limit on direct investment, according to OFDI, was $1.5 million, this company would have to produce a capital inflow of $0.5 million into the United States. This remittance could take one of two forms: (1) a decrease in direct investment, either through a repatriation of earnings in the form of dividends or a decrease of loans to the foreign subsidiaries, or (2) proceeds of foreign borrowings.

When proceeds of foreign borrowings were used to meet the requirements of OFDI, a further problem arose when the debt was paid back. When funds were transferred abroad to pay for the borrowings, OFDI considered this capital outflow an increase in direct investment, except under certain circumstances. Assuming everything remained constant, the repayment of the debt required additional capital inflows into the United States to compensate for the repayment outflow. In many cases this meant a need to refinance the debt. The exceptions to this OFDI rule were the cases in which repayment of principal did not commence until seven years after the debt-issue date or when convertible bonds, with an initial maturity of more than seven years, were converted into equity in a U.S. company.

Calculations

As an example, in 1971 the *estimated* limit on direct investment for the Burroughs Corporation had been established at 40% of 1970's earnings. This percentage was determined on the basis of calculations done according to OFDI guidelines. There were a number of valid ways for Burroughs to compute

[1] Direct investment has been arbitrarily defined as investment where more than 10% of the ownership belongs to the U.S. investor.

the limit on direct investments but the 40%-of-previous-year-earnings method offered the best solution.[2]

Accordingly, a tentative estimate of Burroughs's direct investment situation vis-à-vis OFDI requirements for 1971 was:

TRANSFER OF CAPITAL		
Estimated increase in receivables from affiliated companies		$31.5 million
Repayment of borrowings:		
Euro-dollar term loan:	$10.8 m	
Other:	10.0 m	20.8
Total transfer of capital		$52.3
REINVESTED EARNINGS		
Estimated net income for 1971		34.7
DIRECT INVESTMENT		$87.0
ALLOWED DIRECT INVESTMENT		
40% of 1970 net income ($33.0)		$13.2
EXCESS OF EXPECTED OVER ALLOWED DIRECT INVESTMENT		$73.8

[2]The other two most important methods were (1) minimum allowable in which up to $2 million was allowed as direct investment and (2) historical allowable in which a fixed amount based on a percentage of average direct investment in 1965–66 was allowed.

CHAPTER 9

An Integrated Approach to the Finance Function in the Multinational Enterprise

In the preceding chapters we analyzed the major financial problems facing the multinational enterprise: raising funds, protecting against exchange risks, and controlling operations in the midst of inflation and exchange fluctuations. To facilitiate the presentation, each of these problems was discussed in isolation without relating one to the other explicitly. For example, we discussed the issue of financing the firm at the lowest possible cost without analyzing in detail the impact of various financing choices on hedging strategies. In reality, all of these problems are interrelated and the solution to any one of them affects the others. Thus, the objective of this chapter is to develop a framework in which all these interrelationships can be analyzed and simultaneous solutions can be found.

We begin the chapter with an example that allows us to review the problems of the financial officer in the multinational enterprise and the choices that are available for their solution. Criteria are then provided to choose among the various financial options. The chapter concludes with an example in which simultaneous solutions can be found for the various financial problems, given certain criteria.

THE ELEMENTS OF THE FINANCE FUNCTION—A REVIEW

As a review of the financing problems discussed in this part of the book, let us study a problem that raises the main issues encountered by the financial officer and that allows for an exploration of the interrelationships among the various financial problems.

The case involves an American company which builds a factory in Belgium for $40 million. To finance the investment $40 million worth of equity is issued in the United States. Thus, the initial balance sheet of the Belgian operation appears as follows:

Initial Balance Sheet (in million dollars' worth of Belgian francs)

Plant and equipment	$40	Paid-in capital	$40
	40		40

The factory is scheduled to manufacture and to sell 1 million widgets per month. The direct costs of manufacturing the widgets are forecast at $50/widget worth of Belgian francs. All the costs are payable in Belgian francs. The widgets will be sold under an advance contract at $51/widget worth of Belgian francs payable in Belgian francs.

Suppliers and labor will not extend any credit to this company, and the buyer will not prepay for the product. Thus, the first problem the financial officer encounters is how to finance the manufacture of the widgets. The forecast of monthly cash flows appears as follows:

Forecast Cash Flows (in million dollars' worth of Belgian francs)

	Month 1	*Month 2*	. . .	*Month 12*	*Cumulative*
Revenues	—	+51		+51	+561
Expenditures	-50	-50		-54	-604
Net flow	-50	+1		-3	-43

The higher expenditures in Month 12 are due to $4 million of repairs scheduled for that month. This $4 million equals the amount of depreciation and represents repairs to maintain the value of the plant and equipment at $40 million. Thus, of the $11 million of profits for the first year, the company reinvests $4 million. The parent company would like to repatriate as much as possible of the remaining $7 million in profits.

The financial officer must raise $50 million worth of Belgian francs before operations begin. The required maturity of this loan depends on the parent company's willingness to delay repatriation of profits. If dividend payments are delayed until the loan is repaid, there are roughly $7 million in the first year and $8 million in succeeding years available to repay the loan.[1] A seven-year loan maturity is possible under these conditions. As a compromise, assume that a fifteen-year loan is available so that the company repatriates about 50% of the profits every year ignoring net interest charges after taxes. These financing arrangements will modify the cash flows as follows:

Forecast Cash Flows (in million dollars' worth of Belgian francs)

	Month 1	*Month 2*	...	*Month 11*	*Month 12*
Flow before financing	-50	+1		+1	-3.0
$50 million loan	+50				-3.5
	0	+1		+1	-6.5
Cumulative cash flow	0	+1		+10	+3.5

In addition to the problem of finding the optimum way to finance the $50 million, the financial officer is responsible for the management of the exchange risk created by the financing, if any, as well as by the operation as a whole.

Financing Options

If it is assumed that a fifteen-year loan is available in every currency of interest, the following options are available:

1. Borrow Belgian francs.
2. Borrow dollars (the parent's home currency) or any third currency.
3. Borrow dollars or any third currency on a covered basis against Belgian francs.
4. Borrow Belgian francs or any third currency on a covered basis against dollars.

Each of these options, even if available for the same maturity, will carry a different nominal interest rate. To decide among the various options, it is necessary to consider exchange risk in order to arrive at a *net effective cost of funds.* A financial policy designed to minimize the cost of financing will choose the financing option with the lowest net effective cost.

[1] The exact amount of funds available to repay the principal is $7 million less interest payments.

Exposure to Foreign Exchange Risk

As discussed earlier, there are different types of exposure. Below we discuss the exposure involved in each financing option and in the business operation as a whole under each type of exposure.

Transaction Exposure. Regardless of the financial option chosen, this business will produce an annual transaction exposure in the form of dividend remittance. One of the problems of the financial officer is to decide whether to secure in advance an exchange rate for this transaction through an exchange hedge or to wait until the remittance actually takes place.

Whether there is another transaction exposure in this business depends on the financing option chosen.

BORROWING BELGIAN FRANCS. Under this alternative, the proceeds from operations can be used to repay the debt without any transaction in the exchange markets; both are in Belgian francs. There is no transaction exposure arising from the loan.

BORROWING DOLLARS OR A THIRD CURRENCY. If the currency of the loan is other than Belgian francs, including U.S. dollars, a transaction exposure arises. At the time of the repayment Belgian francs must be converted into the currency of the loan. Whether an exchange gain or loss occurs at this time depends on the spot rate prevailing then relative to the exchange rate at the time when the loan was taken down.

BORROWING DOLLARS OR A THIRD CURRENCY COVERED AGAINST BELGIAN FRANCS. Regardless of the currency of the loan, if a forward contract is entered into to sell Belgian francs and purchase the other currency at the time of repayment of the loan, the exchange risk in this transaction is eliminated. The forward rate establishes in advance the rate at which the exchange conversion needed for the repayment will take place. This may involve an additional cost if the foreign currency is selling at a premium against the Belgian franc in the forward market; however, this cost will be known with certainty in advance and can be used in conjunction with the interest rate to estimate the net effective cost of the loan.

BORROWING BELGIAN FRANCS OR A THIRD CURRENCY COVERED AGAINST DOLLARS. In this case we have locked in an exchange rate between the borrowed currency and the dollar. However, the currency that will be available for repayment is Belgian francs, not U.S. dollars. If the currency of the loan is Belgian francs, the forward contract just creates a new exposure because the dollars obtained from the forward purchase must be exchanged back into Belgian francs. If the currency of the loan is a third currency, the cover transaction does not eliminate the transaction exposure; it just changes the nature of this exposure. It changes it from an exposure of Belgian francs against the borrowed currency to an exposure of the Belgian franc against the dollar.

Translation Exposure. At the end of the first year of operations the financial statements of the Belgian affiliate will appear as follows:

Balance Sheet
December 31, 1900
(in million dollars' worth of Belgian francs)

Assets		*Liabilities and Equity*	
Cash	$ 3.5	Borrowings	$46.5
Inventory	50.0	Paid-in capital	40.0
Plant and equipment	40.0	Retained earnings	7.0
	$93.5		$93.5

Income Statement
For the Year Ending December 31, 1900
(in million dollars' worth of Belgian francs)

Sales	$561
Less cost of goods sold	550
Operating profits	11
Less depreciation	4
Net profits	$ 7

Under FASB #8 the cash and borrowing accounts are translated at current exchange rates. The inventory account will be translated at current exchange rates only in case of a large depreciation of the Belgian franc against the dollar. Otherwise, the inventory account will be translated at historical exchange rates. If it is assumed that a large depreciation of the Belgian franc is expected, the balance sheet contains $53.5 million of exposed assets. The amount of exposed liabilities depends on the option taken to finance the operation, i.e. the currency of the borrowings. Thus, if the borrowings are made in Belgian francs, the net exposure in the balance sheet is $7.0 million (equal to $53.5 million assets less $46.5 liabilities).

In the income statement the $11 million of operating profits will be translated at the *average* of the exchange rates prevailing during the period. The depreciation account, however, will be translated at historical rates. Thus, the translation exposure in the income statement is $11 million.

If there is a 10% depreciation of the Belgian franc against the dollar during the year, there will be a total translation loss in the amount of $1.25 million. This is composed of a $0.7 million loss in the translation of the balance sheet (a $7.00 million net asset position assuming financing in Belgian francs) plus a $0.44 million loss in the income statement (an $11 million operating profit depreciated at an average of 4% for the year). After the exchange depreciation, the net profits in terms of dollars will be $5.86 million instead of the anticipated $7.0 million.[2]

Let us now see how the various financing options affect translation exposure. For simplicity's sake we have ignored interest payments. Thus, the exposure of the income statement remains the same throughout the various financing options. In fact, interest payments also will be translated at average exchange rates for the period.

BORROWING BELGIAN FRANCS. The balance sheet exposure in this case is a net asset position of $7 million in Belgian francs. The financing in Belgian francs helps to reduce the net asset position in this currency.

BORROWING DOLLARS OR A THIRD CURRENCY. The net Belgian franc exposure is the same as the total of exposed assets. There are no liabilities in the currency to reduce the asset exposure. If the financing is done in dollars, no other exposure will be incurred for translation purposes. However, if the financing is made in a third currency, say Swiss francs, the company will have a net liability position of $46.5 million in Swiss francs, in addition to the net asset position in Belgian francs.

2

Translation of Balance Sheet

	Exchange Rate			*Exchange Rate*	
	1:1	*1:0.9*		*1:1*	*1:0.9*
Cash	3.5	3.15	Borrowings	46.5	41.85
Inventory	50.0	45.00	Paid-in capital	40.0	40.00
Plant and equipment			Retained earnings	7.0	5.86
Initial (after deprc.)	36.0	36.00			
Acquisition	4.0	3.60			
	93.5	87.75		93.5	87.71

Translation of Income Statement

	Exchange Rate	
	1:1	*1:0.96*
Sales	561	538.56
Cost of goods sold	550	528.00
Operating profit	11	10.56
Less depreciation	4	4.00
	7	6.56
Foreign exchange loss on translation of balance sheet	—	0.70
Net profits	7	5.86

BORROWING DOLLARS OR A THIRD CURRENCY COVERED AGAINST BELGIAN FRANCS. A covered liability is translated at the rate in the forward exchange contract. If the borrowings are in dollars, the forward contract is a dollar rate and the rate will remain constant throughout the life of the contract. If the borrowings are in a third currency, say Swiss francs, the forward rate will lock in an exchange rate in terms of Swiss francs against Belgian francs. In fact, the forward contract converts the Swiss franc debt into a Belgian franc debt. For translation purposes, the initial value of the debt is the dollar equivalent of the Belgian francs required to repay the debt under the forward contract. However, as the parity between the dollar and the Belgian franc changes, the translated dollar value of the debt will be changed. Thus, the net balance sheet exposure is \$53.5 million in net assets if dollars are borrowed and it is \$53.5 million less the dollar value of the debt translated at the exchange rate in the forward contract if a third currency is used. If there is neither premium nor discount in the forward rate, the net exposure in Belgian francs will be \$7 million.

BORROWING BELGIAN FRANCS OR A THIRD CURRENCY COVERED AGAINST DOLLARS. In this case the cover establishes a fixed rate for the value of the debt in terms of dollars. That is, the liability is not exposed to translation gains or losses. The cover has effectively converted the debt into a dollar debt. The net balance sheet exposure in this financing option is \$53.5 million net asset position in Belgian francs. The value of the debt in dollars will be determined by the forward rate against the dollar.

Exhibit 9.1 summarizes the implications of each of the financing options for transaction and translation exposures.

EXHIBIT 9.1. Summary of Exposure Implications of Alternative Financing Options

Financing Option	*Transaction Exposure*	*Translation Exposure*[a]
Borrowing Belgian francs	None	53.5 - 46.5 = 7.0 in BF
Borrowing dollars	At the end of each year: 3.5 long in BF 3.5 short in \$	53.5 net assets in BF
Borrowing a third currency	At the end of each year: 3.5 long in BF 3.5 short in third currency	53.5 net assets in BF 46.5 net liability in third currency
Borrowing a third currency covered against Belgian francs	None	53.5 - 46.5[b] = 7.0[b] in BF
Borrowing a third currency covered against dollars	At the end of each year: 3.5 long in BF 3.5 short in \$	53.5 net assets in BF

[a]Ignores translation of profits. Profits are in Belgian francs regardless of the financing option chosen.

[b]Actual figure depends on the forward rate between BF and third currency.

Economic Exposure. If it is assumed that this is a stable operation in which every year repeats the performance presented above for the first year, this operation will generate $12 million in profits annually, of which $4 million is reinvested to maintain the value of the equipment.[3] The total economic value of this affiliate is the sum of $8 million received *every year* ad infinitum discounted at the appropriate discount factor. If it is assumed that the parent company maintains a constant leverage by refinancing any portion of the debt which is repaid, the $8 million annual cash flow will be distributed $3.5 million to lenders and $4.5 million to the parent company.[4]

Because of the legal characteristics of debt obligations, lenders do not absorb the exchange risk of the borrower. Exchange gains or losses in these financings accumulate to the equity holders. The lender of Swiss francs receives the same amount of Swiss francs lent out initially. If the exchange rate between the Belgian franc and the Swiss franc varies during the life of the loan, any gain or loss accrues to the Belgian borrower. Thus, the economic exposure to exchange risk of the Belgian operation consists of two factors:

1. The transaction exposure of the financing option.
2. Net profits before financing.

In the preceding section we discussed the transaction exposure involved in each financing option. Now we turn to the exposure of profits. If there is a depreciation of the Belgian franc, what would be the effect on these figures? The answer to this question depends on how soon, if at all, selling prices can be renegotiated and on what inflation rate in costs accompanies or follows the depreciation. These issues were discussed in Chapter 8. Operating management is closer to these problems than the financial officer is; hence, the control system advocated in that chapter is appropriate.

If we could assume that all prices (selling prices as well as costs) adjust instantaneously to a depreciation, that they do so by the same relative magnitude as the amount of depreciation, and that the quantity of widgets sold remains constant, there is no economic exposure to exchange risk in the profit component of economic exposure. If, in addition, the financing is carried in Belgian francs, then the Belgian operation has zero economic exposure to exchange fluctuations. Now, these are very strong assumptions. In reality, there will be at least a transition period before prices can be adjusted. In this case the profits during the adjustment period constitute the extent of the economic exposure.

By careful construction of this example we eliminated one source of discrepancy between translation and economic exposure: the use of historical costs in the preparation of financial statements. In our example, inventory turned over every month and annual repairs maintained the value of plant and equipment at a constant level. In practice, these are not likely to be valid assumptions and adjustments will have to be made to the profit figures to reflect

[3]The operating profit of $12 million is based on twelve months of sales in contrast to eleven months for the first year.

[4]If a discount rate of 10% is assumed, the economic value of the whole operation is $80 million. The value of the debt is $35 million and the value of the equity is $45 million.

replacement values in order to reconcile the profits for accounting purposes and the profits for economic exposure purpose.

Exposure Measures Compared. Assume only two financing choices: Belgian francs or dollars. Also assume that operations can be adjusted after two years to produce the level of profits initially forecast. A 100% dividend payout is assumed.

Ignoring the first year, when there are only eleven months of production, the exposures under the two financing options are:

Exposures under Belgian franc financing:

Transaction. For every year the amount of dividends repatriated, $4.5 million.

Translation. At the end of every year net exposed assets plus profits (54.5 - 46.5 + 12.0), $20.0 million.

Economic. During the first two years $4.5 million profit every year. None afterward.

Exposures under dollar financing:

Transaction. For every year the amount of dividends repatriated, $4.5 million, plus debt repayment, $3.5 million. Total is $8.0 million per year.

Translation. At the end of every year net exposed assets plus profits (54.5 + 12.0), $46.5 million.

Economic. During the first two years $4.5 million profits plus $3.5 million debt repayment; in years two through maturity of the loan, $3.5 million debt repayment.

This summary shows economic exposure as a refinement of transaction exposure. The refinement consists of incorporating *monetary* adjustments in operations (i.e., price changes) in the computation of economic exposure. After these changes become operational, the level of profits adjusts to compensate for exchange fluctuations.

The greatest difference in results provided by the various exposure measures is between translation exposure and the other two exposures. Clearly the type of exposure that management focuses upon will determine the amount which they may consider hedging.

REACHING FINANCIAL DECISIONS

How is management to reach a decision that considers all these financial variables and outcomes? Two major factors will determine the decisions: (1) the nature of financial markets and (2) management's attitude toward exchange risk.

Nature of Financial Markets

The financial markets can be divided into two types: efficient markets and inefficient markets. In an efficient market all available information is quickly reflected in the observed prices. There is no reward for individuals who try to anticipate the future. In this market the best forecast of future spot rates available is the current forward exchange rate. The relationship of the forward rate to the spot rate, in turn, equals the interest rate differential between the two currencies involved. Thus, the money markets in which interest rates are determined implicitly anticipate fluctuations in the exchange rates also. Under these conditions, the *expected* net effective cost of all financial options is the same. Currencies carrying a high interest rate tend to depreciate in value and currencies with a low interest rate tend to appreciate in value. After the fact, one financing option will appear to have been superior to the others. However, in these markets it would be impossible to anticipate *consistently* which financial option would be best. In inefficient markets, on the other hand, research on the part of the manager may be rewarded with profits beyond any transaction and search costs. Over the long run, the manager has a chance to profit if the appropriate analysis of currencies is conducted. Clearly, the conditions of the market for any currency may change from time to time.

Management's Attitude Toward Exchange Risk

Once the manager establishes the nature of the relevant financial markets, the choice of specific financial options depends on the manager's attitude toward exchange risk. How much is the manager willing to pay in order to avoid this risk? Below we present four types of attitudes as examples.

Risk Paranoid. To this manager, uncertainty about future exchange rates is unbearable. Regardless of whether the markets are efficient or not, all required financing will be done in the local currency. Often this manager will concentrate on the translation measure of exchange risk and hedge any exposure remaining after local financing.

Risk Neutral. This individual is a perfect example of economic rationality. To this person, $1 saved in interest rates equals $1 of expected exchange losses. In efficient markets, if any bias exists, it is toward borrowing in the lower-interest rate currency. The interest cost saving is certain while the expected exchange loss will take place only in the future. Considerations such as maintaining proper banking relationships may be the ones actually determining the decision. In inefficient markets low-cost options will be selected, regardless of exposure. This manager will concentrate on transaction or economic measures of exposure and will ignore the impact of translation on earnings per share. In inefficient markets some of these exposures may be hedged.

Asymmetrical Risk Aversion. Here, any foreign exchange loss carries a much larger weight in the manager's decision than a foreign exchange gain of the same magnitude. In efficient markets in which expected foreign exchange gains equal expected losses for any financial alternative, the manager will prefer the options in which the cost of financing appears in the form of interest cost instead of exchange losses. Even when a financial choice seems preferable because of inefficient markets, the option will not be chosen unless the chances of a significant exchange loss have a very small probability of occurring. Often the trigger number beyond which exchange losses are not acceptable is measured in terms of exposure for translation purposes. If probable exchange losses exceed a certain amount, hedging strategies will be initiated.

Aggressive Speculator. To this manager, the financial markets are just another opportunity to increase business profits. Financial markets are just one other market in which the firm operates and exploits opportunities. In efficient markets the behavior of this manager is closest to the one for the risk neutral manager described above. In inefficient markets, however, this manager will not be bound by the immediate financial requirements of the business. Depending on the degree of aggressiveness of the manager, exchange positions of varying magnitudes may be established to profit from market inefficiences.

Research has shown that the most prevalent behavior among financial officers of U.S. multinational companies is of the risk asymmetrical type.[5]

IMPACT OF ALTERNATIVE EXCHANGE POLICIES ON FINANCIAL DECISIONS

The four attitudes toward exchange risk just discussed represent pure cases of financial policies. In reality, management often trades off its preferences against the cost of achieving these preferences. Particularly if management considers the exchange markets inefficient, it will find it useful to examine the implications of alternative postures toward exchange risk. If markets are inefficient, dominant strategies can be found. Exchange exposure policies that require the firm to forego dominant financial strategies have their cost increased by the profits or cost savings foregone.

As an illustration of how to evaluate alternative exchange policies while considering the multiple financial problems simultaneously, we will introduce a new example in which more choices must be made than in the one-subsidiary example used in the earlier part of this chapter. The example will include three subsidiaries in three different countries and will provide three different future environments or scenarios in which the implications of different policies can be measured. Obviously, this approach can be easily adapted to a large number of countries and possible future scenarios with the aid of a computer program. However, our concern here is not so much with an exact analysis; it is with a framework that is useful in looking at the combined set of financial problems.

In exchange for the larger variety of choices, we will make some simplifying assumptions that facilitate the presentation. These are:

1. The relevant target of exposure management is exposure as defined by

[5]See Rita M. Rodriguez, "Management of Foreign Exchange Risk in U.S. Multinationals," *Sloan Management Review,* Spring 1978, pp. 31-49.

FASB #8 in the more general case in which inventories are translated at historical rates. That is, exposure in each currency is measured by the sum of cash plus accounts receivable less debt. There is no economic exposure since it is assumed that selling prices and costs can be adjusted quickly in response to exchange fluctuations. Since no dividends are scheduled, transaction exposure arises only from financing in a currency different from the ones generated by business operations. This is ignored directly and is considered indirectly through its impact on balance sheet exposure.

2. The time horizon for the analysis is one year. This avoids complications with calculations of the time-value of money and refinancing decisions. It also avoids dealing with fractions or annual interest figures.

3. Taxes are ignored.

Data for the Analysis

There are three types of data which one must have before starting to analyze the implications of a given foreign exchange policy:

1. A forecast of business operations.
2. Present actual market conditions.
3. A variety of scenarios for the market's situation at the end of the planning period.

Data Forecasting Business Operations and Describing Actual Market Conditions. In this category the officer needs:

1. A forecast of assets and liabilities per currency.
2. A forecast of flow of funds per currency.
3. The rate of return on business assets in each currency.
4. Initial interest rates in the domestic and Euro-markets, spot exchange rates, and forward exchange rates for each currency.

(1) normally appears at the end of a period during financial consolidation. However, it must be linked with the expected *changes* in those asset and liability positions (combining (1) and (2)) in order to consider covering policies. The data from (3) and (4) provide information required to evaluate the costs (and returns) of various strategies while (1) and (2) indicate the amount of funds involved. For our purposes here, one can eliminate the possibility of wrong forecasts on the operations of the business and proceed as if (1)–(3) were known with certainty. A wide range of values could be incorporated in the analysis. Again, this broader analysis involving risk considerations in one or more of the above data sets could be handled operationally on a computer with ease.

Data on Future Market Scenarios. Various strategies can be analyzed under a number of different *scenarios.* These scenarios may be thought of as possible *outcomes* or future *states of the world.* In this example the number of scenarios is reduced to three, which we will call:

1. The *most likely* outcome.
2. *No change* from the present situation.
3. A change *opposite to* the one anticipated in the *most likely* scenario.

Since there is a simplifying assumption of a one-year planning horizon, only the spot rates at the end of the period are needed. Interest rates and forward rates for multiple horizons would be relevant if the firm manager were thinking in terms of sequential financing. That consideration is omitted here for the sake of simplicity.

Steps in the Analysis

1. Choose a foreign exchange policy. Find what transactions this exchange management will generate in answering the three basic problems of the financial officer:
   a. In what currency should excess funds be invested?
   b. In what currency should funds be raised to meet financing requirements?
   c. After (a) and (b) are answered, what more could be done to achieve the desired foreign exchange exposure?
2. Establish the returns and costs of the financial transactions initiated under Step 1 with a variety of scenarios. For each scenario, disaggregate the costs/returns of financial transactions into three major components:
   a. Incremental financing.
   b. Remaining exchange exposure.
   c. Hedging undesirable exchange exposures.
3. Repeat the analysis presented under Steps 1 and 2 for alternative policies. In this example there will be three types of policies:
   a. *Aggressive.* Make the best estimate possible of currency changes and interest rates and act to minimize cost of financing and exchange exposure. Some positions may be "overhedged" when there are likely to be substantial gains from the cover to fully offset the exposure losses.
   b. *Zero exposure.* Reduce the exposure to revaluation effects in all nonparent currencies to the minimum. Finance each subsidiary in local currency and hedge any remaining exchange exposure.
   c. *Do nothing.* Let the chips fall where they may! Finance in the cheapest currencies, accept any exchange losses in the remaining assets, and do no hedging.

4. Select a decision criterion, or criteria (e.g., "maximize expected value").

5. Evaluate the results of the impacts of each policy under alternative scenarios:
   a. How likely is each scenario?
   b. What is the return or cost, given the decision rule from Step 4?

6. Reverse the previous analysis:
   a. What scenario would render a given policy unacceptable?
   b. How likely is that scenario?

Application of the Suggested Framework

Data for the Analysis: The Business and Market Environment. The example is based on data for three subsidiaries of a U.S. company; i.e., the dollar is the base currency. Subsidiaries are located in the United Kingdom, the Netherlands, and France. The outline will follow the form detailed earlier for obtaining and analyzing the various data items. In this section are (1) a forecast of business operations, (2) the actual foreign exchange and money market rates, and (3) the computation of net effective rates under alternative market scenarios.

1. FORECAST BUSINESS OPERATIONS

Balance Sheets—Today

United Kingdom				*Netherlands*				*France*			
Cash	$ 45			Cash	$ 10			Cash	$ 2		
A/R	100			A/R	75			A/R	50		
Inv.	50			Inv.	75			Inv.	50		
P&E	100	Equity	$295	P&E	20	Equity	$180	P&E	5	Equity	$107
	$295		$295		$180		$180		$107		$107

Forecast Balance Sheets—One Year Later

United Kingdom				*Netherlands*				*France*			
Cash	$ 45			Cash	$ 30			Cash	$ 2		
A/R	160	New		A/R	75			A/R	75	New	
Inv.	90	Funds[a]	$ 70	Inv.	75			Inv.	95	Funds[a]	$ 50
P&E	100	Equity[b]	325	P&E	20	Equity[b]	$200	P&E	5	Equity[b]	127
	$395		$395		$200		$200		$177		$177

[a]Financing to be raised, which will be done with some debt issue. The topic of the change in capital structure implied by this action will be discussed in Part Three.

[b]Includes retained profits from the year's operations, as detailed in the next table.

If it is assumed that initial cash balances are minimum amounts required for operations, then the flows of funds through the period are:

Forecast Sources and Uses of Funds

	United Kingdom	*Netherlands*	*France*
Sources:			
Profits	$ 30	$20	$20
Requiring Financing	70	—	50
	$100	$20	$70
Uses:			
↑A/R	$ 60	$ 0	$25
↑Inventories	40	$ 0	45
↑Cash	0	$20	0
	$100	$20	$70

Summary of Forecast Flow of Funds

Excess cash to be invested	Netherlands	$20
Funds to be raised	United Kingdom	70
	France	50

2. ACTUAL FOREIGN EXCHANGE AND MONEY MARKET RATES[6]

	US$	*Pound sterling (£)*	*Dutch guilder (DFl)*	*French franc (FF)*
Spot rates		$2.3820/£	DFl 2.6275/$	FF 4.6925/$
Forward 1-year rates		$2.3025/£	DFl 2.6095/$	FF 4.9525/$
Forward premium (discount) against US$		-3.3%	+0.7%	-5.5%
Interest rates				
Euro-market	12.5%	16.5%	11.7%	17.5%
Domestic	9.0%	14.0%	12.5%	14.0%

Notice that interest parity holds roughly in the external markets. The forward premium or discount of each currency against the dollar approximates the interest rate differential between the two currencies in the Euro-markets or external markets.

[6]These rates represent midpoint rates. In practice, one would deal with bid and offer rates as discussed in Chapter 5. Notice that the quotes are expressed in terms of $/£, DFl/S, and FF/$, the standard procedure in the country of each currency.

3. EFFECTIVE RATES UNDER ALTERNATIVE MARKET SCENARIOS

Effective Rates under "Most Likely" Market

	US$	*£*	*DFl*	*FF*
Spot rates		\$2.20/£	DFl 2.50/\$	FF 4.80/\$
Forecast % revaluation		-7.6%	+4.8%	-2.3%
Effective interest rates				
Euro-market	12.5%	8.9% (16.5 - 7.6)	16.5% (11.7 + 4.8)	15.2% (17.5 - 2.3)
Domestic	9.0%	6.4% (14.0 - 7.6)	17.3% (12.5 + 4.8)	11.7% (14.0 - 2.3)

The *most likely* scenario in these cases implies that the manager's forecast of the exchange markets differs from the one imbedded in current rates. The manager's most likely future spot rate in all these cases is different from the current forward exchange rate; i.e., the manager is disregarding the information contained in current forward rates on the assumption that exchange markets are inefficient and his or her forecast of future spot rates can be better than the market's. If markets are considered to be efficient, the figures for the *most likely* outcome would be the implicit forecast of the forward rate. Effective interest rates are the algebraic sum of the nominal interest rate and the forecast revaluation in the spot rate.[7]

The other two scenarios presented below can be seen as two specific possibilities of the markets, regardless of whether they are efficient or inefficient.

Effective Rates under "No Change" Market

Spot rates—same as actual market rates shown earlier.

Effective interest rates—same as actual market rates shown earlier.

Effective Rates under "Opposite to Most Likely" Market

	US$	*£*	*DFl*	*FF*
Spot rates		\$2.50/£	DFl.2.65/\$	FF 4.60/\$
Forecast % revaluation		+5.0%	-0.9%	+2.0%
Effective interest rates				
Euro-market	12.5%	21.5% (16.5 + 5.0)	10.8% (11.7 - 0.9)	19.5% (17.5 + 2.0)
Domestic	9.0%	19.0% (14.0 + 5.0)	11.6% (12.5 - 0.9)	16.0% (14.0 + 2.0)

Prescriptions and Implications of an Aggressive Policy. Having provided the necessary data for the analysis, we can now study the implications of alternative

[7]This is accurate only if borrowings are made on a discounted basis. In addition, one must take into account the impact of changes in spot exchange rates on interest payments. See Chapter 7.

exchange risk policies. In this section we analyze a specific policy: an aggressive policy. We must first determine the prescriptions of this policy to solve the various financing problems. Then we can estimate the associated returns or costs under alternative market scenarios.

The costs or returns are subdivided into three components which are associated with:

1. Incremental financing.
2. Remaining exchange exposure.
3. Hedging undesirable exchange exposures.

The three components are then combined. By segregating the costs/returns of the finance function into the three major components, one obtains a better grasp of the implications of alternative financing strategies. Given that management may have different risk attitudes toward each of the components in the finance function, the segregation should be useful in choosing the desired financial strategy.

SOURCES OF INCREMENTAL FINANCING. The objectives of the financial officer in managing cash flows are to invest excess funds at the highest possible effective rate and to borrow at the lowest possible effective rate, given exchange risk constraints. Under the aggressive policy, the decision maker will take the estimates of the "most likely" outcome as if this were a certain outcome and act to maximize profits accordingly. In the example this rule would dictate: "Borrow domestic pounds as much as possible, and invest excess funds in domestic guilders as much as possible."

This conclusion is derived from the effective interest rate calculations shown above. The cheapest *source* of financing is the domestic pound at 6.4%. If external markets must be used for borrowing because of foreign exchange controls, the £ is still the cheapest currency at 8.9% vs. 16.5% for the Euro-guilder and 15.2% for the Euro-franc. The effective Euro-pound rate is actually lower than the domestic rate for each of the other currencies. On the other hand, the best *use* of funds is the domestic guilder (17.3%), if it is possible to deposit or lend funds there. Alternatively, the best use of funds in the external markets is the Euro-guilder at 16.5%.

If all these opportunities are available *but domestic markets can be used only by local subsidiaries and transactions between subsidiaries are avoided,* then the Summary of Forecast Flow of Funds would indicate that the parent should direct the subsidiaries to complete the following transactions:

United Kingdom:	-\$70–Raise funds in domestic pounds.
Netherlands:	+\$20–Invest the funds in the domestic guilder market.
France:	-\$50–Raise funds in Euro-pounds.

The transactions will maximize revenues (or minimize costs) in the management of incremental financing needs under the most likely scenario, given the two restrictive assumptions above.

Now one can compute the return (cost) of this policy by combining decisions with the effective interest rates calculated earlier for each scenario.

Returns/Costs of Incremental Financing

	Scenario		
Subsidiary	*Most Likely*	*No Change*	*Opposite to Likely*
U.K. (£)	-$70 @ 6.4% = $4.5	-$70 @ 14.0% = -$ 9.8	-$70 @ 19.0% = -$13.3
Nether. (DFI)	+ 20 @ 17.3% = 3.5	+ 20 @ 12.5% = 2.5	+ 20 @ 11.6% = 2.3
France (Euro £)	- 50 @ 8.9% = -4.4	- 50 @ 16.5% = -8.3	- 50 @ 21.5% = -10.7
	-$5.4	-$15.6	-$21.7

REMAINING EXCHANGE EXPOSURE. The solution to the problems created by incremental financing in some cases helps to reduce the level of exposure to exchange risk; however, in other cases these financing decisions increase this exposure. We must look at the residual exposure and estimate the costs or returns that may be incurred under alternative scenarios because of this exposure. This residual exposure is the combination of two decisions: the decision to invest in the specific countries and the decision to finance the operation in a given fashion.

We assumed earlier that there was no economic exposure to exchange risk in this business and that management concentrated on the exchange exposure as measured by FASB #8. We will further assume now that management places the same value on $1 of reported exchange gains or losses from the translation of financial statements as on $1 gain or loss in cash.

Combining the forecast exposure before financing (cash plus accounts receivable at the end of the period) with the financing decisions taken in the previous section will produce the forecast exposure after financing for the three subsidiaries in combination.

Forecast Exposures to Exchange Risk

	£	*DFI*	*FF*
Forecast exposure before incremental financing (Cash + A/R)	$205	$105	$77
Impact of financing	- 70 - 50[a]		
Total forecast exposure after financing	+$ 85	+$105	+$77

[a]For France.

Now one can join the forecast exposure after incremental financing with the changes in spot rates specified under each scenario. Although the firm has borrowed to meet its incremental financing needs in the currency expected to devalue, pounds, an exposure to fluctuations in the value of that currency remains. In spite of the additional pound borrowings, the company still has a net asset position in pounds. It also has a net asset position in French francs, another currency expected to depreciate against the U.S. dollar. The incremental financings, however, have helped to bolster the asset position in the currency expected to appreciate against the dollar, the guilder. The combination on the initial balance sheet positions and incremental financing, in the absence of any other action in the exchange markets, will provide translation foreign exchange gains and losses which can be computed as follows:

Returns/Costs of Residual Exposure under Alternative Scenarios

Most Likely	*No Change*	*Opposite to Likely*
(£) \$ 85 X −7.6% = −\$6.5	Nothing	(£) \$ 85 X +5.0% = +\$4.3
(DFI) \$105 X +4.8% = + 5.0		(DFI) \$105 X −0.9% = − 1.0
(FF) \$ 77 X −2.3% = − 1.8		(FF) \$ 77 X +2.0% = + 1.5
−\$3.3		+\$4.8

HEDGING UNDESIRABLE EXCHANGE EXPOSURES. Under an aggressive policy, the decision maker will not be happy with positive exposures in depreciating currencies or negative exposures in appreciating currencies. The manager may even want to profit from expected changes in exchange rates. Under the expected outcome, there will be a foreign exchange loss of \$3.3 when the gains and losses in the three currencies are combined, as shown in the preceding table.

Since the forecast for future spot rates which the manager considers most likely differs from the market's forecast (the current forward rate), a hedging strategy can be devised to try to eliminate exchange losses altogether, and even to produce exchange gains.

Under the conventional hedging transactions discussed in Chapters 6 and 7, the amount of the hedge is the same as the amount of the exposure. The purpose is to lock in a specific exchange rate—the forward rate—or interest differential for the translation of the exposure. The cost of this hedge is the premium or discount of the forward rate relative to the spot rate or the interest differential. Regardless of what actually happens to future spot rates, the manager knows with certainty the exchange gain or loss to be reported in the transaction.[8]

The alternative hedging strategies suggested in this section depart from the traditional ones in two ways: The amount of the hedge is different from the amount of the exposure, and positive exposures in appreciating currencies or negative exposures in depreciating currencies are incurred in order to generate exchange gains. The objective here is not to lock in a rate, but to produce exchange gains. However, should the manager's forecast prove wrong, the expected gains can turn into losses if the spot rate actually moves in the opposite direction from the one anticipated.

In the case of sterling, the exposure remaining after the incremental fi-

[8]The *opportunity* exchange gain or loss, however, depends on the actual future spot rate. See Chapter 6.

nancing will produce a loss of \$6.5 under the scenario the manager considers most likely. In this scenario the manager expects a 7.6% depreciation of the pound. This compares with the market's forecast of about 4% depreciation for the pound (a 4% interest differential among Euro-rates and a 3.3% discount on the forward rates). One possibility for producing exchange gains in sufficient amount to compensate for the expected exchange losses in sterling, \$6.5, is to sell pounds forward against dollars at \$2.3025/£, the current forward rate. If the expected spot rate of \$2.20/£ materializes, there will be a gain of \$0.1025/£ (equal to \$2.3025 - \$2.2000). The amount of pounds to be sold forward can be determined as follows:

$$(\text{Amount £ hedged}) \times (0.1025) = \$6.5$$

$$\text{Amount £ hedged} = \frac{\$6.5}{0.1025} = £63.41$$

At the current spot rate of \$2.3820/£, this amount of pounds equals a hedge in the amount of \$151.04. This is an amount substantially larger than the exposure of \$85.

An alternative to just increasing the amount of the hedge in a specific currency is to generate an exchange gain by assuming an exchange position in another currency. In our example the guilder is expected to appreciate. The market expects it to appreciate by only 1% (0.7% in the forward market, 0.8% in interest differentials in the Euro-markets) while management expects it to appreciate by 4.8%. A long position in guilders will generate exchange gains. Let us do this hedge through the money market. In the money market it is necessary to borrow the funds, say pounds at 16.5%, and invest the proceeds in guilders at 11.7%. This interest differential appears to guarantee a loss. However, the manager is expecting a depreciation of 7.6% in sterling and an appreciation of 4.8% in the guilder. This brings the expected effective interest rates to 8.9% (equal to 16.5% less 7.6%) in sterling and 16.5% (equal to 11.7% plus 4.8%) in guilders, for an expected gain of 7.6% on each pound involved in the hedge. How many pounds must be hedged to produce an exchange gain of \$6.5? To take into account the impact of the expected exchange fluctuation on the value of interest paid and received, the following formula can be applied:[9]

$$\text{Amount hedged} = \frac{\text{Expected loss}}{(1 + R_I)(1 + \text{Reval}) - (1 + R_B)(1\ \text{Reval}_B)}$$

where R_I = nominal interest rate on currency of investment
R_B = nominal interest rate on currency borrowed
Reval = percentage revaluation

$$\text{Amount hedged} = \frac{\$6.5}{(1 + 0.117)(1 + 0.048) - (1 + 0.165)(1 - 0.076)} = \$68$$

[9]The intuitive answer to the question of how many pounds will have to be hedged at a 7.6% profit per pound to produce a gain of \$6.5 is \$85, equal to 6.5 ÷ 0.076. This ignores the impact of exchange fluctuations on interest which is measured by the multiplicative relationships in the denominator of this formula.

In this case the amount that the aggressive policy prescribes for the hedge, \$68, is actually less than the amount of the exposure, \$85. In spite of the aggressive nature of this policy, it is safe to assume that the manager would rather use a smaller than a larger amount of hedge to accomplish the same result: eliminating the exchange losses under the most likely scenario. However, it must be noticed that this hedge involves the forecast of two currency values in terms of dollars (sterling and the guilder) instead of only one (sterling against dollars) in the previous approach. Assume that this additional risk just serves to deter the aggressive manager from trying to generate profits larger than the amount of expected exchange losses.

Because the residual exchange position in the guilder is likely to produce a gain, no hedging tactic is prescribed by the aggressive policy in this case.

To simplify the presentation, assume that management considers the expected loss in the residual exposure in French francs, \$1.8, relatively small to warrant the risk of trying to generate exchange gains to compensate for it.[10] However, under the aggressive policy, management is not willing to pay approximately 5.5%, the market's discount on the forward French franc, to protect the exposure against a depreciation which is expected to be around 2.3%.

Now the firm can compute the difference in costs from this decision to cover the pound exposure under the three outcomes. By the calculations of the amount to be hedged, the gain from hedging will be exactly the amount of the pound loss under the most likely alternative, \$6.5. Under the no change outcome, the cost of hedging will be the differential interest rate, (11.7 - 16.5 =) 4.8%, times the \$68 hedged. Under the opposite to likely, the cost of hedging can be found by multiplying the adjusted interest rate differential by the \$68.[11] The results are shown in the table below.

Returns/Costs of Hedging under Alternative Scenarios

Most Likely	*No Change*	*Opposite to Likely*
+\$6.5	-\$3.3	-\$7.9

[10] If the formula presented above is used, to produce exchange gains of \$1.8 under the most likely scenario, it is necessary to borrow francs and invest the proceeds in guilders in the amount of \$78:

$$\frac{\text{Amount}}{\text{Hedged}} = \frac{\$1.8}{(1 + 0.117)(1 + 0.048) - (1 + 0.175)(1 - 0.023)} = \$78$$

[11] $$\text{Gain (Loss)} = \frac{\text{Amount}}{\text{Hedged}} \left[(1 + R_I)(1\ \text{Reval}_I) - (1 + R_B)(1\ \text{Reval}_B)\right]$$

where R_I = nominal interest rate of investment currency
R_B = nominal interest rate of borrowed currency
Reval = percentage revaluation

$$\text{Gain (Loss)} = \$68 \times [(1 + 0.117)(1 - 0.009) - (1 + 0.165)(1 + 0.05)] = -\$7.9$$

If the forecast is correct, there are hedging gains. Otherwise, the hedging operation produces losses.

Notice that in this example the hedging decision moves in the same direction as the incremental financing decision. In both cases, effective rates on a most likely basis suggest borrowing funds in pounds and investing them in guilders. A more difficult situation arises when the hedging decision actually indicates moves opposite to those dictated by the incremental financing decision. This would be the case if the effective interest rates calculated initially included a depreciation instead of an appreciation of the guilder. Under these assumptions, the incremental financing decision might still dictate borrowing funds in pounds and investing them in guilders. However, the expected exchange gain in guilders of \$5.0 in the example would instead become an exchange loss of \$105 (the exposure) times the percentage depreciation. In economic terms one might say that this is an exchange loss worth having if the gain in interest differentials in the financing more than compensates for the loss in exposure. However, the manager might still believe that, although the long exposure in guilders makes sense economically, the implications of the guilder exposure for financial reporting (translating foreign exchange losses) would be unacceptable. In that case hedging would have an additional cost because the cost associated with incremental financing will be higher. Management's ability to explain foreign exchange losses reported explicitly vs. interest differential costs submerged in the financial charges account will dictate the amount of "irrational" hedging that management will contract.

TOTAL COST OF AGGRESSIVE POLICY UNDER EACH SCENARIO. One can now combine the financial costs and returns of the three components under the aggressive policy for each of the three different scenarios to find the total cost or return of this exposure policy under each scenario.

Combined Returns/Costs of Aggressive Policy

	Scenario		
	Most Likely	*No Change*	*Opposite to Likely*
Incremental financing	-\$5.4	-\$15.6	-\$21.7
Remaining exposure	- 3.3	—	4.8
Hedging	6.5	- 3.3	- 7.9
	-\$2.2	-\$18.9	-\$24.8

Final Evaluation of Alternative Exchange Policies. If the analysis shown above is completed for *each* of the policies under consideration, it is then possible to review the outcome of each policy or strategy in comparison with the others on each scenario. The results of these computations for the two other alternatives ("zero exposure" and "do nothing") may be combined with the return/cost figures of the "aggressive" policy to produce the following table:[12]

Returns/Cost of Alternative Exchange Policies

	Scenario		
Policy	*Most Likely*	*No Change*	*Opposite to Likely*
Aggressive	-$2.2	-$18.9	-$24.8
Zero exposure	- 9.6	- 16.0	- 20.6
Do nothing	- 8.7	- 15.6	- 16.9

Under the policy of zero exposure, we assume that the firm will first meet its financial needs in the local financial market, up to the point where zero exposure is achieved using the cheaper of domestic or Euro-currency markets. Beyond that exposure level the firm would finance with the parent's reference currency, dollars. If the required financing leaves an exposure to foreign exchange risk, the exposure will be hedged. An amount equal in size to the amount of the exposure will be used in the hedging operation. Borrowings for hedging purposes will be made in the local or the Euro-market, whichever is less expensive. Proceeds from the borrowings for hedging purposes will be invested in the highest yielding dollars. Since the amount used in the hedging operation is the same as the amount exposed, the cost of hedging is the interest differential. Excess funds are also converted into dollars.

Under the do nothing strategy, funds are raised in the cheapest source and invested in the highest yielding currency, as with the aggressive strategy. In this three-part analysis, do nothing will require proceeding only as far as step one, selecting the optimum incremental financing mix. This policy will not cover any foreign exchange exposure remaining after financing. Foreign exchange risk will enter into the calculations only to the extent required to calculate the net interest yields (nominal interest rate plus foreign exchange expectations). In essence, this strategy is not as passive as it might seem. It presumes consideration of foreign exchange rates when financing is done (like the aggressive strategy) but refuses to consider doing anything about the translation losses on the remaining exposed assets.

From this table summarizing the implications of alternative financing strategies under various outcomes in the market, one has then to reach a decision on the policy to follow. Here the important variables are management's attitude toward *risk* and the *size* of the funds involved. Thus, the management might be willing to gamble on a 50-50 proposition if the sum is $1. The same odds and the same gamble would not be so appealing if there is $1 million involved. The principle applies to the corporation as well as to the individual.

Among the criteria that management may use to select the desired financial strategy is a rule dictating the choice of the strategy with the highest expected value (least cost). To use this expected value decision rule, assign probabilities to each scenario. For example, assign 0.6 to the most likely alterna-

[12]The actual calculation of the results under the do nothing and zero exposure strategies are assigned as questions at the end of the chapter.

tive, 0.3 to no change, and 0.1 to the opposite to likely scenario. With these probabilities, one can compute the expected value for each policy. Under the aggressive policy, the expected return under the three scenarios is -\$9.47, that is [(0.6 × -\$2.2) + (0.3 × -\$18.9) + (0.1 × -\$24.8)]. Similarly, the expected values for the zero exposure policy and do nothing policy are -\$12.62 and -\$11.59, respectively. This analysis indicates the dominance of the aggressive strategy on an expected value standard.

One can alter the probabilities, searching for the break-even point at which there must be a "greater-than-*x*%" expectation for the most likely outcome and below which *x*% the aggressive strategy is no longer dominant.[13] In addition, management may want to examine other probabilities, reviewing how the trade-offs vary under alternative policies and different probability assessments.

For the reasons indicated above on the \$1-vs.-\$1-million gamble, expected value may not be the main criterion. Management might not be willing to live with even a 0.1 probability of a \$24.8 loss, which would be possible given an opposite to likely outcome and the aggressive strategy. It may be that such a loss would not be tolerated, rendering the expected value of this strategy unimpor-

[13] If the ratio of no change to opposite to likely scenario probabilities remains at 3 to 1, then the strategy which would eventually come to dominate would be do nothing. Combining these two scenarios, we can solve algebraically for the probability (*P*) below which the aggressive policy is no longer dominant by using the following system of simultaneous equations:

Expected value of "do nothing:"

$$P\left\{\begin{matrix}\text{Outcome}\\ \text{of ``do nothing''}\\ \text{under most likely}\end{matrix}\right\} + (1-P)\left\{\begin{matrix}\text{Weighted outcome of}\\ \text{``do nothing'' under no change}\\ \text{and opposite to likely}\end{matrix}\right\}$$

Expected value of "aggressive:"

$$P\left\{\begin{matrix}\text{Outcome}\\ \text{of ``aggressive''}\\ \text{under most likely}\end{matrix}\right\} + (1-P)\left\{\begin{matrix}\text{Weighted outcome}\\ \text{of ``aggressive'' under no}\\ \text{change and opposite to likely}\end{matrix}\right\}$$

Using the results from the table summarizing the impact of various strategies under alternative outcomes, we can calculate the weighted values as follows:

Weighted outcome of "do nothing" under no change and opposite to likely:

$$\frac{3 \times (-\$15.6) + (-\$16.9)}{4} = -\$15.9$$

Weighted outcome of "aggressive" under no change and opposite to likely:

$$\frac{3 \times (-\$18.9) + (-\$24.8)}{4} = -\$20.4$$

Substituting in the simultaneous equations above, we get:

$$P(-\$8.7) + (1-P)(-\$15.9)$$

$$P(-\$2.2) + (1-P)(-\$20.4)$$

These are equal at the breakeven *P*. Solving, we get $P = 0.41$.

Below this probability of the most likely outcome, "do nothing" is a superior policy on an expected value basis.

For further discussion of the analysis of risk see Chapter 11 in this book.

tant. Other such *loss functions* could be designed and considered after discussion with management.

SUMMARY AND CONCLUSION

The above framework has been used to evaluate three popular exchange policies for dealing with the financial problems that the multinational enterprise faces. Based on effective interest costs from various financing sources, the raising and deployment of funds were assigned a net cost or profit. Then a charge for gains or losses on remaining exposure to exchange risk was inserted. Finally, a charge for hedging certain unacceptable exposure positions was included where what was unacceptable varied depending on the exchange policy under evaluation. The sum of the costs or returns associated with each of these components produced the total cost or return of the specific exchange policy for each outcome in the exchange markets. Implicitly, the sum of these components assumed that $1 of exchange loss is equivalent to $1 of interest cost. In fact, the utility of exchange losses may be different from that of interest. The aggressive strategy was selected from among three strategies examined as the one that minimized the expected cost of the finance function, given assigned probabilities for different eventual states in the foreign exchange markets.

This example has dealt mainly with the short-term financial planning of the international firm, analogous to working capital management in traditional domestic corporation finance. It is useful to contrast this situation with operations in a single domestic environment in which there are generally no problems in providing financing for a given subsidiary if the parent (or the consolidated firm) has surplus cash. When facing international financing, there are limits on the mobility of funds. There are tariff rules which alter the pricing structure that can be used to move funds from subsidiary to subsidiary. There are differential tax considerations. There are absolute limits on the removal of profits and/or cash transfers between firms. There are local borrowing limits. There are exposure complexities. All of these represent restrictions that simply do not apply in the totally domestic operation. Note that even if the consolidated international firm were in total balance, external transactions for the sake of local tax and tariff considerations and the exposure situation would still be required in many cases.

There are some parallels in domestic conglomerates, where lenders to a given subsidiary and the decentralized incentive system for local managers influence cash transfers within the family, but these situations are not as constraining as most international examples.

In the preceding example we also followed a preestablished sequence of financial problems. We first solved the problem of providing incremental financing, then evaluated the impact on translation of foreign operations, and finally decided whether to cover or not and in what amount. An alternative sequence could result in different results, given that the actions under the alternative strategies would be changed. For example, if instead of the sequence used in the preceding example, the initial decision were based on creating a zero exposure in certain currencies, after which funds could be raised or deployed within a subset of the approved (i.e., nondevaluation-prone) currencies, then the cost/return results would differ in some cases.

In other situations there could be restrictions on quantities of funds which can be invested or borrowed in certain currencies by particular subsidiaries. These outer limits could be built into the analysis, if necessary.

The issue of intercompany transactions among sister companies was avoided, forcing each subsidiary to operate in the open markets and not having access to the domestic markets of other subsidiaries' national economies. In fact, this assumption could be eased in many organizational settings. The complexity of the analysis would be increased, together with problems of incentives and organizational rewards to the various subsidiary managers whose interests in a given situation would often conflict. The arm's-length guideline is a good operational rule for these transactions. The difficulty arises in dividing any extra savings one subsidiary realizes from having access to the domestic market of another subsidiary. Thus, the transfer price problem encountered in many firms (when one division sells a good to another division, and each division manager seeks a price which will maximize the division's profits) is encountered here as well.

Had the initial balance sheets included some debt for these three subsidiaries, then the firm would also have had the option of changing some of its debt exposure. This could have been done either by changing the currency of the debt or borrowing funds in another currency which then would be converted to the same currency as the existing debt. Either of these options might have been used under the zero exposure strategy or under possible interpretations of the aggressive strategy. The all-equity assumption in the initial balance sheets is used here for simplicity. If there had been existing debt and the firm was unwilling or unable to make changes in the currency or to borrow additional amounts for conversion to an asset which would offset the existing debt in that currency, then the all-equity assumption is still valid for considering incremental costs and revenues of various strategies under various outcomes.

Ultimately, the computer models suggested above would permit evaluation of a number of alternative strategies considered by management. In addition, mathematical formulations under certainty could optimize strategies given certain cost and revenue functions together with limits on the amount of funds which may be channeled around the firm. These formulations can be run under different expectations about the effective interest cost figures (pivoting on what happens to the various currencies involved), and management can see how the optimum strategy alters with various scenarios. Each formulation provides an optimum under a given scenario. Management could then evaluate each optimum for its return under the alternative scenarios. An expected value weighting system or a complex utility formulation could be introduced to aid management in finding a reasonable strategy for dealing with its currency environment.

Of course, when the one-period model above is replaced with a multiperiod analysis, the computational difficulties are vastly increased. More serious than the mathematical programming, computer programming, and computer capacity problems are the difficulties in forecasting (1) subsidiary funds flow, (2) currency effective interest rates, and (3) currency spot and forward rates for many periods of varied lengths many years into the future. Although the use of more sophisticated analyses will increase in future years, the practicality of the forecasting is a serious obstacle.

Various mathematical approaches to handling foreign exchange exposure management have been considered for over fifteen years. However, Carter and Rodriguez found that most managers of larger firms (an average of $2 billion in 1976 sales, with about one-third of earnings and assets outside the United States) were aware of the models but were not using them.[14] Of these forty firms, approximately half the international financial officers used computer models. Most of these models, however, were data gathering and compilation models that permitted "what-if" analysis of alternative outcomes and strategies. None involved mathematical programming. Typically, the models were offered by vendors such as banks as part of a package of international financial services. The managers generally felt that understanding the models was of value because it was a form of training for themselves. They also wanted the vendor for currency forecasts. However, they did not trust the models' tax and other routines, and they felt that if one had reasonable forecasts for rates, it was easy to know what actions to take without recourse to the programming models. In addition, a major complaint was the mass of data required to operate the models and the difficulties of updating inputs to the models. Most managers did not expect increased use of optimization models in the future, although one observed, "Everybody wants a security blanket, and a witch doctor can sell them even if the medicine is no good."

Part Two has reviewed the instruments of foreign trade financing, evaluating the costs of funding as well as the difficulties surrounding the definition of foreign exchange exposure. This last chapter has offered a relatively simple approach for combining costs associated with particular exchange policies, evaluating those costs for several popular strategies under alternative outcomes of the world.

Part Three will turn to the problems associated with capital budgeting in the broader sense, analyzing the returns from projects in various nations over a longer period.

Questions

1. How does a strategy for dealing with foreign exchange risk differ from an outcome?

2. Why might a foreign exchange manager reject a strategy even though (s)he concedes it is optimal on an expected value basis?

3. Why may there be different interest rates in the local and the Euromarkets of a given currency? How can a multinational corporation take advantage of these differentials?

[14]E. Eugene Carter and Rita M. Rodriguez, "Foreign Exchange Exposure Models: What 40 U.S. Multinationals Think." *Euromoney*, March, 1978, pp. 95–111.

4. One multinational firm has a policy of making each subsidiary within a given currency area responsible for its foreign exchange losses. What are some of the costs of this strategy? How would you decide upon a better strategy? What example would you suggest as a more desirable policy for the firm?

5. "I don't care what happens to the currency vis-à-vis our parent's currency. My job is to make a profit here." If the head of your subsidiary in a country with a devaluation-prone currency had this reaction, how would you deal with it?

6. Calculate the cost of hedging shown in the text example for the opposite to likely outcome and the aggressive strategy. Show how the cost is computed.

7. Show the costs for a do nothing and a zero exposure strategy for the example given in the text. Note the description of these strategies in the text for an indication of how the calculations should be done.

Bibliography

Carter, E. Eugene, and Rita M. Rodriguez, "Foreign Exchange Models: What 40 U.S. Multinationals Think." *Euromoney,* March 1978, pp. 95-111.

Folks, William R., Jr., "The Optimal Level of Forward Exchange Transactions." *Journal of Financial and Quantitative Analysis,* Jan. 1973, pp. 105-110.

Heckerman, Donald, "The Exchange Risk of Foreign Operations," *Journal of Business,* Jan. 1972, pp. 42-48.

Hoyt, Newton H., Jr., "The Management of Currency Exchange Risk by the Singer Company." *Financial Management,* Spring 1972, pp. 13-20.

Jucker, James V., and Clovis deFaro, "The Selection of International Borrowing Sources." *Journal of Financial and Quantitative Analysis,* Sept. 1975, pp. 381-407.

Lietaer, Bernard A., *Financial Management of Foreign Exchange Risk: An Operational Technique to Reduce Risk.* Cambridge, Mass.: MIT Press, 1971.

Rodriguez, Rita M., "Management of Foreign Exchange Risk in U.S. Multinationals." *Sloan Management Review,* Spring 1978, pp. 31-49.

——, *Foreign Exchange Management in U.S. Multinationals.* Lexington, Mass.: D. C. Heath and Company, 1979.

Rutenberg, David P., "Maneuvering Liquid Assets in a Multinational Company." *Management Science,* June 1970, pp. B671-B684.

Schwab, Bernhard and Peter Lusztig, "Apportioning Foreign Exchange Risk Through the Use of Third Currencies: Some Questions on Efficiency." *Financial Management,* Autumn 1978, pp. 25-30.

Schydlowsky, Daniel, foreign exchange model described in Sidney Robbins and Robert Stobaugh, *Money in the Multinational Enterprise.* New York: Basic Books, Inc., 1973.

Shapiro, Alan C., "International Cash Management–The Determination of Multicurrency Cash Balances." *Journal of Financial and Quantitative Analysis,* Dec. 1976, pp. 893-900.

—— and David P. Rutenberg, "When to Hedge Against Devaluation." *Management Science,* Aug. 1974, pp. 1514-1520.

FARMATEL, S. A.

In October 1972 Mr. de Chomereau, the treasurer of Farmatel, was analyzing the problems associated with the company's financial policies. Farmatel was a French company selling pharmaceutical and chemical products worldwide. During 1972 the foreign subsidiaries had increased their accounts payable to the parent company substantially, and additional large increases were planned in 1973. These increased demands on the parent company's financial resources coincided with an increase in working capital needs and a large decrease in profits at the parent company during 1972. These internal pressures promised that 1973 would be a difficult financial year. In addition, the French government had decided to follow a tight monetary policy to combat the country's high inflation rate. The amount of credit available to the economy was to be limited and the cost of short-term and medium-term credit was to be increased.

Mr. de Chomereau was wondering what might be done to improve the coordination between the financial policies of the foreign subsidiaries and the parent company to achieve a reduction in the amount and cost of financing required for the group. He was particularly puzzled by the fact that he had no financial control whatsoever over these subsidiaries. As the treasurer of Farmatel, his tasks mainly were to manage the cash position and the short- and medium-term financing of the parent in France. The subsidiaries were controlled only by Farmatel product divisions and by Farminter, the subsidiary in charge of the international operations of Farmatel. The major concern of both Farminter and the product divisions was sales growth. As a consequence, not much attention was paid to the financial practices of the subsidiaries even though their actions had a direct bearing on Farmatel's sources and uses of funds.

Company Background

Farmatel was composed of three parts: the parent operating and holding company, the French subsidiaries, and the foreign subsidiaries. Very often the ties between some of the French subsidiaries and the product divisions of the parent company were much stronger than the ties between the product divisions of the parent company. The French subsidiaries retained a higher degree of autonomy than plant or sales branches inside a divisionalized American firm. The firm was research-and-development oriented, and patents protected a high profit margin. As a result, the pressure to control subsidiaries was low. Control was mostly informal through discussions between parent company headquarters and the subsidiaries' management. A high degree of autonomy was given to the subsidiaries' top management and great reliance was placed on tradition. The decision to consolidate accounts in 1968 and the profitability crises of 1967 and 1969, however, were pushing headquarters toward an increased centralization even with widely divergent characteristics among the various subsidiaries (Exhibit 1).

The firm had a fast and profitable growth but relative disorder from the organizational standpoint. Total sales for the group[1] grew tenfold between 1965

[1] Farmatel sales, plus French subsidiary sales, plus foreign subsidiary sales, less intragroup sales. These same principles of consolidation apply to group profit and R&D figures.

EXHIBIT 1. FARMATEL S.A.: Financial Data on Foreign Subsidiaries, 1972

Country of Incorporation	Sales	Profit (Loss)	Dividends to Farmatel	Royalties	Purchases from Farmatel and French Subsidiaries
West Germany	$ 4,500	$ 250	—	$ 180	$ 470
Belgium	2,000	80	$ 60	60	2,100
Spain	5,000	400	—	70	2,500
Italy	8,900	150	30	450	5,100
Portugal	2,000	200	—	110	700
United Kingdom	58,000	3,900	—	2,300	4,200
Argentina	2,900	50	—	200	2,100
Brazil	5,700	(200)	—	—	3,800
Mexico	13,300	507	—	600	2,000
Peru	4,900	50	45	350	1,700
Uruguay	1,000	60	—	55	560
Venezuela	2,900	150	—	—	2,000
India	400	(5)	—	—	60
Japan	10,000	(280)	—	—	7,000
Vietnam	1,500	(150)	—	—	900
Thailand	20	1	—	—	12
United States	5,000	150	30	—	15
	$128,020	$5,313	$165	$4,375	$35,217
Direct Export (Farminter)	$18,000				

and 1972, while profits increased nine times and R&D expenses fifteen times. In 1972 sales were FF 1,320,000,000 ($259,000,000), profits were FF 62,000,000 ($12,000,000), and R&D expenses were FF 121,000,000 ($24,000,000). The financing of the growth had been largely achieved through retained earnings (Exhibit 2). In 1970 long- and short-term debt was less than 30% of total liabilities and equity.

Organization

In 1972 the parent operating and holding company sales were FF 320,000,000 ($63,000,000), French subsidiary sales were FF 370,000,000 ($72,500,000), and foreign subsidiary sales were FF 630,000,000 ($128,000,000). A diagram of the organization of the company is presented in Exhibit 3.

The Operating-Holding Company. Within the operating-holding parent company there were three product divisions: pharmaceuticals, chemicals, and miscellaneous. Each of these divisions was then organized on a functional basis. For instance, the pharmaceutical division was split into sales and manufacturing. The sales function was itself split into two departments: specialties and active principles. Specialties were finished products; active principles were semifinished products that were to be transformed by the subsidiaries.

The French Subsidiaries. These subsidiaries were in pharmaceuticals (ten large subsidiaries), chemicals (six large subsidiaries), and medical instruments and

EXHIBIT 2. FARMATEL S.A.: Unconsolidated Balance Sheets 1969/1973 (million dollars; translation rate: 1$ = FF5.10)

	Assets				
	1969	*1970*	*1971*	*1972*	*1973 Forecast*
Net fixed assets	$112	$108	$115	$122	$127
Long-term loans and equity investment in subsidiaries	68	73	77	101	106
Inventories	20	22	27	40	58
Accounts receivable	19	24	28	39	67
Cash	6	2	1	2	1
Total	$225	$229	$248	$304	$359

	Liabilities and Equity				
	1969	*1970*	*1971*	*1972*	*1973 Forecast*
Common stock	$ 30	$ 30	$ 30	$ 40	$ 40
Reserves and retained earnings	160	165	172	187	191
Long-term debt	12	9	8	27	113 (long-term and short-term debt combined)
Short-term debt	13	14	29	38	
Accounts payable	10	11	9	12	15
Total	$225	$229	$248	$304	$359

SOURCE: Disguised company data.

other business (two subsidiaries). In addition, Farminter, an independent French subsidiary, operated as a sort of International Division for Farmatel. In general, the French subsidiaries reported directly to the top management of Farmatel, but they communicated widely with the corresponding product divisions of the operating-holding company (e.g., subsidiaries in the chemical business with Farmatel chemical product division, and so on) or with the R&D division (for laboratories). Their financial autonomy was variable. Some of them had a fairly independent borrowing policy. Other (especially laboratories) were heavily dependent on Farmatel funds.

The Foreign Subsidiaries. The international operations of Farmatel were organized in an intricate fashion. Direct exports were channeled through Farminter. This subsidiary was the link between the product divisions of Farmatel (or the exporting French subsidiaries) and the foreign clients. To have better access to some markets, Farmatel had created several wholly owned sales subsidiaries in these markets. Some of these sales subsidiaries, like the Brazilian one, had then set up limited manufacturing or packaging operations because of tariff problems, patent necessity, or governmental pressures. The increased coordi-

EXHIBIT 3. Farmatel S.A.: Organization Chart

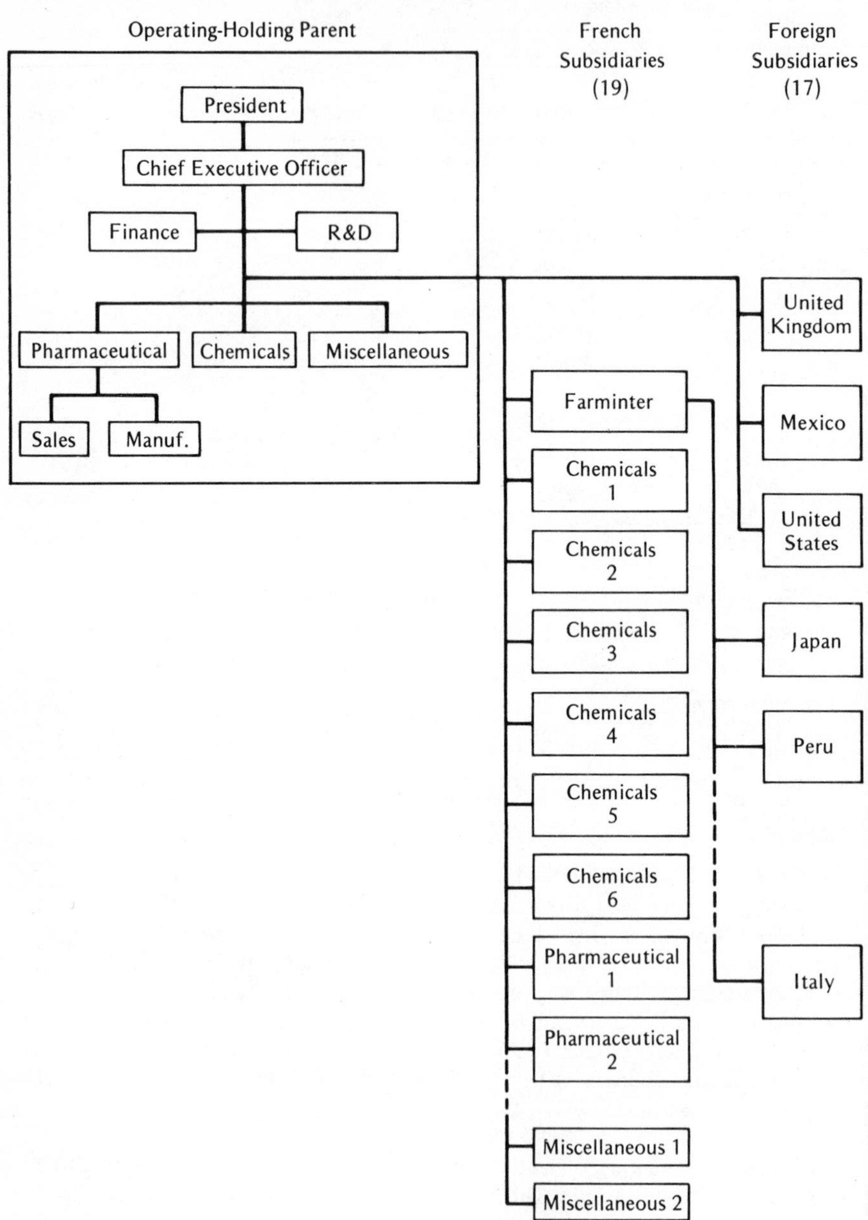

nation requirements had pushed the product divisions at Farmatel to bypass Farminter and to communicate directly with the individual managers of the foreign subsidiaries involved in manufacturing.

The sales departments of the French product divisions and French subsidiaries were responsible for product quality, delivery dates, selling prices, and the terms of sale (e.g., length of accounts receivable of the subsidiaries). The product divisions were anxious to have the foreign subsidiaries absorb a regular and growing volume of production since they were judged mainly in terms of sales growth, and because this contributed to the good relationships between the sales and manufacturing department (which depended on a regular and planned growth in sales).

The nature of the relationship between Farmatel and the foreign subsidiaries depended also on the size and nature of these subsidiaries. Three kinds of subsidiaries could be distinguished:

1. Export sales subsidiaries (mainly in Europe and Japan) sold Farmatel finished products.

2. Captive manufacturing subsidiaries bought active principles from Farmatel and transformed these basic materials into specialty products (Latin America, and so on).

3. Integrated subsidiaries bought bulk chemicals outside the group and transformed them into finished products (e.g., the U.K. subsidiary, which also had its own R&D facility).

The third group of subsidiaries (United Kingdom, United States, Mexico) were often large in size. They were relatively autonomous and managed by general managers who regarded Farmatel as an associate more than a parent company. These managers reported directly to the Farmatel president. Other subsidiaries generally reported to Farminter's president, although the largest ones (Brazil and Japan) were directly supervised by the Farmatel president. Even those subsidiaries reporting to Farminter's president retained a right of appeal to Farmatel.

Control System

The foreign subsidiaries sent detailed reports to Farminter containing:

1. Monthly sales forecasts for the next year.

2. Income statement for the current year and for the next five years.

3. Investment budget—current year and next five years.

4. Balance sheet for the current year and pro forma balance sheets for the next five years.

From these annual forecasts Farminter computed monthly forecasts of purchases by subsidiaries which were used by the manufacturing departments to schedule production. Farminter's second task was to compute variance between actual and budgeted figures each month and to indicate corrective actions to small subsidiaries. The focus of Farminter was mainly on commercial variables, especially sales volume.

The budget evaluation process was very simple with very little feedback from subsidiaries to headquarters during the budgeting phase. In fact, the subsidiaries' budget was not discussed as long as sales and profits showed an increase over the previous year's performance. Partly accounting for this behavior was the fact that no one at Farminter (or Farmatel) was particularly competent in international finance and accounting. The impact on the subsidiaries of different financial policies and accounting principles, of local environmental variables, or of variables such as currency parity changes was rarely considered.

The managers of the large subsidiaries reporting to the president sent the same kind of financial information as the small ones. Their sales were less carefully monitored because they had no direct impact on the sales or manufacturing operations of the parent company. Their forecasts were accepted without discussion as long as profitability and sales were growing.

Financial Policies

Big, integrated subsidiaries were financially independent of the parent company. The managers of these subsidiaries tried not to depend on the parent company for their financing needs to avoid giving Farmatel any leverage on them. Their high profitability and the relatively low payout to Farmatel allowed them to finance their expansion from retained earnings. When external financing was necessary, they dealt with local banks with whom they had developed banking relationships for a long time. This was especially true of the U.K. subsidiary, controlled by Farmatel since 1946.

The smaller subsidiaries, buying finished products or raw materials, were much more dependent on Farmatel. An important part of their financing came from Farmatel's accounts receivable. When they had additional financial needs, they asked Farmatel for a lengthening of their credit terms or for a loan. In these cases the decision taken by Farminter and the product departments was generally positive.

Some conflicts had arisen in the past about devaluation losses. Subsidiaries having an important volume of accounts payable to Farmatel were severely hit when a devaluation in the local currency suddenly increased the local currency value of these accounts. As a result, some had asked to be invoiced in local currency, and this change was accepted. In other cases the burden of the devaluation had been split on a 50/50 basis between Farmatel and the subsidiary.

Mr. de Chomereau's Position

Mr. Boutrolles, the financial vice president, was responsible for determining the long-term financial policy of Farmatel. This policy included financial structure, availability of funds for major R&D investment projects, and dividend policy.

Mr. de Chomereau negotiated with banks about terms of the loans and managed the short-term financial needs of Farmatel.

At the end of 1972 Mr. de Chomereau, the treasurer who reported to Mr. Boutrolles, felt very uneasy about the financial needs for the coming year. The local subsidiaries' increase in the length of accounts receivable was imposing a heavy financial strain on Farmatel. Simultaneously, the working capital requirements of Farmatel had increased due to an increase in inventories and a slight increase in domestic accounts receivable. This situation was expected to continue into 1973. Furthermore, price increases for finished products were blocked by the government, but labor and material costs were increasing steadily. Therefore, the profit margins in 1973 were expected to be lower than in 1972.

Because of governmental restrictions, it was difficult to obtain short-term loans in France. Also, the cost of Euro-dollar or Euro-mark financing was uncertain. Mr. de Chomereau had dealt with the Euro-currency market, but he was apprehensive about the reaction of Mr. Boutrolles to the high interest rate on Euro-dollars or to the eventual exchange loss from possible upvaluation of the deutsche mark or devaluation of the French franc. Furthermore, borrowing on the Euro-markets was complicated by the necessity of obtaining authorization from the French government.

Taking the delicate present financial situation of Farmatel as a stimulus, Mr. de Chomereau had tried to demonstrate to Mr. Boutrolles that the financial autonomy of the subsidiaries was detrimental to the group interest. He pointed out that the sales people were not always acting in the best interest of the company by granting the subsidiaries very favorable financial terms. Mr. de Chomereau asked Mr. Boutrolles whether some form of financial coordination between different units of the group would not be an improvement over the present situation. Mr. Boutrolles' reaction had been relatively cold. He explained to Mr. de Chomereau that their task was already complicated enough, and that to advise the sales department of Farminter on such matters would make this task even more complex. Furthermore, nobody in the finance department had experience and competence in the area of international financial management. He stated that the subsidiaries were growing fast and profitably and that it would be unwise to disturb such a satisfactory situation.

Mr. de Chomereau was annoyed by this answer. He perceived the antagonism of Mr. Boutrolles to his proposal, but he thought that Mr. Boutrolles had failed to give solid contrary arguments against a change in the actual situation. As far as expertise was concerned, he felt that he had some insight in international matters. Anyway, he thought that worldwide financial coordination could be established progressively, allowing him to learn the intricacies of the matter. He decided to write a report using four subsidiaries as an example. This would give Mr. Boutrolles a basis for a realistic decision regarding the foreign operations' financial policy. If Farmatel decided to move toward financial centralization, then other factors should also be taken into account. For example, he thought the possibilities of establishing a holding company in a tax haven should be considered. According to French law, the profits of such a holding company would not have to be consolidated with the parent for tax purposes. Increased centralization also opened the door for a more tax-conscious management of transfer prices.

In the process of writing this report, Mr. de Chomereau became increasingly aware of the complexity of computing gains from worldwide financial centralization. Since the main objective of these computations was to illustrate and reinforce his standpoint, he decided to make some simplifying assumptions:

1. Half of long-term debt for the parent company and the subsidiaries was one-year debt that could be borrowed at the beginning of the year and repaid with interest at the end of the year.

2. Accounts receivable by the parent from foreign subsidiaries were in local currencies.

3. Parental tax rate (50%) should be applied to foreign subsidiaries.

4. Inventories of foreign subsidiaries were not exposed to exchange risk, for a change in parity was in general matched by a roughly equal change in price.

5. Since Farmatel consolidation was not for tax purposes, foreign exchange losses were not tax deductible and foreign exchange gains were not taxable.

With these assumptions in mind, Mr. de Chomereau decided to estimate the optimum financing for 1973 using the cost figures (interest, taxes, and so on) for the end of 1972 and to compute the overall savings for the group of a more centralized financial policy.

Data on the selected subsidiaries and their countries are presented in Exhibits 4 through 7.

EXHIBIT 4. FARMATEL S.A.: Balance Sheets—Selected Subsidiaries (thousands of dollars)

United Kingdom (Pound @ $2.34/Pound)					
Assets	*1972*	*1973 (Forecast)*	*Liabilities*	*1972*	*1973 (Forecast)*
Net fixed assets	$21,300	$22,700	Equity	$28,100	$30,400
Inventories	6,600	6,800	Long-term debt	7,500	7,100
Accounts receivable					
Other Farmatel subsidiaries	5,600	4,700	Short-term debt	4,900	3,000
Others	7,300	7,500			
Cash	2,100	1,200	Accounts payable	2,400	2,400
Total	$42,900	$42,900	Total	$42,900	$42,900

EXHIBIT 4. Continued

Germany (DM @ 3.20 DM/$)

Assets	*1972*	*1973 (Forecast)*	*Liabilities*	*1972*	*1973 (Forecast)*
Net fixed assets	$ 1,300	$ 1,300	Equity	$ 1,300	$ 1,400
			Long-term debt	600	700
Inventories	400	500	Short-term debt	100	100
Accounts receivable	300	400			
Cash	100	100	Accounts payable	100	100
Total	$ 2,100	$ 2,300	Total	$ 2,100	$ 2,300

Italy (Lira @ 582.5 Lira/$)

Assets	*1972*	*1973 (Forecast)*	*Liabilities*	*1972*	*1973 (Forecast)*
Net fixed assets	$ 395	$ 403	Equity	$ 549	$ 669
			Long-term debt	670	644
Inventories	635	687	Short-term debt	275	258
Accounts receivable	1,785	2,077			
Cash	21	17	Accounts payable (Farmatel)	1,342	1,614
Total	$ 2,836	$ 3,185	Total	$ 2,836	$ 3,185

Brazil (Cruzeiro @ 6.21 CR/$)

Assets	*1972*	*1973 (Forecast)*	*Liabilities*	*1972*	*1973 (Forecast)*
Net fixed assets	$ 158	$ 217	Equity	$ 371	$ 209
			Long-term debt		
			Farmatel	161	274
			Others	80	—
Inventories	338	548			
			Short-term debt	110	145
Accounts receivable	950	1,304	Accounts payable		
			Farmatel	709	1,409
Cash	32	48	Others	48	81
Total	$ 1,478	$ 2,118	Total	$ 1,478	$ 2,118

EXHIBIT 5. Cost of Borrowing, end 1972, percent.

	(Prime Borrowers)	
	Short-Term	*Long-Term*
France	8.00	8.40
Germany	8.75	8.50
Italy	8.00	8.50
United Kingdom	9.00	9.50
Brazil	34.00	36.00
Euro-dollar	6.25	7.50
Euro-pound	10.25	9.75

SOURCE: Morgan Guaranty Trust Company, WORLD FINANCIAL MARKETS, various issues.

EXHIBIT 6. Exchange Rates, 1971 and 1972

			1972			
		1971	*I*	*II*	*III*	*IV*
French franc/$	Spot	5.53	5.028	5.002	5.012	5.125
3-month forward		5.44	5.028	4.994	5.002	5.150
Deutsche mark/$	Spot	3.31	3.168	3.150	3.202	3.202
3-month forward		3.31	3.152	3.215	3.178	3.188
Italian lira/$	Spot	612.00	582.50	580.75	581.88	582.50
$/U.K. pound[a]	Spot	2.48	2.615	2.44	2.42	2.34
3-month forward		2.48	2.610	2.42	2.40	2.32
Brazil[b] cruzeiro/$	Spot	5.50	5.845	5.915	6.025	6.215

[a]For the United Kingdom, unlike all other countries, the exchange rate is given in dollar per unit of national currency (and not in units of national currency per dollar).

[b]Between 1967 and 1972, the value of the dollar in terms of cruzeiros went from a basis of 100 to 217 (~ 25% depreciation/year).

EXHIBIT 7. Tax Rates and Exchange Controls (end 1972)

	Corporate Tax	*Tax on Dividends and Royalties Paid*	*Maximum Remittances*	*Other Exchange Control*
France	50%	No	No limit in theory.	Transfer of funds (other than for imports)[a] has to be authorized by Finance Ministry.
Germany	52.53% (undistributed) profit 15.45% (distributed profit)	50% of royalties added to taxable income	Should be "fair"; maximum around 10%.	No
Italy	38.39%	Royalties: 16.5% tax Dividends: 30% tax	No limit in theory.	If remittances less than 8% capital: exchange at official rate; if amount greater than 8%: use "account in lira" (more expensive).
United Kingdom	40%	Royalties: 0% tax Dividends: 15% tax	No limit in theory.	No
Brazil	30% (undistributed profit)	Royalties: 25% tax Dividends: 25% tax Interest: 25% tax	Royalties should be less than 5% of sales. If three year average remittances are greater than 12% of equity, then there is an additional tax on the amount greater than 12%. Tax is usually around 40% to 60%. Management fees should be less than 5% of sales.	In balance of payments "emergency," remittances may be limited to 10% of capital.

[a]Or debt amortization, dividends, royalties.

PART THREE

Capital budgeting is usually concerned with the rate of return from a particular project. This rate of return is often based on the future receipts from the project compared to the investment required to generate those receipts. The future receipts are discounted to reflect the cost of capital for the firm. Thus, the firm obtains funds at some rate, and a delay in the receipt of cash from an investment means that the cash receipts must be large enough to compensate for the time the funds were unavailable.

The next four chapters draw upon the basic capital budgeting analysis contained in most introductory finance texts. Chapter 10 discusses the determination of the cash flows relating to a single investment with emphasis upon the particular aspects which uniquely affect international investments. The appropriate mechanisms for evaluating those cash flows and an analysis of special types of risk attendant to international investments are reviewed.

Chapter 11 analyzes the acceptance criteria for projects. Building upon the traditional capital structure theory and cost of capital in differential capital markets, it presents the considerations for determination of the discount rate or acceptance criterion for risky investments. An extended example of a major project analysis by a multinational corporation concludes this chapter.

Chapter 12 moves beyond the single project to address the issue of strategic investments, in which multi-period considerations are important. These considerations may include keeping the firm's market positions over time or maintaining the firm's ability to compete in a particular industry in later years. The general philosophy of governmental taxation and contributions from economics, organization theory, business policy, business history, anti-trust and general management are brought forth to help in understanding the motivation for foreign investment.

Chapter 13 discusses returns from investments for various markets within the framework of capital markets and portfolio theory. The concepts of portfolio risk for evaluating projects in a capital budgeting framework are introduced, and this framework provides information about international diversification opportunities. Empirical results based on security returns are noted. This chapter integrates concepts from the previous chapters and concludes this section on capital budgeting in the international corporation.

Although many of the examples are based on a U.S. corporation operating abroad, the goal is to present general patterns of analysis which are independent of particular corporate considerations in the United States. Thus, students from other lands may read the text for the suggestions which bear on any business enterprise contemplating investment outside its home country. A summary of some international taxation policies and some particular references to the U.S. system is combined in Appendix 1 at the end of this book.

CHAPTER 10

Cash Flows in Capital Budgeting – The International Elements

Although reported profits are used as a standard for many evaluations of management, most expenses such as materials and wages are paid from cash, not earnings. Accordingly, in the international corporation one begins an appraisal of a given project by noting the *expected cash flows* attendant to the project. The *determination* of those flows in the international firm creates the usual difficulties found in a domestic corporation. However, the international setting is more complex than in the typical domestic project analysis. Although the analytical pattern follows the basic model suggested by corporate financial practice, the multinational firm also must consider factors peculiar to multinational operations and their financing.

OPERATING CASH FLOWS—THE INTERNATIONAL ELEMENTS

Joint Considerations

Revenues from any proposed project must be reviewed carefully if the firm has the ability to realize some of the revenues *independent* of the project. For example, there is no problem if a truck manufacturer has decided to establish a car manufacturing plant in another country. On the other hand, often the proposed investment in the other country will affect the operations of other units in the system of the multinational firm through vertical integration, such as a mining operation in Bolivia for a U.S. metal firm, or a sales subsidiary in France for an Italian car manufacturer. The investment also may be a duplicate of the parent operation in major respects through horizontal combinations, such as a typewriter manufacturer creating a manufacturing and distribution outlet in another land.

When such joint effects exist, the firm evaluates the projects by aggregating total demand for a common product. Then, the executives ask themselves, "How much extra business can we create from this foreign operation? For that portion of the business which is 'taken' from an existing operation, what are the savings involved?"

For example, the ability to compete more effectively in the Brazilian home furnishings market might suggest to Frigidaire that the firm locate a refrigerator manufacturing plant there. This plant will have some sales generated from a new market, some sales taken from other competitors who are already there, and some sales which are substitutions of Frigidaire products which are currently imported. The first two components of sales are clearly incremental revenue. The last component, substitution of Frigidaire-Brazil refrigerators for Frigidaire-World refrigerators, may have differential benefits because of different costs of production and importation. However, unless cost savings are present, these sales are *not* relevant to the project. In the typical case the loss of the sales and profits to Frigidaire-World is a net cost which should be charged to the project.

Economies of Scale

If there is a policy of many small local manufacturing outlets vs. centralized manufacturing and there are substantial production economies of scale, individual projects should be charged for the additional costs involved in the diseconomies. Thus, while Honeywell manufactures computers in many nations, its major models tend to be manufactured in one location and shipped throughout the world. Clearly, management perceives total shipping costs of Honeywell's large 3500s to be less than the costs associated with diseconomies from small unit production if the machines were manufactured in more than one location.

Differences in Cost and Revenue Assumptions

Another special operating cash flow is the supervisory fee or royalty paid to the parent. Often, parents require supervisory fee arrangements with their subsidiaries as one means of remitting funds from foreign projects. In evaluating the cash flows of a project and the cash flows to the parent, several cautionary notes must be considered in relation to a supervisory fee. First, for the *project,* the relevant cash flow is the after-tax cost of what a real payment for the "supervision" would be worth in an arm's-length transaction. An arbitrarily high fee, created to permit remission of the funds from the project to the parent, has no relevance in evaluating the worth of the project *per se* if it is an accounting or political expediency designed for currency remission. Second, for the parent evaluating the cash flow to itself from this project, the supervisory inflow after subtracting any incremental costs is simply one more cash return. On the other hand, taxing and business authorities in the host country may question the propriety of this arrangement unless both sides initially recognize and accept it as a device to permit cash remissions.

Tie-In Sales

A variant of the supervisory/royalty fee is the tie-in sale, in which the subsidiary must buy certain items from the parent. Sometimes this purchase represents an implicit royalty; other times, it is simply a device to insure quality control and/or a low cost to all manufacturing facilities on an integrated, companywide basis (the "economy of scale" argument for a component of the final product, for example). The conclusion on how to treat this item is the same as for the supervisory/royalty fee: It is the value of the product at an arm's-length level for the project.

Operating Cash Flows—An Example

One way to see the effect of several of the above items is to consider the following situation. Zebracorp currently exports 5,000 units per month to Country X at a price of $2.00. The variable cost of producing these units and delivering them to Palma, the capital and major distribution point of the country, is $1.00 per unit. The Minister of Development has approached Zebracorp with a proposal that the firm install a small manufacturing operation in Palma that would cost $300,000. In return for an increase in tariffs against other firms, Zebracorp will agree to sell its product at $1.80, to buy certain raw materials from local suppliers, and to use local managers. Total costs of local labor and materials will be $0.50 per unit. Zebracorp will turn over the investment at the end of five years to a local investor for the sum of $1.00. Under this arrangement, Zebracorp believes it can sell about 10,000 units per month. Other materials can be purchased from the parent at $0.30 per unit, and the parent will receive a direct contribution to overhead after variable costs of $0.10 per unit sold. There is a five-year straight-line depreciation of the $300,000 of equipment. Taxes are 50% of profits in Country X and the parent country also has a 50% tax rate with direct credit for Country X's taxes. There is no restriction on cash flow repatriations and the exchange rates are expected to remain constant.

Should Zebracorp accept the Minister's proposal? We begin by looking at the cash flows in Exhibit 10.1. The rate of return on the proposed project is only 3.3%.

After this analysis, the company decides to reject the project. The Minister then hints that Alphacorp, a major competitor, is probably interested in the proposal. Does this fact change the decision?

If Zebracorp executives believe the Minister's assertion, then they must accept a probable loss in sales of the 5,000 units presently sold. Hence, the

EXHIBIT 10.1 Zebracorp—Palma Project

CASH FLOW GENERATED BY PROJECT:		
Revenues = 10,000 X $1.80	$18,000 per month	
Variable costs = 10,000 X $.80	- 8,000 per month	
Operating profit	$10,000 per month	
Operating revenues per year	$120,000	
Depreciation ($300,000/5)[a]	- 60,000	
Profit for tax purposes	$ 60,000	
Local taxes @ 50%	- 30,000	
Profit after taxes	30,000	
Depreciation[a]	+ 60,000	
Net annual cash flow in Country X		$90,000
Yearly profit on materials sold by parent = (12 X 10,000 X $.10 - 50% of total for taxes)		6,000
Net cash flow to parent with full repatriation		$96,000
CASH FLOW FOREGONE:		
Revenues = 5,000 X $2	$10,000 per month	
Variable costs = 5,000 X $1	- 5,000 per month	
Extra profits	$ 5,000 per month	
Extra taxes @ 50%	- 2,500 per month	
Extra cash flow	$ 2,500 per month	
Extra cash flow per year which is foregone		-30,000
Net incremental cash flow		$66,000
RATE OF RETURN:[b]		
$66,000 per year for 5 years, $300,000 investment		3.3%

[a]Depreciation is a non-cash expense, subtracted to compute taxable income, then added back to compute cash flow.

[b]For those readers unfamiliar with discounting and the calculation of the rate of return, a brief summary of these concepts may be found in the appendix to this chapter.

relevant cash flow in this case is the basic cash flow of the project, $96,000 per year for five years, and the rate of return is now 18%.

RATE OF RETURN:	
$96,000 per year for 5 years, $300,000 investment	18%

FINANCIAL CASH FLOWS—THE INTERNATIONAL ELEMENTS

There are three special elements in the financial cash flows of international projects:

1. The value of capital equipment contributed;
2. The assessment of taxes; and
3. The remission of debt/equity funds provided by the parent.

Contribution of Equipment

When manufacturing is involved in a project, the contribution of used equipment from the parent can be a central item. The equipment may cost $100,000 new, have a depreciated book value for tax purposes of $40,000 to the parent, and have a fair used market value in the project's host country of $60,000.[1] Transferring the equipment to the project at any price above $40,000 forces the parent to incur either a capital gains tax or ordinary income taxes on recapture of depreciation, depending on the situation and the interpretation. On the other hand, transferring at any price below $60,000 means that there is an implicit investment or subsidy in the project by the parent in the amount by which the nominal value differs from $60,000.

The *value* of the equipment to the project may be taken as the fair market price in the host country, $60,000. However, the *cost* of the equipment to the parent is the present book value, $40,000, plus shipping expenses, and plus any tax payment due because of the difference between the book value and the market value in the foreign country. Assume shipping costs paid by the parent are $5,000. This cost implies a $15,000 difference between the book value of the equipment adjusted for transportation costs, $45,000, and the local market value of $60,000. This $15,000 would be treated as excess depreciation subject to recapture by the taxing authorities in the parent's country. Using a 50% tax rate, the parent company would owe the tax authorities $7,500. Thus, the cost of the investment to the parent is $52,500. This figure is composed of the $40,000 book value plus the $5,000 shipping costs plus $7,500 for incremental taxes. Since the host country accepted the value of the equipment at $60,000 as part of the investment, the parent company is making a profit of $7,500 ($60,000–$52,500) which is part of the investment in the new project.

Because the economics of equipment typically are intertwined with production, it may be difficult for the parent to look at a project in this light. However, the incremental cash flow associated with the project investment is the focus of the analysis, and the relevant price to the project is the fair market price, $60,000.

The parent can help the project in another way which eliminates the problem of the taxes imputed to the parent by depreciation recapture on a $60,000 sale. If tax authorities in the two countries permit it, the parent may be able to claim a transfer of the equipment to the project at $40,000 in value (hence, incurring no tax by selling at book value), whereas the local taxing

[1]Other than import duties and shipping charges, the used market price in the host country and the parent's home country should be the same. In the absence of this identity, the relevant price would be the *higher* charge, assuming the parent would operate to maximize its own return from sale of used equipment. From the *project's* standpoint, the relevant price is the *lower* one. That is, the parent manager could first sell the equipment at the higher price, taking a profit. In a second transaction, the project manager then could buy similar equipment at a lower price.

authorities may permit a higher valuation (e.g., $80,000) for purposes of depreciation and/or investment by the parent. A higher value for depreciation purposes permits the project to shelter more of its income from profitable operations from local taxes. A larger base for investment also increases the parent's claim on profits (as a percentage of investment) or loan repayments (in the event much of the investment is called a "loan"). This transaction often is illegal because taxing authorities may require a common basis for valuation.[2]

These considerations may be relevant even when the equipment contributed by the parent is new. This is particularly the case when the parent company is the manufacturer of the equipment and when the specialized nature of the equipment does not allow for a readily available market price. In this case the host country may challenge the true value of the equipment and the home country may question the allocation of revenues between profits and costs.

Taxation

Earlier it was noted that international taxation agreements are extremely complex. There is little merit in learning the details of particular covenants because the tax treaties and enforcement practices change over time. At any point, these policies vary considerably from nation to nation. Information about tax arrangements of a particular country can be furnished by local governmental, financial, and legal sources. In addition, popular business chronicles in many industrialized countries often feature the latest "tax haven." A summary of some tax issues and a bibliography are contained in Appendix 1 to this book.

Some of the basic concepts that one must examine in determining the general philosophy of taxation include the following:

1. The principle of equity;
2. The use of cash vs. accrual systems in the determination of taxable income;
3. The definition of a taxable entity;
4. The treatment of dual taxation;
5. The presence of special tax treaties; and
6. The existence of tax incentive programs.

It is generally accepted that *equity* dictates that persons in similar situations should pay a similar tax. However, the definition of similar situations is largely affected by some of the concepts discussed briefly below.

Foreign income can be taxed on a cash basis or on an accrual basis. On a *cash* basis, foreign income is taxable when it is received in the form of cash for dividends, royalties, etc. On an *accrual* basis, income is taxed according to the period in which sales and associated costs are incurred and the *right* to receive

[2]In the National Industrial Conference Board (1966) study, one of every eight companies interviewed said they contributed machinery to their foreign subsidiaries, usually to Latin American countries and less frequently to European subsidiaries.

cash is confirmed. The actual cash receipts and expenditures may not have taken place or may have taken place several accounting periods before. Given the complexities associated with accrual systems, there is a tendency for countries to tax foreign income on a cash basis instead of on an accrual basis. However, the result also is a function of how the taxable entity is defined.

A broader definition of the corporate *entity* reduces the merits of this argument vis-à-vis the multinational. Thus, if Shell is not just a corporation in the Netherlands, but in fact is a worldwide citizen, then taxes should be due on that worldwide income. Sometimes a broad entity concept is desired by the parent for tax purposes; the use of a branch for foreign operations makes it possible for the U.S. corporation to consolidate branch losses in earlier years, offsetting taxable profits in other operations. At other times, the parent prefers a separate subsidiary in another land, especially when such an arrangement delays or avoids imposition of taxes by the parent's home country. This avoidance is especially valuable when the firm wishes to transfer funds from one nation to another. If the home land taxes profits only when these profits are remitted home, then a "tax haven" subsidiary which receives funds from a foreign operating subsidiary can reinvest these funds in some other land. Had this intermediate corporation not existed, the withdrawal of profits from the operating subsidiary would have created a home-country tax liability, reducing the amount which could be reinvested in the other land.

Once the entity is broadened to include operations in other lands, then there is a jurisdictional question. The policy among nations has been to recognize the injustice of *dual taxation* upon the same entity. Country X will tax the operations of Zebracorp in its land, and perhaps withholding taxes on dividends remitted to the home nation. The home land may permit Zebracorp to receive partial or total credit for the taxes paid to Country X. Typical choices involve the option either (1) to deduct the taxes paid to Country X from gross income taxable at home or (2) to compute the taxes which would have been due at home had all income been received there and then to deduct the taxes paid in Country X from the home-country tax liability. Normally, Zebracorp will prefer the latter course; there is a full credit against the home country's taxes for the taxes previously paid as opposed to a simple deduction against taxable income.

Many nations also operate on the basis of special *tax treaties* which further adjust the amounts which may be paid or withheld in those countries. In these situations the subsidiary may not even have to file a tax return in Country X if the operations are carefully kept within well-defined guidelines. For example, the United States presently has special tax treaties with more than twenty nations which permit this nonfiling.

Finally, tax laws are influenced by *special policies* that are designed to achieve certain goals. The country may wish to sponsor particular types of development by granting major income tax concessions such as lower rates, a moratorium on taxes, or rebates. To meet competition from other nations, taxes may be deferred or reduced on trading companies or export financing corporations. As an example of special governmental tax incentives for exports, Ireland eliminates all corporate income taxes until 1990 on firms' profits from export sales. Since Ireland is a member of the European Economic Community which provides free trade benefits to firms operating in the EEC nations, this benefit is substantial. Alternatively, special taxes may be imposed which force companies to repatriate earnings in consideration of the parent country's balance of payments.

Remission of Funds

For the *project,* the relevant cash inflow is the return from operations after adjustment for local corporate taxes. From the *parent's* view, however, the crucial variable is the remission of funds to the parent treasury in New York or London. Accordingly, from this point of view the cash flows are related to the investment; the supervisory payments net of the costs to provide the supervision; royalties, interest, and dividend remission; and loan principal and equity return.[3] Here, the policies of many multinationals have been about one step (five years) ahead of local taxing authorities.[4] Anxious to preserve capital in their land and concerned about excessive profiteering by the outside parent, local officials began limiting the amount of profits which could be remitted. The multinational parents responded with greater parent loan participation, arguing that loan repayment was not part of profit; loans then were adjusted for very high interest rates. When this practice began to be challenged, the local authorities were confronted with large supervisory fees. And the fight still continues!

In a study by the late Judd Polk and others at the National Industrial Conference Board in 1966, corporation managers noted that the key factor in a country's remittance policy was the *possibility* of remittance, whether or not the managers had expectations of large remittances. The European countries' record of liberal policy on remittance was in their favor, although some experienced executives feared that recent restrictions might recur. Some managers attempted to negotiate formal agreements on withdrawals, although this approach typically applied to earnings and not to capital. Managers of newer companies favored parent loans rather than equity to a greater degree than managers of experienced multinationals, although the risk for long-term loans is similar to that of equity. Managers of the newer firms assumed these "loans" were more easily retrievable, while others felt that easy availability of equity from the parent was a poor motivator for the local manager when compared to a loan obligation with fixed principal repayment. Companies with an "international" appearance were not as concerned about remission as the "nationals with international operations." Some managers viewed earnings on a flexible approach, looking at each land individually. Others regarded the cash generated

[3]Remitting royalties *may* be more lucrative than paying dividends. The royalties are usually considered deductible business expenses for local country taxes. Even if royalties are not deductible, the local country may tax these remissions at a lower rate than dividends because there is a *dividend withholding tax* in addition to the *corporate tax.* Hence, the royalty may be exposed to lower total taxes than the straight dividend from corporate profits. The United States taxes the royalty income in full, whereas dividends received can be given credit for some taxes paid locally. A readable and comprehensive summary of the impact of various channels by which multinational firms may transfer resources among units is contained in Donald R. Lessard, "Transfer Prices, Taxes and Financial Markets: Implications of Internal Financial Transfers within the Multinational Firm," Proceedings of the New York University Conference on Economic Issues of Multinational Firms, edited by Robert G. Hawkins (New York: JAI Press, 1977).

[4]"Government is the pursuit of Jackals by Jackasses." (H. L. Mencken).

by earnings as a pool which should be remitted to a tax haven for the reasons noted earlier.

Today, many local taxing authorities recognize the legitimate concern of parents about remission. On the other hand, they are also concerned about the development of their own nations. Accordingly, the typical investment contract for a major project will specify the capital structure of the firm and will limit supervisory fees or royalties to (say) 5% of gross revenues. However, the availability of alternative arrangements and the specifics of the particular proposal offered are factors that the manager must include in evaluating the project cash flows. The operating tactics used to cope with these restrictions on debt repayment or profit remission are contained as part of the capital structure discussion in Chapter 11.

WHOSE CASH FLOWS?

Although there will be more to say later on the issue of parent return vs. project (subsidiary) return as the relevant criterion, note how this decision is central to the analysis. Without our evaluating the cost of funds (which is done in the following chapter), recall the problem of Zebracorp's investing in Country X for five years. The cash flows generated by the project for Zebracorp as a whole were $96,000 if it is assumed that the current business will be lost unless Zebracorp establishes local operations. At the end of the period the business is turned over to local managers. Suppose the Minister of Development then notes that it would be appropriate if all the cash were left on deposit locally at no interest. At the end of the five-year period the accumulated cash may be remitted to the parent. What is the rate of return of the project to Zebracorp?

If the funds are blocked until later years, the only cash flow to the parent during earlier years relates to the profits in the materials produced, $6,000 per year. Hence, the calculations are:

Zebracorp—Palma Project: Repatriation Pattern and Rate of Return

	Project	*Parent*
Investment	$300,000	$300,000
Cash flow per year (5 years)	96,000	6,000
Terminal cash flow (5th year)	0	450,000
Rate of return	18.0%	10.2%

Notice that we separate the operating cash flows generated by the project and the alternative *channels* by which that cash may be remitted. Tariff and tax considerations may dictate different approaches to the channeling of the cash throw-offs from a project, and it is useful to distinguish between these two types of flows as shown in the example.

If the example is altered to allow for a deterioration in the exchange rate of the local currency vis-à-vis the parent country's currency, and if the analysis is computed in terms of local currency (LC), the cruzeiro, and parent currency (PC), the U.S. dollar, the results again change. Suppose the expected deterioration is 5% per year after the first year.

The value of the raw matrial profits will deteriorate if the prices of raw materials purchased from the parent are fixed in cruzeiros. The relevant cash flow to the parent is *dollar cash flow* above the manufacturing cost. With constant costs of operation, the margin will shrink. The example included payment of $0.30 per unit and variable profits of $0.10 before tax. If the currency in which payment is made deteriorates by 20% over several years, the value of the payment is really only 80% of $0.30, or $0.24. Hence, the unit cash flow contributed assuming production costs continue to be $0.20 per unit is $0.04. Thus, after a 20% decline in exchange rates, the actual margin has declined 60% from $0.10 per unit to $0.04 per unit.[5]

In the example the unit profits to the parent from selling raw materials after allowance for the 5% annual deteriorations in the cruzeiro is computed as follows:

Zebracorp–Palma Project: Parent Raw Material Cash Flows

	Year 1	*Year 2*	*Year 3*	*Year 4*	*Year 5*
Unit payment	$0.30	$0.285	$0.2708	$0.2572	$0.2444
Cost	(0.20)	(0.20)	(0.20)	(0.20)	(0.20)
Unit profit	0.10	0.085	0.0708	0.0572	0.0444[6]
Yearly cash flows (120,000 units, 50% tax)	$6,000	$5,100	$4,248	$3,432	$2,661

Using these figures, one may compute the dollar value to Zebracorp of the project's cash flow even though portions of the flow are not remitted to the parent. These figures are:

Zebracorp–Palma Project: Total Project Cash Flows in U.S. Dollars

Project	*Year 1*	*Year 2*	*Year 3*	*Year 4*	*Year 5*
Operating cash flows	$90,000	$85,500	$81,225	$77,164	$73,306
Cash to parent on raw materials	6,000	5,100	4,248	3,432	2,661
Total	$96,000	$90,600	$85,473	$80,596	$75,967

Dollar return on $300,000 investment = 13.8%

For the parent, one may calculate the dollars on hand each year assuming

[5] As a general formula in any simple inflationary evaluation, if x is the percentage change in gross revenues per unit and y is the initial profit margin, the percentage decrease or increase in profits (z) is (x/y) times 100. Using the example, $x = -20\%$, $y = 33\frac{1}{3}\%$, and $z = (-20\%/33\frac{1}{3}\%) \times 100 = 60\%$.

[6] The earlier rough approach ignored the effects of compounding. Thus, the 5% is applied to a smaller base each year, leaving $0.044 per unit in year 5 rather than the $0.040 calculated.

the funds are blocked until the fifth year except for raw material purchases. These cash flows and the related return are:

Zebracorp—Palma Project: Cash Flows to Parent in U.S. Dollars

Parent	*Year 1*	*Year 2*	*Year 3*	*Year 4*	*Year 5*
Cash to parent on raw materials	$6,000	$5,100	$4,248	$3,432	$ 2,661
Terminal flow ($90,000 × 5 years × 0.94^4)					366,528
Total	$6,000	$5,100	$4,248	$3,432	$369,189

Dollar return on $300,000 investment = 5.4%

Alternatively, the manager may wish to value the return of Zebracorp in terms of local currency, the cruzeiro. Since the payments for new materials were assumed to be made in cruzeiro, the local currency values and the associated investment and cash flow create roughly the same value as the return calculated earlier for a constant exchange rate, 18.0%. However, the flows must be adjusted for the decline in profits to the parent associated with the depreciation of the cruzeiro. The cruzeiro value of those raw material profits will be lower than under no depreciation of the local currency against the parent's currency. As a result, the rate of return should be slightly lower. The local investment is Cr3,000,000 (assuming an initial exchange rate of 10Cr/$), local income is Cr900,000 per year, and the firm generates cruzeiro income for the parent as noted in the table.

Zebracorp—Palma Project: Total Project Cash Flows in Cruzeiros

	Year 1	*Year 2*	*Year 3*	*Year 4*	*Year 5*
Exchange rate	10Cr/$	10.5Cr/$	11.03Cr/$	11.58Cr/$	12.16Cr/$
Raw material cash gain to parent, US$	$6,000	$5,100	$4,248	$3,432	$2,661
Raw material cash gain, cruzeiro value	Cr 60,000	Cr 53,550	Cr 46,834	Cr 39,730	Cr 32,345
Operating cash flows	900,000	900,000	900,000	900,000	900,000
Total	Cr 960,000	Cr 953,550	Cr 946,834	Cr 939,730	Cr 932,345

Cruzeiro return on Cr 3,000,000 investment = 17.5%

Thus, depending on the numeraire (cruzeiro or dollar) and whether one looks at total project cash flows or the cash flows received by the parent, there are sharply divergent returns associated with this simple investment.

Zebracorp—Palma Project: Comparative Rates of Return

	With Cruzeiro Depreciation	*Constant Cruzeiro/Dollar Rate*
Total project returns		
in local currency (Cr)	17.5%	18.0%
in US$	13.8%	18.0%
Return to parent in US$, with profit repatriation blocked until fifth year	5.4%	10.2%

From the point of veiw of the parent company, there are two major problems. First, the currency is blocked. The parent has substantial cash flows from the project which remain idle because of restrictions of the host country's government. Second, in terms of the currency invested by the parent, the loss in dollar purchasing power of the local currency is substantial. This problem is similar to the external purchasing power of nations discussed in Part One.

These problems are acute in this case of a five-year investment horizon. Very often the investment by the parent company has a much longer time horizon, in which case the impact of initial controls on repatriation of cash and changes in the relative value of currencies may be evened out over the long run, as long as local prices are allowed to change. If the parent intends to continue expanding a profitable local operation, a repatriation restriction is irrelevant to the evaluation of the project. The expansion of the operations would require that profits be retained and reinvested in the project anyway instead of being remitted to the parent company. On the other hand, a multinational manager with all foreign investments in countries that restrict repatriation should analyze the liquidity of the parent company, e.g., its ability to pay dividends. The other major problem, the change in the relative value of currencies, also acquires a different dimension when a long period of investment is assumed. Some currencies that were considered to be very weak against the U.S. dollar in the 1960s have turned out to be very strong during the 1970s.

Although these problems will continually confront the parent manager, there are some elements which mitigate their impact. First, convertibility insurance is sometimes available from outside sources, as for example from the Export-Import Bank (Eximbank) and the Overseas Private Investment Corporation (OPIC). Lloyds and other large private insurers will insure against expropriation in some situations. Second, the restricted funds usually can be reinvested in some project. If there is no short-term project, bonds of the local government or local industries can be selected. These bonds are likely to be a little riskier than the currency of the country, but they provide a positive rate of return.

THE TERMINAL RATE OF RETURN

Above we evaluated the Palma project in terms of the rate of return of the specific project. However, a firm does not invest in a single project. It invests in a series of projects over time. From the standpoint of the parent (which requires funds for other projects) or the project (where there are currencies blocked by the host country), management needs to focus on the *reinvestment rate* of the cash flows. In many cases reinvestment will be in the project itself. The host country may have created high tariffs on imported goods, allowing the project's output to sell in a protected market. However, the condition attendant to this agreement may be that all domestic demand must be filled at a "reasonable" price. Alternatively, the original capital structure related to the project in the host country may have contained a large debt base linked to the financial cash flows discussed previously. In either case the cash flow from the project may have to be reinvested in the project both to protect the viability of the project by increasing output to meet domestic demand at a reasonable price and to provide normal funds for expansion given the initial low equity base.

Even if reinvestment in the project is not required because of these above considerations, the host country may block repatriation. Accordingly, a reasonable approach is the use of the Terminal Rate of Return (TROR). This approach is useful in any situation in which there are unequal project lives.[7]

The TROR requires the analyst to state the reinvestment rate for cash flows from a project. In the absence of this explicit statement, the rate of return computations implicitly assume that any cash generated during the life of the project is reinvested at the rate of return calculated for the project. The reinvestment rate assumed to compute the TROR may be the firm's cost of capital or may be a lower rate based on investment of the idle cash in short-term securities. It may change over time, reflecting alternative reinvestment rate assumptions. Whatever the rate, the cash throw-offs from a project are compounded *forward* to some horizon point. The initial investment is compared to this summed horizon value (the sum of each year's cash flows compounded forward to the same point). Then the internal rate of return is computed which will equate the investment to that compounded horizon value.

Algebraically, assume a reinvestment rate, r'. Each period's cash flow is compounded forward to the horizon, n, at this rate. The TROR (r_T) is the rate of return equating the initial investment, Y_0 (< 0), and the sum of compounded horizon values to zero. Thus,

$$0 = Y_0 + \frac{Y_1(1 + r')^{n-1}}{(1 + r_T)^n} + \frac{Y_2(1 + r')^{n-2}}{(1 + r_T)^n} + \ldots + \frac{Y_n}{(1 + r_T)^n}$$

$$= Y_0 + \frac{\sum_{i=1}^{n} Y_i(1 + r')^{n-i}}{(1 + r_T)^n}$$

Assume Zebracorp considers another \$300,000 project in Country Y with a stable currency and similar returns of \$96,000 per year for five years. The taxation policy is the same, but none of the return is related to purchases of

[7] Again, readers who wish to review discounting are referred to the Appendix to this chapter. A more detailed discussion of the terminal rate of return can be found in E. Eugene Carter, *Portfolio Aspects of Corporate Capital Budgeting* (Lexington, Mass.: D. C. Heath and Co., 1974), pp. 31-38.

parts from the parent. Hence, all of the $96,000 is generated by the project in Country Y. If free repatriation is assumed, the rate of return to the parent is the discount rate which equates a $300,000 investment with $96,000 per year for five years, or 18.0%.

If currency repatriation is blocked and cash must be kept idle, the rate of return must be based on a $300,000 investment and $480,000 (5 × $96,000) received at the end of the fifth year. The return is 9.9%.

Finally, assuming the money can be reinvested locally at 5% after taxes, we may compute a terminal rate of return. This is that return for which a $300,000 investment will provide the amount received after five years from the project's operating cash flow and reinvestment cash flows. This amount is:

$96,000 first year invested for 4 years at 5% compounded	=	$116,689
$96,000 second year invested for 3 years at 5% compounded	=	111,132
$96,000 third year invested for 2 years at 5% compounded	=	105,840
$96,000 fourth year invested for 1 year at 5% compounded	=	100,800
$96,000 fifth year received at the end of the year	=	96,000
Total at end of fifth year	=	$530,461
Terminal rate of return on a $300,000 investment	=	12.1%

The Net Terminal Value (NTV) is computed in similar fashion except that the investment is compounded forward at some opportunity (reinvestment) rate and subtracted from the compounded value of the accumulated operating cash flows. However, when the discount rate is related to the cost of capital, this decision rule will provide the same accept/reject signal as a normal net present value evaluation. In the case of the project with low reinvestment rates the results may differ.

In evaluating a single project, a manager may need to use various assumptions for projects located in different countries as well as study a given project under alternative hypotheses about repatriation and reinvestment. Consider how the relative rankings of the projects vary (1) when there is free repatriation, (2) when the currency is blocked, and (3) when the currency is blocked but with a reinvestment assumption. A sample of such calculations is shown in Exhibit 10.2. The outlay for each of three projects is held constant at $1,000, the horizon period is five years, and the reinvestment rate is 10%. Although these examples are simplified to provide level cash flows in most cases and changing parity rates are ignored, observe that (1) the pattern of analysis is valid (i.e., reinvestment rates are important) and (2) depending on the assumptions made regarding repatriation and reinvestment, the return to the parent from an investment will vary sharply.[8]

Notice in this example the following:

First, under a simple rate of return calculation, the project with a very short life and high flows in early years is favored.

Second, when the currencies are blocked, all project returns decline.

[8]The zeros in later years for Projects B and C are for ease of calculation. They can be replaced with small values and the earlier flows adjusted to provide similar rankings.

EXHIBIT 10.2. **Alternative Criteria for Determining Project Returns**

Cash Flows	Projects A	B	C
Outlay	($1,000)	($1,000)	($1,000)
Year 1	0	700	400
Year 2	200	700	400
Year 3	300	0	400
Year 4	400	0	400
Year 5	800	0	0
Total inflows	$1,700	$1,400	$1,600
Terminal value of inflows @ 10%	$1,869	$1,957	$2,042
Rate of return (Cash received yearly, reinvested at rate of return)	14%	(25%)	22%
Rate of return (Blocked until year 5, no reinvestment)	(11%)	7%	10%
Terminal rate of return (Blocked until year 5, reinvested at 10%)	13%	14%	(15%)

NOTE: The preferred choices are circled. Figures are rounded to the nearest whole percentage.

These declines are especially sharp for Projects B and C where the blocking period relative to the productive life of the investments is large.

Third, under TROR the final reversal of project rankings is obtained. A project which was never dominant under the other two evaluations becomes the most desired project.

Because the terminal rate of return calculations eliminate one of the main objections to the rate of return analysis (i.e., in the latter calculation the reinvestment rate is the same as the project's rate of return[9]), and because the rate of return can be more appealing to corporate executives than net present value even though the latter is technically superior, this measure will be included in future examples in this text. However, a full portfolio evaluation of the firm's projects requires more than a simple project accept/reject decision. As the firm moves toward this portfolio evaluation, its managers must begin to consider risk, a topic which colors any but the most superficial analysis of project analysis in other nations. It is especially critical in the less developed nations with a history of rapidly changing governments.

TYPES OF PROJECT RISK

Whatever the return of a project, the corporate officers are likely to be very concerned with the risk associated with that return. The safest of government bonds still has risk. First, for a long maturity bond, changes in prevailing

[9]For example, create a cash flow and compute the ROR. Delay receipt of $1.00 from one year's cash flow to a later year and compound it at the rate of return of the project. This action will provide a new cash flow which has the same rate of return as that of the original project. Hence, the implicit worth of the earlier receipt is the ROR; i.e., the implied opportunity cost of the funds is independent of the firm's cost of capital.

levels of interest rates mean changes in the price of the bond before maturity. The price will decline if prevailing interest rates rise. Only with a price decline can a new purchaser of the bond receive a return from the coupon and from price appreciation as the bond approaches maturity which is equivalent to the yield from a new issue brought out in the time of higher rates. Similarly, the longer the maturity, the greater the risk of tax changes affecting the net yield vis-à-vis other financing instruments. There are risks of the government itself which will affect the safety of the bond. Hence, even a relatively safe investment such as a government bond has risk.

When one focuses upon the operating projects of the typical corporation, the risks are compounded. First, there are the risks normally evaluated in domestic capital budgeting problems: *business* and *financial* risks. Second, there are risks associated with *inflation* and *currency* considerations. Finally, there are basic *political* risks relating to expropriation and other government policies.

Business and Financial Risk

The corporate financial officer must evaluate risk associated with a particular line of business as well as with the capital structure of the firm. For example, the purchase of an established department store in a growing metropolitan area normally would be considered as having less risk than the decision to invest in an imaginative new computer terminal. This is a type of business risk: It relates solely to the particular characteristics of the industry and the firm in question. Cyclical businesses (capital goods industries such as steel, for example) have a higher business risk than noncyclical businesses. New businesses in an industry generally have higher risk than established firms because of the extra risk attendant to choice of location and development of an effective organization.

The return to the equity holders is related to the business risk of the firm plus any financial risk. The latter is incurred by the presence of senior financial securities (i.e., debt) in the capital structure. As a greater amount of debt or preferred stock is added to the capital structure, common equity holders require a higher return since their financial risk is increased by larger principal and interest payments which increase the probability of financial insolvency. The business risk associated with a firm and an industry will have some influence on the capital structure. Even the best established firms in a high-risk industry are unlikely to have the same proportion of debt at a cheap price as a firm in a low-risk industry with many marketable current assets, for example. In addition to these industry characteristics, there are different financial policies followed by the corporate officers. Some nearly identical firms may have relatively high debt (i.e., added financial risk) while others in the same industry and with an equally seasoned business have a more conservative structure, perhaps with no debt. This issue of risk and capital structure will be reviewed in Chapter 11.

Inflation and Currency Risks

In Chapter 8 we considered the impact of inflation and exchange fluctuations on operating cash flows. When the manager is analyzing a project proposal located in another land a similar analysis must be performed.

First, consideration should be given to increased wages and general operating costs as well as the ability to pass on cost increases in the form of higher prices. The market for the finished product may permit price increases exceeding the net cost increases. Alternatively, allowable price increases may be less than cost increases. However, in the absence of a monetary correction policy as in Brazil, the taxation assumptions are important. The problem is that depreciation is usually based on historical cost. The increase in earning power of an asset caused by the inflationary effects on the currency are taxed heavily. Thus, part of the recovery of the currency erosion might be recovered by higher selling prices. Yet this recovery is accomplished by higher profits which are taxed using the original cost basis of depreciation (see Chapter 8).

Second, differential rates may apply. Labor costs may increase at an expected rate of 5% per year and raw materials at 4%; many of the fixed costs of the firm, such as depreciation or amortization of R&D costs, may not change if replacement of fixed assets is not contemplated in the near future. Accordingly, the rate of price increase needed to sustain standard profits usually will be much less than the inflation rate associated with many of the costs because the costs apply to a fraction of the revenues whereas the sales price increase applies to all the revenues.

Third, the terminal value of the project should reflect gains on the eventual sale of assets at the higher inflated price for used equipment, assuming maintenance was adequate.

One of the main reasons that inflation in another economy is likely to pose substantial problems in the capital budgeting decisions is the potential effect of inflation on the *currency exchange rates.* With a relatively high inflation rate and goods whose quantity demanded is sensitive to price changes, the country *must* devalue its currency for reasons such as purchasing power parity discussed in Part One. A country's relatively high inflation makes its goods less competitive on the world market and forces the country's balance of payments into continuous deficits. The country loses reserves and faces eventual depreciation of its currency. However, over the short term, relative rates of inflation and exchange depreciations often differ. In addition, the inflation rate relevant to exchange rate fluctuations is an average of the inflation rates that prevail in different sectors of the economy. The specific investment project will be exposed to only a portion of the various sectors in the economy.[10]

The complexities of this issue can best be seen in an extended example such as the Chaolandia Super Widgets case at the end of Chapter 11. These items all relate to the effect of inflation on the cash flows, or the numerator in the rate of return analysis. The impact of inflation on the discount rate, or denominator, is discussed in Chapter 11.

Political Risks

There are really only two political risks, both usually associated with investments in developing countries having unstable governments. These risks are related to *exchange* and *expropriation* (fractional or total!).

[10]One survey of devaluations and upvaluations as they affect reported earnings is contained in Robert A. Olstein and Thornton L. O'Glove, "Devaluation and Multinational Reporting," *Financial Analysts Journal,* Sept.-Oct. 1973, pp. 65–84. This article also reports proposed changes in reporting standards, and contains a table of firms which derive at least 20% of their revenues from non-U.S. sources.

In addition to the problem of a deteriorating exchange rate discussed above, another currency exchange problem associated with political risk is a temporary block on the currency. Black market operations, whatever the moral attitude the corporation may hold toward them, are usually not available for the relatively large size and highly visible transactions associated with a corporation from a major developed nation attempting to terminate its operations in a small developing land. Ownership may continue, but there is simply no way to remove funds from the country. This situation confronted many Indians in the wake of General Amin's actions in Uganda in 1972-74. Some of them felt they still owned their businesses, and nothing the Ugandan government did directly contradicted this premise. The Indians, many of whom were Ugandan citizens, operated from Kenya after widespread racial violence against them in Uganda, yet they had no means by which they might remove funds from their Ugandan operation.

There are brokers of varying degrees of reputability and legality who engage in the trading of blocked accounts. The most obvious way to eliminate blockages in such countries as Greece, Turkey, and the Soviet Union is to arrange swaps between two corporations, each lending to the other in the land where its own funds are restricted. In other times, a parent may charge a high rate of interest on loans to a subsidiary in a country that blocks currency repatriation.

War and revolution also add great uncertainty to the eventual repatriation of funds. Even after the Russian Revolution, Exxon (then Jersey Standard) continued to invest. The Russians seized the firm's $160,000 investment in Azerbaijan in 1920. Exxon invested another $8.8 million over the next five years, confident that the investment was still theirs. Sometimes, executives are overly enthusiastic about a business environment, ignoring both political liberties and international relationships. Many American executives rejoiced in Nazi Germany. Henry Ford continued to invest. Thomas Watson of IBM liked the environment for business. Corn Products president George Moffett said it was less onerous than the New Deal: "In Germany . . . there is no uncertainty, no political caprice, and no nonsense. You reach an agreement with the government and it sticks. You have a problem and you go to the government and get a clear, immediate answer, whereas in America you may spend weeks trying to find out where you stand with the New Deal and then just as you seem to have reached an understanding there is an overnight change in policy . . ." These comments may refer more to the New Deal (with complaints that are familiar today when business executives deal with the Soviet bloc countries), but the attitude toward Germany was startling. Poor forecasting and an insensitivity to the environment for many German citizens are not unique to American corporate presidents. Ultimately, most American assets in Germany not destroyed in the war were returned, even though remissions were blocked and the assets could not be sold for exchangeable currency during the war. A similar sequestering occurred for U. S. assets of foreign nationals whose countries were occupied by the Nazis, even before the United States declared war on Germany. Similar situations during the Spanish civil war or the Chilean situation today, for example, may raise the same questions about the relationship of the political risk to the citizen's environment.

These repatriation blocks can be evaluated in context of the example shown in Exhibit 10.2, where the effect on the terminal rate of return from blocking with and without reinvestment assumptions can be determined. When such risk is substantial, then the effect of such a block on the return must be considered.

Note that these blocks have generally been interpreted as public policy applicable to many firms. There may also be specific limitations on transfers from a particular firm. As we define the area of expropriation below, this limitation may be more appropriately considered as firm-specific in the nature of a host country's involvement in the operation of the individual firm.

From the standpoint of the corporation, we define expropriation broadly, with pure nationalization of ownership and complete involvement in the operation by the national government being one relatively infrequent extreme example. Generally, expropriation refers to an increased and substantial operating involvement by the host government that causes a downward revision to the initial understanding in the parent corporation's management role and cash flows from the operation. What is expropriated is the owner's right to operate fully the corporation.

The risk and expected value of particular states of the world may be very hard to assess. For example, even at the extreme of nationalization, the risk may range from complete uncertainty to a high probability of a takeover. Even given a takeover, there may be substantial variation in the possible compensation, ranging from nothing to market value paid immediately. In addition, assessing the probabilities tends to be very difficult and highly subjective. Nevertheless, the following comments are offered to cope with broadly defined expropriation. Additional approaches to the problem may be found in many of the references cited in the bibliography to this chapter.

The more direct political risk is expropriation. This may be gradual with increasing demands for participation by locals or by the host government in the profits and ownership of the business. Initially, it may take the form of a high sales tax or the right to buy into the equity of the firm at some price. Often the price is extremely low and related to the book value of the firm. Later, formal plans for takeover may include a five-year phasing of nationals into key operating positions. The more dramatic course is a pure takeover, as, for example, the American copper operations in Chile or the international petroleum corporations in Libya. In its extreme form, expropriation is a one-hour affair in which military forces with heavy armaments surround the offices and the corporate managers are given thirty minutes to evaluate the situation. They are provided with transportation to the airfield where a DC-3 removes them from the land after an unusual avoidance of baggage clearance and customs formalities. When the situation warrants, the corporation's officers will consider the worst-case assumption, calculating the maximum loss if expropriation occurs in various years.

There is a variety of techniques that the firm may employ to alter the probabilities of expropriation no matter what the transition in governments might bring. One way of categorizing actions designed to lessen the probabilities or the effect of expropriation is shown in Exhibit 10.3. First, there are influences on the government in a positive vein. Second, there are negative inducements for the government to avoid expropriation. Finally, there are outside options which sometimes alter the probabilities, but more often they alter the effect.

EXHIBIT 10.3. Coping with Political Risks: Expropriation

Positive Approaches		*Negative Approaches*
Prior negotiation of controls and operating contracts	Direct	License/patent restrictions under international agreements
Prior agreement for sale		Control of external raw materials
Joint venture with government		Control of transportation to (external) markets
Use of locals in management	Indirect	Control of downstream processing
Joint venture with local banks		Control of external markets
Equity participation by middle class		
Local sourcing		
Local retail outlets		

External Approaches to Minimize Loss

International insurance or investment guarantees
Thinly capitalized firms:
- Local financing
- External financing secured only by the local operation

The positive approaches (left column) involve indicating to the host government the firm's interest in the nation on a longer-term basis. Careful negotiation may result in contracts addressing the firm's obligation to employ locals and to accommodate various control agreements relating to management, profitability, and investment.[11] Perhaps the agreements provide for eventual termination of the foreign ownership. There can be a joint venture with the host government, either now or in later years, with arrangements made for the government to have a long-run minority or majority position. These contracts indicate the firm's commitment to meet the government in achieving political, developmental, and financial goals for the project. Indirectly, the firm can provide for reinforcing the government's nonfinancial goals by sourcing capital equipment and operating supplies locally; by using locals for unskilled, skilled, and managerial roles; and by spreading equity throughout the local citizenry.[12]

[11] Sometimes national employees do not identify as fully with the country as expected. The late president of National Cash Register, Stanley C. Allyn, told of the NCR office in the path of the Wehrmacht as it rumbled into Paris. One tank swerved from the column and headed for the office. Out jumped a pistol-bearing German soldier who hammered on the door. Meeting the local French official, he remarked, "I'm from the Berlin office. Sorry I can't stay long, but I was wondering: Did you make quota last year?" See Mira Wilkins, *The Maturing of Multinational Enterprise: American Business Abroad from 1914 to 1970* (Cambridge, Mass.: Harvard University Press, 1974).

[12] The last policy is usually operated in the form of substantial investments by a few big banks controlled by the wealthier citizens of the country. An alternative approach, somewhat limited in the absence of a well-developed equity market, is to encourage investment by as many of the middle class as possible. The disadvantages of this indirect pressure on the government are the costs of handling small investors (many of whom may be relatively unsophisticated financially) coupled with the stockholder resentment created when a dividend is passed. The indirect pressure on the government, of course, is that nationalization or other forms of political involvement in the management of the firm force the government to contend not just with workers who may be unhappy under govern-

Among the negative approaches is control of the operation by restricting inputs or outputs. By having the local venture provide only one step in the process of selling a product (basic raw material development, or selling imported goods manufactured elsewhere, for example), nationalization of the operation prevents the government from retaining a viable business. Where there is a sizable producing operation which depends on external markets, control of those external markets, of the transportation to those markets, or of intervening processing required to provide the final good to those markets all constrict the government.

For example, Mideast oil producers were limited in their abilities to nationalize local oil operations when most of the downstream refining capacity and market outlets were controlled by their local partners (the international oil companies) who presumably would not be pleased by an expropriation. To the extent that the international oil producers could supply their refineries from other sources and no other refineries were available (the situation prevailing in the late 1950s and 1960s), the ability of the Mideast nations to profit from expropriation was reduced. In later periods, it was the limited availability to the oil companies of alternative economic sources of crude oil which increased the Mideast nations' position even though most of the tanker fleets were either owned or under long-term charter to the oil companies. The benefit of nationalization to the oil-producing nations, of course, was greater influence in the whole production process from crude oil to consumer petroleum products.

Control of transportation, the situation of United Fruit (now United Brands) vis-à-vis various small Latin countries (also known in former days as "banana republics" for their main United Fruit product), prevented those nations from nationalizing plantations. Put simply, the bananas would rot before optional transportation could be developed, and unless all these nations acted in concert, the effect on United Fruit from one nationalization would have been relatively insignificant.[13]

A corporation which controls critical licenses or patents has influence on the government, for operating illegally without these licenses brings sanctions upon the nation. Many Western nations and companies have been reluctant to invest in the Eastern bloc for many years because of Soviet indifference to international copyright and patent agreements.

Finally, as suggested at the bottom of Exhibit 10.3, the company has outside options. First, investment guarantees from OPIC (the Overseas Private Investment Corporation) or another source mean that any expropriation can be recovered to some degree. The determination of value may be very different for the corporation (which viewed the operation as a going concern) and the insurance agency (which may view it at book value). Such insurance programs have a negative effect on the host governments, for inhospitable investment

ment operation (the Chilean copper case), but also with a wide range of investors who either lose their investment or anticipate poor results from increased government involvement. Hence, the joint venture or involvement of local middle-class equity participation may be a direct way of responding to a government's goals, but it also may be a very indirect way of forcing the government to reckon with higher domestic costs from an expropriation move.

[13]The merits of concerted action were learned well in the Middle East by the Organization of Petroleum Exporting Countries.

environments are well noted by these insurance organizations and are transmitted to potential investors who inquire about insurance and risks. Such insurance may eventually be developed through the United Nations or regional insurance banks, for the collective benefits to most developing countries would seem to be considerable.

Another strategy, followed by many investors in unstable environments, is to pay whatever price is required for local financing or for unguaranteed outside financing supported by the local investment. In the event of nationalization, the corporation negates any debt obligation, leaving the local lenders to fight with the local government about repayment. Alternatively, as occurred in the Freeport Cuban nickel operation, the major banks can be left to argue with the new government while the corporation goes on its way (home).[14]

Finally, bribes are also possible. The OECD members adopted a voluntary code of behavior in June 1977, stating that firms should not make contributions to political office seekers or pay bribes unless legally permitted. This code of behavior also suggested disclosure of sales and profits by geographic area, and urged firms not to exploit any dominant market positions. The impact of these strictures remains to be seen, but it is likely to be negligible. Like Codes of Ethics for U.S. Congressmen, the problem is *enforcement,* not *standards,* and there is no legal implication of this OECD code unless each member nation passes legislation along these lines. Even then, enforcement is hampered unless there is an exchange of information and other cooperation among the nations. It is also useful to draw a distinction between bribes and extortion. Money changes hands, but the question is who initiates the exchange, if anyone knows. Years ago Guatemalan dictators regularly gave large land holdings to various army generals to insure their continued support. The generals had no use for the land, and neither did anyone else. However, they were able to sell it at high prices to United Fruit, who feared their displeasure. This tale, of course, is not unique in time, place, or corporation.

As we have indicated in earlier chapters and will suggest again later, it is naive to assume that the "best" outcome for the parent corporation many miles away from a foreign subsidiary necessarily coincides with economic betterment of the citizens of that country, let alone the enhancement of their political and social environment. Firms can make large profits under ruthless dictatorships, and they may indeed make less money when long-run development of the economic infrastructure of a nation dictates certain national policies that conflict with the maximized present value of cash flows to XYZ Multinational. On the other hand, one also should recognize that many actions taken by the host government for the social or economic enhancement of the local environment may be sadly misguided or patently corrupt.

[14]These examples, of course, actually reverse the conventional corporate finance evaluation where additional debt *increases* the financial risk to the equity holders. In these situations, local debt or unguaranteed debt permits the equity holders both to improve their return because of the leverage and to have less risk from expropriation. On the other hand, the higher debt burden increases the risk that inability to meet debt payments will force loss of equity in the business. In many cases, however, the increased risk of insolvency in no way compares with the benefit of avoiding substantial losses from expropriation.

THE EVALUATION OF RISK

After observing the types of international financial risk, the management must reach a decision on how to cope with that risk. In terms of the analysis suggested, contingency planning of a "what-if" variety can (1) reduce the probabilities of expropriation or repatriation restrictions beyond those known when the investment is made and can (2) show the probable effects on the terminal rate of return should such blockages be encountered.

Chapter 11 discusses the determination of the appropriate acceptance criteria when risk is present. In addition to identifying the type of risk discussed earlier (business and financial risk, inflation and currency risk, and exchange and expropriation risk), it is necessary to determine the composite risk that is present in a project. After looking at historical information about the type of business in general and the profitability of business in that country in particular, the firm's managers form judgments about the probable performance of a project in that country. Through interaction of the various factors, the final dispersion of terminal rate of return, earnings per share, sales, and the like can be determined most effectively by a risk analysis simulation. This technique is reviewed as part of Chapter 11, and an extended example of its use is part of that chapter as well.

SUMMARY

We may separate the determination of the project's cash flows into operating cash flows and financial cash flows. In the *operating* cash flow determination, the importance of determining the relevant cash flows when there are substantial interdependencies or joint effects with the parent sponsor of the project was stressed. These interdependencies include vertical and horizontal combinations, alternative cost and revenue assumptions for the finished products, and economies of scale in production or distribution. The use of royalties or supervisory fees as they affect the return also must be considered.

In evaluating the *financial* cash flows, one aspect is the impact on the value of investment when there is a contribution of equipment from the parent. A brief introduction to the major concepts of taxation argued that the enlarged concept of the corporate entity has made governments increasingly believe that corporations in their land should pay taxes on profits earned anywhere in the world with some adjustment for local taxes paid in other lands. In response, a major motivation for tax havens has been to avoid the taxes on funds removed from one foreign subsidiary to be invested in another foreign subsidiary. Finally, there are special national or supernational policies designed to encourage foreign trade or to protect a balance of payments position.

The issue of the *remission* of funds and the concern of companies for the return of cash to the parent has been raised but not resolved. This concern led to the discussion of whose cash flows are relevant: the parent's or the project's. This issue will return later, but there are sharply divergent returns depending on the numeraire selected for evaluating the cash flows and on the cash flows received by the project vs. the parent.

In evaluating the returns, the familiar concepts of rate of return and net present value were used. These standards were supplemented by the *terminal rate of return* which permits an explicit consideration of the reinvestment rate for projects. This assumption is especially important when there are blocked funds which cannot be removed from a host country until a later period. The returns of a project vary depending on which standard of evaluation is considered. Tables of present values of one unit of a currency received at various periods and at different discount rates are shown in Appendix 2 of this book.

An introduction to project *risk* reviewed the business and financial risk concepts found in traditional corporate finance. Another type of risk results from the link between differential inflation rates and currency exchange rates. Political risks, relating to blocks on exchange or outright expropriation, are a third type of uncertainty. Finally, a variety of positive, negative, and independent actions which may be taken by the corporation to reduce these risks was offered.

Questions

1. What factors make the cash flows from a project create different values for the parent and for the subsidiary which undertakes the project?

2. How does the terminal rate of return differ from the rate of return? How would you use it in a project which has revaluations (appreciation or depreciation) likely for the local currency against the parent's currency? Does it make a difference if the funds are blocked or remitted?

3. "I don't worry about anticipating currency changes; all I care about is the absolute level of inflation. I just reduce the value of the funds by that amount to get the equivalent in German marks." (German corporate executive). Do you agree with this analysis?

4. How would you attempt to cope with the political risks in a country when the government has a record of rapid changes in personnel?

5. "They claim we exploit them since we demand a one-year payout on all projects. But, you know, we have had so many things nationalized in Latin America in the last thirty years with all these revolving governments that a short life is all we can fairly anticipate. Now, one country may feel we exploit them if they do not have nationalization in a given decade, but we have to look at our portfolio of returns from all the nations over many years. So we have no choice." Comment.

Bibliography

Carter, E. Eugene, *Portfolio Aspects of Corporate Capital Budgeting.* Lexington, Mass.: D. C. Heath and Company, 1974.

Carter, William Gilbert, "National Support of International Ventures." *Columbia Journal of World Business,* Sept.-Oct. 1972, pp. 6–12.

Eiteman, David K., and Arthur I. Stonehill, *Multinational Business Finance.* Reading, Mass.: Addison-Wesley Publishing Co., 1973, Ch. 10.

Hawkins, R. G., N. Mintz and M. Provissiero, "Government Takeovers of U.S. Foreign Affiliates." *Journal of International Business Studies,* Spring 1976, pp. 3-16.

Labys, Walter C., "International Commodity Markets, Models and Forecasts." *Columbia Journal of World Business,* Winter 1976, pp. 36–45.

Lessard, Donald R., "Transfer Prices, Taxes and Financial Markets: Implications of Internal Financial Transfers within the Multinational Firm," Proceedings of the New York University Conference on Economic Issues of Multinational Firms, edited by Robert G. Hawkins. New York: JAI Press, 1977.

Mikesell, Raymond F., et al., *Foreign Investment in the Petroleum and Mineral Industries.* Resources for the Future, Inc., Baltimore, Md.: John Hopkins Press, 1971.

Olstein, Robert A., and Thornton L. O'Glove, "Devaluation and Multinational Reporting." *Financial Analysts Journal,* Sept.-Oct. 1973, pp. 65–84.

Polk, Judd, et al., *U.S. Production Abroad and the Balance of Payments.* New York: National Industrial Conference Board, 1966.

Robock, Stefan H., "Political Risk: Identification and Assessment." *Columbia Journal of World Business,* July-Aug. 1971, pp. 6–20.

Truitt, J. Frederick, "Expropriation of Foreign Investment: Summary of the Post-World War II Experience of American and British Investors in the Less Developed Countries." *Journal of International Business Studies,* Fall 1970, pp. 21-34.

Wilkins, Mira, *The Maturing of Multinational Enterprise: American Business Abroad from 1914 to 1970.* Cambridge, Mass.: Harvard University Press, 1974.

Appendix: Discounting—Net Present Value and Internal Rate of Return

Once the cash flows are determined for the project and for the parent, we seek a means to evaluate what value to assign to the cash flows considering the time value of money. Net Present Value (NPV) and Rate of Return (ROR) are two means by which to discount cash flows.

Suppose one has X dollars (e.g., \$10) and the discount rate is r (e.g., 10%). At the end of one year the value Y_1 of the holding is:

$$Y_1 = X(1 + r) \qquad Y_1 = \$10\,(1 + 0.10) = \$11.00$$

At the end of two years:

$$Y_2 = Y_1\,(1 + r) = X\,(1 + r)^2 \qquad Y_2 = \$10\,(1 + 0.10)^2 = \$12.10$$

Y_2 represents the *terminal value* of investment X at the end of the second year compounded annually at the rate, r. One can reverse the procedure. Given Y_2 dollars at the end of two years and the rate of discount, r, then X, the amount of money equivalent to Y_2 dollars two years hence, can be found.

$$X = \frac{Y_2}{(1 + r)^2} \qquad X = \frac{\$12.10}{(1 + 0.10)^2} = \$10$$

and X is the *present value* of Y_2.

In capital budgeting, one estimates the Y values (yearly net cash flows) for the investment. A discount rate is selected which is the opportunity cost of funds to the firm (the cost of capital), r. Then X, the *net present value* of the stream of cash flows, can be computed. This stream includes the initial investment, Y_0, which is negative, and the other Y_i's which may be negative or positive.

$$X = Y_0 + \frac{Y_1}{(1 + r)} + \frac{Y_2}{(1 + r)^2} + \cdots + \frac{Y_n}{(1 + r)^n}$$

If the present value is positive ($X > 0$), then the investment is considered desirable because it covers the cost of funds to the firm.

The rate of return is also called the discounted rate of return, internal rate of return, or return on investment. The ROR is the rate at which the future cash flows can be discounted to equal the investment. It is obtained by using the same equation but a slightly different analysis. Instead of assigning a discount rate, r, the equation is solved for that rate for which the present value of the stream of cash outflows and inflows of an investment equals 0. That is,

$$0 = Y_0 + \frac{Y_1}{(1 + r)} + \frac{Y_2}{(1 + r)^2} + \cdots + \frac{Y_n}{(1 + r)^n}$$

Y_0 is negative, representing the cash investment by the firm in the project.

These two standards will not always rank projects in the same way. Further, it is possible for a project to have more than one rate of return. One difficult assumption is that the project cash flows evaluated under a ROR calculation are presumed to continue to earn at that rate when reinvested. However, in evaluating single projects in the international setting, a general adjustment is useful which eliminates the limitations of some of the assumptions contained in these two models. This adjustment, the Terminal Rate of Return, was discussed in Chapter 10.

CHAPTER 11

The Appropriate Acceptance Criteria for Capital Expenditures

The previous chapter outlined how a manager determines the relevant cash flows in international investments. The manager also needs to consider the return that should be demanded for a single project. First, there are the traditional corporate finance precepts on the cost of capital. But then, whose capital structure is relevant: the parent's or the subsidiary project's? In resolving this issue, consolidated statements and their effect on the expectations of lenders and investors must be considered. We also consider the practical tactics of international business operations. From these topics which deal with the cost of capital and capital structure considerations, we turn to the specifics of a project, introducing both the techniques by which the probable risk associated with a project can be determined and the appropriate criteria for valuing that risk. This discussion is followed by a comprehensive risk analysis of a project, Freeport Mineral's decision to invest in an Australian nickel mine. Finally, we address the dilemma recurring in both these chapters: The corporation operates under certain policies to protect itself from excessive risk; yet these policies themselves contribute to a climate that often breeds the outcome of the most feared risk–expropriation.

THE COST OF CAPITAL

The cost of capital is the variable that financial theory uses as the minimum rate a project must yield in order to be accepted by a firm. Since the cost of capital usually refers to the average cost of funds (debt and equity) used to finance the firm, the project must yield at least that amount to be a worthwhile operation.

Chapter 10 discussed the concept of business (operating) and financial risk and built upon the traditional analysis offered in corporate financial theory. Debt has a lower cost than equity since it has priority claim in liquidation as well as first claim on earnings in each period. Equity requires a higher return because the investors face the business risks related to the corporation as well as the financial risks associated with the presence of debt.

For the firm, this combination of factors allows a cost of capital curve which may appear as presented in Exhibit 11.1. The overall cost of capital of the firm is a function of the cost of debt and equity and their relative proportions. The cost of capital initially declines as the relatively cheaper debt is substituted for the more expensive equity. At some point the steadily increasing equity cost combined with the increasing cost of debt will cause the cost of capital to flatten and then to rise. There is continuing controversy over whether there is a unique point or a range of points at which the cost of capital curve is the lowest. Similarly, there is concern over how these curves differ for alternative industries (different business risks) and for more complicated financial structures than the simple debt-equity model suggested here. The most famous critics of this tradi-

EXHIBIT 11.1. The Cost of Capital

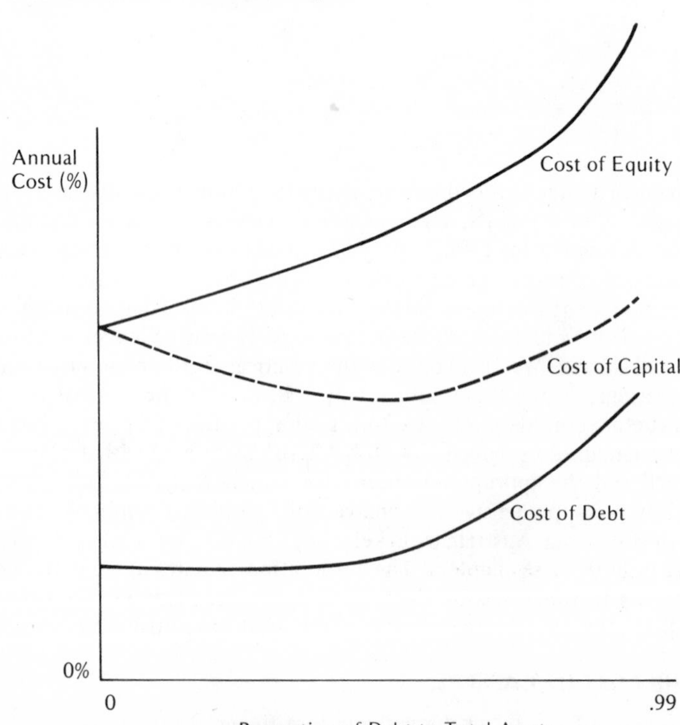

tional model, Modigliani and Miller, would suggest that the only benefit of debt financing is the tax deductibility of the interest. However, later versions of their theory would still have the cost of capital curve turning upward at some point as the risk of financial insolvency increases.[1]

The job of the financial manager is to choose the best capital structure for the firm in the long run and then to time the issues of debt, equity, and preferred stock to minimize the company's cost of capital over time. There are periods in the market when a debt or equity issue is relatively favorable; therefore, the financial officer should seek to avoid the periods of highest cost for issuing these securities. Expectations may change, of course. In the last few years, many firms that refused to issue debt at an interest cost of 9% were rapidly seeking funds eighteen months later at 9½%. The difference was that the 9% rate appeared at a time of rising rates which eventually reached over 10% for seasoned corporate debt issues. When the market turned down to "only" 9½%, many managers were happy to have these lower rates. The 9½% rate became more reasonable once the higher rates had been seen.

By focusing upon the capital structure concept, an executive can avoid the error of evaluating capital projects on the basis of the particular financing alternative considered at a point in time. Thus, if the company is issuing debt with an after-tax cost of 4%, it might use a discount rate of 4% in evaluating projects. Some years later, an exceedingly high debt ratio induced by following this policy over time would force an equity issue. Assume that the manager believes equity costs 15%. The implication is that the projects being evaluated that year should meet a 15% hurdle rate. Such a mentality plays havoc with any sort of decentralized organization in which divisions must compete against each other for scarce funds. The motivation of a divisional manager would be to submit all the low return projects in debt financing years, saving the higher return projects for equity financing years and/or urging a competing division manager to meet the equity hurdle rate.

The conclusion is that the firm should decide on a cost of the combined components of the capital structure over time. This cost is used as the hurdle rate each year regardless of the particular financing which is undertaken that year.

Obvious as this conclusion is to most practicing financial executives, its subtlety is often missed when evaluating major projects or proposals which have particular mortgage debt attached to them. In most cases a lender considers the overall capability of a business and not just the security of a mortgage on a proposed new building. Similarly, the presence of a mortgage on a building may in turn affect the potential availability of debt from other lenders. Hence, to give the new building the benefit of all the debt (resulting in a lower hurdle rate for the new building as a project) ignores the effect of reduced debt availability for the remainder of the corporation.

The cost of capital for the *firm* is one of the most unsettled issues in both theory and practice. When one turns to the assessment of the appropriate cost

[1] For those readers interested in the assumptions beyond this analysis and for additional references, see an introductory text such as Weston and Brigham, *Managerial Finance,* 5th ed. (Hinsdale, Ill.: Dryden Press, 1975) or Van Horne, *Financial Management and Policy,* 4th ed. (Englewood Cliffs, N. J.: Prentice-Hall, Inc., 1977). In particular, see Van Horne, Ch. 9, for a discussion of the Modigliani and Miller position.

of capital for a *project,* the confusion increases. Essentially, the cost of capital to the firm is related to the return and risk of the firm's project investments. How does one determine the appropriate cost of capital for projects of varying risk classifications? The issue is important, for that cost of capital is reflected in the discount rate used in evaluating the project.

One can focus on the *weighted cost of capital appropriate for this investment.* When the corporation is a holding company, in effect it may be viewed as a relatively passive investor owning separate corporations. The weighted cost of capital may be computed for those subunits as separate entities either by looking at how the local market evaluates publicly traded competitors of those subunits or by discussing with lenders and investors the appropriate capital structure of those entities.

Viewing the weighted average cost of capital shown in Exhibit 11.1, one might note that it has both theoretical and empirical foundations. The theoretical foundations are based on the existence of a rational or *perfect* capital market. The empirical foundations are still subject to debate. On the other hand, in international capital markets we should assume *imperfect* capital markets. There are segmented capital markets, there is disequilibrium in the markets, and there are special financing arrangements unique to many projects depending on their location. When these imperfections in the capital market do exist, the determination of the lowest cost of capital is not possible theoretically. However, the manager still must find a hurdle rate by which to accept or reject projects in foreign countries. An approximation to the cost of capital under those imperfect conditions must be found. The way that local investors react to similar projects will provide some guidance in this endeavor, although this reaction is not necessarily a theoretically optimal decision rule.

An alternative to the concept of the average cost of capital is the concept of *return to equity,* one of the components of the total cost of capital. This approach can be particularly useful when special financing arrangements are attached to the specific project.

An example of a situation in which management usually concentrates its analysis on the return on equity is the shipping industry. In this case the yard which manufactures the ship traditionally supplies a substantial amount of the total funds required secured only by the ship. The return to the equity holders is a function of the ship's cost, the revenues and operating expenses, and the timing of the particular financing scheme offered by a given shipyard. This last item is often a source of erroneous conclusions. Holding the cost, revenue, and operating cost assumptions constant, it is obvious that the shorter loan (faster payback) option will have a lower return to equity in normal settings. Essentially, the cheaper debt financing will be paid off sooner, meaning that the ship will be financed increasingly by larger portions of equity over its life. Without debt on which to lever the return to equity in later years, the return to equity will be lower than otherwise would be the case. The analysis is valid, however, only if one assumes that no other financing is available in later years. One can argue that short-term financing might be used in later years to replace some or all of that debt. Alternatively, one needs to consider if the low-debt balance sheet afforded by the rapid repayment of debt under the shorter-lived debt option would not permit more debt from other lenders for financing additional projects.

In some situations the particular financing may be dominated uniquely and completely by the particular project at hand. Special joint ventures or subsidiaries in which the parent firm offers no guarantees may be regarded as unique projects with their own cost of capital. For example, Freeport Minerals traditionally operates in this manner. Nationalization of its huge Cuban nickel plant caused the parent to lose its equity in the subsidiary and several banks to lose huge amounts of loans to the project secured by that plant. However, the effect on the other lenders to Freeport and the rest of Freeport's operations was minimal. This case is probably atypical. Often the corporation will fulfill a moral obligation (perhaps induced by enlightened self-interest in assuring itself a welcome for future financing options) to pay off liabilities of legally separate entities. This behavior was seen when American Express repaid debts of its legally separate warehousing subsidiary in the wake of the salad oil scandal.

In the following discussion we will focus upon a number of returns when looking at cases, for the manager will appropriately review several different returns. On one hand, the overall operating return will be considered. In addition, the return to equity which may be affected by unique financing arrangements in particular settings will be reviewed, and judgments must be reached about whether returns to equity under sharply divergent financing arrangements are comparable. Will equity shareholders and other lenders perceive their risk as unchanged regardless of the local financing arrangements which are employed for a particular project? The terminal rate of return introduced in Chapter 10 allows us to interpose a particular reinvestment rate, but it mixes the operating and reinvestment returns in stating a project return. Accordingly, net present value and rate of return results will be useful as well.

WHOSE COST OF CAPITAL?

In evaluating the cost of capital, particular projects may sometimes be evaluated on the basis of their appropriate capital structure when standing alone. This option is easy when the projects are operations in a major industry with publicly traded competitors. For the typical international project, one must evaluate the particular risk characteristics of the cash flow, a topic discussed later.

There is a form of fallacious analysis that is sometimes encountered, which essentially is based on the use of pyramiding as shown in Exhibit 11.2. Advocates of this position say the following: "We shall invest in that project in Country X, and we know our parent has a cost of capital of (say) 12%. Accordingly, we shall borrow as much local money as possible and then invest the balance ourselves. As long as we can earn our 12%, we are in fine shape."

Ignoring major risk considerations and differential inflation rates, assume the proposed project is comparable to other projects of the firm. What is the fallacy of this argument? Exhibit 11.2 indicates the problem. Assume the parent and all subsidiaries are able to obtain 50% debt and 50% equity with debt carrying a consistent cost of 4% after tax. Call the parent a holding company and let two of the subsidiaries act as holding companies. That is, they do nothing but invest their capital (raised by debt and equity issues) in the equity of other firms. In this example they have invested directly in only one other firm. In

EXHIBIT 11.2. Pyramid Corporate Structure

Holding Corp

$2M debt at 4% 2M equity at 20%	12% cost of capital

Subsidiary 1

$4M debt at 4% 4M equity at 12%	8% cost of capital

Subsidiary 2

$8M debt at 4% 8M equity at 8%	6% cost of capital

Consolidated

Debt	$30M
Equity	2M

Subsidiary 3

$16M debt at 4% 16M equity at 6%	5% cost of capital

the typical pyramiding example the units invest in a variety of firms. An analysis of the conclusions drawn from this exhibit may suggest why such "diversification" is used.

Consider the final operating company, Subsidiary 3. The lender to this firm is content, assuming the $16M in debt is reasonably secured by real assets. The lenders to the other firms are not concerned, for the firms only have a 0.5 debt-to-total-capitalization ratio. However, if these lenders go beyond the simplest of analyses, they see that their ultimate real assets for security are downstream. Furthermore, the lender to Subsidiary 3 would have first claim on the assets under normal circumstances. To take the first case, consider the lender to Holding Corp. When this lender considers the consolidated statement, it is apparent that the real "firm" has $30M in debt and only $2M in equity. This lender's $2M of debt stands behind an additional $28M of debt, and all of the indebtedness is secured by the $32M of assets of Subsidiary 3. (For kindness' sake in this example, assume that the assets of Subsidiary 3 do exist and are reasonably valued, a situation that does not always occur.)

This exaggerated situation points out the fallacy of merely charging the subsidiary with the cost of capital of the parent when that investment is really equity. In fact, the subsidiary should be charged with the appropriate cost of equity for going into *that* business in *that* land. Typically, this charge for equity will be higher than the parent's cost of capital. Accordingly, the cost of funds to the usual subsidiary will be increased.

The local capital structures may differ sharply from the parent capital structure arrangements. For example, the debt load afforded most Japanese firms is grossly above the comparable debt load of an American firm in the same industry. Exhibit 11.3 shows tabulations of debt ratios in different nations. In part, this additional debt is because of the involvement of the government of Japan on both sides. The Bank of Japan (government-owned) provides debt via commercial banks to major industries on the government's favored list, as we elaborate upon in Chapter 16. Lenders know that the government is committed to protecting business. Hence, the risk of bankruptcy is reduced given the

EXHIBIT 11.3. Debt Ratios in Selected Industries and Countries[a]

	Alcoholic Beverages	*Auto-mobiles*	*Chemicals*	*Electrical*	*Foods*	*Iron and Steel*	*Non-ferrous Metals*	*Paper*	*Textiles*	*Total*
Benelux	45.7	—	44.6	37.5	56.2	50.0	59.2	35.9	54.2	47.9
France	35.8	36.0	34.3	59.1	24.7	33.7	55.0	35.5	20.9	37.2
W. Germany	59.2	55.1	54.8	67.5	42.5	63.8	68.1	71.8	44.9	58.6
Italy	64.9	77.3	68.2	73.6	66.4	77.9	67.5	—	66.6	70.3
Japan	60.9	70.3	73.2	71.1	78.3	74.5	74.5	77.7	72.2	72.5
Sweden	—	76.4	45.6	60.1	46.8	70.0	68.7	60.7	—	61.2
Switzerland	—	—	59.7	50.8	29.2	—	26.3	—	—	41.5
United Kingdom	43.8	56.5	38.7	46.9	47.6	44.9	41.7	46.6	42.4	45.5
United States	31.1	39.2	43.3	50.3	34.2	35.8	36.7	33.9	44.2	38.7
Total	48.8	58.7	51.4	57.4	47.3	56.3	55.3	51.7	49.4	

[a]The numbers in the matrix represent average total debt as a percent of total assets based on book value. Each company is weighted equally, i.e., the individual company debt ratios are summed and divided by the number of companies in each sample.

SOURCE: Stonehill, Arthur and Thomas Stitzel, "Financial Structure and the Multinational Corporation." CALIFORNIA MANAGEMENT REVIEW, Fall 1969. Vol. 12, No. 1, pp. 91–96. U.S. corporations are the ten largest in each industry (four only for automobiles), ranked by 1965 sales and reported in MOODY'S INDUSTRIAL MANUAL (New York: Moody's Investor Service, Inc., June 1966). Japanese corporations are the largest publicly owned corporations in each industry as reported in KAISHA SHIKIHO (Quarterly Reports on Corporations) (Tokyo: Toyo Keizai Shinpo Sha, July 1967). European corporations are all the publicly owned corporations reported in BEERMAN'S FINANCIAL YEARBOOK OF EUROPE (London: R. Beerman Publishers, 1967).

government commitment to preserve the major corporation as an economic force in Japan and throughout the world. The local capital structure considerations may provide a lower capital cost in some cases than the parent's home country would permit. Typically, the local capital structure will provide a higher cost to the project if the home country is an industrialized nation and the local country is a less developed land.[2]

Thus, one returns to the basic conclusion that the relevant starting cost of capital for business and financial risk should be based on what the subsidiary would have to earn operating on its own in its own environment. Bearing in mind currency and political risks and possible imperfections in the capital markets which permit lower capital costs of the parent to be passed through, one can consider whether this investment is desirable from the standpoint of the parent.

INFLATION AND THE SELECTION OF THE DISCOUNT RATE

Coping with inflation within the capital budgeting framework is one of the most difficult topics to evaluate. *As a general rule, inflation that is widely accepted will be built into the cost of debt and equity for the firm.* Hence, the weighted cost of capital reflects such anticipated price changes, and the cash flow assumptions also can accommodate these expectations. Unless the manager has superior forecasting ability, it is unrealistic to add a further increase to the discount rate derived from the cost of capital to adjust for inflation. To the extent that lenders anticipate price increases, the cost of debt will reflect the cheaper currency in which they are repaid. Equity holders, too, should have a nominal return consistent with inflation and anticipated real returns, and the sensible calculation of the cost of equity should reflect this valuation.

A local lender has no interest in lending money at 8% if there is 7% inflation. Assuming the real rate on debt is 8%, this individual knows that a borrower can invest those funds in an asset which will likely rise in nominal value by 15%. To give up the choice of doing this personally, the lender demands a return which will provide purchasing power parity (i.e., at least 7% increment), plus compensate for not having the use of the money (the real interest rate). Hence, the stated rate will reflect both inflationary expectations and the price of money. A similar calculation is also performed by equity investors so their required rate of return includes inflationary expectations as well.

A proper evaluation of the cost of capital must be based on current and future costs for debt and equity raised in the proportions of the optimal capital structure of the firm. Only current and future costs of funds include the expected inflation rates relevant to future capital projects. The historical cost of funds of the firm, sometimes called the imbedded cost of capital, measures historical inflationary conditions, not the inflation expected to prevail in the future.

In the inflationary conditions *both* the cash flow figures and the cost

[2]From their survey in 1968, Stonehill and Nathanson found that 64% of their respondents who used a cost of capital concept did *not* vary it for foreign investments. In terms of income, the largest group counted cash flow plus retained earnings as "income." See Arthur Stonehill and Leonard Nathanson, "Capital Budgeting and the Multinational Corporation," *California Management Review,* Summer 1968, pp. 39–54.

of capital estimates in capital budgeting should reflect expected inflation rates. Otherwise a misleading conclusion may be reached. For example, reflecting the impact of inflation on the cash flows without adjusting the cost of capital for the effects of inflation will make almost any project appear desirable. The increase in nominal value of the assets alone is bound to produce this result.

Fundamentally, using the local weighted cost of capital in evaluating projects is beneficial because that cost accounts for much of the inflationary pressures if properly computed. This viewpoint prevents the foreign corporation with a domestic cost of capital of (say) 12% from concluding that it would be much better off in Country X where almost any project earns 20%. This behavior is prevented simply by forcing the multinational corporation to reflect that much of the earnings in Country X are inflationary, and a local cost of capital would probably be at least 15%.

To avoid the difficulties involved in measuring the impact of inflation on the evaluation of projects, many companies ignore inflation altogether. This is done on the assumption that the rate of inflation on the sectors where the project will operate is the same as for the economy as a whole. We think this assumption is incorrect in many instances. Inflation rates in the economic sectors in which the project will operate often will be different from the average for the economy as a whole. However, the overall rate of inflation in the economy is the one that investors will consider in trying to maintain the purchasing power of their money. To incorporate the impact of inflation correctly the cash flows should reflect the rate of inflation specific to the project, while the cost of capital reflects the overall inflation rate expected in the economy. The impact of inflation on both cash flow figures and the cost of capital should be considered separately and explicitly.[3]

THE ISSUE OF CONSOLIDATED STATEMENTS

In the context of a cost of capital analysis, if the consolidated risk position of the firm is changed by the addition of a major subsidiary in a high-risk area, then the minimum expected return to shareholders and to lenders should be increased. However, this conclusion is based on the awareness of lenders.

Sometimes, the awareness of investors can be myopic. For example, throughout the period when lease payments of U.S. companies had to be re-

[3]Foster presents a model relating inflation rates to net present value, allowing for three differential inflation rates. These are changes in general price levels (adjusting the discount rate), increases in some revenues becuase of the ability to pass on higher costs, and increases in variable costs. He notes that the general rate of inflation may differ from the revenue or cost increases. In the case of costs, labor market imperfections or considerations of capital intensive options may allow a lower rate of increase in costs. For revenues, the question is the elasticity of revenues with the general price increases. This elasticity reflects the ability to pass along general price increases. Foster also introduces the capital costs for fixed-debt obligations and adjusts for taxes in his formula. Again, as noted earlier in a criticism of ship financing, a fixed-debt formula relies on an "imbedded" debt cost, and does not insure that the capital structure remains in balance. This particular version of Foster's formula forces a unique matching of projects and debt which is not always practically or theoretically desirable. See Earl M. Foster, "The Impact of Inflation on Capital Budgeting Decisions," *Quarterly Review of Economics and Business,* Autumn 1970, pp. 19–24.

ported only as a footnote to the financial statements, many advocates of leasing emphasized that leasing expanded the debt capacity of the firm. This argument was based largely on the assumption that the lenders did not adjust for the lease commitments, which were every bit as mandatory for the going concern as debt payments. Since at the time lease payments did not have to be shown in the body of the balance sheet, leasing was referred to as "off-balance sheet financing." In fact, many lenders acknowledged that they adjusted for lease commitments; yet the adjustments made were often cursory if they existed at all, and they differed from analyst to analyst within the same lending institution. (Since 1977 new capital lease payments of U.S. companies must be capitalized and reported in the main body of the balance sheet.)

Ignoring subsidiaries that were not consolidated into the financial statements also appears to have made possible rather spectacular bankruptcies. Nearly half a century ago, Ivar Kreuger, the Swedish "match king," and Samuel Insull, the American utility executive, both relied on massive pyramiding of corporate holding companies along the lines described by Exhibit 11.2. Ultimately, of course, the smallest downturn in the operating concerns destroyed the financial viability of the holding companies, a risk that the lenders to the holding companies might have been expected to foresee, but one that they did not anticipate. (In addition, Kreuger had substantial elements of fraud through grossly overvalued assets.)

The myopia of investors in the Insull and Kreuger pyramiding examples and other more recent cases can be attributed, at least in part, to reporting standards that at the time did not require the consolidation of subsidiaries' financial statements. Disclosure of the combined income generated by subsidiaries, and the combined total assets and leverage of the system was not required in these cases. Currently, the U.S. rules for consolidation of financial statements of subsidiaries depend on the percentage ownership of the parent of the subsidiary. The requirements range from declaring only dividends (i.e., a one-line income item, dividends from subsidiaries) to a pro rata inclusion of profits and losses, to a full merging of the balance sheets and income statements with a minority interest shown where the subsidiary is not 100% owned:

U.S. Rules for Consolidation of Financial Statements

Percentage of Beneficial Ownership by Parent in Subsidiary	*Consolidation for Financial Reporting Purposes*
0–20%	Dividends as received
20–50%	Pro rata inclusions of profits and losses
50–100%	Full consolidation[a]

[a]Consolidation may be avoided in the case of some majority-owned foreign operations if the parent can convince its auditors that it does not have control of the subsidiary or there are substantial restrictions on the repatriation of cash.

Ownership of less than 50% does not require consolidation of the balance sheet and the subsidiary's leverage; i.e., off-balance sheet financing is possible.

OPERATING TACTICS FOR THE CAPITAL STRUCTURE

The actual capital structure the parent chooses for the subsidiary may be dictated by legal formalities, by the request of the host government, and by the protection afforded the parent if its investment is a loan. These are issues of practical tactics.

One popular rule of thumb is for the parent to borrow locally as much as possible. This strategy is followed in order to limit the loss if nationalization takes place, to reduce the foreign exchange loss from currency devaluations in the host country (assuming the loans are denominated in the local currency), and to serve as a motivational device for the local manager (who can be told that the capital costs are dictated by that environment and not by simple parent policy).

However, the cost of this insurance must be considered. In some situations the interest rate differential exceeds any reasonable expectation for currency realignment. A high local interest rate may compensate in part for the lender's reluctance to leave money in the local currency which is likely to depreciate. Beyond this level, the rate charged may reflect the scarcity of the capital markets and the deliberate monetary policy of the host country attempting to encourage the inflow of foreign exchange. Hence, the cost of the insurance is the differential over the life of the loan for local financing vs. alternative external financing proposals.

As an example, if currency rates are stable and there are no major inflationary effects, borrowing locally at 20% vs. externally at 10% means the borrower pays a 10% yearly premium on the amount borrowed to avoid expropriation risk on that part of the investment or to protect against the unlikely event of a devaluation of the local currency. If the plant is expropriated, that loan is just never repaid to the local sources. Of course, the expropriating government may make some token payment, and that payment will be given to the local lenders.

In addition to borrowing locally, many firms prefer local investors for reasons of risk coping discussed in Chapter 10. The local government may appreciate the efforts of the company to bring in local interests as well as recognize the anger of those local interests in the event that the operation is nationalized with little payment to the investors. However, the limitations of local capital markets coupled with the high costs of dealing with many small investors often limit this approach. In this situation the local government may prefer the multinational which brings in all the hard currency needed for the project instead of absorbing local funds.

Just as supervisory fees and royalties are sometimes used to minimize disputes over the remission of some funds, many parents prefer to term their equity investments in the local operation a loan. The loan repayments are considered by the parent to be required by the conditions of the financing agreement. Accordingly, remission of interest plus principal is expected to have a better chance of approval from the local government than dividend repatriation.

When local governments complain about excessive amounts of parent loans to the subsidiary, these loans are sometimes converted to direct loans against inventory and accounts receivable. Although this policy reduces the security for the local senior lenders, it does give the parent a legitimate basis for lending. A disadvantage of this strategy is that with a growing business the inventories and accounts receivable are likely to expand. This expansion requires a greater debt commitment by the parent at the time when a withdrawal is desired. However, the growing business may be in a better position to substitute local debt for parent debt at this point, so that the financing may be reasonable.

From the standpoint of taxes the U.S. parent with a favorable outcome of a project may expect to reduce most of the investment by tax-free loan repayments and then pay a capital gains tax on the sale of the small equity investment in the firm if and when that sale is made. However, Section 482 of the 1962 Revenue Act places the burden of proof on the parent to show that these are bona fide loans. The IRS can argue that much of the loan principal being remitted is a dividend payment, and as such is subject to tax.

In terms of the total debt on the consolidated corporate balance sheet, intercompany loans are eliminated. Thus, the effect on the debt-to-equity ratio of the consolidated firm is nil. However, from the standpoint of the debt-bearing capacity of the local firm, local lenders may be more skeptical of a parent's high debt obligation. Placing the parent's debt in a subordinated position dispels this local concern.

DETERMINING THE DISCOUNT RATE IN A RISKY PROJECT

After a risk analysis simulation is completed, or perhaps from some other analysis, the management may have a distribution of returns on some criterion as shown in Exhibit 11.4. To calculate net present values with risky projects, one has two options. One may adjust the returns to a *certainty equivalent* figure, as discussed in the appendix to this chapter. Alternatively, given the uncertainty attached to the returns of a project (the numerator in present value calculations), one can search for the discount rate (the denominator in present value calculations) that would incorporate the riskiness of the project. Methods of searching for this discount rate adjusted for the *total* risk of the project are presented below.[4]

One approach is to evaluate the project in terms of what capital structure would be appropriate for a project with that risk profile. A capital structure appropriate for the industry, the country, and the risk attitude of management can be selected. Inductively, this same logic can be applied to projects within a given subsidiary firm; if the project carries more risk than the normal project of the firm, the relevant cost of capital is higher. This reasoning leads to what is called the *risk-adjusted discount rate.*

An alternative to these approaches, which theoretically should achieve a similar result, is to focus on discounting the project's flows at a rate appropriate for an *all-equity* investment of that riskiness, which is then *adjusted for various*

[4]Notice that these techniques measure the *total* risk of the project. Modern capital theory suggests that only the systematic risk, or the variation of the project with the market referred to as beta, be included in the discount rate. This alternative is discussed in Chapter 13.

EXHIBIT 11.4. Probabilities of Rates of Return of Project A

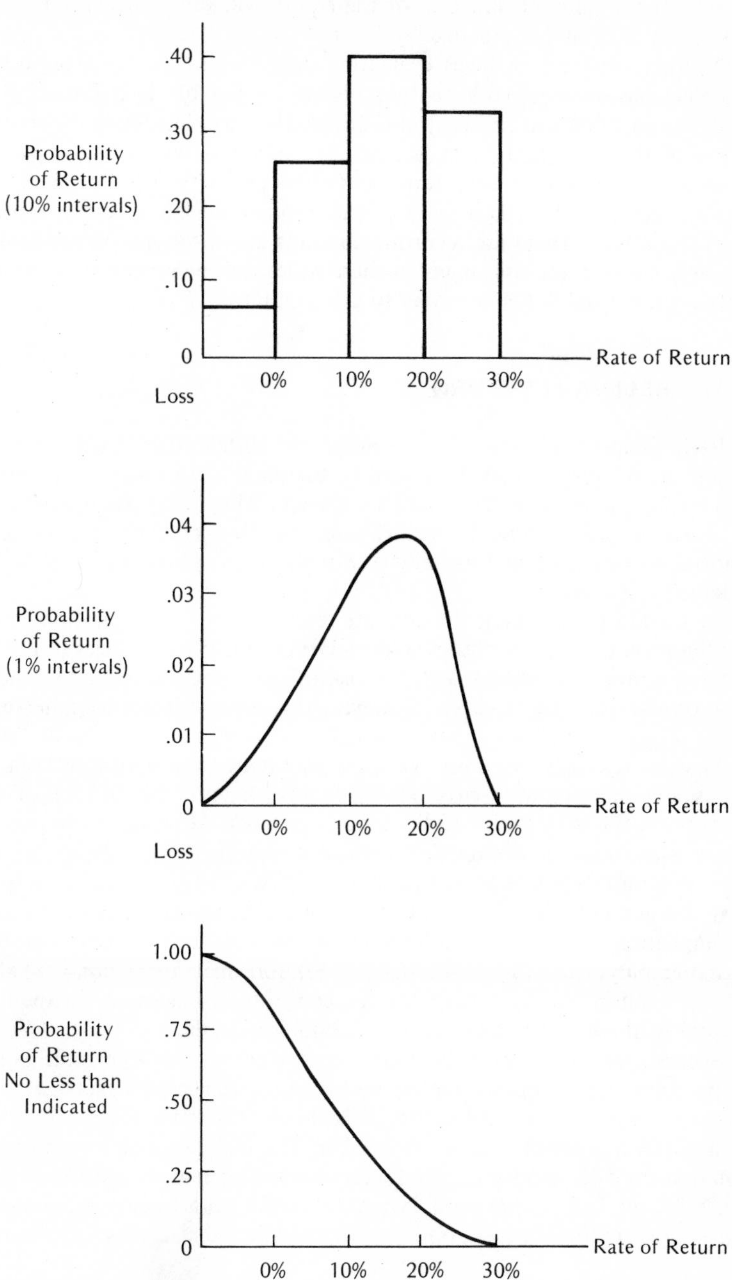

loads of debt. If this adjustment is made, then (1) the amount and cost of the debt and (2) the amount and cost of the equity will vary somewhat from the weighted cost of capital in practice.[5]

Another approach involves evaluating the standard deviation or variance of a project based on the risk analysis results. In Exhibit 11.5 Project B has one distribution of returns and Project C has another. By calculating the standard deviation of the returns, the manager has an index with which to compare the distribution of the two projects' returns. (Others prefer the coefficient of variation of the return, which is a ratio of the standard deviation to the expected value of the return. There are recurring conflicts about the use of standard deviation as a measure for risk; many of these issues and the process of computing variance are discussed in the appendix to this chapter.)

THE RELEVANT RETURN

Both Chapters 10 and 11 have noted the differentials when comparing the return to the project and the return to the parent and when comparing the returns in the project's or the parent's currency. When there are dramatic currency shifts or major delays in repatriation, the divergence of returns can be substantial, as discussed in Chapter 10. Finally, then, whose return should be considered?

At the most basic level, the ultimate return and risk considerations should be for the parent company's stockholders. Hence, dollar remittances to the U.S. parent and a return consistent with the risk of operating the foreign subsidiary are appropriate for this example. However, two general issues complicate this view.

First, increasingly the investors in the parent are from a worldwide family. If the shareholder group wants only U.S. investments, the impact of their nationality on the external portfolio is not significant. However, these non-U.S. investors may want a worldwide purchasing power return; therefore, their concern is a currency basket weighted in some way with the dollar only one part of the contents. In addition, just as many U.S. shareholders have increasingly emphasized a variety of non-economic issues (South African operations, minority employment, the environment), so, too, may these non-U.S. shareholders demand increasing concern by the company management for the firm's operations worldwide, especially in the shareholders' lands.

Second, and more directly, many companies in the true multinational tradition accept their role as worldwide investors. Hence, the fact that funds are blocked in removal from Country X is about as relevant as knowing that a plant in California is not readily marketable. The fact that assets are restricted in a nation on a temporary or a long-term basis is merely an additional inconvenience for the U.S. corporation, just as a low-skill labor force, poor commuter facilities, bad railroad connections, or limited banking associations may be

[5]Whatever the intellectual justification, higher hurdle rates are used for riskier projects. In Fremgen's survey, 54% of the 179 respondents indicated their firms used higher discount rates when evaluating riskier projects. See James M. Fremgen, "Capital Budgeting Practices: A Survey." *Management Accounting,* May 1973, pp. 19–25.

EXHIBIT 11.5. Probabilities of Rates of Return, Projects B and C

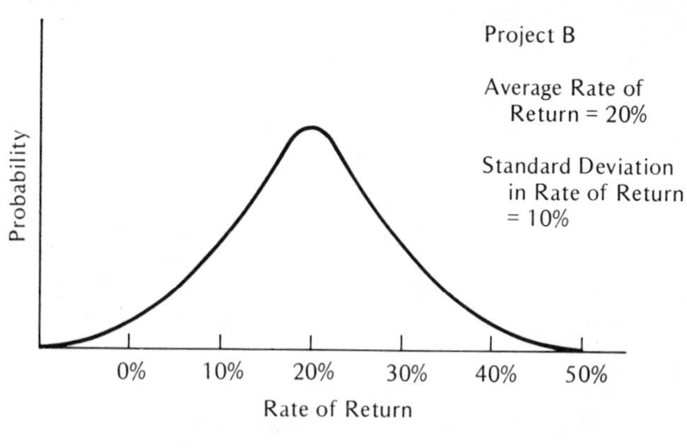

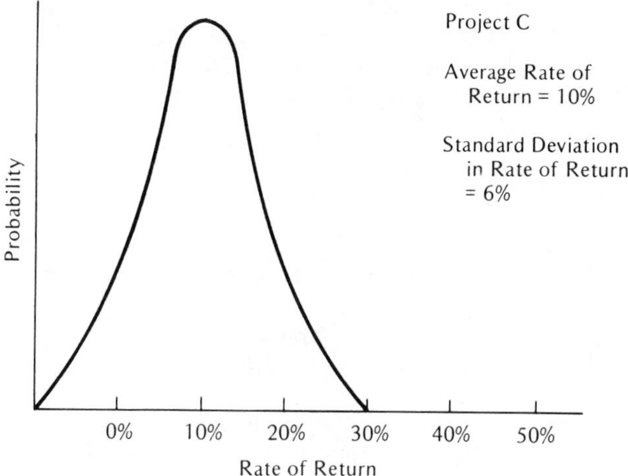

part of operating in some parts of the United States. Obviously, blocked funds are more serious than weak communications or nonmarketable plants in California, but the difference is one of degree, not substance. The nonmobility of assets and the restrictions on business practice are a fact of corporate life not unique to operations in particular countries.

Hence, to the extent that the corporation views itself as a true multinational, the effect of restrictions on repatriation may not be severe. If the firm anticipates continued investment in a country which is in a growing market, the restriction is not even an issue to be addressed in the "good-citizen or bad-citizen" framework noted above. Rather, the commitment is made for long-term continuing investments in the country, and the restriction on repatriation is generally irrelevant.

In most cases the firm will verify that the project return and the parent return are both agreeable. However, these are but two goals, and the firm will probably have a number of other goals or constraints of a financial nature, plus nonfinancial standards. Among the financial considerations beyond the return of the project and the return to the parent are liquidity, reported earnings, and alternative uses of cash.

Liquidity

Even if the returns are satisfactory, the parent may have stringent needs for cash in particular years which a given international project cannot meet. Hence, this constraint may be binding.

Reported Earnings

The consolidation standards may mean that the huge reported losses in the early years of a project will be too large to be acceptable to the current managers, who fear adverse shareholder reaction. Alternatively, relatively high reported earnings may be linked to a need for cash remissions if the parent wishes to maintain a particular dividend payout ratio of (say) 40% of reported earnings. Hence, the earnings reported may relate directly to the liquidity issue.

Alternative Uses of Cash

If the parent plans to invest the funds in the local country, then the project return and reinvestment rate may dominate. At the other extreme, reinvestments outside the local country mean the parent return in the parent currency will prevail. Hence, a multinational may emphasize different return standards for various nations depending on how a given project fits the corporation's portfolio of projects now and in the future.

Thus, return and risk are but two financial aspects of international investments, and other financial values operate as constraints. In extreme cases these other values become dominant goals.

AN EXTENDED EXAMPLE—FREEPORT MINERALS[6]

Background

Originally a major sulphur producer, Freeport Minerals decided in 1970 to diversify its operations in the wake of a breakdown in what had been an extremely profitable oligopolistic sulphur market. In 1966 the firm had 85% of its income from sulphur. By 1968, with sulphur prices at $40 per ton, there was evidence of a large number of entrants into the market who depressed prices. By 1970 sulphur sold for $20 per ton. Accordingly, Freeport decided to begin operating in other mineral areas and hoped to derive only 15% of its income from sulphur by 1975.

[6]This case was prepared entirely from public sources, and Freeport's management was not consulted.

The nickel industry was dominated by International Nickel (INCO) whose operations were mainly in the United States and Canada. Freeport also was interested in nickel and had several profitable ventures in this field. One of the opportunities which became available was the Greenvale proposal in Australia. This project would cost approximately $264 million to develop based on 1971 cost estimates. This amount included $111 million for a nickel processing plant, $45 million for a special railway, and $15 million for the mine development. The remainder of the outlays was allocated for preoperating expenses (including interest during the construction period), inflation, and working capital.

The basic project was expected to produce revenues of $72.2 million per year for twenty years based on anticipated ore reserves, a price of $1.35 per pound for nickel, and yearly production of about 22.300 tons of nickel plus a small amount of cobalt. Given figures for operating costs consistent with the company's knowledge and confirmed by the experience of other firms in Australia, Freeport constructed a forecasted income statement for the project. Using accelerated depreciation, depletion standards consistent with Australian tax policies, and a tax rate of 38%, the projections of the Greenvale project are shown in Exhibit 11.6.

Two major financing options were under consideration:

1. A loan for $135 million in U.S. dollars at 8%, payable in level installments of principal over a ten-year life period commencing at the end of 1975. This would be from a group of major insurance companies.

2. A yen loan of $160 million at 6% with eighteen annual level principal payments commencing at the end of 1975. This offer was from one of the major customers of the nickel, a Japanese business association (zaibatsu). Although this loan would require concessions from the pricing base and would be accompanied by a long-term contract, the management of Freeport thought the loan was a generous one.

When these financing options were considered, the resulting financial cash flows are as shown in Exhibit 11.6. Freeport was uncertain where the cash throw-offs would be reinvested. If the money were brought to the United States, additional taxes would have to be paid. However, by adjusting the ownership of the firm among various other corporate interests, U.S. taxes on the profits could be avoided until the funds were returned to the United States.

Risk Analysis

A risk analysis of the Freeport project can be prepared, with the following variables seeming to be most subject to change or to random outcome:

Construction Cost. The firm would commit $264 million for the project, but there was some chance that the cost might be considerably higher. The project already included $43.4 million for escalation and contingencies. In the event all of these funds were not needed, they would be returned prior to initial production. In the event other funds were required, they would be paid at an

EXHIBIT 11.6. Freeport Minerals Greenvale Project—Income Statement, Cash Flow Statement, and Measures of Return (millions of U.S. dollars)

	1975	1976	1977	1978	1979	1980	1981	1982	1983	1984	1985	1986	1987	1988	1989	1990	1991	1992
Income Statement																		
Revenues	$72.2	$72.2	$72.2	$72.2	$72.2	$72.2	$72.2	$72.2	$72.2	$72.2	$72.2	$72.2	$72.2	$72.2	$72.2	$72.2	$72.2	$72.2
Less Total Operating Costs	36.1	36.1	36.1	36.1	36.1	36.1	36.1	36.1	36.1	36.1	31.7	31.7	31.7	31.7	31.7	23.0	23.0	23.0
Less Interest (8% U.S. loan, 10 years)	10.8	9.7	8.6	7.6	6.5	5.4	4.3	3.2	2.2	1.1								
Profit Before Taxes	25.3	26.4	27.5	28.5	29.6	30.7	31.8	32.9	33.9	35.0	40.5	40.5	40.5	40.5	40.5	49.2	49.2	49.2
Taxes	0	10.0	10.5	10.8	11.2	11.7	12.1	12.5	12.9	13.3	19.8	19.8	19.8	19.8	19.8	19.1	19.1	19.1
Net Profit	25.3	16.4	17.0	17.7	18.4	19.0	19.7	20.4	21.0	21.7	24.7	24.7	24.7	24.7	24.7	30.1	30.1	30.1
Financial and Operating Cash Flows																		
Net Profit	$25.3	$16.4	$17.0	$17.7	$18.4	$19.0	$19.7	$20.4	$21.0	$21.7	$24.7	$24.7	$24.7	$24.7	$24.7	$30.1	$30.1	$30.1
Depreciation	14.2	14.2	14.2	14.2	14.2	14.2	14.2	14.2	14.2	14.2	9.8	9.8	9.8	9.8	9.8	1.1	1.1	1.1
Tax Savings (Accelerated Depreciation for Tax Purposes	3.0	1.9	1.0	.2	(.7)	(.7)	(.7)	(.7)	(.7)	(.7)	(.3)	(.3)	(.3)	(.3)	(.3)	—	—	—
After-Tax Interest[a]	10.8	6.0	5.3	4.7	4.0	3.3	2.7	2.0	1.4	.7	—	—	—	—	—	—	—	—
Operating Cash Flow	53.3	38.5	37.5	36.8	35.9	35.8	35.9	35.9	35.9	35.9	34.2	34.2	34.2	34.2	34.2	31.2	31.2	31.2
Principal and After-Tax Interest (8% U.S. Loan, 10 years)	24.3	19.5	18.8	18.2	17.5	16.8	16.2	15.5	14.9	14.2								
Equity Cash Flow (U.S. Loan)	29.0	19.0	18.7	18.6	18.4	19.0	19.7	20.4	21.0	21.7	34.2	34.2	34.2	34.2	34.2	31.2	31.2	31.2
Principal and After-Tax Interest (6% Japanese Loan, 18 years)	14.9	14.5	14.2	13.9	13.5	13.2	12.9	12.5	12.2	11.9	11.5	11.2	10.9	10.6	10.2	9.9	9.6	9.2
Equity Cash Flow (Japanese Loan)	38.4	24.0	23.3	22.9	22.4	22.6	23.0	23.4	23.7	24.0	22.7	23.0	23.3	23.6	24.0	21.3	21.6	22.0

Measures of Return

	Operating Cash Flow	Equity Cash Flow $135 million, 8% U.S. Loan, 10 years	Equity Cash Flow $160 million, 6% Japanese Loan, 18 years
Rate of Return[b]	11.0%	14.4%	19.9%
Terminal Rate of Return (10% Reinvestment Rate)	10.7%	12.1%	16.5%
Net Present Value at 10%	$18.9M	$49.6M	$80.9M

[a] Because of start-up expenses, projections assume there are no savings to tax-deductibility of interest in 1975, and no taxes are payable in that year.

[b] All return calculations assume average investment is made two years before initial operating cash inflows.

early point in the development of the project as the increased construction costs or plant difficulties appeared. Basically, management was confident that the construction costs would be between $205 and $325 million.

Production. Although confident of the mineral reserves, a major uncertainty related to the year when the production would be on stream. Accordingly, there was a possibility that only partial production would begin in 1975, perhaps at 80% of the planned level. Final production would certainly increase from the starting point to the full level over four years.

Mineral Content. There was some small doubt about the richness of the mineral deposits. This quality figure might deviate somewhat from the expected nickel content, although the range was probably not much more than ±10%.

Price. From other analysis, the management could believe that the starting price was likely to be higher than the $1.35 estimated. This price might grow from the time of the initial investment by about 5% to 6% per year based on forecasts of the world's economy. Because nickel was a key commercial ingredient, world industrial activity was a barometer of nickel demand. Relating this price increase to world industrial production, the growth rate was tempered by a possibility of additional nickel production entering the market and decreasing prices.

Operating Costs. The possible escalation in labor rates and materials costs during the life of the plant were expected to be related to the strength of the Australian economy, which itself was linked to world industrial production. Operating costs were expected to increase by slightly less than the price of world nickel, subject to the performance of the Australian economy.

For the financing options, there were also uncertainties. Although the loans were firm commitments subject to the firm's meeting various financial tests each year, Freeport management was concerned about the exchange rates of the currencies. Specifically, the U.S. dollar might deteriorate over time while the yen might appreciate. For its financing analysis, management decided to assume that the dollar might depreciate or appreciate relative to other currencies. Since the revenues were always denominated in dollars, this factor would have little influence on the profile of the project other than the impact of operating costs which would be paid in Australian dollars. On the other hand, continuing appreciation of the Japanese yen over the life of the project could prove costly. The management felt that the yen might well appreciate by an average of 2% per year for the next eight to ten years, but management was not willing to forecast beyond that. Furthermore, it was hard to anticipate the yearly links in appreciation of the yen; lower than average appreciation in one year might simply be a temporary delay offset by higher appreciation in a later year. Basically, they believed that the yen was likely to remain strong vis-à-vis the dollar for at least ten years. They felt that the basic interest rate differential of 2% on the yen loan vs. the dollar loan reflected the assessment of lenders as well.

For the immediate future, however, there was a much higher probability of a sharp yen appreciation, perhaps by as much as 10% within a year or so. In addition, one economist in the firm was convinced that this action could be a chain, resulting in a high probability of another 10% appreciation in a few years.

A risk analysis combines these uncertainties and the interrelationships into a computer model.[7] Using these relationships and a random number sampling function within the model, the financial results can be presented showing these risk elements. When combined with the accounting relationships for income statements, balance sheets, and discounted cash flow, the results are useful to management in evaluating the possible risk associated with a project. The inputs for the Freeport model are given in Exhibit 11.7.

Exhibit 11.8 presents the results of the simulation analysis performed under the assumptions described. Distribution of rates of return are presented for operating cash flows and for returns on equity. The returns on operating cash flows have been calculated under two assumptions: (1) The cash generated by the project is reinvested at the same rate as the rate for the project and (2) the cash generated by the project is reinvested at 10%. The return on equity is calculated under the two alternative sources of financing: U.S. dollars at 8% and yen at 6%. The returns on equity are also calculated under the two assumptions about reinvestment rates.

The rate of return on operating cash flows shows a tighter distribution when the 10% terminal rate of return is assumed than when the cash generated by the project is reinvested at the same rate as the project. This is because the average rate of return on operating cash flows, ignoring the terminal rate of return, is well above 10%. Simulation outcomes in which the operating cash flow rate of return is below 10%, had such outcomes been present, would have been improved by the assumption of a 10% reinvestment rate. Initial rates of return above 10% are reduced by the assumption of a 10% reinvestment rate, as discussed in Chapter 10.

The rate of return to equity shows a much wider range of possible returns under the yen financing than under the U.S. dollar financing. Therefore, each possible outcome has a lower frequency under the yen financing than under the dollar financing. In both sources of financing, the spread of returns to equity is narrowed considerably when the assumption of a reinvestment rate of 10% is incorporated, for the same reason as in the case of operating cash flows.

Is the lower average return to equity shown on the dollar financing caused by the short life of the loan (ten years vs. the eighteen-year life of the project and the eighteen-year yen loan)? In evaluating this issue, management must consider the alternatives available at the end of the ten years or available in steps beginning after a few years of mineral production. Looking at the conventional debt coverage ratios, one sees that in the earliest years the average coverage on the yen loan is significantly better than the dollar loan, as shown in Exhibit 11.9. However, if the debt/capitalization rate is considered and reinvestment opportunities are ignored, the firm appears more conservative under the dollar option because the loan was lower initially and is repaid more rapidly. This table also shows the adjusted returns to equity *if the dollar loan is converted to eighteen years,* with all the other assumptions maintained. From

[7]For a discussion of risk analysis and simulation techniques, see E. Eugene Carter, *Portfolio Aspects of Corporate Capital Budgeting* (Lexington, Mass.: D. C. Heath and Company, 1974), Chapters 2 and 3.

EXHIBIT 11.7. Freeport Simulation Variables

Random Variable	*Symbol*	*Frequency*	*Distribution of Random Variable*	*Range of Random Variable*	*Calculation*
Construction	A	1st Year	Poisson	Mean = .4	$A = 205 + (120 \times (X))$ X = Random variable
Production	B	1st year	Uniform	.7 – 1.0	B = Random variable *Year* 1 $B(1) = B \times$ expected value 2 $B(2) = (B + ((B - 1)/4)) \times$ expected value 3 $B(3) = (B + ((B - 1)/2)) \times$ expected value 4 $B(4) = (B + 3 \times ((B - 1)/4)) \times$ expected value 5–18 $B(5)$ through $B(18)$ = expected value
Mineral Content	C	1st year	Normal	Mean = 1 Standard Deviation = .05	$C = X$ X = Random variable
Price	D	Annual	Normal	Mean = 1.06 Standard Deviation = .03	$D(Y) = D(Y - 1) \times (X)$ X = Random variable Y = Year
Operating Costs	E	Annual	Uniform	.95 – 1.00	$E(Y) = E(Y - 1) \times (X_1) \times (X_2)$ X_1 = Random variable from price index, X X_2 = Random variable .95 – 1.00 Y = Year
Yen Appreciation	F	Annual	Normal	Mean = 1.02 Standard Deviation = .002	See below

Calculation of Yen Appreciation:

Appreciation	*Probability in Year 1*	*Probability of Year 3 Appreciation*[a] *0%*	*10%*
0%	.50	.50	.50
10%	.50	.25	.75

From Year 4 onward, a normal distribution with a mean of 2% and a standard deviation of .2% is assumed to reflect the probabilities of appreciation in any year.

[a]Given that appreciation in Year 1 to the left has occurred.

EXHIBIT 11.8.a. Freeport Minerals Greenvale Project-Distribution of Returns

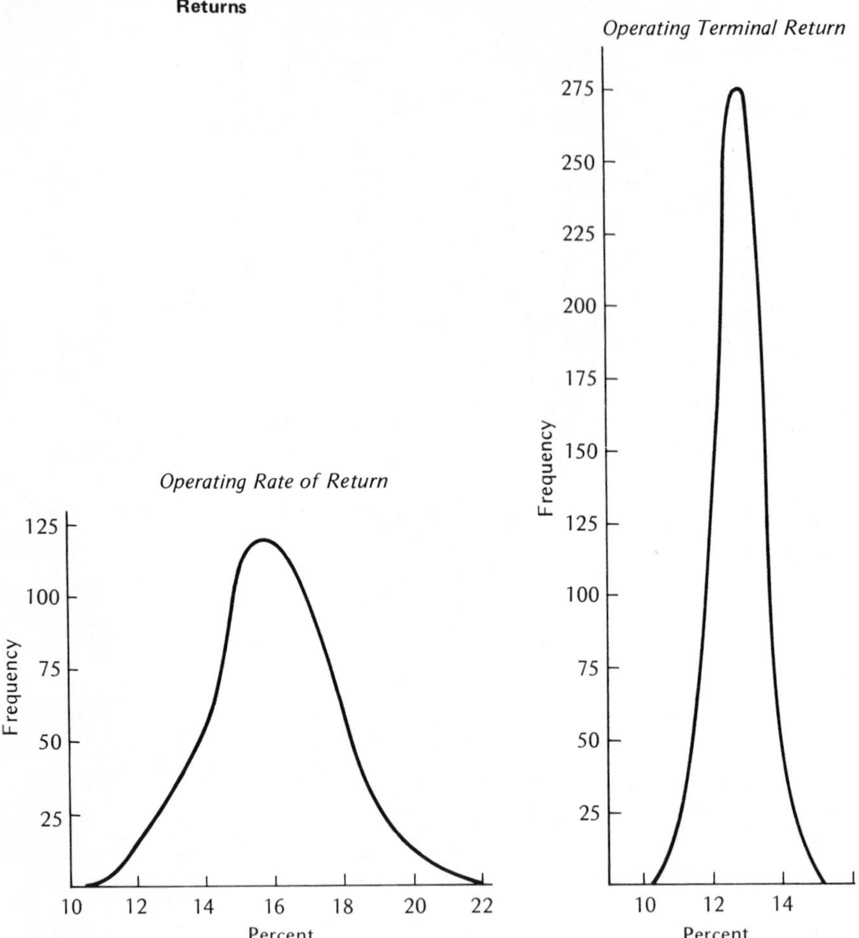

this basic result, one sees again the inappropriate nature of the short-lived debt assumption if dollar refinancing options or the eighteen-year dollar loan are available.

There are two additional advantages retained by the yen loan in this analysis when the criterion is equity rate of return. First, the *loan is larger,* and with no other financing available, the capital structure is different under the two assumptions. Given a fixed operating return above the cost of debt, leverage assures that the return to equity will be larger for the greater-debt situation if the debt rates are similar. Second, the appreciation of the yen averages more than 2% per year for ten years, meaning that the cost of the yen loan for those years will be slightly greater than the 6% nominal rate plus 2%. However, in later years (eleven through eighteen) this appreciation is not present, consistent with the expectations of Freeport management discussed earlier. Hence, the *average rate of the yen loan is lower* than the U.S. dollar loan for the full eighteen years.

EXHIBIT 11.8.b. Continued

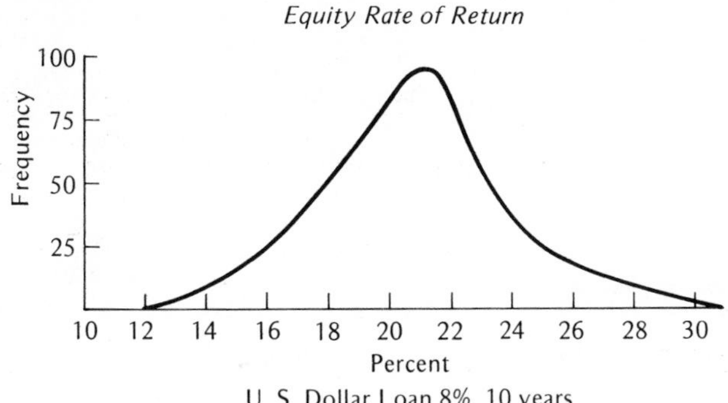

U. S. Dollar Loan 8%, 10 years

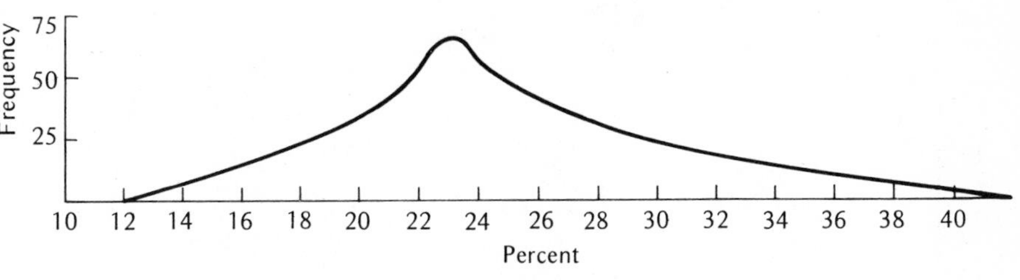

Japanese Yen Loan 6%, 18 years

EXHIBIT 11.8.c. Continued

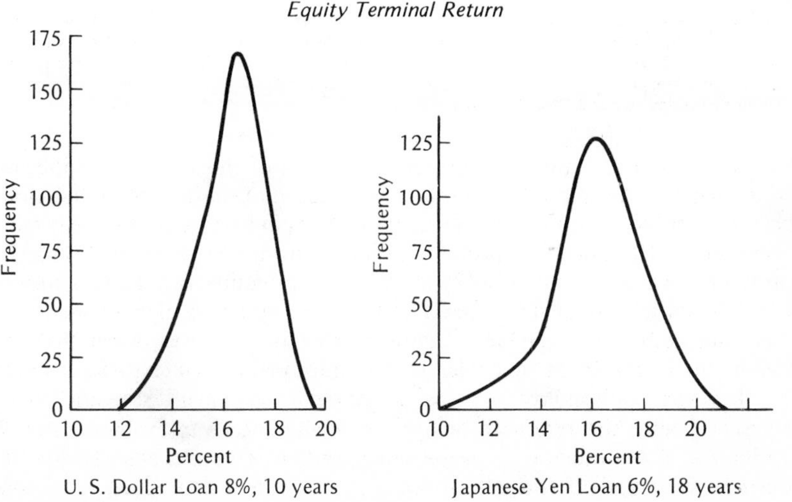

EXHIBIT 11.9. Freeport Minerals Greenvale Project—Ratios of Alternative Loan Agreements

	Debt Service Coverage Ratios[a]			*Debt/Capitalization*		
	(Outcomes Under Certainty)					
	1975	*1980*	*1986*	*1975*	*1980*	*1986*
$135M U.S. Dollar Loan (10 years)	2.3	3.2	—	.51	.25	0
$160M Japanese Yen Loan (18 years)	2.7	3.1	6.6	.61	.44	.24
$135M U.S. Dollar Loan (18 years)	3.6	4.0	7.3	.51	.37	.20

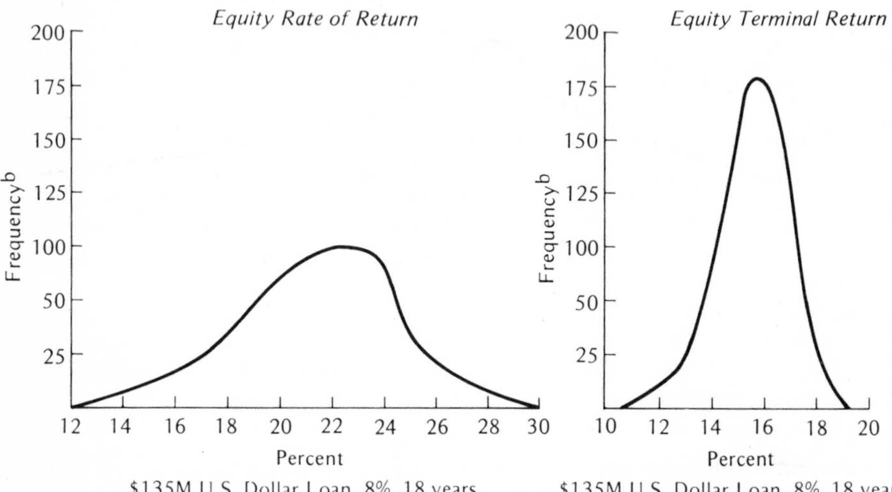

$135M U.S. Dollar Loan, 8%, 18 years $135M U.S. Dollar Loan, 8%, 18 years

[a]Debt service coverage ratio is net income after tax plus interest divided by the sum of loan principal repayment plus interest. An alternative definition, giving results slightly different from those here, is net operating income after tax divided by principal repayment plus after-tax interest.

[b]Frequency is per 1,000 simulation trials.

The capital structure/cost of capital analysis of this chapter is applicable to this problem. An important unstated assumption of the cost of capital model is that the capital structure, once selected, remains in balance over the entire life of the project. Thus, in any period, the cash flow from a project must (1) pay the returns on debt and equity and (2) retire debt and equity in the *exact* proportion as the initial capital structure. Over time, the return to all components will be as indicated in the capital structure discussion. However, when there are different debt repayment schedules or no additional refinancing options available, then the applicability of a particular debt repayment schedule to the analysis will alter the return to equity. An analyst needs to examine carefully whether the assumptions of a proportional capital structure over the life of a project is warranted. If not, the infusion of subsequent debt issues is relevant.

In this case Freeport management needs to review its expected financing options for the next five to ten years. If these choices are sufficiently uncertain or costly, then payment of a higher rate for a long-term loan may be warranted; a long-term loan which matches the life of the project serves to keep the capital structure in balance. Hence, it may be regarded as a form of insurance. In the event the Japanese loan were not available, then the company might be willing to pay (say) 9% for a U.S. dollar eighteen-year loan for example.

In addition to this consideration, Freeport needs to review the dispersion in returns it wishes to tolerate. The dispersion of possible outcomes for the rate of return and the terminal return to *equity* is *greater* under the Japanese loan than under either the ten-year or eighteen-year U.S. proposals, as would be expected given the appreciation uncertainties. Whether management wishes to live with this dispersion is a question Freeport has to resolve. There is also the dispersion of *operating* returns. Freeport management must review the dispersion and return relative to other corporate opportunities which are available, as well as the dispersion from existing operations.

Conclusion

This approach to uncertainty provides additional information to Freeport management on the distribution of returns from its project. There may be an analysis of other variables (first-year earnings per share contribution, expected cash flow for each year, and so on). From this basic computation, management may wish to complete *sensitivity analyses* on the variables which are random: the investigation of a faster growth in expected value of nickel prices or the impact of a greater dispersion of construction costs on the returns. *Other variables could be randomized* and the impact of their uncertainty on the returns could be calculated. Most important, the possibilities of *more sophisticated financing arrangements* could be studied, such as sequencing of different loans, the sharing of equity participation, and so forth.

The Greenvale project is not necessarily unwise as an investment. The use of computer risk analysis simulation merely permits a greater awareness of the uncertainties surrounding the project than otherwise available. This uncertainty may dictate contingency planning for certain outcomes and may suggest that certain financing strategies are more sensible than others.

The final chapter in Part Three analyzes the issue of *portfolio* evaluation of capital projects. Freeport management needs to consider not just the Greenvale project, but the impact of other nickel projects as well as the other operations of the corporation. From the parent's viewpoint, the variance in returns from Greenvale is one input to the variance in the corporation's return. That corporate variance is a function of the interralationships among the various projects in which the parent has invested. An extended analysis of Freeport's position is possible with the Freeport Minerals case at the end of Chapter 13.

PUBLIC POLICY AND THE ECONOMICS OF THE FIRM

Even these basic examples have illuminated the essential conflict between the developing nation's government—concerned with the growth of the country's economy and the welfare of its people, and the multinational corporation preoccupied with earning a fair return on the shareholder's investment consistent with general corporate responsibility and a justifiable level of risk.

On the one side, the firm may segment proposed investments based on risk and rate of return. Classically, the firm will demand a higher return where there is greater risk whether that risk be economic or political. Accordingly, limitations on the firm's freedom to repatriate funds, the imposition of blocked or semiblocked currency restrictions, and the polite inquiry by the potential host country's negotiators about eventual sharing of the ownership of the proposed venture with the local government or other nationals all cause the assessment of the project's risk to increase.

On the other hand, the local country is interested in a partner that will improve the country itself. The corporation is expected to bring in not just hard currency but a new business which will produce a good product at a fair price with suitable employment policies. It is only natural that the local negotiators will take strong interest in the intentions of the firm. They may understandably impose safeguards to prevent the rapacious devouring of the resources of the land by a corporate octopus whose single goal is to remove as much profit as rapidly as possible.

Thus, the firm wants stability and a hospitable environment, and it is willing to continue investment in the country given that environment. The host country, concerned about the nature of some corporations, wants an enduring commitment not only to profits but also to a reasonable corporate citizenship in terms of pricing, employment, and proper corporate demeanor. Worries on the part of the firm cause it to inquire about repatriation agreements. Worries on the part of the local negotiators cause them to seek plans for substantial national representation on the board or for restrictions on the pace at which the firm can remit its profits.

These issues, once raised, reinforce the concerns of the firm's envoys about nationalization or expropriation at the most serious level or minority voting blocks and repatriation restrictions at the least obnoxious level.

Hence, the cycle begins, and the cobweb created by this action-reaction-intensified action-intensified reaction creates not only ill will but very rigid contracts! The result is the situation viewed today: The local countries resent major corporations (often American) that have high returns from foreign operations which are remitted rapidly. The American corporation, in turn, worries about the increasing risks from longer-term investments in nations where political instability and currency shocks are a yearly, if not monthly, fact of life.

Stated simply, worries about risk induce greater profiteering, usually translated into "high returns remitted rapidly." This action, in turn, supports the local countries' contention that the multinationals are tempted to bleed their lands for a larger corporate goal of maximizing profits.[8]

[8]The possibility of a war between the host and parent governments further aggravates the situation. On the other hand, the American subsidiaries of the German I. G. Farben produced chemicals for the Allied war effort while General Motor's German subsidiaries manufactured trucks for the Wehrmacht in World War II. See *The New York Times,* March 13, 1974, p. 36. During World War I, the Germans dealt very carefully with the U.S. assets impounded in Germany, for they had far *more* assets in the United States. Most of the units continued to operate autonomously, even though the sequestered assets could not be sold and their earnings could not be remitted to the German owners.

To this end, private and public insurance schemes designed to minimize these possible shocks help the corporations feel more comfortable with the environment. However, limitations on the types of risk which are covered, together with careful considerations of the legality of the agreement, induce a cautionary attitude on the part of the multinational. The continuing hesitancy of OPIC to pay Kennecott and Anaconda for Chilean losses because of legitimate factual disputes has done nothing to reassure corporations.

There is also the conflict between the desire to be a good local citizen (whether from local economic self-interest or survival or from the view of responsible business practice) and the need to use global transfers of skills and resources which form the basis for the multinational firm. Hymer reviews many of the assumptions justifying the existence of a multinational firm, observing that one can reasonably argue whether the economies of scale offered by the multinational firm might be as well realized by crossing industries, placing the giant firm within a given political/societal border.[9] Among other issues, there are difficulties imposed on local fiscal and monetary policy of a given nation-state by the existence of the multinational firm, since there is no multinational fiscal/monetary authority.

SUMMARY

This chapter reviewed the corporate financial theory on the *cost of capital* and the impact of business and financial risk on the return to shareholders. The use of *different discount rates* for projects of varying degrees of risk was suggested as plausible, providing that discount rates were based on what firms active in that type of project would require as a capital structure in the open market or on what is reasonable based on the general riskiness of the project.

We examined the fallacy of *pyramiding* in which the local capital structure is used in conjunction with a low cost of equity from the parent-investor to justify a very low discount rate for a project in a foreign land. The appropriate discount rate for a project in another nation is generally no less than the discount rate implied by domestic financing of that project using domestic capital sources if available. The divergence of capital structures from nation to nation was noted.

Inflation, if anticipated, is built into the cost of capital for a project when domestic sources are used as the initial standards for evaluation. Local lenders have very high charges for debt because they often anticipate substantial inflation which will reduce the effective returns on the debt issue.

Practical *operating tactics* for investing in some lands include financing with local debt and equity financing, denominating the parent's investment as a loan instead of equity, and using royalty and supervisory fees paid to the parent.

After noting the alternative means by which managers may evaluate the risk of a project, once again the issue appeared of *whose returns* are to be considered. The tradition of concern with the welfare of shareholders is blunted by two considerations. First, many shareholders are not citizens of the parent

[9]Stephen Hymer, "The Efficiency (Contradictions) of Multinational Corporations," *American Economic Review,* May 1970, pp. 441–448.

country, especially in the case of a U.S. parent. Second, a socially responsible corporation committed to a given region or area as a true multinational may not be preoccupied with bringing funds home.

An extended example involving Freeport Minerals was presented. Using risk analysis and some basic capital structure insights, we offered an illustration of how management of the firm might consider the riskiness of a proposed Australian nickel project.

Finally, the problem of insecure corporations confronting worried governments of developing countries was addressed. Each is concerned about undesirable actions of the other; yet each protective reaction by one reinforces the anxiety felt by the other. Supernational insurance schemes were suggested as one means to stop this cycle of mutual action and reaction.

Questions

1. "If the parent's cost of capital is 15%, its equity investment in a subsidiary only needs to be charged to the subsidiary at 15%." Why or why not?

2. "Regardless of the interest rate, we always borrow in a cheap currency with a likely devaluation, since that minimizes our financing costs." Give an example in which this strategy would fail. Do you think it is a good rule of thumb?

3. What data would you desire in order to evaluate the risk of a project in a particular country? Why would one corporation find a given level of risk acceptable while another one might reject it? Does this indicate the irrationality of corporate management?

4. With worldwide operations, IBM has about 300 American nationals working for it outside the United States. Do you think this policy is a good one? What firms could use it more profitably than other firms, or do you believe it makes sense for all firms?

Bibliography

Adams, William T., "The Emerging Law of Dispute Settlement Under the United States Investment Insurance Program." *Law and Policy in International Business.* Vol. 3, No. 1, 1971, pp. 101-156.

Carter, E. Eugene, *Portfolio Aspects of Corporate Capital Budgeting.* Lexington, Mass.: D. C. Heath and Company, 1974.

Chenery, H. B., "Comparative Advantage and Development Policy." *American Economic Review,* March 1961, pp. 18-51.

Eiteman, David K., and Arthur I. Stonehill, *Multinational Business Finance.* Reading, Mass.: Addison-Wesley Publishing Co., 1973, Chs. 9 and 10.

Foster, Earl M., "The Impact of Inflation on Capital Budgeting Decisions." *Quarterly Review of Economics and Business,* Autumn 1970, pp. 19-24.

Hackett, John T., "The Multinational Corporation and World Wide Inflation." *Financial Executive,* February 1975, pp. 64-73.

Hymer, Stephen, "The Efficiency (Contradictions) of Multinational Corporations." *American Economic Review,* May 1970, pp. 441-448.

Johnson, H. G., "A Theoretical Model of Economic Nationalism in New and Developing States." *Political Science Quarterly,* June 1965, pp. 169-185.

Polk, Judd, et al., *U.S. Production Abroad and the Balance of Payments.* New York: National Industrial Conference Board, 1966.

Shulman, J. S., "Transfer Pricing in the Multinational Firm." *European Business,* Jan. 1969, pp. 46-54.

Weston, J. Fred, and Bart W. Sorge, *International Managerial Finance.* Homewood, Ill.: Richard D. Irwin, Inc., 1972, Ch. 3.

Appendix: The Evaluation of Project Risk

The technique of risk analysis has been available for many years. Essentially, the technique requires estimates of the distribution of possible outcomes of a project's major components (e.g., sales, market share, advertising costs, wage rates, and so on). The crucial variables are linked together in a model (e.g., if market share increases by 8% in year 4, sales will increase by an expected value of $3,000,000 with a standard deviation of $50,000). Then the model is embedded in a computer program. Computer simulation can determine the range of possible outcomes on various criteria for the project.[1]

If the criterion is rate of return and the company is considering Project A and Project B as two mutually exclusive alternatives, there might be a distribution of returns as shown in Exhibit 1. Notice the greater risk in Project B. Although Project B has a higher rate of return than Project A, one management might prefer Project B, arguing that a higher risk is fully justified by the return, and another management might prefer the safer (and lower) return of Project A.

In addition, risk analysis reveals to the manager that some projects are not what they seem at first. Thus, in comparing the rate of return or net present value of two projects on the basis of the most likely single value (mode) for each of the many underlying variables, a manager might find one project has the higher value with certainty. However, on the basis of simulation, the executive might learn that the other project has a higher mode for rate of return or net

[1] Simulation involves repeated chance trials using calculations from a random number generator adjusted to provide various probability distributions.

EXHIBIT 1. Cumulative Rate of Return Distribution

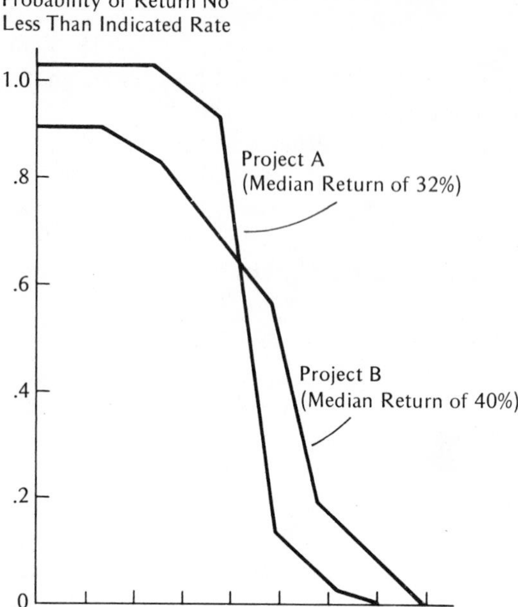

present value because of the form of the underlying distributions which must be combined.

Finally, risk analysis and simulation may be used as part of sensitivity analyses which enable one to explore the effect of shifts in any or all of the underlying variables.

In addition to the problem of obtaining estimates of the variables, a basic drawback of risk analysis is in the indeterminacy of the technique. In some cases a project will be eliminated if it is completely dominated (i.e., there are other alternatives which have a higher return for any level of risk). However, in most cases the manager now sees risk added to the analysis and the choice is based on an attitude toward risk. This weakness indeed may be a strength, for it allows the manager to include attitudes and values which are not so readily obtained by explicit questioning from a staff management scientist.

From a risk analysis simulation, a manager can derive a distribution of probable returns for a proposed project. These distributions may be very varied, but a standard deviation and variance for each distribution can be calculated.[2] From these measures of dispersion, some managers impute requirements for the discount rates. For example, they may consider the coefficient of variation, the

[2]Variance in algebraic terms is computed as follows. Let

Y_i be a return in category i,

P_i be the probability of category i occurring,

ratio of the standard deviation of the value to the expected value. Thus, if the standard deviation of a project is 7% and the expected terminal rate of return is 18%, the coefficient of variation of the terminal rate of return is 7/18, or 0.4. When this project is compared with another project, the focus is not on return or variation *per se*, but the ratio. Another project with a return of 5% and a standard deviation of return of 2% would also have a coefficient of variation of 0.4. Similarly, a project with a 25% terminal rate of return but a standard deviation of 13% would have a coefficient of variation of 0.2, making it less desirable than the first project. The problem with this measure is that management's attitude toward risk is not necessarily uniform with regard to the ratio. An equally good measure may be to require that a project have a return minus the standard deviation which is at least 10%. Or perhaps a relevant measure is the return minus some constant times the standard deviation. Alternatively, management may focus simply on the probability of a loss. If the probability of a loss is greater than *N*%, no return will be sufficiently high to invest. Another standard is to say that the return must be reduced by a constant times the probability of a loss, and the resulting figure must be greater than say, 10%. All these rules are only armchair standards for coping with risk.[3]

Risk aversion is a measure of one's disinclination to take risks. Risk aversion is expressed by index numbers that measure the willingness of an individual to gamble in given situations. If one assumes that most individuals prefer less risk to more risk for a given level of expected return, then one can see how the level of risk an individual is willing to accept in exchange for a potentially higher expected return changes with income or with wealth.

Consider the choice between a risky asset and a fixed income asset. One can transform the expected income into some combination of the risky invest-

---

$\bar{Y}$ be the average of all Y_i values, weighted by the probability of occurring

$$\left(= \sum_{i=1}^{N} P_i Y_i, \text{ where } \sum_{i=1}^{N} \text{ means } P_1 Y_1 + P_2 N_2 + \cdots + P_N Y_N \right)$$

Then the variance is equal to

$$\sum_{i=1}^{N} P_i (Y_i - \bar{Y})^2$$

[3]Conrath found that executives analyzed projects consistent with a decision rule that P (loss) < 10% and E (Return) = 30% + 3 × P (loss). See David W. Conrath, "From Statistical Decision Theory to Practice: Some Problems with the Transition," *Management Science,* April 1973, pp. 873–883. Alderfer and Bierman found that subjects in a gambling situation consistently had a strong aversion to loss and preferred an alternative with a lower mean and higher variance but with a lower probability of loss to another alternative with a higher mean, lower variance, and higher probability of loss. See Clayton T. Alderfer and Harold Bierman, Jr., "Choices with Risk Beyond the Mean and Variance," *Journal of Business,* July 1970, pp. 341–353. From a field study of eight firms, Mao concluded that the negative semivariance (the variance of outcomes below the mean) was a far better measure of risk than variance. James C. T. Mao, "Survey of Capital Budgeting: Theory and Practice," *Journal of Finance,* May 1970, pp. 349–360.

ment and the fixed income investment. Then, if one increases the *absolute* dollar amount invested in the risky asset as wealth increases, there is decreasing *absolute* risk aversion. If the *percentage* of total wealth invested in the risky asset increases with wealth, then there is decreasing *relative* risk aversion. Pratt and others have indicated that it is plausible that individuals would show decreasing absolute risk aversion.[4] Intuitively, one can find reasonable explanations for either increasing or decreasing relative risk aversion as wealth rises.

To replace the dependency on variance and its inadequacy as a measure of risk, one may substitute a more formal approach of charging each period's cash flow with the cost of reducing risk in that period. This adjusted cash flow then may be included in computing the adjusted terminal rate of return after this insurance premium has been included. This approach parallels the idea of a certainty equivalent which has been discussed in business decisions by Raiffa and others.[5] A rational and consistent decision maker will be indifferent between some certain value and a distribution of uncertain returns. For example, one may choose to accept $0.50 rather than a gamble with equal probabilities of nothing and $1.00. Depending on whether one is risk averse or risk prone, one might accept (for example) $0.45 or $0.55, respectively, rather than accept the gamble. Similarly, one can generalize this concept to (1) uncertain payments at some future time period and (2) a distribution of outcomes more detailed than the two possibilities (0 or $1) shown here. In analyzing a capital budgeting project or a portfolio, the manager must obtain a distribution of cash flows which may be expected in each year. Then, what payments would be acceptable with certainty in place of that uncertain cash flow in that year? This certainty equivalent value is then discounted at the appropriate rate.[6]

Apart from management specification problems, the disadvantage of this approach is selecting the combinations of portfolio cash flows and finding the probability of their outcome. The certainty equivalent of a portfolio distribution in the nth year is *not* the sum of the certainty equivalents of the projects within that portfolio unless the projects, individually and in total, are so small as to warrant the assumption of a linear utility function for the manager over that interval.

[4] See J. W. Pratt, "Risk Aversion in the Small and the Large," *Econometrica,* Jan.-April 1964, pp. 122–136.

[5] See Howard Raiffa, *Decision Analysis: Introductory Lectures on Choices Under Uncertainty* (Reading, Mass.: Addison-Wesley, 1968).

[6] The rate would be a risk-free rate (U.S. government bonds, for example) since the risk of the project has already been considered. In making this decision operationally, several simplifications can be employed which somewhat distort the results from the theoretical values. Thus, one may assume a_i, a coefficient for transforming the expected value of the cash flows in year Y_i to the certainty equivalent a_iY_i. Under this simplification, the net present value of the certainty equivalents of an N-year project is

$$\sum_{i=1}^{N} \frac{a_i Y_i}{(1+r)^i} \qquad [0 \leqslant a_i \leqslant 1]$$

Essentially, the selection of a_i is designed to compensate for the parameters of the cash flow distribution other than the expected value.

CHAOLANDIA'S SUPER-WIDGETS

In early 1979 the manager of Aggressive Enterprises in Chaolandia submitted the following project for approval by the parent company. Chaolandia was a developing country and Aggressive Enterprises operated there in the form of a locally incorporated subsidiary.

Product. Super-widgets. Aggressive Enterprises had been manufacturing widgets in Chaolandia. The new project would allow the country to produce more powerful widgets, super-widgets.

Investment Requirements. It was estimated that 100,000 Chaolandia pesos (CP) would be required for plant and equipment. There was no parent investment for working capital. However, 20,000 CP of the 100,000 CP required for plant and equipment could be provided by the parent out of obsolete equipment it maintained in its warehouse. Chaolandia's government was agreeable to this transfer. The government also agreed to a five-year straight-line depreciation method for the 100,000 CP of plant and equipment.

Project Life. Although the market for super-widgets was expected to continue expanding at least for the next twenty years, Chaolandia's government insisted in making arrangements for the government purchase of the company after five years. In this case the government proposed to purchase the super-widget plant for 155,000 CP at the end of five years, in December 1984.

Demand. At a price of 400 CP per unit, demand for super-widgets was estimated as follows:

	Domestic	*Exports*
	(units)	
1980	100	50
1981	150	75
1982	200	100
1983	200	100
1984	200	100

The domestic demand was considered to be price inelastic. That is, for the likely prices in the future, the quantity demanded appeared to be independent of the price charged. However, this was not the case with exports. Export demand was considered to be price elastic. It was thought that for each 1% increase in prices, the export quantity demanded decreased by 1.2%. Chaolandia's exports could affect the sales of some of the other divisions of Aggressive Enterprises. However, this impact was expected to be nominal at least during the first five years of the project.

Prices. The engineers had estimated that an initial price of 400 CP was appropriate, given the competition. However, historical inflation in the country made it possible to count on an annual 10% increase in prices. The 400 CP for 1980 already incorporated the rate of inflation between 1979 and 1980.

Variable Costs were estimated by the Engineering Department as follows:

Raw material	Domestic	50 CP per unit
	Imported	25 CP per unit
Labor		25 CP per unit

Domestic costs had recently been increasing at an annual rate of 12% because of inflation. Import prices were subject to fluctuations in the exchange rate. Cost estimates for 1980 already incorporated the rate of inflation between 1979 and 1980.

Fixed Costs were estimated as follows:

Supervisory fees to the parent	10,000 CP annually
Selling and administrative expenses	30,000 CP annually
Depreciation	20,000 CP annually

Selling and administrative expenses were also subject to a 12% inflation rate per annum. The supervisory fees were a form of royalty and they did not involve additional expenditures at home.

Exchange Rate. The economics department of Aggressive Enterprises had estimated the following exchange rates:

	CP per $
1979	4.00 CP
1980	4.00
1981	4.40
1982	4.40
1983	4.90
1984	4.90

There was no control on repatriation of earnings.

Taxes.

Chaolandia's Taxes:	25% income tax and no loss carry forward 25% withholding tax on dividends
Parent Country Taxes:	Income: 50%, allowing tax credit for taxes paid abroad Capital gains: 30%

Remittances. It was expected that all the profits after taxes would be remitted to the parent company.

Cost of Capital Applicable to Chaolandia. 20%. Super-widgets production in Chaolandia was not expected to alter the risk profile of Aggressive Enterprises.

1. Would you accept the project? What assumptions do you consider to be critical in your analysis? Use Exhibits 1 and 2 for your projections.

2. How would you analyze the project if earnings repatriation were prohibited during the initial four years of the project?

EXHIBIT 1. Super-Widgets Project: Pro Forma Statement (Chaolandia pesos)

Receipts	*1980*	*1981*	*1982*	*1983*	*1984*
1. Sales (units)					
2. Domestic					
3. Exports					
4. Total					
5. Price per unit					
6. Gross revenue					
Expenses					
7. Raw material					
8. Domestic					
9. Imports					
10. Labor (per unit)					
11. Total variable cost per unit					
12. No. of units					
13. Total variable costs					
14. Supervisory fees					
15. Selling and administrative					
16. Depreciation					
17. Total expenses					
18. Profit before taxes					
19. Local taxes					
20. Profit after taxes					
21. Withholding taxes					

EXHIBIT 2. Super-Widgets Project: Cash Flow Analysis (parent country dollars)

	1979	1980	1981	1982	1983	1984
Exchange Rate:	4.00	4.00	4.40	4.40	4.90	4.90
Cash Inflows						
1. Profit after taxes						
2. Depreciation						
3. Others:						
4.						
5.						
6. Total cash inflows						
Cash Outflows						
1. Initial investment						
2. Taxes:						
3. Chaolandia						
4.						
5. Parent country						
6. On dividends						
7. On fees						
8. On capital gains						
9.						
10.						
11. Total cash outflows						
12.						
13. Net cash flows						
14. Discount factors at 20%						
15. Discounted flows						
16. Net present value						

3. How would you analyze the project if Aggressive Enterprises intended to continue operating Super-widget for the next twenty years (i.e, the government would not purchase it at the end of fifth year) and a control in earnings repatriation existed? Assume earnings repatriation at the present time is limited to 12% of annual earnings.

4. Chaolandia's government and financial institutions have offered several alternatives to finance the project. These alternatives include several degrees of leverage with local funds. These local funds, however, are much more expensive than the price Aggressive Enterprises has in the home country. How would you analyze the project if an independent financial package had to be created for its financing, and the relevant question became: What is the return on Aggressive Enterprises' equity?

CHAPTER 12

Corporate Strategy and the Decision to Invest Abroad

Although this book emphasizes the *financial* considerations of investments, prior to such analysis must come resolution of the issue of the corporation's *strategy*. Also called the question of policy or corporate philosophy of operations, the topic concerns such issues as:

> "What is our primary expertise to be in ten years?"
>
> "Where do we want to operate by geographic region and by product line?"
>
> "Without changes in our operating policies and business lines, where will we be in twenty years?"

Thus, the heuristic the firm employs to reduce the number of projects subjected to detailed analysis is a screening process based on an answer to the question:

> "In terms of our corporate strategic plan, would this operation fit our future image of the firm?"

Only if there is an affirmative answer should the firm pursue an analysis of the project. This issue is explored after reviewing economic and behavioral factors which influence the decision to invest abroad.

THE STIMULUS FOR INTERNATIONAL INVESTMENT

Economic Motivations[1]

Comparative Advantage. A major economic motivator is comparative advantage. This basic concept of economics suggests that each productive asset is most effective in terms of the value of total output for the society if used in those tasks for which its relative advantage over other alternatives is greatest.

As an example, assume that there are two countries, A and B, both with one hundred labor weeks of time available at equal labor rates. A product can be produced in either nation, but it must have two processes completed for the finished version. The units per process for each nation are:

		Units Produced per Week	
		Process X	*Process Y*
Country A	100 weeks	10/wk	5/wk
Country B	100 weeks	6/wk	2/wk

Comparative advantage suggests that each nation's workers should be used where they have the largest relative advantage or smallest relative disadvantage. In this example Country A is more efficient in terms of units per week for both Process X and Y. This fact relates to *absolute efficiency.* However, its *relative efficiency* is greater for Process Y, since the ratio $5/2$ is greater than $10/6$. A policy of completing as many units as possible of Process Y in Country A would result in production of 500 units. Those units are treated with Process X in Country B, and the remaining seventeen weeks of unused time in Country B are used to produce an additional 25½ finished units (completing both Process X and Process Y for these extra units), for a total finished production from both nations of 525½. Given the problem as defined, this is the maximum output possible.[2]

Translated to international corporate operations, the impact of comparative advantage may be related to labor skills or unit costs, to transportation expenses for reaching the total market, and to capital markets, for example. In

[1] A review of the major economic elements which may contribute to a direct foreign investment decision is found in Richard E. Caves, "International Corporations: The Industrial Economics of Foreign Investment," *Economica,* Feb. 1971, pp. 1–27.

[2] A strategy of completing all Process X in Country A would provide 1,000 units, but this is beyond the capacity of Country B for Process Y since the maximum in Process Y from Country B at 2 units per week is 200 units in 100 weeks. Thus, Country A would complete Process X on these 200 units and complete both Process X and Process Y on an additional 266.7 units in the remaining 80 labor weeks, for a total finished production of *466.7 units.* If one were to produce finished products separately in each country (the "no-trade" situation in international exchange, for example), then Country A could produce 333.3 units and Country B could produce 150 units, for a total of *483.3 units.*

spite of much rhetoric about cheap foreign labor and its effect on American jobs, there are several aspects to the issue of relative labor costs and unit costs. These unit costs, in turn, are a function of capital (machinery and human training) and wage rates in conjunction with productivity. The wage rates paid in many countries appear low when compared with the wages paid in the United States. This fact is likely to make these other countries more attractive as an investment site for the multinational company when the goods to be produced require a large amount of labor. However, when the goods to be produced require a considerable amount of capital investment relative to labor, then the lower wages play a less important role in the final decision. Other factors such as the skill of the labor force may make investing in high-wage countries more desirable, as discussed in Part One.

When there are limited economies of scale in producing a product which has relatively high transportation costs, the firm may favor establishment of several plants around the world. This policy allows lower transportation costs to customers and lower total unit costs. In this case lower costs would result from distribution benefits: Average miles per unit delivered are lower. In addition, special economies in transportation may exist if there is governmental aid or differential geographic elements (e.g., navigable waterways or mountainous terrain and no railroads).

In the capital markets, freedom of transactions among currencies means that rates adjusted for risk should reach equilibrium. However, limitations on capital export and import, alternative expectations about currencies, special tax considerations, and the political risks noted in Chapter 10 suggest rate differentials in capital markets. When the local government commits public policy toward encouragement of a particular enterprise, then special tax concessions and other arrangements mean that, even if the markets were in equilibrium, the special arrangements may offer attractive financing incentives for the multinational corporation. The studies relevant to this issue in the international securities example will be discussed in Chapter 13.

Operational Constraints. A second economic incentive for international operations is simply binding operational constraints or incentives. Independently of comparative advantage, certain raw materials may be available only in a particular region. Proximity to those supplies may force a location of manufacturing operations at those points. Government policies may force production operations in many lands in order to sell in those countries. Finally, the local government may tie availability of the resource (bauxite, nickel, and so on) to the establishment of a local plant beyond the scope required by the firm's operation. Hence, these economic constraints, induced by nature or by government, to some degree determine the location of international operations.

Multiple constraints may occur, of course, and are often the bane of multinational officers' existence. These constraints become intensified in times of political turmoil. For instance, German pilots flying for Pan American's Colombian subsidiary were paid about one-third the U.S. pilots' wages. Yet, in 1939 the U.S. government ordered the firm to purge the Colombian affiliate of all German pilots, compensating them for the operating losses. In a similar vein, several Latin American governments looked with resentment upon the U.S. government's attempts to prevent the Latin American subsidiaries of

American multinationals from selling to Cuba during the American embargo of that nation. Usually, such shipments went ahead with minor U.S. government protests.

Taxation. A basic economic incentive to location decisions is taxation. Because management is charged with the responsibility of maximizing shareholder returns in the long run, lower corporate taxes in particular areas of the world become important.

The form of tax benefit differs. The absolute rate of taxes on profits may be low. The definition of taxable income may be more advantageous to the firm in some nations than in others; for example, the United Kingdom has periodically allowed free depreciation on some assets in particular industries, permitting firms to take as much depreciation as desired in a given year to offset all profits until the asset is fully depreciated. Finally, some nations may have very low taxes on the receipt of dividend income or a very low withholding tax applied to dividend or interest payments outside the nation. Such an arrangement encourages the multinational firm to use this land as a base for a financing subsidiary which receives dividends from operating subsidiaries and remits payments to other firms in the same corporate family. These issues, and the basic rules of U.S. taxation of international income, are addressed in Appendix 1.

Financial Diversification. One economic motivation often linked to the "acceptance of a good investment" philosophy is financial diversification, or spreading the firm's risk throughout a wider range than any one nation will permit. By diversifying over basic markets, products, regions, and governments, the firm hopes to avoid dependence on the outcome of a single unique investment. This is the same intent as that which compels an investor to allocate a securities portfolio over many stocks.

Oligopolistic Markets. An oligopolistic market structure often is associated with a decision to invest abroad. When there is limited product differentiation, economies of scale, and a small number of sellers, then an oligopolistic market structure induces a follow-the-leader strategy among the competitors. To prevent one member from dominating local or world markets, the other members of the industry are compelled to match one company's expansion lead. Often, this is simply a "me, too" attitude. However, this attitude can also be rationalized as the result of an effective reduction in the risk that management perceives in the investment. An investment that once appeared extremely risky because of the large number of unknowns involved could be perceived by the firm as less risky if a major competitor is investing in that area. In other cases the reaction is part of a well thought out strategy based on industry economics in which the competitors believe the cost structure and economies of scale in marketing, production, sourcing, and so on, would permit one member to dominate if that firm could seize a large enough total market share.[3]

[3]For a detailed analysis of the impact of oligopolistic markets on the multinational enterprise, see F. T. Knickerbocker, *Oligopolistic Reaction and Multinational Enterprise* (Boston: Division of Research, Harvard Business School, 1973).

Potential Loss of Markets. Finally, there is the opportunity to invest because failure to invest would result in losses. Some business opposition to a particular antipollution device may be based on the belief that it is uneconomic to the firm. However, if the mayor of a city makes it clear that unless the firm installs a residual fluid discharge precipitator he will close the plant, then the return on the investment in the precipitator is very high. Similarly, a firm may establish foreign operations in order to supply the foreign market (or the original domestic market) when there is a belief that the market will be lost unless such an operation is established.

Anti-Trust: Strategy and Stricture

One important factor affecting the decision to invest in domestic markets or in foreign lands is anti-trust legislation. The United States has played a leading role in development and enforcement of this type of legislation. However, in recent years other nations and international agencies appear to be generating similar concerns.

Although anti-trust case law evolves over time, in the United States after World War II a series of decisions and consent decrees left American business restricted in the manner of investing abroad. The Department of Justice sought to prohibit actions by American firms abroad through joint ventures or wholly owned subsidiaries that would operate to the detriment of competition in the American market.

Cartels were a major target of the anti-trust division of the Department of Justice. Although legitimate controls on patents and trademarks were allowed, joint venture agreements that restricted the ability of Company A's subsidiary, Company B (owned in conjunction with another subsidiary or an independent firm), to compete in Company A's home territory were prohibited, as were restrictions on Company B's selling in territories of other Company A subsidiaries. Company A might *restrict* Company B's uses of patents or trademarks, but it could not prohibit Company B's *sales* activities.

Sometimes firms argued that the operations were part of the same large company, and there was no prohibition against divisional coordination in a corporation. In the American Timkin case, common control, patents, and policies did not change the fact that the subsidiaries had minority owners and legally were separate corporations subject to American restrictions on their activities.

Alcoa is famous in American anti-trust law for both the domestic and the international aspects of the case. Essentially, Alcoa had a near monopoly of the American aluminum market, and a successful case of the anti-trust division won a decision. The final judgment by Judge Learned Hand in district court (caused by the disqualification of too many supreme court justices because of prior interests) made clear that even if Alcoa had behaved in a simple competitive spirit and had not sought dominance, a monopoly *per se* was evil and could be broken up. (Judge Hand made clear that Alcoa was not so pure of spirit.) After the war, government aluminum plants were sold to other firms so that Alcoa's market dominance was reduced. Aluminium Limited of Canada was owned by many of the same shareholders, largely the Mellon and Davis families.

Aluminium Limited made agreements with European firms to restrict imports to the United States. The firm had business headquarters in New York and its shareholders were mainly U.S. citizens. Judge Hand stressed that Aluminium Limited was guilty under U.S. anti-trust law and declared that *any* corporation *anywhere substantially* affecting U.S. commerce could be challenged. In 1950 the Alcoa shareholders had to give up their ownership in one of the two companies.

Other firms were attacked for activities that the firm's managers argued were in pursuit of the 1918 Webb-Pomerene Law, which allowed U.S. exporters jointly to sell abroad. Many firms invested abroad under this law and argued that they were protected from anti-trust prosecution. This argument was generally rejected.

Judge Wyzanski, in the Minnesota Mining case of 1950, found the firm guilty of anti-trust violations, even though the firm argued that nationalistic feeling, exchange rate issues, exchange controls, and the like had caused the firm to sell in third country markets its British-subsidiary produced goods rather than American goods. In essence, Judge Wyzanski argued that the greater profitability of British production for the third market was no defense since the market could have been served at a profit from the United States. He implied that *branches* were acceptable but that separate corportions were vulnerable for restraints on activities completely outside the United States if those activities could rebound to American commerce.

Mira Wilkins argues that in the long run this period of strict anti-trust enforcement probably helped American business, for firms were less willing to become involved in joint ventures with Americans or with Europeans, who themselves had no interest in appearing in U.S. courtrooms.[4] Accordingly, the American firms were more wary about going abroad. When they did go abroad, they approached it on their own and with determination. The American firms certainly learned that cartel-inducing agreements had to be avoided.

There are also concerns about anti-trust enforcement by other nations. For example, the European Economic Community under Articles 85 and 86 of the Treaty of Rome has restrictions on corporate practices and anti-competitive structures that relate to the United States Sherman Act, Clayton Act, and Federal Trade Commission Act. However, several aspects of the Articles limit impact on the European firms:

1. Enterprises are broadly defined. In contrast to some of U.S. cases noted above, European anti-trust enforcement does not apply to practices between wholly owned subsidiaries or between officers of the same company.

2. Only activities involving more than one nation are regulated. Although nominally U.S. anti-trust activity applies to anti-trust violations in interstate commerce, the U.S. Acts have broad impact; thus, the Clayton Act deals with acquisitions in "any line of commerce in any section of the

[4] Wilkins, *The Maturing of Multinational Enterprise: American Business Abroad from 1914 to 1970* (Cambridge, Mass.: Harvard University Press, 1974), pp. 295–300.

country." Furthermore, officials can cite the impact of intrastate commerce upon interstate commerce.

3. Exemptions for "good" cartels are permitted upon application to the EEC Commission or upon qualification under one or more blanket agreements provided in the interests of rationalizing certain industries. Such encouragement toward cartelization is based upon a need for the smaller EEC companies in certain industries to reach certain minimum size order for economies of scale to permit more effective competition with large corporations outside the EEC.

4. Small agreements or mergers are generally ignored completely. The U.S. Anti-trust Division for its own efficiency will often ignore smaller cases, but they are still violations of the law and will be prosecuted as such on occasion.

5. Mergers themselves have rarely been challenged. The one case pursued by the EEC Commission involved Continental Can. The decision affirmed the right to challenge mergers, but it did not support the charge of monopolization. Some years ago the Commission circulated a proposal regarding prior notification of any merger (including joint ventures) between firms whose combined sales exceeded $1 billion. The proposal has never been acted upon.[5]

Organizational and Behavioral Elements

Before turning to descriptive studies which analyze why firms have gone abroad in the past, it is helpful to review the ideas from organization theory, which influence the investment process. One comprehensive structure developed to explain organizational decision making is *The Behavioral Theory of the Firm* by Richard M. Cyert and James G. March.[6] In their work, Cyert and March treat the organization as a *coalition* of decision-making individuals. How these individuals reach decisions within the organizational framework is then described by relational concepts.

Elements of the Decisions. Cyert and March find three major components in the decision process—goals, expectations, and choice.

The *goals* in a decision are formed through formal and informal bargaining among the participants, and these goals evolve through time. A goal can be characterized by its dimension—the target of the goal, and its aspiration level—how far the goal is to be carried out. The dimensions of the goal are highly influenced by the nature of the changing membership in the coalition of individuals. For example, the decision of a new president of General Motors to emphasize the production of small cars to offset the impact of imported compacts shows the

[5] Jones lucidly summarizes many of the other similarities and contrasts in U.S. and EEC anti-trust law. See Robert T. Jones, "Executive's Guide to Antitrust in Europe." *Harvard Business Review,* May–June 1976, pp. 106–118.

[6] Richard M. Cyert and James G. March, *The Behavioral Theory of the Firm* (Englewood Cliffs, New Jersey: Prentice-Hall, Inc., 1963).

goal of offsetting foreign competition. The level of aspiration may fluctuate from holding market share to eliminating foreign competition.

Expectations formed by the coalition members are a function of the information gathered. Accordingly, changes in the system of sampling information, in the presentation of information to the firm, and in the range of information available affect firm expectations. If the GM president had a new information system installed, receiving daily selling data by model instead of weekly reports ten days after each week ended, then the expectations of the firm (i.e., its view of the automobile world) would probably be different at any given point in time from what would otherwise be the case.

Cyert and March analyze *choice* as occurring in response to a problem and affected by standard operating rules for coping with an uncertain environment. They assume multiple and changing goals, and the choice process is to obtain an "acceptable decision which meets the minimum level for various goals." Thus, the GM president may have seen a problem as "stop the erosion of GM world market share by foreign compacts." GM administration may have an alert system which triggers the response, such as any 10% decline in sales volume maintained more than two quarters in a row. A general task force may be assigned to review the situation and make recommendations, the normal response to a volume decline. The recommendation may be for a restyling of a certain body shell, even though all participants know there may be other options which additional intensive study might reveal as a superior choice. However, this restyle recommendation is consistent with the time frame, certain cost structures, and no more than a certain level of production disruption.

Relational Concepts. There are four relational concepts which Cyert and March believe affect the goals-expectations-choice decision framework:

Quasi-resolution of conflict occurs in the Cyert and March framework because departmentalized rationality usually prevails over the single-mindedness of centralized decision making. By having local rationality (in which subunits operate with subgoals), by using acceptable level decision rules (minimum-or-better standards rather than maximization), and by the occurrence of sequential attention to goals at various tiers in the organization, potential conflict is reduced. Decisions are made to accommodate and to resolve disagreement among coalition members for the time being. In this approach no formal or long-term conflict resolution is involved.

The *search* for problem solutions is influenced by the decision process in that search is motivated, simple-minded, and biased. A problem evokes a search process to find an acceptable level solution. A solution is sought by seeking alternatives within the neighborhood of the problem itself and in the area of the most obvious alternative. If this procedure fails, the search process is broadened until an acceptable alternative is found.

Organizational learning is the process by which organizations adapt over time. Firms adapt in *goals* based on past performance, past expectations, and past performance of comparable organizations. There is adaptation in *attention rules;* coalition members learn to study parts of their environment and to ignore other information. Organizations adapt in *search rules,* for if a search is unsuccessful, the search rules themselves are altered until a solution is found.

Uncertainty avoidance behavior is practiced by organizations which use short-run *fire-fighting techniques* to solve problems after they occur rather than to anticipate them. Cyert and March argue that firms typically do not anticipate the future by seeking a maximum expected value or a minimum level of operations. Rather, they ignore the problem and focus on *short-run feedback* as a response to problems which develop. They seek a *negotiated environment* in which standard pricing policies for members of the industry, normal business practices, and other such phenomena allow the firm to reduce the uncertainty present in its competitive environment.

One can expand on this basic Cyert and March framework to evaluate capital budgeting decision. Thus, a study by Carter suggested the following:[7]

Multiple Organizational Levels for Decisions. Within *The Behavioral Theory,* the emphasis upon unilevel or multilevel coalitions served to avoid a discussion of the influence that tiers of individuals have upon decision making. For example, the final consensus is the result of highly filtered goals in which a participant received a somewhat ordered goal system from above, modified it according to his/her interests and biases, and transmitted it lower in the organization. *The requirement that decisions pass through many organizational levels itself influences the outcome of those decisions.* Whatever the goals of the board of GM, the interaction of engineers, marketeers, stylists, and so forth will all affect the decision process as decisions move through the organization.

Bilateral Bargaining. Related to the multiple level consideration is the two-party (superior-subordinate) formation of expected project performance. The final expectations of the coalition are the result of *sequential* bargaining at *various levels* in the firm rather than the result of any group consensus. The automobile engineer concedes a certain engine performance in the compact car in order to gain approval of the marketing department; together they recommend a particular model for production to the group vice president for that automobile division.

Uncertainty and Goals. Goals found in a firm are related to the degree of uncertainty present in the firm's general environment and to the uncertainty present in a particular project's forecasts. In strategic decisions the firm may use a partial adjustment in goals to handle uncertainty. *The number of goals adjusts to accommodate the degree of uncertainty.* Thus, a simple goal of maximum rate of return may dominate a decision on which GM division would bring out a previously approved new model. On the other hand, a potential decision for GM to build a mass transit system in Seattle is likely to trigger many more issues as part of the discussion. How much does GM want to be in mass transit? What timetable is appropriate for this new venture? Will it detract from automotive and truck production?

Stimulus for Search. Many factors besides a problem generate search. Some of these stimuli might be:

1. The desire of an executive to meet a certain goal which is related to personal well-being.

[7]E. Eugene Carter, "The Behavioral Theory of the Firm and Top-Level Corporate Decisions," *Administrative Science Quarterly,* Dec. 1971, pp. 413-28.

2. A top executive's decision to have the firm enter a new area even though profits and sales are satisfactory in the current field. For instance, GM has an interest in mass transit. Hence, the problem is less important than a general philisophy of management to diversity.

3. A change in managers. The new manager may have fundamentally different beliefs on what the firm should be doing.

4. Opportunity-oriented search. The fact that a business operates in certain economic, geographic, and industrial markets means that particular opportunities will occur. The nature of the business means that certain opportunities will come to management regardless of any search effort.

The Pollyanna-Nietzsche Effect. Managers may operate as if a *decision resolves all uncertainty* present in the data on which the decision was based. A think-positive mental attitude can be used to stimulate successful performance by the organizational participants. Thus, the new GM president could forget the uncertainty surrounding a task force's recommendation of a restyled model intended to lessen the foreign car penetration of GM's world market share. The president could act as if the project will stop these competitors.

From this discussion of *The Behavioral Theory of the Firm,* one can judge the impact of these concepts upon the international operations of the firm. For example, the impact of changes in the coalition members on the goals and choice process of the firm is important. England and Lee found that there were different priorities among Japanese, Korean, and American managers in the degree to which they pursued organizational harmony, growth vs. earnings, and so on.[8] The main maximization criteria for American managers were productivity, organizational efficiency, and profit maximization. For Japanese managers, the main criteria were productivity and organizational growth. Carter concluded that American managers were significantly less interested in cash flow as a decision criterion than European managers, but all managers tended to emphasize growth in earnings per share.[9] Thus, as the firm expands beyond its national borders, inclusion of other executives from different cultures will alter the decision criteria and the decision process.

Interviewing managers of eighty-seven firms in five countries across four industries, Stonehill et al. found that the main goal of corporate officers was to maximize corporate earnings in total (France, Japan, and the Netherlands) or on a per share basis (the United States).[10] These authors suggested that national cultural factors and institutional restrictions (tax codes, lack of fully developed equity markets, restrictions on credit availability, income distribution, accounting regulations, and the like) would continue to encourage managers' concern with facors other than maximizing shareholder wealth, the normative goal of most finance textbooks. Consistent with the Cyert and March

[8] George W. England and Raymond Lee, "Organizational Goals and Expected Behavior Among American, Japanese, and Korean Managers–A Comparative Study," *Academy of Management Journal,* Dec. 1971, pp. 425–438.

[9] E. Eugene Carter, *Portfolio Aspects of Corporate Capital Budgeting* (Lexington, Mass.: D. C. Heath and Company, 1974), pp. 144–147.

[10] Arthur Stonehill et al., "Financial Goals and Debt Ratio Determinants: A Survey of Practice in Five Countries," *Financial Management,* Autumn 1975, pp. 27–41.

concepts, the executives favored goals that enabled them to retain control and to have their enterprises prosper. These authors also found that the major determinant of debt ratios was financial risk (measured by fixed charge coverage) rather than a national or industry factor of risk. This goal was only slightly more important than insuring the availability of capital to the firm.

These factors diminish the impact of a financial evaluation based only on a rate of return criterion. These organizational realities are important and often have great effect on the type of projects evaluated and the standards applied. Financial evaluations are important for a final decision, for the financial results provide one basis for the decision. The arguments within the organization will be whether a project has a *reasonable* return *given* the organizational and environmental constraints. The impact of organizational or behavioral characteristics of the firm on its standards and strategy is considerable. Those organizational elements influence the nature of the financial evaluations, but they do not negate them.

EMPIRICAL DATA

Studies of the Motivation to Invest Abroad

In one major analysis of the decision of U.S. firms to invest abroad, the National Industrial Conference Board (1966) survey found that the main criterion dominating the decision was a concern for markets.[11] The companies also usually referred to some goal of return on investment, but the measurement of this return was very simple and was often expressed as a percentage of sales. Leading U.S. consumer goods firms especially were oriented in this manner.

Such a strategy is not inconsistent with the economic goals noted earlier: Loss of markets may be the loss of a financial return, and the decision to invest abroad is made either to prevent economic losses or to profit from opportunities which are available in other lands.

Similarly, market dominance may be a reasonable companion to profitability under some circumstances. Gale presents a cross-sectional regression analysis based on 106 companies for which he evaluated the impact of market share, firm size, and concentration as explanatory variables for rate of return. Defining rate of return as net income on book equity over a five-year period (1963-1967) and adjusting for leverage of different firms, he confirmed his hypotheses that positive relationships between market share and profitability

[11]Other researchers confirm this motivation. Spitäller reviews various quantitative studies of both long-term portfolio capital and foreign direct investment. He concludes that the decision to invest abroad is primarily affected by the size of the foreign market, but he notes that the results are also consistent with the argument for differential rates of return. However, because of the aggregative nature of the data by which other researchers supported the importance of differential rates of return, Spitäller suggests that the other researchers did not consider the "unity of the investment decision of the international firm. This unity implies that the foreign investment decisions of a firm are interdependent." Hence, the broader strategy issue also appears in this conclusion. (See Erich Spitäller, "A Survey of Recent Quantitative Studies of Long-Term Capital Movements," *International Monetary Fund Staff Papers,* March 1971, pp. 189-217.)

were greater for: (1) high concentration industries vs. low concentration industies, (2) moderate growth industries vs. rapid growth industries, (3) relatively large firms vs. smaller firms, and (4) large firms in high concentration industries with relatively moderate growth vs. all other firms. He notes that "the findings of this study would seem to confirm our belief that interaction effects . . . play an important role in the determination of firm and industry performance." Thus, his conclusion is consistent with the strategy of a firm's seeking access to particular markets in the expectation of greater long-run profitability from obtaining a dominant market share.[12]

A subset of this emphasis on the market strategy has often been referred to in the context of the *product life cycle* (or, in a related term that is less favorable and uses more ideologically loaded words when applied to the United States, American economic imperialism). Stated briefly, the product life cycle as presented by Vernon suggests that the corporation will be forced to seek untapped markets because of increasingly broad penetration of a market and development of competitive pressures sufficient to lessen the return on the company's incremental investment.[13] Thus, the produce life cycle approach is a dynamic oligopoly theory, in which declining margins in one land induce the firm to go abroad. It may initially export, and then follow this policy with full manufacturing abroad as the export market is threatened by competition.

Aharoni found that the decision process of major corporations to invest in Israel was dominated by a combination of the product life cycle and the absorption of organizational uncertainty as projects filtered upward.[14] The absorption of organizational uncertainty, observed in many firms by various researchers, is the filtering process by which successive individuals in the decision-making process condense and delete risk elements associated with a project or decision. This study reinforces the blending of financial/economic factors and organizational/behavioral characteristics in the foreign investment decision process.

Hymer found the decision for foreign investment motivated by one or more forms of *monopolistic advantage.*[15] The monopoly forms which give the firm an advantage abroad include technology, capital markets access, sourcing leads, management, or some other variable.

Aliber, among others, emphasized the advantage the major multinational has in access to capital markets. Such access permits a lower discount rate when evaluating projects, placing the firm at an advantage over the domestic corporation in many nations which do not have such a capital market.[16]

[12] Bradley T. Gale, "Market Share and Rate of Return," *Review of Economics and Statistics,* Dec. 1972, pp. 412–423.

[13] Raymond Vernon, "International Investment and International Trade in the Product Life Cycle," *Quarterly Journal of Economics,* May 1966, pp. 190–207.

[14] Yair Aharoni, *The Foreign Investment Decision Process* (Boston, Mass.: Graduate School of Business Administration, Harvard University, 1966).

[15] Stephen Hymer, "The International Operations of National Firms: A Study of Direct Investment," unpublished doctoral dissertation, Massachusetts Institute of Technology, Cambridge, Mass., 1960.

[16] Robert Aliber, "A Theory of Direct Foreign Investment," in Charles Kindleberger, ed., *The International Corporation: A Symposium* (Cambridge, Mass.: MIT Press, 1970), pp. 17–34.

Two top officers of General Electric have justified the firm's investment abroad on five grounds:

1. To stabilize markets rather than engage in cutthroat competition;
2. To diversify holdings;
3. To enforce patents;
4. To meet national feelings;
5. To increase U.S. exports.

These justifications, cited in Wilkins, are consistent with the arguments discussed earlier.[17] Perhaps the most interesting new goal is that of patent enforcement. The argument is that a local firm, even as a subsidiary of a foreign company, is better able to watch and to stop patent infringement than the parent. One doubts how important the fifth reason is for management.

A History of Aggregate U.S. Foreign Direct Investment

Although the data are notoriously bad because of incomplete reporting and odd translation procedures, a tabulation of U.S. foreign direct investment by region and by industry is shown in Exhibits 12.1 and 12.2. In the early part of the century investment was in mining ventures, and most investment was in the Western Hemisphere. More than one-third of the investment was in Mexico, Cuba, and the West Indies, and one-fourth of the investment was associated with utility, agricultural, and railroad projects.

After World War I there was a discernible movement toward manufacturing with aggregate foreign investment in manufacturing rising to 24% of the total by 1929. Together with growth in petroleum and utility projects, the percentage loss was absorbed by railroads and mining ventures. Note that these declines are relative, except for a few nationalizations, reflecting fewer new investments in mining and railroads. Mexico's early relative importance diminished and was offset by greater investments in Central and South America.

During the Great Depression the book value of foreign investment declined from $7.6 billion to $7 billion, reflecting write-offs of assets. In addition, Mexico nationalized all U.S. petroleum investments in 1938. Interestingly enough, the United States was seen as a relatively desirable market in this period, for there was a net investment inflow each year from 1933 to 1939, probably stimulated by economic turmoil and increased probabilities of war in Europe.

In the two decades from 1950 to 1970 there was a 10½% compounded growth in foreign investment in the first half and 9½% in the last half, exceedingly high figures considering the relatively large base. Investment moved sharply to manufacturing and sales, which together accounted for nearly half of all direct investment by 1970. Utilities diminished in importance, and certainly by the

[17]Mira Wilkins, *The Maturing of Multinational Enterprise: American Business Abroad from 1914 to 1970* (Cambridge, Mass.: Harvard University Press, 1974), p. 68.

EXHIBIT 12.1. Sector Distribution of U.S. Foreign Direct Investment, 1914–1970

	Total (in billions)	*Manufacturing*	*Petroleum*	*Sales*	*Mining*	*Utilities*	*Other*
1914	$ 2.7	18%	13%	6%	27%	5%	13% agriculture, 9% railroads, 9% other
1919	3.9	20	15	6	22	4	15% agriculture, 8% railroads, 10% other
1929	7.6	24	17	5	16	13	13% agriculture, 4% railroads, 8% other
1940	7.0	27	19	7	11	23	6% agriculture, 7% other
1950	11.8	32	29	7	9	12	11 other
1960	31.8	35	34	8	9	8	6 other
1970	78.2	41	28	8	8	4	11 other

SOURCE: Calculations based on Mira Wilkins, THE MATURING OF MULTINATIONAL ENTERPRISE, Harvard University Press, 1974, various tables; Cleona Lewis assisted by Karl T. Schlotterbeck, AMERICA'S STAKE IN INTERNATIONAL INVESTMENTS, The Brookings Institution, 1938; U.S. Department of Commerce, SURVEY OF CURRENT BUSINESS, and other publications, various issues.

All figures are book values as of date indicated.

EXHIBIT 12.2 Geographic Distribution of U.S. Foreign Direct Investment, 1914–1970

	Europe	*Canada*	*Mexico*	*Cuba and West Indies*	*Central and South America*	*Asia*
Total						
1914	22%	23%	22%	11%	16%	5%
1919	18	21	17	15	20	5
1929	18	22	9	14	26	6
1940	20	30	5	10	25	6
1946	14	35	43	43	43	?
Manufacturing						
1950	24	50		20		2
1960	34	44		14		3
1970	42	31		14		5

SOURCE: Calculations based on Mira Wilkins, THE MATURING OF MULTINATIONAL ENTERPRISE, Harvard University Press, 1974, various tables; Cleona Lewis assisted by Karl T. Schlotterbeck, AMERICA'S STAKE IN INTERNATIONAL INVESTMENTS, The Brookings Institution, 1938; U.S. Department of Commerce, SURVEY OF CURRENT BUSINESS, and other publications, various issues.

All figures are book values as of date indicated.

late 1970s petroleum had also declined because of Mid-East nationalization. Data for manufacturing firms show that Europe became the dominant spot for U.S. investors, reflecting the booming markets after World War II, coupled with a desire of U.S. firms to take advantage of lower tariffs among EEC countries for internally manufactured goods after the Common Market emerged.

A NORMATIVE MODEL FOR EVALUATING DIRECT INVESTMENT

A large number of the factors considered in the decision to invest abroad have been reviewed in the preceding pages. Some of these factors were related to economic considerations, such as market structure. Other factors were related to the fashion in which business firms make decisions. In this section we attempt to unify these considerations into a simple framework which may be useful to the financial manager evaluating investment proposals. Only the skeleton of the analysis is given, but the specific details of any situation should be placed easily in this analytical construct. The approach consists of three steps:

1. Statement of alternative strategies according to specific criteria.
2. Evaluation of each strategy in terms of risk and return.
3. Selection of the strategy or combination of strategies that suits management's preferences and capabilities.

Statement of Alternative Strategies

In order to limit the number of product and country combinations which a multinational company will consider, it can develop a series of criteria to select alternative strategies. These criteria could be designed by the managers who are acquainted with the characteristics that make a strategy worthy of further consideration. Consider four criteria: (1) product life cycle stage, (2) market characteristics, (3) replacement vs. expansionary projects, and (4) financing constraints.

Using *product life cycle stages* as a criterion, Stobaugh classifies countries according to market size, investment climate, availability of local resources, and distance to major producing centers.[18] Products, in turn, are classified according to freight costs, economies of scale in production, and consumers' need for the products. Under this scheme, a table is prepared containing an index number for each product in each country. The strategies implied by this table are usually based on expanding operations into those products and countries where the index numbers are high and where the competitors are not yet established.

One way of using *market characteristics* to select strategies would be to classify the products according to potential market growth and present market penetration. This decision rule will select products in those countries where a large market share is held or where promising growth exists. An alternative way to use market characteristics is to classify products according to income or price elasticity and to favor those countries where income levels are such that the product has the best chance to enjoy a large market.

A *replacement/expansion* approach to selecting potential strategies divides investments into those which represent replacement of old projects (e.g., a plant to substitute a fully depreciated one) and those which involve an expansion. This latter group could be subdivided into projects which are expansions of old ideas and those which are new ideas altogether. Again, a table of index numbers could indicate relative desirability of projects.

The outcome of the exercise of screening the company's products and the world according to certain criteria is to derive a list of strategies (combinations of products and countries) which management can evaluate. A composite index might be created by summing the weighted index scores of each country/product combination for all the tables above. The index number of some of these combinations will further reduce the number of strategies that management considers. Hence, a reduced composite score for countries and products might suggest the family of strategies for final review.

Strategy Evaluation

Traditional financial theory evaluates projects along two dimensions: return and risk. In this context, risk has usually been measured by the size of the standard deviation of the return of the project before financing considerations.[19] Once management has decided upon a reduced number of strategies (combinations of products and countries) it wishes to consider further, it estimates the return and the risk associated with each of those strategies or combinations of strategies. If

[18] Robert Stobaugh, "Where in the World Should We Put That Plant?" *Harvard Business Review,* Jan.-Feb. 1969, pp. 129-136.

[19] This measure of risk refers to *total risk.* Under the capital asset pricing model, the relevant risk is only that portion of total risk that is linked to the covariability of the asset with some market. This is discussed in Chapter 13.

management does not wish to prepare a full risk evaluation for each broad strategy or potential product/country offering, alternatively it may attach a premium or discount to the return required from each strategy. Suppose the required return in traditional investments domestically is 15%. If the project is a new product in a less developed country (LDC) the required return may be raised to 26%. Once these adjustments are determined, they could be presented in the tabular form of Exhibit 12.3. For any given proposal, the adjustment to the required rate is taken from the table. From the example of the new product in an LDC, if it has low income elasticity of demand, high growth, a large market, and a stable government, then the premium is + 4 + 2 + 3 + 2, or 11%, for a total required return of 26%.

This analysis assumes simple additive relationships for risk, although a correlation among various risks is presumed to exist. For example, in every case the premium requested for political instability is higher when the product has a low income elasticity or a low growth potential. The rationalization for this assignment of required premiums may be that management believes that, regardless of the overall political stability of the country, local authorities are more likely to interfere with the operations of a foreign-owned plant producing staple commodities with low income elasticity in a stagnant economy of low growth potential than with the operations of a plant producing a product with the opposite characteristics. This is a crude approach to the assessment of these premiums. More sophisticated mathematical approaches are easy to envision once the basic concept is accepted. The output of this analysis will be a quick screening of proposed strategies which can be used in the appraisal process for major product lines in different lands by a decentralized firm.

EXHIBIT 12.3. Increases in Return Required to Adjust for Risk

		Product							
		New				*Old*			
		Income Elasticity		*Growth Potential*		*Income Elasticity*		*Growth Potential*	
Country		*High*	*Low*	*High*	*Low*	*High*	*Low*	*High*	*Low*
Less Developed Countries									
Effective Mkt. Size	Large	+2	+4	+2	+4	+1	+3	+1	+3
	Small	+4	+6	+4	+6	+3	+5	+3	+5
Political Instability	High	+5	+8	+5	+8	+5	+7	+5	+7
	Low	+2	+3	+2	+3	+1	+2	+1	+2
Developed Countries									
Effective Mkt. Size	Large	+1	+3	+1	+3	0	+1	0	+1
	Small	+2	+4	+2	+4	+1	+2	+1	+2
Local Competition	High	+2	+4	+2	+4	+1	+2	+1	+2
	Low	+2	+3	+2	+3	0	+1	0	+1

As stated before, the management of a company would decide what critical variables should be represented in the rows and columns of Exhibit 12.3. In any case, each combination of product and country could be described either by two variables, the expected return and its standard deviation, or by the premium figures in the table that reflect adjustments to desired return for risk.

Selection of a Strategy

The final step is for management to relate these choices to what they wish the company to be in the future. In Exhibit 12.3 each entry was considered to be independent of every other entry when the evaluation was made. However, management may find it can reduce the average risk by combining some strategies. At this point, *constraints* imposed on the company as a whole must be brought to bear. One such constraint may be the percentage of earnings tolerated as subject to repatriation controls before the capitalization rate of the stock is penalized. Other constraints that management might want to introduce at this level are the availability of management resources and various qualitative considerations such as contribution to the development of other countries or of management itself.

Finally, an appropriate variable to be introduced at this point is *size*. Once management has decided upon the appropriate mix of products and countries for a certain budget size, the next step is to repeat the process for the next budget size. The outcome of this analysis might be to choose a similar strategy with a comparable return-risk configuration. Alternatively, management might choose a strategy which produces a risk-return balance different from the previous budget size. Each of these strategies for each budget size can be plotted in a diagram as shown in Exhibit 12.4. A simplified final table of options described according to the risk return characteristics could be completed as in Exhibit 12.5.

SUMMARY

A variety of theories emphasize different factors in corporate investment decisions beyond the simple goals posited in normative financial theory. In the international environment, considerations such as comparative advantage, taxation policy, operational constraints or incentives relating to resources, the basic profit opportunities of a foreign investment, diversification strategies, and a strategy to limit losses are economic variables which may influence a decision to invest abroad. In addition, certain organizational and behavioral theories discuss the motivation of managers in the corporate decision process, such as the goals-expectations-choice trichotomy of *The Behavioral Theory of the Firm.* This theory can be extended to the capital budgeting process to include such concepts as the impact of multiple levels on the decision process, the bilateral bargaining between the sponsor of the project and the managers responsible for

EXHIBIT 12.4. Risk/Return/Budget Size Evaluation

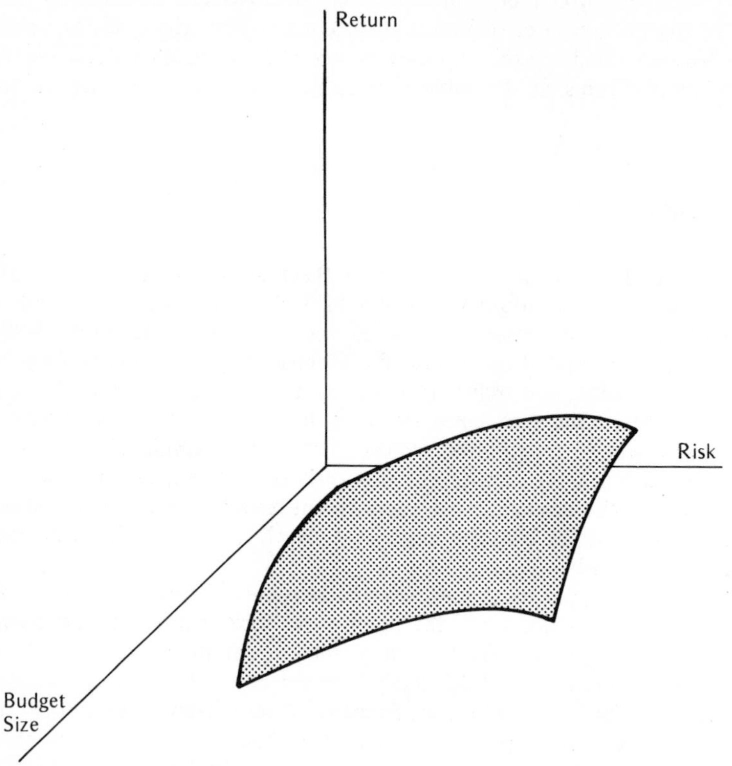

its approval, the influence of uncertainty on the goals of the firm, the variety of motivations for the search process, and the impact of the Pollyanna-Nietzsche effect in which uncertainty is forgotten after a decision is made. We also reviewed the anti-trust elements of international investment and the history of American foreign direct investment.

Several descriptive studies of the motivation of firms abroad note the importance of market share and growth opportunities coupled with uncertainty absorption created by multiple layers of management. The product life cycle, in which maturation of the markets at home induces the corporation to move abroad, is consistent with the motivation found in some studies.

In suggesting an operational strategy for the firm to employ in its decisions, we introduced an index evaluation of projects on various criteria. The index might include such variables as the income elasticity and growth potential of new or old products, the market size, the political instability of the governments, and so on. The initial screening is based on particular financing strategies, the product life cycle, general market evaluations, or whether the investments are replacement or expansionary products. The variations in these outcomes for

EXHIBIT 12.5. Comparative Budgets: Summary Results[a]

Country	*Budget 1* Products (1 . . . M)			
Developed	R^1_{11} σ_{11}	R^1_{12} σ_{12}	. . .	R^1_{1M} σ_{1M}
LDC	R^1_{21} σ_{21}	R^1_{22} σ_{22}	. . .	R^1_{2M} σ_{2M}

Country	*Budget 2* Products (1 . . . M)			
Developed	R^2_{11} σ^2_{11}	R^2_{12} σ_{12}	. . .	R^2_{1M} σ_{1M}
LDC	R^2_{21} σ_{21}	R^2_{22} σ_{22}	. . .	R^2_{2M} σ_{2M}

Country	*Budget* N Products (1 . . . M)			
Developed	R^N_{11} σ_{11}	R^N_{12} σ_{12}	. . .	R^N_{1M} σ_{1M}
LDC	R^N_{21} σ_{21}	R^N_{22} σ_{22}	. . .	R^N_{2M} σ_{2M}

[a] For R^k_{ij} and σ^k_{ij}, i is a Developed (1) or LDC (2) environment, j is a Product (1 through M), and k is a Budget level (1 through N).

various budget sizes are noted. When these screenings are completed, management reviews the expected return and variation in that return for the projects which passed the above filtering and are under final consideration.

The extraction example of Freeport is one type of international project which can be discussed in detail, using the case following Chapter 13. Another typical situation is international sourcing and joint venture capital budgeting; the issues surrounding this decision can be viewed in the Cummins Engine case at the end of this chapter. Finally, the capital budgeting analysis surrounding selling in a local market with or without export has many facets, most of which can be seen in the Chaolandia Super-Widgets case at the end of Chapter 10 and the International Tire Company case at the end of this chapter. Although each of these situations poses slightly different problems, most of the same issues relating to corporate and international financial analysis inevitably are present.

Questions

1. "They have cheaper wage rates than we do. Therefore, they can undersell us in everything. We must have tariffs or quotas to limit the amount of foreign imports." What economic concepts are ignored in this objection?

2. How do relatively cheap capital in one nation and relatively cheap labor in another nation affect the allocation of industry between them? What does the international mobility of capital suggest for your conclusion?

3. The auto industry is often cited as an example of an oligopolistic industry. If true, what would this structure suggest for the international movements of the firms? Does this conclusion seem to occur?

4. Explain the product life cycle as applied to foreign investment decisions. How would you restate this cycle in terms of *The Behavioral Theory of the Firm* concepts?

5. How might an entrepreneur differ from a corporate manager in motivation to establish international operations? What does the lack of concentrated stock ownership in the hands of management suggest about the motivations of the corporate managers in U.S. firms?

Bibliography

Aharoni, Yair, *The Foreign Investment Decision Process.* Boston, Mass.: Graduate School of Business Administration, Harvard University, 1966.

Aliber, Robert, "A Theory of Direct Foreign Investment," in Charles Kindleberger, ed., *The International Corporation: A Symposium.* Cambridge, Mass.: MIT Press, 1970, pp. 17-34.

Bhattacharya, Anindya K., *Foreign Trade and International Development.* Lexington, Mass.: D. C. Heath and Company, 1976.

Carter, E. Eugene, "The Behavioral Theory of the Firm and Top-Level Corporate Decisions." *Administrative Science Quarterly,* Dec. 1971, pp. 413-428.

——, *Portfolio Aspects of Corporate Capital Budgeting.* Lexington, Mass.: D. C. Heath and Company, 1974.

Caves, Richard E., "International Corporations: The Industrial Economics of Foreign Investment." *Economica,* Feb. 1971, pp. 1-27.

Clark, Peter B., and Richard D. Hass, "The Portfolio Approach to Capital Movements: A Comment." *Journal of Political Economy,* May-June 1972, pp. 612-616.

Daniels, John D., *Recent Foreign Direct Manufacturing Investment in the United States: An Interview Study of the Decision Process.* New York: Praeger Special Studies, Praeger Publishers, 1971.

Dunning, John H., ed., *Economic Analysis and the Multinational Enterprise.* London: Allen and Unwin, 1974.

Eiteman, David K., and Arthur T. Stonehill, *Multinational Business Finance.* Reading, Mass.: Addison-Wesley Publishing Co., 1973.

England, George W., and Raymond Lee, "Organizational Goals and Expected Behavior Among American, Japanese, and Korean Managers—A Comparative Study." *Academy of Management Journal,* Dec. 1971, pp. 425-438.

Fatemi, Nasrollah S., Gail W. Williams, and Thibaut DeSaint-Phalle, *Multinational Corporation,* 2nd ed. New York: A. S. Barnes and Co., 1976.

Gale, Bradley T., "Market Share and Rate of Return." *Review of Economics and Statistics,* Dec. 1972, pp. 412-423.

Hymer, Stephen, "The Efficiency (Contradictions) of Multinational Corporations." *American Economic Review,* May 1970, pp. 441-448.

——, "The International Operations of National Firms: A Study of Direct Investment." Doctoral dissertation, Massachusetts Institute of Technology, Cambridge, Mass., 1960, published by MIT Press, Cambridge, Mass., 1976.

Jones, Robert T., "Executive's Guide to Antitrust in Europe." *Harvard Business Review,* May-June 1976, pp. 106-118.

Knickerbocker, F. T., *Oligopolistic Reaction and Multinational Enterprise.* Boston, Mass.: Graduate School of Business Administration, Harvard University, 1973.

Kobrin, Stephen J., "The Environmental Determinants of Foreign Direct Investment: An Ex Post Empirical Analysis." *Journal of International Business Studies,* Fall 1976, pp. 29-42.

Mazzolini, Renato, "Creating Europe's Multinationals: The International Merger Route." *Journal of Business,* January 1975, pp. 39-51.

——, "Behavioral and Strategic Obstacles to European Transnational Concentration." *Columbia Journal of World Business,* Summer 1973, pp. 68-78.

Meeker, Guy B., "Face-Out Joint Venture: Can It Work for Latin America?" *Inter-American Economic Affairs,* Spring 1971, pp. 25-42.

Nehemkis, Peter, "Business Payoffs Abroad: Rhetoric and Reality." *California Management Review,* Winter 1975, pp. 5-20.

Polk, Judd, et al., *U.S. Production Abroad and the Balance of Payments.* New York: National Industrial Conference Board, 1966.

Root, Franklin, R., *International Trade and Investment,* Part Four, 4th ed. Cincinnati, Ohio: South-Western Publishing Co., 1978.

Scaperlanda, Anthony E., and Laurence J. Mauer, "The Determinants of U.S. Direct Investment in the E.E.C." *American Economic Review,* Sept. 1969, pp. 558-568.

Spitäller, Erich, "A Survey of Recent Quantitative Studies of Long-Term Capital Movements." *International Monetary Fund Staff Papers,* March 1971, pp. 189-217.

Stobaugh, Robert, "Where in the World Should We Put That Plant?" *Harvard Business Review,* Jan.-Feb. 1969, pp. 129-136.

Stonehill, Arthur, et al., "Financial Goals and Debt Ratio Determinants: A Survey of Practice in Five Countries." *Financial Management,* Autumn 1975, pp. 27-41.

Tomlinson, James W., *The Joint Venture Process in International Business.* Cambridge, Mass.: MIT Press, 1970.

Vernon, Raymond, "International Investment and International Trade in the Product Life Cycle." *Quarterly Journal of Economics,* May 1966, pp. 190-207.

——, ed., *The Product Life Cycle and International Trade.* Boston, Mass.: Division of Research, Harvard Business School, 1972.

Wells, Louis, "Text of a Product Cycle Model of International Trade: U. S. Exports of Consumer Durables." *Quarterly Journal of Economics,* Feb. 1969, pp. 152-162.

Wilkins, Mira, *The Maturing of Multinational Enterprise: American Business Abroad from 1914 to 1970.* Cambridge, Mass.: Harvard University Press, 1974.

THE INTERNATIONAL TIRE COMPANY

In January 1968 the Executive Committee of the International Tire Company was considering a proposal for the expansion of manufacturing capacity by 50% at the company's tire facility in Shawinigan, Quebec. In December of 1967 revised forecasts at Canadian headquarters indicated that 1969 demand would substantially exceed previous projections. Shawinigan capacity would fall 2,200 tires short of daily Quebec requirements in a matter of months, and some 4,950 units per day short by 1970. It was in response to this revised projection that the proposal for expansion at Shawinigan had been prepared by International's Canadian Division and submitted to the U.S. parent for approval. Capital requirements for the Shawinigan expansion were estimated at C$9.1 million.[1]

THE PARENT COMPANY

Since its founding in 1899 the International Tire Company had experienced continuous growth both at home and abroad. In 1966 sales soared past the $2 billion mark for the first time. Foreign operations began with an export department in 1913 and had expanded to a network of manufacturing facilities in 52 foreign locations and of product distribution in 140 countries.

Building on its wartime experience, the company became a major factor in the synthetic rubber, plastics, and fiber industries and an important supplier of defense products. By late 1967 International's broad product line totaled some 48,000 items. These items supplied 70% of all required materials for the tire operation. This placed the company among the lowest cost of the domestic tire producers. Exhibit 1 contains a summary of the firm's consolidated financial performance during the 1959-1967 period. Exhibit 2 compares the operations of International with those of other major tire producers.

Not all members of the tire industry shared International's fortune. Over 300 U. S. tire manufacturers operated in 1915. During the 1930s sharply reduced demand and large fluctuations in raw material costs drove the producers into a price war from which they did not recover until well into the 1940s and which only the strongest industry participants survived. In the late 1950s the major producers cut prices on high-margin tires in their first and premium lines. The high prices in these lines had provided an umbrella for smaller producers to compete during the postwar period. As a result, smaller firms, hard pressed by the slashing of profits, fell prey to acquisition by the larger companies. By the early 1960s only 14 companies were producing vehicle tires. In 1968 U. S. tire plant capacity totaled over one million daily units, mostly composed of passenger car tires. The Big Four–Akron Rubber Co., International, Ohio Diversified, and Eastern Tire–controlled some 68% of this total

[1]The official par value of 1.08108 Canadian dollars per US$ was established on May 2, 1962, following a twelve-year period of floating of the rate. The Canadian government announced on June 1, 1970, that it was once again floating the Canadian dollar.

EXHIBIT 1. The International Tire Company: Summary Financial Data, 1959–1967 (millions of dollars)

	1959	*1960*	*1961[a]*	*1962[a]*	*1963*	*1964*	*1965*	*1966*	*1967*
Net Sales	$1,328	$1,301	$1,406	$1,520	$1,594	$1,771	$1,997	$2,063	$2,344
Net Income	72	70	66	69	87	96	122	122	141
Percent of sales	5.4%	5.4%	4.7%	4.6%	5.5%	5.4%	5.6%	5.5%	6.0%
Retained Earnings	43	41	36	39	52	57	70	68	94
Depreciation	51	54	55	57	59	61	68	74	79
Per Share:									
Dividends	1.10	1.10	1.10	1.10	1.21	1.32	1.43	1.54	1.60
Net income	2.50	2.44	2.30	2.43	3.03	3.31	3.87	3.88	4.75
Total Assets	924	968	1,024	1,100	1,223	1,386	1,559	1,705	2,071
Current Ratio	3.2	3.1	2.9	3.9	3.2	2.7	2.7	2.6	2.6
Fixed Assets (net)	301	322	333	378	397	472	537	616	751
Capital Expenditures	91	78	69	105	79	139	138	154	219
Long-term Debt	85	84	79	157	157	173	223	261	447
Foreign Subsidiary Income	18.6	24.4	13.5	16.9	24.0	25.2	30.1	29.2	33.7

[a]In fiscal 1961 and 1962, foreign earnings were substantially reduced by losses due to devaluation of foreign currencies.
SOURCE: International Tire Company, ANNUAL REPORTS.

EXHIBIT 2. Consolidated Sales and Profits of Major Rubber Companies 1955–1967

	U.S. Producers				*Foreign Producers*		
	Akron Rubber Co.	*International*	*Ohio Diversified Co.*	*Eastern Tire Co.*	*Dunlop*	*Pirelli*	*Michelin*[a]
			Sales (million dollars)				
1955	1496	1227	796	991			
1957	1505	1168	767	958			
1959	1706	1328	842	1064			
1961	1752	1406	893	1107			
1963	2212	1594	959	1196			
1965	2724	1997	1143	1453			
1966	2902	2063	1106	1392	923	739	
1967	3219	2344	1254	1572	1,080	894	
			Profits After Taxes (million dollars)				
1955	69	67	49	35			
1957	72	59	39	25			
1959	78	70	33	34			
1961	78	66	29	28			
1963	110	87	38	33			
1965	130	122	53	50			
1966	141	122	39	36	28		7
1967	163	141	50	62	34		8
			Profit-Sales Ratio (percent)				
1955	4.6	5.5	6.2	3.5			
1957	4.8	5.0	5.1	2.6			
1959	4.6	5.3	3.9	3.2			
1961	4.4	4.7	3.2	2.5			
1963	5.0	5.4	4.0	2.8			
1965	4.8	6.1	4.6	3.4			
1966	4.8	5.9	3.5	2.6	3.1		
1967	5.1	6.0	4.0	3.9	3.1		

[a]Michelin figures are for tire sales only, not total consolidated sales.
SOURCE: International Tire Company and industry reports.

capacity. Estimates of productive capacity for the major producers are presented in Exhibit 3.

The Tire Market

The original equipment (O/E) market accounted for about one-third of the industry's shipments of tires. Demand in this sector was primarily a function of new vehicle production. Despite low margins of 2–4% sales, two economic factors encouraged the tire manufacturers to woo Detroit: (1) Since Detroit's relationships with suppliers remained fairly stable over the years, tire producers benefited from the predictability of large orders for the uniform product and (2) companies associated with Detroit enjoyed advantages in the lucrative

EXHIBIT 3. Major Producers' Daily Worldwide Tire Capacities—1968 Estimates (thousands of tires)

	Akron Rubber Co.	*International*	*Ohio Diversified Co.*	*Eastern Tire Co.*	*Dunlop*	*Pirelli*	*Michelin*	*Total Area*
United States	281	218	108	140	23	–	–	1,084
Europe and United Kingdom	83	74	20	35	103	73	201	722
Latin America	25	18	8	3	–	11	–	68
Asia	115	14	52	11	30	–	–	260
Other	48	30	13	19	29	7	1	164
Total	552	354	201	208	185	91	202	2,298

Note: The capacity figures do not include minority interests. "Total Area" figures include capacities of other, mainly local, producers.

SOURCE: International Tire Company, company estimates.

replacement market because most satisfied car owners replaced tires with the same brand as the original set.

The tremendous bargaining power of Detroit enabled it to keep the lid on O/E tire prices and to impose on suppliers constraints such as minimum levels of inventories and minimum numbers of nationwide dealerships and servicing centers. As a result, only the five largest producers were able to reap the rewards of association with Detroit. International Tire held approximately 25% of the original equipment market.

The replacement sector typically accounted for two-thirds of the unit volume and a higher than proportionate share of sales and profits. Passenger car tires were about 85% of total replacement tire production. Demand fluctuations resulted primarily from changes in the number of cars two years old on the road, average annual mileage per vehicle, and typical mileage traveled per tire.

Although the average miles driven annually per car remained relatively constant, tire life decreased somewhat during the 1960s. Despite improved tire construction, the faster rate of replacement occurred because of higher driving speeds, heavier cars, greater popularity of power systems, the imposition of federal and state tire safety laws including tread depth minima, and a generally more safety-conscious public. Annual increases in replacement shipments during the 1960s averaged about 7%. The main uncertainty concerning future growth in the market centered on the tire life of the newly accepted belted tire.

Two sectors existed within the replacement market. The major and associated brands of tires bearing the name of the parent company or its affiliates were marketed through company owned stores and independent dealers. Private label brands were distributed to mass merchandisers, department stores, oil companies, and automotive supply chains. Exhibit 4 presents an analysis of International's sales by markets.

Recent Market Developments

The mid-1960s marked the beginning of a new era in tire marketing philosophy. The cheap tire image acquired by the industry during the 1958–1964 struggle for market share gave way to new lines geared to a style- and performance-minded public. Extensive promotion by the major companies met with imme-

EXHIBIT 4. The International Tire Company: Sales Breakdown 1964 (millions of dollars)

Total Domestic Tires and Associated Goods				$ 941
Passenger Car Tires			$506	
Original Equipment		$110		
Replacement		396		
Major Brand	$275			
Associate Brand	95			
Private Label	26			
Noncar Tires			286	
Original Equipment		88		
Replacement		198		
Associated Goods			149	
Foreign Sales (mostly tires)				468
Canada		105		
Overseas		363		
Domestic nontire sales				297
Metal		127		
Aerospace		55		
Chemical		60		
Consumer		55		
Total Company Sales				$1,706

SOURCE: A security analyst's report.

diate success, indicating consumer acceptance of considerably higher-priced products. The next innovation, the belted-bias tire, was perhaps the most significant product change in the industry since the tubeless tire was brought out in 1950. Shipments of belted tires were expected to comprise 90% of all original equipment automobile tire shipments by 1970. The result of this new image and consumer attitudes was summarized in the estimate that the price per unit net of discounts had increased from $21.50 in 1964 to almost $30.00 by 1968. This higher realization price, however, had not been reflected in the profitability of the company. A slower growth in tire markets, sluggishness in car shipments, higher interest charges, and the increasing cost of wage settlements combined to keep the profitability of the tire and rubber industry below the average for all manufacturing companies.

A crucial issue for tire producers was the effect of the belted tire on the replacement market. Alarmists pointed to the longer life of the belted tire as depressing replacement sales and pushing the consumer to cheaper tires when replacing. Others noted the increased consumer consciousness of safety and pointed to the umbrella effect of pricing the belted tire in the $40.00 range to increase sales of the four-ply conventional bias tires priced in the $30.00 range. Still others discounted the belted-longer-life thesis, arguing that the increasing mileage per car, heavier vehicles, and higher speeds of travel would send consumers back to the quality replacement market even sooner than before.

A second crucial issue concerned the extent to which the *radial* tire would penetrate the U.S. market. Recently, Ohio Diversified and certain other domestic companies turned their efforts to the coming of the Radial Age. The economics of the radial, however, had proved a bit difficult to swallow. Estimates of conversion costs ran as high as $2.5 million for a plant that could produce 30,000 tires per day. To justify conversion costs, the radial had to sell at premiums of 50-60% above the conventional four-ply tire to make it profitable.

The belted tire was thus seen as a compromise between the conventional tire and the radial. On the other hand, lessening consumer acceptance of the belted tire and growth of radial imports led many observers to project a shift in demand by 1974-1975 to some 65-70 million radial units. Michelin's talk of setting up production in Canada was viewed as the possible stimulus required to push the 1970s market over to the radial.

Although International had introduced a limited number of radial-ply models, company planners agreed with those in the industry who felt that the public was not prepared to pay higher cost of these tires. Estimates were that demand for radials would remain well below 5% of the total North American market for several years. In view of this fact, production was arranged to provide the market with the rapidly proliferating belted line.

THE CANADIAN MARKET

The original incentive for the major auto tire producers to enter into Canadian manufacturing operations was provided by the tariff imposed by Canada in 1906. This tariff levied a 30% charge on all tires imported from the United States and other favored nations. By 1926, International, Akron Rubber, Dunlop, Eastern, Ohio Diversified, and National Brands of Canada had divisions in Canada.

Except for the setback during the Great Depression, demand for tires had grown rapidly and steadily. By 1953 Canadian shipments had reached C$130 million, of which exports accounted for C$5 million. During the 1959-1967 period shipments of tires more than doubled to C$282 million, falling back somewhat in 1967. Although tires were not included among the duty exemptions under the Auto Pact,[2] industry sales benefited from the increase in Canadian production and sales of vehicles sparked by the Pact. Exhibit 5 traces the pattern of production and sales of tires during the 1960s. Exhibit 6 presents data on the shipments of motor vehicles in Canada during the same period.

Possibly the most conspicuous element in the Canadian tire industry's competitive environment was the stability of the market shares held by the various participants over the past many years. From 1946-1968 International's share was estimated to have fluctuated within a range of only 4%, as seen in Exhibit 7. All four major U.S. producers sold to both the original equipment and replacement markets and their product, pricing, and distribution policies were basically identical. Dunlop, the one non-U.S. affiliate producing in Canada, was fighting to maintain its market share in the highly competitive market. Experiencing difficulty with its Canadian industrial products division, the British

[2]The Auto Pact was, in essence, an agreement made between the United States and Canada which stated that cars produced on either side of the border could be shipped across the border free of tariffs. The Pact was signed in 1964. Tires *on* these cars were free of duty.

EXHIBIT 5. Production, Domestic Sales, Exports, and Prices of Canadian Tires, 1961–1967

	Production	Replacement Sales	Original Equipment Sales[a,b]	Total Domestic Sales	Exports[b]	Price Index
			Passenger Car Tires (units)			
1961	7,961,644	5,957,367	1,815,918	7,773,285	129,000	100.0
1962	9,180,939	6,456,358	2,346,732	8,803,090	314,000	89.4
1963	10,545,390	6,846,454	3,042,599	9,889,053	506,000	90.0
1964	11,431,427	7,506,674	3,219,567	10,726,241	558,000	87.8
1965	12,052,428	8,029,602	3,949,546	11,979,148	388,000	90.6
1966	13,527,315	8,864,539	3,742,720	12,607,259	401,000	92.1
1967	13,998,051	9,532,558	4,119,175	13,651,733	634,000	93.7
			All Tires (units)			
1961	9,264,705	6,835,194	2,233,100	9,068,294	198,000	100.0
1962	10,760,709	7,461,550	2,872,362	10,333,912	429,000	86.6
1963	12,358,248	7,871,728	3,678,682	11,550,410	686,000	87.5
1964	13,361,712	8,678,970	3,922,148	12,601,118	646,000	87.1
1965	14,149,481	9,277,735	4,758,142	14,035,877	461,000	89.8
1966	16,018,557	10,202,837	4,734,641	14,937,478	531,000	92.1
1967	16,532,592	10,946,761	5,141,209	16,087,970	825,000	93.8

[a]Original equipment sales include tires sold to be installed in cars later exported to the United States.

[b]Tires mounted on cars shipped under the Auto Pact are free of duty in the United States. Loose tires, however, regardless of whether they are for the original equipment market, are subject to import duty.

SOURCE: Rubber Association of Canada.

EXHIBIT 6. Motor Vehicle Shipments in Canada, 1961–1967 (thousands of units)

	Shipments of Local Manufacture (1)	Exports (2)	Exports to United States (3)	Imports (4)	Canadian Market (5) (1) + (4) - (2)
1961	321.9	9.5	—	160.9	419.3
1962	426.1	11.9	—	94.7	508.9
1963	530.2	15.5	.3	59.6	574.3
1964	558.2	38.3	11.0	92.5	612.4
1965	705.6	77.9	31.7	136.5	764.2
1966	699.6	189.5	146.8	188.7	698.8
1967	725.5	342.4	311.0	313.7	696.8
1968 (est.)	891.7	522.1	472.5	437.0	806.6

SOURCE: Motor Vehicle Manufacturers' Association of Canada, WARD'S AUTOMOTIVE YEARBOOK.

EXHIBIT 7. Capacity of Major Tire Manufacturers in Canada for Selected Years (total daily tires)

	1946	1955		1963		1968 (est.)	
	%	%	Tires	%	Tires	%	Tires
International	20.3	19.5	6,500	21.1	10,800	23.5	20,850
Ohio Diversified Co.	10.9	10.0	3,300	9.8	5,000	9.2	8,200
Akron Rubber Co.	36.5	30.0	10,000	33.8	17,350	35.2	31,200
Eastern Tire Co.	17.9	19.5	6,500	19.1	9,800	17.8	15,800
Other	5.8	10.2	3,400	6.4	3,300	5.2	4,640
Total U.S. Manufacturers	91.4	89.2	29,700	90.2	46,250	91.0	80,690
Dunlop	8.6	10.8	3,600	9.8	5,000	9.0	8,000
Total Capacity	100.0	100.0	33,300	100.0	51,250	100.0	88,690

SOURCE: International Tire Company, company estimates.

subsidiary seemed content to upgrade its distribution to the replacement market and to leave the bidding for the original equipment stakes to the others.

THE CANADIAN DIVISION

Relation to the Parent

Long-term planning for production and capital investment in the three tire plants under its control was initiated by the Canadian division on the basis of five-year forecasts updated yearly. These five-year forecasts contained detailed projections of the market demand by geographical area and product line. Comparisons were then made between demand and current approved capacity. The differences between these two figures served as a basis for proposals for expansion containing a detailed workup of plant, equipment, and personnel resources required to meet the five-year projections. Included with these proposals was a statement of funds needed in support of the recommendations. These figures and recommendations were then submitted to corporate headquarters and planning staffs in the United States for evaluation. As the time for an actual expansion drew near, the whole evaluation procedure was repeated. At this time, the study was made in a much more detailed fashion, and the final result of the evaluation was submitted to the Corporate Executive Committee for approval.

Following a major investment, the staff at headquarters kept separate control of the operation for some time prior to its integration into the whole of the Canadian Division's operations. Approximately one year after start-up a complete report of resources used and revenues realized was submitted to the parent's Budget Committee for comparison with the projections contained in the initial proposal.

Intercompany transfers were very small. Plants obtained raw material from the cheapest source of supply rather than being forced to buy from other of International's affiliates. In most cases of significant dollar volumes, the parent would conduct feasibility studies to determine the lowest price at which it could supply the input from its integrated operations in the United States.

Because of transport costs and duty charges, however, the only significant volume of intercompany sales was in nylon tire fabric produced in Canada and which comprised 5% of International's Canadian tire textile needs. Tire-grade natural rubber was purchased on the world market. The majority of the other inputs were obtained from local manufacturers. Synthetic rubber, which accounted for approximately 20% of total cost, was imported to a large extent from the United States, though not necessarily from International's subsidiaries.

Long-standing corporate policy required all foreign capital expansion projects to be financed in the local capital markets. International called for standard percentages of foreign earnings to be remitted annually. In 1963, amid rumors of an upcoming voluntary restraint program on U.S. capital outflows, International began to pay more attention to the remissions of its non-U.S. subsidiaries. For several years the Canadian remittances had fallen below the established level. In a move to correct this position, two offerings of debt totaling $27.5 million were placed with several Canadian insurance companies in 1963. The net proceeds of this offering were to be applied to future capital remissions and local expansion.

Canadian Division Expansions

The Canadian Division was incorporated in the early 1900s with the construction of International's first manufacturing facility outside the United States at London, Ontario. This plant serviced the entire expanding Canadian market through 1960 when another plant was built in Victoria, Alberta, to cater to the western market. A third plant was built in 1964 in Shawinigan, Quebec, because of unexpected growth in eastern replacement markets and unusual projections as to the effects of the rumored upcoming Auto Pact on original equipment demand. These factors led to market estimates through 1969 substantially above International's existing Canadian tire capacity. In particular, General Motors had announced plans to construct a C$35 million, 100,000 vehicle annual capacity, assembly plant to be located in Ste. Therese, Quebec. Operations were to begin in early 1965. General Motors also announced a new policy that all tire needs would be purchased from Quebec sources only. Other factors reinforcing International's decision to build in Quebec were the shortage of available space at London, the relatively low Quebec wage rates, and the political situation in Quebec which threatened to boycott Canadian goods imported from other provinces. Akron Rubber's decision to construct in Quebec was announced about the same time.

When the Shawinigan plant was built, the 1965 production was 2,750 tires per day. By October 1967 operations at Shawinigan were expanded to full-capacity production of 4,400 units. Then in November the unforeseen occurred: Detroit announced adoption of belted tires for two thirds of their 1968 models. An urgent request for approval for conversion of facilities to the production of 1,760 belted tires was rushed through the Executive Committee. The total cost of this conversion was C$825,000, financed with Canadian funds. This conversion had hardly been approved when revised forecasts indicated the upcoming shortage which the Executive Committee was now considering.

THE PROPOSED SHAWINIGAN EXPANSION

The January 1968 request for immediate expansion of the facilities at Shawinigan from 4,400 to 6,600 tires per day reflected once again market growth rates exceeding those forecasted only 18 months before. The scheduled 4,180 original equipment tires—over 60% of the total tentative production—indicated the influence of the Auto Pact on the Canadian original equipment market. Although all Canadian producers had increased their capacities several times since 1964, the strain on Canadian tire production facilities vs. the periodic slight overcapacity situation in the United States resulted in large cyclical flows of imports from the United States. To quote one International executive, "From 1965 on this industry didn't take a breath. We (the Canadian division) made every tire we knew how to, and what we didn't make we brought in."

The Alternatives

The forecast detailing the need for immediate expansion of Shawinigan by 2,200 units dealt with four alternatives to expansion at Shawinigan. These alternatives were: (1) expansion at London, (2) construction of a new plant in Ontario, (3) imports from the United States, and (4) construction of a new plant in Nova Scotia to obtain more geographic dispersion of production facilities.

These alternatives were evaluated according to capital requirements, operating costs, freight charges, duty rates, return on capital invested, and time necessary to come on stream. The analysis indicated that if the expansion in capacity were to be made in Canada, the most economical way to achieve this would be by expanding Shawinigan. Including working capital, the total cost was estimated at C$9.2 million. The entire financial package would be obtained from Canadian sources. Payback period for the project was calculated to be 9.4 years. Exhibit 8 contains the financial flows statement submitted to the Executive Committee in support of the proposal.

The Canadian Economy

Adding momentum to the upward market trend was the general expansion of the Canadian economy which had been in a lull for several years and had just begun its turnaround in 1967-1968. Projections for the 1968-1969 economy pointed to a year of increasing expansion. A major contributor to the new prosperity was the forecasted 1968 record high level of $13 billion in exports which would provide a surplus of over $1.1 billion in the merchandise accounts. Of the $13 billion, $2.6 billion were to be in exports of automotive products to the United States, up from $1.6 billion in 1967 and $76 million in 1964.

The Labor Market

In early 1967 the United Rubber Workers of Canada began agitating for increased recognition. Primary demands were for wage parity with the auto workers and for master contracts to cover all Canadian plants of each rubber

EXHIBIT 8. The International Tire Company: Shawinigan 1968 Expansion Proposal: Financial Flows (millions of Canadian dollars)

	1969	1970	1971	1972	1973	1974
Capital Appropriation	7.4					
Working Capital	1.8					
Total investment	9.2					
Net Sales	10.2	10.2	10.2	10.2	10.2	10.2
Costs	(8.3)	(8.1)	(8.1)	(8.1)	(8.1)	(8.1)
Profit Before Tax	1.9	2.1	2.1	2.1	2.1	2.1
Taxes (53.1%)	(1.0)	(1.1)	(1.1)	(1.1)	(1.1)	(1.1)
Profit After Tax	.9	1.0	1.0	1.0	1.0	1.0
Depreciation	.4	.4	.4	.4	.4	.4
Cash Flow	1.3	1.4	1.4	1.4	1.4	1.4
After-Tax Rate of Return	9.8%	10.8%	10.8%	10.8%	10.8%	10.8%
Payback Period: 9.4 years						

SOURCE: International Tire Company, company estimates.

producer. Commenting on the woes of the Canadian rubber industry, the president of the Rubber Association of Canada noted that productivity in Canadian tire plants was 20–30% below the American level. Main reasons cited were: (1) The smaller market allowed only shorter runs and (2) the wide variety of tire types produced in the limited number of plants created serious scheduling problems and inefficiencies.

By mid-1967 labor demands focused on inclusion of a cost-of-living clause in a master contract which would cover all Canadian plants of the individual company. Confronting the companies' refusal to give in on a master contract with common expiration dates, the URW began walkouts at Akron Rubber's New Sarnia and International's London plants. Union unrest continued to mount and culminated in a two-month strike at New Sarnia, severely hurting Akron Rubber's 1967 Canadian earnings. As the companies strove to meet their Canadian commitments despite the loss in productive facilities, imports from the United States rose to unprecedented levels. The settlement calling for a 30% increase in wages over the next three years contributed to price increases totaling 15% for the last three quarters of 1967.

Industry's Expansion Plans

Akron Rubber Canada had opened 1968 with the announcement of a C$12.7 million investment for its Sherbrooke, Quebec, plant. The undertaking was the single largest capital project ever authorized in the Canadian rubber industry. The main purpose appeared to be rationalization of production to allow concentration at the New Sarnia plant on belted-tire production. In response to the auto makers' demand for belted tires on its 1968 models, Akron Rubber also announced a $2.2 million expansion at the New Sarnia plant. The additions at New Sarnia and Sherbrooke formed the nucleus of a proposed C$66 million expansion plan for all Akron Rubber Canadian facilities over the next several years. The total program would allow the company to cope with the shift to belted tires as well as the significant growth in demand of all rubber products.

Following the same philosophy, Eastern Tire announced C$17.2 million in 1967-1968 expenditures to build capacity at its Ontario facilities. Ohio Diversified indicated it would invest C$9.9 million at the Windsor, Ontario, plant. Dunlop proposed a more modest C$5 million expansion to support its share in the growing market.

Imports and Foreign Competition

During the 1960s total imports of tires into Canada rose from about 6% to over 15% of the total market for all tires in 1967. In passenger car tires, import units rose from 85,000 in 1961 to 1,570,000 in 1967. Roughly three-quarters of the imports were brought in by U.S. affiliates to buffer their own shortages as Canadian demand increased faster than capacity. Exhibit 9 gives detailed data on tire imports into Canada.

The major portion of non-U.S. imports stemmed from France, Italy, and Japan—presumably the efforts of Michelin, Pirelli, and Bridgestone. While the European imports were directed mostly at the quality markets—chiefly radials—the Japanese were aggressively marketing on a price basis a full range of the popular tire types.

EXHIBIT 9. Canadian Tire Imports, 1960–1967, Imports by Country, 1965–1967

	Tire Imports (thousands of Canadian dollars)		
	Passenger Car Tires (1)	*Truck, Bus, and Grader (2)*	*All Tires (3)*
1960	—	—	9,776
1961	1,342	4,223	9,356
1962	943	4,615	9,267
1963	1,371	6,485	11,852
1964	2,840	8,436	16,356
1965	3,915	7,576	16,624
1966	3,946	8,137	17,721
1967	19,240	14,850	41,860

	Imports by Country of Origin	
	1966	*1967*
United Kingdom	471	489
Austria	107	174
France	3,596	3,465
West Germany	107	456
Italy	623	730
Netherlands	215	358
Japan	980	2,187
United States	10,358	31,579
Total	16,991	41,114

SOURCE: Rubber Association of Canada.

The other major factor in the competitive environment was the Michelin plant due to open in 1971. Estimates of its capacity ranged from 12–20,000 units per day. This capacity was reported to be directed at the steel-radial, truck-bus market of which 85% was to be sold in the United States across the 5½% duty barrier. Despite the distance between U.S. markets and the Nova Scotia plant, this strategy was apparently superior to locating a plant in the United States and shipping the 15% across the 17½% barrier into Canada. Among the key determinants of Michelin's locational strategy were the reportedly substantial incentives given to the French company by the Canadian government. These incentives included financial packages amounting to 60% of the capital cost plus the right of free entry into Canada of all Michelin tires produced abroad. Michelin would thus have the advantage of rationalizing its Canadian production while gaining free entry for its entire line which could then be passed into the Canadian and U.S. markets. Speculation abounded that it would be only a few years before Michelin set up full production of all product lines in Canada.

Extremely perplexing to local manufacturers was the ability of the Europeans and Japanese to compete in the Canadian market on an export basis. All the major locals had third-country plants; yet all had found that tariffs and transport costs made importing unprofitable. The major producers inferred that extensive export subsidies were being given by the foreign governments to local exporters but were not accorded U.S. affiliates based in the same country.

The Final Decision

At this point, the alternatives that the Executive Committee faced were (1) to expand Shawinigan, (2) to export from the United States to Canada, or (3) to not expand production in any place.

There were four major factors against the expansion of U.S. production to cater to the Canadian market: (1) Canada imposed a tariff on all imported tires (see Exhibit 10); (2) transport costs over 300 miles, other things equal, were considered to increase costs above competitive levels; (3) U.S. facilities were presently operating close to full capacity; and (4) wage levels were higher in the United States than in Canada (see Exhibit 11). On the other hand, there

EXHIBIT 10. Tariff on Tire Imports for Selected Countries (percent)

	1963	*1968*	*1969*	*1970*	*1971*	*1972*
United States	8.5	7.5	6.5	5.5		4.0
Japan	25.0	20.0	—	17.5	15.0	12.5
Canada	22.5	21.5	(—— 20.5 and 17.5 ——)			
United Kingdom	24.0	19.0	—	16.5	14.0	12.0
EEC:						
Italy	18.0	14.4	—	12.6	10.8	9.0
France	18.0	14.4	—	12.6	10.8	9.0
Germany	18.0	14.4	—	12.6	10.8	9.0
Spain	28.5	—	—	—	—	28.5

SOURCE: Statement of the Rubber Manufacturers Association.

EXHIBIT 11. Estimated Hourly Employment Costs of Tire Production Workers in Major Tire Producing Countries—1970

United States	$6.00	France	$2.35
Japan	$1.75	West Germany	$2.85
United Kingdom	$2.25	Spain	$1.05
Italy	$2.25	Canada	$5.00

Note: Employment cost figures include fringe benefits.
SOURCE: Statement of the Rubber Manufacturers Association on November 25, 1970.

were two factors against the expansion of Canadian facilities: (1) U.S. labor was becoming increasingly vociferous against the expansion abroad of multinational companies which were alleged to take jobs away from American workers and (2) rumors were repeated that the Canadian government might take a much tougher stand against foreign ownership.

CUMMINS ENGINE COMPANY, INC. (THE KOMATSU VENTURE)[1]

In early March 1972 John T. Hackett, Executive Vice President of Cummins Engine Company, Inc., was reviewing the company's strategy in general and a new venture in particular. He was expected to make a recommendation to the Board of Directors on both matters the following week.

CUMMINS'S OPERATIONS

Cummins had been continuously under the aegis of the J. Irwin Miller family, the financiers who supported Clessie Cummins, founder of the company, during the long initial period of losses between 1919 and 1938. In 1971 J. Irwin Miller was Chairman of the Board of Cummins, and his family controlled 46% of Cummins's shares.

Cummins Engine was the world's largest independent producer of high-speed diesel engines (i.e., equipment containing the engine was not produced by Cummins). Its products were geared to that sector of the power industry in which the engine was a differentiated component of the final product. This was especially the case in the heavy-duty truck market. In heavy-duty trucks the engine, though only 20% of the initial cost, was the single most important item in the total cost of operating the truck. It was in this high-power, highly economic-sensitive market that Cummins was best equipped to compete. Diesel engines and related parts comprised 91% of Cummins's 1971 consolidated net sales of $492 million.

Engines were usually sold to equipment manufacturers, some of which were Cummins's major competitors who also produced diesel engines themselves. However, Cummins's reputation was such that the majority of these competitors, including General Motors, International Harvester, and Mack Trucks, also offered Cummins engines in their models to satisfy customers who specified Cummins power. Exhibit 1 shows the shares of the engine market taken by Cummins and its competitors.

EXHIBIT 1. **U.S. Diesel Engines: Manufacturers Market Share, 1966–1970**

	1966	*1967*	*1968*	*1969*	*1970*
Cummins	39.7%	40.0%	41.3%	36.6%	41.9%
Detroit Diesel	28.5	30.7	27.3	25.9	21.9
Mack	15.3	14.7	15.8	16.7	16.4
Perkins	4.0	2.8	4.0	7.3	6.3
IHC	2.5	2.2	3.9	2.9	2.9
GMC	0.7	1.4	3.2	6.5	6.5
Ford	0.4	1.1	2.2	2.6	2.6
Others[a]	8.9	7.1	2.3	1.5	1.5
	100.0%	100.0%	100.0%	100.0%	100.0%

[a]Principally Caterpillar Tractor.
SOURCE: Automotive Manufacturers Association.

[1]This case is a consolidation of two cases that appeared in the first edition of this text, Cummins Engine Company, Inc. (A) and Cummins Engine Company, Inc. (B).

Cummins had made special efforts to penetrate the off-highway markets in recent years. The basic truck engines had been altered, permitting Cummins to make important inroads into the construction, industrial marine, and agricultural markets. In 1971 off-highway applications accounted for approximately 29% of Cummins's U. S. engine sales.

The major sector for Cummins in the off-highway market was construction equipment. This market consisted of crawler tractors, scrapers, dump trucks, cranes, etc. In the United States and Europe the major manufacturer was Caterpillar, which also manufactured its own engines and held 36% of the total market.

NEW STRATEGY

A new strategy was founded in an analysis of the company's objectives and the potential ways of achieving these objectives, given the characteristics of the environment in which Cummins would operate in the future. The corporate goals of Cummins were: (1) 15% annual growth in profits; (2) 15% return on shareholders' equity; and (3) maintaining highest standards of responsibility to all parties (individuals, community, shareholders, government). Achievement of these objectives in the 1950s and part of the 1960s evidenced the success of Cummins during that period. However, an analysis of the future showed that the potential growth of the power market, and diesel power in particular, would be less than in previous decades. Cummins's management estimated that no more than 8% or 10% of profit growth could be expected from this market in the future. Chances were high that if Cummins remained committed just to the diesel engine business, future results would fall short of company objectives. Management's response to this challenge was clear in the new strategy: Move into the most profitable parts of the engine business and move outside the engine business into other fields.

In finding ways to maximize Cummins's returns from the engine business, two major elements were studied: the strength of the company and the characteristics of the environment. Cummins's management knew that its technological leadership in the engine field and the superb network of distributors to service the ultimate customer were the two major factors placing Cummins in its prominent position. The actual manufacturing of the engines, though requiring skill, could be done equally well by many other producers. Therefore, Cummins's resources should be concentrated in designing and marketing engines—the areas in which Cummins had an advantage over other producers in the market. If Cummins were to concentrate in doing what they knew best, manufacturing should be done by Cummins's suppliers and *not* Cummins itself. An analysis of the economic environment led to similar conclusions. Cummins's present operations consisted of combining labor, capital, and technology to produce engines. A forecast of the behavior of these factors in the future showed a rising cost of money and labor and an accelerated pace in technological innovation. The rising cost of money indicated that this resource should be saved for high-return enterprises only. The rising cost of labor suggested that this resource should be used only at the highest potential level. Finally, the fast change in technology dictated a large degree of flexibility at all times to adjust to continuous changes. The combination of these three elements lead Cummins's management to conclude that Cummins should leave the capital-intensive process of manufacturing to somebody else. It should save its resources for high-yield operations and remain flexible in adopting new manufacturing technologies.

The second leg of the strategy, acquisition of companies in industries related to engines, was also based on the analysis that suggested the reduction in emphasis on manufacturing in the engine business. The rationale for going into engine-related fields was that Cummins could make use of its present network of distributors as well as its technological leadership to increase the return in these areas in which large commitment of capital in production was not necessary. The implementation of this part of the strategy led to the creation of Cummins Sundstrand, Inc., and Diesel ReCon, Inc., in 1971. Cummins Sundstrand sold and serviced transmissions produced by Sundstrand. Diesel ReCon operated an engine remanufacturing operation and was jointly owned by Cummins and thirty-five independent U. S. distributorships.

The third leg of the strategy, investment in emerging industries, was where the hopes for high growth in the long term were centered. Several industries were screened to meet Cummins's criteria for growth potential. Among these, the leisure business was chosen as the one with the highest expected growth. Following this concept, K2 Corporation, a leading manufacturer of fiberglass snow skis in the United States, was acquired in 1970.

THE KOMATSU VENTURE

The opportunity to start implementing the new strategy had finally been offered in early 1972, after a year of negotiations. Cummins Engine contemplated allowing a Japanese manufacturer, Komatsu, Ltd., to manufacture its super-powerful K-engine series. Under the plan, the recently designed K engines would be produced only in Japan. Cummins would first purchase the engine components and assemble them, but eventually the complete engines would be bought from the Japanese manufacturer at a prearranged price. This would be the first time that Cummins would depend on an external supplier for its products—in this case a new product that promised to be highly successful.

The K Engine

The concept of the K engine had been born in response to Cummins's perceptions of demand in the power market. It was estimated that the need for increased horsepower, especially in the United States, would soon exceed the predictable power growth of the company's products. It was forecast that very substantial markets would open up in the 400-600 horsepower and 800-1,200 horsepower markets during the 1970s.

March 1970 marked the birth of the K engine. At that time management gave approval to the new engine. Gross assumptions about the cost of building a new plant in the United States to produce the new engine and about the market that the K engine would command promised a return of 32.1% at the time.

While research and development improved the performance of the K engine, Mr. Hackett's financial department analyzed the project in detail. Confidence in the new project was bolstered when it was found that an extensive analysis of various assumptions about market volume and prices showed rates of return considerably higher than the company's required 15%. At the same time, a latent issue came to the forefront of the analysis: The K project would require an investment of $44 million to produce in the United States.

The large investment requirements of the new project clearly conflicted with the strategy of conservation of capital. Management reaction to this requirement was predictable within the context of the new strategy: A way to reduce the investment requirements had to be found. In the search, two new factors were brought to bear: (1) The company was committed to worldwide participation and (2) Cummins's largest competitor in the off-highway market, Caterpillar, was starting to make moves into the U.S. on-highway market. A combination of these two factors directed attention to one of Caterpillar's largest international competitors: Komatsu, Ltd., in Japan, with whom Cummins was well-acquainted. Through ten years of license agreements, Cummins had found that Komatsu not only had the capacity to undertake sizable orders for engine manufacturing, but it was also capable of producing engines to meet Cummins's high standards. It was soon clear that an extension of the relationship with Komatsu in the context of the K engine would accomplish two objectives: reduce the size of the required investment in the United States and strengthen the ties of a friendship that could pay high dividends later in terms of world markets. From a very early stage it was decided that steps should be taken so that Komatsu would manufacture some of the components of the new engine.

Komatsu, Ltd.

When first established in 1921, Komatsu, Ltd., was a local firm located in the Ishikawa Prefecture at the midpoint of the island. In 1971 Komatsu had sales of $785 million, and it ranked thirtieth among Japanese companies. Its main product, bulldozers, commanded a market share of 60% in Japan, even in the face of Caterpillar's expansion into Japan since 1963.

Komatsu was a vertically integrated equipment manufacturer. Its production facilities were as modern or more so than Cummins's facilities. The foundry factory, in particular, was far superior to what was commonly encountered in the United States. At the same time, the machining operations were as advanced as the technology used by Cummins itself. Labor-capital ratios were similar to those found at Cummins.

In addition to the prominent position of Komatsu in the Japanese capital markets, there were three factors that made Komatsu a desirable business partner to Cummins:

1. Its management under the leadership of Yoshini Kawai had shown insightfulness in anticipating market forces and boldness in approaching new business deals. Komatsu had consistently anticipated major changes

in trends in the Japanese markets that occurred after World War II and after the Korean War. Komatsu's management was one of the first groups of Japanese industrialists to carry on trade transactions with the Communist-bloc countries.

2. Komatsu had placed great emphasis in differentiating itself from top-level foreign brands through the quality of its products. The entry of Caterpillar into Japan through its joint venture with the Mitsubishi Heavy Industries Co. had been highly instrumental in inducing Komatsu to concentrate on better quality control.

3. Komatsu was placing an increasing emphasis on foreign markets. This effort in Komatsu had been combined with a strong resistance against foreign capital in Japan. Export sales had increased to $134 million by 1971 from $25 million in 1966. In 1971 Komatsu had made an organizational reshuffle on a big scale under the Overseas Division and had established as one of its goals to become a world enterprise in the true sense of the word.

Negotiations with Komatsu

The license agreement between Cummins and Komatsu was born of mutual incentives. Komatsu provided Cummins with access to the Japanese market. Cummins provided Komatsu with advanced technology. This technology allowed Komatsu to achieve a great success in some of its machinery. More recently, Cummins was a source of information on a new concept that was receiving increasing attention in Japan: sociability of the engines in terms of pollution controls. Cummins also provided Komatsu with a link to the U.S. market.

In spite of the ongoing relationship between Komatsu and Cummins, no great rapport had been developed between the two companies. Visits in 1971 by Mr. Miller, Chairman of the Board, and Mr. Schacht, President, to Japan showed that the major reason for the lack of a strong relationship between the two companies was poor communication. In the past Komatsu perceived that Cummins treated them as one more supplier to be used only when needed. Both Miller and Schacht agreed that Komatsu was in part justified in feeling that way. In these visits both Cummins men placed great emphasis on correcting Komatsu's views.

While Cummins top officials worked on the diplomatic side with Komatsu, John Hackett's financial department continued analyzing the K engine project under the two alternatives of manufacturing in the United States and subcontracting to Komatsu. The alternative of sourcing from Komatsu was based on having the Japanese company produce the components with the heaviest capital requirements in manufacture. Eight major components that required 75% of the investment were chosen as the basis for negotiations with Komatsu.

The general procedure followed was to compare Cummins cash outlays for each alternative on a present value basis and to determine the price that could be paid for the Japanese components so that the net present value of the two cash streams would be equal. The alternative of manufacturing in the United States had the largest outlay because of the initial investment. Sourcing from Japan required taking into account outlays for supporting costs such as supervision, transportation, travel, etc., plus the basic investment outlay for higher inventory and additional equipment to handle the shipments.

Negotiations during 1971 soon showed that Komatsu was not going to produce the components for less than the maximum price determined by Cummins. So negotiations proceeded on this basis and by the end of August 1971 Cummins top management gathered in Japan to complete the contract. However, on August 27 the Japanese government decided to allow the yen to float. Negotiations which were on the basis of a dollar price came to a standstill and Cummins management decided to come home to reconsider the whole affair. The initial term of the contract provided for Cummins to cover up to 3% of any exchange rate fluctuations; anything above that would have been absorbed by Komatsu. Prices and quantities would be fixed through 1976. If Cummins decided to pull out in 1976, it would pay Komatsu the net book value of the new equipment. If not, new price and quantity negotiations would occur based on the prior agreement.

Back in the United States, Hackett decided to reevaluate the project. New cost figures and more details about the engine were available from the research and development department. The analysis on which the previous negotiations had been based had been made with tentative figures only. John Walters, a recent MBA, was given the task of reviewing the project and making recommendations as his first assignment.

Walters first updated the data on the original project. Sales volume estimates were higher now but so were capital requirements and operating cost estimates. Walters thought that the inflation in the United States should be included in the estimates of costs of producing in the United States. In addition, regulations introduced by President Nixon such as the investment tax credit and the accelerated depreciation had to be taken into account. The analysis of the revised proposal to produce in the United States now showed a rate of return of 26.4%.

The next step was to compare the cash flows of producing in the United States with the alternative of sourcing from Japan to find the transfer price that would equate the two costs. Excerpts of Walters's final presentation on March 9, 1972, are presented in the Appendix.

The March 9th Meeting

After Walters concluded his presentation to Cummins top executives, several issues were raised in the succeeding discussion. Walters's analysis supported the option of sourcing from Japan. This was the approach that Cummins management perceived Schacht and Hackett preferred. However, during the two years that the new arrangement with Komatsu was being considered some executives made it clear that they did not favor this approach. The reasons for their disfavor were raised again in the March 9th meeting.

Henderson, executive vice president of manufacturing, voiced his concern about the quality control of products produced by Komatsu. Although on several occasions it had been shown that Komatsu's quality standards were at least as good as Cummins, operating people in the company were doubtful. In the past, all engine components had been manufactured under the supervision of Cummins's engineers who placed great emphasis on quality control. Using Komatsu as a source, production people contended, could endanger this position. However, it was also true that U.S. plant managers tended to mistrust anything not produced by Cummins, and they found some support for their views in Cummins's experiences with Krupp and Jaguar–joint ventures that had gone sour in the past because of technical difficulties.

Another problem appeared to be labor. At present, the workers at Cummins's major manufacturing facilities in Columbus, Indiana, were on a strike that was already three weeks old. Although Komatsu was not one of the major issues, the topic of foreign sources was.

It also was seen that the introduction of foreign sources would bring problems in terms of control and pricing. It would be difficult to compare profit margins of two products when one required the heavy investment of Cummins's Columbus headquarters and the other let another manufacturer provide the investment.

Appendix: Excerpts from John Walter's Presentation on the Komatsu Venture

Objectives

The objectives of this presentation are the following:

1. To review the alternative of having Cummins manufacture the complete K engine.

2. To analyze the alternative of sourcing major components in the K engine from Komatsu and to select an indifference transfer price which Cummins could pay Komatsu.

3. To evaluate the net financial effect of sourcing at the currently negotiated transfer price.

Assumptions

The set of assumptions which are common for the two alternatives are the following:

Market for Engines. The various models and horsepowers combined were estimated to provide the following market for the K engine:

Year	*No. of Units*	*Avg. Price*
1973	336	$8,060
1974	1,516	8,720
1975	2,917	8,770
1976	3,967	8,820
1977	4,971	8,760
1978	6,128	8,600
1979	7,316	8,610
1980	8,521	8,590
1981	9,814	8,520
1982	11,182	8,450
1983	12,459	8,420
1984	13,847	8,390
1985	15,174	8,370
Total	98,148	$8,510

These market figures have to be adjusted by a "draw factor." The K engine with low horsepower will overlap some of the high horsepower engines in the NH and V lines. Since we are looking for the incremental value of the K engine to Cummins, this draw effect must be eliminated from the K engine cash flows. This adjustment must be made to the revenues from the K engine and to the investment required. Only capital necessary to produce incremental K engine sales should be included in the analysis.

Other Assumptions. Manufacturing expenses, marketing expenses, engine warranty, service parts, support of research and development, and working capital requirements were allocated according to Cummins's past experience and cost accounting procedures. A tax rate of 48% was assumed, and allowance was made for investment tax credit and accelerated depreciation tax rules. The terminal value of the investment is the book value after straight-line depreciation. Working capital is returned 100%.

The Alternative of Manufacturing at Cummins

This alternative is based on capital requirements that will take into account any excess capacity in the present facilities. Investment in new facilities is made only when production demand for the K engine cannot be met with present plant and equipment.

Material and labor cost per unit take into account estimates by the research department, and assume a learning process in which costs per unit decline with time. The cumulative capital investment required from 1972 through 1985 would be $44 million. If one excludes the capital expenditures saved since some of the NH and V engines will not be produced now (the draw effect), the cumulative capital investment for the period is $39 million. The results from the previous assumptions about producing at Columbus provide a return on investment of 26.4% with a payback period of 7.8 years, shown in Exhibits A.1 and A.2 Exhibit A.2 also shows that the most critical assumption is the selling

EXHIBIT A.1. Producing All Engines in the United States: Cash Flow

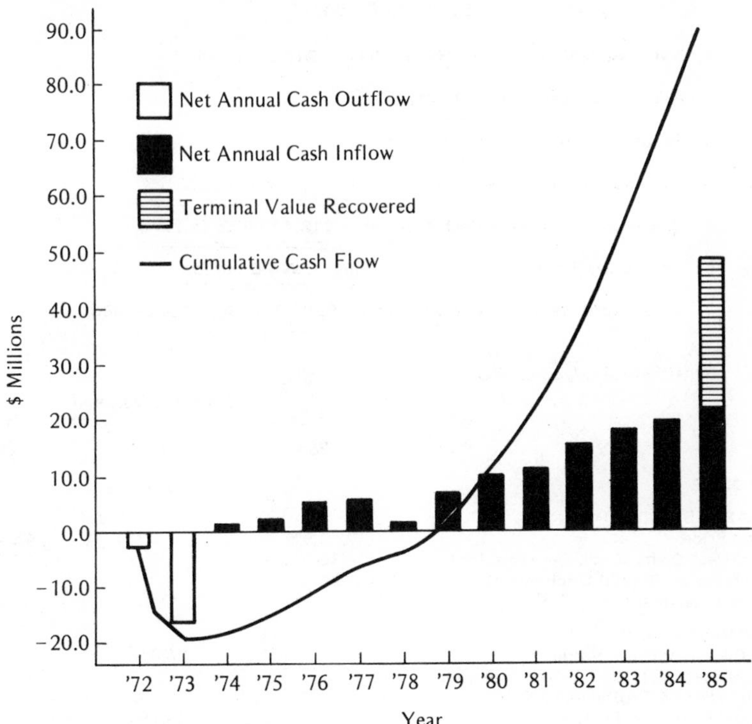

price. A 25% decrease in selling price would bring the rate of return in the project down to 3.9%. Second in importance is an increase in direct cost of 25%. This increase would reduce the return on the project to 14.3%.

The Alternative of Sourcing from Komatsu

Komatsu is being considered as a source of eight major components of the K engine family. If these components were produced domestically, they would require, through 1976, 77% of the total capital investment, 44% of the total material content, and 31% of the total labor content of the base K engine assembly.

The approach to the evaluation of this alternative was based in defining a transfer price that would leave Cummins indifferent financially between sourcing and not sourcing from Komatsu. This indifference point was defined as that transfer price which equated the net present value of cash flows under the sourcing alternative and the net present value of cash flows under the non-sourcing alternative. The following steps were followed: (1) cash flows associated with the *costs* of producing the eight major components domestically were estimated; (2) cash flows of the *costs* of sourcing were estimated; and (3) the indifference transfer prices which make the net present values of the two

EXHIBIT A.2. Producing All Engines in the United States: Summary Analysis

Summary Results

1. Net Present Value at 15% Hurdle Rate = $16.9 million
2. Return on Investment = 26.4%
3. Payback Period = 7.8 Years (in 1979)
4. Maximum Annual Cash Outflow = $15.8 million in 1973
5. Maximum Cumulative Cash Outflow = $18.4 million in 1973
6. Total Cash Flow (Excl. Terminal Value) = $94.6 million
7. Total Profit Before Tax and Interest = $230.3 million (1972–1985)

Sensitivity Analysis on ROI

	Change in Variable		
	-25%	*0*	*+25%*
BASE CASE		26.4%	
VARIABLES			
Selling Price	3.9%		42.4%
Unit Direct Costs (Excl. Depreciation)	36.9%		14.3%
Unit Volume (Capital Unchanged)	20.5%		31.6%
Capital Investment	30.7%		23.2%
TERMINAL VALUE			
Base Case–Net Book Value		26.4%	
Fixed Assets @ 15% of Gross Investment with Working Capital @ 100%		26.3%	
5 Years' Extended Profits		28.4%	
P/E Ratio at 12 X Earnings		33.9%	

alternative cash flows equivalent were found. That is, given that the gross revenues would be the same under both alternatives, the analysis of the transfer price was based on a comparison of costs under each alternative.

Exhibit A.3 shows the "outlay cash flow" under the alternative of producing the eight major components in the United States. If these eight components were produced in the United States, the total capital outlay required would be $18.4 million. The net present value of all outlays involved to manufacture these parts through 1985 discounted at 15% was $30.3 million.

If the decision to source from Komatsu is made, some special outlays will be necessary. These would include allowances for quality management, engineering, and inspection; receiving costs; miscellaneous research and development and manufacturing engineering; and an allowance for extra program management. The other assumption made was that Komatsu's costs would decline according to a learning curve, like Cummins's production costs in the United States. Therefore, the transfer price should also decline through time. Then, given the number of components required each year, the cash cost of producing them at home, and the cash cost excluding transfer price to source them from Komatsu, the appropriate transfer price was found by searching for a price that will provide a net present value of $30.3 million when discounted at 15%, the same as if Cummins produced the components itself. Exhibit A.4 presents

EXHIBIT A.3. Producing Components in the United States: Cost Cash Flows

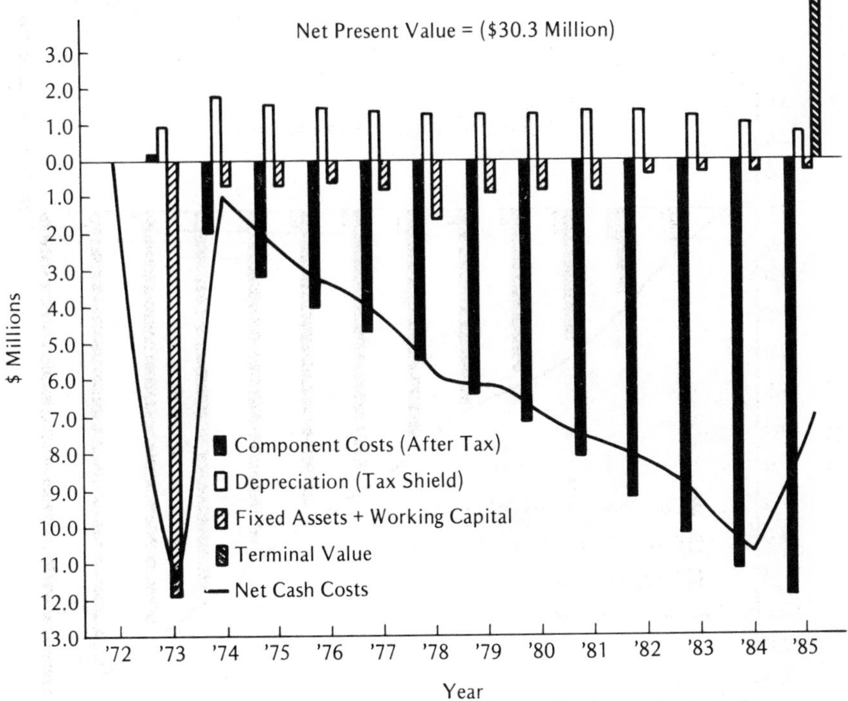

the cash flows for Cummins under the alternative of sourcing from Komatsu once the transfer price has been estimated. The net present value of the two alternatives is the same, by definition: $30.3 million.

Financial Implications

Because of the method used to estimate the transfer price for the sourcing alternative, the net present value of the two alternatives is the same. Cash costs devoted to the formation of capital assets for the production of the eight components under the alternative of total manufacture in the United States can be channeled completely into working capital and direct costs of the eight components in the sourcing alternative. Therefore, the transfer price for the components will contain a unit cost premium above their equivalent domestic direct unit cost. As a consequence, although the internal rate of return of the two alternatives is the same by definition, their impact on reported profits is not the same. Given that the quantity sold and the selling price per engine are independent of the mode of production, if the direct costs are larger under the sourcing alternative than under total domestic production, reported profits will be lower for the sourcing alternative. The impact of the two alternatives on reported after tax profits is presented in Exhibit A.5.

EXHIBIT A.4. Sourcing from Komatsu: Cost Cash Flows

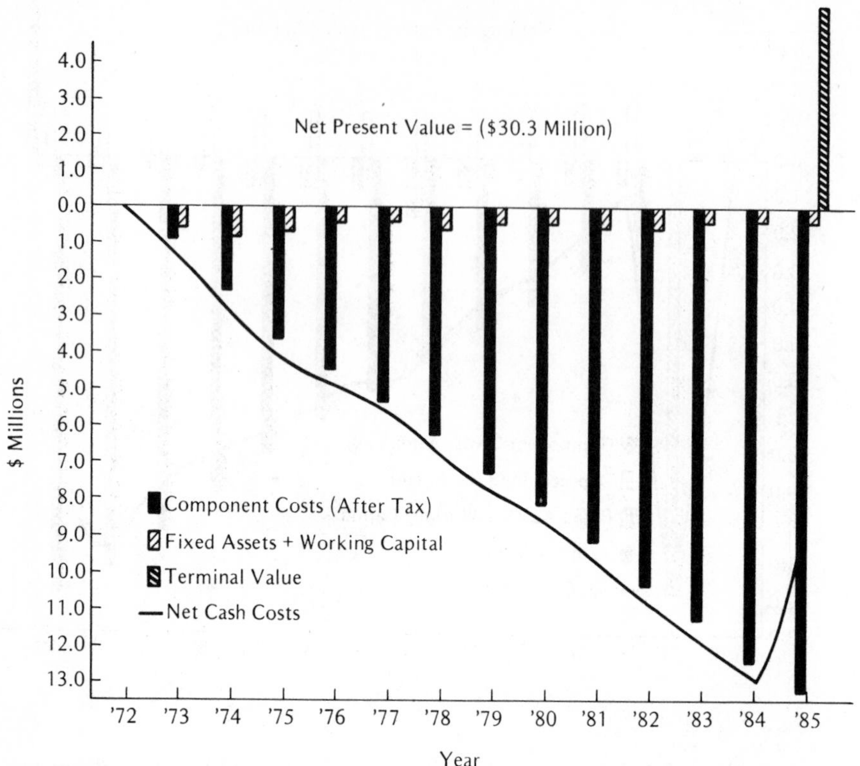

In evaluating these two alternatives, one more important financial point should be taken into account. The alternative of sourcing from abroad requires a much lower initial investment in the project than the alternative of manufacturing the components in the United States. Therefore, the alternative of sourcing will allow the company to undertake other projects, in addition to the K engine, with the same budget.

EXHIBIT A.5. Profits After Taxes: Producing All in United States Versus Sourcing Components (before interest charges)

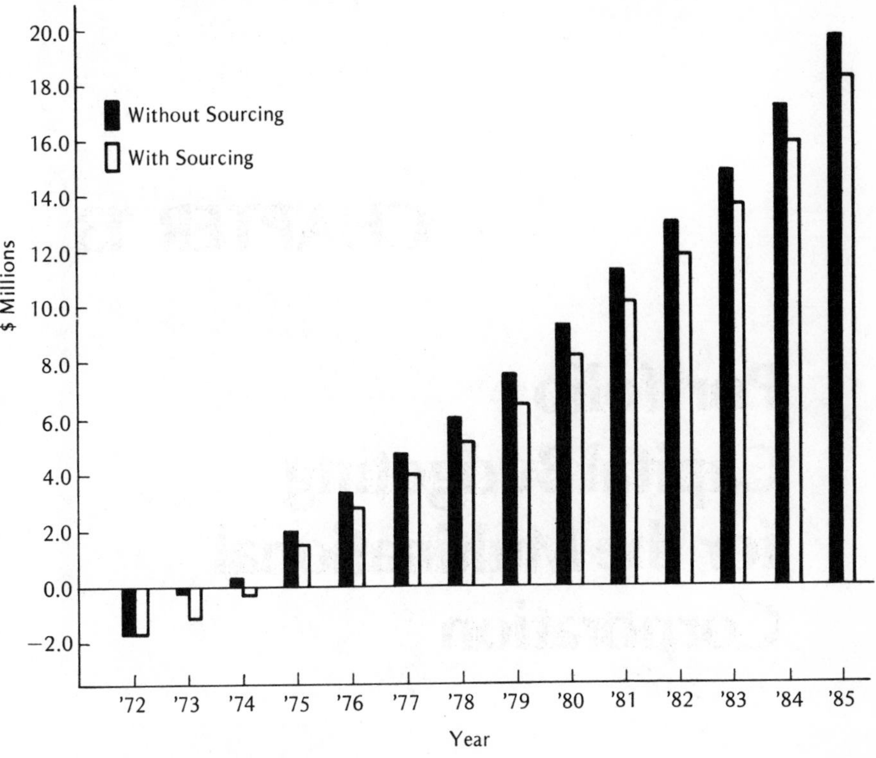

CHAPTER 13

Portfolio Capital Budgeting for the Multinational Corporation

Because of risk and multiple goals, the firm is concerned with project interdependencies now (current) and over time (intertemporal). The firm's investment in a product line now may provide opportunities for future investments which the firm might not have seen and/or which the corporation would not have had the ability to develop in the absence of today's project. Hence, these interdependencies over time are part of the strategic budgeting process discussed in the preceding chapter.

The study of the impact of project interdependencies and diversification on the firm's capital budgeting procedure was delayed until research into security portfolios was transferred to nonfinancial businesses. Thus, this chapter begins with a review of the evidence of how diversification affects the international security portfolio. Then the second part of the chapter applies the principles of portfolio theory to the capital budgeting decision in an international setting. In this context a technique for responding to the complexities of risk, multiple goals, and diversification interdependencies is presented.

DIVERSIFICATION: THE INTERNATIONAL SECURITY PORTFOLIO EVIDENCE

There is now evidence relating to the benefit of international security portfolio diversification. Much of the effort has been related to equities and corporate bond performance in various nations, and there are serious limitations to the findings. However, the criticisms of the research methodologies do not mean that the conclusions are inaccurate; rather, the criticisms at worst say that there is a Scotch verdict: The conclusions are not proved.

The concept having major impact on the evaluation of security portfolios was developed by Markowitz[1] and Tobin.[2] This framework suggests that the risk averse investor can diversify over a security universe by selecting those securities which provide portfolios with maximum expected return for a given variability in that return, or, alternatively, seek portfolios which have minimum variability for a given level of expected return. There is a family of portfolios tracing a curve with each portfolio having greater expected return and greater variance or lower expected return and lower variance than any of its neighbors. (For a graphical presentation, see Exhibit 13.3.) The investor can select the risk-return trade-off. These are *efficient portfolios;* all other portfolios are either inefficient (offering lower expected returns for the same variability, for example) or infeasible (having greater expected returns and the same variability since by definition the efficient set of portfolios has maximum return for a given variability). If borrowing and lending opportunities are available, it may be possible for the investor to move to a position of greater utility based on one of the efficient portfolios and suitable amounts of borrowed or loaned funds; hence, the Tobin term "separability," in that the decision on the optimum portfolio and the decision on how much to borrow can be made independently; the borrowing or lending strategy still utilizes one of the efficient portfolios in the final decision.

These models for investment decision have been applied in the U.S. security market. In addition, extensions of the analysis in a slightly different framework have been used to evaluate performance of mutual funds *ex post* by comparing them to a market portfolio combined with borrowing-lending options open to a naive investor. This investor buys a well-diversified market portfolio and then borrows or lends to move to a suitable composite asset position. As these results have been extended to the international securities market, the researchers have often faced severe difficulties and lack of conformity to an economically competitive market.

There are various articles reviewing the effects of diversification using international security and bond portfolios. Building on the basic Markowitz and Tobin framework, Grubel[3] showed the effects of diversification using market indices in eleven countries, arguing that U.S. investors could gain from such inter-

[1] Harry Markowitz, *Portfolio Selection: Efficient Diversification of Investments* (New York: John Wiley and Sons, 1959).

[2] James Tobin, "Liquidity Preference as Behavior Toward Risk," *Review of Economic Studies,* Feb. 1958, pp. 65–86.

[3] Herbert G. Grubel, "Internationally Diversified Portfolios: Welfare Gains and Capital Flows," *American Economic Review,* Dec. 1968, pp. 1299–1314.

national diversification. Then, using indices of stock market performance for twenty-eight countries, Levy and Sarnat[4] evaluated the benefits of diversification across national borders using data from the 1951–1967 period. They found that investments in the U.S. and Japanese stocks would have been 50–70% of optimal portfolios, largely because of the negative correlations during this period between the stock market indices in these two lands. Predictably, because of the high positive correlation of Western European countries and the U.S. stock market performance in the same period, investment in the securities of the European nations was small. Investments in developing countries were usually recommended in the final portfolio because of diversification effects, even though the standard deviation of investment returns in underdeveloped countries' securities was often very large.

Using ten nations and an evaluation of the arithmetic average of yields on long-term government bonds in those countries, Miller and Whitman[5] similarly considered the benefits of diversification, although they ignored covariances between the returns on European and American securities. The separation theorem implies that choice between risky and riskless assets can be made independently, *not* that choices among two segregated portfolios of risky assets can be made independently, the pattern followed by Miller and Whitman.

Evaluating weekly, one-month, and two-month rates of return of industry subindices for securities traded in the United States, the United Kingdom, and West Germany from January 1, 1965, to June 30, 1967, Grubel and Fadner[6] found that positive correlation among various pairs of assets was an increasing function of holding period (implying that random short-run effects may cause lower correlations in those periods) but that average correlation levels were still greater for within-country comparisons than for between-country comparisons. For the period in which they evaluated the securities, they acknowledged that the currencies' exchange rates were stable. The instability of the more recent years might create even less correlation of between-country industry index comparisons, suggesting even greater benefits from the intercountry portfolio diversification, given that lower correlation improves the portfolio in a risk/return sense for a constant expected return.

Agmon[7] argues for a weak support of the one-market approach to the world security markets, although the author cautiously notes that his results are not inconsistent with a segmented market. A one-market view holds that arbitrage between national security markets is sufficient to create an equilibrium. Although the Agmon study has been criticized for having results that were not inconsistent with the segmented market hypotheses (which the author acknowledged) and for other statistical difficulties, the remaining problem which seems

[4] Haim Levy and Marshall Sarnat, "International Diversification of Investment Portfolios," *American Economic Review,* Sept. 1970, pp. 668–675.

[5] Norman C. Miller and Marina v. N. Whitman, "A Mean-Variance Analysis of United States Long-Term Portfolio Foreign Investment," *Quarterly Journal of Economics,* May 1970, pp. 175–196.

[6] Herbert G. Grubel and Kenneth Fadner. "The Interdependence of International Equity Markets," *Journal of Finance,* March 1971, pp. 89–94.

[7] Tamir Agmon, "The Relations Among Equity Markets: A Study of Share Price Co-Movements in the United States, United Kingdom, Germany and Japan," *Journal of Finance,* Sept. 1972, pp. 839–855.

to plague most of the international studies is that the results they obtain are not sufficient to prove or to disprove any case; they can be consistent with a number of different hypotheses about the structure of the international capital markets and their risk interdependence or risk independence.[8]

Lessard presents results for sixteen major countries' market returns for recent years using monthly data of various periods.[9] The results are consistent with either segmented or integrated world markets. From his careful work, he concludes that U.S. investors lost little if they were not diversified across many countries because the U.S. market is such a large percentage of any world market measure. In the absence of severe barriers to international investment, most other investors, except for Canadians, endured greater risks for a given return ex post if they constrained themselves to a domestic portfolio rather than investing in a fully diversified world portfolio. In an equally-weighted-by-country world market index, a relatively low proportion of domestic variance in a national market index was explained by a world market factor. Individual *securities* typically had more of their variance explained by country factors than by industry elements using an equally weighted market index. Using weekly stock market indices data for twelve countries from 1963–72, Panton, Lessig, and Joy found using cluster analysis that these indices have substantial co-movement and that the co-movements persist over time.[10]

There are other problems with most of these studies. The first criticism is that a national index of security prices may not be an efficient portfolio from the standard risk/return model of Tobin and Markowitz, although it may approach it. Second, the national index is only one portfolio, not the set of efficient (national) portfolios. Third, there is a question of whether inclusion of some of the securities of another nation would aid the diversification more than inclusion of the whole portfolio (i.e., the index) of another nation's security universe. Fourth, any evaluation of portfolio diversification in terms of the random walk hypothesis must reckon with Solnik[11] and McDonald.[12] Among others, these authors note imperfections in the European stock market

[8] For a criticism of the Agmon paper, see Michael Adler and R. Hoersch, "The Relationship Among Equity Markets: Comment," *Journal of Finance,* Sept. 1974, pp. 1311–1317. Then see Bruno Solnik's further efforts in this regard ("The International Pricing of Risk; An Empirical Investigation of the World Capital Market Structures," *Journal of Finance,* May 1974, pp. 365–378) and the resulting criticism by Buckner Wallingford ("Discussion: The International Pricing of Risk," *Journal of Finance,* May 1974, pp. 392–395). Solnik notes the impact of the various national markets, but he argues that his results are consistent with an international capital asset pricing model which takes into account both national and international portfolios; see his "An International Market Model of Security Price Behavior," *Journal of Financial and Quantitative Analysis,* Sept. 1974, pp. 537–554.

[9] Donald Lessard, "World, Country, and Industry Relationships in Equity Returns: Implications for Risk Reduction Through International Diversification," *Financial Analysts Journal,* Jan.-Feb. 1976, pp. 32–38.

[10] Don B. Panton, V. Parker Lessig, and Maurice Joy, "Comovement of International Equity Markets: A Taxonomic Approach," *Journal of Financial and Quantitative Analysis,* Sept. 1976, pp. 415–432.

[11] Bruno Solnik, *European Capital Markets* (Lexington, Mass.: D. C. Heath/Lexington Books, 1973).

[12] John G. McDonald, "French Mutual Fund Performance: Evaluation of Internationally Diversified Portfolios," *Journal of Finance,* Dec. 1973, pp. 1161–1180.

price behavior when analyzed on the same basis as the U.S. studies of the random walk model. Fifth, Solnik cogently argues that the nature of the data available and the quality of the tests that have been used are not sufficient to determine whether markets are completely segmented or integrated[13]; contrary to the Panton et al. study, Solnik notes that there is often low covariance between national markets, which results in international benefits from diversification. Sixth, the question of what numeraire to use for the investor is unsettled; different currencies used as a standard, or different currency bundles, suggest very different conclusions about diversification of portfolios and the international pricing of securities in an efficient markets view of the world.

Finally, the multinational corporate manager is concerned with project diversification, which is not necessarily the same as security diversification.

DOES DIVERSIFICATION EXIST FOR THE NONFINANCIAL BUSINESS?

If we substitute projects for securities in the preceding discussion, we can extend the analysis of security portfolios to capital budgeting.

Consistent with basic capital budgeting theory, higher returns can be obtained only by assuming higher risks. But because of the covariance elements, the portfolio that allows the firm to diversify results earns a surplus return if there are benefits from diversification: The total risk of the diversified firm is lower than the simple sum of the risks of the component projects on their own. In this sense, the corporation can achieve through diversification among projects the same results as the individual investor who diversified among companies.

Whether or not the corporation can do better than the individual investor depends on the corporation's access to projects which the individual cannot invest in directly. If one believes that the corporation has an advantage over individuals in diversification skills, then the total risk of the corporation for the given level of expected return may be lower than what investors could obtain independently for that expected return. This would be the case because the lower risk is available only to investors in the diversified corporation and not to investors who carve their investments from among the company's projects.

The ability of the corporation to create special diversification opportunities is challenged on two grounds. One, the cost of monitoring and coordinating the broadly diversified firm may exceed any potential benefits from the spreading of risk. Alternatively, some critics discount the existence of benefits from corporate diversification. They argue that the investor can adequately diversify (through investment in a mutual fund). Of course, these two criticisms are not inconsistent with each other. If both are granted, the broadly diversified firm is economically inefficient, for there is a net cost of coordination that is not offset by any diversification benefits unrealizable by individual investors on their own!

The corporation probably can diversify more efficiently than individuals in

[13] Bruno Solnik, "Testing International Asset Pricing: Some Pessimistic Views," *Journal of Finance,* May 1977, pp. 503–512.

the multinational setting. In addition to information advantages regarding international opportunities, the major corporation has the ability to use special experience in an industry, to negotiate tax and repatriation agreements, and to marshal a large pool of resources.

In the following two sections we apply the concepts of portfolio theory to capital budgeting. First, we evaluate the total risk of a portfolio of projects of the firm. Then we review the implications of security diversification for the acceptance criterion of the firm.

PORTFOLIO INTERRELATIONSHIPS—THE VARIANCE OF THE PORTFOLIO

Introduction

In our discussion of risk analysis in Chapter 11 we used variance as a measure of the project's dispersion. Although there are limitations to this approach, it is helpful to focus on variance (or its square root, the standard deviation) as one measure by which the corporate officer may evaluate project risk and portfolio risk.

Variance is a measure of the variability in outcome of a project on some particular dimension. But how does one compute the variance of a portfolio of projects? Suppose that three projects are considered by Freeport Minerals. Each is a nickel plant, with one each in two Australian states and one in Ghana. Each project has an expected return and standard deviation. Freeport wants to invest in two plants, but it is unsure of which two are preferred. The standard deviation of an investment in the two Australian plants may be very close to the sum of each plant's standard deviation; each of them shares most of the same risks with respect to the world nickel market, costs in Australia, the value of the American dollar, inflation, and so on. They have high positive *correlation.*

On the other hand, the standard deviation in return on the same money invested in the Ghana plant and either one of the Australian plants may be substantially less than the simple sum of the two project's standard deviations. There is obvious diversification. Freeport has reason to hope that a labor strike or severe inflation or devaluation in one country, for example, would not necessarily follow in the other. It is true that both pairs of investments are subject to the same technological and world market conditions of nickel, but there is a benefit from spreading the risk geographically.

Finally, Freeport management might elect more diversification by investing in one Australian nickel plant and a zinc operation in Peru. There is then geographic diversification and product diversification.

These examples should present intuitive reasons for rejecting project standard deviation sums as a measure of portfolio risk. The standard deviation or variance pays no heed to any other project. Accordingly, another statistical measure is involved, the covariance. Between each project and every other project, the covariance can be computed, and it is a measure of their *joint* riskiness. Further, the variance of a portfolio of two or more projects can be found by combining the respective variances and covariances.

As an example, assume that three of the projects mentioned have the following mean, standard deviation, and covariance figures:

	Nickel Projects		Zinc Mine
	Australia	Ghana	Peru
Mean return	0.20	0.25	0.20
Standard deviation	0.10	0.25	0.12
Covariances	Australia–Ghana: 0.020	Ghana–Peru: 0.006	Australia–Peru: 0.0024

From these figures one can compute the various portfolios returns and variances from investing in the combinations of projects shown in Exhibit 13.1. These calculations assume that there are equal dollar investments required in each investment. The portfolio return is

$$R = \sum_{i=1}^{n} a_i r_i$$

where $i = 1$ to n reflects the projects in the portfolio, a_i is the fraction of the budget invested in each project (and $\sum_{i=1}^{n} a_i = 1$), and r_i is the return of project i.

The standard deviation of the portfolio return is

$$S = \sqrt{\sum_{i=1}^{n} a_i^2 S_i^2 + \sum_{i=1}^{n} \sum_{j=1}^{n} a_i a_j S_{ij}} \quad (i \neq j)$$

where S is the standard deviation of the portfolio, a_i and a_j are as defined before, S_i is the standard deviation of project i, and S_{ij} is the covariance between projects i and j. The covariance (S_{ij}) between projects is the correlation between projects i and j (ρ_{ij}) times the standard deviation of each project, or $\rho_{ij} \times S_i \times S_j$.

Using these same formulas, one can compute the portfolio figures by using the assumption of a normal distribution for other criteria: terminal return, net present value, earnings per share in a given year, growth rate in sales, and so on.[14]

[14]The formulae for combining the figures are slightly altered from this model in some cases; one cannot use the basic rate of return equations shown here which parallel the investment security example. See E. Eugene Carter, *Portfolio Aspects of Corporate Capital Budgeting* (Lexington, Mass.: D. C. Heath and Company, 1974), pp. 83–88, for an explanation of this difference.

EXHIBIT 13.1. Portfolio Returns and Variances

Australian/Ghanaian Nickel Operation

Return: $= .5(.20) + .5(.25) = .225$ or $\underline{\underline{22.5\%}}$

Standard Deviation:

$$= \sqrt{.25(.10)^2 + .25(.25)^2 + 2 \times .25 \times (.020)}$$
$$= \sqrt{.028125}$$
$$= .168 \text{ or } \underline{\underline{16.8\%}}$$

Zinc Mine/Australian Nickel Operation

Return: $= .5(.20) + .5(.20) = .20$ or $\underline{\underline{20\%}}$

Standard Deviation:

$$= \sqrt{.25(.10)^2 + .25(.12)^2 + 2 \times .25 \times (.0024)}$$
$$= \sqrt{.0073}$$
$$= .085 \text{ or } \underline{\underline{8.5\%}}$$

Zinc Mine/Ghanaian Nickel Operation

Return: $= .5(.25) + .5(.20) = .225$ or $\underline{\underline{22.5\%}}$

Standard Deviation:

$$= \sqrt{.25(.25)^2 + .25(.12)^2 + 2 \times .25 \times (.006)}$$
$$= \sqrt{.02223}$$
$$= .149 \text{ or } \underline{\underline{14.9\%}}$$

All Three Projects

Return: $= .33(.20) + .33(.25) + .33(.20) = .215$ or $\underline{\underline{21.5\%}}$

Standard Deviation:

$$= \sqrt{.11(.10)^2 + .11(.25)^2 + .11(.12)^2 + 2 \times .11 \times (.02) + 2 \times .11 \times (.006) + 2 \times .11 \times (.0024)}$$
$$= \sqrt{.015807}$$
$$= .126 \text{ or } \underline{\underline{12.6\%}}$$

Joint and Interactive Simulation

Risk analysis on the basis of individual projects can be done as described in the Freeport example in Chapter 11. A joint simulation of projects must be completed, however, in order to derive covariances among the projects.[15] In a joint simulation the outcome of each project is computed for a given trial, a sample of projects, and stored in relation to the outcome of all the other projects on that trial. Then the sampling process is reinitialized and the simulation repeated. Hence, when projects are dependent on some common variable (such as GNP, growth in a particular area of the economy, and so on), this assurance of a common value for those underlying factors is critical. From these data it is possible to compute the mean, variance, and covariance of the projects on each criterion since the simulation trials store values of each project's outcome in conjunction with all other projects' outcomes on a given trial.

Given multiple goals of managers, a useful approach is an interactive computer model. Assume the manager is concerned about ten major criteria: sales, earnings per share, and cash flow for each of three years; and the net present value. By providing a range of computing options which enable the manager to see the results of various portfolio combinations, the model permits selection of the final portfolio in a rapid manner. Nothing in this model would prevent using any of the mathematical programming formulations for starting portfolios. The manager would want to resimulate the final portfolio to obtain a detailed distribution of returns and outcomes since the model operates on the normality assumptions which are probably not valid for the actual outcomes.

As an example, there may have been a general decision made by the firm about the type of projects which are to be reviewed; the joint simulation is then completed. These variance-covariance data are inserted into the interactive model and the executive faces a computer terminal, provided with information such as shown in Exhibit 13.2.

[15]The most evasive measure on any standard to be evaluated is likely to be the estimate of covariance between projects. If correlation of returns among the projects is known, one can compute the covariance, and vice versa. Using the assumptions of normality, there are two other ways of estimating the portfolio figures.

First, one may ask managers to specify correlation between projects. This task is difficult to accomplish even if the manager is thoroughly familiar with the concept. If it is possible in a given situation, such correlations can generate the covariance matrix. On the other hand, if the existing firm is huge in relation to any proposed project, the loss in accuracy in the variance of firm and project portfolio is nominal when the correlations between new projects are ignored. Rather, all that must be estimated is the correlation of each new project with the existing firm's asset base or some market standard.

A second approach is to use equivalent formulae which allow an estimate of the maximum variance in portfolio net present values from some compendium of project present value variances, ignoring the covariances between projects or between projects and the firm/"market."

Under either alternative, there is a nontrivial problem created given the possible combinations that can occur for a portfolio of projects. Thus, if one calculates all possible combinations of projects, and analyzes the outcomes, the task is enormous. A portfolio of one to twenty potential projects would involve computing over one million combinations unless some simplifying rule is used.

EXHIBIT 13.2.

WHEN THE COMPUTER TYPES -OPTION?- PLEASE ANSWER WITH ONE OF THE RESPONSES SHOWN BELOW

OPTION	DESCRIPTION
=======	===
NP	STARTS A NEW PORTFOLIO
PC	PORTFOLIO CONTENTS
EC	LIST PROJECT ENTRY COSTS
IP	LIST ILLEGAL PROJECT COMBINATIONS
A	ADD A NEW PROJECT TO YOUR PORTFOLIO
D	DELETE A PROJECT FROM YOUR PORTFOLIO
P	PORTFOLIO STATISTICS
SP	SHORT PORTFOLIO OUTPUT
C	COMBINE PROJECTS
MR	RANK PROJECTS BY MEAN VALUES
VR	RANK PROJECTS BY VARIABILITY (STD. DEV.)
END	STOPS PROGRAM

WHEN THE COMPUTER TYPES -CRITERION?- PLEASE ANSWER WITH ONE RESPONSE SHOWN BELOW

CRITERION	DESCRIPTION
==========	===
S1	SALES IN YEAR 1
S2	SALES IN YEAR 2
S3	SALES IN YEAR 3
CF1	CASH FLOW IN YEAR 1
CF2	CASH FLOW IN YEAR 2
CF3	CASH FLOW IN YEAR 3
EPS1	EARNINGS PER SHARE IN YEAR 1
EPS2	EARNINGS PER SHARE IN YEAR 2
EPS3	EARNINGS PER SHARE IN YEAR 3
NPV	NET PRESENT VALUE

In this program, the executive has a number of filtering options available:

1. The program may be used to determine *portfolio* data. It presents the capital outlay and the results on any of the criteria for any combination of projects legally allowed. The program would include interest cost for any debt used.

2. *Confidence levels* using normality assumptions may be printed for the portfolios chosen by the executive on any criteria. These confidence intervals are derived by using the standard deviations of the portfolio to compute 25%/75%, 10%/90%, 5%/95%, and 1%/99% ranges for the criteria required by the executive.

3. *Comparison options* permit the executive to study the effectiveness of the proposed portfolio vis-à-vis the current operation in meeting various

goals for future years. Based upon statistical compilations in the program, the executive could view the probability that earnings per share in the second year would be no less under the proposed portfolio than expected second-year earnings per share of the existing firm alone. These probabilities are explicitly presented for each of the ten criteria.

4. *Portfolio-project comparisons* allow the executive to view how the proposed portfolio would be altered on each of the ten criteria by adding or deleting a particular project. These results are similar to those obtained for the existing firm/portfolio comparison. The comparison would indicate the amount by which the expected values and standard deviations of the portfolio would be changed by addition or deletion of a project.

5. *Mean search* routines permit the executive to seek altered values from the expected outcome of the portfolio on any criterion. When using this option, the manager may indicate the criterion and the number of proposals desired (N). The program will return the N projects with the greatest effect in increasing or decreasing the expected value under consideration. The program would review all projects, those currently in the proposed portfolio, or those currently out of the proposed portfolio as requested. The manager's specification will depend upon whether the desire is to eliminate projects from the portfolio which have an unfavorable impact on a criterion (e.g., a binding budget constraint and low earnings per share in the first year) or to add projects which would increase an outcome (e.g., projects to boost sales in the second year).

6. *Variance search* routines require the manager to input the same information as under the mean search routine. The program searches for those projects in and/or out of the current portfolio which most increase or decrease the variance on a given criterion.

Naturally, nothing requires the use of these goals. The manager might favor these goals plus an average growth in earnings per share for the next five or ten years, or plus a certain percentage of sales/earnings from major regions of the world or major product lines.

Multiperiod decisions when the future portfolio opportunities are not known compound the problem. One option is to build in probable funds requirements and returns for future projects, penalizing the projects under current review if they do not generate sufficient cash flows in particular future periods. In addition, only by earmarking particular debt sources for unique opportunities can the viability of special financing options applicable only to given projects be included in such a model. The benefits of pooled resources providing better debt rates than the simple sum of the individual projects can be taken into account with the subsequent resimulation of the desirable portfolio after use of the inter active model.[16]

[16]These issues are discussed in detail in Carter, *Portfolio Aspects of Corporate Capital Budgeting,* Ch. 8.

THE CAPITAL ASSET PRICING MODEL

An alternative to evaluating the covariance between projects to obtain a portfolio that meets a suitable risk/return profile for the corporation is to obtain the discount rate appropriate for specific projects with given risk characteristics. We discussed this topic earlier in Chapter 11. However, at that time we concentrated on the total risk of the firm and ignored the issue of possible security diversification by stockholders. The ability of stockholders to diversify their investments reduces the total risk these individuals see in specific companies. When this fact is taken into account, the discount rate that the firm uses as an acceptance criterion must be modified accordingly. One model that incorporates these concepts is the capital asset pricing model (CAPM).

Briefly, the CAPM suggests that the relevant discount rate for a project is based on the covariance between that project and the *market portfolio* (i.e., some well-diversified efficient portfolio that holds all corporate project portfolios). This covariance is combined with estimates of the expected *market return* and the return from a *risk-free asset* to determine the required return for the project.

The prescriptions of the CAPM are based on the conclusion that, optimally, the investor will purchase combinations of the market portfolio and the risk-free asset. The line connecting these possible combinations is called the *market line.* This market line, shown in Exhibit 13.3, provides the trade-offs between risk and return available to the investor. An investor who placed half the funds in the risk-free asset and half in the market portfolio would have an expected return which is half the sum of these two expected returns. Furthermore, given zero correlation between the risk-free return and the market return, the standard deviation of return (the risk) would also fall halfway between the two standard

EXHIBIT 13.3. The Market Portfolio and the Market Line

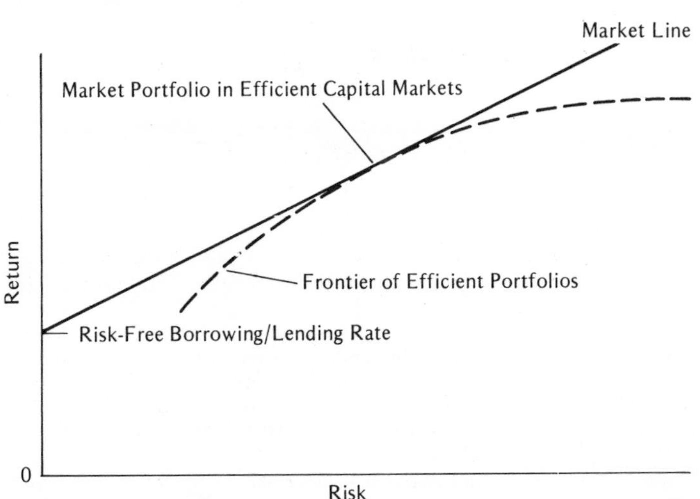

deviations. Other proportions between the risk-free asset and the market portfolio would fall on the line traced in Exhibit 13.3.[17]

Given forecasts of the market return and variability, the risk-free rate, and the various project returns under different market outcomes, then the minimum required rate of return can be determined. If the project returns more than this minimum, it is a desirable investment.

Although derived from slightly different precepts, the capital asset pricing model approach parallels the beta analysis which has had an impact in security portfolio selection. This analysis says that one can compare the return of a portfolio (R_P) to the risk-free return (R_F) and the market return (R_M) through the following formulation:

$$(1) \qquad (R_P - R_F) = a + \beta(R_M - R_F)$$

Beta (β) is the measure of the volatility of the security or portfolio (i.e., mutual fund) with respect to the market return. Beta is the covariance of the security with the market divided by the variance of the market return. Alpha is a measure of any excess return for the mutual fund or security above what is required given its volatility. A negative alpha implies that the return of the fund or security over the periods evaluated was not sufficient to compensate investors for its volatility.

For *project* evaluations, the alpha is removed and one rearranges terms to solve for R_E, the required return on equity in the project. This gives the result that[18]

$$(2) \qquad R_E = \beta(R_M - R_F) + R_F$$

or, since $\beta = \dfrac{\sigma_{EM}}{\sigma_M^2}$,

$$R_E = \frac{\sigma_{EM}}{\sigma_M^2}(R_M - R_F) + R_F$$

$$= R_F\left(1 - \frac{\sigma_{EM}}{\sigma_M^2}\right) + R_M \frac{\sigma_{EM}}{\sigma_M^2}$$

Using the traditional approach to cost of capital presented in Chapter 11, we see that the required project return will be a weighted function of the returns

[17]If one does not believe that the capital markets are efficient, then the market line traced as a ray from the risk-free rate will not necessarily be tangent at the market portfolio but would be tangent at some other point. However, the strategy outlined here is still open to a naive security or project investor: The investment is split between some broad market investment and a risk-free security.

[18]σ_{EM}/σ_M^2 represents the covariance between the equity and market returns divided by the variance of the market return.

and proportionate financing of debt and equity in the project's financing, or

$$R_{\text{Project}} = R_E \left(\frac{E}{D+E}\right) + R_D \left(\frac{E}{D+E}\right) \tag{3}$$

where R_E is found as shown in the previous paragraph by using the covariance of the project and the market and an estimated beta.

Even if beta can be estimated from similar projects or the returns of similar firms in the market, if there is any leverage the observed beta will not be the same as the beta for a firm/project with different leverage. Then the manager must decide how to compute a cost of capital for a project with leverage which differs from the standard computed above.

One approach is to first compute the beta for the equity in a no-debt project (β_E). Suppose that one uses the Modigliani-Miller argument that the only increase in value for a levered firm comes from the tax deductibility of debt interest. The value of this tax shield can be subtracted from the total market value of the levered firm's debt and equity, or the similar firm which represents the proposed project. In the case of perpetual debt the cumulative value of the tax savings from the debt interest is the tax rate, T, of the firm times the value of the debt $[TD]$. In other cases the present value of all the future interest payments after tax discounted at the pre-tax debt rate must be computed directly. These calculations provide the value of the firm under 100% equity financing once the increment in observed market value derived from the tax deductibility of interest is eliminated. Using historical data for the existing firm/project or comparable firms, one could obtain data on the return in total value for the firm in each period.

For example, if the value, V, is the sum of equity and debt, and it is also equal to the value under all equity, V_A, plus the tax savings of perpetual debt (TD) by assumption, then the value of the all-equity firm is equal to the observed equity value plus $(1 - T)\,D$, or

$$V = E + D = V_A + TD \tag{4}$$

$$V_A = E + (1 - T)D \tag{5}$$

The return in each period for the all-equity firm is the *change* in this total value plus the income, which is the Dividend (Div) and Interest income (C), divided by beginning value, or

$$\frac{V_{A_{t+1}}}{V_{A_t}} = \frac{E_{t+1} + Div + C + (1 - T)D_{t+1}}{E_t + (1 - T)D_t} \tag{6}$$

If this valuation is completed for each historical or hypothetical future period, its volatility can be evaluated in the capital asset pricing model equation shown in (2). This analysis provides the estimate of the β_E, for by definition the value of the all-equity firm and its volatility coincide with the value of the equity and the volatility of the equity.[19]

Again, assume the perpetual debt case and the Modigliani-Miller conclusion that the increment in value from leverage arises only from the tax deductibility of interest. Then the cost of capital will be the cost of equity with no debt (using the β_E, R_M, and R_F from the earlier estimates) times the product of one minus the tax rate times the proportion of debt in the firm/project, or

$$(7)\quad R_P = [\beta_E(R_M - R_F) + R_F]\left[1 - (\text{Tax Rate})\left(\frac{\text{Additional debt}}{\text{Value of no-debt project}}\right)\right]$$

This assumes that the cost of debt, R_D, is the same as R_F and that there is perpetual debt. This calculation also ignores the effect of bankruptcy on the value of the firm (i.e., value will increase up to 99% debt), but the assumption may not be unreasonable for acceptable levels of debt, especially if assets can be sold in bankruptcy at their market value. Also ignored is the common situation in which the bankruptcy of the firm depends on total risk of all projects, not just one project. The usual assumptions of the CAPM (homogeneous expectations, no transaction costs, perfectly divisible securities, no taxes, fixed quantities of all assets, a sufficiently large number of investors so that all are price takers, and no cost of information which is fully and immediately available to all investors) are sufficient for the one-period proofs to hold.

These assumptions may be violated in international markets. For example, manipulation is a regular feature of many foreign stock markets for several reasons. First, accounting standards are usually lower throughout the world than in the United States, as noted in Chapter 8, so that data are not available or are not believable. Rumors can be started with little to refute them. Second, low margin requirements, if any, permit a small amount of money to be leveraged by an operator. Finally, the size of the float of securities as well as the smaller size of many companies means that a small amount of money can move a large proportion of the company's average daily stock volume, permitting highly volatile price changes whose benefits largely accrue to the manipulators. Although the French Commissions des Operations de Bourse has reduced speculative operations on the Paris Bourse, London continues to be a major problem area, in part because the London stock exchange and an informal group policing operations lack subpoena powers to learn who actually bought and sold a stock, for example. The other nations' exchanges, especially Italy's, are particularly susceptible to manipulation.[20]

The theoretical impact of this model is substantial. What makes its application difficult in practical situations is the determination of reasonable forecasts for the market return and the risk-free return in the future. Whatever the estima-

[19] Alternatively, one can estimate β_E from the observed β's of the levered firm if leverage was constant for the entire period. In this case the direct estimate of β_E is $\beta_E = \beta / [1 + (1-T)D/E]$. See Mark E. Rubenstein, "A Mean-Variance Synthesis of Corporate Financial Theory," *Journal of Finance*, March 1973, pp. 167–181.

[20] For example, see William M. Carley's "Foreign Stock Markets Often Do Very Little to Curb Manipulation," *The Wall Street Journal*, October 6, 1976, p. 1ff.

tion problems in the risk-free return evaluation, the biggest question is: What is the market return? When it is in the international setting, is it the return in the home country's security market? Management desires project returns; therefore, some judgment must be made about the market return in different periods. If this figure is used as the estimate of the future market return, then the links between variability in that market return in future years and the equity returns of the projects under review must be determined when the appropriate debt load for the project is included.

The portfolio simulation approach outlined earlier produces covariances as a by-product of the individual project simulations in the portfolio process. These covariance estimates refer only to the projects that the firm is contemplating. It can be argued that in most cases these projects would constitute only a subset of all the projects included in the market portfolio to which the investor has access. In this case the total risk of a portfolio of projects, although making allowance for covariances, would still contain a portion of risk which the investor could diversify away by investing in the market portfolio. However, to the extent that the corporation has access to special projects which are not available in the market portfolio, the analysis of the total risk of the special portfolio contributes new insights. Some of the risk of these special projects may be correlated with the market portfolio, but the rest constitutes a unique source of diversification that only the specific corporation can contribute. Finally, the simulation approach makes it possible to incorporate into the analysis multiple goals other than variance in returns which management may feel relevant.

In practice, both types of analyses, the simulation approach and the CAPM framework, can complement one another.

CAPITAL BUDGETING IN PORTFOLIO—CONCLUSIONS

These four chapters have surveyed the major aspects of the international capital budgeting decision. First, the determination of the relevant cash flows for the single project was approached. The terminal rate of return where funds were blocked and limited opportunities were available for reinvestment and the relevance of repatriated funds or local funds were reviewed. If the firm is a multinational, repatriation may be less important than if the firm views itself as a national with foreign interests. Depending on this self-image, the importance of the pool of funds or simply local endeavors will vary considerably. Several approaches to evaluating inflation and currency realignments were noted.

The local cost of capital is the relevant discount rate for most decisions. If there are benefits of diversification accruing to the multinational corporation beyond the benefits which can be derived by small investors acting on their own (and probably there are), then these benefits result in an overall corporate cost of capital which is lower than the weighted sum of the individual costs. Supervision and coordination costs require some use of these excess resources, but the balance is a joint benefit accruing to the shareholders of the multinational firm.

There are general motivations beyond pure diversification which might compel the firm to operate in other than its native land. Even if one rejects the diversification argument, there are economic incentives (taxes, special opportunities, restricted access to resources in the absence of foreign operations, comparative advantage, and the product life cycle) as well as organizational issues which may play a major role in the decision to operate in other lands.

Finally, there are multiple goals in any firm. A multiple goal risk analysis by project and portfolio can be applicable to project evaluation. The evidence for diversification through security investments in other lands is limited by methodological constraints. Believing in the benefits of diversification for the corporation, a manager may use applications of portfolio theory to the international capital budgeting problem.

Chapter 13 has suggested that international capital markets are segmented, that is, not in equilibrium because of a lack of extensive arbitrage; Part Four will have a review of the elements of these capital markets.

Questions

1. What are the arguments for the existence of a corporation's ability to be an efficient diversifier? Do you believe the arguments?

2. Why does a joint simulation produce the covariances between projects?

3. Under what conditions is variance a bad measure of risk?

4. Why is the market line shown in Exhibit 13.3 linear? If the borrowing and lending rates were different, how would that change the analysis required for an investor's decision?

5. How can a firm obtain a reasonable estimate of the local cost of capital for a project? Why might a multinational corporation have an advantage over a local firm in terms of the cost of capital?

Bibliography

Adler, Michael, and R. Hoersch, "The Relationship Among Equity Markets: Comment." *Journal of Finance,* Sept. 1974, pp. 1311-1317.

Agmon, Tamir, "Country Risk–The Significance of the Country Factor to Share Price Movements in the United Kingdom, Germany and Japan." *Journal of Business,* Jan. 1973, pp. 24-32.

——, "The Relations Among Equity Markets: A Study of Share Price Co-Movements in the United States, United Kingdom, Germany and Japan." *Journal of Finance,* Sept. 1972, pp. 839-855.

——, and Donald R. Lessard, "Investor Recognition of Corporate International Diversification." *Journal of Finance,* Sept. 1977, pp. 1049-1056.

Black, Fischer, "International Capital Market Equilibrium with Investment Barriers." *Journal of Financial Economics,* Dec. 1974, pp. 337-352.

——, "The Ins and Outs of Foreign Investment." *Financial Analysts Journal,* May-June, 1978, pp. 25-32.

Carter, E. Eugene, *Portfolio Aspects of Corporate Capital Budgeting.* Lexington, Mass.: D. C. Heath and Company, 1974.

Cohen, Kalman J., Walter L. Ness, Jr., Hitoshi Okuda, Robert A. Schwartz, and David K. Whitcomb, "The Determinants of Common Stock Returns Volatility: An International Comparison." *Journal of Finance,* May 1976 (Proceedings), pp. 733-751.

Cohn, Richard A., and John J. Pringle, "Imperfections in International Financial Markets: Implications for Risk Premia and the Cost of Capital to Firms." *Journal of Finance,* March 1973, pp. 59-66.

Friend, Irwin, and James L. Bicksler, eds., *Risk and Return in Finance, Volumes 1 and 2.* Cambridge, Mass.: Ballinger Publishing Company, 1977.

Grauer, F. L. A., R. H. Litzenberger, and R. E. Stehl, "Sharing Rules and Equilibrium in an International Capital Market Under Uncertainty." *Journal of Financial Economics,* June 1976, pp. 233-257.

Grubel, Herbert G., "Internationally Diversified Portfolios: Welfare Gains and Capital Flows." *American Economic Review,* Dec. 1968, pp. 1299-1314.

——, and Kenneth Fadner, "The Interdependence of International Equity Markets." *Journal of Finance,* March 1971, pp. 89-94.

Hughes, John S., Dennis E. Logue, and Richard James Sqeeney, "Corporate International Diversification and Market Assigned Measures of Risk and Diversification." *Journal of Financial and Quantitative Analysis,* Nov. 1975, pp. 617-637.

Lessard, Donald, "International Portfolio Diversification: A Multivariate Analysis for a Group of Latin American Countries." *Journal of Finance,* June 1973, pp. 619-633.

——, "World, Country, and Industry Relationships in Equity Returns: Implications for Risk Reduction Through International Diversification." *Financial Analysts Journal,* Jan.-Feb. 1976, pp. 32-38.

Levy, Haim, and Marshall Sarnat, "International Diversification of Investment Portfolios." *American Economic Review,* Sept. 1970, pp. 668-675.

McDonald, John G., "French Mutual Fund Performance: Evaluation of Internationally Diversified Portfolios." *Journal of Finance,* Dec. 1973, pp. 1161-1180.

Makridakis, Spyros G., and Steven C. Wheelwright, "An Analysis of the Interrelationships Among the Major World Stock Exchanges." *Journal of Business Finance and Accounting,* Summer 1974, pp. 195-215.

Markowitz, Harry, *Portfolio Selection: Efficient Diversification of Investments.* New York: John Wiley and Sons, 1959.

Miller, Norman C., and Marina v. N. Whitman, "Alternative Theories and Tests of U.S. Short-Term Foreign Investment." *Journal of Finance,* Dec. 1973, pp. 1131-1147.

——, "A Mean-Variance Analysis of United States Long-Term Portfolio Foreign Investment." *Quarterly Journal of Economics,* May 1970, pp. 175-196.

Panton, Don B., V. Parker Lessig, and O. Maurice Joy, "Comovement of International Equity Markets: A Taxonomic Approach." *Journal of Financial and Quantitative Analysis,* Sept. 1976, pp. 415-432.

Pogue, Gerald A. and Bruno Solnik, "The Market Model Applied to European Common Stocks: An Empirical Approach." *Journal of Financial and Quantitative Analysis,* Dec. 1974, pp. 917-944.

Polk, Judd, et al., *U.S. Production Abroad and the Balance of Payments.* New York: National Industrial Conference Board, 1966.

Ripley, Duncan M., "Capital Control Policies and Foreign Shares Prices." *Journal of Finance,* June 1975, pp. 865-868.

——, "Systematic Elements in the Linkage of National Stock Market Indices." *Review of Economics and Statistics,* Aug. 1973, pp. 356-361.

Senbet, Lemma W., "International Capital Market Equilibrium and the Multinational Firm Financing and Investment Policies." *Journal of Financial and Quantitative Analysis,* Sept. 1978.

Solnik, Bruno, *European Capital Markets.* Lexington, Mass.: D. C. Heath/ Lexington Books, 1973.

——, "An International Market Model of Security Price Behavior." *Journal of Financial and Quantitative Analysis,* Sept. 1974, pp. 537-554.

——, "The International Pricing of Risk: An Empirical Investigation of the World Capital Market Structures." *Journal of Finance,* May 1974, pp. 365-378.

——, "Note on the Validity of the Random Walk for European Stock Prices." *Journal of Finance,* Dec. 1973, pp. 1151-1159.

——, "Testing International Asset Pricing: Some Pessimistic Views." *Journal of Finance,* May 1977, pp. 503-512.

Stehle, Richard, "An Empirical Test of the Alternative Hypotheses of National and International Pricing of Risky Assets." *Journal of Finance,* May 1977, pp. 493-502.

Subrahmanyam, Marti G., "On the Optimality of International Capital Market Integration." *Journal of Financial Economics,* March 1975, pp. 3-28.

Tobin, James, "Liquidity Preference as Behavior Toward Risk." *Review of Economic Studies,* Feb. 1958, pp. 65-86.

Wallingford, Buckner A. H., II, "Discussion: The International Pricing of Risk." *Journal of Finance,* May 1974, pp. 392-395.

FREEPORT MINERALS[1]

In June 1971 Freeport's treasury office was approaching the final stages in the deliberations to choose a package to finance the Greenvale project, a nickel mining and processing venture in Australia. Although the Freeport name had traditionally been associated with the sulphur industry, a diversification move initiated around 1968 had taken the company into new areas, one of which was Greenvale.

The choice of a financial package for the Greenvale project was not an easy one. In addition to the intricacies associated with each specific source of funds, the terms on which these funds were available were interrelated. The decisions appeared to be grouped into three major areas: (1) the selection of sales contracts for the processed ore; (2) the choice of the desired amount of leverage; and (3) the determination of the institutional source and currency denomination for the debt.

The success of the Greenvale project and its financing were critical to Freeport, for the project was large and it was a major step in Freeport's policy of diversification from sulphur mining and processing to other mineral exploitation.

COMPANY BACKGROUND

Freeport Minerals is a multinational resource processing company that produces a variety of minerals and chemical commodities for sale to large industrial customers. In 1968 sulphur contributed over 80% of Freeport net income, and Freeport produced 26% of total world production.

Until 1968 the producers of sulphur had been a classical oligopoly, able to control sales and production and to enjoy high prices. The relatively low price elasticity of demand for sulphur, the low degree of sophistication involved in the technology, and the few differences in production costs among the producers ($17-$20/ton) made self-control essential to the prevention of "undesirable policies" in the industry.

However, the rising demand for sulphur (about 10% annually) and the high selling price made the industry attractive to new entrants. As a result, the world sulphur oligopoly began to break down in 1968. First, Canadian producers of natural gas began to sell huge quantities of sulphur obtained as a by-product of their main activity. Then, the Mexican producers of sulphur, protected by their national tariffs and quota walls, started selling their excess sulphur at marginal prices in the U.S. market. As a result, the f.o.b. price of a ton of sulphur went from a high of $40/ton in 1968 to a low of $20/ton in 1970.

Freeport's response to this sudden increase in supply was to close its marginal mine. As a result, Freeport's sales of sulphur decreased by 18% from 1968 to 1970. The impact of the sulphur price decline on Freeport's profits was so dramatic that profits halved between 1968 and 1970 (Exhibit 1).

[1]This case has been prepared totally from publicly available sources. Freeport's management has not been consulted in the preparation of the case.

The Diversification Moves

When the sulphur oligopoly broke down and diversification became the strategy for moving away from the depressed sector, its other operations became very important to Freeport. Top management began expanding into areas where Freeport had some competitive advantage. The main diversification axis was to be copper and nickel extraction and processing. The company looked forward to becoming a significant producer of these minerals within a decade.

The impact of the diversification moves on Freeport's investments, sales, and earnings by 1971, and the forecast for 1975, are presented in Exhibit 2.

Freeport Financial Situation in 1971

Despite the enlargement of its product portfolio, Freeport was in a strong financial position in 1971. With \$3.8 million of long-term debt and \$234 million of stockholders' equity, the firm had the financial capabilities to continue its aggressive expansion and diversification program. However, the drop in profitability between 1968 and 1971 had been very painful, and the company was fighting to come back to its 1968 profit level. The stock price moved from \$40/\$50 in 1968 to \$16/\$20 in 1971, following Freeport's traditionally stable P/E ratio of 17.

Freeport always had a conservative financial policy. From 1965 to 1968 the slow expansion of the firm had been financed mainly through retained earnings (40% of total earnings) or issuance of new shares. In the financing of projects, Freeport had always tried to accomplish two objectives: (1) maximize external borrowings (20% equity being the upper limit) and (2) avoid lending to the subsidiary or guaranteeing the subsidiary's debt. The borrowings of Freeport's subsidiaries had been based either on the inherent value of the operation from advance sales contracts or on government guarantees. Freeport had often used AID risk insurance to protect itself against losses due to war or expropriation or problems in converting currencies. This policy had proven to be especially sound in 1959, when the huge Cuban operations of Freeport were nationalized. Freeport wrote off \$9 million, the amount of the equity. However, Citibank in New York, one of the major lenders to the Cuban subsidiary, suffered one of the biggest losses in its history.

Freeport consolidated its subsidiaries by using the equity method: Only the equity stake in the subsidiaries appeared in the Freeport balance sheet and income statement. The liabilities of the subsidiaries never appeared on the parent's balance sheet. Freeport management placed considerable weight on the maintenance of a debt-free balance sheet in order to keep flexibility for eventual financing of major ventures. (See Note 2 to Exhibit 1.)

THE GREENVALE PROJECT

The Joint Venture Freeport Mineral Exploration

Freeport decided to make Australia the focus of its mineral exploration efforts. The basis for this decision was the continent's political stability and favorable

EXHIBIT 1. **Freeport Minerals: Financial Data (thousands of dollars)**

	Total Assets	*Stockholders' Equity*	*Gross Sales*	*Net Income*
1970	$280,366	$233,648	$136,558	$15,881
1969	293,976	233,221	175,209	28,516
1968	290,001	229,460	189,683	40,395
1967	275,629	210,446	173,105	32,357
1966	238,905	196,145	143,576	32,174
1965	209,442	178,945	106,752	21,660
1964	227,191	165,945	78,782	15,349
1963	174,511	156,904	66,329	12,816
1962	182,370	148,829	56,904	12,727
1961	211,001	145,150	52,724	12,856
1960	203,689	140,605	52,997	13,194[a]
1959	167,406	154,428	53,234	14,478
1958	164,494	148,915	55,342	13,084[a]
1957	93,891	76,167	63,283	12,973
1956	87,514	70,608	68,078	13,378

[a]Excludes an extraordinary item in 1960 of $9,630,000 (after taxes), representing a write-off of the Company's investment in Cuban American Nickel Company and an extraordinary item in 1958 of $67,100,000 (after taxes), representing a profit from the sale of oil and gas interests in the Lake Washington field.

Statements of Income

	Year Ended Dec. 31, 1970	*Year Ended Dec. 31, 1969*
Gross sales	$136,558	$175,209
Other income, net	3,018	1,739
	139,576	176,948
Costs and expenses:		
Production and delivery costs	86,190	111,568
Exploration and development costs	5,915	8,426
Depreciation and amortization	14,279	14,588
Selling, general, and administrative expenses	7,342	7,392
Taxes (Note 1)	9,969	6,458
Total costs	123,695	148,432
Net income	$ 15,881	$ 28,516
Net income per share	$1.02	$1.84

THE ACCOMPANYING NOTES ARE AN INTEGRAL PART OF THESE STATEMENTS

(Exhibit 1 continues on the following page.)

EXHIBIT 1. Balance Sheets (cont.)

Assets	*Dec. 31, 1970*	*Dec. 31, 1969*
Current assets:		
Cash and marketable securities	$ 50,558	$ 50,613
Accounts receivable	24,050	22,234
Inventories, at average cost	26,623	25,448
	101,231	98,295
Investments in affiliates (Note 2)	5,484	3,677
Property, plant, and equipment, at cost	281,047	277,425
Less, allowance for depreciation and amortization	(116,677)	(104,007)
Net property, plant, and equipment	164,370	173,418
Other assets	9,281	8,576
Total Assets	$280,366	$293,966

Liabilities	*Dec. 31, 1970*	*Dec. 31, 1969*
Current liabilities:		
Accounts payable & accrued expenses	$ 7,331	$ 9,734
Accrued royalties payable	7,293	12,849
Accrued income & other taxes	525	2,679
First mortgage bond payments of National Potash Company—due within one year	968	913
	16,117	26,175
First mortgage bonds of National Potash Company, less portion included in current liabilities (Note 3)	3,813	4,781
Deferred employee benefits	1,402	1,215
Reserve for future income taxes, and deferred investment tax credits (Note 1)	25,386	18,584
Stockholders' equity		
Common stock, par value $5, authorized 40,000,000 shares, issued 15,526,080 shares December 31, 1970, and 15,522,520 shares December 31, 1969	77,631	77,613
Excess of amount paid in over par value of common stock	11,131	11,104
Retained earnings	144,886	144,504
	233,648	233,221
Total Liabilities and Stockholders' Equity	$280,366	$293,966

Note 1: Income taxes provided in 1967 and prior years reflect tax losses relating to Cuban American Nickel Company, formerly a subsidiary, whose Cuban assets were confiscated by the Fidel Castro government. The Internal Revenue Service has questioned some of these deductions. Discussions in an effort to resolve these differences by settlement are progressing. If settlement cannot be reached, it is estimated that a maximum deficiency approximating $9,000,000 (after applying $5,000,000 of available tax credits) plus interest, payable in the future, might be asserted. The Company intends to resist any such assertion if made and, in the opinion of its counsel, the Company should prevail.

Note 2: At December 31, 1970, investments in affiliates comprised $1,396,000 in Freeport Indonesia, Incorporated, and $4,088,000 applicable to various other investments.

The net assets of Freeport Indonesia at December 31, 1970, as shown on its financial statements, amounted to $8,539,000, including current assets of $2,979,000, property, plant, and equipment of $35,346,000, less current liabilities of $719,000 and long-term liabilities of $29,067,000. Freeport Sulphur Company's equity in these net assets amounted to $8,144,000. The difference between this equity and the investment of $1,396,000 principally represents costs of exploration and preliminary work incurred by Freeport Sulphur and written off against its earnings in prior years as expenditures were incurred.

Reference is made to comments in the accompanying letter to stockholders regarding the Freeport Indonesia project for development of the Ertsberg copper deposit.

In connection with the financing of that project, Freeport Sulphur Company was committed at December 31, 1970, to provide a maximum of $13,000,000 in additional equity funds, of which $11,500,000 is presently estimated to be required.

Note 3: The first mortgage bonds, principally 4 percent, are due in annual installments through November 1, 1974. They represent indebtedness of National Potash Company, without recourse to Freeport Sulphur Company, incurred in 1956, 1957, and 1958 when Freeport Sulphur owned a one-half interest in National Potash. National Potash became a wholly owned subsidiary of Freeport Sulphur in 1966.

SOURCE: Company Annual Report.

EXHIBIT 2. Freeport Minerals: Product Diversification

Diversification by Product, 1971[a]

Product	Investment		Sales		Earnings Contribution	
	Million $	*%*	*Million $*	*%*	*Million $*	*%*
Sulphur	$124.4	44%	$ 72.5	51%	$ 9.9	54%
Phosphates (with captive sulphur	74.0	26	38.5	27	2.7	14
Kaolin (processing)	29.1	10	17.0	12	1.8	10
Potash (mining)	29.2	10	9.0	7	1.7	9
Oil and Gas	19.6	7	4.0	3	0.0	0
Other (Nepean, Erstberg)	9.1	3	—	—[b]	2.3	13
Total	$285.4	100%	$141.0	100%	$18.4	100%

Expected Contribution to Net Income by Product and Subsidiary, 1975[a]

	Direct Ownership	*Million $*	*%*
PARENT COMPANY			
Sulphur		$ 8.0	14.6%
Phosphates		9.4	17.0
Kaolin		4.5	8.2
Potash		1.8	3.3
Oil and Gas		0.0	0.0
Investment income (including Nepean)[a]		1.3	2.4
		$25.0	45.5%
FOREIGN SUBSIDIARIES			
Erstberg (copper)	87%	$15.9	28.8%
Greenvale (nickel)	50	11.6	21.0
Mt. Keith (nickel)	50	d.s.	—
New Caledonia (nickel)	49	d.s.	—
Palm Valley (Australia) (nickel)	9.5	d.s	—
Metal Exploration Ltd. (nickel)	22	2.6	4.7
		$30.1	54.5%
Total		$55.1	100.0%

[a]Foreign subsidiaries are based on equity participation and dividends received. Exploration and mining abroad is done via local subsidiaries.

[b]Nepean is also a nickel joint venture with Metal Exploration.

d.s. = development stage.

SOURCE: Lombard, Nelson, and MacKenna, "Freeport Minerals Company," June 22, 1972.

geology for nickel, a premium commodity in which Freeport's staff had accumulated considerable experience, including a decade in pre-Castro Cuba. As a first step, the company bought a 22% equity position in Metals Exploration N.L., an Australian company, for $2 million. Metals Exploration N.L. was a young company created by a group of Australians including several university teachers in geology or chemistry. The goal of the company was to identify metal deposits in Australia, and Greenvale was one of their findings. The Greenvale project became a 50/50 joint venture of Freeport Queensland Nickel Inc. (a wholly owned subsidiary of Freeport Minerals) and Metals Exploraton Pty. Ltd. (a wholly owned subsidiary of Metal Exploration N.L.)

The Nickel Industry

Structure. The major characteristics of the nickel industry were high concentration, a high degree of vertical integration, and high barriers to entry. The industry was a worldwide oligopoly with the following world market share in 1966 and 1971:

Nickel Production: Market Shares of Major Companies

	1966	*1971 (estimates)*
International Nickel INCO (Canadian)	51.5%	42%
Le Nickel (French)	14.2%	11%
Falconbridge (Canadian)	11.6%	13%
Sheritt Gordon (U.S.)	4.4%	
Hanna (U.S.)	3.6%	34%
Japanese firms	8.0%	
Others	6.7%	

This very high degree of concentration had technological and historical explanations.

Until the end of the nineteenth centry the Rothschild-controlled firm, Le Nickel, had the monopoly of the nickel produced in the world. In 1902, helped by J. P. Morgan, Oxford Nickel and Guardian Nickel merged to form International Nickel (INCO) that was to dominate the industry until today.

From 1929 to 1940 INCO had a 90% share of the world nickel market, and Le Nickel had 10%. In the postwar era INCO's dominance decreased. New companies like Hanna and Sheritt Gordon appeared, but INCO was able to conserve a dominant position. The nickel oligopoly was successful in maintaining high barriers to entry and in controlling output. The price of nickel was kept at a high level that allowed nickel producers to be fairly profitable. Since 1965 INCO's return on equity had stabilized at a steady 16%.

Barriers to entry in the nickel industry were economies of scale (the smaller producers, like Hanna, were much less profitable than INCO, which had three big refineries); high capital requirements (a fully integrated nickel operation of the minimum scale required between \$50 million and \$200 million); control of raw materials by producers that were vertically integrated; technological patents and know-how; and long-term contracts with nickel buyers.

Prices. In a nutshell, the prices in the nickel industry were determined by INCO and expressed in U.S. dollars. INCO's large share of the market placed it in the position of being the price leader in the industry. The fact that a large proportion of INCO's nickel was sold in the United States and that many of its mines were located in the United States made the U.S. dollar the currency of the nickel market that INCO dominated.

The nickel producers appeared to predict future demand with a high degree of certainty. They increased capacity in proportion to market share in order to match capacity and demand. Apparently a kind of implicit agreement did exist between producers not to increase market share by a savage price war that would be detrimental to everybody's profitability. Any price cut would be followed by others, and the only result would be the same market share at a lower price. The INCO prewar price of $0.35/lb. lasted from 1929 to 1946. The price of nickel had been determined by INCO's costs, with a comfortable margin allowing some higher cost producers to survive. An implication of this fact was that all suppliers quoted prices in U.S. dollars. Short-term supply and demand fluctuation had a weak effect on nickel prices and were absorbed by inventory change, rationing, or production cutbacks. Historical prices of nickel ingots through 1967 and the reasons associated with the price changes are presented in Exhibit 3. Since then prices had increased rapidly to $1.35/lb. in 1971.

Demand. Although subject to the characteristic fluctuations of demand for raw materials, the demand for nickel was relatively steady because nickel was used mainly as an intermediate product; stainless steel, for example, is an alloy of steel and nickel. Nickel thus was sold to steel producers or other industrial firms. One of the problems of nickel was that copper, aluminum, and (to a lesser extent) cobalt or even plastic were good substitutes. However, in the short term, the responsiveness of demand to changes in prices of nickel was rather small. Short-term price elasticity of demand for nickel had been estimated at -1.026 by a team of economists. The substitution of alternative minerals for nickel required some amount of time and commitment to different technologies. But in the long term the response of demand to changes in nickel prices could be expected to be much larger. World consumption of nickel was expected to grow 6-7% annually.

Recent Developments. Until 1970 INCO had acted in a benevolent and relatively paternalistic way toward other nickel companies. Each year INCO published an analysis of world nickel consumption. This analysis became the basis for the plans of other producers in the industry. INCO freely distributed reports on its R&D activities and organized conferences around the world for potential nickel users. INCO's promotion was directed toward increasing primary demand, not toward increasing the company's market share. The industry never formed a trade association; INCO was it. However, in the early 1970s the giant of the nickel industry began to show some signs of aggressiveness.

In 1971 INCO took the plunge. Its market share slipped to 42%. Sales had dropped 20% from the 1969 high in 1970. Profits declined by 50%. The major causes were the expansion of competitors and general overcapacity in the industry. One of the reasons for this overcapacity was that during the 1960s INCO had not tried to fight competition by maintaining low selling prices as it did in the 1920s. Behind the comfortable shelter of industry high prices, smaller competitors had begun to survive profitably. The situation of shortages of nickel supply in the 1960s made it impossible for INCO to control competition. The prolonged world economic slump in the early 1970s reduced demand for steel and other nickel-bearing alloys, and INCO as well as its competitors were saddled with overcapacity.

EXHIBIT 3. Freeport Minerals: Fluctuations in Nickel Ingot Prices, 1946-1971

Date	*Prices (¢/lb)*	*Relevant Events*
11/25/46	31.25–35.0	Contract price on large quantities raised to level of base price, which had been unchanged at 35¢ since 1929.
1/1/48	35.0–33.75	U.S. tariff reduction from 2½¢ to 1¼¢ is directly passed on to customers, leaving price received by INCO unchanged.
7/22/48	33.75–40.0	"In 1938 each ton of ore mined produced 43 lbs, of nickel compared to 27 lbs. in 1948. Increased demand has made it necessary to mine considerably lower grade ores, leading to a price increase to 40¢ a lb." At an annual meeting INCO announced expansion plans in anticipation of growing demand.
5/31/50	40.0–48.0	INCO cites cumulative cost increases and reiterates policy of keeping price close to costs in order to encourage demand growth while covering costs of expansion.
12/13/50	48.0–50.5	Wage increase, negotiated on the same day, preceded the price increase.
6/1/51	50.5–56.5	One-year union contract concluded May 26. Wage increase and 10% reduction of work week.
6/14/53	56.5–60.0	Legal ceiling raised after discussions between INCO and U.S. government. INCO cites exchange rate depreciation of U.S. dollar as necessitating change in order to keep their price on U.S. sales constant in Canadian terms.
11/24/54	60.0–64.5	Increase "intended to offset higher costs."
12/6/56	64.5–74.0	"The increases were to meet higher costs, especially for the new project in Manitoba." INCO reiterates policy of "stable and reasonable prices, which are of major importance in the development of new and expanded uses and markets for nickel."
7/1/61	74.0–81.25	Increase unexpected in view of Canadian dollar devaluation and weakening of stainless markets at a time when steel as a whole was improving. Increase came shortly after the Castro government nationalized Cuban plants accounting for 9% of world production. Customers reported angered by the move.
5/24/62	81.25–79.0	Falconbridge initiates cut; INCO "taken completely by surprise, but followed the next day." Price cut offset the effect of devaluation of the Canadian dollar to 92.5¢. Falconbridge's motive linked to expiration of U.S. government contract accounting for some 25% of its annual output.
9/28/65	79.0–77.75	U.S. import duty is suspended for three years. Producers pass the saving on to customers.
11/1/66	77.75–85.25	"Chairman Henry S. Wingate said the boost was necessary to finance the immediate development of a low-grade nickel property in Manitoba and to compensate for the higher costs of labor following a 95¢ per hour wage hike." Opposition from U.S. and Canadian governments ineffective in deferring increase.
9/15/67	85.25–94.0	Sheritt-Gordon led with an increase to 98¢ on powder and briquettes; INCO and Falconbridge reacted by going to 94¢ on cathodes. Cathodes compete with powder only when sheared at a cost of 2¢, but a spread between the two prices is still evident.
1971	135	

SOURCE: 1946–1967: "Economic Analysis of the Nickel Industry," Charles River Associates, Incorporated, Dec. 1968.
1971: Commodity Research Bureau, Inc., COMMODITY YEARBOOK, 1975.

INCO's response to these events was a change in strategy and an internal reorganization. Henry S. Wingate, chairman and chief executive of INCO, a lawyer who had run the company for eighteen years, proceeded to chop employment by 18% and cut production to 80% of capacity in 1971. "Now that there is the need of getting out and selling nickel, we are not quite so altruistic," declared an INCO executive.[2]

Characteristics of the Greenvale Project

The Nickel Deposits and Processing. In 1967 geologists discovered a deposit of high-grade nickel laterite at Greenvale in Queensland, Australia, over 100 miles inland from Townsville on the northeast coast. Experts conducted drillings in the area in the subsequent three years and estimated a reserve of at least 44 million tons of ore averaging 1.57% nickel and 0.12% cobalt. The ore at Greenvale extended like a flat blanket varying from 5 to 60 feet thick parallel to the surface over an area of 800 acres with about 20 feet of overburden.

The mine would require an employment force of 100 to haul and crush ore at an annual rate of 2.5 million tons. This ore would be transported to the processing plant in Townsville on the coast via a new 140-mile railway which was to be built by the companies and owned and operated by the Queensland government. The Townsville plant would employ 600 people and was scheduled for completion in mid-1974. Mine site construction had already begun. Ore mining was scheduled to start in late 1973, and production in late 1974. Full production capacity was to be reached in the beginning of 1975.

Capital Requirements. The estimated capital requirement for the full development of the Greenvale project totaled $264 million. This total cost broke down into:

Greenvale Capital Requirements

Greenvale mine development	US$ 15.0 million
Railway	44.6
Nickel processing plant	110.8
Preoperating cost	16.5
Interest during construction	19.1
Working capital needs	14.7
Escalation and contingency	43.4
	US$264.1 million

THE FINANCING DECISIONS

It was clear to Freeport that the profitability of this project depended heavily on the financing package obtained. An estimate of cash flows based on certain financing assumptions subject to modification is presented in Exhibit 4.

[2] "Inco: A Giant Wakes Up and Starts Fighting," *Business Week,* May 26, 1973, p.44.

The decision appeared to be a three-tiered one. First the type of sales contract would have to be determined. The longer the time coverage of the sales contract, the easier it would be to obtain favorable financing. Without any long-term sales contract it would be extremely hard to obtain financing at reasonable terms. The selection of a financial package was, in turn, a two-stage decision. The amount of leverage that the project could carry had to be established. Then, the source of the debt portion of the financial package had to be chosen.

Sales Contracts

Freeport's tradition had been to cover the entire output of a project with advance sales contracts before it approached the sources of financing. These contracts were required to pursue the company's policy of maximizing the amount of debt in the financing of its projects.

Long-term sales contracts for selling nickel are founded on a basis of mutual advantage. A contract gives the purchaser the advantage of a relatively regular supply at a discount from the market price while it guarantees a minimum price for the supplier. The floor price in the contract is generally 10% less than the market price when the contract is signed. The price of the nickel, when above the minimum agreed price, increases with the level of the market price. However,

EXHIBIT 4. Freeport Minerals: Greenvale Nickel Venture: Cash Flow Projection

	Assumptions:		
Ore Reserves	44.0 million tons		
Extraction Rate	2.5 million tons, wet, per annum		
Price			
Nickel Sinter	$3,020 per ton	(135¢ per lb)	
Cobalt	$3,584 per ton	(160¢ per lb)	
Product			
Nickel	22,321 tons X $3,020 =	$67.4M	
Cobalt	1,340 tons X $3,584	4.8M	
REVENUES—PER ANNUM		$72.2M	
COST			
Mining per wet ton	$2.00		
Transport, 1.57 cents per wet ton mile	$2.20 over first ten years		
Refining, per ton metal	$800 (less depreciation from 1985 onwards)		
Royalty	10¢ per ton over first ten years, 15¢ per ton thereafter.		
Administrative	$1.0 million per annum		
CAPITAL			
Equity	$87 million		$264 million
Borrowings at 9% repaid by 1984	$177 million		
DEPRECIATION			
Mine, $1.1 million p.a. over 18 years	$20 million		
Railway, $4.4 million p.a. over 10 years	$44 million		
Refinery, $8.7 million p.a. over 15 years	$130 million (including all preconstruction interest)		

EXHIBIT 4. (cont.)

Pro forma Statements (millions of dollars)

	1975	1976	1977	1978	1979	1980	1981	1982	1983	1984	5 years 1985/89	3 years 1990/92
CAPITAL												
Equity	$ 87.0	$ 87.0	$ 87.0	$ 87.0	$ 87.0	$87.0	$87.0	$87.0	$87.0	$87.0	$ 87.0	$ 87.0
Borrowings	177.0	159.3	141.6	123.9	106.2	88.5	70.8	53.1	35.4	17.7		
Less Repayments	17.7	17.7	17.7	17.7	17.7	17.7	17.7	17.7	17.7	17.7		
	159.3	141.6	123.9	106.2	88.5	70.8	53.1	35.4	17.7	—		
REVENUES	72.2	72.2	72.2	72.2	72.2	72.2	72.2	72.2	72.2	72.2	361.0	216.6
COSTS												
Mining	5.0	5.0	5.0	5.0	5.0	5.0	5.0	5.0	5.0	5.0	25.0	15.0
Depreciation	1.1	1.1	1.1	1.1	1.1	1.1	1.1	1.1	1.1	1.1	5.5	3.3
Transport	5.5	5.5	5.5	5.5	5.5	5.5	5.5	5.5	5.5	5.5	27.5	16.5
Depreciation	4.4	4.4	4.4	4.4	4.4	4.4	4.4	4.4	4.4	4.4	—	—
Refining	10.1	10.1	10.1	10.1	10.1	10.1	10.1	10.1	10.1	10.1	50.5	30.3
Depreciation	8.7	8.7	8.7	8.7	8.7	8.7	8.7	8.7	8.7	8.7	43.5	0
Royalty	.3	.3	.3	.3	.3	.3	.3	.3	.3	.3	1.5	.9
Interest at 9%	15.9	14.3	12.7	11.2	9.6	8.0	6.4	4.8	3.2	1.6	—	—
Administration	1.0	1.0	1.0	1.0	1.0	1.0	1.0	1.0	1.0	1.0	5.0	3.0
TOTAL COSTS	52.0	50.4	48.8	47.3	45.7	44.1	42.5	40.9	39.3	37.7	158.5	69.0
PROFIT BEFORE TAX	20.2	21.8	23.4	24.9	26.5	28.1	29.7	31.3	2.9	34.5	202.5	147.6
Taxation												
38% of Profit before Tax Plus Mine Depreciation[a]	0	(8.7)	(9.3)	(9.9)	(10.5)	(11.1)	(11.7)	(12.3)	(12.9)	(13.5)	(79.0)	(57.3)
NET PROFIT	20.2	13.1	14.1	15.0	16.0	17.0	18.0	19.0	20.0	21.0	123.5	90.3
Depreciation	14.2	14.2	14.2	14.2	14.2	14.2	14.2	14.2	14.2	14.2	49.0	3.3
Tax Savings[a]	3.0	1.9	1.0	.2	(.7)	(.7)	(.7)	(.7)	(.7)	(.7)	(1.5)	—
After-tax Interest	15.9	8.9	7.9	6.9	5.9	4.9	4.0	3.0	2.0	1.0	—	—

OPERATING CASH FLOW (excluding Financing)	50.3	41.1	37.2	36.3	35.4	35.4	35.5	35.5	35.5	35.5	171.0	93.6 + working capital in 1992
Principal + Interest ($177M for 10 yrs. at 9%)	(33.6)	(26.6)	(25.6)	(24.6)	(23.6)	(22.6)	(21.7)	(20.7)	(19.7)	(18.7)		
EQUITY CASH FLOW	16.7	14.5	11.6	11.7	11.8	12.8	13.8	14.8	15.8	16.8	171.0	93.6 + working capital in 1992

Rates of Return

	Net Present Value 10%	*15%*	*Internal Rate of Return*	*Terminal Rate of Return at 10%*
Operating Cash Flow and $264M Outlay	$23.6M	–$56.9M	11.2%	10.9%
Equity Cash Flow and $87M Outlay	62.1M	9.8M	16.4%	13.6%

[a]Taxes are based on the use of 150% declining balance rates for tax purposes. No tax is assumed payable in the first year because of various expensed start-up costs, some of which are carried over to 1976. Hence, the tax savings are carried over to 1976.

SOURCE: Based on raw calculations in Roach, Williams and Co. (Share brokers), REPORT ON METALS EXPLORATION, Melbourne, Australia, 1970.

the discount from the market price increases with the level of the market price; e.g., if market prices double, the discount might be 25%. There is, in general, no ceiling price.

The annual quantity that the purchaser is obliged to buy at the given price is fixed in the contract. The supplier is *not* obliged to supply this quantity. If the quantity of nickel available is lower than forecast, or if the percentage of pure metal is lower and the supplier cannot ship as much metal as anticipated, there is no penalty. On the other hand, the metal cannot be sold to other users until the contract requirements are fulfilled. In these sales contracts the purchaser is responsible for the transportation of the metal. In 1971, Freeport could obtain long-term sales contracts for the Australian nickel only with Japanese and German clients.

The Amount of Leverage

Freeport was seasoned in dealing with international bankers who specialized in project financing. When a bank is asked to finance a project like a mining venture, it tries to assess the degree of risk involved in the project. The assessment of risk is translated to a required coverage of interest costs and amortization of the loan by the projected cash flows. If the project is very risky, the bank will require a high coverage ratio (i.e., a high ratio of annual cash flows to annual interest cost plus loan amortization). This coverage ratio may be close to 1 for low-risk ventures and rise to 5 for very risky projects based on average cash flows and coverage.

As the horizon of the loan is lengthened, the project's risks become more difficult to assess. As a result, the required coverage ratio may be 3 if the average loan maturity is fifteen years and 4 if the average loan maturity is eighteen years.

To evaluate the riskiness of a project the bank considers the following types of risk:

Construction Risk. This risk refers to the technological factors involved in the project. If a project involves a special quality of ore which requires a new processing technology never before tried, the construction risk will be relatively high. The experience and skill of the firm in the type of project are important in this regard. As far as mining is concerned, an open pit operation is less risky than an underground operation.

Resource Risk. This risk concerns the possibility of finding less ore than expected or of finding a poorer ore than anticipated. The first risk (volume) is very important in operations like petroleum. The second one (quality) is crucial in metal exploration. In this case to find a 1.8% ore instead of the 2.2% expected is not uncommon and makes a large difference in the revenues of the project.

Operating Risk. This risk involves the eventual problems that might appear in the exploitation of the venture as well as possible variations in operating expenses. The eventual problems of exploitation are a function of the supply of raw material (volume and quality of ore) and environmental factors such as transportation and logistic problems. The predictability of the operating expenses depends on the nature of these expenses and on the economic variables that affect them.

Market Risk. This risk depends on the predictability of the volume and price of sales. This, in turn, depends on the possibility of obtaining long-term sales contracts and on the terms of the contracts. The future of the market is important. Factors such as the structure of the market and the strategy of major firms in the market affect this type of risk a great deal.

Political Risk. This risk encompasses the possibility of partial or complete nationalization or any other political event affecting the project's cash flows.

Force Majeure Risk. This risk covers events such as earthquakes or epidemics that cannot be anticipated easily.

Sources of Debt Financing

Suppliers' Credit. This subordinate credit was limited to the amount of procurement abroad. This is a cheap source of funds. Interest rates in 1971 were about 8%. The maturity of the loans is about ten years from project completion, and initial repayment was often delayed for five years. De facto, international agreements have had the result of equalizing the interest rate and maturity of the loans offered by various countries. The currency of the loan is always the currency of the supplier. In 1971 price differences between the United States, Germany and Japan were about 5% higher in Japan and Germany.

In the case of Greenvale only about 30% of the railway construction costs and of the nickel processing plant could be sourced outside Australia at reasonable prices. For the other 70% of the required assets, high tariffs and transportation costs made Australian prices almost 40% cheaper than comparable products bought abroad. Generally, long-term credit was not available from the Australian suppliers. Thus, at best, 30% ($46.6M) of the total equipment cost might be imported and financed with suppliers' credit. The balance, $108.8M, would be purchased in Australia with ninety-day or six-month credit terms.

Purchaser's Credit. This credit was given by the purchasers of nickel, the same people who signed the long-term contracts mentioned earlier. Therefore, some trade-offs had to be made between the floor price and the discount from marketplace on one hand and the interest rate on the other. In the case of Freeport one could assume that starting with a long-term sales contract with a floor price of $1.35 and a floating price equal to the market price less a 10% discount (e.g., initial market price is $1.50) then Freeport had two financing options:

1. $1.30 floor price and 15% discount from market for an 8% loan.
2. $1.25 floor price and 20% discount from market for a 6.5% loan.

The maturity of these loans could be as long as twenty years after completion of the project. However, the amount of these loans was limited to 50%

of total investment. The currency of the loan was always the one of the purchaser. These loans sometimes could be subordinated to senior loans.

Local Markets. The Australian financial market was a source of funds. However, its capacity was limited. In 1971 the very maximum that could be raised for a single project was 100 million Australian dollars (A$ = US$1.12). In a *bank* loan the maximum maturity would be seven to ten years after commitment. Interest rate would be floating at 1% premium over the Australian overdraft rate, which was 8.5% early in 1971. An *insurance company* loan carried a longer maturity of up to fifteen years from commitment at a fixed rate of 9.5%. However, insurance companies would agree to lend funds only if they obtained an equity stake in the project. In the case of Freeport one-sixth of the loan was the minimum equity contribution, which was made in cash.

Euro-dollars. Euro-bonds were out of the question for such a mining operation. That year a firm had to be a General Motors-type of risk to obtain funds in the Euro-bond market. The only alternative left in the Euro-markets was a long-term Euro-dollar loan. The maximum maturity for such a loan was ten years from commitment. The maximum loan might be $200 million at a 1–1½% floating rate over the six-month London interbank rate. This type of loan could be arranged in currencies such as the guilder or deutsche mark; however, the quantity available for a single project in such markets was low (about $50 million). In any case there were substantial issue costs involved.

PART FOUR

In the post-World War II Western world one of the most striking phenomena has been the growth in the Euro-dollar market. In Chapter 14 we study the nature of these funds, seeking to understand several theories of how they came about and to know who uses them for what purpose. The development of international banking is discussed in this context. In Chapter 15 the various types of international bonds, of which the Euro-bonds are a major segment, are discussed. There are bonds denominated in several currencies, parallel bonds, convertible Euro-bonds, and other varieties which have grown at different rates and which create different risks to the holder. Finally, since the multinational firm undertakes financings within the boundaries of the countries in which it operates, in Chapter 16 we sketch the characteristics of the markets in major developed nations.

These three chapters provide an institutional coloration to the international financial analysis presented in previous chapters. Inevitably, the particular data contained in the comparative statistics will become outdated; however, the analytical construct developed to analyze these data will remain valid.

Part Four has been designed to provide financial managers with an understanding of the financial markets in which multinational companies operate. We have therefore included both institutional factors and basic economic relationships.

CHAPTER 14

The Euro-Currency Markets

Euro-currencies, monies traded outside the country of their origin, are the core of the international financial markets. This chapter will discuss the short-term portion of these markets. The following chapter will consider international bonds, including Euro-bonds. Much of the text will focus on the Euro-dollar market since the dollar is the currency with the largest amount of trading in the Euro-currency markets, and Europe is where most of this trading takes place.

Since the word Euro-dollar has usually been surrounded by a degree of mysticism, the presentation begins by discussing what a Euro-dollar looks like and how it is traded. The characteristics of these markets are described: instruments used, origin of the markets, determinants of rates and country composition. The chapter concludes with a discussion of international banking and its role in the Euro-currency markets. The appendix to this chapter reviews the literature on the impact of Euro-dollars creation on the balance of payments and money supply.

WHAT ARE EURO-DOLLARS?

Euro-dollars are financial assets and liabilities denominated in dollars but traded outside the United States. In fact many writers attribute the beginnings of the Euro-dollar market to some degree to the Russians. After World War II

Eastern European nations and the Soviet Union obtained dollar balances in trade, and these were placed on deposit with Soviet banks in the West, such as Narodny Bank in London. These banks, in turn, reloaned the dollars to other European banks, thus trading dollars outside the United States and starting the process of Euro-dollar creation.

Although traded outside the United States, every Euro-dollar deposit has its origin in and continues to be associated with a deposit in a bank in the United States. To understand this process one must understand the technical aspects of international transfer of funds. Financial officers of multinational companies do not usually cross countries' borders with suitcases packed with paper or metal money.[1] With almost the single exception of the fund smuggler, international capital transactions are not realized through paper or metal money. Instead, these transactions use bank deposits which can be moved by using bank transfers. These transfers are usually executed via telex or some other fast means of communication.

Cash flows in a commercial bank are identified by four major pieces of information: (1) currency, (2) institution and location, (3) maturity date, and (4) interest rate. For example, the complete description of a cash flow could read as follows: "$1 million inflow for June 30 carrying 10% per annum to be received in the London branch from deposits drawn on Chase Manhattan." This inflow could be from the repayment of a dollar loan made to a customer earlier by the British branch at 10% per annum. The bank also knows that the payment will be made by the customer's requesting Chase Manhattan to transfer funds from the customer's account to the London bank's account.

To have a better grasp of how these bank transfers take place and how Euro-dollars come into existence, look at a few transactions:

1. ABC Corporation which maintains a deposit with Chase Manhattan decides to transfer some of its dollar deposit to Barclays in London. Chase Manhattan sends a telex to Barclays informing it of Chase's transfer of funds to Barclays's account with Chase according to the request of ABC Corporation.

Questions are then asked:

a. Does Barclays wish to leave its newly acquired deposit with Chase Manhattan or does it prefer to keep it with some other bank? Assume that Barclays keeps the new deposit with Chase.

b. At what maturity and therefore interest rate does Barclays wish to place the deposit funds? Perhaps Barclays replies that it wants a seven-day certificate of deposit at the going rate at which Chase is accepting inter-bank deposits.

Meantime, in London, a similar set of questions is being raised between Barclays and ABC Corporation. ABC Corporation wants the deposit kept at Barclays as it first indicated; however, the maturity and the interest rate on the deposit must be established. Assume that ABC

[1]This is not to say that some colorful examples of the suitcase version do not exist. The Swiss Alps have witnessed many of these transfers.

Corporation wishes to maintain a seven-day deposit at the going rate for deposits with Barclays.

A Euro-dollar deposit has been created. The deposit in London is denominated in dollars; Barclays has now acquired the power to deal in dollars outside the United States.

2. Barclays decides to exercise its power to deal in dollars. Shortly after Barclays received the deposit from ABC Corporation it also received an application for a Euro-dollar loan from XYZ Corporation. XYZ Corporation needs the money for only seven days. However, XYZ Corporation would like to have the Euro-dollar funds transferred to Switzerland where it eventually intends to use the funds. In Switzerland, XYZ Corporation conducts its banking business with the Union Bank of Switzerland.

Barclays extends the Euro-dollar loan to XYZ Corporation at the prevailing rate for the desired maturity. Now Barclays must transfer its dollar balances to the account of XYZ Corporation with the Union Bank of Switzerland. Accordingly, Barclays sends a telex to Chase Manhattan requesting that its deposit with Chase be transferred to Union Bank of Switzerland for their account with XYZ Corporation. Union Bank of Switzerland will now engage in the same kind of inquiry as when the Euro-dollar deposit was first created at Barclays.

a. Does Union Bank of Switzerland wish to maintain the deposit with Chase Manhattan or another banking institution?

b. For what maturity is the deposit to be maintained and, therefore, what interest rate?

Euro-dollars are now being traded outside the United States. However, the link with Chase is maintained. Throughout the two transactions Chase had some kind of deposit or liability. The only change at Chase was in the name of the owner of that deposit from Corporation ABC, to Barclays, to Union Bank of Switzerland. Notice, however, that Corporation ABC now thinks it has a Euro-dollar deposit with Barclays and that XYZ Corporation thinks it has a Euro-dollar loan from Barclays and a Euro-dollar deposit with the Union Bank of Switzerland.

What happens if, when Union Bank of Switzerland is notified of the impending receipt of a Euro-dollar deposit, it requests that the deposit be transferred to Union Bank's account with Credit Lyonnais in Paris? That is, Union Bank of Switzerland wishes to place a dollar-denominated deposit with Credit Lyonnais; i.e., an interbank loan. Then, Chase Manhattan will inform Credit Lyonnais that Union Bank of Switzerland is transferring a dollar deposit to their account. The next set of questions then will be:

a. Where does Credit Lyonnais want to have the dollar deposit, at Chase or at another bank?

b. For what maturity and at what interest rate is it to be deposited?

Assume that Credit Lyonnais wishes to have an overnight deposit with Chase. The deposit at Chase now has had its ownership transferred once more from Union Bank of Switzerland to Credit Lyonnais. However, a deposit is still maintained at an American bank, Chase, in this case. Had anyone in the chain decided to use Citibank rather than Chase Manhattan as the recipient of their deposit, Chase Manhattan would have moved out of the chain of transactions, but a deposit would still be maintained with an American bank, Citibank in that case.

Every time a bank transfer of funds takes place in the Euro-dollar market, two questions must be answered to complete the transfer: "Where?" and "What maturity?" The answer to the "where" in the Euro-dollar market must always involve an American bank, although the convoluted nature of the transaction may also involve many other foreign banks, as in the case of Union Bank of Switzerland and Credit Lyonnais in the example. However, there may be transactions in the Euro-markets where a transfer of funds is not necessary, for example, if the XYZ Corporation had chosen to maintain its borrowed funds with Barclays instead of transferring them to the Union Bank. In these cases the American bank will not get involved until a transaction transferring funds to another bank occurs. But the period during which the American bank is not involved is bound to be short-lived.

Before leaving this introduction to Euro-dollars, notice that the word itself is presently a misnomer which has historical roots. As to the first part of the word, "Euro," Euro-dollars can actually be traded anywhere as long as it is outside the United States. The bulk of the Euro-dollar transactions are consummated in Europe, but a sizable amount is also transacted in other parts of the world. Actually, one of the developments of the 1970s has been the emergence of the Asian dollar market (notice that the Euro- prefix has been dropped in this case). The second part of the word, "dollar," is also misleading. One should rather speak of the Euro-*currency* market since many currencies besides the dollar can be found as the denominator of financial assets and liabilities traded outside the country of that currency. Thus, there is a market in Euro-French francs, Euro-guilders, etc. However, Euro-dollars proper dominate the market, accounting for about 75% of the total Euro-currency liabilities of the banks.

In the same manner that Euro-dollars are tied to a deposit in the United States, Euro-guilders are tied to deposits in the Netherlands, Euro-Swiss francs to deposits in Switzerland, and so on. A given individual may think that (s)he is holding Swiss franc deposits in London at Barclays because (s)he has the legal right to withdraw Swiss francs from Barclays; however, the actual funds at Barclays must be held at a Swiss bank. Barclays can comply with the request from the customer to withdraw Swiss francs only by asking a Swiss bank to transfer funds from Barclays's account to the account of the customer or to whatever bank the customer chooses to transfer the Swiss francs.

MULTIPLE CREATION AND CONTRACTION OF EURO-DOLLARS

Euro-dollars, once they come into existence, can reproduce themselves. In the previous example, assuming that each of the Euro-dollar transactions is for the same amount, by the time that Credit Lyonnais accepts the Euro-dollar deposit the original Euro-deposit of the ABC Corporation has tripled.

The upper half of Exhibit 14.1 (section A) shows how the initial Euro-dollar deposit multiplies in our example. The exhibit assumes each transaction is for $1 million. The initial transfer of a deposit from Chase to Barclays by the ABC Corporation creates a new Euro-dollar deposit of $1 million (transaction A.1). Now Barclays extends a Euro-dollar loan in the amount of $1 million to the XYZ Corporation (transaction A.2). Funds are initially made available to the XYZ Corporation in the form of dollar deposits with Barclays; i.e., Barclays has increased both its dollar loans and its dollar deposits by $1 million.[2] This raises the total Euro-dollar liabilities of non-U.S. banks to $2 million. Had the XYZ Corporation held the Euro-dollar deposit with Barclays, this would have stopped, at least temporarily, the multiple creation of Euro-dollars. Barclays exhausted its dollar-lending capacity. Yet, the XYZ Corporation chooses to withdraw its deposit from Barclays and to deposit it with the Union Bank of Switzerland (transaction A.3). After this transaction the amount of Euro-dollar deposits is still $2 million. However, the Union Bank has acquired Euro-dollar balances that it can lend out. In the example, Union Bank's dollars are lent to Credit Lyonnais, presumably because Credit Lyonnais is paying a higher interest rate for deposits than Barclays (transaction A.4). This is an interbank Euro-dollar loan. This creates an additional Euro-dollar deposit in the amount of $1 million, the Euro-deposit in Credit Lyonnais. The total of Euro-dollar deposits outstanding in the system is now $3 million.

From the point of view of each individual bank in the system, the particular bank has not been adding to Euro-dollar accounts, but only relending the dollars, which for them is simply investing the deposits they receive. However, the aggregate effect is to expand the Euro-dollars beyond the original amount.

From the pattern just described we can see how the expansion of Euro-dollars may occur. In this example where the banks did not maintain any reserves against their deposits, the potential expansion of Euro-dollars is infinite. Each bank that receives a $1 million Euro-dollar deposit can lend $1 million which becomes a new Euro-dollar deposit in another bank. If the banks maintain certain reserves against their Euro-deposits, say 10%, the theoretical limit for the expansion of Euro-dollar deposits in the example would be $10 million. As explained in any introductory text in money and banking, a 10% reserve requirement implies a multiplier for the initial deposit of 10; i.e., the multiplier is the reciprocal of the reserve requirement ($1 \div 0.10 = 10$).

Notice that this credit creation process refers to *new* dollar liabilities created and traded outside the United States. A draft on a U.S. bank which is traded outside the United States is not a Euro-dollar in most definitions since there is no new credit involved; it is similar to a share of General Motors exchanged between non-American owners. The example shown above also makes the bank a passive respondent to a dollar depositor. The foreign bank has to do something with the dollars which it seemingly reluctantly has accepted. In reality the bank actively will solicit customers for dollar loans even though there are no dollars on deposit. When the loans are made, the customer eventually will demand the dollar proceeds of the loan, and the bank will have to seek dollar deposits; i.e., to borrow dollars.

[2] Since at this stage there is not a transfer of funds, Chase is not affected by the transaction.

EXHIBIT 14.1. Multiple Creation and Contraction of Euro-Dollars

Transactions	Changes in Balance Sheets of Banks							
	Chase Manhattan		Barclays		Union Bank of Switzerland		Credit Lyonnais	
A. EURO-DOLLAR CREATION								
1. ABC Corporation transfers deposit from Chase to Barclays		Deposit (ABC) -1,000,000 Deposit (Barclays) +1,000,000	$ Balance (Chase) +1,000,000	$ Deposit (ABC) +1,000,000				
2. Barclays makes Euro-dollar loan to XYZ Corporation			$ Loan (XYZ) +1,000,000	$ Deposit (XYZ) +1,000,000				
3. XYZ Corporation withdraws deposit from Barclays and deposits it in Union Bank of Switzerland		Deposit (Barclays) -1,000,000 Deposit (Union Bk) +1,000,000	$ Balance (Chase) -1,000,000	$Deposit (XYZ) -1,000,000	$ Balance (Chase) +1,000,000	$ Deposit (XYZ) +1,000,000		
4. Union Bank places (lends) its deposit with Credit Lyonnais		Deposit (Union Bk) -1,000,000 Deposit (Cr Lyon) +1,000,000			$ Balance (Chase) -1,000,000 $ Balance (Cr Lyon) +1,000,000		$ Balance (Chase) +1,000,000	$ Deposit (Union Bk) +1,000,000
Total Euro-Dollar Deposits Outstanding: $3,000,000								
B. EURO-DOLLAR CONTRACTION								
1. XYZ Corporation exchanges Euro-dollar deposit into Swiss francs						$ Deposit (XYZ) -1,000,000 SF Deposit (XYZ) +1,000,000		
2. Union Bank of Switzerland brings its exchange position to zero. (After XYZ converted its dollar deposit into Swiss francs, Union Bank was left long in dollars and short in francs.)					$ Balance (Cr Lyon) -1,000,000 SF Balance (Cr Lyon) +1,000,000			$ Deposit (Union Bk) -1,000,000 SF Deposit (Union Bk) +1,000,000
3. Credit Lyonnais brings its exchange position to zero	SF Balances (Cr Lyon) -1,000,000	Deposit (Cr Lyon) -1,000,000					$ Balance (Chase) -1,000,000	SF Deposit (Chase) -1,000,000
Total Euro-Dollar Deposits Outstanding: $1,000,000								

Typically, there are no legal reserves against Euro-dollar deposits. Thus, it would appear that Euro-dollar deposits could expand to infinity. However, there is a built-in check to this expansion. Most corporations obtaining a Euro-loan do so with the purpose of spending the proceeds—not just to maintain the loan proceeds indefinitely as a deposit in a Euro-bank. As expenditures are made, this will often require a foreign exchange transaction to convert the dollars borrowed into local currency. This exchange transaction will not only eliminate further possibilities for expansion of Euro-dollar deposits, but it may actually contract the volume of outstanding Euro-dollar deposits.

In the lower portion of Exhibit 14.1 (section B) we can see the impact of XYZ Corporation converting the proceeds of the Euro-dollar loan into local currency, Swiss francs. Assuming that the XYZ Corporation wants the loan to pay a liability denominated in Swiss francs, the dollar proceeds must be exchanged into Swiss francs before payment can be made. In the example the foreign exchange transaction is made with the Union Bank of Switzerland, (transaction B.1). This transaction immediately reduces the amount of Euro-dollar deposits outstanding by $1 million. It also eliminates the possibility of the Union Bank making a Euro-dollar loan and expanding Euro-dollar deposits. However, in our example the Union Bank had already proceeded to lend its Euro-dollar funds to Credit Lyonnais before the foreign exchange transaction took place. That loan must be reversed.

The exchange transaction by the XYZ Corporation leaves the Union Bank exposed to exchange risks. A dollar asset, the balances with Credit Lyonnais, is now matched by a liability in Swiss francs, the XYZ deposit. To eliminate this exposure, Union Bank must convert the dollar asset into Swiss francs (transaction B.2). Assuming the exchange transaction is made with Credit Lyonnais, the exchange risk is transferred to Credit Lyonnais which sees its dollar deposit converted into a Swiss franc deposit. Again, the exchange transaction reduces the amount of outstanding Euro-dollar deposits by another $1 million. Total outstanding deposits have contracted to $1 million, the original Euro-dollar deposit by ABC Corporation. This is the same result as if Union Bank had not gone ahead and lent out its Euro-dollar balances before XYZ's exchange transaction. That is, the conversion of an Euro-dollar deposit into non-dollars stops the process of multiple creation of Euro-dollars. In addition, if the institution with whom the deposit was held had already gone ahead and lent out the Euro-dollars, the exchange transaction will also contract the volume of Euro-dollar deposits outstanding.

For Credit Lyonnais to eliminate the exchange position created by Union Bank's exchange transaction, it has to convert its dollar balance held with Chase into Swiss francs. (For simplicity's sake we assume this exchange transaction is done with Chase, which maintains Swiss franc balances with Credit Lyonnais.) This now kills the deposit maintained at Chase, and the life created by the original deposit transfer to the Euro-market is terminated. The net result of all the transactions combined is now $1 million of Euro-dollar deposits and a reduction of foreign exchange balances of a U.S. bank by $1 million.[3]

[3]If the XYZ Corporation wanted to use the loan proceeds in the United States, the effects would have been similar, except for the loss of reserves by Chase. Assuming XYZ maintains an account with Chase, the ownership of the Chase deposit would have been transferred from Barclays to XYZ. The Euro-dollar deposits outstanding after this would also be $1 million, the initial Euro-dollar deposit.

It is important to note the contributing factor that stopped the expansion of Euro-dollars and even worked to contract the size of outstanding Euro-dollar deposits in this example. This is the factor that makes it impossible for the Euro-dollar market to grow without any bounds, with the attendant implications for world monetary liquidity and U.S. monetary policy. Commercial banks do not take foreign exchange risks (i.e., they maintain a zero net exchange position) in their *lending* operations. This is in contrast to the foreign exchange operations where they do take exchange risks. In the lending operation the currency of the loans and the deposits used to finance these loans is the same. If this relationship is altered, banks take steps to restore the zero exchange position. This is the process that eliminated the Euro-dollar deposit at Credit Lyonnais above.

If, instead of Credit Lyonnais doing the exchange transaction with Chase, it did it with the French central bank and the central bank kept the dollar balances with Chase, the U.S. bank would not loose foreign exchange. The central bank's keeping of the dollar balances would be done as an intervention in the foreign exchange market. In contrast to a commercial bank, the central bank would want to assume this exchange position for policy reasons. Actually if the central bank chose to maintain its Euro-dollar deposits with a Euro-bank instead of Chase, the whole cycle of Euro-dollar expansion could be started again as a new Euro-dollar deposit is created. Because of the possible multiple creation of credit, most central banks restrain themselves from depositing dollar reserves in the Euro-markets. Instead these reserves are kept invested in the domestic money market; e.g., U.S. government securities.

Thus, to establish the extent of multiple expansion of Euro-deposits, one must determine what happens to the dollars created by Euro-loans. Does the borrower turn them over to someone who exchanges them for another currency, perhaps ultimately increasing the foreign currency reserves of a central bank? If so, does the central bank place the dollars on deposit with a U.S. bank in a time deposit account, or buy government bonds, or place them as a Euro-dollar deposit?

Obviously, the potential multiple creation of Euro-dollars has a great impact on the total size of the Euro-dollar market. Similarly, the market as a whole is of great relevance in analyzing countries' balance of payments and money supplies. These relationships are examined in the appendix to this chapter. Generally, students of this topic have concluded that the multiplier effect of Euro-dollars in practice is closer to one rather than the infinite multiplier theoretically possible under the current situation of no required reserves.[4]

Euro-dollars are *time* deposits, not demand deposits as we think of bank checking deposits. They are *not* money in the purest sense, since they are not perfect means of payment, one of the definitions of money found in any basic economics textbook. Banks in the Euro-dollar scheme, aiding in the redepositing process that is critical to the creation of the multiple Euro-dollars, are mainly non-bank financial intermediaries, not primary creators of money. (They often act as financial intermediaries in the United States as well, as when they offer a savings account or sell a certificate of deposit in order to fund a loan.) It is because the Euro-dollar loan is not likely to be idle (soon moving out of the Euro-

[4]For example, see John Hewson and Eisuke Sakakibara, *The Euro-currency Markets and Their Implications* (Lexington, Mass.: D. C. Heath, 1975).

dollar system) and because the Euro-dollar deposit carries interest that the multiplier is likely to be rather low. If the Euro-dollars could not leave the system so easily (U.S. demand deposits, for example), then the multiplier would be much higher.

In this sense, the expansion of Euro-dollar deposits can be compared to the impact on U.S. money supply of a deposit transferred from a U.S. commercial bank to a domestic savings and loan institution, a non-bank institution. The savings bank can extend a loan like the Euro-bank can. Similarly, the recipient of the savings bank loan will most likely not redeposit the loan proceeds with another savings bank which could then make another loan. Instead, the borrower is likely to spend the loan in the operations of a business. The recipients of these payments likely will deposit the funds in a commercial bank, thus terminating the potential expansion of credit in the nonbank financial intermediaries.[5]

EURO-CURRENCY INSTRUMENTS

In the preceding discussion we introduced the two major types of instruments used in the Euro-markets: Euro-deposits and Euro-loans. In this section we discuss their characteristics in some detail.

Euro-Deposits. The bulk of Euro-deposits has a maturity of less than a year. Depositors in the Euro-markets may have their funds in regular time deposits (which may be overnight, call money, or other terms) or in certificates of deposit, usually for longer (three-six month) maturities. In contrast to the U.S. practice, the Euro-banks do not maintain demand deposits (checking accounts) for customers. Accordingly, the transfer of funds usually takes the form of a cablegraphic transfer. Mail is then used to confirm the transactions that have taken place over the telex or cable. In the Euro-dollar market, one is dealing with large amounts ($100,000 to begin with), and time is very important. The float time of a transfer of funds must be reduced to a minimum so that the owner of the funds does not lose sizable amounts of interest.

Negotiable certificates of deposits for Euro-dollars were introduced in 1966. The bank allows the holder of a three-twelve months or longer deposit to remarket it, should that be desired. Some of these deposits are also formally designated as floating rate accounts; the interest paid on them will increase or decrease together with the interbank rates. In addition, the London market features "forward forward" CDs, by which a bank commits itself to issue a certificate of deposit in so many months for a certain duration for a particular pre-set interest rate, usually based on a standard yield curve calculation. Thus, the bank may agree to a one-year certificate of deposit to be issued in six months. If the six-month rate is 9% and the eighteen-month rate is 10%, then the one-year CD to commence in six months would have a rate of around 10½%, so that the yield on the 9% CD for six months and the 10½% CD for months seven

[5] An analysis of the impact of nonbank financial institutions on domestic multiple creation of credit can be found in John G. Gurley and Edward S. Shaw, "Financial Intermediaries and the Saving-Investment Process," *Journal of Finance,* May 1956, pp. 257–276. Further discussion of this topic appears in the appendix to the chapter.

through eighteen would average out to the same as the 10% for the spot eighteen-month CD.

Euro-Loans. Usually, Euro-loans range from a $500,000 base up to $100 million or more, typically in $1-million units. The usual maturity ranges from thirty days to five or seven years. When the lender is known to the bank, loans of under twelve-months' maturity are often established very easily. The lender will simply call to request a loan; if the rate and terms quoted by the bank are satisfactory, the loan is immediately accepted. When a parent guarantee is required, as is sometimes the case for a foreign subsidiary requesting a loan, the guarantee can often be based on a telephone conversation. Confirming wires or letters are sent later.

The interest rates on Euro-dollar loans are often floating rates, especially for the intermediate and longer maturities (three years or longer). In contrast to the bank lending practice in the United States, European Euro-dollar lenders establish a rate at some fixed percentage over a given interbank lending rate, usually the London interbank offer rate (LIBOR) at which they borrow a substantial part of their funds. This rate is the charge that banks make for loans to each other. Hence, the borrower may find a loan quoted at "1½% over LIBOR, established at six-month intervals, until maturity." These floating rate revolving loans (also called "revolvers" or "roll-over credits") protect bank profits against increases in the interest rate on Euro-dollar deposits (the source of financing for the loan) such as might be induced by currency speculation or changes in yields on various currencies.

Some borrowers operate with lines of credit, which are usually given for a period not to exceed twelve months but may be renegotiated at the end of the period. A commitment fee of ¼–½% may be placed on the unused portion of the line of credit. The rate on each take-down of the loan is established at the time of the take-down and will typically be based on an interbank rate plus a previously set premium.

The rates for the loans to prime borrowers have ranged from LIBOR + ¾% for seven-eight-year maturity to as little as LIBOR + ⅜% for a five-year maturity. Nonprime borrowers pay a higher spread of 2–3% depending on maturity and credit worthiness. In periods of high liquidity in the market, as in 1977, the spreads charged to less than prime borrowers tend to approach those charged to prime ones.

Usually, there is no amortization of the loan, as is common in the United States; instead, the entire amount is repaid at the maturity date. The loan is also not secured except by the general credit of the firm, although there are often constraints on additional debt incurred by the firm.

WHY EURO-CURRENCY MARKETS?

There is a simple reason: government regulations. At the beginning of the chapter Euro-dollars were defined as financial assets and liabilities denominated in dollars but traded outside the United States. The Euro-dollar market offers the opportunity for trading dollars outside the control of government regulations imposed on residents (defined according to law) within the boundaries of the United States. When these regulations start to constrain the dollar money market in the United States, then the trading requirements can be satisfied by creating another dollar money market outside the United States—the Euro-dollar market. Below are presented the most important regulations that have contributed to the growth of the Euro-dollar market. Similar regulations. perhaps with different objectives, can be found to have aided the development of other Euro-currency markets.[6]

United States interest rate ceilings and reserve requirements have always been important tools to pursue monetary policy objectives. By the Federal Reserve's Regulation Q, United States banks were limited in the interest rate they could pay on deposits. The restriction did not apply to Euro-dollar deposits, even when they were in the European branches of American banks. Hence, once the ceiling imposed by Regulation Q was reached, there was an incentive for citizens of all lands to pull funds from the United States and invest them in higher yield Euro-dollar deposits.

The flight of dollar deposits from U.S. banks to Euro-banks coincided with the discovery of a profitable use of those dollars back in the United States. Regulation M in the United States specifies the amount that U.S. banks are required to keep as a reserve against deposits. However, until 1969 this regulation did not affect the amount of reserves to be kept by American banks against deposits from foreign banks or from their own foreign branches. Hence, dollar-denominated accounts in European branches (Euro-dollar accounts) had no reserve requirements, and the branch could deposit (lend) the funds with its parent who was then free to lend against the full face amount of the account. In contrast, had the same customer deposited the funds in the American head office in the first place, the bank would have been forced to keep a certain percentage of the funds on reserve against the deposit.

This process became more of a necessity to U.S. banks in the soaring expansion of the Euro-dollar market in 1969 and 1970. Tightening credit terms in the United States reduced the availability of funds in this country. Meanwhile the foreign branches of U.S. banks were paying far higher rates (up to 13% vs. 6-7% in the United States) on dollar deposits abroad, pulling the depositors away from the domestic accounts. The reason for these high rates was simply that these Euro-dollars were especially valuable for lending purposes to U.S. banks.

The sequence, then, began with U.S. banks dearly needing funds to lend to customers, for ceilings on interest rates here (Regulation Q) encouraged non-residents who had dollar deposits to move them to the Euro-dollar market (where the ceilings did not apply) or to other currencies. Realizing these facts, American banks sought to borrow Euro-dollar funds from their own branches and from other European banks for relending to regular commercial customers. This increased borrowing from the Euro-dollar market pushed up interest rates in that market further. This process not only allowed the banks to reattract funds which would otherwise be lost because of interest rate differentials, but it

[6]Although most of these regulations are not binding as of the time of this writing, they illustrate how the Euro-markets developed. Since governments reserve their rights to impose or reimpose regulations, a review of the past can also serve to illuminate the impact that future regulatory developments may have on the financial markets.

meant the funds could be reloaned without the reserve requirements faced by the banks for U.S. dollar deposits.

The differential in required reserves was eliminated for U.S. banks by a revision of Regulation M by the Federal Reserve Board in September 1969. This revision required U.S. banks to maintain a reserve against liabilities to foreign banks (including U.S. banks' foreign branches) in a progressive fashion. After some changes, the reserve requirements imposed on Euro-dollar borrowings from foreign branches or any foreign bank were made comparable to the reserve requirements on large certificates of deposit, about 4%. However, on August 1978, an interesting twist of events took place in the regulatory history of the Euro-dollar market: The Federal Reserve Board reduced to zero the reserve requirements on Euro-dollar borrowings by U.S. banks. The 1969 change in Regulation M was aimed at eliminating any advantage that Euro-dollar borrowings might provide U.S. banks over domestic borrowings. The change of August 1978 was designed to create such a privileged position for Euro-dollar borrowings. In an aggressive maneuver the Federal Reserve Board was attempting to recreate the credit conditions of 1969, when U.S. banks turned in large numbers to the Euro-dollar market as a source of funds. If U.S. banks could be induced to repeat that performance, a supporting force would be placed behind the value of the dollar, which had declined steadily during most of 1978. As this book went to press, the results of this policy were not yet fully known.

As to Regulation Q, the ceilings on interest rates paid to large depositors have been eliminated for all intents and purposes. However, Regulation Q is still in existence and, in principle at least, ceilings could be imposed again at the will of the Federal Reserve Board.[7]

Another set of regulations which contributed heavily to the rapid growth of the Euro-dollar market was developed to control capital outflows from the United States and improve the balance of payments situation of this country. These regulations were: (1) the controls on foreign direct investment, (2) the interest equalization tax, and (3) the voluntary credit restraint program. The controls on foreign direct investment made it necessary for multinational companies to finance growth of foreign direct investment from sources outside the United States. The interest equalization tax imposed a penalty on U.S. residents who bought securities issued by foreigners. Finally, the voluntary credit restraint program limited the amount of credit that U.S. banks could extend to foreigners. In summary, all these restrictions attempted to rechannel a demand for funds from the financial markets in the United States to elsewhere. This elsewhere was conveniently satisfied by the Euro-dollar market. Except for some reporting requirements, all these regulations were eliminated in January 1974.

In addition to the regulations imposed by the United States, controls im-

[7] Regulation Q and its changes also affected the ownership of Euro-dollar accounts. Oscar Altman of the IMF estimates that two-thirds of the 1962 Euro-dollars were owned by central banks, yet only one-third of the 1967 base was owned by this group. Prior to 1962 Regulation Q ceilings on dollar interest rates also applied to central bank deposits. Hence, these banks liked the higher rates on dollar deposits which they would realize in Euro-dollars. When the ceiling was removed in applicability to their accounts, there was less need for them to seek Euro-dollars. It is also true that the nonofficial Euro-dollar market grew much faster in this period than the official holdings. See Oscar L. Altman, "Euro-dollars," *Finance and Development,* March 1967.

posed or likely to be imposed by other countries on the use of the local currencies also encouraged growth of the Euro-dollar market. Thus, even if RCA or Nestlé operating in Italy could arrange Italian lira loans, there was the possibility of present or future restrictions on the use of those loans outside Italy. For example, if these firms wanted to purchase raw materials from a German supplier, they might discover that the Bank of Italy was limiting the amount of liras which could be removed from the country. The Euro-dollar (or the Euro-lira) loan, in contrast, would have no such restriction. Since the dollar is the most liquid and most readily acceptable currency, Euro-dollars became the most popular Euro-currency even for non-American firms operating in other lands.

EURO-CURRENCY RATES

Euro-currency rates, like rates in any other financial market, are determined by supply of and demand for funds in the particular market and in related markets. More specifically, Euro-currency rates are affected by the rates in the corresponding home currency, by spot and forward exchange rates, by domestic and Euro-rates in other currencies, and by the inflation rate in various countries. In a complete explanation of Euro-rates the markets where all these other rates are determined should also be considered.[8] However, this is a very complex process and the validity of the relationships would depend on the degree of efficiency in the markets, a subject where a good deal of controversy still exists. (See Chapter 5.) Thus, we will limit the scope of this presentation to the relationship between domestic and Euro-rates. With any degree of inefficiency in the markets the strongest line of causality is likely to run from domestic rates to Euro-rates.

Given the similarities, for example, between a Euro-dollar deposit and a domestic deposit for the same maturity, we would expect the interest rate on the two deposits to be the same. However, as discussed in the preceding section, governments regulate domestic money markets while Euro-currency markets remain free of regulations. The costs created by these regulations are reflected in the rates and create a spread between domestic rates and Euro-currency rates. Let's see how these factors affect the rate in one specific currency, Euro-dollars.

From the lender's point of view, the individual has the money market in the United States available as an alternative to a Euro-dollar deposit.[9] Thus, the money market rates in the United States provide a floor for Euro-dollar rates. When the domestic rates go up, so do the Euro-dollar rates, and vice versa. Supporting this relationship is the fact that Euro-banks can usually pay a higher rate for dollar deposits than domestic commercial banks since Euro-banks do not have to meet reserve requirements or insure their deposits against default. Domestic rates provide a floor as long as the United States does not restrict

[8] For a detailed discussion of Euro-rates including these factors, see Gunter Dufey and Ian H. Giddy, *The International Money Market* (Englewood Cliffs, N.J.: Prentice-Hall, Inc., 1978), Ch. 2.

[9] Euro-dollars can come to the U.S. money market with a vengeance when the rate is attractive; some of the more aggressive acquisition funding by Jimmy Ling and Las Vegas financier Kirk Kerkorian was done through Euro-dollar credits.

foreigners' investments in the domestic market. If such regulations were imposed, as when Switzerland charges negative interest rates on foreign deposits, the domestic rate would become a ceiling instead of a floor to the Euro-rate.[10]

From the final borrower's point of view, in the absence of regulations, the major difference between the local U.S. market and the Euro-dollar market is that commercial banks in the U.S. market usually require minimum compensating balances, which effectively raise the cost of funds borrowed, while Euro-loans do not require these balances to be kept with the bank. Therefore, the borrower is usually willing to pay a slightly higher nominal interest rate on loans in the Euro-markets. When capital flow controls imposed by the government make it difficult to borrow in the domestic markets, borrowers would be willing to pay a substantially higher interest rate for Euro-currencies than for domestic funds.

Given the conditions that have prevailed in the U.S. domestic markets, Euro-dollar rates have usually maintained a spread over domestic rates. Exhibit 14.2 compares rate on ninety-day certificates of deposit in the United States with Euro-dollar rates for similar maturity. Throughout the period presented in the chart the CD rate has provided an effective floor to the Euro-dollar rate, which has remained consistently above the CD rate.

Now that we have established that U.S. rates provide a floor to Euro-dollar rates and that the latter tend to maintain a spread over the former, the next question is: "What determines the fluctuations in the size of the spread of Euro-dollar rates over U.S. rates?" The answer is government regulations. The bottom line in Exhibit 14.2 shows the spread between the two rates after accounting for reserve requirements on CDs.

Formerly, the banking system regulations that most affected the Euro-dollar rates were Regulations Q and M. Regulation Q, by imposing ceilings on the rates that U.S. commercial banks could pay on deposits, converted the Euro-dollar market into a buffer market where commercial banks went to raise funds whenever these funds could not be secured in the domestic markets. Regulation M, as mentioned before, made the use of the Euro-markets more profitable because the funds raised there for domestic use were not subject to the same reserve requirements as domestic funds. Because of changes in the regulations, these forces did not affect the markets from late 1969 to the fall of 1978. Euro-dollar borrowings by U.S. banks became subject to reserve requirements in 1969, and the ceilings imposed by Regulation Q were lifted in 1973. The regulations designed to control capital outflows from the United States were also eliminated

[10]This discussion ignores U.S. withholding income tax on income paid to foreigners. This tax will tend to push Euro-dollar rates below the level of rates in the U.S. money market. However, deposits in commercial banks have been exempted from this tax since 1966 (Public Law 89-809, Sec. 102). This law exempts bank depositors from U.S. withholding tax as long as the foreign owner is not engaged in business in the United States and uses the proceeds outside the United States. The exemption was initially issued for a limited amount of time but it has continued to be renewed every time that its expiration date has approached.

In principle, the interest earned on Euro-dollar deposits should also be subject to income tax in the country of residence of the deposit owner. However, in practice, this is rarely the case since the name of the owner of the deposit is not reported to the country of the owner's residence and the depositor usually turns out to be remiss in declaring it for tax purposes.

EXHIBIT 14.2. Euro-dollar and Domestic U.S. Rates Compared

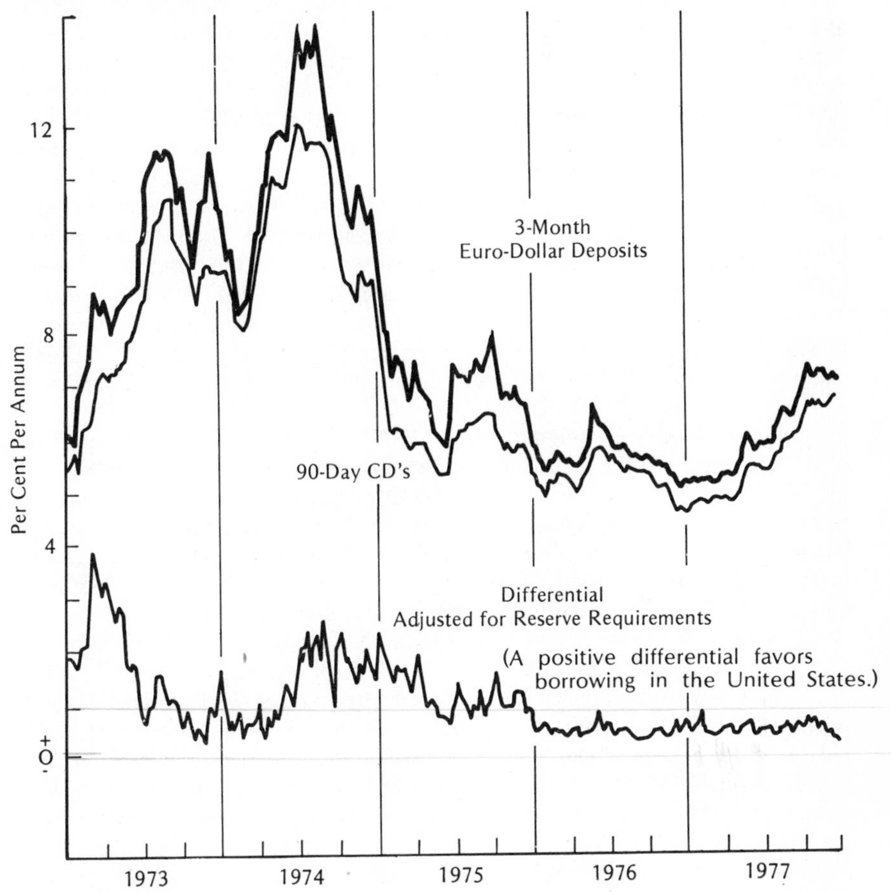

SOURCE: Board of Governors of the Federal Reserve System, Division of International Finance, SELECTED INTEREST AND EXCHANGE RATES, January 3, 1978.

in January 1974. However, the reserve requirements imposed on the borrowings of Euro-dollars by U.S. banks were reduced to zero on August 1978. This again made Euro-dollar borrowings more desirable and allowed U.S. banks to pay a higher interest rate on borrowed Euro-dollars than domestic dollars.

The controls on the U.S. balance of payments in existence until 1974 effectively segmented the domestic and the Euro-dollar markets to the extent that domestic funds could not be used to finance foreign operations. Any time that foreigners or expanding U.S. businesses abroad increased their demand for funds over and above the capacities of foreign domestic markets, the major alternative available for raising the needed funds was the Euro-dollar market. This established an upward bias to the Euro-dollar rates over the U.S. domestic rates. In addition, every time there was an international monetary crisis involving speculation on the depreciation of the U.S. dollar against other major currencies, the spread of Euro-dollar rates over U.S. domestic rates widened. See, for example, the first quarter of 1973 in Exhibit 14.2. In the presence of controls on capital outflows from the United States, the borrowing of dollars to finance the purchase of so-called harder currencies could be made only in the Euro-dollar market; therefore, there was an increase in rates in that market.

With the elimination of the controls to protect the U.S. balance of payments in early 1974, and the changes in the other relevant regulations for U.S. banking before then, it was expected that the spreads between Euro-dollar rates and U.S. domestic rates would narrow substantially or disappear. The only justification left for a spread appeared to be sovereign risk. Some lenders might prefer to keep their dollar deposits in the United States rather than in London, where they might become subject to confiscation by the British government. Obviously, this risk could work both ways. However, large spreads of Euro-rates over domestic U.S. rates prevailed and even increased during 1974 and part of 1975.

The oil crisis, toward the end of 1973, resulted in a quadrupling of oil prices and immersed the industrial world in economic recession during 1974. But in the United States, the fear of inflation dominated the concern for economic recession and monetary authorities reinforced the tight monetary policy already begun in 1973. As a result, extremely high levels of interest rates came to prevail in the dollar markets. And, although controls on capital outflows had been eliminated earlier in the year, U.S. banks were under considerable pressure to conserve their funds for domestic lending instead of channeling them to foreign borrowers. Simultaneously, the value of the U.S. dollar, which had rallied at the end of 1973 with the realization that the United States was less dependent on foreign oil than most other industrialized countries, came under pressure as the U.S. trade deficit grew and trade surpluses in countries such as Germany continued during 1974. But, given the monetary conditions in the domestic dollar market, foreigners wishing to borrow dollars to invest in other currencies were effectively forced to do so in the Euro-dollar markets. As a result, the spread of Euro-dollar rates over domestic rates widened once more.

Another factor reinforcing the increase in interest differentials between Euro-currency and domestic rates during 1974 and 1975 was the scare of a collapse of the Euro-dollar market. On top of the fears for the Euro-markets generated by the recycling of massive amounts of petro-dollars came the insolvency of banks such as Herstatt in Germany and Franklin National in New York. These scares added a further upward pressure to Euro-rates as funds invested in dollars were diverted from the Euro-market into the domestic U.S. money market and invested in government securities.

As the United States started pulling out of its recession ahead of other industrialized countries in 1975, the dollar began to strengthen. However, the fears about the Euro-markets, which started in 1974, were slow to disappear during 1975. In addition, there was concern that the new economic expansion would be short-lived and lead to the same type of conditions that had prevailed in 1974. Thus, the spread of Euro-dollar rates over domestic rates remained relatively high in 1975.

It appears that the continued lower interest rates during 1976 and most of 1977 served to assuage the fears of 1974–75. In addition, Euro-markets began increasing in liquidity with a combination of increased funds from petro-dollar investments and decreased demand for funds from a world experiencing sluggish economic growth. In the United States domestic dollars, confronted with a relatively easy monetary policy, moved freely between the Euro-markets and the domestic markets. The result of these forces translated into reduced spreads between Euro-dollars and domestic rates during 1976–77. Not even the decline of the dollar toward the end of 1977 and during 1978 saw this spread increase again.

Before ending this brief discussion of factors affecting Euro-rates we should note another factor we have, up until now, left out of the discussion in order to simplify the presentation. Although we have been talking about a *rate*, it would be more appropriate to talk about deposit and lending *rates*, since the spread between these two rates is also affected by the conditions we have described.

COUNTRY COMPOSITION OF EURO-CURRENCY MARKETS

The growth in the Euro-currency markets in recent years has been phenomenal. Figures prepared by the Bank for International Settlements (BIS) from data furnished by banks in eight major European countries–only a portion of the market–show this growth very clearly. In less than ten years the Euro-currency markets have multiplied by more than ten fold, from $37.7 billion in 1968 to $373.8 billion in 1977.[11] The dominant currency, as mentioned earlier, is the U.S. dollar. Although losing some ground to other currencies, mainly German marks and Swiss francs, in 1977 the dollar still accounted for 70% of the external assets of these eight banks.

A more comprehensive set of data provided by BIS includes the banks of the Group of Ten countries, Switzerland, and offshore branches of U.S. banks. Exhibit 14.3 shows for the end of 1977 the external assets and liabilities of this group against itself and against other areas of the world. More than half of the positions of the Group of Ten countries are against itself. However, as a group they contribute more deposits (liabilities of the banks) to the Euro-currency markets than what they receive in loans (assets of the banks) from these markets. This is mostly accounted for by Switzerland. In 1977 Switzerland contributed $74 billion to the external deposits of the group; however, it borrowed only $16 billion from the group as a whole. This role of Switzerland has been a constant feature of the Euro-currency markets. In 1977 the United States and the United Kingdom also were net contributors of deposits to this group.

In addition to the Group of Ten and Switzerland, the net providers of funds to the Euro-currency markets are the oil-exporting countries. All these countries, including the so-called high absorbers, deposited more funds in these markets than they borrowed from it. The net deposits from the oil-exporting countries combined were almost as large as for the Group of Ten plus Switzer-

[11] See Bank for International Settlements: *Forty-Eighth Annual Report,* Basle, June, 1978, p. 98. The eight reporting countries are Belgium-Luxembourg, France, Germany, Italy, the Netherlands, Sweden, Switzerland, and the United Kingdom.

EXHIBIT 14.3. External Positions of Banks in the Group of Ten against Itself and Other Country Areas, All Currencies, End of 1977[a] (millions of U.S. dollars)

Liabilities/assets vis-à-vis	*Liabilities*	*Assets*	*Net Position Assets Less Liabilities*
Group of Ten[a]			
Belgium-Luxembourg	27,416	38,664	-11,248
France	39,378	34,515	-4,863
Germany, Federal Rep.	23,981	36,202	12,221
Italy	13,354	20,664	7,310
Netherlands	24,207	17,354	-6,853
Sweden	3,224	7,742	4,518
Switzerland[b]	73,684	15,628	-58,056
United Kingdom	85,074	68,752	-16,322
Canada	12,484	11,604	-880
Japan	7,263	29,450	22,187
United States	73,930	39,087	-34,843
Total, Group of Ten	383,995	319,662	-64,333
Other countries in Western Europe	38,745	56,492	17,747
Australia, New Zealand and South Africa	2,438	13,722	11,284
Eastern Europe[c]	7,785	32,908	25,123
Caribbean area	51,527	74,657	23,130
Latin America	34,894	71,077	36,183
Middle East			
Oil-exporting countries:			
a) Low absorbers: Kuwait, Qatar, Saudi Arabia and the United Arab Emirates	32,520	3,832	-28,688
b) High absorbers: Bahrain, Iran, Iraq, Libya and Oman	18,826	10,354	- 8,472
Other countries	22,435	8,087	-14,348
Total, Middle East	73,781	22,273	-51,508
Other Africa	11,005	14,034	3,029
Other Asia	37,783	40,948	3,165
International institutions	6,511	2,719	- 3,792
Unallocated	9,819	8,758	- 1,061
Grand total	658,283	657,250	~0

Note: A full country breakdown of the reporting banks' liabilities and assets is available only for banks in Belgium-Luxembourg, France, the Federal Republic of Germany, Italy, the Netherlands, Sweden and the United Kingdom and for the offshore branches of U.S. banks. For banks in the other reporting countries—Canada, Japan, Switzerland, and the United States—the country breakdown is less than complete. The liabilities of banks in the United States exclude U.S. Treasury bills and certificates held in custody by the banks on behalf of non-residents.

[a] The Group of Ten classification in this table includes also Switzerland and the offshore branches of U.S. banks in the Bahamas, Cayman Islands, Panama, Lebanon, Hong Kong, and Singapore.

[b] Positions vis-à-vis the BIS are included under Switzerland, except for the U.S. banks, which report them under the residual for "Other countries in western Europe."

[c] Excluding positions of banks located in the Federal Republic of Germany vis-à-vis the German Democratic Republic.

SOURCE: Bank for International Settlements, FORTY-EIGHTH ANNUAL REPORT, Basle, June, 1978, pp. 94–95.

land in 1977. Of course, this position has developed only since 1973, after the large increases in oil prices.

The three largest recipients of Euro-currency loans from the banks in Exhibit 14.3 are the European countries outside the Group of Ten, Eastern Europe, and Latin America. Among the larger net borrowers in the European countries in 1977 are Denmark, Finland, Norway, and Spain. The heaviest borrowers in Eastern Europe are Poland and Russia. In Latin America the leading borrowers are Brazil and Mexico. The large volume of Euro-credits to all these countries is well known. Among other important net borrowers are Turkey, Peru, Liberia, and Zaïre. Some of these loans have been a source of concern to the banking community. Finally, among the Asian countries well-known borrowers are Hong Kong, Indonesia, South Korea, and the Philippines.

Much of these Euro-currency borrowings outside the Group of Ten is relatively recent, since 1974. To a large extent, these countries have been the ultimate recipients of the excess funds accumulated by the oil-exporting countries. The Euro-currency markets have succeeded in recycling petro-dollars very effectively. This subject is discussed further in the international banking section.

INTERNATIONAL BANKING

To understand the pattern of credits that existed in the Euro-currency markets by 1977 it is necessary to review the development of international banking. The growth of Euro-currency markets and international banking has been closely intertwined.

U.S. Banks

All the U.S. regulations discussed earlier in this chapter as contributing to the growth of the Euro-dollar market, also affected the U.S. commercial banking system, either directly or indirectly. Some of the regulations, such as Regulation Q, established the need for banks to have access to the Euro-dollar market to raise necessary funds to finance domestic operations. This need drove many banks to expand their international operations by establishing a physical presence in the Euro-markets. Thus, branches of U.S. commercial banks became some of the major institutions in the Euro-markets.

The presence of branches of U.S. commercial banks in the Euro-markets is also tied to the traditional role of commercial banks in catering to the needs of their customers. After World War II there was a dynamic increase in world trade and foreign investment. American banks in the past had had correspondent banking relationships with foreign banks which were designed to satisfy their clients' needs for banking services abroad—normally restricted to financing trade and perhaps to providing working capital. However, as American business moved overseas, the banks followed their clients and set up branches to serve them directly rather than pass business to their correspondents. This close contact enabled the banks to offer a broader range of services than was previously available. Furthermore, banks of all nationalities began to compete fiercely for the business of emerging multinational corporations. This competition became more acute between 1965 and 1973 when U.S. corporations were restricted on the amount of funds they could raise in the United States to invest abroad. Given that the voluntary credit restraint program in the United States during that same period made it virtually impossible for U.S. banks to use funds raised in the United States to lend abroad, the Euro-currency market was the only viable alternative for financing the funds needs of the banks' customers. This obviously increased the role of these banks in the Euro-currency markets.

The response of U.S. banks to the combined forces of the need for external funds to finance domestic operations and the need to cater to the multinational corporation abroad can be seen in the increased presence of U.S. banks abroad. In 1960 there were only 8 banks in the United States with branches abroad. The number of foreign branches of U.S. banks in that year was 131 with combined assets of $3.5 billion. However, by 1977 there were 730 foreign branches of U.S. banks with total assets of $228 billion. The nature of these branches could be inferred partly from their location and size of the total business conducted. In 1977 these branches were heavily concentrated in international financial centers in the Caribbean (132 branches) and the United Kingdom (58 branches). The combined assets of these branches accounted for 65% of the foreign branches' total assets. Particularly the branches in the Caribbean serve mostly "to book" transactions that originate elsewhere: therefore, the name "shell" branches.[12]

Since access to private deposits is very limited, particularly for the newcomers in the 1960s, other banks are the major source of funds for these branches. This source of funds is technically called the *interbank market.* On the average, foreign branches draw 50% of their funds from the interbank market. The rest comes from a mixture of sources whose weight has varied from year to year but which is composed of other branches, foreign official institutions, and some local deposits.

A concurrent trend with the movement abroad in U.S. banking has been diversification of services. In the late 1960s, with the advent of the one-bank holding company and the diversification opportunities it offered in the United States, several important banks began to take a worldwide view of diversification. Leasing, factoring, cash and securities handling services, mortgage banking, computer-based financial advisory services, and so on, were undertaken by many banks in the United States. For banks with domestic subsidiaries active in these areas, establishing an overseas subsidiary was a logical step. Many major U.S. banks started to consider diversification into medium- and long-term finance, directly or as an intermediary, as one of the most logical extensions of their activities. After all, for decades European banks had been able to satisfy a client's total financing needs in house rather than refer the customer to an investment banker for the long-term position.

The critical regulatory check on U.S. banks' diversifying abroad is the Federal Reserve Board and its interpretation of legislation. The keystone of this legislation for international diversification is Section 25(A) of the Federal

[12] Andrew F. Brimmer and Frederick R. Dahl, "Growth of American International Banking," Paper presented before joint session of the American Economic Association and the American Finance Association. San Francisco, California, Dec. 28, 1974, p. 45, and Federal Reserve Bank of Chicago, "International Letter," July 7, 1978, p. 3.

Reserve Act, the so-called Edge Act. Since branches abroad are permitted to carry on only the activities permitted to their parent banks in the United States, diversification overseas is generally achieved through the medium of a U.S. subsidiary established under the Edge Act. The subsidiary in turn holds equity in foreign businesses. Passed shortly after World War I to permit U.S. banks to compete abroad on an equal footing with the more diversified foreign banks, the Edge Act could theoretically be interpreted to justify any activity overseas as long as it was carried on by the local banks of a particular market. In practice, however, the Federal Reserve Board interprets the permissible activities of an Edge Act subsidiary as including only those that are "finance related," thus excluding control of industrial or other nonfinancial investments. The number of Edge Act subsidiaries has grown considerably as a result.

Spurred by the developments in the Euro-dollar market and in the U.S. banking scene, as well as by the increased exposure to European "one-stop shopping" banks, U.S. banks began to pursue diversification actively since 1972, especially in Europe. Major U.S. banks—such as Manufacturers Hanover Trust Company, Bankers Trust Company, First National Bank of Chicago, Bank of America, Marine Midland, as well as some smaller banks—have established investment banking subsidiaries in London to furnish their organizations with expertise in underwriting, placement of securities, and syndication of loans. Further, these vehicles undertake varied functions ranging from leasing to venture capital. However, medium-term loan business and participation in some Euro-bond underwriting are the mainstays for most of these new subsidiaries. The emphasis of these operations appears to be on tapping the fixed fee income attached to the manager function. With declining spreads in a highly competitive market, the income generated from the management function becomes of vital importance to the lending operation.

The importance of international business to U.S. commercial banks can be seen in the following data: For thirteen major U.S. banks, the growth in international earnings accounted for 95% of total earnings growth from 1970 to 1975. These international earnings compounded at 36% per annum in these years. By 1976 21% of their total assets were international vs. only 8.5% in 1970. About half of the assets and liabilities were in Europe, largely Euro-dollar credits and debits.[13]

The European Banking Response

The arrival of American banks in Europe led to the breakdown of the correspondent bank system. The American banks even began to compete for local clients in Europe and for deposits on a small scale. European banks responded first by forming a number of consortia among themselves with the goal of coordinating broad areas of activity. This appeared to provide a broader branch network for many European banks with virtually no overseas branches. Finally, given the limitations of these joint arrangements, many of these banks began opening offices abroad on their own in search for new markets.

Given the source of the initial challenge, American banks, it appeared

[13]Salomon Brothers, *United States Multinational Banking,* New York, 1976.

logical to direct some of the expansion of these European banks into the domestic American markets. In the 1970s this expansion accelerated. By mid-1978 the total assets of foreign banks in the United States amounted to $104 billion, compared with only $27 billion in 1972. The role of foreign banks in the United States is particularly large in the area of commercial and industrial loans, where they accounted for 11% of all such loans outstanding in the United States in 1978.[14]

Facilitating this expansion was the fact that foreign banks operating in the United States were subject to much fewer regulations than domestic banks. For example, foreign banks could engage in national banking while domestic banks could not. However, the International Banking Act of 1978 changed this situation by effectively bringing foreign banks under the regulation and supervision of federal agencies. Under this Act foreign banks were placed in a position comparable to domestic banks. Thus, although the Act permits the establishment of branches by foreign banks in multiple states, only one of them is allowed to accept deposits. (This limitation does not apply to branches in existence before July 1978.) The Act also gives the Federal Reserve Board authority to impose reserve requirements and other regulations on foreign banks.

International Bank Loans

The kind of development that characterized international banking during most of the period 1974–77 can be summarized by the following comment from the Bank for International Settlements:

> 1977 was another year of strong growth in the international financial markets. Despite slackening in the pace of world economic recovery, slower growth in international trade and shrinking balance of payments financing requirements, the combined volume of net credit outstanding through the international banking sector . . . may be estimated to have expanded in dollar terms by around $100 billion . . . the growth of the markets has become increasingly supply determined. Interbank competition for new business has stiffened and the banks' lending margins have been squeezed, sometimes to a degree that can hardly be considered in the interest of the stability of the market as a whole.[15]

Given the sizable international banking network that American and other banks had developed by 1974, the world recession and the financial problems following the oil crisis of 1973 could be seen either as a great challenge or a call to come back home. International banking chose to call it a great challenge.

Under the new conditions the loan market shifted from U.S. multinationals and other prime credit risks to governments in developed countries experiencing balance of payments difficulties and to governments in developing countries experiencing all kinds of economic problems. Many of the latter

[14] Federal Reserve Bank of Chicago, "International Letter," March 31, 1978.

[15] Bank for International Settlements, *Forty-Eighth Annual Report,* Basle, June 1978, p. 86.

countries had only limited, if at all, access to the Euro-currency markets before 1974. But now they appeared to be the only significant source of growth. To a highly competitive banking system dependent on a very high volume of business for survival, these countries became more interesting business propositions after 1973 than in earlier days. As a result, an increasing amount of credit began to be channeled to developing countries and developed countries in difficulties. (The figures obtained for 1977 were presented in Exhibit 14.3.)

In fact, the Euro-currency markets were channeling the increasing surplus of funds of oil-exporting countries to the less fortunate countries. OPEC contributed the funds; the banking system bore the credit risks, often for a very small lending margin. By 1977 this situation had begun to worry many monetary authorities, particularly in the United States.

Morgan Guaranty data indicated that net international borrowing by non-OPEC LDCs totaled $180 billion by the end of 1976, including public agency debt and private banking debt. Can these LDCs service their debt? On the average, debt service/GNP ratios were deteriorating. Private debt averaged 28% of the total indebtedness of LDCs and about 10% of the indebtedness of low-income LDCs. Different banks participated to a different extent on these loans. Thus, 44% of Citicorp's international portfolio was to LDCs in 1975, yet only 16% of this figure was to middle- and low-income LDCs. In contrast, BankAmerica had 37% of its LDC loan portfolio to middle- and low-income LDCs.[16]

How does the bank protect against default? First, if it is in a minority position, often there are cross-default provisions in any loan agreement, providing that default on a loan to XYZ bank will constitute default on IMF or other international body loans. Thus, nations inclined to let a large private bank lose are forced to recognize that their ability to approach international lending agencies also will be jeopardized. Second, default *per se* does not coincide with a liquidation sale. What happens is a rescheduling of debt. In twenty years through 1975 eight countries rescheduled a total of twenty-three times. These included Argentina, Chile, and Indonesia (four times each); Peru (three times); and Brazil, Turkey, and Zaïre (twice each).

Such rescheduling should not be automatic reassurance that "things always can be worked out." One particularly difficult case has lessons for LDC lending in general. A small nation was very dependent on one major raw material export, accounting for 63% of exports on the average. With income of only $90 per capita, a typical downturn in the price of the metal export placed the country in deep trouble. It was already paying an extra ¾% over other LDCs on loans, and the country was headed by politicians, not by the technocrats who are more reassuring to lenders. Government deficits were 32% of the total budget for the first half dozen years in the 1970s; worse, they never were forecast accurately. The estimated deficit for 1973, for example, turned out to be one-third the actual deficit. Private, hard-currency external debt was 70% of total debt in 1973, with 99% of it maturing in under ten years (vs. a figure of 55% for India, for example). In the first half of one year, debt service was 9% of the government budget, but the final figure was 60% higher than forecast a few months earlier. The government budget traditionally had 20% of the total allocated at the discretion of the president. Much of the new debt was for

[16] See Salomon Brothers, *United States Multinational Banking,* New York, 1976.

nonprojects: current deficits, old debt repayment, general operations including an international airline deficit, and military hardware. This figure reached 100% of the new debt in 1974. Finally, there were consistent examples of clerical incompetence and technical default: Payments were not made on time or they were made to the wrong bank office, often in the wrong amount. At one point the Minister of Finance simply refused to receive anyone at his office or home for six weeks.

Why did banks continue to lend? One important factor must be that Citibank, one of America's leading banks and probably the leading bank in international operations, together with its affiliates accounted for 60% of the Euro-currency borrowings of the country in 1972–73. Other banks, reminiscent of the stock market attitudes of many U.S. investors, thought that Citibank knew what was happening and one would never lose money following such a bank. Most of the lending was accounted for by twenty-six large banks, including eight from Japan and three major U.S. banks. Many of the banks wanted loans even under bad terms in order to develop a local name that would provide future good business. Some banks ignored project appraisals, arguing that all payments depended on the government; such an attitude resulted in funding bad projects. The spreads on the loans were good, and some banks felt the risk was well rewarded. When difficult times arrived in 1973, new loans were made by some international lending agencies, allegedly acting on behalf of many lenders. The final agreement, however, provided that the agency had first claim on all payments. The private lenders complained but could do nothing.

This example is Zaïre. Neither the country nor the banks are unique, however, and the payments deficits induced by the oil imports and nationalistic projects in LDCs dependent on a limited number of price-volatile exports are a major problem for the *developed* countries and their banks as well.[17]

Exercises on the Euro-Dollar Market

The following transactions are designed to follow the path of some of the flows that take place in the Euro-dollar market. A series of "T-accounts" with initial balances has been provided to facilitate following the transactions described below.

Assume: 1. All foreigners keep their balances in the United States with the Chase Manhattan Bank.

2. All banks keep 10% of their deposits in reserves.

[17] P. A. Wellons, *Borrowing by Developing Countries on the Euro-Currency Market*, Development Centre of the Organization for Economic Co-operation and Development, Paris, 1977.

At the end of each transaction determine the impact on:

1. Each of the parties involved.
2. The U.S. money supply.
3. The U.S. balance of payments.
4. The money supply of each foreign country involved.
5. The balance of payments of each foreign country involved.

Transaction No. 1. The German Central Bank, which maintains part of its foreign exchange reserve in the form of Treasury bills, decides to sell $100 worth of Treasury bills to Mr. Smith, an American resident. Mr. Smith pays with a check drawn on his account with Chase Manhattan.

Transaction No. 2. The German Central Bank transfers its deposits to a German commercial bank. (Sometimes this is done as part of domestic monetary policy in which case the Central Bank exchanges dollar deposits for deutsche marks with the commercial banks. The objective is to reduce credit in the domestic market and give incentives for capital outflows.)

Transaction No. 3. A French importer asks for a Euro-dollar loan from the German commercial bank. Assuming that the commercial bank keeps a precautionary reserve of 10%, it can make a loan in the amount of $90.

Transaction No. 4. The French importer uses the Euro-loan to pay a debt owed to a German exporter.

Transaction No. 5. The German exporter deposits the dollar balances with the German commercial bank.

Transaction No. 6. Citibank wishes to borrow Euro-dollars from the German commercial bank to take care of anticipated loan demand.

Transaction No. 7. Citibank wishes to make a loan. In order to convert the deposit at Chase into lendable funds, it asks Chase to provide cash or deposits with the Federal Reserve Bank. Since Chase was fully loaned-up, it has to sell some loans in order to collect the required amount of cash.

Chase Manhattan Bank

Cash Loans	10 90	Demand Deposit, Smith	100

German Central Bank

Foreign Exchange	1000	Liabilities	1000

German Commercial Bank

Cash Loans	10 90	Deposits	100

French Importer

Inventory	90	Accounts Payable	90

German Exporter

Accounts Receivable	90	Equity	90

Citibank

Cash Loans	10 90	Demand Deposit	100

Bibliography

Aliber, Robert Z., "International Banking: Growth and Regulation." *Columbia Journal of World Business,* Winter 1975, pp. 9-15.

Altman, Oscar L., "Euro-Dollars." *Finance and Development,* March 1967.

Bank for International Settlements, *Annual Report,* annual issues.

"Banking in the Middle East: A Survey." *The Banker* (London), March, 1978, pp. 55-92.

Bell, Geoffrey, *The Euro-Dollar Market and the International Financial System.* New York: Halsted Press/John Wiley and Sons, 1973.

Dufey, Gunter, and Ian Giddy, *The International Money Market.* Englewood Cliffs, N.J.: Prentice-Hall, Inc., 1978.

Edwards, Franklin R. and Jack Zwick, "Activities and Regulatory Issues: Foreign Banks in the United States," *Columbia Journal of World Business,* Spring, 1975, pp. 58-73.

Einzig, Paul, *The Euro-Dollar System.* 5th ed. New York: St. Martin's Press, 1973.

——, *Parallel Money Markets.* Two vols. London: Macmillan/St. Martin's Press, 1971 and 1972.

Ferris, Paul, "The Multi-Banks of Europe: A Dramatic Experiment." *Worldwide P and I Planning,* May–June 1971, pp. 20–27.

Findlay, M. Chapman III, and E. J. Kleinschmidt, "Error-Learning in the Eurodollar Market." *Journal of Financial and Quantitative Analysis,* Sept. 1975, pp. 429–446.

Freedman, Charles, "A Model of the Eurodollar Market." *Journal of Monetary Economics,* April 1977, pp. 139–161.

Friedman, Milton, "The Euro-Dollar Market: Some First Principles." *The Morgan Guaranty Survey,* Oct. 1969, pp. 1–11.

Hendershott, Patrick H., "The Structure of International Interest Rates: The U.S. Treasury Bill Rate and the Eurodollar Deposit Rate." *Journal of Finance,* Sept. 1967, pp. 455-465.

Hewson, John, and Eisuke Sakakibara, *The Euro-Currency Markets and Their Implications.* Lexington, Mass.: D. C. Heath, 1975.

Hinshaw, Randall, "The Euro-Dollar Market: A Comment," *Journal of Money, Credit and Banking,* Aug. 1972, pp. 688-690.

Klopstock, Fred H., "Money Creation in the Euro-Dollar Market—A Note on Professor Friedman's Views." *Monthly Review,* Jan. 1970, Federal Reserve Bank of New York, pp. 12-15.

——, *The Euro-Dollar Market: Some Unresolved Issues.* Princeton, N.J.: Princeton University, March 1968.

——, "The Euromarkets Tighten Their Links with New York." *Euromoney,* Aug. 1975, pp. 25-30.

Kwack, Sung Y., "The Structure of International Interest Rates: An Extension of Hendershott's Tests." *Journal of Finance,* Sept. 1971, pp. 897-900.

Lee, Boyden E., "The Euro-Dollar Multiplier," *Journal of Finance.* Sept. 1973, pp. 867-74.

Lewis, Kenneth A. and Francis F. Breen, "Empirical Issues in the Demand for Currency: A Multinational Study." *Journal of Finance,* September 1975, pp. 1065-1080.

Little, Jane Sneddon, *Euro-Dollars: The Money Market Gypsies.* New York: Harper and Row, Inc., 1975.

——, "The Impact of the Euro-Dollar Market on the Effectiveness of Monetary Policy in the United States and Abroad." *New England Economic Review,* Federal Reserve Bank of Boston, March-Apr., 1975, pp. 3-19.

Lutz, Friedrich A., "The Euro-Currency System." *Banca Nazionale del Lavoro,* Sept. 1974, pp. 183-200.

Makin John H., and Dennis E. Logue (editors), *Eurocurrencies and the International Monetary System.* Washington, D.C.: American Enterprise Institute for Public Policy Research, 1976.

Mayer, Helmut W., "Some Theoretical Problems Relating to the Euro-Dollar Market." *Essays in International Finance,* No. 79. Princeton, N.J.: Princeton University, 1970.

McKinnon, Ronald I., "The Eurocurrency Market." *Essays in International Finance,* No. 125. Princeton, N.J.: Princeton University, 1977.

Mikesell, Raymond F., "The Euro-Dollar Market and the Foreign Demand for Liquid Dollar Assets." *Journal of Money, Credit and Banking,* Aug. 1972, pp. 643-683.

—— and J. Herbert Furth, *Foreign Dollar Balances and The International Role of the Dollar.* New York: Columbia University Press, 1974.

Parker, Carol, "The Lure of Luxembourg." *The Banker* (London), May 1977, pp. 37-42.

Potter, David R. W., "The London Dollar CD—Liquid Tool for International Cash Management." *Columbia Journal of World Business,* Summer 1973, pp. 5-10.

Pringle, Robin, "The British Big Four Stake Their Claim." *The Banker (London),* August 1977, pp. 113-126.

Rich, Geörg, "A Theoretical and Empirical Analysis of the Euro-Dollar Market." *Journal of Money, Credit and Banking,* Aug. 1972, pp. 617-635.

Ricks, David, and Jeffrey S. Arpan, "Foreign Banking in the United States." *Business Horizons,* Feb. 1976, pp. 84-87.

Riehl, Heinz, and Rita M. Rodriguez, *Foreign Exchange Markets.* New York: McGraw-Hill Book Company, 1977.

Robichek, Alexander A., and Mark R. Eaker, "Debt Denomination and Exchange Risk in International Capital Markets." *Financial Management,* Autumn 1976, pp. 11-18.

Salomon Brothers, *United States Multinational Banking.* New York, 1976.

Stem, Carl H., "The Euro-Dollar Market and the Foreign Demand for

Liquid Dollar Assets: A Comment." *Journal of Money, Credit and Banking,* Aug. 1972, pp. 691-703.

"Survey–The Euromarkets." *The Banker* (London), January 1978, pp. 43-81.

Wellons, P. A., *Borrowing by Developing Countries on the Euro-Currency Markets.* Paris: Development Centre of the Organization for Economic Co-Operation and Development, 1977.

Appendix: Multiple Creation of Euro-Dollars and the Impact of This Market on the U.S. Balance of Payments and the Money Supply

Chapter 14 has illustrated how Euro-dollars can be created in a multiple fashion. This raised a series of questions which will be addressed in this appendix.

FRACTIONAL RESERVES AS THE "SOURCE" OF EURO-DOLLARS

The example showed how the Euro-dollars can be expanded, but the more relevant question is, "*Are* they created in this way?" There can be leakages from the system. The creation of a reserve is one leak; if there were no reserves (and foreign banks in most cases are *not* required to have *any* reserves to back their Euro-dollar deposits), then the theoretical expansion of Euro-dollar deposits from a $1,000,000 deposit is infinite.

In the United States, with a closed banking system, there is a very large impact from the creation of an autonomous deposit. All funds usually end up in a bank. Purchase of shares in a mutual fund will mean that the fund deposits the cash in a bank or buys shares in corporate stock from individuals who deposit their funds in a bank. An individual who buys newly issued stock from a corporation will see the check used ultimately to pay suppliers for goods, to purchase a new plant for the corporation, or to carry out some other project. Again, the recipient probably will deposit the funds in a bank at some point.

However, for the Euro-dollar to multiply, the funds must *not* come back to the U.S. banking system. Thus, if anyone chooses to buy goods from a corporation which deposits the funds in (say) a California bank, then the Euro-dollar expansion from the original $1,000,000 deposit ends.

If the multiplier (or, in Jane S. Little's apt phrase, the measure of fertility) is fairly low, then for practical purposes the European banks resemble our savings and loan associations which cannot create money, for the funds they lend from depositors' accounts typically do not come back to them anywhere in the system. Rather, the funds likely end up in the bank accounts of the suppliers, carpenters, and others associated with the home. Some small amount may come to the savings and loan association, but the bulk of the funds "created" by the new mortgage does not.

Some people have referred to the loan-creation and money-creation possibilities of banks in a fractional reserve system (including the Euro-dollar system) as the creation of money by a bookkeeper's pen. However, those observers who believe the multiplier in the Euro-dollar market is low note that the pen runs out of ink very quickly. The question is not the theoretical expansion of the Euro-dollars but the actual one, and the evidence cited by most scholars indicates that the multiplier is fairly low. The great problem is that, unlike the American banking system, the Euro-bank system is not closed. Too much money returns to businesses who deposit it outside the system. They may be banks in other lands who turn the dollars over to their central bank in exchange for reserves. This central bank (or the foreign exchange trader to whom the local bank had gone for currency) may then deposit it in the United States. Latin American banks or banks in other lands may want the dollars for loans to their customers, who use these funds to pay their American suppliers. In either case the money has lost its immediate potential to expand the Euro-dollar accounts.

Fred Klopstock estimated that about 30–40% of the Euro-dollar deposits were created by the multiplier.[1] Other researchers have found different estimates for the Euro-dollar multiplier. For example, Makin (1972) estimated the high figure of 18.45, while Lee (1973) estimated 1.51. There are statistical and economic difficulties with most of these models, not the least of which is that they usually presume a fixed percentage of total deposits held in reserve by the banks as well as a fixed demand for currency by firms or individuals. Certainly the first assumption is unrealistic in the Euro-currency market where there are no reserve requirements. It also is true that the nature of the market is such that a new, exogenous inflow as a Euro-dollar deposit lowers the equilibrium interest rate. On the other hand, a lower equilibrium rate means that other deposits will leave the Euro system. Hence, the multiplier *could* theoretically be less than one. In a careful estimate of the multiplier, Hewson and Sakakibara (1975) use monthly data from 1968–72. Noting that the range for the multiplier from their econometric results is from 0.63 to 1.61, they conclude that the multiplier on Euro-dollars is probably not much different from 1.[2] An excellent summary of the research on the size of the multiplier is presented in Appendix 2 to Chapter 3 of Dufey and Giddy (1978). Thus, the leakages of dollars from the system and the existence of reserves in some cases appear to defeat the rapid expansion shown as theoretically possible.

Where, then, has the sharp increase in Euro-dollars come from? For the most part, it has resulted from a drain of local dollar reserves from banks and the public (citizens and corporations) throughout the world. By competing on the basis of rates and services, the European banks have attracted dollars. In some cases firms have converted other currencies to dollars to take advantage of the Euro-dollar rates. This process uses dollars which are in Europe, perhaps as a

[1] For bibliographical references in this appendix, see the bibliography to this chapter.

[2] See Hewson and Sakakibara (1975), Ch. 6, pp. 117–139.

result of the huge commitments of the United States after World War II or as a result of the more recent payments deficits.

EURO-DOLLARS AND THE U.S. DEFICIT IN THE BALANCE OF PAYMENTS

Theoretically, there is no need for the United States to have a deficit in order for Euro-dollars to grow and vice versa. Any person (other than a resident American) owning dollars who wishes to switch them to a non-U.S. bank creates a Euro-dollar. However, the ultimate growth of the U.S. payments deficit helped create the rapid expansion in Euro-dollars.

By 1958 most of the European countries had made their currencies freely convertible into the dollar, and that made the dollar useful to many firms and individuals as a liquid asset. The movement by central banks and others in the early 1960s to earn higher rates of interest on their dollars than American banks were permitted to pay under Regulation Q pulled funds into Euro-dollars.

In addition, there is also speculation that the flow of U.S. funds abroad stimulated much of the interest in the Euro-dollars. For example, the soaring price of oil meant many U.S. dollars went to the Mideast, and many of these dollars no doubt found their way into the Euro-dollar markets. Furthermore, prior to 1969 the American banks had a great interest in seeing customers take their dollar deposits from the United States to their European branches because of the reserve requirements discussed earlier. Hence, the American firm requesting a loan may have learned that the compensating balances should be kept by its subsidiary in London at the London branch of the American bank.

Ultimately, the question pivots on what was the Euro-dollar deposit replacing and where did the Euro-dollars go. Mikesell (1972) studied different sources and uses of Euro-dollars. The effect of these sources and uses depends on the combinations which are involved. Although the empirical tests Mikesell used are not without problems, he generally concluded that the basic increase in Euro-dollars is associated with an improvement in the official reserves transaction balance of payments of the United States. That is, the balance in the combinations favored a pattern in which the account of desired dollar claims was positive. In addition, he found that increased U.S. dollar borrowing, in the Euro-dollar market were associated with an improvement in the basic balance. Finally, he noted that these two conclusions were not dependent on the contributions of U.S. residents, i.e., the shifting of the resident's deposit to a foreign bank. That is, the favorable effect of the U.S. dollar borrowings and the increase of the Euro-dollars on the balance of payments was independent of the contribution made by the increase in Euro-dollars generated by United States residents.

Exhibit A.1 shows one observer's analysis of the potential effect on the U.S. balance of payments from various combinations of Euro-dollar sources and uses.

It is certainly not necessary for the United States to have a balance of payments deficit in order for Euro-dollars to grow, as the exhibit makes clear. For example, Germany's balance of payments *surpluses* from 1970–72 totaled $14 billion, yet Euro-mark deposits tripled in the same period.

In terms of the Euro-dollars' effect on the balance of payments, Jane S.

EXHIBIT A.1. Sources and Uses of Euro-Dollar Funds According to their Potential Impact on the International Strength of the U.S. Dollar

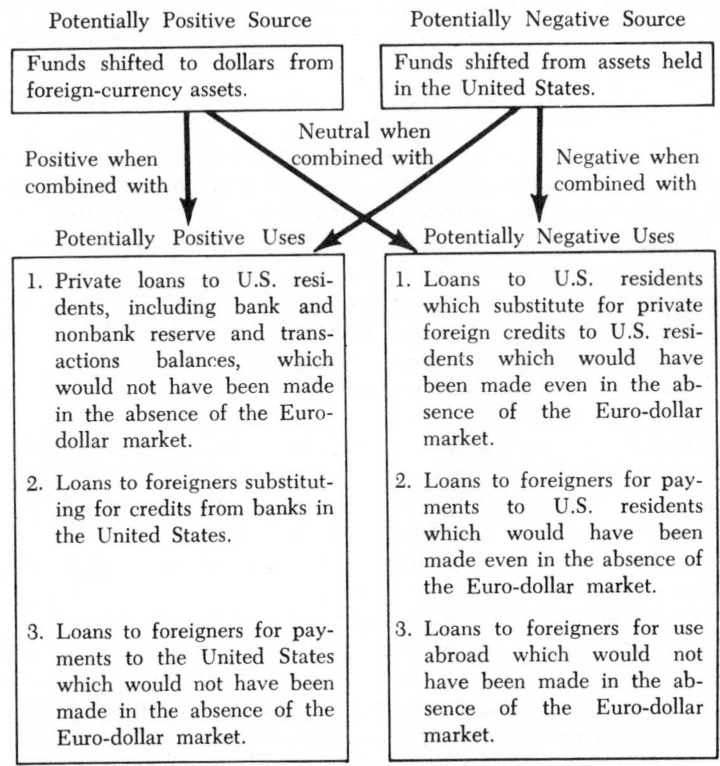

Potentially Positive Source
Funds shifted to dollars from foreign-currency assets.
Potentially Negative Source
Funds shifted from assets held in the United States.
Positive when combined with
Neutral when combined with
Negative when combined with
Potentially Positive Uses
1. Private loans to U.S. residents, including bank and nonbank reserve and transactions balances, which would not have been made in the absence of the Euro-dollar market.
2. Loans to foreigners substituting for credits from banks in the United States.
3. Loans to foreigners for payments to the United States which would not have been made in the absence of the Euro-dollar market.
Potentially Negative Uses
1. Loans to U.S. residents which substitute for private foreign credits to U.S. residents which would have been made even in the absence of the Euro-dollar market.
2. Loans to foreigners for payments to U.S. residents which would have been made even in the absence of the Euro-dollar market.
3. Loans to foreigners for use abroad which would not have been made in the absence of the Euro-dollar market.

SOURCE: Jane S. Little, EURO-DOLLARS: THE MONEY MARKET GYPSIES, Harper & Row, New York, 1975, p. 184.

Little concludes that the Euro-dollars had a slight positive effect on the balance of payments through 1969 but by the end of 1973 had turned clearly negative; i.e., they aggravated the deficit that would have occurred anyway.

The *ultimate* effect of the increase in Euro-dollars on the current account or the long-term capital account of the United States might take several forms. The availability of dollar credits to foreign importers might increase U.S. exports. Greater international liquidity in general might have an ultimately favorable effect on U.S. exports. Some purchasers of American corporations' Euro-bonds may have raised their dollars for this purpose by Euro-dollar loans. On the other hand, U.S. borrowings from the Euro-dollar accounts hurt the current account because of interest payments on those borrowings. In addition, because of the freedom from exchange controls and restrictions, it is likely that the Euro-dollar market has contributed to the various periods of speculation against the dollar in favor of stronger currencies. Speculators borrowed dollars to purchase harder currencies with the expectation of the devaluation. The Euro-dollar market facilitated this activity.

EURO-DOLLARS AND THE MONEY SUPPLY

Much of the growth in Euro-dollar accounts in 1966 and 1969 came with the desire of U.S. banks to skirt restrictions on the amount they could pay for funds in order to obtain money for loans to customers. As a result, these banks borrowed from their own branches and from other Euro-banks in massive amounts in 1969 and 1970 as we noted. Between January 1969 and August 1970 the amount borrowed from the branches rose from $7 billion to over $15 billion. By December 1971 this amount was back to less than $1 billion, largely because of the change in regulations, the high rate on Euro-dollars vis-à-vis domestic sources, and the easing of interest rates in the United States.

This violent swing in the demand for Euro-dollars was reflected in the widening of the spread in the Euro-dollar rates vs. domestic rates. Typically, the difference paid on deposits had been around 1–2%. With the ceiling on U.S. rates, however, the spread between the rate on ninety-day Euro-dollar deposits vs. three-month certificates of deposit rose beyond 3%, and the spread peaked in mid-1969 at 6¼% for U.S. CD's (the Regulation Q ceiling) vs. 11% in the ninety-day Euro-dollar market.

Naturally, such an expansion of demand for Euro-dollars spilled over into the cost for other funds. Hence, European central banks began to resent the policies of the U.S. Federal Reserve Board which induced the U.S. banks to escape those Fed rules by Euro-dollar activities. *The Board action in the Euro-dollar market lessened the effectiveness of European central bank monetary policy.*

This demonstrates the basic complicating effect of Euro-dollars on a nation's monetary supply and policies. Transfers from one Euro-dollar holder to another do not change the U.S. money supply. However, while the movement of dollar accounts (or any other currency) already outside the nation's borders does not affect that nation's money supply directly, the multiplier effects of redepositing can expand total *world* money supply which has effects on every nation's credits, costs, prices, and output. The extent of this impact depends on the size of leakages from the system which, as explained before, are considered to be large.

Similarly, there may also be differences in domestic reserve requirements: Liabilities to other banks may have different reserve requirements from deposits held by nonbanking sources (as was the situation in the United States prior to October 1969). Furthermore, different time deposit reserve requirements in various nations can have dramatic effects on the total world supply of credit. For example, the U.S. banks have reserve standards whereas the Euro-dollar banks have no technical reserve requirements.

The difficulty of monetary control in a Euro-currency environment is amply confirmed by Hewson and Sakakibara (1975). Applying their general free-exchange econometric model to the German attempt to hold down the DM in the 1968–73 period, they confirmed that effective control of external liabilities of German banks was almost completely offset by nonbank inflow increases, especially through the Euro-markets.[3]

[3]See Hewson and Sakakibara (1975), pp. 41–65.

CITICORP LEASING INTERNATIONAL, INC.

Citicorp Leasing International, Inc. (CLI), is a Delaware corporation and a wholly owned subsidiary of the First National City Corporation (FNCC), the parent company to Citibank.

CLI began operations in late 1969 with a staff of three people located in London. In July 1971, top management decided that a period of reevaluation was due. Events had been taking place at too fast a speed for CLI's management to be fully aware of their implications. There were five specific areas that CLI wished to consider more closely: (1) its borrowing policy in the Euro-dollar markets, (2) the future of the Euro-dollar markets, (3) its foreign exchange management policy, (4) the future of international leasing, and (5) relationships with the parent corporation and with Citibank in particular.

INTERNATIONAL LEASING

Leasing is usually transacted by a national company operating within the boundaries of one country's tax, legal, and commercial environment. Such companies operating in the local indigenous market tend to concentrate on the middle-market equipment and/or small-ticket market. The industry generally defines a small ticket to be less than $50,000 value, the middle market to be from $50,000 to $1,000,000, and big tickets to cost over $1,000,000. Their financial packages, patterns, and lease agreements are standardized. On the other hand, an international leasing company will usually reside in a different country from the lessee. It will, in many ways, be more typical of an equipment finance company than a leasing company. The finance packages offered will range from a true lease to a chattel mortgage, depending on the needs of the customer. In all cases the transactions are very specialized and generally limited to large-ticket equipment. The complexity frequently requires establishing a shell corporation specifically for the purposes of the transaction.

Government Policies

For international transactions, exchange control regulations and tax treaties are of critical importance. Juggling a transaction between countries with different tax and legal requirements gives considerable flexibility to the lessor and lessee. If a country has exchange controls, the central bank will usually favor a request by a domestic company to finance equipment in a foreign currency either by means of a lease or by borrowing.

Because of international tax disparities, the structuring of a lease involving two countries with favorable tax treaties can result in significant savings to the lessee. An example is the treaty between the United States and Australia vs. the United Kingdom and Australia. Unlike the U.S.-Australia treaty, the U.K.-Australia treaty provides for no withholding taxes on lease payment to the U.K. leasing company. Packaging a lease with the lessor in the United Kingdom rather than the United States frees those funds that might be withheld.

International leasing may offer flexibility in the currency of a lease transaction which is priced according to the interest rates of the particular currency. For example, a lessee has the option to select lease payments in dollars or another currency, therefore taking a position on interest rates and foreign exchange rates.

An international leasing company is able to take immediate advantages of favorable depreciation schedules in different countries. For example, the United Kingdom allows 100% write-off the first year for a ship while Canada provides 40% declining balance. When leasing to a U.K. ship owner who cannot utilize such favorable depreciation allowances, the company can arrange for the lessor to be one who can fully utilize the government's incentive and pass portions of the benefits on to the lessee in the form of lower finance charges.

Another advantage of an international leasing company is the ability to structure a transaction in order to take advantage of legal regulations regarding the depreciation of the equipment which may differ between countries. Such an example is the case when the lessee has an option to purchase the equipment upon termination of the lease at the fair market value. In the United States such a contract is considered a true lease providing the lessor with depreciation. In the United Kingdom the same contract would be considered a hire-purchase or conditional sale, thus providing depreciation to the lessee. Being able to take advantage of situations which are treated differently in two countries is the primary challenge of an international leasing company.

The Market

The U.S. National Planning Association estimates that during 1971 $11.3 billion worth of equipment was placed on lease in the United States alone: $7.9 billion was leased by the manufacturers of equipment and the balance, $3.4 billion, by third-party lessors, independent leasing companies, and financial institutions. It is estimated that outside the United States $2 billion worth of equipment was placed on lease by third-party lessors in 1971. The third-party lessor market outside the United States is estimated to be growing at the rate of 20% per year. In terms of cumulative book value of equipment placed on lease, the entire world market is estimated at $120 billion, one-half of which is in the United States. Most of this value is equipment placed on lease by manufacturers.

Of the equipment placed on lease by third-party lessors outside the United States, nearly one-half is believed to be large-ticket and middle-market equipment. Excluding the United States, Europe is the largest single geographical area for leasing in the world market. Leasing activity in less developed countries is usually not extensive and for the most part is confined to small-ticket items.

The competition to an international leasing company is primarily the equipment manufacturers' own leasing programs and other forms of financing provided by commercial and merchant banks, mostly U.K. merchant banks. In contrast to domestic leasing, which in most developed countries is intensely competitive, few leasing companies compete on an international basis. Those that do tend to concentrate either in small- to medium-ticket items or else in large-ticket items. Even though several of the large international leasing companies have the skills necessary to handle complex international transactions, there is little competition for particular deals. This is due both to the specialization in the type of client each leasing company deals with and to the time required to negotiate a particular transaction—often from four months to a year.

CLI OPERATIONS

Leasing Operations

CLI is the largest truly international leasing company in the world. It operates in the medium- to long-term leasing markets (financings of between three and fifteen years) and its transactions cover the full range of capital equipment. CLI's lessees are concentrated in the manufacturing and transportation industries. The company holds a lead position in the European and the Canadian computer leasing markets and has opened major international markets in aircraft and ship financing.

Even though CLI handles all types of leases, the company engages primarily in direct equipment leasing involving "noncancelable full-payout net finance leases." In this type of lease the total rent payable under each full-payout lease is calculated to return to the company the cost of the equipment, plus a lease charge which covers all direct expenses, overhead, and profit to the company. The lessee is required usually to pay local taxes, license fees, and insurance and to maintain and repair the equipment.

Leasing business is developed by direct solicitation of lessees through CLI's own sales force, by arrangements with manufacturers and vendors of equipment, and by referrals to the company by banks and others involved in advising industry on equipment financing programs.

CLI's management attributes its success to three major factors: (1) the relationships with multinational companies which the affiliate bank, FNCB, provided, (2) the dynamic management group which has realized the opportunities available in the industry, and (3) the growth of the industry in general. Financial statements for the company are presented in Exhibits 1 and 2. Exhibit 3 presents selected financial statistics for CLI and some other U.S. leasing companies.

Organization

FNCC operates two independent leasing companies: Citicorp Leasing, Inc., which deals only with the U.S. market, and CLI, which handles only foreign transactions. CLI's head office is located in London where a staff specialized in the various aspects of the business offers support to offices located throughout the world. Operations are organized on a geographical basis. Regional offices are maintained in London, New York, and Tokyo, each led by a vice president with general line responsibilities. Each of these regional offices is responsible for the region's local vehicles (branches and fully owned subsidiaries of CLI) located in various countries within the region. Throughout the organization, CLI's management is in the hands of a team of enterprising young specialists, most of whom are in their late twenties and early thirties.

EXHIBIT 1. **Citicorp Leasing International, Inc.: Consolidated Balance Sheet—June 30, 1971 (thousands of dollars)**

Assets			*Liabilities and Equity*		
Cash and Deposits		$ 12,426	Short-term Borrowings		$ 88,831
Accounts Receivable		915	Accounts Payable		2,364
Other Current Assets		1,532	Accruals		2,332
Lease Receivables	89,036		Advance Rentals		715
Unearned Lease Income	(27,452)		Other Taxes Payable		53
			Long-term Debt		19,796
Net Receivables		61,584	Foreign Exchange Reserve		470
Residual Valuation		8,477	Deferred Taxes		721
Mortgage and Loan Financing		12,418	Total Liabilities		$115,282
		97,352			
Nonpayout Lease Equipment:					
Investment Equipment	27,615		Capital	9,940	
			Retained Earnings	190	
Accumulated Depreciation	(3,941)		Total Equity	10,130	
Net Investment		23,674			
Investment and Advances for Subsidiaries and Affiliates		1,355			
Other Fixed Assets (Net)		3,031			
Total Assets		$125,412	Total Liabilities and Equity		$125,412

Planning and Control

Corporate Strategy. The strategy that CLI has followed in the past two years has been one of opening offices in major financial centers (London, Tokyo, and New York) and in places where Citibank's banking experience appeared to indicate a potentially prosperous market. The function of each of these offices is to generate as much leasing business as possible. The only constraints imposed by the corporate level on these endeavors are the credit risks of the lessee (which are usually prime credit risks) and the requirement of arranging financing and lease repayments in the same currency. These constraints work to make the large multinational and national companies the primary potential customers of CLI. These customers very often have access to the same terms and sources of funds as CLI.

The affiliation of CLI with Citibank has proven to be extremely helpful in obtaining an initial feel for potential markets throughout the world. After opening an office in a country, this relationship also provides access to the prime customers of the bank. On many occasions the bank itself has referred customers interested in international leasing to CLI.

Given this favorable initial assignment, the major problem that CLI has encountered in tapping the market has been the tax and legal institutions of various countries. Particularly in the case of developing countries, this fact has meant that on some occasions a considerable amount of time has been spent in working with the government to develop previously nonexistent leasing regulations. In the case of developed countries, the major limitation has been finding customers with whom a mutually advantageous contract can be formulated.

EXHIBIT 2. Citicorp Leasing International, Inc.: Consolidated Profit and Loss Statement—June 30, 1971 (thousands of dollars)

INCOME			
Leasing and Loan Income			
Lease Income	$6,076		
Interest Income	1,307		
Other Income	691		
		$8,074	
Nonpayout Revenue (net)			
Lease Revenue	4,810		
Less Depreciation Expense	(2,091)		
		2,719	
Total Income			$10,793
EXPENSES			
Interest and Finance	6,137		
Staff Payments	1,093		
Personnel	138		
Marketing	418		
General Operating	553		
Premises	240		
Other	384		
Total Expenses			8,963
EARNINGS BEFORE TAX			1,830
Tax Reserve			456
EARNINGS AFTER TAX			1,374
Net Income (loss) in unconsolidated subsidiaries			(619)
NET PROFIT FOR PERIOD			$ 755

The Budget. Each branch, each region, and each specialized marketing group at the head office—such as aircraft, shipping, and so on—is a profit center of CLI. As such, each develops a yearly budget and a five-year plan. The budgeting process requires estimates regarding the size of the market, the market share, the types of equipment that are expected to be leased (large-ticket, small-ticket, etc.), terms of the leases, tax treatment, and average cost of funds.

The final budget that CLI submits to FNCC is the result of a summary consolidation of budgets prepared by each profit center. This budget is then submitted to the board of directors of FNCC. The approved budget becomes the basis on which capital and human resources are deployed. In terms of capital, this means contributions of FNCC to CLI's capital and CLI contributions to the local subsidiaries' capital. In tems of human resources, the budget indicates the personnel to be maintained at each budget center. This final budget becomes an informal instrument of performance evaluation.

Financial Management

The final decision on the sources, terms, and rates of borrowings necessary to fund the leasing operation is made at the head office on the recommendation of the vice president of finance. In addition to providing the funds for international

EXHIBIT 3. Comparative Capitalizations[a]

	P/E[b]	Capital[c]		Short-Term Debt		Long-Term Debt		Other Liabilities		Total Liabilities and Equity	
		Million $	%	Million $	%	Million $	%	Million $	%	Million $	%
CIC Leasing	27.4	2.5	8	12.0	38	14.5	46	2.5	8	31.5	100
Greyhound Computer Corp.	9.1	67.5	36	6.5	4	106.5	57	4.5	3	184.5	100
Leaseway	31.9	53.0	25	65.0	30	94.0	44	2.0	1	214.0	100
U.S. Leasing	28.2	44.0	30	83.5	57	18.0	12	1.5	1	147.0	100
Gelco IVM Leasing	34.9	4.0	6	1.5	2	57.5	90	1.5	2	64.5	100
Diebold Computer Leasing	11.3	34.5	21	24.0	15	101.3	63	1.7	1	161.5	100
Data Processing Fin. & Gen.	7.5	62.0	30	30.0	15	111.0	54	1.5	1	204.5	100
Computer Investors Group	10.7	10.0	20	13.0	27	25.5	53	—	—	47.5	100
American Fin. Leas. & Serv.	15.3	11.0	24	1.0	3	32.5	72	.5	1	45.0	100
Citicorp Leasing Int. Inc.	—	11.3	9	88.8	70	19.8	15	5.5	6	125.4	100

Comparative Profit & Loss Statements[a]

	Revenue Income		Interest Expense		Administrative Expenses		Other[d] Expenses		Net Income After Taxes	
	Million $	%	Million $	%	Million $	%	Million $	%	Million $	%
CIC Leasing	3.7	100	1.1	30	1.2	32	.6	16	.8	22
Greyhound Computer Corp.	43.7	100	9.6	22	8.9	20	21.9	50	3.3	8
Leaseway	79.1	100	9.5	12	17.9	23	43.8	55	7.9	10
U.S. Leasing	18.3	100	7.3	40	6.2	34	1.7	9	3.1	17
Gelco IVM Leasing	8.4	100	3.8	45	2.6	32	1.3	15	.7	8
Diebold Computer Leasing	30.9	100	11.1	36	1.0	3	17.4	56	1.4	5
Data Processing Fin. & Gen.	49.2	100	11.4	23	2.0	4	33.4	68	2.4	5
Computer Investors Group	10.6	100	3.1	30	1.1	10	5.1	48	1.3	12
American Fin. Leas. & Serv.	8.5	100	2.8	33	1.8	21	2.4	28	1.5	18
Citicorp Leasing Int. Inc.	12.8	100	6.1	47	2.8	21	2.5	19	1.4	13

[a]Data correspond to fiscal years between 1969 and 1971. Year selected in each case was the latest one available in 1971.
[b]P/E as of September 30, 1971.
[c]Capital consists of equity, retained earnings, and deferred taxes.
[d]Other consists of taxes, depreciation, reserves, and expenses not directly related to leasing activity.

leases, the office of the vice president of finance serves as a source of financial information for the rest of the company.

It is the policy of the company not to take a position in the foreign exchange market. Generally, the borrowings to finance a lease transaction and the lease repayments are denominated in the same currency. In the case of international leases, the U.S. dollar is the most common currency in which leases and borrowings are denominated. Local subsidiaries will usually denominate the lease of small-ticket items in the local currency and finance the lease with local funds.

In the past it has been the company's policy to match the maturity of fixed rate leases with the maturity of fixed rate borrowings. In the case of floating rate leases, the maturity of the borrowings is fixed for an intermediate period –usually six months–during which time the rate in the lease is fixed. The objective of this policy is to guarantee a profitable spread. However, a large proportion of the leases the company has made are on a fixed rate basis. The average maturity of the leases is eight to ten years.

In spite of the overall policy of matching maturities of leases and borrowings, during 1971 the company made the decision to finance most of its fund requirements with short-term money. Taking into consideration on one hand the large percentage of total costs that interest represents and on the other hand the existing relationship between short- and long-term rates and their projections for the future, the company decided it would be profitable to take advantage of this opportunity. Schedules of debt repayments both due within a year and due in more than a year are presented in Exhibit 4. The rates obtained on these borrowings were the rates available to the best borrowers in the market at the time. These rates were available on the credit of CLI itself. Though CLI might realize some possible advantages because of its affiliation with FNCC, by and large borrowings were arranged without guarantees. For recent Euro-dollar rates, see Exhibit 5.

EURO-DOLLAR MARKETS

Recent Market Behavior

Euro-Bond Market. The vice president of finance felt that the general lull in activity in the new Euro-bond issues in July would help the tone in that market and would probably bring rates down somewhat. Only ten issues were expected for July, five of which were in U.S. dollars. It was expected that the amount raised in the long-term Euro-markets in July would be $180 million compared to the $655 million raised in February when the market clearly became congested. On the other hand, speculation of a dollar devaluation and a deutsche mark revaluation could keep Euro-bond rates high. Suspicion about the future of the dollar was particularly evident at the beginning of the year when, in spite of a large spread between Euro-bond and U.S. domestic bond yields, a large backlog of new issues in the market was created. The anticipations of a revaluation of the deutsche mark materialized with the floating of the deutsche mark and some other currencies, including the guilder, in May. Since that date the Bundesbank had introduced restrictive measures to prevent any new offering denominated in deutsche marks.

EXHIBIT 4. **Citicorp Leasing International, Inc.: Dollar Borrowings Outstanding as of July 11, 1971**

	Amount	*%*	*Interest*	*Interest Due*[a]	
		SHORT-TERM			
Demand	$ 3,500,000	7.375			
Demand	350,000	7.375			
July 26	2,975,000	8.125	$ 39,697	M	
July 27	5,250,000	7.50	64,494	M	
July 27	700,000	7.50	8,600	M	
July 29	7,000,000	7.125	40,105	M	
Aug. 3	350,000	7.187	6,203	M	
Aug. 10	280,000	8.25	5,724	M	
Aug. 30	2,003,750	7.625	25,862	M	
Aug. 31	3,500,000	7.50	43,701	M	
Sept. 7	1,575,000	6.375	49,842	M	
Sept. 8	700,000	6.375	21,914	M	
Sept. 13	210,000	6.625	6,879	M	
Sept. 21	125,909	7.75	2,413	M	
Sept. 22	437,500	6.5625	14,114	M	
Sept. 22	1,400,000	6.675	43,827	M	
Sept. 29	542,500	7.50	14,312	Sept. 29, 1971	Q
Sept. 30	175,000	6.6875	5,757	M	
Oct. 7	4,708,907	7.375	85,741	M	
Oct. 13	7,000,000	7.125	244,636	M	
Oct. 26	9,625,000	7.1875	508,219	M	
Oct. 27	87,500	7.375	3,167	M	
Dec. 21	86,625	7.875	1,687	Sept. 21, 1971	Q
Dec. 29	542,500	7.75	14,805	Sept. 29, 1971	Q
Mar. 21, 1972	88,725	8.375	1,843	Sept. 21, 1971	Q
Mar. 29, 1972	542,500	7.875	15,052	Sept. 29, 1971	Q
June 21, 1972	91,350	8.375	1,907	Sept. 21, 1971	Q
June 29, 1972	560,000	7.875	15,538	Sept. 29, 1971	Q
July 7, 1972	1,225,000	8.125	98,077	July 7, 1972	A
	$55,632,766				
		LONG-TERM			
Sept. 21, 1972	$ 93,800	8.375	$ 1,947	Sept. 21, 1971	Q
Sept. 29, 1972	568,750	7.875	15,779	Sept. 29, 1971	Q
Dec. 21, 1972	96,250	8.375	1,998	Sept. 21, 1971	Q
Dec. 29, 1972	393,750	8.125	16,798	Sept. 29, 1971	Q
March 21, 1973	98,000	9.0	2,206	Sept. 21, 1971	Q
March 29, 1973	603,750	8.125	17,330	Sept. 29, 1971	Q
June 21, 1973	101,500	9.0	2,268	Sept. 21, 1971	Q
June 29, 1973	612,500	8.25	17,829	Sept. 29, 1971	Q
Sept. 21, 1973	105,000	9.0	2,346	Sept. 21, 1971	Q
Oct. 1, 1973	630,000	8.375	18,621	Sept. 29, 1971	Q
Dec. 21, 1973	107,275	9.0	2,397	Sept. 21, 1971	Q
Dec. 31, 1973	647,500	8.75	20,025	Sept. 29, 1971	Q
March 21, 1974	110,250	9.125	2,499	Sept. 21, 1971	Q
March 29, 1974	665,000	8.875	20,870	Sept. 29, 1971	Q
May 13, 1974	875,000	8.0	17,328	Aug. 13, 1971	Q
June 21, 1974	113,050	9.125	2,563	Sept. 21, 1971	Q
Sept. 23, 1974	116,200	9.125	2,633	Sept. 21, 1971	Q
Dec. 23, 1974	119,350	9.125	2,705	Sept. 21, 1971	Q
March 21, 1975	122,500	9.375	2,856	Sept. 21, 1971	Q
June 4, 1975	7,000,000	8.75	305,763	Dec. 4, 1971	S/A
June 23, 1975	82,950	9.375	1,946	Sept. 21, 1971	Q
May 17, 1976	175,000	9.0	15,566	May 17, 1972	A
June 1, 1976	175,000	8.875	3,346	May 30, 1972	A
June 4, 1976	3,500,000	9.0	157,377	Dec. 4, 1971	S/A
	$17,112,375				

[a]M—monthly
Q—quarterly
S/A—semi-annually
A—annually

EXHIBIT 5. Short-Term and Long-Term Euro-Dollar Interest Rates, 1967–1971

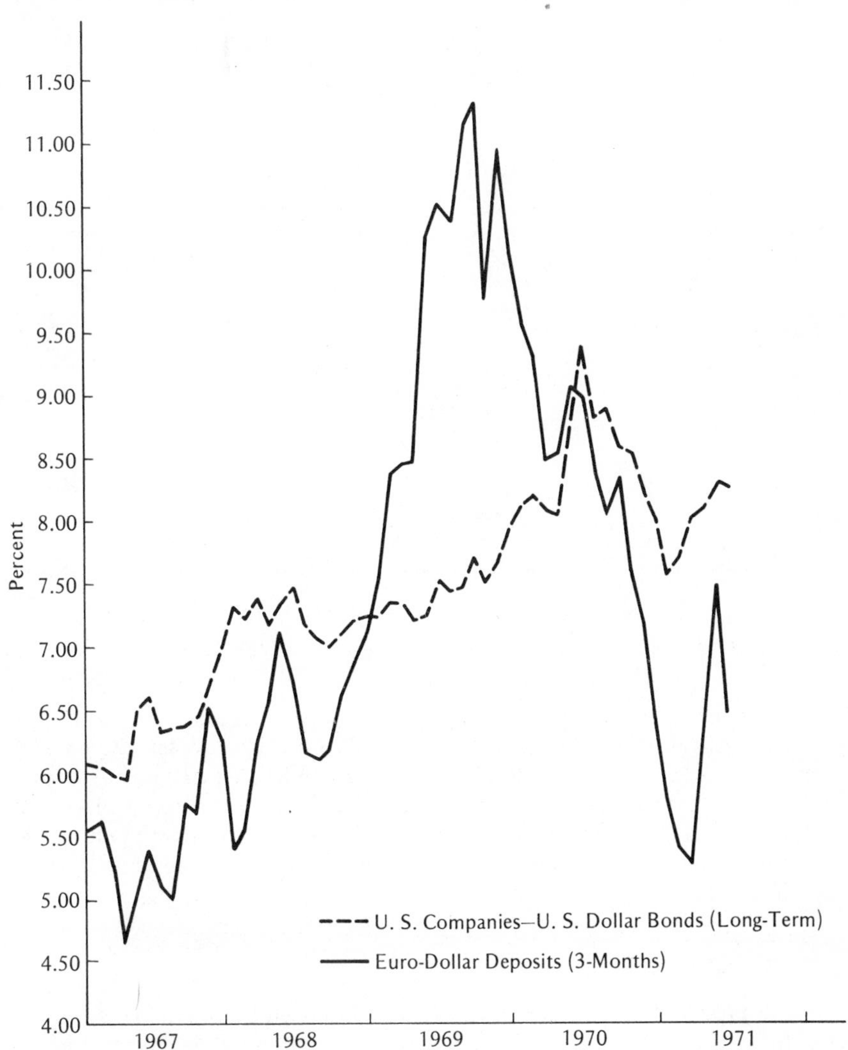

SOURCE: Morgan Guaranty Trust Company of New York, WORLD FINANCIAL STATISTICS.

Euro-dollar Rates. By mid-July 1971 the short-term Euro-rates appeared to be about near the year's low (Exhibit 6). After a continuous decline during the first three months of the year, short-term Euro-rates had increased considerably in the succeeding three months. By July, however, these rates appeared to be back to the low levels of March. The earlier decline in rates appeared to be associated with the improved conditions in the U.S. domestic market where short rates continued declining and with a reflow of funds from U.S. banks to their

EXHIBIT 6. United States: Domestic and Euro-Dollar Money Rates

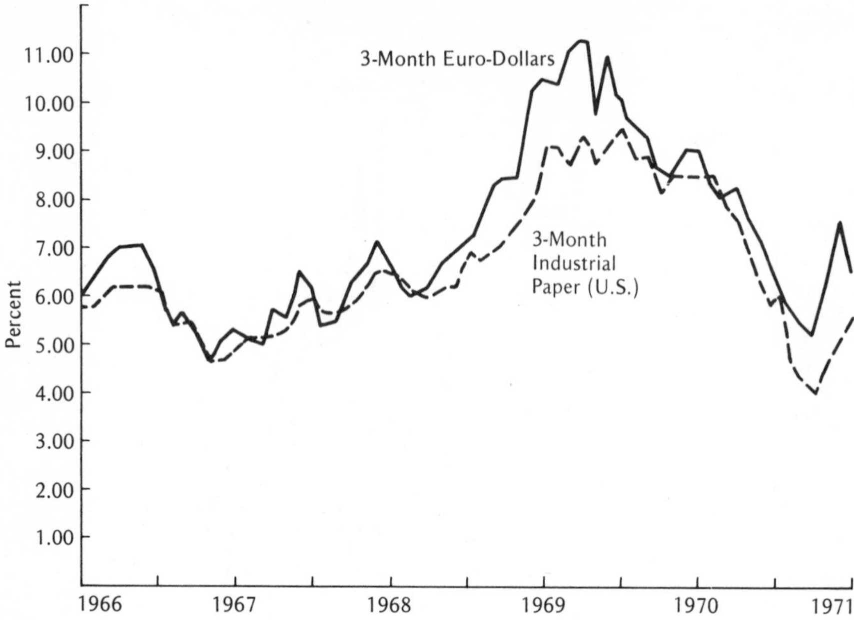

SOURCE: Morgan Guaranty Trust Company of New York, WORLD FINANCIAL STATISTICS, various issues.

foreign branches in January. By April, however, apprehensions about a possible currency crisis, followed by the actual monetary crisis in May, sent Euro-dollar rates to much higher levels. Recent EEC talks which had led to hopes of a possible monetary integration appeared to have brought some peace to the market. It was anticipated, however, that during the last few days of the month rates would edge up as a result of month-end operations by banks and a renewed pressure on the dollar.

Other Considerations

The vice president of finance thought that even though European investors paid attention to the rates paid by Euro-dollar deposits or bonds, one of the primary considerations in their minds was the strength of the U.S. economy. At the present time there were four factors that lurked on the horizon of the U.S. economy. On the domestic front, in spite of mounting unemployment, inflation appeared to continue unabated. In the international sphere the continuous deficits in the U.S. balance of payments and the recent floating of the deutsche mark and other currencies all combined to produce increased pressures on the dollar. Finally, in the political arena the following year, 1972, was to be an election year and it was suspected that President Nixon would run for re-election.

Given the parallel between Euro-dollar rates and U.S. domestic rates, CLI's finance vice president decided to analyze the relationship between these two sets of rates. Data collected by him are contained in Exhibits 6 and 7.

EXHIBIT 7. U.S. Nonfinancial Business Corporations: A Percentage Allocation of Sources and Uses of Funds, 1956–1971 (percentages)

	1956–1966			*1967*			*1968*			*1969*			*1970*			*1971 (I&II)*		
SOURCES OF FUNDS																		
Total	100.0			100.0			100.0			100.0			100.0			100.0		
Internal	67.5			63.6			57.1			50.4			58.3			54.0		
Net Saving		31.4			32.5			26.9			17.3			12.5			15.6	
Capital Consumption		68.6			67.5			73.1			82.7			87.5			84.4	
External	32.5			36.4			32.9			49.6			41.7			46.0		
Credit and Equity Market		57.0			83.2			65.4			66.7			88.2			78.4	
Stock			14.1			7.8			-2.6			11.0			17.5			22.2
Bonds			42.5			50.2			42.6			30.9			52.3			55.6
Mortgage			17.9			15.4			19.1			12.3			13.7			17.8
Bank Loans and Other			25.5			26.6			40.9			45.8			16.5			4.4
Other																		
Profits Tax Liabilities						-81.0			13.1			-9.7			-62.3			29.0
Trade Debt			59.0			84.5			63.1			101.0			103.8			46.0
Other Liabilities			41.0			96.5			23.8			8.7			58.5			25.0
USES OF FUNDS																		
Total	100.0			100.0			100.0			100.0			100.0			100.0		
Real Investment	73.0			74.5			70.5			71.9			79.8			68.9		
Plant and Equipment		87.0			86.8			88.6			89.0			93.0			91.9	
Residential Construction		5.3			3.2			3.0			3.3			3.9			4.7	
Inventories		7.7			10.0			8.4			7.7			3.1			3.4	
Financial Investment	25.6			15.1			23.7			23.5			18.5			23.3		
Liquid Assets		11.4			14.5			33.6			4.7			45.6			18.9	
Trade Credit		55.5			53.1			54.3			62.0			31.8			36.1	
Consumer Credit		4.1			6.2			6.6			4.7			7.2			5.8	
Miscellaneous Assets		29.5			26.2			5.5			28.6			15.4			39.2	
Discrepancy	1.4			10.4			5.8			4.6			1.7			7.8		

SOURCE: Federal Reserve Board of Governors, FLOW OF FUNDS ACCOUNTS, various issues.

CHAPTER 15

The International Bond Market

The distinctive characteristic of the international bond market is that these bonds initially are sold outside the country of the borrower, often in several countries. Therefore, funds in the international bond market are generally raised in currencies other than the one of the borrower.[1] Once this basic characteristic is established, one can go further and subdivide the international bond market into the Euro-bond market and the foreign bond market. This classification is based on the currency in which the lender buys the bonds and the borrower repays the debt. When the bonds are sold principally in countries other than the country of the currency in which the issue is denominated, it is called a *Euro-bond issue.* When the bonds are sold primarily in the country of the currency of the issue, it is called a *foreign bond.* Both Euro-bonds and foreign bonds may include options as to the currency in which the final payment may be made. In addition, the Euro-bond market offers several alternatives in the currency composition of the unit of account of the issue.[2]

[1] An exception is the American firm borrowing Euro-dollars, for example.

[2] Some portions of this chapter draw heavily on *The European Market for International Bonds,* prepared by Yoon S. Park under the supervision of Professor Eli Shapiro and distributed by the Intercollegiate Case Clearing House, Boston, Mass. An expanded version of that material appears as Chapter 2 in Yoon S. Park, *The Euro-Bond Market: Function and Structure* (New York: Praeger Press, 1974).

BACKGROUND

Until 1963 foreign security issues in Europe remained relatively underdeveloped because of the fragmentation and relatively small size of European capital markets, the high interest rates prevailing in most of these markets, and numerous government controls. By 1963 foreigners were tapping the U.S. capital market for over $1 billion per year. As Exhibit 15.1 shows, from 1955 to 1962 new issues of foreign securities in the United States were greater than those in all European countries combined.

EXHIBIT 15.1. Foreign Issues in European Countries and the United States, 1955–1962 (millions of U.S. dollars)

	1955	*1956*	*1957*	*1958*	*1959*	*1960*	*1961*	*1962*	*Total 1955–1962*
European countries	$392	$235	$219	$ 349	$384	$308	$592	$444	$2,923
United States	200	403	539	1,144	568	440	290	587	4,171

SOURCE: Jean Mensbruggle, "Foreign Issues in Europe," IMF STAFF PAPERS, July 1964, p. 329.

A number of European governments and business enterprises floated bond issues in New York instead of in European capital markets because New York offered them lower interest costs and a more efficient underwriting system than those available elsewhere. However, the introduction of the Interest Equalization Tax (IET) in July 1963 effectively discouraged U.S. residents from buying foreign securities. The IET reduced the after-tax return to U.S. purchasers, diminishing their desire to acquire such securities. This forced non-U.S. borrowers to turn increasingly to European capital markets in spite of the limitations that borrowing in these markets entailed.

Other measures related to the U.S. dollar gave further impetus to the growth of the international bond market. These forces were the emergence of a large Euro-dollar market and the controls on foreign direct investment imposed on U.S. companies on a voluntary basis in 1965 and on a mandatory basis in 1968. The emergence of a sizable Euro-dollar market provided the raw material for large bond financings to take place. The controls on U.S. foreign direct investment forced U.S. companies to approach the European markets to raise the bulk of the funds required to finance their foreign operations.

The result of the combination of all these forces was a fantastic growth in the international bond markets, as shown in Exhibit 15.2.

FOREIGN BONDS

A foreign bond is an international bond sold by a foreign borrower but denominated in the currency of the country in which it is placed. It is underwritten and sold by a national underwriting syndicate in the lending country. For example, a U.S. company might float a bond issue in the Swiss capital market, underwritten by a Swiss syndicate and denominated in Swiss francs.

EXHIBIT 15.2. New International Bond Issues Outside the United States (millions of U.S. dollars)

	1966	1967	1968	1969	1970	1971	1972	1973	1974	1975	1976	1977	Total 1966–1977
Euro-Bonds[a]	$1,142	$2,002	$3,573	$3,156	$2,966	$3,642	$6,335	$4,193	$2,134	$ 8,567	$14,328	$17,735	$ 69,773
Foreign Bonds	378	403	1,135	827	378	1,538	2,060	2,626	1,432	4,884	7,586	7,185	30,432
Total International Bonds	$1,520	$2,405	$4,708	$3,983	$3,344	$5,180	$8,395	$6,819	$3,566	$13,457	$21,914	$24,920	$100,205

[a]Includes European Unit of Account, European Monetary Unit, and multiple currency option issues.
SOURCE: Morgan Guaranty Trust Company, WORLD FINANCIAL MARKETS, New York, various issues.

EXHIBIT 15.3. Foreign Bond Issues Outside the United States (millions of U.S. dollars)

	1968	1969	1970	1971	1972	1973	1974	1975	1976	1977
Foreign Bonds, Total (Ex. 15.2)	$1,135	$827	$378	$1,538	$2,060	$2,626	$1,432	$4,884	$7,586	$7,185
By Category of Borrower										
U.S. Companies	139	223	55	200	215	546	77	61	28	40
Foreign Companies	56	128	83	212	345	396	455	1,386	1,654	1,158
State Enterprises	12	107	16	163	249	446	568	1,314	2,439	1,909
Governments	317	98	53	254	177	297	138	765	1,307	1,834
International Organizations	611	271	171	709	1,074	941	194	1,358	2,158	2,244
By Currency of Denomination										
German Mark	674	531	89	308	500	362	253	1,089	1,288	2,096
Swiss Franc	238	196	193	669	815	1,526	911	3,297	5,359	3,463
Dutch Guilder		}	17	17	31	0	4	182	597	211
Japanese Yen		} 100	15	92	311	271	0	67	226	1,271
Other	223	}	64	452	403	467	264	248	116	144

SOURCE: Morgan Guaranty Trust Company, WORLD FINANCIAL MARKETS, New York, various issues.

The bond issue is sold to investors in the Swiss capital market, where it will be quoted and traded. (A summary of foreign bonds issues outside the United States is found in Exhibit 15.3.)

Until 1973 the largest issuer of foreign bonds was international organizations, such as the World Bank. During that period the second largest issuer of foreign bonds was U.S. companies. However, since then, with the weakening of the dollar, U.S. companies have been reluctant to issue foreign bonds in currencies such as the Swiss franc and the German mark. International organizations have continued to account for between one and two billion dollars worth of issues annually. But it is governments and state enterprises that have dominated the foreign bond market since 1973. In 1977 they accounted for over 50% of bonds issued in this market. This compares with only an 18% share of a much smaller market in 1970.

A combination of relative interest rates and availability of funds has determined the participation of various currencies in the foreign bond market. Thus, the growth of foreign bonds denominated in Swiss francs and yen has been supported by the governments of the respective countries. By maintaining relatively low interest rates, the Swiss government since 1971 and the Japanese government since 1977 have encouraged foreign borrowers to use their markets as a source of funds. This serves to mop up excess liquidity in the domestic money markets—a liquidity largely created by the intervention of these governments in the exchange markets to support the value of the dollar against their currencies. In exchange for the apparently lower interest rate, foreign borrowers have been forced to convert the domestic currency (francs or yen) into dollars (i.e., sell marks or yen and purchase dollars). This exchange has helped absorb some of the dollars that these governments have acquired from their intervention in the exchange markets. By returning some of the domestic currency to the central banks, this exchange also helps to control money supply growth.

Among the elements that comprise the borrowing cost, the interest rate is but one of the factors. Other components of cost are the commission rates and the exchange risks. In a foreign bond loan, the risk of a currency revaluation is borne by the borrower—appreciation resulting in a loss, depreciation in a gain. For example, an American firm operating mostly in U.S. dollars floats a mark foreign bond issue in Germany. If the mark appreciates by 10% next year, both the interest and principal payments become 10% more expensive to the company than before the appreciation, as discussed in Chapter 7.

STRAIGHT EURO-BONDS

The Euro-bond is an international bond "underwritten by an international syndicate and sold in countries other than the country of the currency in which the issue is denominated."[3] From a miniscule size of $164 million in 1963, the bond market exhibited a phenomenal growth that reached $6,335 million in 1972 and over $17 billion in 1977. From 1966-1977, almost $70 billion was borrowed through Euro-bonds. U.S. companies alone borrowed over $10 billion

[3]Morgan Guaranty Trust Company, *World Financial Markets,* last page of each issue.

on the Euro-bond market by the end of 1977, but the bulk of the borrowing occurred prior to 1974. See Exhibit 15.4.

The Euro-bond market has emerged as the most important segment of the international capital market. Before 1963, most international long-term issues were raised through foreign bond issues in certain national capital markets, primarily in the United States and Switzerland, but also in Germany, the Netherlands, and the United Kingdom. Of these, only Switzerland and Germany remain as important markets for foreign bonds today. The dominant form of international new issue activity has shifted to the Euro-bond market.

The Euro-bond market, although centered in Europe, is truly international in the sense that the underwriting syndicates typically comprise investment bankers from a number of countries, the bonds are sold to investors around the world, and the flotations are not governed by national regulations.[4] However, in spite of the cosmopolitan nature of the Euro-bond market, a Euro-bond is a simple instrument for borrowers and investors to understand. It is denominated in a given currency and there are no major regulations with which to contend.[5]

As described before, the impetus for the fast growth of the international bond market was largely provided by the regulations imposed on the international capital flows in the United States. The Interest Equalization Tax (IET) drove foreigners to raise funds outside the United States. The controls on foreign direct investment, initially voluntary but made mandatory in 1968, sent U.S. companies to raise funds in foreign markets for their foreign operations. The growth of the Euro-bond market very clearly reflects the impact of these two regulations. Exhibit 15.4 shows the increasing participation of U.S. companies and non-U.S. companies in the Euro-bond market in response to these regulations throughout 1972. On January 1974 the IET and the controls on direct investment were lifted by the U.S. government, and the participation of U.S. companies in this market declined drastically. However, non-U.S. companies have become an increasingly significant portion of new issues in the Euro-bond market.

State enterprises, which were also subject to the impact of IET, comprise another significant portion of the Euro-bond market. Governments kept a relatively low profile in the Euro-bond market through 1974. However, since then both governments and state enterprises have become significant issuers of Euro-bonds. In 1970 these two categories accounted for 31.9% of issued Euro-bonds. By 1977 the percentage had risen to 43.1%. Entities such as the Mexican and Brazilian governments, the government and the government enterprises of Finland and Sweden, and the provinces of Canada have been particularly large issuers of paper.

International organizations have played only a minor role in this market

[4]Some countries—like Italy, France, and Belgium—put informal pressure on their *domestic* banks to slow down their underwriting of Euro-bond issues. However, no country can regulate the *whole* Euro-bond market.

[5]An impetus to the deutschemark-denominated Euro-bonds similar to the IET effect on dollar Euro-bonds came when the German government placed a 25% tax on interest payments on German corporate bonds held by foreigners. Thus, bond purchasers were moved to seek deutschemark-denominated bonds outside the West German government's regulation, which tended to decrease interest rates for Euro-bonds denominated in deutsche marks.

EXHIBIT 15.4. New Euro-Bond Issues (millions of U.S. dollars)

	1966	1967	1968	1969	1970	1971	1972	1973	1974	1975	1976	1977
Euro-Bonds, Total (Ex. 15.2)	$1,142	$2,002	$3,573	$3,156	$2,966	$3,642	$6,335	$4,193	$2,134	$8,567	$14,328	$17,735
By Category of Borrower												
U.S. Companies	439	562	2,096	1,005	741	1,098	1,992	874	110	268	435	1,130
Other Companies	376	575	603	817	1,065	1,119	1,759	1,309	640	2,903	5,323	7,284
State Enterprises	118	442	349	682	594	848	1,170	947	542	3,123	4,138	4,707
Governments	108	303	500	584	351	479	1,019	659	482	1,658	2,239	2,936
International Organizations	101	120	25	68	215	98	395	404	360	615	2,193	1,678
By Currency of Denomination												
U.S. Dollar	921	1,780	2,554	1,723	1,775	2,221	3,908	2,447	996	3,738	9,125	11,628
German Mark	147	171	914	1,338	688	786	1,129	1,025	344	2,278	2,713	4,109
Dutch Guilder	—	—	—	17	391	298	393	194	381	719	502	361
Other[a]	74	51	105	78	112	337	905	262	179	610	443	935
Canadian Dollar								0	60	558	1,407	674
French Franc								166	0	293	39	0
European Unit of Account								99	174	371	99	28

[a]Includes European Unit of Account (through 1972), European Monetary Unit, and multiple currency option issues.
SOURCE: Morgan Guaranty Trust Company, WORLD FINANCIAL MARKETS, New York, various issues.

in comparison with the foreign bond market. The smaller participation of the latter two entities in the Euro-bond market is partly a reflection of the nature of the IET inasmuch as these institutions were exempted from the tax imposed on foreign issues in the United States. For example, the International Bank for Reconstruction and Development (World Bank) was allowed to raise funds through bond issues in the United States without the lenders being subject to the penalties of the IET.

The development of the Euro-bond market as a substitute for the U.S. domestic market also is reflected in the dominant role that the dollar has played in the Euro-bond market. Until 1967 the Euro-dollar bond often accounted for as much as 90% of the Euro-bond market. After that year the strength of the mark relative to the dollar gave a larger role to the mark in the Euro-bond market. Still, Euro-dollar bonds have generally retained a minimum of approximately 50% of the total new issues in the Euro-bond market. (See Exhibit 15.4.)

Euro-bonds also have proven to be a versatile instrument. Not only have maturities been tailored to the needs of the borrowers under the regulations,[6] but Euro-bonds have also appeared with a variety of features designed to make the instrument more desirable to the investor and practical to the borrower. Examples of this versatility are the emergence of convertible Euro-bonds, floating rates, commercial paper and sweeteners such as warrants.

The convertible Euro-bonds have typically been issued by U.S. companies and denominated in U.S. dollars. After being firmly established in 1968, the ebbs and flows of this market have paralleled those of the U.S. stock market. The years of 1968, 1969, and 1972, when the stock market reached record performance, have seen large amounts of convertible Euro-dollar bonds sold successfully in the market. The sagging stock market in 1970–71 and 1974 was a clear setback to the convertible Euro-bond market.

Following the pattern of many direct Euro-dollar loans, initially there was an interest in floating rate Euro-bonds. One was introduced in 1971 with a fifteen-year maturity and an interest rate adjusted every six months. But the market did not develop in these bonds and the initial issues became very illiquid. However, since 1975 there appears to be a renewed interest in these bonds.

Euro-dollar commercial paper was first issued in 1970, permitting short-term users of Euro-dollar funds to create formal indebtedness, bypassing the banks in the Euro-dollar loan market. Thus, the general credit of the firm permitted it to avoid short-term Euro-dollar loans from banks or medium- to long-term financing from the Euro-bond market if it was willing to roll over its commercial paper and was able to sell it. Usually, an underwriter was involved in the issue of commercial paper.

Some Euro-bond issues have carried warrants, as in the United States. Generally, interest in these features has declined with the stock market indices, since the value of the warrant is related to its strike price compared to the current market price. Firms are reluctant to use warrants when the stock is severely depressed unless the strike price (the price at which the warrant can be exercised

[6]For example, the controls on U.S. foreign direct investment did not count as a capital outflow the repayment of debt with maturity longer than seven years and repayment of principal after that year. Accordingly, the typical Euro-bond had a maturity of more than seven years and specified a balloon payment at the end of the period for the principal.

to acquire common stock) is far above market. Such a spread, of course, lessens the value of the warrant to the bond purchaser.

EURO-BONDS INVOLVING MORE THAN ONE CURRENCY

The straight Euro-bonds described in the previous section have dominated the Euro-bond market. However, bonds that involve more than one currency in the denomination of the bonds have comprised an increasing portion of the Euro-bond market. These other Euro-bond issues appear in Exhibit 15.4 as "other" in the classification of Euro-bonds by currency. These alternate arrangements as to currencies have responded to two primary needs. First, they are an incentive to the lender. Second, they are a way to average the uncertainty involved in the foreign exchange risk of a single currency. The latter factor has been of particular relevance since 1972 when foreign exchange markets have exhibited a much higher instability than in the preceding period. Below is a summary of the major characteristics for the most important types of Euro-bonds with currency mixes.

Multiple Currency Bonds

The multiple currency bond, in one of its most widely used forms, entitles the creditor to request payment of the interest and the principal of the bond in any predetermined currency as well as in the currency of the loan in accordance with a previously established unchangeable parity. Thus, the obligation is expressed in various national currencies at the choice of the lender.

This option strengthens the exchange guaranty for the lender because (s)he loses only if *all* currencies included in the multiple currency contract depreciate against the other currencies *not* included in the contract. Suppose, for example, that a Lebanese lender bought a multiple currency bond with three currency options: British pounds, French francs, and U.S. dollars. When all three currencies depreciate against the Lebanese currency, (s)he loses in the same proportion as the currency which has depreciated the *least* among the three currencies.

If any one currency in the contract appreciates, the lender gains by that much because payment always can be required in the currency which offers the greatest advantage. With a multiple currency clause, therefore, when all currencies in the contract depreciate, but in different proportions, the obligation of the borrower fluctuates in the same proportion as the currency which has depreciated the *least.* However, when all currencies in the contract appreciate but in different proportions, the obligation appreciates in the same degree as the currency *most* appreciated.

Thus, a multiple currency bond presents a disadvantage to the borrower, for (s)he must cover the currency expected to appreciate the most and still cannot profit from depreciation of a particular currency. For this reason, the multiple currency bond is utilized by borrowers who for one reason or another fear difficulties in the placing of the bond; the high interest rates which were offered for such bonds in the past few years suggest that poor credit risk issuers who have no cheaper alternatives resort to these issues. The first multiple currency bond in the postwar period was the 1957 Petrofina $25 million issue, repayable in Dutch guilders, Belgian francs, German marks, U.S. dollars, or Swiss francs at the 1957 exchange rate. Ordinarily the choice is restricted to two currencies.

European Monetary Unit (EMU) Bonds

In late 1970 the European Coal and Steel Community borrowed EMU 50 million (which was equal to U.S. $50 million prior to the 1971 devaluations) for a fifteen-year maturity. The value of the debt was fixed at the time of issue at a permanent exchange rate in terms of the six EEC currencies. As a result, the lender is protected against depreciation since the least depreciating currency can be designated as the repayment currency by the lender. Should appreciation take place in several of the currencies, then the lender may demand payment in that currency which has appreciated the most.

In this sense, the EMU (also called the European Currency Unit) bond is a multiple currency bond which is based on six major reference currencies. Although the borrowing rates are slightly lower than those for the typical Eurobond, dollar-denominated issue, the difficulty in the EMU bond is that the borrower bears the exchange risk for six major currencies.

Unit of Account Bonds

Because of the Euro-dollar, an international money and capital market came into being in Europe. This development would have been considered utopian a few years before. However, strong as the dollar might have been as a foreign currency, it always was a national currency, the trend, value, and confidence of which was mainly determined by factors such as the situation of the U.S. balance of payments, internal economic developments, the political situation, and the monetary policy of the United States. A national currency does not in all circumstances offer the necessary basis for the development of an international capital market.

It is precisely with these considerations in mind that in 1961 the European Unit of Account (EUA) began to be utilized for the issue of international bonds. The unit of account is neither a means of payment nor an instrument of exchange, although it may become so under special circumstances, as for example when a transfer is made from one account to another on the books of a bank.[7] Mainly, however, it serves as a yardstick helping to determine the value of the obligations entered into, with the aim of maintaining the value of the respective liabilities and claims as constant as possible with respect to the original value.

The unit of account is not a modern invention. As long ago as the late Middle Ages, when every kingdom, every principality, and even small towns had

[7] At present, the Bank for International Settlements, the European Monetary Agreement, and the European Coal and Steel Community employ the European unit of account as the basic currency unit.

separate currencies, units of account such as the Mark-Banco of Hamburg and the Florin-Banco of the Amsterdam Wissel-Bank were used in settling accounts in international trade.[8]

The value of the European unit of account initially was that of the unit of account of the European Payments Union (EPU),[9] i.e., 0.88867088 gram of fine gold which was equivalent to one U.S. dollar prior to the 1971 devaluation. This value could be changed only under very strict conditions as to the fluctuations in the seventeen reference currencies to which it was limited.[10]

In 1972 a new formula for the value of the EUA was announced. The number of reference currencies was reduced to nine, the currencies of the enlarged Common Market. In order to qualify as a reference currency two conditions must be met: (1) The currency must have a par value (to be defined below); and (2) The exchange rate of the currency must be kept within the margins of the so-called snake. From time to time these currencies have left and reentered the snake. However, the British pound and the French franc had been outside the snake for several years by 1978.

How does this bond work? The table below gives the value of the EUA in terms of the reference currencies in 1978:

Reference	*Value of EUA 1*
Belgian franc	48.6572
Danish krone	8.56656
French franc	(a)
German mark	3.15665
Irish pound	(a)
Italian lira	(a)
Luxembourg franc	48.6572
Dutch guilder	3.35507
Sterling	(a)

[a] At the time these currencies did not qualify as reference currencies since they were floating outside the "snake."

These bonds in practice are traded in German marks. Thus, to purchase an EUA $1,000 bond selling at face value, the buyer would pay DM3156.65. At maturity the buyer will receive exactly DM3156.65 plus interest, unless there has been a change in parity.

Central to the value of an EUA bond is the definition of parity and the conditions under which it is changed. For parity values to be changed the following conditions must be met: (1) All the reference currencies must change their "par value" since the last change of the EUA, and (2) A majority of reference currencies must change their value in the same direction. In this case the EUA

[8] Fernand Collin, *The Formation of a European Capital Market and Other Lectures.* Brussels, 1964, p. 11.

[9] An institution that existed between 1950–58 to help settle balances among its seventeen member nations. This institution was created to help solve the problems created by the lack of convertibility of the participants' currencies.

[10] The currencies involved were those of the original seventeen members of the EPU, which comprised the six members of the European Economic Community, the seven members of the European Free Trade Association, and Iceland, Greece, Ireland, and Turkey.

will move in the direction of the majority, to the extent of the smallest percentage change. It must be noted that a currency may leave and rejoin the snake without a change in par value for purposes of the EUA.

The concept of par values is difficult to understand under the current regime of floating rates. The difficulty is surmounted by leaving the definition of par values to the central banks involved. Thus, in the case of the German mark, the market value of EUA 1 at the time of this writing is around DM2.6. However, for purposes of EUA bonds, the par value is as defined above, DM3.15665. Since this definition of the value of EUA's is used for several other transactions among the members of the Common Market, the par values of the reference currencies are determined more by political considerations than by market forces. As a consequence, the value of the EUA for the last few years in terms of the reference currencies has remained constant, despite wide variations in the market exchange rates.

What are the exchange risks associated with the EUA bond? At the time of issue, the borrower may demand payment of the proceeds in the currency of his choice. Obviously, the borrower will select the currency that gives him or her the best premium over the market. With the par values presented above, in 1978 that would be the German mark. For interest payments and principal repayment, the choice of currency belongs to the lender. Again, the lender will choose that currency most to his or her favor. Given the par values presented above and market rates in 1978, the lender would choose German marks.

In terms of his or her own currency a borrower loses from a devaluation of his or her own currency or an upvaluation of the EUA; the borrower gains from an upvaluation of his or her own currency or a devaluation of the EUA. The opposite is true for the lender, in terms of his or her own currency.

With current par values the borrower benefits when first issuing the bond, but at the time of repayment he or she is penalized, as long as par values are maintained. The opposite is true for the borrower. Given the present disparities between par values and market rates, this situation is equilibriated by EUA bonds carrying 1/2% to 1% higher interest than German mark bonds. Of course, if par values are changed the perceived benefits and drawbacks will be changed.

By 1978 there were approximately 70 EUA bond issues outstanding. The market was very thin and the largest market maker was said to be Kredietbank Luxembourgeoise.

Dual-Currency Convertible Bonds

A new instrument in the international bond markets was developed in 1977 by non-U.S. companies issuing convertible bonds denominated in currencies different from their own. For example, a Japanese company may issue a dollar convertible bond. In this case the currency of denomination of the bond is the dollar, but the currency of the shares into which the bond is convertible is the yen. The conversion rate is expressed in terms of a fixed number of shares. Thus, when the yen appreciates against the dollar the convertible bond also may appreciate because the dollar value of the yen shares into which the bond is convertible is worth more.[11] The opposite may happen when the yen depreciates against the dollar. If the convertible bond is redeemed as a bond the borrower bears the exchange risk between the dollar and the yen. However, if the conversion feature is exercised by the lender, the borrower is responsible only for the number of shares promised in the conversion rate. Obviously, the value of a convertible bond at any point in time depends on the combined effects of exchange rate fluctuations, the performance of the stock price, and market interest rates.

In early 1978, Japanese companies were issuing convertible bonds in Swiss francs and German marks to take advantage of the relatively low interest rates in these currencies. Companies in Switzerland, the United Kingdom, and the Netherlands have floated significant amounts of dollar convertible bonds in the recent past. Companies in Singapore and Sweden have also participated in this market. The dollar convertible bonds have done very well. The appreciation of the yen against the dollar in 1978 brought the price of many of the dollar convertible bonds issued by Japanese companies above their par value.

Parallel Bonds

A parallel bond is a multinational issue (usually a large issue) comprised of several bonds floated simultaneously among various countries, with each participating country raising funds in its own currency. The terms and conditions of all the bonds are made uniform as far as possible and are different only where absolutely necessary.

The chief proponent, H. J. Abs, of Deutsche Bank, held that parallel bonds "would accumulate the available resources of the European capital markets involved. As each issue would be made out in the currency of the country concerned the bond would be acceptable to all groups of investors. Each individual bond could be raised within the limits of each country's financing capacity in different amounts."[12] The parallel bond is similar to the foreign bond discussed earlier, only more complex. It is a combination of a group of foreign bonds among several countries, with synchronization of timing and issue terms. Since the parts of the parallel bond are floated at the same time, the terms of issue would probably need to be tailored to meet conditions in the least favorable market at that time. The main argument for this type of bond is the ability to borrow a large amount of funds simultaneously. However, the record has shown that other types of securities, particularly the dollar Euro-bond, can be floated in relatively large amounts without the possible disadvantages of the parallel bond mentioned above. Thus far, very few parallel bond issues have been floated.

[11]The extent of the appreciation of the bond depends on whether the convertible is selling primarily as a bond or as equity. The closer the selling price is to its equity value, the closer the reflection of the appreciation of the yen in the price of the convertible.

[12]H. J. Abs, "Parallel Loans to Mobilize Continental Funds," *The Times* (London), March 11, 1964, p. 18.

INTERNATIONAL BOND-MARKET INSTITUTIONS

Financial Intermediaries

Since foreign bonds are underwritten in the country of the currency of the bond denomination, the institutions involved in issuing these bonds are those that handle bond issues in the given country. The characteristics of some of the major capital markets and their institutions will be discussed in the following chapter.

Euro-bonds, on the other hand, are underwritten by an international syndicate. The cornerstone of the Euro-bond market is the thirty to forty financial institutions in Europe and the United States which manage the major share of all new international bonds. Since Euro-bond issues attract few institutional investors,[13] it is especially important for the underwriting investment bankers to have experience in preparing an issue for placement with banks and residents in a large number of countries.

The general pattern of a Euro-bond syndicate follows the traditional American system, i.e., the three-tier structure of the managers, the underwriting group, and the selling group. The investment banks acting as managers select an underwriting group of important concerns with contacts in a number of countries, and the selling group is ordinarily several times larger and has a wider geographical representation. The underwriters of a typical Euro-bond issue ordinarily comprise well-known European banking institutions and leading U.S. investment banks, with a total number of participants that usually surpasses the traditional two or three in the United States by a substantial number. The selling group easily can be fifty or more so that the retail market in every country can be reached.

The underwriting costs for Euro-bond issues are somewhat higher than for bond flotation in the U.S. domestic market. Whereas the total underwriting cost for an average issue in the United States may be about 2% of issue value, the comparable cost for a Euro-bond issue with a maturity of 15 years or more is ordinarily 2.5%, consisting of a 1.5% selling commission, a 0.5% management fee, and a 0.5% underwriting fee. Additional incidental expenses payable by the issuing or borrowing company may run as high as $100,000, with the actual cost partly dependent on the amount of financial advertising. Issues with shorter maturities often cost less.

One difficulty with the European underwriting system is that it usually does not involve a firm commitment on the part of the syndicate members to take precommitted amounts of the issue; rather they operate on a best-efforts basis. This factor means the lead investment banker has a limited basis for estimating how firm the interest is on the part of the syndicate members prior to the actual issue. Although the European situation typically has a provision

[13]The European institutional investors such as the pension funds and the insurance companies prefer a debenture denominated in the currency of their own country rather than in dollars, because their liabilities are payable in their domestic currency.

relating to loss of commissions if issues are returned to the market during the life of the syndicate, this penalty arrangement is difficult to enforce, with the result that the syndicates are usually ended promptly, with the lead investment banker and some others bearing the responsibility of stabilizing the market in the bonds after issuance.[14]

When there is a large amount of the issue unsold, unlike the United States where the underwriters typically must "swallow" the unsold portion, in the European case the underwriters have the right to raise the coupon or sell the remaining issue at deep discount, to reduce the size of the issue, or simply to cancel it in the event the syndicate does not wish to absorb the balance.

Although about half the U.S. firms chose to list their Euro-bond issues on the New York Stock Exchange in the 1965-69 period, more than 80% listed the issues on the Luxembourg Stock Exchange. Multiple listings are possible. In contrast, the next highest incidence of listing was the London Stock Exchange, where only 6% of the issues were listed.[15] This emphasis on the Luxembourg exchange is related on the part of the issuer to less stringent listing requirements. From the point of view of the bond buyer, securities regulations and disclosure of issuer's information (which in Luxembourg are similar to the U.S. Securities and Exchange Commission regulations) offer additional protection. The issues are traded in the secondary market by about twenty-five major traders, with daily turnover between $60 and $100 million.

Since the Euro-bond transactions are conducted throughout the major world financial centers, there have been problems in settling transactions such as delays in receipt of bonds purchased or payment for bonds sold, frequent reshipment of securities, and the tying up of substantial amounts of dealer's capital. In order to solve these problems, New York's Morgan Guaranty Bank created a Euro-bond clearing house. In early 1969 Barclays Bank announced plans to start its own clearing operations, but it dropped the idea two months later. Resenting the dominance of the clearing operation by one bank (and an American one at that), late in 1969 fifty-five banks from America and Europe met to form CEDEL, a new clearing organization. Clearing operations commenced in September 1971 with over seventy subscribing shareholders. Friction between the two systems eventually led to Morgan Guaranty's decision to open ownership of its operation, and it sold 97% of its interest in late 1972 to various institutions in twenty countries. This opened the door for a number of arrangements between the two systems so that physical delivery of bonds can be made more easily.

In 1978 a group of European banks was developing a computer-assisted trading and information system, called Eurex. It was expected that this service would improve the efficiency and depth of the Euro-markets. In this system subscribers will have access to up-to-date Euro-bond prices and will be able to conclude transactions through the network provided by the computer system.

[14] See Gunter Rischer, "The Role of Underwriters in the Euro-capital Market," *Euromoney,* June 1972, pp. 4–10.

[15] Compiled by Yoon S. Park from White, Weld and Co., *International Bond Market Letter.* New York, various issues.

Borrower's Financial Subsidiaries

Taking the United States as an example, although one incentive to raising money in the Euro-bond market for U.S. corporations was to comply with various U.S. voluntary and mandatory credit restraint programs in the late 1960s, another incentive was simply to avoid exchange control on funds used abroad. Thus, a large base of funds can be raised at one move and the funds redistributed wherever the firm needs them. The alternative is separate issues in a number of countries, with possible current or future exchange restrictions on the movement of funds among those countries.

As noted earlier in the text, countries differ in their policies about withholding taxes on dividends and interest to residents and nonresidents. Most Western European countries have one withholding tax for residents and nonresidents alike, ranging from 5% in Luxembourg to 41.25% in the United Kingdom. Others (Canada, Germany) have withholding only on interest paid to nonresidents. Still other nations (Denmark, the Netherlands, Sweden) have no withholding tax. Most nations have tax treaties with other nations which may reduce the withholding tax,[16] and in virtually all cases the holders of the bonds can have credit against their local income taxes for the amount withheld. The difficulty is that many of the Euro-bond purchasers have no intention of declaring the income to their local tax authorities; hence, the credit is worthless. Most Euro-bond issues have a clause which provides that the borrower will increase the interest payment to offset any future withholding tax on interest to nonresidents should it be legislated.

The interest of U.S. corporations in domestic financing subsidiaries (often incorporated in Delaware) stems from the Section 861 provisions of the Internal Revenue Code. When 80% or more of the gross income of a U.S. corporation is from foreign sources, then there is no withholding required for payment of dividends or interest to nonresidents.[17] Hence, when the financing subsidiary raises funds in the Euro-bond market, it can meet a non-U.S. income rule, permitting it to pay the debtors (and investors) their return without withholding. Unlike a foreign finance subsidiary, the domestic subsidiary can have its gains and losses consolidated with the parent. When foreign taxes are due on the income the foreign operating subsidiary pays the finance subsidiary, there is a credit against U.S. tax liability for such tax payments. Again, because of tax treaty arrangements, it is likely that there will be no tax by foreign governments on the remission of interest from the foreign operating subsidiaries to the U.S. domestic finance subsidiary (which in turn pays its debtholders and investors). Should the proceeds of the domestic finance subsidiary's fund raising be used in the United States, then the interest paid to it by the (U.S.) operating subsidiaries

[16] For example, under a treaty, Great Britain's withholding on dividends and interest for payments to Americans is reduced from the standard 41.25% to 0.

[17] With the elimination of the Interest Equalization Tax and other capital controls in 1976, the Internal Revenue Service (IRS) has stopped giving rulings guaranteeing that Euro-bond issues of U.S. companies under the 80% clause are exempt from withholding taxes. Thus, as of 1978 there was no total assurance that withholding taxes on Euro-bond issues of U.S. companies would not be subject to withholding taxes in the future under a separate decision from the IRS.

will be U.S. income, and the payments to the foreign debtholders and investors would be subject to U.S. withholding.

If the proceeds of the Euro-bond issue are to be used in the United States, then overseas finance subsidiaries are desirable. The IRS rule is that it is U.S. source income (hence, payments are subject to U.S. withholding) only if more than 80% of its gross income is from the conduct of a trade or business in the United States. Hence, it is possible that the management may arrange for the interest income to be received by the finance subsidiary, yet not deemed U.S. source income if the activities of the finance subsidiary itself are entirely outside the United States; it is not conducting a trade or business in the United States but merely receiving interest from loans to U.S. firms (the operating subsidiaries). Among the finance subsidiary locations, Delaware and Luxembourg have been used most widely. At first, U.S. corporations favored Luxembourg as the site for their financial subsidiaries but switched their preferences to the United States, especially to Delaware, in 1966.

A Delaware subsidiary is subject to very low state taxes and few restrictions on its legal ability to change operations. Also, it is possible to consolidate a Delaware subsidiary with the parent company for U.S. tax purposes, thereby taking advantages of tax-deductible losses that the subsidiary may incur in initial operations.

Luxembourg offers many advantages as the site for the financial subsidiary. For nominal fees, a holding company (which is in effect a financial subsidiary) can be established which is exempt from both Luxembourg income tax and withholding tax on interest and dividend payments.

INTEREST RATES ON INTERNATIONAL BONDS

The interest rates on foreign bonds are directly correlated with the rates prevailing in the given country adjusted by whatever regulation affects foreign bonds in particular. These regulations have often been modified to cater to government objectives regarding the balance of payments. Thus, when the United States tried to reduce its deficit in the balance of payments, it imposed the Interest Equalization Tax that raised the cost of issuing foreign bonds in this country. Conversely, Germany, which has been fighting continuing pressures to appreciate its currency, has at times given incentives to foreign borrowers to use the German bond market as a source of funds.

In the Euro-bond market, the rates of a one-currency bond are directly related to the long-term rate level in the home country of the currency, the Euro-rate for short maturities of that currency, the rates in other currencies, and currency regulations and restrictions. For example, the Euro-dollar bond rate depends on the U.S. long-term rate, the Euro-dollar rate (and therefore on U.S. short-term rates), and the long-term rate in other countries. Given the controls on capital outflows from the United States that prevailed between 1965 and the end of 1973, the U.S. long-term rate actually served as a floor for the Euro-dollar bond rate. Lenders could always invest in the United States. However, borrowers were forced to raise the funds used for expansion of foreign operations in the Euro-bond market. Depending on the size of this demand for foreign financing, the Euro-bond rate could go substantially over the domestic U.S. bond rate. However, long-term rates in other currencies have served as a check on how high the Euro-dollar bond rate can go.[18]

One must also notice that there is clearly a feedback cycle between Euro-dollars and dollar-denominated Euro-bonds, even though one is generally short-term and the other medium- to long-term. Because of rate differentials observed or anticipated in the short run, Euro-dollar holders may want to shift into Euro-bonds for a brief period, for example. In addition, monetary authorities in some countries encourage the use of Euro-dollar accounts in the initial floating of Euro-dollar issues since that policy avoids pressure on the domestic currency if used instead. Thus, under a steady flow of Euro-bond issues, there is a continuous amount of Euro-dollars so used; a peak period of issue would intensify the demand for Euro-dollars. Counteracting this effect is the substitution between them; hence, an increase in the supply of dollar-denominated debt issues with demand fixed will lower equilibrium interest rates.

In spite of the fast growth of the Euro-bond market, this market is still small compared to the U.S. bond market. As a result, the Euro-bond market does not have great depth and breadth. It is not unusual to hear an investment banker advising a customer to decide whether a Euro-bond issue would be desirable so that "if a favorable market develops they would be ready," since such a good market can disappear in a period of a couple of weeks. Thus, another large determinant of the level of Euro-bond rates is the volume of new issues coming to the international market in any one period.

In general, Euro-bond interest rates have been rising steadily since 1963, in line with the overall rising interest rate trend in Western Europe and the United States. This trend of rising interest rates was further accelerated from 1969-74 mainly because of the all-time high interest rates on the U.S. bond market and around the world.

Bibliography

Borsuk, Mark, "The Future Development of Offshore Capital Markets in Asia." *Columbia Journal of World Business,* Spring 1974, pp. 48-60.

Dufey, Gunter, "The Euro-Bond Market: Its Significance for International Financial Management." *Journal of International Business Studies,* Summer 1970, pp. 65-81.

Enzig, Paul, *The Euro-Bond Market.* New York: St. Martin's Press, 1969.

Korsvold, Paul E., "International Capital Markets." Unpublished draft, May 1973.

[18]A stepwise regression by Park using monthly data from 1968-72 found 78% of the variance in the Euro-dollar bond rates explained by the U.S. triple-A bond rate. Park, *The Euro-Bond Market: Function and Structure,* pp. 86-88.

Park, Yoon S., *The Euro-Bond Market: Function and Structure.* New York: Praeger Press, 1974.

Salomon Brothers, *United States Multinational Banking.* New York, 1976.

Wai, U Tan, and H. T. Patrick, "Stock and Bond Issues and Capital Markets in Less Developed Countries." *IMF Staff Papers,* July 1973, pp. 253-317.

CHAPTER 16

Comparative Capital Markets

In the preceding two chapters we noted the relationship that interest rates in the international financial markets bore to rates in the domestic market of the currency in question. This chapter presents a framework for analyzing domestic capital markets. The analysis will focus on the relatively well-developed financial markets in Europe, the United States, and Japan.

It is impossible to discuss in any depth the characteristics of specific financial markets in one chapter. However, we would like to provide a general approach to the analysis of financial markets. The data on specific countries are used only as illustrations of an analytical approach. The framework provided should be helpful in understanding the financial markets of any country.

The same set of actors appears in every financial system. At one extreme is a group of individuals and institutions that consume less than they generate in income. The income not consumed is saved. At the other extreme is a set of individuals and institutions that find the income they generate insufficient to cover the level of expenditures they desire. The expenditures over and above the income generated by these units is used for current consumption or for investment in real goods, in contrast to financial investment.

The role of financial markets is to channel the excess funds of savers into the hands of those who have needs for funds beyond their income. Two groups of institutions facilitate this flow of funds from savers to investors. One group comprises *financial institutions* such as commercial banks that accept deposits from savers and lend funds to investors, usually business enterprises. The other set of institutions comprises the *security markets* where savers and investors in real goods meet directly: the equity and debt markets.

This simple explanation of financial markets is depicted graphically in Exhibit 16.1 in which the arrows indicate the flow of funds from savers on the left to the final users of funds on the right, all under the umbrella of the monetary authorities. Obviously, this is an extremely simplified presentation of financial markets. In reality, there is a large degree of interaction among the various groups presented in the exhibit. Also, flow of funds in directions opposite to the ones presented in the diagram can occur.

Exhibit 16.2 shows the role that the various institutions mentioned in Exhibit 16.1 actually played during 1976. The left panel of the exhibit shows the percentage of total financial assets purchased by each sector. The right panel shows the percentage of total financial assets issued by each sector–liabilities of that sector. The two sectors with very distinctive positions in each panel of the exhibit are the nonfinancial business enterprises, which are much more heavily represented as issuers of liabilities, and the household sector, which is more

EXHIBIT 16.1. Diagram of Flow of Funds in Financial Markets

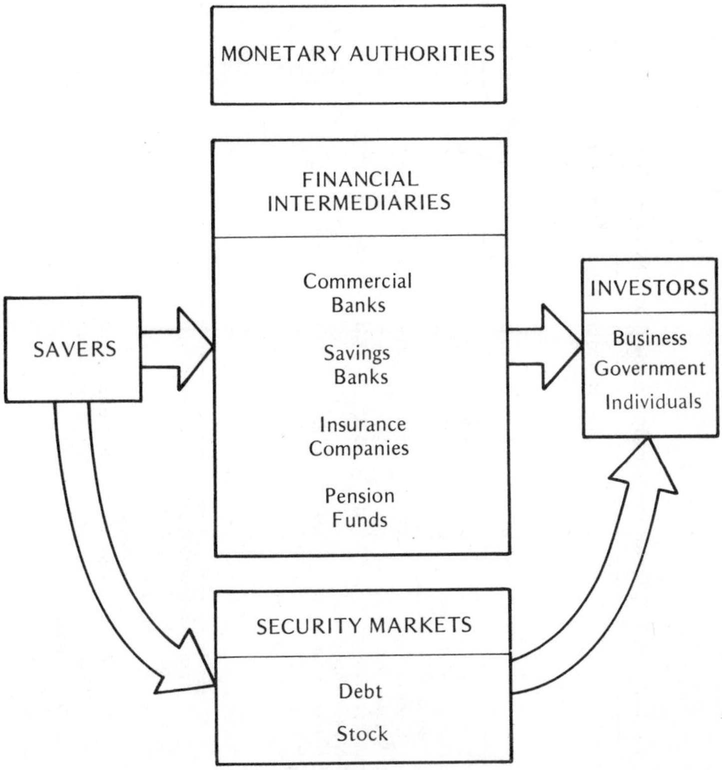

EXHIBIT 16.2 Sector Participation in the Flow of Funds, 1976

	Assets Acquired by Sector as a Percentage of Total Flow of Funds in Each Country							*Liabilities Issued by Sector as a Percentage of Total Flow of Funds in Each Country*						
	Germany	*U.S.*	*France*	*Italy*	*Netherlands*[c]	*U.K.*	*Japan*	*Germany*	*U.S.*	*France*	*Italy*	*Netherlands*[c]	*U.K.*	*Japan*
Central Bank	3.5%	1.7%	0.4%	11.8%	1.6%	N.A.	1.2%	2.3%	1.7%	1.1%	11.4%	.7%	N.A.	1.2%
Commercial Banks	38.1	14.2	26.8	31.2	24.4	24.8	14.7	37.1	13.9	26.7	29.4	23.6	24.0	14.7
Nonbank Financial Intermediaries	8.0	26.0	20.9	6.1	17.8	15.4	16.4	7.5	25.1	20.7	6.1	17.1	16.9	16.4
Federal and Local Government	(1.0)	10.4[a]	4.4	14.5	7.9	5.7	15.3	12.2	20.2[a]	6.3	29.2	12.4	14.5	27.5
Nonfinancial Business Enterprises	13.0	10.5	5.7	8.8	34.3	8.8	21.9	25.5	15.1	21.4	21.3	27.0	14.5	27.0
Households	27.6	29.3	27.0	23.2		20.8	28.7	2.6	16.7	12.6	0.4		8.0	10.3
Rest of the World	10.8	5.9	14.8	4.4[b]	14.1	24.5	1.8	12.7	7.4	11.2	2.1[b]	19.2	22.1	2.8
	100.0%	100.0%	100.0%	100.0%	100.0%	100.0%	100.0%	100.0%	100.0%	100.0%	100.0%	100.0%	100.0%	100.0%

[a] Includes federally sponsored credit agencies.
[b] Includes discrepancies.
[c] 1975 figures.
N.A. = Not available

Figures may not add to 100% because of rounding errors.

SOURCE: Organization for Economic Cooperation and Development, OECD FINANCIAL STATISTICS, OECD Publications Center, Washington, D.C., November 1977.

heavily represented as a purchaser of financial assets. Commercial banks are both major purchasers of financial assets and issuers of liabilities. To a lesser extent this is also true for the nonbank financial intermediaries. Federal and local governments appear as net issuers of liabilities in 1976. This is in marked contrast with earlier periods when this sector often played a lesser role in the financial markets of these countries. The participation of the rest of the world sector differs from country to country.

SAVINGS

Two major questions arise when studying the savings of a country: (1) What is the level of savings relative to national income, and (2) In what form are these savings? The answer to the first question will determine the amount of funds available for investment in productive capacity. The answer to the second question gives an indication of the sectors that benefit from these savings and the financial intermediaries available in the country.

For the countries presented in the tables in this chapter, total savings, personal and business, account for between 30% and 40% of the respective national incomes. Italy, France, and the United Kingdom had approximately 30% of their national income accounted for by savings. Germany, the United States, the Netherlands, and Japan had savings of about 40% of national income. Other things constant, the countries with higher rates of savings are likely to have more sophisticated financial markets and higher economic growth to the extent that savings are channeled into real investments.

From Exhibit 16.2 we noticed that the largest purchaser of financial assets is the household sector. Exhibit 16.3 shows how the household sector distributed financial assets among various types of securities. In every country cash and short-term deposits account for 50% or more of the financial assets acquired by households. In the United States the household sector was actually selling its holdings of short-term securities and equity shares and using the proceeds to acquire highly liquid deposits. In the United Kingdom households were selling shares for the same purpose. The figures show a high desire for liquidity on the part of households in all the countries shown in the exhibit. This is partly determined by the level of liquid balances that individuals deem necessary for transaction purposes and the level of interest rates, but the data are also influenced by the lackluster performance of the stock markets in most countries in the period leading to 1976.

In spite of the high desire for liquidity referred to above, households in all these countries found some funds available to channel into long-term financial investments. Financial investments in long-term securities took the form of bonds and loans in Germany. In the United States and the United Kingdom the long-term financial investments were generally in life insurance companies and pension funds. France and Japan had a rather small percentage of their financial savings placed in long-term financial securities. The explanation for this pattern of distribution of financial savings is best understood by analyzing the type of financial intermediaries available in each country.

EXHIBIT 16.3. Household Sector: Financial Assets Acquired and Liabilities Issued during 1976

	Distribution of Acquired Financial Assets							*Distribution of Issued Liabilities*						
	Germany	*U.S.*	*France*	*Italy*	*Nether-lands*[b]	*U.K.*	*Japan*	*Germany*	*U.S.*	*France*	*Italy*	*Nether-lands*[b]	*U.K.*	*Japan*
Monetary Gold and Foreign Exchange	—	—	—	—		—	—	—	—	—	—		—	—
Cash and Transferable Deposits	5.9%	4.7%	17.2%	33.7%		8.4%	12.6%	—	—	—	—		—	—
Other Deposits	47.7	64.3	70.2	50.2		40.5	59.4	—	—	—	—		—	—
Short-term Securities	0.7	(7.2)	—	5.1		—	11.2[d]	—	—	—	—		—	—
Short-term Loans	—	—	—	—		(0.2)	—	31.7%	28.6%	16.5%	100.0%		9.3%	77.8%[e]
Trade Credit	—	—	—	—		—	—	—	1.4	—	—		6.7	19.7
Bonds	21.3	8.4	3.1	2.7		12.1	—	—	—	—	—		—	—
Shares	[a]	(2.3)	1.9	1.7		(7.6)	1.2	—	—	—	—		—	—
Savings Bonds and Other Debt Certificates	—	2.7	—	—		—	—	—	—	—	—		—	—
Long-term Loans	24.4	5.1	—	—		1.2	—	65.7	64.6	80.6	—		84.3	—
Equity on Life Insurance and Pension Funds	—	31.6	3.6	—		45.0	12.8	—	—	—	—		—	—
Others	0.1	(7.4)	3.9	6.7		0.6	2.7	2.6	5.3	2.4[c]	—		(0.2)	2.5
	100.0%	100.0%	100.0%	100.0%		100.0%	100.0%	100.0%	100.0%	100.0%	100.0%		100.0%	100.0%

[a]Less than 0.1%.
[b]Breakdown not available.
[c]Plus accounting registration differences
[d]Includes bonds.
[e]Includes long-term loans.

Figures may not add to 100% because of rounding errors.

SOURCE: Organization for Economic Cooperation and Development, OECD FINANCIAL STATISTICS, OECD Publications Center, Washington, D.C., November 1977.

FINANCIAL INTERMEDIARIES

At the apex of the organization of any country's financial markets are the monetary authorities that regulate the flow of funds from savers to final investors. These authorities supervise the functioning of the financial intermediaries and the actual workings of the money and capital markets. In the following sections we review briefly the role of monetary authorities and then turn to a general analysis of the financial intermediaries. The financial intermediaries are separated between commercial banks and nonbank financial intermediaries. Of these two, commercial banks in every country play a much larger role than all other financial intermediaries combined. Thus, commercial banks are studied in more detail in the following discussion.

Monetary Authorities

The primary institution regulating the flow of funds in financial markets is the central bank of the country. In some cases the central bank handles the monetary affairs of the country single handedly. In other cases other institutions such as the Treasury also play an important role in the determination of the availability and distribution of credit.

Monetary authorities in every country have the economic goals of maintaining full employment, controlling the rate of inflation, maintaining external equilibrium, and furthering economic growth. Given the conflicting nature of these goals, monetary authorities usually must choose what priority to assign to each. The ranking of these priorities changes from time to time. Some of the trade-offs that governments make in the selection of these goals were discussed earlier in the text in the analysis of the external position of a country. An understanding of what priorities a government places on various goals at a certain point in time is extremely useful in anticipating the actions that the monetary authorities will take to control the credit flows in the country.

The traditional controls of central banks are open market operations, the level of the discount rate, reserve requirements, and selective controls. Among the countries studied in this chapter, only the United States and the United Kingdom make extensive use of open market operations to control the financial markets. The money markets in the other countries are not sufficiently broad and deep to allow a heavy reliance on open market operations to accomplish desired objectives. That leaves the other three tools as the major weapons that most central banks use in pursuing their monetary goals.

Among the seven countries, the monetary authorities of three merit special attention because of their peculiar characteristics. At one extreme is Switzerland, where the central bank (40% owned by private interests) exerted only limited influence on the financial markets until the early 70s. Then monetary policy was largely determined by the commercial banks. It is only in very recent years that problems with the exchange rate in the international markets and with inflation in the domestic markets have induced the Swiss central bank to take a more active posture. In contrast, France and Italy are characterized by a number of governmental institutions that act with the central bank to exert a very powerful control over the financial markets.

In France the powers of the Bank of France (the central bank) are reinforced by the presence of two other regulatory bodies: the National Credit Council and the Banking Control Commission. Although the latter two organizations include members from business, labor, and banking, they are truly headed by the Bank of France in conjunction with the Treasury. The decisions of these organizations are carried out through the French Banks Association. All banks in France, including the three major banks which are state owned, belong to this association. In addition to highly centralized credit decisions, the Bank of France possesses a powerful arsenal of tools to enforce its decisions. These tools go so far as to include a review of each company's outstanding debt once a year. Not only the total credit needs but also the type of credit are considered in this review.

Italy is another country where monetary authorities assume a very strong stance. Credit policies are formulated by the Interministerial Committee for Credit and Savings. These policies are then implemented through the Bank of Italy (the central bank) and the Treasury. The Bank of Italy retains a large degree of discretionary authority and its supervision of the monetary system is tight. Specific credits are monitored and the issue of securities is controlled. Another important characteristic of the Bank of Italy's policy has been the incorporation of development goals into monetary policy. This has given rise to a discriminating set of policies that differentiates on a regional as well as an industrial basis in its granting of credit. For example, the south of Italy always gets preferential treatment under any monetary policy.

Commercial Banks

There are two major characteristics that distinguish commercial banks in Europe and Japan from the banks in the United States. Whereas national banking and even branching in some states is forbidden in the United States, the other nations studied in this chapter are characterized by the existence of commercial banks with branches all over the country. The other major difference is the ability of commercial banks in these countries to underwrite securities. In the United States commercial banking and investment banking cannot be performed by the same financial institution. In the European countries and in Japan commercial banks not only can underwrite securities, but they are also usually active in buying and selling industrial bonds and equities for their own account. These equity holdings give commercial banks an opportunity to participate in the decisions of private companies, and often they help to establish a very special relationship between the commercial banks and the industrial sector: e.g., the zaibatsu (informal conglomerates) in Japan.

In spite of very large numbers of banks and branches in the European countries and Japan, the commercial banking business in those countries is highly concentrated in the hands of a few banks. In Germany, where there are more than 300 commercial banks with over 5,000 branches, the three largest banks (Deutsche Bank, Dresdner Bank, and Commerzbank) account for about 40% of total commercial bank assets. A similar story can be found in Switzerland where three banks (Swiss Bank Corporation, Credit Suisse, and the Union Bank of Switzerland) represent a growing 40% of the total assets of Swiss banks.

In France the three largest banks (Banque Nationale de Paris, Credit Lyonnais, and Societé General) are state-owned and account for 75% of total bank assets. In the Netherlands, the Big Two [Algemene Bank Nederland (ABN) and Amsterdam-Rotterdam Bank (AMRO)] now hold more than 50% of all commercial bank assets. In the United Kingdom, the concentration in banking is slightly less, with the largest amount of business being controlled by the ten clearing banks.

In terms of direct loans, commercial banks traditionally have specialized in short-term credits. The most common form of these credits outside the United States are overdrafts (purposely exceeding a checking deposit balance) and discounting of trade-related financial paper. The system of compensating balances of borrowers held with commercial banks common in the United States is usually not found in European commercial banks; however, compensating balances are very popular in Japan. The traditional high reliance of commercial banks on short-term credit as their primary earning asset can be seen in Exhibit 16.4, in which one of the largest items in the acquisition of financial assets is often short-term loans.

In spite of the traditional reliance of short-term credits, commercial banks in all the countries studied have begun to play an increasingly significant role in the medium- and long-term funds market. In Exhibit 16.4 70.2% of acquired assets in Germany and 42.2% of acquired assets in France were in the form of long-term loans in 1976.[1] These two countries contrast with Italy, the United Kingdom, and Japan. In Italy, in spite of the large variety of commercial banks (by historical origins and geographical coverage), all banks still concentrate on short-term loans in the form of overdrafts and trade paper discounts. In the United Kingdom commercial banks until 1971 considered themselves only as suppliers of working capital. Since the banking reform of 1971 these banks have sought to be one-stop supermarkets for all types of borrowers. However, the share of long-term loans in their portfolio of acquired assets has risen only from 0.7% in 1971-73 to 3.8% in 1976. In Japan only 10% of total loans carry a maturity of over a year.

The growth of medium- and long-term credit in France (42% of the average total financial assets acquired in 1976 as compared to 31% during 1971-73) shows the impact of French governmental credit policies and development plans. Most of the medium-term lending of French banks can be rediscounted with Credit National, one of the public credit institutions. These credits have a maturity of up to seven years and have to be approved by both Credit National and the Bank of France. If these institutions do not approve the loan, the commercial bank cannot rediscount the loan with them. Other things constant, this would make the particular loan less desirable to the commercial bank—the objective of the monetary authorities.

In analyzing the prevalence of short-term maturities in the loans extended by commercial banks, one must take into account the fact that most of these short-term credits are usually refinanced before or shortly after the loan expires. This process converts short-term loans into *de facto* long-term credits. This sequence of events is further supported by the situation prevalent in several

[1] The majority of the loans classified in the exhibits in this chapter as long-term have a maturity not exceeding five to seven years.

EXHIBIT 16.4. Commercial Banks: Financial Assets Acquired and Liabilities Issued during 1976

	Distribution of Acquired Financial Assets							Distribution of Issued Liabilities						
	Germany	U.S.	France	Italy	Netherlands[e]	U.K.[a]	Japan	Germany	U.S.	France	Italy	Netherlands[e]	U.K.[a]	Japan
Monetary Gold and Foreign Exchange	—	—	d	—	—	—	—	—	—	—	—	—	—	—
Cash and Transferable Deposits	—	8.1%	3.0%	16.7%	12.8%	0.5%	(0.2)%	4.3%	15.0%	12.3%	63.9%	26.2%	19.1%	25.9%
Other Deposits	—	—	27.5	15.7	38.2	59.2	(0.1)	64.7	50.5	74.6	39.6	59.9	65.7	47.1
Short-term Securities	(3.0)%	4.6	(2.2)	0.6	3.2	(4.5)	—	—	5.4	1.4	—	—	13.0	—
Short-term Loans	11.2	22.2	22.7	42.5	10.3	37.8	65.7[b]	—	—	—	5.9	2.4	—	1.2[b]
Trade Credit	—	—	—	—	—	—	—	—	—	—	—	—	—	—
Bonds	14.4	27.1	0.6	18.4	3.7	0.4	29.6	25.1	0.9	7.0	—	6.3	0.5	13.0
Shares	1.7	—	1.1	0.6	0.1	0.2	2.3	1.2	2.0	0.7	—	0.9	1.5	0.5
Savings Bonds and Other Debt Certificates	—	—	—	—	25.8	—	—	—	—	—	—	4.0	—	—
Long-term Loans	70.2	17.1	42.2	5.4	5.9	3.8	—	0.1	—	1.9	—	0.4	0.2	—
Equity on Life Insurance and Pension Funds	—	—	—	—	—	—	—	—	—	—	—	—	—	—
Other	5.2	21.0	2.7[c]	—	—	2.6	2.6	4.7	26.2	2.1[c]	(9.3)	—	d	12.2
	100.0%	100.0%	100.0%	100.0%	100.0%	100.0%	100.0%	100.0%	100.0%	100.0%	100.0%	100.0%	100.0%	100.0%

[a]Central bank is included in the banking sector.
[b]Includes long-term loans.
[c]Plus accounting registration differences.
[d]Less than 0.1%.
[e]1975 figures.

Figures may not add to 100% because of rounding errors.

SOURCE: Organization for Economic Cooperation and Development, OECD FINANCIAL STATISTICS, OECD Publications Center, Washington, D.C., November 1977.

countries where the commercial banks have close ties with the industrial sector through their direct or indirect holdings of equity in industrial companies.

The position of power that commercial banks enjoy in the financial markets is further reinforced in those countries where they are allowed to undertake traditional investment or merchant banking activities. This is particularly so in Switzerland where the political and monetary stability together with the unequaled tradition of secrecy have attracted a large volume of foreign funds into the country. This has made the country one of the world's major sources of capital and the Swiss commercial banks some of the most powerful private financial institutions in international markets. Any major financing in Switzerland must be handled through one of the Big Three (the three largest banks). They do most of the underwriting and placing of bond issues and they are active in the trading of securities. These banks also control a queuing system whereby companies must wait before they can issue securities. The mechanics of the queuing system are not described anywhere, but the queue is tightly controlled by the commercial banks. Furthermore, the commercial banks, usually through holding companies, also maintain long-term positions in commercial and industrial enterprises.

In Germany the commercial banks have not enjoyed the same continuous inflow of foreign funds. However, German commercial banks are in a position similar to that of the Swiss banks in the area of underwriting. German banks handle both the listing and the initial transactions of new issues and maintain a secondary market for the securities they handle. The queuing system to issue securities is also present in Germany and it is controlled by the major German commercial banks. In the Netherlands and France the commercial banks also enjoy the ability to underwrite securities. However, French commercial banks until recently took no direct equity positions in the industrial sector. In the early 1970s the three state-owned French banks did expand into the holding of equities. This policy is in addition to the traditionally large trust department each of these banks has.

A country that traditionally kept commercial banking and investment banking separate as in the United States is the United Kingdom. However, since the 1971 U.K. bank reform the commercial banks have started to compete with the merchant banks (investment banks) by advising on corporate issues and bringing the issues to the market. These activities have usually been carried out by buying an interest in an established merchant bank or by creating new merchant banks. In Japan commercial banks can participate only in the underwriting of government securities, a large proportion of which is kept for portfolio purposes. The underwriting of industrial securities in Japan is left to the "security houses."

The major sources of funds for commercial banks in all the countries are deposits. However, the bond market also plays an important role in raising funds for commercial banks in Germany and Japan. (See Exhibit 16.4.)

Nonbank Financial Intermediaries

As mentioned before, not only are commercial banks the largest financial intermediaries in every country but they also perform a large number of functions. Both of these factors limit the role that nonbank financial intermediaries play in the financial markets of these countries. However, the nonbank financial intermediaries play a significant role in the medium- and long-term sectors of the financial markets, although not in the short-term sector which is the main province of the commercial banks. Exhibit 16.5 presents data on the distribution of financial assets acquired and liabilities issued by nonbank financial institutions in 1976.

Nonbank financial intermediaries can be disaggregated into two major categories according to their primary source of funds: (1) Those that receive funds on a contractual basis, such as insurance companies, and (2) Those that receive funds on a noncontractual basis, such as savings banks.

The contractual type of nonbank financial institution is composed of insurance companies and pension funds. Outside the United States and the United Kingdom pension funds are nonexistent or very unimportant in the countries shown in Exhibit 16.5. The importance of insurance companies in all the countries can be gauged by the percentage of total liabilities issued in the form of insurance policies and pension fund contributions. This category in Exhibit 16.5 shows that insurance companies controlled a large amount of household incremental savings in the Netherlands, almost 80% of total liabilities issued by nonbank financial institutions. In the United States and the United Kingdom pension funds and insurance companies also accounted for a significant amount of total liabilities issued by nonbank financial institutions. In Japan, where insurance companies are a growing institution, 14% of total liabilities of nonbank financial institutions were in insurance policies. This leaves Germany, France, and Italy among the countries in Exhibit 16.5 with little apparent representation in the insurance industry. The absence of liabilities issued by insurance companies in Germany is misleading and must be explained in terms of data deficiencies; footnote (a) to Exhibit 16.5 shows the presence of insurance companies, yet there is no figure for insurance equity. Insurance companies in Germany include more than 300 firms and are very active. On the other hand, France and Italy are representative of many countries where there is no insurance industry as known in the United States. Instead, the government provides insurance compensation for its citizens. The source of funds for this compensation is the annual fiscal budget; therefore, in these countries a pool of investible funds generated from payments on insurance policies does not exist. The amount required for compensation is determined according to the law of the country and is raised on an annual basis. Obviously, in not every country are these social services provided by the government or by private institutions.

The remaining nonbank financial institutions, excluding insurance companies and pension funds, can be further divided between those whose sources of funds are of a long-term nature and those whose sources of funds are mostly short-term deposits. There is a high correlation between the degree of government control over these institutions and their ability to generate long-term sources of funds.

Exhibit 16.5 shows that the two countries with the largest percentages of their liabilities generated in the form of long-term funds, other than equity on life insurance and pension funds, are France and Italy. The study of the nonbank institutions in these countries throws light on the system that is prevalent in several European countries. In France government control begins with the postal savings and the savings banks. These institutions are required to deposit the

EXHIBIT 16.5. Nonbank Financial Institutions: Financial Assets Acquired and Liabilities Issued during 1976

	Distribution of Acquired Financial Assets							Distribution of Issued Liabilities						
	Germany[a]	*U.S.*[b]	*France*	*Italy*	*Netherlands*[d]	*U.K.*	*Japan*	*Germany*	*U.S.*	*France*	*Italy*	*Netherlands*[d]	*U.K.*	*Japan*
Monetary Gold and Foreign Exchange	—	—	—	—	—	—	—	—	—	—	—	—	—	—
Cash and Transferable Deposits	(2.7)%	0.4%	0.2%	9.2%	0.7%	2.5%	1.9%	—	41.9%	1.3%	0.9%	—	—	14.0%
Other Deposits	17.6	(0.9)	(2.7)	(3.4)	3.2	2.8	(0.2)	—	1.6	43.5	3.3	17.0%	37.9%	52.0
Short-term Securities	0.3	4.8	7.6	(2.4)	0.3	0.6	[e]	—	—	1.6	—	—	0.8	—
Short-term Loans	—	9.9	7.9	1.8	1.9	0.6	59.9[f]	0.4%	(3.7)	5.7	1.4	3.1	3.5	2.2[f]
Trade Credit	—	0.2	—	—	—	—	—	—	—	—	—	—	—	—
Bonds	29.6	34.1	14.5	(0.4)	6.1	36.5	22.8	—	14.6	13.6	70.8	—	[e]	2.7
Shares	5.0	7.2	3.3	2.4	4.1	14.9	4.9	0.8	(0.5)	3.9	6.2	—	3.6	0.2
Savings Bonds and Other Debt Certificates	—	—	—	—	81.7	—	—	—	—	—	—	—	—	—
Long-term Loans	51.8	39.0	69.2	93.3	0.6	41.7	—	98.4	1.3	11.9	8.8	0.1	1.3	—
Equity on Life Insurance and Pension Funds	—	—	—	—	—	—	—	—	29.6	—	—	79.7	52.4	14.3
Others	—	5.1	—	—	1.4	—	10.7	—	15.2	18.4[c]	8.6	—	0.6	14.5
	100.0%	100.0%	100.0%	100.0%	100.0%	100.0%	100.0%	100.0%	100.0%	100.0%	100.0%	100.0%	100.0%	100.0%

[a]Insurance companies, building corporations and other large corporations.
[b]Nonbank financial institutions plus federally sponsored credit agencies.
[c]Plus accounting registration difference.
[d]1975 figures.
[e]Less than 0.1%.
[f]Includes long-term loans.

Figures may not add to 100% because of rounding errors.

SOURCE: Organization for Economic Cooperation and Development, OECD FINANCIAL STATISTICS, OECD Publications Center, Washington, D.C., November 1977.

enormous funds they collect, most of the household sector savings deposits, with the Caisse des Depots et Consignations (CDC) at a fixed rate of interest. CDC, in turn, channels the bulk of these funds into government projects which include lending to semipublic credit institutions. These semipublic credit institutions then extend long-term loans to industry either directly in the form of loans or indirectly through the discounting of medium-term credit granted to industry by commercial banks. These semipublic credit institutions also raise a substantial portion of their funds in the bond and equity market. Initially, these institutions were created after World War II to channel savings into desired areas during the reconstruction period. Now they are the primary source of medium- and long-term credit in the country. In addition to Credit National, which is the largest of these institutions and lends to industry in general, there is a series of institutions that specialize in granting credit to specific sectors. Examples of these other institutions include Credit Foncier, which is primarily concerned with financing residential construction, and Credit Agricole, which provides loans to farmers.

In Italy the institutions that raise funds in the long-term sector of the market are also of a public or semipublic nature. These institutions specialize in three major types of credits: industry and public works, mortgages, and agricultural credit. The main source of funds of these institutions is the bond market which they dominate. Exhibit 16.5 shows that 70.8% of the liabilities issued by nonbank financial institutions in Italy in 1976 were in the form of bonds. These bonds were issued mostly by these semipublic institutions which also have access to commercial banks and to direct loans from the government for their sources of funds. The bonds are issued under very attractive terms to the bondholder. Being of a semipublic nature, the major criterion in their lending is development of the country. The larger the contribution a company can prove it can make in the development of a region, the better the credit terms provided.

In these examples of France and Italy one can see the strong influence that their governments can exert directly on the financial markets. The channeling of credit to different economic sectors can be controlled with relative ease in these countries. It only requires changing the lending criteria of the semipublic credit institutions which the government controls. This is usually justified on the ground of social or economic externalities.

Savings banks and specialized banks abound in all these countries. Savings bank lending policies can be strictly controlled by the government, as seen in France. In the other countries the savings banks tend to operate more like commercial banks specializing in specific types of credits, such as consumer credit or any other credit demanded by the bulk of the bank's depositors.

The allocation of credit by these nonbank financial intermediaries can be associated with the origin of their sources of funds. Those countries with a large reliance on contractual sources of funds invest a larger percentage of their funds in bonds and shares. Exhibit 16.5 shows that the three countries with the largest amount of funds raised in the form of equity in insurance companies and pension funds (the United States, the United Kingdom, and the Netherlands) are also the countries with the largest percentage of total assets acquired represented by bonds, shares, and other debt certificates. The other countries in the exhibit lend their funds mostly in the form of short- and long-term loans.

The form in which these financial intermediaries raise their funds and channel them into the hands of the final investor is a major determinant of the depth and breadth of the security markets in a country. The countries without privately funded insurance companies and pension funds deprive themselves of a major participant in the security markets. It is in the countries with large institutional investors that we find developed security markets. The best examples of this situation are the United States and the United Kingdom.

SECURITY MARKETS

Issuers of Securities

In the preceding discussion we made reference to security markets in the context of the investment that financial intermediaries make in these markets. A more direct appraisal of the breadth and depth of the security markets can be obtained by studying the amount of gross issues by sector presented in Exhibit 16.6. A detailed analysis of these markets would require a study of the stock of securities available in these markets as well as a disaggregation of securities by ownership. In this chapter we will look only at the gross issues.

Even using the 1976 exchange rates to convert the figures of gross issues from local currencies into U.S. dollars, we see that the volume of gross issues in the United States at $192 billion is by far the largest among the countries. With almost half of the volume of the United States, Japan's gross issues follow with the amount of $89 billion. The size of gross issues in Germany, Italy, and the United Kingdom ranges between $10 and $40 billion. The smallest markets appear in France and the Netherlands. Notice, however, that this ranking in size is not adjusted for the size of the economic system of each country.

In every country debt issues represent the large majority of total issues of securities. The only country in the exhibit with a significant percentage of total issues in equity is France, 18.2%. This is largely because of a system prevailing in that country that allows for a large number of small businesses to gather under the umbrella of a single organization that issues securities on its name, usually with a government guarantee. In the remaining countries in the exhibit the size of the equity issues varies from an insignificant 0.6% of total gross issues in the Netherlands to just under 10% in the United Kingdom. However, it is important to note that while equities characteristically play a less important role than debt in the security markets, the relative significance of equity issues within each country varies from year to year depending on the health of the stock market. In every country most of the shares were issues by private nonfinancial companies.

The public issues of bonds can be divided between those issued by governments or their agencies and those issued by private institutions. Government issues usually have a larger representation in the market than do issues of the private sector in the United States and the United Kingdom. In Germany and Japan the government sector used to be a relatively small issuer of bonds until recently; however, changes in the world economy have led to greater government investment. This increased need for funds has enlarged the government participation in the market of these two countries dramatically. In France and Italy both private and government sectors are heavy users of the bond market as a source of funds. Within the issues of bonds by the private sector, nonfinancial businesses rank higher than financial firms only in the United States. In all the other

EXHIBIT 16.6. Gross Issues of Equity Shares and Bonds by Sector, 1976 (in percentages)

	Germany		U.S.		France		Italy		Netherlands		U.K.		Japan	
Shares	5.9%		5.8%		18.2%		12.4%		0.6%[a]		9.9%		4.2%	
Private Nonfinancial		4.4%		5.4%		15.6%				0.1%		7.2%		3.7%
Financial Institutions		1.4		0.4		2.6				0.5		2.7		0.5
Bonds: Public Issues	72.4		94.2[a]		81.1		79.4		14.4		89.5		95.7	
Central Government		15.4		49.9		16.5		24.1%		8.1		78.3		34.2
Central Government Enterprises		—		0.6		—		—		—		—		—
State & Local Government		2.4		9.4		6.5		—		1.4		10.1		10.7
State & Local Enterprises		—		8.9		—		—		—		—		—
Public Nonfinancial		2.0		—		11.0		9.5		} 1.5		0.1		9.6
Private Nonfinancial		0.2		15.6		13.4		1.0		}		1.0		6.4
Financial Institutions		50.6		4.9		33.2		44.9		2.3		[b]		34.6
Rest of the World		1.7		4.8		0.5		—		1.1		—		0.2
Bonds: Private Placements	—		—		0.4		8.2		3.9		0.5		0.1	
Debt Certificates	21.8		—		—		—		81.2		—		—	
	100.0%		100.0%		100.0%		100.0%		100.0%		100.0%		100.0%	
Total Gross Issues (in U.S. billion dollars translated at 1976 exchange rates)	$41.2		$192.1		$10.8		$19.0		$12.8		$19.2		$88.7	

[a] Includes private placements.
[b] Less than 0.1%.

Figures may not add to 100% or subtotal because of rounding errors.

SOURCE: Organization for Economic Cooperation and Development, OECD FINANCIAL STATISTICS, OECD Publications Center, Washington, D.C., November 1977.

countries in Exhibit 16.6 financial institutions are the heaviest issuers of bonds within the private sector. This is a reflection of the earlier discussion of financial intermediaries that found the bond market one of the major sources of funds for these firms. Among these countries the financial intermediaries issuing bonds are usually nonbank intermediaries. This is so with the exception of Japan where commercial banks obtain approximately 10% of their sources of funds from the bond market.

Buyers of Securities

Exhibit 16.7 presents the distribution of holdings of outstanding equity shares and bonds by sector. The ultimate provider of funds to the security markets, the household sector, is an important holder of securities in all the countries in this exhibit. This importance is particularly large in the cases of the United States, the United Kingdom, and the Netherlands. In these countries individuals are the single largest holder of outstanding securities.

The contribution to the security markets of contractual-type of financial institutions, insurance companies and pension funds, can be seen in the three countries where these institutions are particularly important, the United States, the United Kingdom, and the Netherlands. In these countries these institutions are the second largest holder of equities, exceeded only by the household sector. They are also large holders of bonds. In the case of the United Kingdom the bond holdings of insurance companies and pension funds exceed even the holdings of the household sector. Other financial institutions are also important holders of bonds.

In Japan and Germany the households also are important holders of securities. However, the importance of financial institutions is often as large or larger than households'. For example, commercial banks are one of the largest holders of equity shares in Japan and the largest holder of bonds in Japan and Germany. Commercial banks are also particularly important holders of bonds in Italy. The importance of commercial banks to industry in these countries is not limited to their contribution of funds in the form of loans. When the industrial sector members raise funds in the capital markets, they meet commercial banks in these markets also. The holdings of equity, in particular, contribute to the control of industry by banking.

Finally, an interesting phenomenon in Japan, Germany, the Netherlands, and Italy is the large holdings of equity shares by nonfinancial business enterprises. These are firms owning shares in other businesses. This points to the more integrated type of industry that exists in these countries in comparison to the United States and the United Kingdom where anti-trust legislation frowns on this type of crossholding of ownership.

SUMMARY

This chapter can only begin to outline the relationship among the participants in the capital markets of selected nations. The variable nature of governments is critical, for some keep influence and control of monetary and fiscal

EXHIBIT 16.7. Distribution of Holdings of Equity Shares and Domestic Bonds: End of 1976

	Germany	*U.S.*	*France*[c]	*Italy*	*Netherlands*[a]	*U.K.*[b]	*Japan*
			EQUITY SHARES				
Holders of Shares:							
Central Banks	—	—	—	0.5%	—	—	—
Commercial Banks	7.5%	0.1%	—	3.5	4.2%	0.7%	23.5%
Insurance Companies and Pension Funds	2.1	20.3	—	1.4	29.3	31.8	22.5
Other Financial Institutions	3.4	4.8	—	1.3	1.0	1.0	11.5
General Governments	7.1	—	—	—	24.5	3.4	0.9
Nonfinancial Business Enterprises	16.0	—	—	52.2	}41.0	4.0	36.6
Households	16.7	71.5	—	25.8		53.8	35.0
Rest of the World	5.4	3.3	—	15.2	—	5.2	—
Not Disaggregated	41.8	—	—	—	—	—	(29.9)
	100.0%	100.0%	100.0%	100.0%	100.0%	100.0%	100.0%
			DOMESTIC BONDS				
Holders of Bonds:							
Central Banks	0.4%	3.3%	—	20.3%	0.5%	—	9.2%
Commercial Banks	43.4	12.1	—	53.5	9.6	12.0%	25.6
Insurance Companies and Pension Funds	11.7	27.1	—	1.0	10.1	35.5	1.3
Other Financial Institutions	3.2	6.5	—	0.9	11.0	13.8	22.3
General Governments	2.9	2.4	—	2.8	2.7	0.1	14.2
Nonfinancial Business Enterprises	4.8	0.7	—	}21.4	}66.1	1.3	4.8
Households	22.1	45.3	—			24.0	22.0
Rest of the World	5.3	2.7			—	13.3	—
Not Disaggregated	6.3	—	—		—	—	0.5
	100.0%	100.0%	100.0%	100.0%	100.0%	100.0%	100.0%

[a]End of 1974.
[b]End of 1975.
[c]France: data are not available.
Figures may not add to 100% because of rounding errors.

SOURCE: Organization for Economic Cooperation and Development, OECD FINANCIAL STATISTICS, OECD Publications Center, Washington, D.C., November 1977.

policy at a minimum while others own the major credit institutions and hold household deposits. The nature of the channeling process, by which excess income from various sectors such as households is moved to the users of capital, is important to note when a manager is seeking funds in various nations. In addition, the varied structures outlined in this chapter may well suggest to the citizen of any country the directions in which his or her nation may evolve in coming years.

These figures do not change with great speed, but they can move with the business cycle. In addition, delays in reporting from various national authorities mean that the data are often nearly two years late. However, the basic relationships and the major differences among countries tend to persist.

The appendix to this chapter provides a short checklist of variables to consider when evaluating the financial markets in any nation. The checklists for evaluating developed and developing countries following Chapter 3 also are relevant to this topic.

Questions

Collect the relevant data to analyze the financial markets of a developed country. (The outline in the appendix to this chapter can be useful in this endeavor.) Sources of data can be obtained from the bibliography and from publications of the central bank and commercial banks in the country you are analyzing.

1. Describe the behavior of the major sectors in the financial markets in the last five years.

2. What are the implications of the patterns of behavior you find in these sectors for the following:

   a. Effectiveness of monetary policy.

   b. Availability and cost of various types of financial investment instruments.

   c. Availability and cost of various sources of funds.

   d. Development of security markets.

   e. General levels of interest rates.

   f. Spread between short- and long-term rates.

   g. Volatility of interest rates.

   h. International capital markets.

3. What is your forecast for the level of interest rates during the next twelve months? Why?

Bibliography*

The Banker's Guide to World Financial Centers," *The Banker (London),* May 1978, pp. 51-140.

Business International Corporation, *Financing Foreign Operations,* current issues, New York.

Organization for Economic Cooperation and Development, *OECD Financial Statistics,* OECD Publications Center, current issues, Washington, D.C.

Appendix: Outline for Analyzing Financial Markets

Savers:

- I. Short-term financial investment
- II. Long-term financial investment
  - A. Contractual, e.g., insurance premiums
  - B. Noncontractual
    - 1. Nonmarketable, e.g., time deposits
    - 2. Marketable, e.g., commercial paper

Financial Intermediaries:

- I. Sources of funds
  - A. Deposits
  - B. Contractual payments
  - C. Marketable securities
- II. Uses of funds
  - A. Short-term financial investments
    - 1. Marketable instruments
    - 2. Nonmarketable instruments, e.g., loans
  - B. Long-term financial investments
    - 1. Marketable instruments
    - 2. Nonmarketable instruments

Borrowers:

- I. Nonfinancial business enterprises
  - A. Internal funds
  - B. External funds
    - 1. Short-term sources of funds

*See also the bibliography to Chapters 14 and 15.

   a. Loans
   b. Trade credit
   c. Public offerings
  2. Long-term sources
   a. Loans
   b. Private placements
   c. Public offerings

II. Public enterprises
(choices are similar to above nonfinancial business enterprises)

III. Government
(choices are similar to above nonfinancial business enterprises)

ALTOS HORNOS DE VIZCAYA, S.A

In early April 1971, Juan Luis Burgos Marin, financial director of Altos Hornos de Vizcaya (AHV), was considering a new proposal presented to him to raise funds in the Euro-dollar market. A lawyer and economist by training, Mr. Burgos had been with AHV for the previous twelve years.

AHV was founded in 1848, and it grew to be the largest Spanish basic steel producer, with sales of U.S. $264 million in 1970. It had borrowed from foreign banks in the past, but these borrowings had been associated primarily with imports of raw materials and equipment which were strongly encouraged by the export institutions of the exporting countries. The proposal that Mr. Burgos was considering now was different. It involved borrowing directly from foreign banks without the intervention of export-oriented organizations. The proposal to obtain a Euro-dollar loan had been presented to Mr. Burgos by Credito Latino, an international brokerage company which specialized in raising unsecured funds in the Euro-dollar market.

THE SPANISH STEEL INDUSTRY

Production

Following the pattern common to other European countries, Spain began manufacturing steel in the nineteenth century and by the first part of the twentieth century it had developed sufficient steel-making capacity to satisfy internal demand. By 1929 the output had reached one million tons, but thereafter the industry stagnated. First came the Civil War (1936-38), followed by an international boycott of the Spanish regime. The reconstruction of the steel industry was not able to begin until 1949 when urgently needed capital goods could once again be imported. The following year the government, in order to increase production, formed a national steel company, the Instituto Nacional de Industria de la Empresa Nacional Siderurgica (ENSIDESA), with the purpose of constructing and operating an integrated steel plant in Aviles, in northwestern Spain. Other steel manufacturers of mixed ownership, namely Altos Hornos de Vizcaya and Uninsa, also began to expand their capacity. By 1964 Spain was producing 3.1 million tons of steel annually.

Accion Concertadas

In 1964 the Spanish government launched its First Development Plan (1964-67) in order to stimulate the domestic economy. The Plan authorized agreements, "Accion Concertadas," between the government and companies in basic industries. Companies would receive government support and fiscal incentives provided they cooperated with the government toward the attainment of the goals of the Development Plan. Altos Hornos de Vizcaya and Uninsa signed such agreements in March 1965 to cover the period 1965-72. ENSIDESA, being wholly owned by the government, gave its silent consent.

The major objective of the Accion Concertadas between the three major steel producers and the government was to insure a smooth and balanced expansion of Spanish steel capacity. The companies committed themselves to certain plant additions and modifications during the period 1964–72, thereby specifying their capacity and technology. AHV was to produce about 40% of total production by 1971. Prices for finished products were to be set by the Ministry of Trade, as were prices of intercompany purchases of semifinished products.

In return for such cooperation, the companies received government support and fiscal incentives, among which were:

1. Government agencies would grant loans for 70% of the value of capital expenditures for agreed-upon plant expansions, subject to an upper limit of $62 million.

2. The government would extend its guarantee to loans obtained by the companies in order to meet the objectives of the Plan.

3. Companies would obtain up to a 95% rebate on import taxes for capital goods, raw materials, and interest payments abroad. Application for rebate had to be made to the Ministry of Commerce and approval was granted on an individual basis. (The normal tax rate on interest payments to foreigners was 24%.)

4. A five-year depreciation period would be allowed for the new plant and equipment.

Since 1965 the steel industry had been growing dynamically; production of steel had risen to 7.4 million tons in 1970, and construction already undertaken by the three producers promised to result in a capacity of 12 million tons by 1975. The capacity planned for 1975 was 90% of the expected domestic demand at that date. (See Exhibits 1 and 2.) The table below highlights this development and compares Spanish steel production with the United Kingdom and Mexico:

Steel Production (thousands of metric tons)

	1953	*1968*	*1970*	*Kilograms per Capita 1970*
United Kingdom	17,891	26,277	28,000	465
Spain	897	4,940	7,400	252
Mexico	462	3,285	3,832	179

Steel Prices

The Ministry of Trade set Spanish steel prices below those operative in the European Economic Community (EEC) and other European countries. Even after the 6% hike which started in July 1971, prices were expected to remain an average of 10–15% below those of Common Market countries.

EXHIBIT 1. Spanish Supply and Demand for Steel: Forecast for 1971–1980

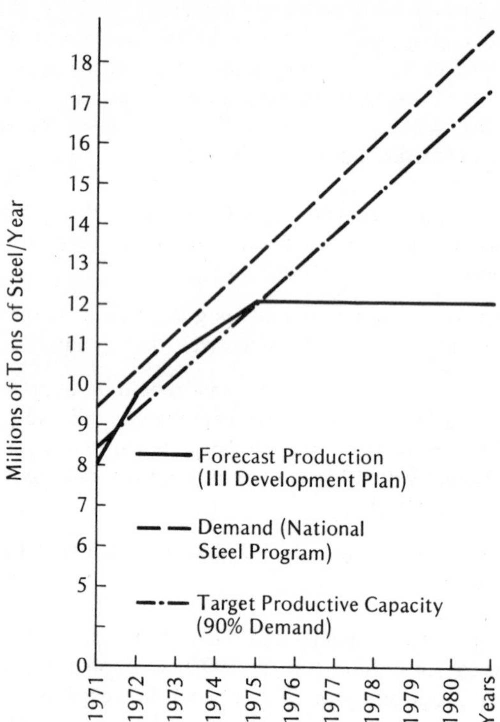

The Spanish steel industry also was well protected from the dumping of steel product imports by regulations which stipulated that:

1. Quotas for products not produced or produced in insufficient quantity by local manufacturers had to be agreed upon by the manufacturers and the Ministry of External Trade.

2. Imports outside the quota system were liable to an import tax, unlike products inside the quota. Moreover, if the selling prices of these products were below that charged by local manufacturers, an antidumping clause could be invoked by the Spanish Steel Federation to forbid further imports.

Sources of Raw Materials

Iron and coal were the two major raw materials used in the production of steel. Iron was Spain's main extractive industry, and the supply of iron ore was expected to be sufficient to satisfy the needs of the steel industry in the future. The nationalized HUNOSA coal mining company was preparing a $400

EXHIBIT 2. **Spanish Steel Product 1930–1970**

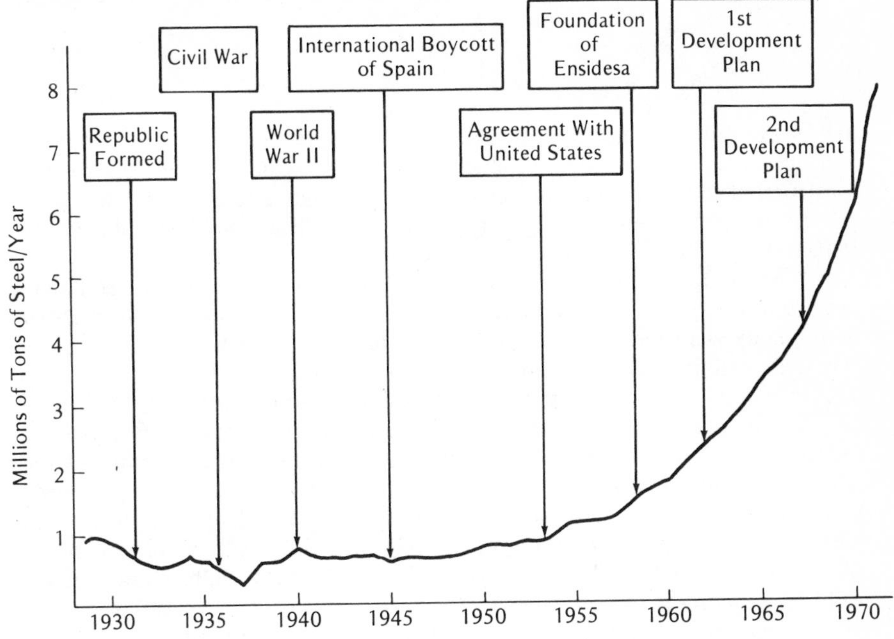

million expansion and modernization program that would make the steel makers less dependent on imported coal.

COMPANY BACKGROUND

Ownership

In 1970 the largest single shareholder of AHV was the largest steel company in the United States, U.S. Steel Corporation. In 1964 U.S. Steel had subscribed to 27% of the shares of AHV. In addition, U.S. Steel had extended a long-term unsecured loan to AHV in the amount of $10 million and had agreed to a technical assistance pact with AHV. U.S. Steel was involved in every aspect of the company's operations, and it was represented on the Board of Directors and on each daily operational committee through its permanent mission of resident U.S. Steel executives and technicians.

The next important single shareholder was the Bank of Spain (the central bank) which owned approximately 6% of the equity. This figure, however, did not fully indicate the large support that the government offered to AHV in the form of loans and guarantees amounting to more than $120 million. Commercial banks and industrial banks together owned approximately 7½% of the equity. This again did not reveal the strong commitment of these institutions to AHV in the form of loans. The remaining 59½% of the equity was in the hands of 36,000 private and institutional shareholders. The shares of AHV were listed and traded on the Madrid, Barcelona, and Bilbao Stock Exchanges.

Operations

AHV was a fully integrated steel producer. It processed coal, iron ore, and scrap iron up to semifinished steel products such as wire, rods, and girders for the construction industry. Hot- and cold-rolled strip and galvanized products were offered for general engineering purposes and for the automobile industry. In 1970 AHV produced 1.7 million tons of steel.

The company had two main plants. The most important was at Bilbao in northern Spain and the second was at Sagunto on the Mediterranean coast. Both plants were located at a port, which facilitated the importation of raw materials—mainly coal and semifinished goods. Raw materials constituted 56% of cost of goods sold: 22% was imported and 34% was produced in Spain.

In the past twelve years AHV had invested over $260 million in expanding capacity and modernizing existing facilities, and it now possessed some of the most technically advanced machinery in Europe. This machinery contributed to the productivity of labor which accounted for 15% of cost of goods sold. With a labor force of 14,000 people, AHV was the largest employer in the Bilbao area. It paid the highest wages and salaries in both Bilbao and Sagunto and had a record of smooth labor relations. Its wage contracts were negotiated every two years and included incentive schemes to increase productivity.

AHV had investments in affiliated companies which provided control of the major suppliers and distributors. The most recent acquisition had been S. A. Basconia which had been purchased during 1969 and which was AHV's largest customer, buying 12% of total sales. The other affiliates had been acquired in the 1940s. Among these, Agruminsa was AHV's principal supplier of raw materials.

AHV'S FINANCIAL FORECASTS

Forecasted Need for Funds

In spite of the continuous growth in AHV's sales, a slowdown in the economy during 1969 resulted in sales falling short of projections and a corresponding squeeze on working capital. Suppliers' credit as well as overdraft facilities had been extended to finance the unexpected build-up in inventories. (See Exhibits 3 and 4.) Moreover, a temporary decree by the Ministry of Finance forced importers to place an advance deposit with the Bank of Spain to cover the cost of imports. This policy was designed to curb the importation of unnecessary consumer goods which threatened to harm Spain's balance of payments, but it also adversely affected raw material imports.

In addition to this short-term working capital consideration, AHV also needed $20 million to finance the final phase of the expansion plan to which it was committed. The rebuilding of the blooming-slabbing mill was nearly completed, but work on enlarging a hot strip mill and a cold rolling facility was

EXHIBIT 3. Altos Hornos de Vizcaya, S.A.: Comparative Balance Sheet (thousands of U.S. dollars)

Assets	1968	1969	1970
Cash	$ 1,107	$ 1,929	$ 360
Miscellaneous Receivables	22,438	14,154	21,520
Inventory	43,096	47,980	112,921
Current Assets	$ 66,641	$ 64,063	$134,801
Land, Plant & Machinery	$353,709	$393,437	$402,671
Less Accumulated Depreciation	(84,980)	(96,279)	(111,748)
Net Plant	268,729	297,158	290,923
Investments in Affiliates	20,185	40,066	39,983
Other Assets	6,217	4,909	6,224
Total Assets	$361,772	$406,193	$471,931

Liabilities & Capitalization	1968	1969	1970
Notes Payable[a]	$ 43,494	$ 21,969	$ 45,073
Import Financing	4,534	3,783	14,426
Suppliers Account Payable	32,100	39,793	76,590
Accrued Expenses	11,208	16,356	20,136
Current Liabilities	$ 91,336	$ 81,901	$156,225
Deferred Liabilities	389	877	2,271
Funded Debt[b]	194,347	243,079	226,725
Common Stock	47,288	47,288	49,838
Reserves and Retained Earnings	28,412	33,048	36,872
Total Long-Term Capitalization	$270,047	$323,415	$313,435
Total Liabilities & Net Worth	$361,772	$406,193	$471,931

[a]Of the $45 million of notes payable in 1970, approximately $32 million have been contributed by three banks: Banco de Vizcaya, Banco de Bilbao, and Banco de Urquijo, who control 8% of the outstanding shares. These overdraft facilities, although technically listed as short-term, are of a longer-term nature as they have been rolled over again and again in the past.

[b]The repayment schedule of funded debt outstanding at the end of 1970 is as follows:

Year	Amortization (000s)	%
1971	$ 15,165	6.7
1972	21,381	9.4
1973	20,249	8.9
1974	32,478	14.3
1975	20,197	8.9
1976	19,451	8.6
1977	20,079	8.9
1978	16,847	7.4
1979	17,190	7.6
1980–2009	43,688	19.3
Total	$226,725	100.0

(continued)

EXHIBIT 3. continued

The sources of funded debt outstanding at the end of 1970 are as follows:

Lender	*Amount (000s)*	*%*
Spanish Government Agencies, including Banco de Credito Industrial (BCI), Instituto Nacional de la Vivienda (INV), and Banco de Credito a la Construccion (BCC)—(on long-term credit basis)	$ 99,254	43.8
Peseta Bonds owned by leading Spanish banks, insurance companies, pension funds, and other private and institutional investors (average life of 13 years)	$ 77,615	34.2
U.S. Steel Corporation	$ 10,050	4.4
Export-Import Bank of the United States (five loans of up to 11 years maturity)	$ 12,176	5.6
Other Foreign Banks	$ 27,630	12.2
Total	$226,725	100.0

EXHIBIT 4. Comparative Income Statement for the Year Ending December 31 (thousands of U.S. dollars)

	1968	*1969*	*1970*
Revenue			
Net Sales	$152,336	$193,996	$264,022
Less Cost of Goods Sold	123,530	149,727	205,504
Gross Profit	$ 28,806	$ 44,269	$ 58,518
Less Selling, General, and Administrative Expenses	3,843	4,305	6,361
Interest and Discount	10,881	17,883	20,884
Depreciation	10,771	11,959	16,480
Taxes	776	1,199	2,065
Welfare	4,200	5,626	6,242
Operating Profit	$ (1,665)	$ 3,297	$ 6,486
Other Income	1,901	1,784	1,050
Net Profit	$ 234	$ 5,081	$ 7,536
Cash Flow	$ 11,005	$ 17,040	$ 24,016
Dividends	$ –	$ 2,364	$ 2,492

planned to commence in September 1971 and be completed by the end of 1972. The company's plans for future expansion were restricted to routine replacement and maintenance and to the expenditure of between $1.5 million and $2.0 million on modernizing and acquiring subsidiaries over the next ten years.

Although AHV did not intend to expand the capacity of its existing plants, the National Steel Plan called for the construction of a fourth integrated steel plant in Spain with an annual capacity of around 5 million tons. This fourth plant was necessary to close the gap between local consumption and production which was expected to develop after 1975. (See Exhibit 1.) AHV had submitted the only feasibility study which the government had received for such a plant. The proposal to build the new plant at Sagunto was expected to be approved by the end of 1971. The plant would be located next to AHV's existing factory, but it would be an entirely separate entity. The likely details of the plan were:

1. The plant would necessitate a total investment of $1.4 billion—the largest single industrial project ever undertaken in Spain.

2. The capitalization of the new company would be:

   25% equity, privately held

   35% official government credit in long-term loans (fifteen years at 5.5%)

   22% foreign currency loans

   18% bonds

3. The new plant would begin operations on a small scale in 1975 and be fully operative in 1980. This target date required that construction work begin during 1972.

The management of AHV desired very much to participate in the ownership and development of the new company to as great a degree as possible. Informed opinion suggested that AHV might be allowed to contribute between 30% and 50% of the equity of the new company.

Known Sources of Funds

To meet part of the anticipated demands for funds, Mr. Burgos counted on three known sources: Credit from Banco de Credito Industrial (BCI, a Spanish government agency in charge of industrial credit), U.S. Steel payment for part of the shares previously subscribed, and larger profits due to an increase in prices.

Between 1971 and 1972 BCI was to grant a total of $32,358,000 in the form of long-term loans to AHV. These funds would be received by AHV in three equal shares. The first part had been received in January 1971. The second part was scheduled to be received in September of the same year, and the final part would be received in 1972. These loans were made according to the Accion Concertadas Agreement. However, the 1972 loan was to be the final loan from BCI under the terms of this agreement.

Only 25% of the shares to which U.S. Steel had subscribed in 1964 had been fully paid. U.S. Steel had recently indicated it intended to pay for the remaining shares toward the end of 1971 or early 1972. This would provide an additional $13,385,000 cash inflow.

The expected increment in profits because of price increases was based on the authorization of the Spanish Ministry of Trade to raise the prices of iron and steel products by 6%, effective from July 1971, for all companies in the steel industry. It was expected to generate an additional $10 million of increased revenue during the second half of 1971 alone.

Other Potential Sources of Funds

Mr. Burgos realized that a gap existed between the forecast demand for funds and the available sources of funds. A financial package to bridge this gap had to be designed. Potential sources of funds included bond issues, commercial bank credits, and the recent proposal from Credito Latino to borrow Eurodollars. Mr. Burgos had decided not to consider an equity issue at the time. That was to be saved for the future, probably in connection with the financing of the new plant on the Mediterranean.

Local Funds. The aggressive expansion program nearing completion in 1971 had required an enormous injection of capital. The government's official credit agencies had supplied the bulk of these funds under the terms of the Accion Concertadas. Other major sources were foreign banks in the United States and Europe, which financed the importation of capital goods, and the company's traditional bankers who also were shareholders. Since Spanish bankers represented approximately 35% of the board members, creditors were not unhappy about the structure of the firm's capitalization. Such a situation in which banks had considerable influence in the affairs of industrial companies was not uncommon in Spain, and this close association permitted a relatively high debt to equity ratio. (See notes to Exhibit 3.) However, Mr. Burgos felt that it would be hard to obtain any more credit from these commercial banks for purposes other than current operations.

Only 10% of the book value of fixed assets and only a small proportion of inventory had been pledged against loans received by AHV. Management had followed a policy of granting chattel mortgages only when absolutely necessary, which had been infrequent because the state's guarantee usually acted as a superior security to the lender. Covenants and conditions attached to outstanding loans and bond issues were unlikely to restrict future borrowings; the requirements regarding working capital, dividend payments, and capitalization ratios gave ample leeway for management to operate as it wished. This also was the feeling of the bond underwriters with whom Mr. Burgos had talked. It appeared that an issue of $10-20 million, thirty-year, peseta bonds at an interest rate between 9% and 10% in 1971 could be successfully placed with institutional investors and private individuals in Spain.

Foreign Funds. AHV's experience in borrowing from foreign banks had been limited to financings related to the importation of capital goods and raw materials. For example, it had received a £6 million loan from a London bank in connection with the building of a new blast furnace at Bilbao, and a New York bank had granted a long-term loan to finance the import of coal from the United States. Mr. Burgos was therefore interested in exploring the services that Credito Latino could offer him.

Credito Latino was an international brokerage company which specialized in bringing borrowers in developing countries and lenders of Euro-dollars together. After sufficient inquiry, Credito Latino quoted a $10-$20 million loan at a floating rate of 1.5% over the six-month Euro-dollar interbank rate, plus a commission of 1% flat. The terms were a two-year grace period with equal semiannual repayments of capital thereafter through the seventh year from the closing date. No compensating balances would be required. Placement was to be on a best-efforts basis, and any contract between AHV and Credito Latino could be rescinded by either party without penalty after a period of three months.

The Final Decision

Before reaching a final decision regarding the best financing package, Mr. Burgos decided to obtain some more information. He asked his assistant to compile some economic data that would serve as a basis to forecast future developments in the market. These data are contained in Exhibits 5 through 9.

EXHIBIT 5. Six-Month Euro-Dollar Deposit Rates, 1963–1971[a] (at or near end of month)

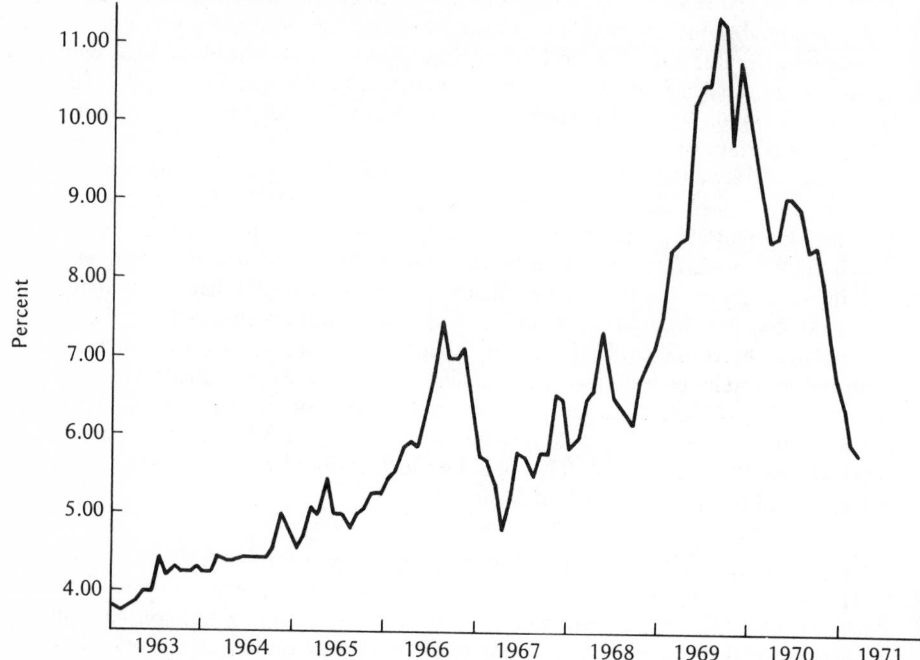

[a]Prime bank's bid rates in London.

SOURCE: Morgan Guaranty Trust Company, WORLD FINANCIAL MARKETS, New York, various issues.

EXHIBIT 6. Interest Rates in Spain
Commercial Banks Lending Rates, 1969–1971 (percent)

	Discount Paper		*Medium-Term (18–36 Months)*		*Long-Term (Over 3 Years)*			
					Commercial Banks		*Industrial Banks*	
1969	*Legal Maximum*	*Lowest*	*Legal Maximum*	*Lowest*	*Highest*	*Lowest*	*Highest*	*Lowest*
3° Q	6.50%	6.00%	7.50%	7.25%	9.50%	9.00%	9.50%	8.50%
1970								
1° Q	6.50	6.00	7.50	7.25	9.50	9.00	9.50	8.50
2° Q	7.50	7.00	8.50	8.25	10.50	10.00	10.50	9.75
3° Q	7.50	7.00	8.50	8.25	10.50	10.00	10.50	9.75
4° Q	7.50	7.00	8.50	8.25	10.50	10.00	10.75	9.75
1971								
1° Q	7.25	7.00	8.25	8.00	10.50	10.00	10.75	10.00

Bank of Spain Rediscount Rates

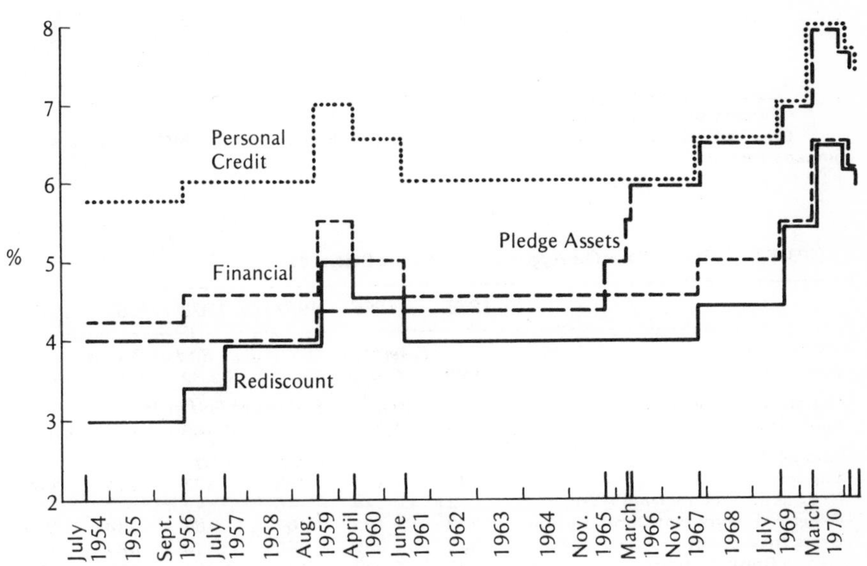

SOURCE: Banco de España, BOLETIN ESTADISTICO.

EXHIBIT 7. **Stock Market Price Index AHV and Spanish Market**

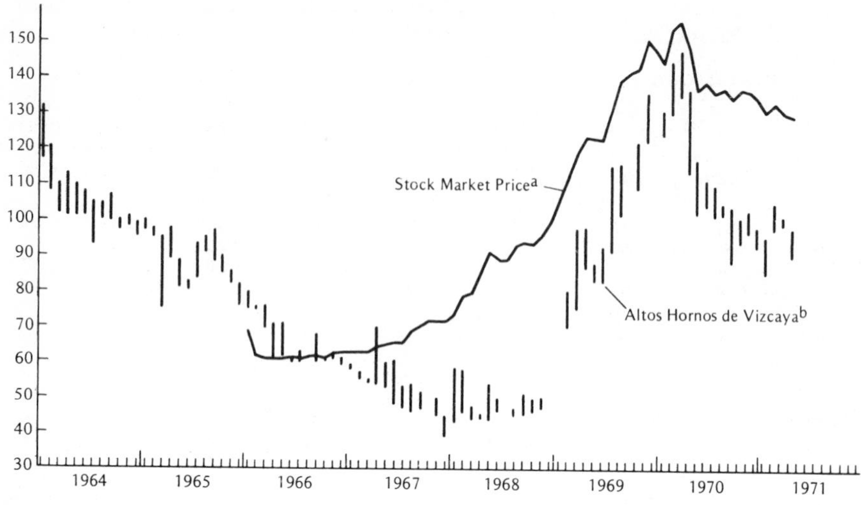

[a]Based on index of mutual funds securities.
[b]Percent of nominal value.
SOURCE: Stock Market—Banco de España, BOLETIN ESTADISTICO. AHV stock—company records.

EXHIBIT 8. **Spain: Selected Aggregate Economic Statistics**

	1965	*1966*	*1967*	*1968*	*1969*	*1970*
Exchange Rate			*Pesetas per U.S. dollar: End of Period*			
Selling Rate	59.99	60.00	69.70	69.82	70.06	69.72
International Liquidity			*Million U.S. dollars: End of Period*			
Bank of Spain	1,422	1,253	1,100	1,149	1,281	1,817
National Accounts			*Billion Pesetas*			
Exports	143	174	180	233	271	340
Net Factor Income from Abroad	-1	-4	-5	-7	-	-
General Government Consumption	112	133	167	187	214	250
Gross Investment	338	390	380	414	482	517
Private Consumption	887	1,013	1,140	1,251	1,379	1,530
Less: Imports	-192	-228	-230	-273	-324	-368
Gross National Expenditure = GNP	1,287	1,477	1,632	1,805	2,011	2,258
Gross Domestic Product	1,288	1,482	1,637	1,812	2,023	2,270
National Income	1,118	1,275	1,401	1,552	1,710	-
International Transactions			*1963 = 100*			
Volume of Exports	126.8	153.3	170.0	220.6	261.5	306.9
Volume of Imports	149.7	172.1	171.3	185.7	215.4	224.9
Export Prices	103.6	111.2	112.9	114.3	114.3	123.2
Import Prices	103.2	106.7	105.4	112.7	117.3	126.1
Wholesale Prices	113.4	116.3	116.9	119.6	122.6	124.6
Wages	136	158	182	194	213	250
Industrial Production	127	146	155	165	191	207

SOURCE: International Monetary Fund, FINANCIAL STATISTICS, July 1972.

EXHIBIT 9. **Spain: Balance of Payments[a] (millions of U.S. dollars)**

	1966	*1967*	*1968*	*1969*	*1970[p]*
A. Goods, Services, and Unrequited Transfers					
Exports f.o.b.	1,308	1,419	1,667	1,994	2,457
Imports f.o.b.	-3,300	-3,200	-3,241	-3,865	-4,337
Receipts for Services and Transfers					
Travel	1,292	1,210	1,212	1,311	1,681
Government Services	55	55	49	55	55
Other Private Services	265	293	430	546	749
Unrequited Transfers	424	457	464	562	674
Payments for Services and Transfers					
Travel	-90	-99	-102	-116	-138
Government Services	-38	-59	-60	-77	-90
Other Private Services	-475	-526	-644	-775	-956
Unrequited Transfers	-5	-6	-17	-30	-15
Total	-564	-456	-242	-395	80
Trade Balance	-1,992	-1,781	-1,574	-1,871	-1,880
Balance of Services	1,009	874	885	944	1,301
Private Unrequited Transfers	417	446	448	550	659
Government Unrequited Transfers	2	5	-1	-18	-
B. Miscellaneous Capital of Nonmonetary Sectors Private Capital, Excluding U.S.					
Government Loans					
Direct Investment Liabilities	134	186	152	200	222
Portfolio Investment Liabilities	58	56	41	10	-13
Loans Received	99	149	141	152	343
Commercial Credits Received	39	31	11	19	88
Commercial Credits Extended	-99	-20	-35	-29	-37
Other	43	40	69	93	90
Official Capital, Excluding Long-Term Loans from Abroad					
Loans Extended	-5	-1	2	3	2
Other	-7	14	-5	-9	-1
Total	262	455	376	439	694
C. U.S. Government Loans and Other Central Government Long-Term Borrowing Abroad (Net Repayment–) U.S. Government Loans					
Private Sector	27	60	57	37	3
Central Government	4	-5	-2	-5	-8
Other Long-Term Borrowing by Central Government					
IBRD	43	31	37	23	9
Treasury Issue Abroad	—	—	60	—	—
Other	3	-6	53	12	-24
Total	77	80	205	67	-20
D. Net Errors and Omissions	34	-217	-267	-342	60
E. Total (A through D)	-191	-138	72	-231	814
F. Allocation of SDRs	—	—	—	—	42
G. Total (E plus F)	-191	-138	72	-231	856

(continued)

EXHIBIT 9. continued

	1966	*1967*	*1968*	*1969*	*1970*[p]
H. Monetary Movements (Increase in Assets–)					
Commercial Banks	20	12	-18	-33	6
Payments Agreements	-23	-32	-15	4	-9
Monetary Gold	25	1	-1	1	286
SDRs	—	—	—	—	-43
Reserve Position in the Fund	-25	166	—	—	-45
Foreign Exchange Assets	196	-9	-38	-190	-689
Other Liabilities	-2	—	—	449	-362
Total	191	138	-72	231	-856

[a]Positive figures are credits; negative figures are debits.

[p]Preliminary.

SOURCE: International Monetary Fund, BALANCE OF PAYMENTS YEARBOOK, February 1972.

FNCB FINANCE, INC.[1]

In early January 1974 a sense of urgency gripped Benjamin Lagdameo, managing director of FNCB Finance, Inc. Only six months remained before the preferential trade treaty between the Philippines and the United States, called the Laurel-Langley Agreement, would end. This economic agreement enabled American citizens, individuals, and corporations to own properties and operate in the Philippines on the same basis as Filipino citizens.

In 1968 Citicorp, through its wholly owned subsidiary First National Overseas Investment Corporation (FNOIC), organized FNCB Finance, Inc., under a joint venture arrangement with five leading business families in the Philippines. FNOIC owned 75% of the new consumer finance company's common stock valued at ₱1,000,000,[2] while the five local partners shared equally the remaining 25%. Within the short span of five years, FNCB Finance grew phenomenally to become the largest and most diversified finance company in the country. However, upon the termination of the Laurel-Langley Agreement on July 4, 1974, FNCB Finance would fall under the ownership provisions of the country's Finance Company Act of 1969, which stipulated a maximum of 40% foreign participation in finance companies. Therefore, FNOIC would have to sell a 35% share of FNCB Finance common stock to Filipino citizens by July 4, 1974, to comply with the Finance Company Act.

The senior management of FNCB Finance had to secure the final approval of FNOIC before a divestment program could be put in motion. Since 1972 various divestment proposals had passed between Manila and New York. In May 1973 an official of Citicorp visited the country to discuss the entire divestment program with local management. However, three critical issues remained unresolved:

1. At what price should the shares to be divested by sold? FNOIC had manifested its concern for an optimum price. On the other hand, local management was wary of the capacity of the country's capital market to absorb the entire issue estimated to cost ₱20–30 million.

2. How could FNOIC retain management control after divestment?

3. How should the post-divestment ownership of the company be structured? Local management proposed that the existing local partners be given the priority to increase their participation to 40%. On the other hand, FNOIC wanted a broad public offering.

BACKGROUND

FNCB Finance, Inc.: A Five-Year Overview

In only five years FNCB Finance had become the largest finance company in the Philippines. Established in 1968, FNCB Finance penetrated the upper end

[1] A note on the Philippine economy and financial institutions follows this case.

[2] In 1968 the exchange rate between the Philippine peso and the U.S. dollar was ₱3.93 per U.S. dollar. In January 1974 the rate was ₱6.78.

EXHIBIT 1. FNCB Finance Inc.: Financial Highlights, 1969–1973 (thousands of pesos)

	1969	*1970*	*1971*	*1972*	*1973*
Total Assets	₱13,600	₱48,254	₱119,658	₱205,304	₱256,199
Earning Assets	13,312	43,988	116,959	194,049	248,775
Gross Income	979	5,677	18,009	34,812	44,049
Gross Expenses	595	1,651	3,858	6,950	11,500
Interest Charges	387	2,551	9,007	21,081	25,743
Net Income (Loss)	(2)	968	3,353	4,417	4,513
Paid-in Capital	1,000	1,000	1,000	2,000	4,000
Total Stockholders' Equity	987	1,955	5,309	9,726	14,503
Shares Outstanding	10,000	10,000	10,000	20,000	40,000
Earnings (Loss) per Share in Pesos	(.22)	96.83	335.33	220.85	112.83

of the consumer finance market with installment sales financing, appliance loans, and small business loans. In 1970 the company began diversifying its financial services by going into commercial lending, financing of receivables, inventory financing, and leasing.

Exhibit 1 shows the growth of FNCB Finance. Net profits increased 67% per annum to ₱4.5 million in 1973. The company's net worth leaped from the initial ₱1 million investment to ₱14.5 million because of retained earnings. Earning assets reached ₱248.8 million in 1973.

The company's impressive growth was noticed not only in financial circles but also in the entire business sector. It earned the reputation of being the country's most innovative and most aggressive finance company. This growth could be attributed to several factors: the FNCB name and logo which elicited investor and creditor confidence, a youthful and aggressive management team, a diversified package of financial services, and an extensive network of eighteen branches. Continuous rapid growth had been forecast to continue in the next five years despite uncertainties in the economic environment. Total assets had been projected to grow to ₱608.8 million by 1975.

Finance Industry Structure and Competition

The Securities and Exchange Commission of the Philippines listed more than 400 finance companies doing business in the country in 1973. The Association of Finance Companies of the Philippines estimated that more than 50% of these companies were small, "fly-by-night" outfits operating in the provinces.

The finance industry was considered by analysts and economists to be highly concentrated. In 1973 four dominant finance companies had a total of ₱466.6 million in earning assets, about 60% of the industry. It was estimated that FNCB Finance held 25.6% of the market, Filinvest Credit Corporation 18.2%, Industrial Finance Company 13.3%, and Commercial Credit Corporation 2.9%. Except for FNCB Finance and Filinvest Credit, the companies were controlled by family business conglomerates, which had substantial interests in banking, manufacturing, and insurance.[3]

The broad Finance Company Act definition had provided finance com-

[3]Chase Manhattan Bank had a minority interest in Filinvest Credit Corporation.

panies substantial elbow room on the lending side. Traditionally, these companies concentrated their lending activities in consumer finance. Industry sources estimated that consumer finance comprised more than 70% of the total loan portfolio. Consumer services included appliance loans (55%), car loans (15%), small business finance (10%), travel loans (7%), and others (13%). Consumer loans usually carried maturities of forty-eight months and were amortized monthly. FNCB Finance in 1971 altered industry practice by offering longer maturities of up to twenty-four to thirty-six months and lowering effective interest rates. Most of the consumer finance companies realized effective yields of up to 52% including service charges, while FNCB Finance charged effective yields of only 22%. Consumer finance had proven to be a risky product line. High delinquency rates had plagued the industry and write-offs eroded margins. Consumer loan delinquencies had been observed to be sensitive to the effects of natural calamities and to changes in economic aggregates such as inflation, unemployment, and wage rates.

To minimize risks and improve quality of earnings, the large companies had gradually diversified their earning assets from traditional consumer lending into commercial and business financing, leasing, and other bank lending activities. This broadening of earning assets had placed the leading finance companies in direct competition with commercial banks, which had traditionally dominated the country's financial system, and with investment banks, which were engaged in loan syndication and project financing. The finance companies enjoyed a competitive edge over commercial banks because of less government regulation and higher spreads or margins due to high legal interest rate ceilings. However, they were as severely limited as the investment banks on the sourcing side. As nonbank financial intermediaries, the finance companies and investment banks could not accept savings and time deposits. They were forced to compete aggressively in the highly volatile and interest-sensitive money market through the issuance of high-yield commercial paper to which commercial banks also had direct access. Approximately 80% of finance companies' fund sources were accounted for by money market activities. Long-term sources of financing were scarce. The country had a small equity market. Of the four leading finance companies, only Filinvest and Industrial Finance Corporation were traded even lightly on the local stock exchanges. However, because of the rapid expansion of earning assets, the finance companies were compelled to lengthen the maturities of their fund sources. Filinvest had readied a ₱10 million bond offering while FNCB Finance had contemplated a ₱10 million convertible debenture issue.

Competition was expected to accelerate in the immediate future as new entrants stampeded into the industry. The following factors supported this imminent development:

1. Barriers to entry were low. Any group could organize a business with only ₱500,000. A medium-sized company could be capitalized at only ₱1 million.

2. Industry profitability had been very attractive. In 1972 the leading finance companies had an average return on investment of 17.6%.

3. Government regulation had been relatively loose. Most of the new and

prospective entrants were commercial banks and other financial institutions on the lookout for diversification vehicles.

This environment sharpened competitive threats. Unless the total market were substantially expanded, the point of industry saturation could be reached within a short time. However, the proliferation of finance companies and the aggressive diversification of their earning assets would probably invite stricter and more rigid government regulation. Industry analysts expected tighter controls over liquidity, lending policies, sourcing of funds, and capital adequacy. These moves could sharply curtail the rapid industry growth.

Divestment Programs of American Corporations

The Securities Exchange Commission of the Philippines reported in a December 1972 survey that a total of 306 corporations owned or controlled by Americans were directly affected by the termination of the Laurel-Langley Agreement. The survey revealed that 122 of these companies possessed real estate properties while 33 others engaged in the exploitation of natural resources or in the operation of public utilities. It estimated that a total of ₱627 million had to be divested or completely disposed of in order to comply with the constitutional provision requiring a maximum of 40% foreign ownership. Recent estimates, however, placed the figure at a staggering ₱2 billion. Total American investments in the country were estimated to be ₱1 to ₱1.5 billion at cost.

To insure an orderly divestment and to prevent an outflow of American investments, the Philippines' SEC and the Board of Investments issued guidelines regarding the manner of divestment. These alternatives are briefly summarized below:

1. Corporations desiring to stay in the Philippines may dilute their capital participation to 40% by enlarging Filipino ownership in the total equity of the company.

2. Corporations may sell excess capital directly to the general public.

3. Corporations may gradually or swiftly pull out of the country by transferring total ownership to Filipino investors.

4. Firms may maintain their total investment in the country by reducing their equity in one corporation and investing in new industries where permitted by local regulations. Firms may therefore reinvest proceeds in pioneering or promoted industries.

5. Land-owning corporations wishing to maintain the existing capital structure may sell their real estate properties to any Filipino national and lease back the same for a maximum allowable period of twenty-five years, renewable for another twenty-five years.

In anticipation of the Laurel-Langley Treaty's expiration and to suit their particular strategies, some American-owned or -controlled companies had already sold their equity holdings. For example, in 1973 Exxon Philippines agreed to sell its entire investment to the government-organized and -controlled Philippine

Petroleum Corporation (PPC). PPC later merged with Filoil, a Filipino-owned oil refining and marketing company. Jerome Brothers, original American owners of 84% of Legaspi Oil Ltd., sold their equity position to a Filipino-Japanese joint venture, so that the country's second largest oil refiner was now owned 44% by the Ayala Corporation (the largest Filipino holding company), 40% by Mitsubishi Corporation, and 16% by the fifteen original Filipino shareholders. RCA Global Communications of New York transferred ₱20 million of its assets in the Philippines to its local subsidiary, Philippine Global Communications. A Filipino group later bought 60% of PhilCom's equity to complete the Filipinization of the company.

FNCB FINANCE DIVESTMENT STUDIES

FNCB Finance Divestment Study in 1972

In early 1972 Xavier Loinaz, FNCB Finance President, initiated moves to prepare the company for actual divestment. At that time, renewal of the Laurel-Langley Agreement was considered unlikely. A strong nationalistic fervor, fanned by student and labor unrest, was sweeping the country. The U.S. Embassy in Manila was a favorite target of violent student rallies and of the militant section of the media.

General Considerations. The extensive study undertaken by the Corporate Planning Group of First National City Bank observed that divestiture would bring mixed blessings to FNOIC. On the plus side, FNOIC counted the following factors:

1. An outright sale of existing equity might yield capital gains subject to a lower tax than regular income. Finding an optimum price was difficult because FNCB Finance shares were not traded in the stock market and the company was young. A very high price would maximize capital gains to FNOIC but would jeopardize saleability.

2. Aggregate investment would be reduced, thereby minimizing exposure risks in the country.

3. Divestment was an excellent opportunity to improve the public image of the finance company, for the ownership base would be broadened.

On the negative side, the following factors were important:

1. FNOIC's effective control over FNCB Finance's operations would be minimized after reduction of its equity participation to a minority position of only 40%. With its 75% holdings, FNOIC exercised absolute authority over all stockholder and Board decisions. Under Philippine corporation laws, a two-thirds stockholders' vote was necessary to amend the articles of incorporation, to declare stock dividends, to issue bonds or stocks, or to sell corporate assets.

2. FNOIC would lose a profitable outlet for funds.

Divestment Objectives. On the basis of the above considerations, FNCB Finance and FNOIC in New York agreed on the following three basic objectives for the divestment package:

1. The divestment strategy should maximize returns on the portion of FNOIC's initial investment to be divested, $90,000.[4]

2. FNOIC's management over corporate affairs and operations should be maintained even after divestment to a minority ownership position.

3. The divestment package should contain features that would enhance the public image of FNCB Finance as a responsive corporate citizen.

Modes of Divestment. The 75% equity position of FNOIC in FNCB Finance could be reduced to 40% through:

1. Direct sale of 35% of total stock; or

2. Sale of the unissued portion of authorized capital to allow dilution of FNOIC's holdings to 40%.

The approaches differed from one another in their impact on the capital structure and leverage of FNCB Finance. A direct sale from the FNOIC holdings would have no impact on capital structure and leverage; there would be a recomposition of ownership. The additional subscription would mean an inflow of cash, thereby increasing paid-in capital and lowering leverage.

The question about the appropriate mode of divestment revolved around the future need for fresh capital in order to meet capitalization and leverage standards. Previously, build-up of stockholders' equity had been achieved by constant retention of earnings. However, FNOIC would derive certain advantages by divesting directly since the funds released to FNOIC after the sale of stock could be earmarked for congeneric projects or repatriated abroad.

Ownership Distribution. Essential to the divestment objectives was the issue of ownership distribution after divestment. A widespread dispersal of ownership would strengthen the probability of FNOIC's retaining effective control with only 40% participation, while the extreme alternative of ownership with existing partners would promote the opposite effect. The business resources and designs of existing partners suggested the possibility of a determined takeover by a single powerful group or bloc of investors. With regard to enhancing the corporate image, divestment to the public would achieve a favorable response. The government had clearly declared its policy of democratizing ownership of corporations. The ownership composition could include a variety of alternatives such as:

1. Divestment soley to existing partners. Partners would increase participation from 25% to 60%.

[4]Thirty-five percent of the initial investment of ₱1,000,000, equal to $255,000 in 1968 at ₱3.93 per U.S. dollar.

2. Divestment solely to new local partners.
   a. New business partners
   b. FNCB Philippines staff
   c. FNCB retirement fund
   d. General public
3. A mixture of the above alternatives.

As an aid to arriving at a decision on the choice of partners, the following pro/con assessment was considered:

	Pro	*Con*
A. Present Partners	Avoid antagonizing present partners Probable business and market development	Loss of control
B. New Business Partners	Business and market development	Unfavorable impact on relationship with existing partners
C. Staff	Enhancement of control through dispersal and staff allegiance	Lack of funding for purchase; recourse to FNCB financing to purchase stock
D. Retirement Fund	Possible retention of effective control through moral suasion on trustees	No positive public relations impact
E. General Public	Highly favorable public relations impact	Long-run possibility of control Unavailability of funds in the market

Senior management was worried about the reaction of the local partners if FNOIC opted for a general public offering. Under the company's Incorporation Papers, the local partners had the right of first refusal regarding the sale of stock. However, it seemed that the partners could be persuaded to respect FNOIC's decision.

Taking the above considerations into account, three ownership composition alternatives had been advanced:

	A	*B*	*C*
FNOIC	40%	40%	40%
Present Five Partners	25	60	40
Total (FNOIC and Partners)	65	100	80
Available Shares for New Partners	35	0	20
Total	100%	100%	100%

Valuation and Pricing of FNCB Finance Stock. Two approaches were used in valuing the FNCB Finance stock. The first approach involved the capitalization of income by using the present value technique. The other method used the price/earnings multiplier method. The following major assumptions were used for both valuation approaches:

1. A time horizon of five years.

2. A 55% average annual growth rate for earnings.

3. A 100% stock dividend in 1972 and a stock split of 100 to 1 to bring the price of the stock within the reach of the general public, reducing par value from ₱100 to only ₱1.00 per share.

4. An annual dividend payout of 25% of earnings.

5. A discount rate of 30%.

6. A terminal value of five times terminal earnings.

Exhibit 2 shows the calculations of the stock price using the capitalization of income approach. Under this approach the expected cash flows associated with owning the stock were projected and its present value found using a discount rate of 30% The capitalization of income method produced a price of ₱28.60 per share. This price represented a 11.1 P/E multiple of 1972 earnings.

The price/earnings multiplier method produced a price of ₱12.85. It was assumed that a multiple of five times earnings was the most realistic multiple for a company such as FNCB Finance. The price of ₱12.85 in 1972, given the cash flows assumed above, implied a discount rate of 47.9%. In other words, given the forecast cash flows, if the investor required a rate of return as high as 47.9%, the maximum price at which the stock could be sold involved only a multiple of five times the projected 1972 earnings of ₱2.57 per share.

A comparison of the P/E multiples of selected financial institutions with stocks traded in the local exchanges is shown in Exhibit 3. However, comparison was hampered by the fact that there were wide fluctuations in P/E ratios from year to year and from company to company. The behavior of the multiples spanned only four to five years, too brief a history to provide meaningful statistical results. Notwithstanding these constraints, it was found that the P/E ratios ranged from a low of 2.5 to a high of 23. The average multiple of three of the five companies ranged from 7 to 8. From these P/E statistics it was inferred that a price of ₱12.85 per stock or a P/E ratio of 5 for FNCB Finance stock represented a moderate value. It was also felt that the higher price of ₱28.60, or a multiple of 11.1, would not be considered overvalued by the market.

To further buttress the valuation, a comparison of return on investment (ROI) for the five companies and expected ROI for FNCB Finance under each pricing alternative was made. For comparability, the definition of ROI for FNCB Finance was based on *projected* earnings per share for each of the following five years (Exhibit 4) over the suggested offer prices of ₱12.85 and ₱28.60. In the case of the other financial institutions, the ROI was expressed in terms of the historical average market price paid by investors in a given year and the earnings per share for that year. The tables on page 627 show the resulting ROIs.

At ₱12.85 per share, investors in FNCB Finance would realize an annual average ROI of 59.8%, surpassing the highly profitable Filinvest Credit Corp.

EXHIBIT 2. FNCB Finance, Inc.: Computation of Price Per Share Under Capitalization of Income Approach

Based on 2,000,000 Shares Outstanding, a 30% Capitalization Rate and Terminal Liquidation Price of 5 X 1976 Earnings

1. GIVEN

	1972	*1973*	*1974*	*1975*	*1976*
a. Earnings Per Share (EPS)	₱2.57	₱4.38	₱6.84	₱9.99	₱14.64
b. Cash Dividend Per Share (DPS)	₱0.64	₱1.09	₱1.71	₱2.50	₱ 3.66

2. ASSUMPTIONS
   a. Acquisition date: October 1,1972
   b. Dividends payable year end

3. COMPUTATION
   Determination of price per share based on the present values of dividend per share and terminal price per share.

   a. Present value of DPS as of date of acquisition:

   (1) PV of DPS at year end 1972

Year	*DPS*	*Discount Factor at 30%*	*PV*
1972	₱0.64	1.00000	₱0.64
1973	1.09	.76923	0.84
1974	1.71	.59172	1.01
1975	2.50	.45517	1.14
1976	3.66	.35013	1.28
			₱4.91

   (2) Present value of DPS as of date of acquisition (Oct. 1, 1972) (Derived by multiplying the PV of DPS at year end 1972 by the discount factor of 30% for one quarter)

   ₱4.91 X .93651 = ₱4.60

   b. Present value of terminal price per share (TPS) as of date of acquisition:
   (1) TPS (year end 1976): ₱14.64 X 5 = ₱73.20
   (2) PV of TPS as of year end 1972: ₱73.20 X .35013 = ₱25.63
   (3) PV of TPS as of date of acquisition (October 1972):
   ₱25.63 X .93651 = ₱24.00

   c. Total present value of DPS and TPS as of date of acquisition:

   ₱4.60 + ₱24.00 = ₱28.60

4. PRICE/EARNING RATIO
   Derived by dividing total PV of DPS and TPS by the 1972 earnings projection:

$$\frac{28.60}{2.57} = 11.1$$

with an ROI of 41.8% and the rest with less than 20%. At the higher price of ₱28.60 per share, the investors would achieve an ROI of only 26.8%. This would still be better than the four other financial institutions but less attractive than the record of Filinvest, the most aggressive competitor.

Given the results of the comparison of P/E multiples and the ROI analysis, the study concluded that market realities demanded the lower valuation of ₱12.85 per share. At this price, the entire issue would be very competitive and would still allow for impressive capital gains to FNOIC. The divested stock would bring in $957,000 after deducting the original investment of $90,000 and

EXHIBIT 3. Price/Earnings Ratios of Publicly Traded Stock of Financial Institutions

Company/Year	*Average Price*	*Earnings per Share*	*Price/Earnings Ratio*
Industrial Finance Corporation[a]			
1971	–	–	–
1970	₱18.50	₱1.06	17.5x
1969	16.25	2.54	6.4x
1968	16.25	2.54	6.4x
1967	16.875	3.84	4.4x
1966	19.00	3.54	5.4x
			7.6x (Ave.)
Filinvest Credit Corporation[a]			
1971	No sales as of May 31	–	–
1970	No sales	₱4.40	–
1969	₱12.50	4.40	2.8x
1968	11.75	7.79	1.5x
1967	11.50	3.97	2.9x
1966	12.00	4.15	2.9x
			2.5x (Ave.)
Private Development Corp. of the Phil. (PDCP)			
1971	N.A.	N.A.	–
1970	₱15.75	₱2.63	5.99
1969	14.00	2.38	5.88
1968	15.25	1.95	7.82
1967	14.25	1.74	8.19
1966	12.30	1.55	7.94
			7.16 (Ave.)
House of Investment (HI)			
1971	No sales as of June 30	–	–
1970	₱11.00	N.A.	–
1969	11.00	₱0.58	19.0x
1968	10.50	0.32	32.8x
1967	9.65	0.65	14.8x
1966	10.00	0.35	28.6x
			23.8x (Ave.)

[a]These firms are more closely akin to FNCBFI than PDCP and HI since they engage in some financing company activities directly or through subsidiaries. PDCP performs development and investment banking functions, while House of Investments is an investment and management company with some investment banking functions.

SOURCE: MANUAL OF PHILIPPINE SECURITIES: THE INVESTOR'S GUIDE, 1971 Edition.

taxes. On a discounted cash flow basis, the after-tax proceeds would yield an ROI of about 75%. (See Exhibit 5.)

The management of FNCB Finance considered the suggested offering price to be extremely conservative. They felt that the head office would surely turn down a P/E multiple of five times projected 1972 earnings. Even a P/E of 11.1 would be difficult to justify. One senior officer even felt that the stock could be sold at a P/E multiple higher than fifteen times, on the basis of the continued use of the FNCB name and logo after divestment, the phenomenal earnings record of the company, and the extensive branch network of the company.

EXHIBIT 4. FNCB Finance Inc. History (1970–71) and Forecast, (1972–1976)

	1970	*1971*	*1972*	*1973*	*1974*	*1975*	*1976*
				(thousands of pesos)			
Revenues	5,685	17,909	34,944	55,911	83,865	117,412	164,370
Expenses	4,185	12,752	26,640	41,754	61,719	85,081	116,960
Net Earnings (after tax)	960	3,355	5,138	8,752	13,685	19,975	29,289
Cash Dividend (25%)	—	839[a]	1,284	2,188	3,421	4,994	7,323
				(pesos)			
Earnings per Share	₱0.48	₱1.68	₱2.57	₱4.38	₱6.84	₱9.99	₱14.64
Dividends per Share	—	₱0.42[a]	₱0.64	₱1.09	₱1.71	₱2.50	₱ 3.66
Earnings Growth Rate	—	250%	53%	70%	56%	46%	47%
Book Value per Share			₱3.58	₱5.98	₱10.19	₱16.50	₱25.7

[a]Proposed dividend payout payable in 1972. 1970–71 share data adjusted proposed stock split and dividend.

ROI Expected from FNCB Investment by Potential Investors Based on Offer Price

Offer Price	*1972*	*1973*	*1974*	*1975*	*1976*	*Annual Average*
₱12.85	20.0%	34.1%	53.2%	77.7%	113.9%	59.8%
₱28.60	9.0%	15.3%	23.9%	34.9%	51.2%	26.8%

ROI of Similarly Traded Financial Institutions Based on Average Market Prices per Year

Company	*1966*	*1967*	*1968*	*1969*	*1970*	*Annual Average*
Industrial Finance Corp.	19%	23%	16%	23%	6%	17.4%
Filinvest Credit Corp.	35%	35%	66%	35%	38%	41.8%
Filipinas Mutual Fund	18%	10%	11%	13%	18%	13.0%
Private Dev. Corp. of the Phillipines	13%	12%	13%	17%	17%	14.4%
House of Investment	4%	7%	3%	5%	—	4.8%

SOURCE: MANUAL OF PHILIPPINE SECURITIES, THE INVESTOR'S GUIDE, 1971 edition.

Retention of Management Control. Another major concern of FNOIC was the retention of FNCB management after divestment. The following options aimed at maintaining management control were available:

1. *Voting Trust.* Philippine corporation laws allow the use of a voting trust for a maximum period of five years. Under a trust agreement, a Filipino trustee becomes a registered stockholder. A trustee can dispose of the shares under

EXHIBIT 5. FNCB Finance, Inc.: Return on Investment to FNOIC

Proceeds from Divestment

1. No. of shares to be divested	700,000 shares	
2. Estimated price per share	₱12.85	
3. Estimated proceeds of divestment (1 X 2)	₱8,995,000	$1,328,656[a]
4. Associated cost of investment	₱ 350,000	$ 89,744
5. Estimated income from capital gains (#3 – #4)	₱8,645,000	$1,238,912
6. U.S. tax (30% X #5)	₱2,593,500	$ 371,674[b]
7. Estimated net income from capital gains after U.S. tax	₱6,051,500	$ 867,238
8. Estimated after-tax divestment proceeds (#4 + #7)		$ 956,982

Return on Investment

1. Cost of investment	$90,000
2. Approximate date of investment	August 1, 1968
3. Assumed date of divestment	October 1, 1972
4. Estimated after-tax divestment proceeds	$957,000
5. Holding period	4 years and 2 months

Computation:
1. P.V. of outflow: $90 thousand
2. P.V. of inflow

Inflow		*Discount Factor at 75%*		*Present Value as of Jan. 1, 1969*		*Discount Factor at 75% (2 months)*		*Present Value as of Aug. 1968 (inflow)*
$957K	X	.10622	=	$102K	X	.88889	=	$90.7K

3. Approximate ROI: 75%

[a]Exchange rate assumed at ₱6.77/$1.00

[b]Computation of net U.S. tax liability (or excess tax credit):

U.S. tax (30% X #5 above)	₱2,593,500	$371,674
Tax credit (based on the 35% Phil. tax rate payable in connection with capital gains): .35 X #5 above	₱3,025,750	$433,619
Net U.S. tax liability (or excess tax credit)	(₱ 432,250)	($ 61,945)

trust only upon the specific instructions of the trustor. The trustee will always vote with the trustor. This device was constrained by the limited time period and by the stipulation that the stocks under trust could not revert to the trustor.

2. *Proxy.* Proxies could be obtained from investors but only for a short period. Creation of an irrevocable proxy was looked upon with disfavor by the local courts.

3. *Pooling Agreement.* Under this option, certain stockholders or a block of stockholders could pool their votes. Pooling agreements had been sustained by the local courts as legal and binding provided it could be demonstrated that

the agreement was not entered into for the purpose of committing fraud, jeopardizing creditors, or exploiting the corporation to the prejudice of the minority stockholders.

4. *Memorandum and Royalty Agreement.* Under this approach, the use of the FNCB name and logo could be exchanged for a royalty fee and for amendments in the Articles of Incorporation insuring the retention of FNCB management. These measures would be in effect until such time as FNOIC withdrew use of the FNCB name and logo. FNOIC, through the present FNCB Finance management, would have to convince the five existing partners to enter into a Memorandum and Royalty Agreement before divestment. Specific measures deemed desirable by FNCB could be included in the agreement. For instance, it could be legally stipulated that in exchange for the use of the name FNCB, the president of the company would be an FNOIC nominee.

Subsequent Events: 1972–1973

Third–Fourth Quarter 1972. During this period the management of FNCB Finance scrutinized the findings of the study. Unfortunately, the divestment program was overtaken by external events which depressed the company's overall performance in 1972. In mid-1972 floods devastated metropolitan Manila and the central provinces of Luzon, the largest island in the Philippines. Agricultural production slumped, prices of prime commodities soared, and the entire economy slowed. The misfortunes were compounded by continuous political unrest. Student demonstrations mounted while political violence continued unabated. President Ferdinand Marcos declared martial law throughout the country on September 21, 1972. Although there were no major political disturbances, general uncertainties loomed on both the political and economic horizons. The historic event induced a cautious wait-and-see attitude on the part of business and the public.

Effective immediately, an increase in the gross receipts tax from 1% to 5% was ordered and made retroactive. All of these unforeseen events combined to depress the profitability of FNCB Finance in 1972. Actual profits in 1972 of ₱4,417,000 missed the budget projection of ₱5,138,000 by 16%. However, profits still posted a 31.7% gain over 1971. The effects of the natural calamities were expected to last for more than a year unless dramatic changes in the economy occurred. Saddled with these difficulties, FNCB Finance's management focused attention on improving profitability. In the meantime, the divestment issue was relegated to the background.

January-December 1973. On March 16, 1973, President Marcos issued a decree which directly affected the current divestment issue. In a move primarily aimed at attracting more foreign investment, President Marcos liberalized direct foreign investment and allowed full and retroactive repatriation of capital, profits, and capital gains. Under the revised rules, the proceeds from the divestment could be repatriated to Citicorp in nine equal annual installments after liquidation of the investment. The improved foreign investment climate made attractive the reinvestment of the proceeds in new Citicorp ventures in the Philippines.

THE 1973 DIVESTMENT PACKAGE

In March 1973 the president of FNCB Finance under whose initiative the divestment study was made was promoted and reassigned to the Citibank Head Office in Manila. Benjamin Lagdameo, the managing director, assumed all the president's responsibilities, including the drafting of a complete divestment package. A major question anticipated by Mr. Lagdameo was the pricing of the shares. He was fully aware of two conflicting forces—the high pricing expectations of Citicorp and the doubtful ability of the capital market to absorb such a potentially large offering. He was deeply concerned with the possibility of being unable to meet the July 4, 1974, deadline. After talking with local investment houses and meeting with consultants, Mr. Lagdameo initially pegged the price at twelve times forecast 1973 earnings of ₱5.5 million. His staff devised the following tentative divestment pachage for presentation to the Citicorp officers scheduled to visit the Philippines in July 1973.

Mode of Divestment

Outright sale of 7,000 common shares held by FNOIC (35% of 20,000 shares before the stock split).

Ownership Distribution

Post divestment ownership of the company will be composed of:

FNOIC	40%
Five Present Partners	40%
General Public	15%
FNCB Philippines Staff	5%

Under this ownership scheme, dependence on the domestic capital market would be minimized. The main burden would be placed on the shoulders of the five Filipino partners.

Pricing. The shares would be sold at twelve times revised projected earnings of ₱5.5 million. Each share would be priced at ₱3,300. The entire issue would amount to ₱23.1 million.

Retention of Management. To maintain FNCB management after divestment, a Memorandum Agreement would be entered into with the five Filipino partners. For the use of the FNCB logo and name, the corporation would be obligated to pay a royalty fee of 10% on net income each year. Amendments to the incorporation papers would be introduced. These amendments would give FNCB veto powers over certain corporate acts.

Marketing. The shares to be divested would be sold on a negotiated private placement basis. Top-level negotiation with the five partners would be undertaken. If the five partners were unable to increase their participation to 8% each, a different financing scheme would be discussed. For the public offering, the entire branch network would be mobilized. High net worth individuals who had invested heavily in the company's commercial paper would be approached. This marketing strategy would strengthen the presence of FNCB Finance in each area because local investors would own a part of the company. A list of prospective investors had been prepared by each branch. For the staff offering, a stock option plan with financing would be devised. If it were to be a broad public offering, an underwriting alternative would appear desirable even at a 5% cost.

CITICORP'S REACTION

One afternoon in July 1973 Ms. Gail Johnson, AVP of FNCB New York, met with Mr. Lagdameo and his staff. A presentation was made summarizing the main features of the divestment program and outlining the advantages of each. Immediately after the presentation, Ms. Johnson threw sharp questions about the pricing and the retention of FNCB management. She suggested that the pricing might be on the low side considering the fact that Citibank shares were being traded on the New York Stock Exchange at a P/E of 20. She said that the phenomenal profit record of the company in its short history and the support provided by FNCB justified a higher valuation. She also mentioned the company's extensive branch network, slated to increase, as another plus factor. She felt that a P/E multiple of 15 was a minimum. Mr. Lagdameo cautioned her about the difficulties of unloading the shares at a multiple higher than 12. He stressed the lack of equity sources and the doubtful capacity of the local market to absorb the entire issue within a short time period. At fifteen times projected 1973 earnings of ₱5.5 million, a staggering ₱28.9 million would have to be raised. Mr. Lagdameo felt that a multiple of 12 should be the maximum offering price. He contended that blue chip corporations with extensive track records were selling in ranges of five to ten times earnings. The shares could be sold at a P/E multiple of 12 only on a negotiated basis. If the shares were underwritten, they could be sold only at a lower price. Ms. Johnson considered Mr. Lagdemeo's points and assured him that these would be taken into account in shaping a head office decision. She also suggested that a public offering of the entire 35% might be advisable. This would insure maximum dispersal. Mr. Lagdameo cited the fact that the original incorporation papers gave the five present Filipino partners the right of first refusal, and a public offering might encounter the opposition of the Filipino partners.

After the meeting with Ms. Johnson, Mr. Lagdameo reassessed the entire situation. He reevaluated the pricing issue, taking into account the points raised by Ms. Johnson. He feared that the proposal might encounter rough seas in New York because of the pricing. To solidify the initial pricing proposal and to provide a more thorough pricing analysis, Mr. Lagdameo requested another Citicorp subsidiary in the Philippines, Citicorp Investment Co., to independently value the shares to be divested.

CIC undertook a comparative study of the valuation of financial institutions openly traded in the local exchanges. The report stated that the shares might not be successfully sold at a multiple of 12. It took note of the fact that FNCB Finance lacked a meaningful track record to convince prospective investors of its future earnings capacity. Company projections of future earnings would be casually considered or even dismissed by sophisticated investors. According to CIC, the P/E multiples of selected financial institutions had clustered around 4-6 in 1972. Based on these observations, CIC recommended a much lower price of six times projected 1973 earnings. It concluded that the shares might be sold at eight times earnings on a negotiated basis.

Appendix: Note on the Philippines

The Philippines, which had a GNP of approximately $10 billion in 1973, is primarily an agricultural country; 60% of its GNP is from this sector. Industrialization has proceeded at a reasonably fast pace. Between 1967 and 1973 the composite index of industrial production grew by 60%. Export accounts depend heavily on the world performance of wood, sugar, copper, coconut products, and hemp. With the rapid increase in world prices for these products in the recent past, the country has been able to replenish its international reserves. Like the rest of the world, the country has been plagued with an increasing rate of inflation.

ECONOMIC PROSPECTS

The bright spots in the country's economy in 1973 may be obscured in the future by the problems of inflation and the energy crisis. GNP growth is expected to slow and to stabilize at 6-8%. The deceleration may be attributed to the following:

1. Weakening of the external sector which has provided the impetus to economic growth in 1973. Recession among the developed economies of the United States, Japan, and Europe, the country's major export customers, will depress export earnings. The biggest exports, except sugar and copper, face downturns in the world market, especially coconut and wood products. Imports of oil, machinery, and chemicals are projected to rise. Economists forecast a deficit of $500 million in the trade account. To finance the deficit, the government is expected to increase Euro-dollar borrowings.

2. Intensification of inflation. Philippine inflation, which is of the cost-push variety, will not abate. Price hikes averaging 18% a year or more are forecast. The biggest headache will be the oil import bill. Even if the value of crude oil imports were maintained at its 1972 level, the import bill would still rise to $450–500 million.

The economy can fall back on the foreign exchange reserves accumulated in 1973 to surmount expected problems in the external sector. The economy will be buoyed by the following:

1. Accelerated agricultural production and recovery from lethargic growth in 1973 because of government efforts in rural development and the channeling of more funds into the agricultural sector.

2. Economic and financial reforms aimed at hastening development. Centralized economic planning will be emphasized. Foreign investments will be encouraged. Financial reforms aimed at developing long-term finance and improving the financial system will be put into effect.

SAVINGS AND CAPITAL FORMATION

The key to a deeper understanding of the economy is a grasp of the pattern of savings and capital formation. Savings, which forms the primary source of domestic capital, is that portion of current income not consumed. For the household, savings is income deposited in financial institutions, hoarded, or invested in tangible assets such as houses, cars, real estate, and so on. For the corporation, it is retained earnings. For the government, it is that part of income spent on public works and other social overhead. Various studies have identified the following characteristics of domestic savings:

1. Gross domestic savings has averaged 16% of GNP and net savings (derived by deducting a capital consumption allowance from gross earnings) 10% of national income.

2. Growth of savings has been relatively high:

1946–49	15.6%
1950–54	12.8%
1955–59	12.5%
1960–64	17.8%
1965–69	20.5%

3. The rate of savings is expected to decelerate sharply because of inflation and perceived weakness of the Philippine peso. In 1973 consumer prices are estimated to have risen by 33%, and savings contracted. Another problem has been the historical weakness of the peso which went through sharp devaluations in 1962 (by almost 100%) and in 1970 (by almost 67%).

4. Household savings have been channeled to financial claims (60%) such as deposits, stocks, bonds, insurance claims, etc., and to tangible assets (40%).

5. The pattern of household savings has depended on income distribution and family expenditures. Given the sharp income inequality, a very small percentage of households can save. The economic elite have excess income to enable them to channel savings away from tangible to financial assets. As the masses increase their income, investments in tangible assets should expand. With the government's goal of narrowing income inequality, it is expected that there would be an increase in holdings of tangible instead of financial assets.

6. As a result of the pioneering efforts of enterprising Filipino individuals, the number of financial institutions has increased and has contributed to the greater mobilization of domestic savings. However, data on lending

practices of financial institutions show that savings are channeled into short-term credit and into consumption and real estate loans.

The country's inability to generate sufficient capital and its reliance on foreign investments can be traced to the misfortunes of poverty. Despite the gains made in the economy by 1973, a large majority of the population remains poor. Statistics from the Family Income and Expenditures Survey of the Bureau of Census show:

a. 86% of total households are dissaving or spending more than their income by as much as ₱800 per annum.

b. 7% manage to break even or barely save. This category contributes approximately 1% of total household savings.

c. 4% save around ₱500–₱1,000 per annum. About 97% of all families account for only 23% of total household savings.

d. 3% save an average of ₱5,000 per annum. This elite group of 3% of all families accounts for 77% of total household savings.

FINANCIAL INSTITUTIONS

Despite the condition of underdevelopment, the country has developed a number of financial institutions with a degree of sophistication. Around the Central Bank, which directly supervises most of the financial institutions in the country, revolve most of the financial institutions known in developed capital markets. Among these institutions the commercial banks dominate the financial markets, with only limited room left to the traditional depository and contractual nonbank institutions.

Commercial Banks

The country's commercial banking system has three subsets—the government-owned commercial banks, the private domestic commercial banks, and the local branches of four foreign banks. The government-controlled commercial banks are the Philippine National Bank, which is the largest in terms of total resources (₱3 billion), and the Philippine Veterans Banks, which provide financial services to the country's veterans. The private domestic commercial banks number 35 and have 786 branches. They comprise the largest subset, accounting for approximately 50-60% of total resources. The four foreign banks are the First National City Bank of New York (the largest private commercial bank), the Bank of America, the Chartered Bank, and the Hong Kong-Shanghai Bank. These four banks have historically provided the impetus for the development of innovative financial services and have exerted a stabilizing factor, especially during periods of threatened financial crisis.

Lending activities are almost entirely directed to the private sector (98%). The following industries are the major recipients: trade (49%), manufacturing (23%), banks and other financial institutions (13%), real estate and consumption (3.8%). The primary emphasis on short-term financing of trade and commerce proceeds from the commercial import-export focus of economic activity. Bank reserves and capital are inadequate to allow commercial banks to move into medium- and long-term financing. Only the government-owned commercial banks are able to provide medium- and long-term finance, but it has been limited to agriculture and real estate. The private commercial banks engage in long-term finance on a case-by-case basis, but only in consortia. To strengthen the banks and to enable them to move into longer-term financing, the government began reforming the commercial banking system in 1973. It forced the consolidation of small- and medium-sized banks and the expansion of the capital bases of larger banks. Minimum paid-in capital was raised from ₱10 million to ₱100 million. Equity participation up to 40% by foreign banks was encouraged. The reforms led to mergers, usually between a domestic and a foreign bank. With the strengthening of the capital base, it is hoped that the banks will be able to absorb long-term risks.

The Central Bank closely regulates all facets of commercial banking. Periodic examination and auditing of banks are conducted to promote efficiency and to check on compliance with regulations. The Central Bank also imposes maximum allowabie interest rates in most of the commercial banks' transactions. The major exception to this regulation is money market rates. Because of the country's weak currency, a tight rein over the banks' foreign exchange transactions is imposed. Commercial banks are not allowed to engage in investment banking.

A historical look at the consolidated sources and uses of funds of the commercial banking system demonstrates the pattern of credit, investment allocation, and resource generation. (See Exhibit 1.) Historically, the major funds use has been in loans and investments, averaging 60–70% of total resources.

EXHIBIT 1. Commercial Banks: Sources and Uses of Funds (millions of pesos)

	1955	*1960*	*1965*	*1970*	*1974*
Sources of Funds					
Deposits	966.0	1,732.0	4,002.1	7,658.7	14,663
Demand	513.2	744.9	1,545.7	2,458.9	5,565
Savings	285.3	714.7	1,402.5	3,757.2	} 7,567
Time	167.5	242.4	1,053.9	1,469.6	
Marginal Deposits					1,531
Capital Accounts	158.0	283.9	828.3	1,470.7	2,688
Due to Banks	121.5	30.0	110.8	511.5	695
Unclassified Liabilities	167.4	290.9	1,789.8	4,398.2	6,673
Foreign Liabilities					4,822
Uses of Funds					
Cash	25.0	44.3	112.0	294.0	1,556
Checks and Other Cash Items	8.7	28.5	94.6	351.4	1,035
Claims:					
Loans and Discount	217.5	939.5	2.655.8	6,422.2	} 17,583
Investments	226.9	131.9	615.1	1,762.3	
Due from Banks	226.2	159.9	368.5	508.6	} 1,800
Due from Central Bank	136.5	150.5	132.0	841.3	
Unclassified Assets	572.1	882.2	2,753.0	3,886.3	3,023
Foreign Assets					4,544
Total Balance Sheet	1,412.9	2,336.8	6,731.0	14,066.1	29,541

SOURCE: Central Bank, STATISTICAL BULLETIN.

Loans have been the larger of the two assets, but investments in bonds, stocks, and marketable securities have been expanding steadily from 11% of total resources in 1960 to approximately 18-22% in recent years, indicating the growth of both capital and money markets. Foreign assets comprise another sizable portion of funds use. On the sources side, deposit liabilities dominate commercial bank resources, ranging from 50-75% over the period 1955-74. Within this particular source, there have been shifts in relative importance among savings and time deposits and demand deposits. Savings and time deposits have been growing faster than demand deposits, at 20% compared to 13%. Demand deposits comprise 12-18% of total resources, while savings and time deposits oscillate between 18% and 25%. Unclassified liabilities, which largely represent commercial paper borrowings in the money market, have generated 15-20% of resources. In recent years this source has increased in relative importance such that it generated 20-30% of resources from 1967 to 1974. Foreign borrowings make up another major source of funds, averaging 5-15%. Capital accounts account for 8-15% of total commercial bank resources.

Nonbank Financial Institutions

All other financial institutions tend to specialize in lending to specific sectors of the economy. Depending on the government's attitude toward their contribution to economic growth, some of these institutions are either directly owned by the government or subsidized in some manner.

FINANCIAL MARKETS

Financial institutions provide the necessary intermediation between suppliers and demanders of finance in two financial markets—the capital market for long-term equity and the money market for short-term debt instruments. The capital market has not achieved a high degree of sophistication.

Capital Market

The country's capital market has been both narrow in terms of types of long-term securities offered and shallow in terms of participants. Few corporate stocks and government securities have been issued. Corporate bond issues have been extremely rare. Participants have been limited to well-to-do individuals, the government, and insurance companies. Pension funds and mutual funds have not been very successful and insurance companies have limited equity markets. As such, a viable institutional market has failed to develop. The failure of the country's capital market to progress can be traced to the following factors:

1. The general condition of economic underdevelopment. The low level of capital investment has not spurred demand for capital.

2. The limited pool of savings and savers. Participants in the financial system have been limited to the few middle- and upper-class savers.

3. The low degree of investor sophistication in terms of analysis.

4. The short-term orientation of the financial institutions' investment priorities.

At its present undeveloped stage, the country's capital market consists of both the primary market for the issues of stocks and the secondary market for the buying and selling of securities. Participants in the primary market are corporations, individuals, financial institutions, and the government. In the secondary market the major actors are the stock exchanges, investment banks, and dealers and brokers.

The securities market consists of the buying and selling of corporate and government securities listed on the four stock exchanges operating in the country. A small over-the-counter market for companies not listed on the exchanges but properly approved by the Securities Exchange Commission also exists. The entire securities industry is closely regulated by the Securities and Exchange Commission, a government agency created in 1936.

In December 1973 a total of 160 companies were listed on the Manila Stock Exchange and 177 on the Makati Stock Exchange. Multiple listing is allowed. Both stock exchanges follow different modes of classification. The Manila Stock Exchange classifies the companies according to Big Board and Small Board. Companies listed on the Big Board are regular dividend-paying companies and generally have higher-priced shares. A total of 88 companies were listed on the Big Board. Companies listed on the Small Board are non-dividend-paying and highly speculative stocks, mostly mining and oil exploration companies. A total of 72 companies were listed on the Small Board. The Makati Stock Exchange categorized the listed companies according to mining (18), mining exploration (52), commercial and industrial (79), and oil exploration (28). Most of the issues in the categories other than commercial and industrial are highly speculative.

The securities industry enjoyed a banner year in 1973. In terms of volume of transactions, it was the strongest bull market in the history of the local capital market. The Manila and Makati Stock Exchanges witnessed volume surging to a total of ₱5,925.1 million, a phenomenal increase of 874% over 1972 and 29% over 1969, another bull year. Over-the-counter transactions increased slightly, by 17.1% to ₱19.3 million. A total of 678.56 million over-the-counter shares were traded. Volume on the Manila Stock Exchange hit ₱3,642.9 million and on the Makati Stock Exchange ₱2,282.2 million. In a single month, August 1973, volume was ₱1,132.55 million on both exchanges. Most of the transactions were in the highly speculative mining and oil sectors. On the Manila Stock Exchange transactions in mining and oil amounted to 94% of total volume, or ₱3,423.22 million. Transactions in the commercial and industrial sector accounted for only 6% or ₱219.75 million. The historic 1973 bull market was largely a result of the improving business climate and the rising prices of metals which accounted for 18% of total exports in the world market. Various financial and monetary measures implemented by the government created a favorable business climate for the infusion of foreign investment capital.

Money Market

The money market is a recent development in the country's financial system. However, it has assumed great significance in mobilizing savings and short-term investments. Major participants in the money market are individual savers, corporations whose savings or liquid surpluses are tapped by bank and nonbank financial institutions, and corporations in need of funds for short-term investments. Savings are funneled into the financial system via the buying and selling of commercial paper, government securities, and other short-term notes. In its evolution, the money market has developed four submarkets:

1. The government securities market for Treasury bills and Central Bank certificates of indebtedness.

2. The interbank call money market. This submarket aids banks in need of temporary funds to bolster reserves according to Central Bank requirements.

3. The market for banker's acceptances and time certificates of deposit.

4. The intercompany market where corporations' commercial paper is issued, bought, and sold.

As an entirely new development, the money market has been insulated from government regulation, particularly from the rigid interest rate system. Interest rates have violently fluctuated within each submarket. In 1973 the interbank rate moved within the range of 1-14%, compared to the 3-30% range in 1972, reflecting the higher level of liquidity in the banking sector. Prime commercial paper rates in the intercompany submarket ranged over 2.5%-18% vs. 5.5%-29% in 1972. The higher level of interest rates prevailing in the money market resulted in disintermediation from savings and time deposits as investors sought higher returns. The increasing popularity of the money market, the resulting disintermediation, and the potential for abuse have caused concern among monetary authorities. The Central Bank is expected to move in to tighten its supervision over money market activities of the financial institutions. An impending move is to raise minimum investments in the money market from ₱1,000 to ₱50,000. This will minimize disintermediation and induce small investors to invest in other financial assets.

PROSPECTS AND NEW DIRECTIONS

The various changes made in the country's aggregate financial system constitute a prelude to more radical reforms. New directions will be charted in the following areas:

1. Higher yields on financial instruments to provide an incentive to savings and investments in financial assets.

2. Creation of a long-term debt market.

3. Creation of a new equity issues market.
4. Reallocation of savings.

These moves will be aimed at making financial intermediation more efficient, encouraging savings, and strengthening financial markets.

More Attractive Yields

To make financial instruments more attractive to savers, the government is expected to loosen the rigid interest rate structure by lifting controls on various rate ceilings. One possibility being explored in financial circles is the installation of a floating interest rate similar to the Brazilian model. For instance, the interest rate on a savings deposit at 6% would be adjusted to minimize inflationary disincentive. If the inflation rate is 15%, interest on the minimum balance of the savings deposit is adjusted to 15% and interest on the average balance is kept at 6%. This will assure the depositor a fair income not fully eroded by inflation. However, the borrower would have to bear higher interest costs. Measures for minimizing this negative impact on borrowers are also being contemplated. Parallel to making financial instruments more attractive is reducing the attractiveness of alternative investments in real assets like real estate and luxury housing. Heavy taxes on real estate are a bright possibility.

Creation of a Long-Term Debt Market

The lack of medium- and long-term finance has been a problem for the financial system and for the economy's ability to generate needed capital. To rectify this situation, the government is expected to hasten the creation of a long-term debt market. It may further encourage the formation of investment banks and induce then to concentrate their activities in the underwriting of equity and bond issues. It will surely resort to taxation which will provide preferential treatment to medium- and long-term lending. A withholding tax on a graduated scale may be imposed on interest income, e.g., 15% on six-month bills and only 5% on two-year or more bills and bonds. The government may also spur the creation of funds which can be set aside for investment in corporate securities.

Creation of a New Equity Issues Market

The stock market has failed to be a significant conduit for long-term finance to corporations. Because ownership of corporations has been concentrated in the hands of a few wealthy individuals, corporations face a thin capital base and is expected to establish foundations for a strong capital market. Measures being contemplated are: (1) tax incentives designed to broaden participation in the stock market; (2) regulations to induce corporations to open their equity to the public, and (3) regulations to force investment houses to concentrate in underwriting of new equity and bond issues.

Reallocation of Savings

The country's financial system has been faulted for its tendency to allocate financing to short-term trade credit, government, real estate, and consumption. This has made the financial system vulnerable to the exigencies of government deficit spending and inflation. For instance, as prices skyrocketed because of inflation, the increased need for working capital had to be satisfied by bank credit. Thus, the capital requirements of the manufacturing and industrial sectors were left on the limb. To correct the imbalance, the government may undertake the following:

1. Allow financial institutions to expand in other forms of finance on a minority basis. This will diversify the allocation of credit.
2. Establish and strengthen a housing finance system to respond to the needs of consumers for housing and real estate. This will free the commercial banks from such financing.
3. Provide tax incentives to long-term industrial finance.

APPENDIX 1

International Taxation

One of the most complex aspects of international business is the area of international taxation. Understanding the rules surrounding domestic treatment of foreign income is the first difficulty. That obligation is compounded by the need for a thorough understanding of tax policies in the other nations which are potential bases for operations. The written code and the practical effect of the rules force most firms to rely extensively on local legal and tax representatives to explain the alternatives for business organization, dividend policy, capital structure, and so on. Several references are included in this appendix for the reader who desires more background information on the taxing policies in many nations. The excellent bibliography of international tax sources by Elisabeth Owens includes a detailed breakdown of publications concerning taxes in many specific nations.[1]

[1] Elisabeth A. Owens, *Bibliography on Taxation of Foreign Operations and Foreigners* (Cambridge, Mass.: International Tax Program, Harvard Law School, 1968), under revision.

THE PHILOSOPHY OF TAXATION

Nations have a variety of reasons for enacting any particular tax. Sometimes taxation is for social reasons: to punish particular behavior, to encourage other actions, or to redistribute income. Sometimes taxation is enforceability: A customs duty with an honest customs service and one port makes that tax more operational than some income taxes. Sometimes taxation is related to an international pattern, and reciprocity or comparable incentive policies dictate a particular code.

Many European nations have used a value added tax (VAT) as a major source of revenue. Tax analysts consider this a national sales tax as opposed to an income tax. The tax is applied to the value of a product at each point in manufacture and is based on the selling price of the good. Each firm can credit against the tax the amount of VAT passed onto it by other suppliers and manufacturers. The advantage of the tax is that it encourages honesty. It is based on revenues, not profits; and since deductions from the applied tax must be supported, each manager in the chain is encouraged to seek accurate figures from the suppliers. VAT can be adjusted or forgiven to stimulate or to discourage export sales, thus responding to balance of payments or domestic inflation problems. The problem with VAT is that there is a possibility of misallocation of resources, since VAT is a sales tax instead of an income tax. However, most nations that adopted a VAT have used it to replace an existing sales (turnover) tax. Some critics argue that the immediate imposition of such a tax causes an increase in inflation, but this charge can be blunted where governments pursue effective fiscal and monetary policies. VAT also is criticized for being a regressive tax, borne with regard to consumption rather than income. Most nations would like to rely on an income tax for individuals and corporations since it can be shown with minimal assumptions that an income tax on profits will reduce total output less than a sales tax or gross turnover tax will.

One major issue is *equity*. Most taxing authorities believe that people who have comparable incomes should pay the same tax and people who have different incomes should pay different taxes. When applied to personal income, this philosophy usually results in a variety of deductions from income for various minimum expenditures that are considered appropriate. There often is an allowance for extraordinary expenses that may occur, such as large medical bills. In the international scene this policy means that a corporation doing business abroad should pay taxes somewhere, regardless of its multinational status. The firm should be taxed on all income regardless of where earned, but there should be offsets for income taxes which different jurisdictions may impose. The basic concern, however, is that taxes should be paid on income as earned, and the taxation system should be equitable, however difficult that term is to define.

Equity is a difficult issue when comparing tax rates on personal income in various countries. First, incomes have to be adjusted for *comparable purchasing power,* and the bundle of goods for a standard of living is related to the starting point. An Englishman who requires Jacob's water biscuits daily will find the cost of living substantially higher in Italy than a comparable Italian would face. Second, the tax rates have to be compared both *internally* and *externally.* British executives are quick to note high British taxes. For example, investment income can be taxed at 98% (with an asset tax which in some cases runs the total tax over 100%). The marginal tax on a $21,000 family income is 60% vs. 25% in the United States. On the other hand, an internal U.K. standard would have an argument for a progressive income tax by noting that less than one in twenty British taxpayers has an income above $8,600 per year. Furthermore, the British executive is far more able than a U.S. counterpart to have "perks" paid for by his/her firm, such as automobiles.[2]

A second issue in taxation is the *social or economic goals* that are encouraged or discouraged by the tax policy. Much of the concern over the U.S. tax policy relates to the loss or creation of jobs for U.S. workers. Various studies exist on U.S. exports and investment abroad and their effect on the balance of payments, the first level of jobs, and the ultimate level of jobs according to various assumptions of what the U.S. government would do in the absence of such jobs. Worldwide, one would expect that free trade would result in greater total output, but the total level of employment and the allocation of that employment *among* nations and among skill levels within nations are at the center of the controversy. No firm statement can be made, for the research tools necessary to understand this subject are not sufficiently refined and the date are not always available. A brief exchange of two proponents of different views is contained in the references to this appendix as part of the U.S. Congressional hearings on taxation of foreign income.

NATIONAL CORPORATE TAXATION POLICIES

Whatever the issues of philosophy, when the corporation faces the corporate tax scheme in a particular nation, there are special factors to be considered.

First, *taxes may be absolutely low* on corporation profits. The lands noted for especially hospitable taxes include Switzerland, Liechtenstein, Luxembourg, Panama, the Netherlands Antilles (Curaçāo), the Bahamas, and Bermuda. Withholding taxes on intercorporate dividends are typically nonexistent in these nations, unlike some major industrial lands where high corporate tax rates and dividend withholding rates restrict the ability to move intercorporate funds about. Exhibit A.1 summarizes some of these effective tax rates.

Second, the *definition of taxable income* may be highly divergent among various nations. For example, constructive receipt is important. One nation may deem profits to be taxable as received on a cash basis whereas another

[2]Most countries of Western Europe have permitted revisions of various business accounts since World War II for tax purposes to adjust for inflation. Most of these adjustments have involved a single index applied to depreciable assets, although some countries included other accounts such as land and inventory. Countries such as Austria, France, and Italy provided annual adjustments if inflation exceeded a certain level; most other countries had a single adjustment to these accounts. Often smaller businesses did not take advantage of these optional adjustments, for typically a one-time tax was imposed on the step-up in basis, which ranged from ½% to 10%. The Scandinavian countries, Canada, the United Kingdom, and the United States have not permitted such adjustments, but instead have relied on changes in their codes involving accelerated depreciation, special investment credits, and the like to offset inflation. See George E. Lent, "Adjusting Taxable Profits for Inflation: The Foreign Experience," in Henry J. Aaron, *Inflation and the Income Tax* (Washington, D.C.: The Brookings Institution, 1976), pp. 195–213, for more discussion of this adjustment for inflation within nations.

EXHIBIT A.1. Foreign Taxes on Subsidiaries of U.S. Corporations

Country	*Statutory Corporate Income Tax Rate*	*Withholding Tax on Dividends to U.S. Parent*	*Maximum Foreign Net Tax on Earnings Remitted to the United States*	*Withholding Tax on Interest to U.S. Parent*	*Withholding Tax on Patent and Royalty Payments*
EUROPE					
Belgium	48%	15%	55.8%	15%	0
Denmark	37%	5%[a]	40.2%	0%	0
France	50%	5%[a]	52.5%	10%	5%
Germany	46–63%[b]	15%[c]	54.1%	0%	0%
Greece	44%	38%	65.3%	43.4%	0%
Ireland	45%	35%	64.3%	35%	0%
Italy	36%[d]	5%[a]	39.2%	15%	0%
Netherlands	48%	5%[a]	50.6%	0%	0%
Norway	23–51%[e]	5%[a]	26.9%	15%	15%
Spain	36%	16.5%	46.6%	24%	15.4%
Sweden	56%[f]	5%[a]	58.2%	0%	0%
Switzerland	~10%[g]	15%[h]	23.5%	5%	0%
United Kingdom	52%		~56.2%	0%	0%
THE AMERICAS					
Argentina	33%	17.5%	44.7%	11.25%	18%
Brazil	30%	25%	47.5%	25%	25%
Canada	40%[i]	15%	49.0%	15%	15%
Colombia	40%	20%	52.0%	0%	47.2%
Mexico	42%[j][k]	20%	53.6%	42%[k]	42%[k]
Venezuela		15%	57.5%		
OTHERS					
Australia	46%	15%	54.1%	0%	20%
Japan	30–40%[e]	10%[a]	37.0%	10%	10%
South Africa	43%	15%	51.6%	10%	12.9%

SOURCE: Based on FOREIGN AND U.S. CORPORATE INCOME AND WITHHOLDING TAX RATES, Ernst and Ernst, New York, 1978, and J. Peter Gaskins, "Taxation of Foreign Source Income." FINANCIAL ANALYSTS JOURNAL, Sept.-Oct. 1973, p. 57.

Many of these figures are based on tax treaties between the U.S. and the country listed. In some cases, the rates may not apply to a specific corporation.

[a] The withholding rates for these countries are all 15% except when a firm is owned almost completely by the U.S. parent, e.g., 90% or more in most cases. Some cases require a lower percentage of ownership, such as the Netherlands (25%), Norway (50%) and Sweden (50%).

[b]The effective German corporate tax rate on distributed profits (e.g. dividends) is about 46 percent and the effective corporate tax rate on undistributed profits is about 63 percent. These taxes are made up of a deductible municipal income tax averaging 15 percent, and federal taxes of 36 percent on distributed profits and 56 percent on undistributed profits.

[c]The rate increases to 25% if the recipient owns at least 10% of the equity and reinvests more than 7½% of the dividends received.

[d]Includes net effect of deductible local income taxes of about 14.7% gross.

[e]First figure is tax on distributed income; second figure is tax on undistributed income. "Maximum foreign net tax" column calculations assume all profits are distributed.

[f]Includes net effect of local income taxes averaging 26% which are deductible from income taxable at the 40% national rate.

[g]The federal income tax rate varies from 3.63% to 9.8% depending on the ratio of profits to net worth. In addition to the federal tax, each canton imposes its own income tax. The cantonal rates vary from 5% to 40%.

[h]The U.S.-U.K. Income Tax Treaty has been renegotiated. The treaty entitles a U.S. shareholder to a refund from the U.K. Inland Revenue of a portion of the advance corporation tax payable by the U.K. corporation when paying a dividend, less a withholding tax on the sum of the dividend and the refund.

Example:

	U.S. Corporation owning 10% or more of U.K. Corporation
Dividend paid	$65.000
Refund of advance corporation tax	17.500
	82.500
Less: Withholding tax @5%	4.125
Total received	$78.375

The proposed new treaty, which has been ratified by the British Parliament will be effective from various dates, some predating ratification.

[i]Manufacturing profits. On other corporate profits, tax is 46%. Province taxes which vary from 0% to 7% are not included.

[j]The Mexican corporate tax begins at 5% and reaches 42% on all income over $66,000.

[k]The Venezuelan corporate tax rate on businesses not involved in the exploitation of minerals or hydrocarbons is 15% of income up to $23,000 progressing to 50% of income over $6,512,000.

nation would treat the same profits as taxable as earned on an accrual basis. One nation may provide greater latitude on the creation of reserves, permitting an offset of taxable revenues by these allocations for future contingencies. Some countries may give full credit for taxes on the income paid in other countries or have no tax on intercorporate dividends or earnings. Especially rapid depreciation or depletion arrangements also affect the definition of taxable income.

Third, *tax treaties* with other nations may influence the total taxation bill of the parent corporation. The United States has tax treaties with more than thirty nations, primarily with members of the European Economic Community and other industrialized nations. As a result, special allowance for avoiding withholding on dividends and interest paid by firms to nationals of the involved countries, special tax reductions on intercorporate dividends, and the like contribute to a simplification of the regulations which will affect any firm. The effects of some of these treaties are suggested in Exhibit A.1, for the normal withholding on dividends from corporations in most of those nations would be 30-40%.

The ability to use low-tax countries solely as tax havens is limited. Many industrialized countries such as the United States are increasingly cautious about the definition of income and where it is held. Often, income is taxed regardless of remission, as emphasized in the 1962 U.S. tax reform measures. In addition, some of these countries, especially smaller developing nations, resent the label of a tax haven while at the same time desiring the economic contributions of major corporate investment. These lands are turning to industrialization, to the development of tourism, or to other tangible assets as an alternative to the tax haven option. Although pleased to provide help to corporations desiring to avoid the export controls imposed by their home countries, these nations believe their appeal simply as a tax-reducing location is not desirable. Other countries revel in their tax status; the Cayman Islands even has an official Tax Haven Committee to boost its image of low taxes.

The complexities of a particular tax code are too involved for any person but the specialist. However, as an aid to understanding the possible patterns in taxation for foreign income, the remainder of this appendix will outline some of the major issues in U.S. taxation of foreign source income. It is based in part on Michael J. McIntyre's *United States Taxation of Foreign Income with Special Emphasis on Private Investments in Developing Countries.*[3] Some of the evolution of the U.S. tax code is contained in the Sola Chemical case discussed earlier in this text.

U.S. TAXATION OF INTERNATIONAL INCOME OF CORPORATIONS—BACKGROUND

The U.S. taxing authorities focus upon the *status* of the taxpayer (resident or citizen vs. all others) and the *source* of the income. Citizens and residents generally are taxed on worldwide income, but with a credit for income taxes paid to other jurisdictions. Nonresidents are generally taxed only on

[3]Cambridge, Mass.: International Law Program, Harvard Law School, 1975.

their U.S. income. There are special rules to limit tax avoidance. A corporation's status is determined by incorporation and not by nationality or residence of shareholders. Corporations incorporated in the United States are U.S. corporations; all other are foreign corporations, even though all the shares may be owned by a U.S. corporation or citizens.

If *less than 50%* of the gross income of a *foreign* corporation is from conduct of a trade or business in the United States, then all its dividend and interest payments are considered foreign source income to the recipient, and special calculations may apply as noted below. Dividends paid by a *U.S. corporation* are considered foreign source income to the recipient only if *80% or more* of that corporation's gross income is from foreign sources. Special rulings apply for mineral companies and other firms in particular industries.

TAX POLICIES—AN OVERVIEW

The basic guideline within the tax system is that the United States claims jurisdiction over *all income* of its citizens and residents *wherever earned.* There is a credit for the income taxes paid to other nations, ranging up to the level of taxes that would have been paid had that income been earned in the United States. Alternatively, these foreign taxes may be deducted from taxable income. Furthermore, the foreign corporation often has deferral of taxes on its income from foreign sources until the income is remitted as dividends. On the other hand, whereas a U.S. firm can exclude from its taxable income 100% of dividends from a U.S. company in which it owns 80% or more of the stock, and 85% of the dividends otherwise, there is no exclusion of dividend income received by a U.S. corporation from a foreign corporation. There is no Investment Tax Credit or Asset Depreciation Ranging (ADR) treatment accorded a foreign corporation when its income is computed for tax credits applicable to the owning U.S. parent corporation. As noted later, it is very difficult to determine income in the international context. While about one-fifth of all U.S. corporate profits is earned abroad ($22 billion) and the U.S. taxes paid on foreign profits are about 5% ($1.1 billion), both the timing of the profits, their definition, and the tax rates applicable to them are highly debatable. None of this foreign definition seemed particularly important when foreign earnings were a small part of the U.S. firm's total earnings, but now the issue is vital given the basic guideline of full U.S. jurisdiction over all income. The variations in taxation arise from issues such as *how* the income is earned, *where* it is earned, and how the earning business is *structured.*

SECTION 162

Since 1958 this section of the U.S. Internal Revenue Code has denied tax deductions for payments made to foreign government officials or employees in the form of bribes. The source and amount of any illegal income must be declared and the tax must be paid. The U.S. Code has similar provisions for domestic bribes. Other nations follow different patterns; foreign bribes are deductible as business expenses under British Inland Revenue regulations.

Under Sections 884 and 888 as revised in 1976, a firm participating in an international boycott in order to do business in another foreign country loses the foreign tax credit, the Domestic International Sales Corporation (DISC) tax benefits, and a deferral of tax on earned income on any boycott income. Income resulting from illegal payments is treated as a new class of Subpart F income (see below) to shareholders of controlled foreign corporations. Such income is considered to be immediately distributed and taxable, whether or not the corporation makes such a distribution.

SECTION 482

A part of the U.S. Internal Revenue Code that has continuing impact on the decisions of individuals and firms is only one sentence in length. However, Section 482 permits the Treasury to allocate income and expenses among firms that are owned or controlled by the same interests if such an allocation is necessary to prohibit an evasion of taxes or to reflect income clearly. Tax credits and allowances also may be apportioned among firms which are not organized or incorporated in the United States. The key in application is the value realized in an arm's-length transaction (i.e., a fair price between an informed and willing buyer and seller). This value is difficult for courts to determine. Various safe harbors are available, and the purpose of the enforcement is only to affect U.S. tax liabilities; hence, according to enforcement officials, it is not designed as a general harassment of multinationals. Once the IRS makes an allocation under Section 482, however, the burden of proof is on the taxpayer to show that both the allocation method and the result of the allocation are arbitrary. The IRS provides detailed rules on how to allocate income among related parties in the most common situations.

SECTION 861

Allocation of expenses among subsidiaries is always a problem, especially when there is a clear joint product and when taxes are involved. For example, in 1974 the Internal Revenue Service made a well-publicized attack on the allocation of corporatewide research and development (R&D) under Section 861. Even though the outlays were made in the United States, the IRS argued that many of the benefits accrued to foreign operations. Hence, it wished to have more of the cost of research and development allocated to foreign operations. The effect of such an allocation is to reduce foreign income (and taxes that were usually credited against the U.S. tax liability) while increasing U.S. taxable income.

Revisions in the Code now mean that firms that have large amounts of interest, research and development, and general administrative costs will find themselves eligible for fewer foreign tax credits. Usually, firms have tried to allocate as much of these expenses to the high tax environment as possible, and typically this has meant charging the United States (parent) corporation with most of these expenses. The foreign subsidiaries were charged only with the marginal costs for their operations. In 1977 IRS rulings elaborated on how they would expect pro ration to take place. A brief explanation of these rulings and an exercise are included with the questions at the end of this appendix.

SECTION 882

A foreign corporation carrying on business in the United States is taxed at the U.S. rate on business profits. This provision of the Code is designed to prevent the creation of foreign subsidiaries by U.S. corporations to carry on various business activities in this country. It is also consistent with the policy of taxing the receipt of income from all activities carried on in this country.

TAX CREDITS (SECTIONS 901, 902, AND SO ON)

Although there is the possibility of treating foreign taxes as a deduction from income, most corporations will elect to take the foreign income taxes as a direct credit against their U.S. tax liability. Only income taxes or in lieu income taxes are eligible for credit. The indirect credit rules generally apply only to corporations, and for the credit to be applicable, the U.S. corporate parent (P) must have 10% or more of the stock of the foreign corporation (S1). The credit is applicable only in the year in which the dividends are received by P.

There is also a pyramid effect, since P can credit foreign income taxes paid by a subsidiary (S2) owned by S1 and by another subsidiary (S3) owned by S2. This three-tier rule relates to receipt of dividends by P. Each participant (P, S1, and S2) must own at least 10% of the stock in the next firm. Furthermore, P must have at least 5% direct or indirect ownership of the corporation that paid the tax for it to be creditable. Thus, P, owning 50% of S1 which owned 25% of S2 which in turn owned 15% of S3, would be able to take credit for taxes paid by S1 (50% beneficial ownership) and S2 ($0.5 \times 0.25 = 12\frac{1}{2}\%$ beneficial ownership) but not for S3 ($0.5 \times 0.25 \times 0.15 =$ less than 5%) even though each firm in the chain owned at least 10% of the next lower firm.

The basic procedure is to *gross up* the dividends received in the United States to taxable income prior to the payment of a portion of the foreign income and dividend withholding taxes. The ratio of the dividends declared by the foreign subsidiary to foreign profit after tax is a multiplier applied to the income taxes paid in the foreign land. To this product is added any withholding taxes on dividends imposed by the foreign land, and the sum of these two items is the maximum total tax credit for that year. Thus, dividends received are increased by some portion of foreign income and dividend withholding taxes, and the U.S. tax is computed as if that figure were entirely U.S. corporate operating income. Against the tax liability calculated is then credited some of the foreign tax payments, reducing the payment to the Internal Revenue Service. See the calculations for Subsidiaries A and B in the exercises following this appendix.

There is generally an *overall* limitation that lumps all foreign source income together. The ratio of that income to total taxable income (foreign and domestic) times the applicable U.S. tax rate provides the maximum credit. This calculation is done to assure that the total tax credits do not exceed what would have been paid in the United States had the entire income been from domestic sources. This calculation is beneficial to firms for which high tax payments in some countries would yield larger credits than could be used. Credits from these countries may then be combined with those from other lands where the tax rates might be lower to give the total credit. For example, assume that the domestic tax rate is 50% and that P has local taxable income of $100 in A and $100 in B. Local taxes are $60 in A and $30 in B and the balance is remitted to P as dividends with no withholding. Then the maximum credit against U.S. taxes would be 50% of $200, or $100, and all $90 of the tax payments could be credited against the U.S. tax liability. This is the "grossing up" process, for the U.S. income is increased to the level before the foreign taxes, and then the U.S. tax calculation is based on that higher level. If the calculations were on a *per country* basis, there would be a full credit for the 30% liability paid in B, but only $50 from the A tax payments would be creditable since the U.S. taxes on that income would have totaled only $50.[4]

Note that the limitation on credit is based on the U.S. tax rate applied to the foreign source income as defined by the U.S. Tax Code. Thus, the foreign tax rate may be less than the U.S. rate, but an allowance for deductions that the foreign government did not permit (hence lowering U.S. calculated taxable income) can mean that not all the foreign taxes are creditable even though they were applied at a nominally lower rate. For example, a $30 foreign tax on $100 of foreign income seems fully creditable if the balance was remitted as a dividend. If the additional deductions of expenses reduce the income to only $50, then a 50% U.S. tax rate means a maximum credit of only $25. Furthermore, investment in the stock of the parent or a loan to the parent by a controlled foreign corporation is also now included as a dividend payment for tax purposes in order to prevent tax avoidance through remission of profits by this investment or loan. There is a two-year carry back and a five-year carry forward for credits in the event of excess credits in any year.

LIMITATIONS ON DEFERRALS

Foreign operations of U.S. corporations are taxable as the income is earned. As noted, a foreign corporation that is completely owned by a U.S. parent may defer U.S. taxes on its foreign source income (as defined above) until remission of dividends to the parent. Because of abuses, the 1962 tax reform program limited deferral in a number of cases largely related to so-called Subpart F income (Sections 951-964). Essentially, a tax is payable on undistributed base company income (defined below) of controlled foreign corporations. This income is treated as a constructive dividend even though the foreign corporation has not remitted the funds to the shareholders. The taxes are imposed on the shareholders of controlled foreign corporations. The definition of control is largely based on the number of shareholders, nationality, and the

[4]Formerly, firms could calculate tax liabilities on a per country basis, which was useful when losses in one country would use up possible tax credits from other countries on an overall calculation.

percentage of ownership. The tax applies only to certain companies (more than 50% of ownership is by U.S. persons where "person" can be a corporation) and only to certain shareholders (more than 10% interest) where applicable. In making the determination of whether more than 50% of the voting control is by U.S. persons, only shareholders with 10% or more of the stock are counted in this figure. Thus, even though more than 50% of the stock might be owned by U.S. citizens/residents, if a sufficient number of these persons have less than 10%, the firm would not be a U.S.-controlled foreign corporation. As an extreme example, eleven U.S. shareholders owning 9% of the stock each would not have a controlled foreign corporation.

Base company income generally can be described as income from operations carried on by a foreign subsidiary for tax minimization purposes. Base company income includes foreign personal holding company income[5] (which mainly deals with income from various investments), base company sales income, and base company services income. Foreign base company sales income includes income from the sale of goods produced and sold outside the country of incorporation and the net income from property which is either bought from or sold to a related person (i.e., a parent or another subsidiary) or sold on behalf of a related person. See McIntyre for a detailed definition of income in these categories.[6] Subsidiary D in the exercises shows the tax treatment for this corporation.

For many purposes, some of the advantages of deferral can still be realized in the area of sales income through use of a Domestic International Sales Corporation (DISC) which is described below. Another interesting exclusion from this foreign base company income is income from sales or services performed in the country of incorporation. Thus, if the firm were to incorporate a subsidiary in every nation in which it does business, then the foreign base company income rules would not apply to those sales. In addition, if less than 10% of the gross income of a foreign-controlled corporation were base company income, then none of the income would be so considered. (If more than 90% of the gross income were base company income, then all the income would be so treated. Between these two points the income would be prorated and base company income would be taxable whether or not distributed.) If the foreign-controlled corporation were to pay taxes of at least 90% of the U.S. level on the income or make a substantial dividend distribution to its shareholders, or a minimum combination of foreign taxes and dividend distribution existed, there would be no special tax. Financial income (dividends, interest, and capital gains) from less developed countries and shipping income from operations of vessels or aircraft in foreign trade are excluded if earnings are reinvested in shipping

[5] Foreign personal holding company income restrictions are designed to prevent individuals from using the tax deferral provisions to avoid taxes on dividends, interest, and capital gains from various transactions. A *controlled* foreign personal holding company is a firm in which more than 50% of the ownership is by five or fewer U.S. citizens or permanent residents and in which 60% or more of the gross income in the first year and 50% or more in subsequent years is foreign personal holding company income. This income is automatically base company income to a controlled foreign corporation even though it is *not* a foreign personal holding company.

[6] *United States Taxation of Foreign Income with Special Emphasis on Private Investments in Developing Countries.*

activities. Several of these provisions are direct consequences of the 1975 Tax Reduction Act.[7]

Most firms operate with branches in the earlier years of foreign operations when losses are expected since the losses of branches can be consolidated with the U.S. parent. However, the 1976 Tax Reform Act permits the Internal Revenue Service to recover taxes on foreign losses which offset U.S. profits if the foreign operations later produce profits on which taxes are otherwise deferred.

DOMESTIC INTERNATIONAL SALES CORPORATIONS (SECTIONS 991-994)

These special U.S. corporations were permitted by 1971 legislation designed to encourage export sales by U.S. firms. Essentially, the firms can defer tax on 50% of their *gain* in export earnings. The shareholders of a DISC are treated as if they have received the remaining 50% of the income (whether or not the earnings were distributed) and are taxable as individuals or corporations on that income. The DISC itself is not taxable. The shareholders are entitled to the foreign tax credit for foreign taxes on a DISC. In addition to certain restrictions on the asset base, the main requirement for DISC treatment under the Code is that 95% of the gross income must be from export activities.

A major benefit of the DISC legislation is the encoded "safe harbors" which specify how profits can be determined for a DISC. A "safe harbor" means there is no IRS challenge if the figures are accurate. Under Section 482, as noted, the amount of income could be a source of dispute since the major activity of a DISC is likely to be reselling of purchased manufactured goods from its parent to export customers. However, the legislation creating DISCs permitted the taxable income to be the greater of (a) 4% of total export receipts plus 10% of the DISC's promotion expenses, (b) 50% of the combined income of both the selling firm (the parent in most cases) and the DISC plus 10% of the DISC's promotion expenses, or (c) the actual taxable income under normal Section 482 accounting standards.

Under the 1976 Tax Reform Act, DISC tax benefits are now available for the gain in average annual export profits over a 1972–75 base period. The export profit base level is 67% of the annual average export profit in the 1972–75 period. Tax on half the profit over that base level is deferred. The base on which the moving average is calculated will move forward one year each year after 1980. New exporters or exporters with foreign profits of less than $100,000 will not have any DISC restriction because their base will be considered zero

[7]Special provisions of the 1975 Tax Reduction Act were designed to restrict the use of foreign tax credits (instead of deductions) for royalties paid to foreign governments by international oil companies. Specifically, the Act denies credits if two conditions occur: the price on which the taxes are based is not the market price (i.e., if artificial "posted" prices are used for tax levies) and the oil company has no "economic interest" in the oil (i.e., if it does not own the oil). However, there is substantial question about the meaning of "economic interest" and the impact of this provision is unclear. Various other provisions also tightened the foreign credit benefits for the international oil companies.

until 1980. Exported military products are eligible for half the normal DISC benefit.[8]

POSSESSIONS CORPORATIONS (SECTION 936)

There are special provisions made for corporations carrying on business in U.S. possessions such as the Canal Zone, Guam, American Samoa, and others. Puerto Rico is also eligible for special treatment under its commonwealth status. To be treated as a possessions corporation, 50% of the gross income must be from the active conduct of a trade or business in a possession and 80% of the gross income must be from sources within a possession. The possessions corporation is then given the option to receive a special tax credit equal to the U.S. tax on its income from active conduct of a business in the possession. Any income tax paid to a foreign or possession government by a corporation electing this treatment is neither deductible nor creditable against U.S. taxes. However, dividends from a possessions corporation are eligible for the 85% or 100% corporate dividend exclusion by a receiving corporation.

For example, under the 1976 Tax Reform Act, U.S. corporations were allowed to repatriate profits from their Puerto Rican subsidiaries at any time free of additional U.S. taxes. Previously, U.S. firms had either reinvested their subsidiaries' profits in Puerto Rico, or at least outside the United States, since the only way profits earned in the Commonwealth could be remitted tax free to the U.S. corporate parent was by ending the Puerto Rican corporation. However, the new benefit was somewhat offset by the Puerto Rican government's imposition of a new 10% tax on profits sent from the country.

CAPITAL GAINS

Gains from the sale of stock in a foreign-controlled corporation are normally taxed at ordinary income tax rates. Gains from an LDC (less developed country) corporation are sometimes eligible for the favorable 30% corporate capital gains tax rate if the ownership has been for at least ten years, at least on the portion of the gain in value attributed to operations prior to 1976.[9]

[8]Prior to 1980 a U.S. corporation whose entire operations were carried on outside the United States but in the Western Hemisphere with 90% of its gross income from active conduct of a trade or business and with 95% of its gross income from outside the United States could be taxed under a special arrangement as a Western Hemisphere Trading Corporation (WHTC), providing an effective tax rate of as low as 34%.

[9]To encourage investment and sales to so-called less developed countries (LDCs), special tax provisions have been permitted for firms doing business in those lands. Essentially, LDCs include all countries with the exception of most of Western Europe, Australia, Canada, Japan, New Zealand, South Africa, the Soviet bloc, and China. An LDC corporation is a firm involved in active trade or business which has 80% of its gross income from LDC sources and 80% of its assets involved in its trade or business in an LDC. The firm need not be incorporated in an LDC, but it cannot be incorporated in the United States.

EXCHANGE GAINS AND LOSSES

The tax treatment of foreign exchange gains and losses is a grey area. Most of the rules involve case law, and the rulings have been contradictory. Part of the question involves *when* a transaction takes place. When there are parent loans to a subsidiary, does the loss from repayment in an upvalued currency occur when the subsidiary repays the parent, when the parent repays the loan to the bank, pro rata with repayment, or when? The other major part of the question involves whether the loss is a *capital* loss or an ordinary loss. One critic has noted that the choices open to the corporation managers on how to translate their foreign operations really permit them to play a "heads-I-win, tails-you-lose" game with the Treasury. Furthermore, as Musgrave notes, the managers may use different methods for various subsidiaries operating abroad.[10]

Branch operations are consolidated into the U.S. parent's return under two methods. Under a *net worth* method, the balance sheet is valued with the current accounts at year-end (current) rates and the remainder of the accounts at the historic rates. Thus, a loss on a short-term loan that must be repaid one month after the close of the tax year in an appreciated currency will be realized in this period even though there is no payment until the next year. Under the *net income* method, funds remitted during the year to the parent are valued at the rate in effect at the time of remission; unremitted income is valued at the year-end rate. Exchange gains and losses are shown only as included in net income, which usually occurs when repayment is made. Usually, a *two-transaction* approach is required. Thus, if goods are purchased and paid for after an upvaluation of the remitting currency, there is a loss on the payment of the account payable, and there is a separate adjustment later if the inventory proves to be worth more than its cost basis in the parent currency.

WITHHOLDING TAXES

If there is a desire to avoid withholding on payments of dividends and interest to investors and debtholders in other lands, the use of various foreign finance subsidiaries becomes important. For example, Rosenberg and Singer show how to create such a subsidiary depending on where the funds are used and where the investors/lenders are.[11] Under U.S. regulations, an "80-20" corporation will be free from a requirement to collect withholding on interest payments. This firm can meet that requirement as long as *less* than 20% of its gross income is from the United States, from which the 80-20 name is derived. Dividends or interest payments to this finance subsidiary from overseas subsidiaries would be subject to various withholding provisions in those countries depending on their tax treaties (or lack thereof) with the United States and with each other. These payments are excluded from U.S. taxes assuming consolidated returns are filed

[10] Peggy B. Musgrave, "Exchange Rate Aspects in Taxation of Foreign Income," *National Tax Journal,* Volume 28, 1975, pp. 404–413.

[11] Herbert C. Rosenberg and Stuart R. Singer, "Selecting an International Finance Subsidiary: A Review of Available Methods," *Journal of Taxation,* May 1969, pp. 296–298.

and the income of the foreign subsidiaries is included with the U.S. parent; other treatments possible include the 85% and 100% exclusions in some cases.

On the other hand, if the firm wanted to borrow funds from its finance subsidiary for operations in this country, then technically there should be withholding of taxes on interest payments since 50% or more of the financial subsidiary income would be related to the conduct of a trade or business in the United States (i.e., all the interest receipts would be from the operating parent). Withholding can be avoided here by creating the financial subsidiary in the Netherlands Antilles, for example, where the treaty provisions with the United States specifically omit withholding on interest payments by that finance subsidiary to foreign shareholders even if all the subsidiary's income is from a U.S. source. When there is a split need for funds, the authors advocate 80–20 corporations in both the United States and the Virgin Islands, with the former used for lending to the foreign subsidiaries and the latter for lending to the U.S. operations.

Much of the need for the 80–20 corporation has disappeared with two changes in the U.S. tax law. First, withholding on dividends and interest payments to non-U.S. residents has been eliminated. Second, the Securities and Exchange Commission now permits direct offerings of Euro-bonds by American corporations as long as there is a specific statement that they are not to be sold in the United States. Previously, managers often used 80–20 corporations to avoid filing a prospectus with the United States SEC in connection with major offerings of securities to non-U.S. residents.

TAX CHANGES—A PROBLEM OF ANALYSIS

Many tax bills have been introduced to change the foreign tax credit system, permitting only deductions for foreign taxes rather than a credit. Other bills have been suggested to avoid the deferral or postponement of taxes, taxing foreign income as earned rather than as remitted. Probably the most aggressively pursued target of some tax reformers is the whole less developed country area. In 1975 the holding company option, in which LDC income could continue to receive special tax benefits through several layers of corporate parents, was eliminated.

Most of these enacted and proposed reforms have sought to place foreign income of the U.S. corporation on the same basis as domestic income and to treat foreign income taxes the same as U.S. states' corporate income taxes. However, there is a curious asymmetry in most of the reformers' logic, aside from the policy and balance of payments implications of their arguments. If parity is the goal, then the foreign operations of U.S. corporations should be allowed the same benefits as domestic corporations: ADR on depreciable assets; the Investment Tax Credit of 10%; elimination of taxes on intercompany dividend income when there is consolidation for tax purposes, or elimination of income taxes on 85% of intercompany dividend income when there is no consolidation; Subchapter S corporations (permitting partnership treatment of corporate profits for certain corporations which continue to have the benefits of limited liability); and DISC treatment of income from third-country export sales by the foreign operations.

With the changes of taxing foreign income as earned, eliminating the foreign tax credit, and eliminating special LDC treatment, initial total world tax collections would increase by $900 million per year. Adding these changes which place the foreign corporation of a U.S. parent on the same footing as a domestic counterpart, then the total tax collection would *decrease* by over $1,600 million, based on a 1976 U.S. Department of Commerce staff study for the House Ways and Means Committee.

Horst provides another set of figures for the change in domestic and foreign direct investment resulting from an end to deferral of foreign income and repeal of the foreign tax credit for U.S. multinationals.[12] Firms were assumed to deduct foreign income taxes prior to computing U.S. tax liability. He completed the analysis under situations in which the existing debt/equity structure remained as it was (Case 1 in Exhibit A.2) and in which the foreign subsidiary substituted debt for all its equity, a desirable practice since the interest on foreign debt would reduce total system taxes (Case 2). Although this change could cause firms to move investment from foreign operations to domestic operations, based on his initial parameters, the total world investment by these firms would decline by over $1 billion. However, the U.S. tax liability would increase initially by about $3 billion under either Case 1 or Case 2.

Future revisions are likely in the Code, but the form of the revisions is most uncertain. For reasons noted at the start of this appendix, the position of most observers varies considerably depending on what they use as an initial reference point of equity and how they can approach that position from the existing state of the Code.

EXHIBIT A.2. Estimated Impact of Repealing Deferral and the Foreign Tax Credit and Allowing Only a Deduction for Foreign Taxes Paid: On New Domestic and Foreign Investment, New Funds Advanced to Subsidiaries, Consolidated After-Tax Income, and Domestic and Foreign Taxes Paid by U.S. Manufacturers, 1974

		Case 1 (Initial Parameters)		*Case 2 (Reliance on Debt)*	
	Initial Value	*Absolute Change*	*Percentage Change*	*Absolute Change*	*Percentage Change*
Domestic Investment	36,400	9,291	25.5	3,970	10.9
Foreign Investment	18,300	-10,283	-56.2	-4,997	-27.3
New Funds for Subsidiary	2,710	-15,725	-580.3	-8.060	-297.4
Consolidated After-Tax Income	15,149	-2,974	-19.6	-3,107	-20.5
U.S. Taxes Paid	6,005	3,028	50.4	2,953	49.2
Foreign Taxes Paid	5,001	-504	-10.1	-144	-2.9

SOURCE: Thomas Horst, "American Taxation of Multinational Forms." AMERICAN ECONOMIC REVIEW, June 1977, p. 386.

[12] Thomas Horst, "American Taxation of Multinational Firms," *American Economic Review,* June 1977, pp. 376–389.

Exercises on Taxation of Foreign Income

ASSUMPTIONS

A. Parent corporation is subject to a 50% tax rate

B. U.S. corporation owns the following:

Subsidiary A–Fully owned foreign subsidiary located in Europe in a developed country.

B–Fully owned foreign subsidiary located in Europe in a developed country.

C–5% ownership in foreign subsidiary located in Europe in a developed country.

D–Fully owned "foreign controlled corporation" in Europe.

C. Total earnings, taxation, and dividends of each subsidiary:

	(million dollars)			
	A	*B*	*C*	*D*
Earnings before taxes	$100	$100	$100	$100
Income taxes	65	65	45	50
Profit after taxes	35	35	55	50
Dividends declared	35	20	30	0
Withholding tax	3	2	3	0

QUESTIONS

1. What are the taxes payable to the U.S. government?

Subsidiary A:

Dividends received		$ 32
Gross up:		
Direct credit (withholding tax)	3	
Indirect credit (proportion of income taxes) (35/35) X 65	65	68
(proportion is based on profits *after* taxes)		
Taxable income		$100
U.S. taxes	50	
Less tax credits	(68)	
Excess tax credit	$ 18	

Subsidiary B:

Dividends received		$ 18
Gross up:		
Direct credit (withholding tax)	2	
Indirect credit (income tax) (20/35) X 65	37	39
Taxable income		$ 57
U.S. taxes	28.5	
Less tax credits	(39.0)	
Excess tax credit	$ 10.5	

Subsidiary C:

Dividends received		$1.35
Gross up:		
Direct credit	0.15	
Indirect (not available, ownership is less than 10%)	0	0.15
Taxable income		$ 1.50
U.S. taxes	0.75	
Less tax credit	(0.15)	
Taxes due	$ 0.60	

Subsidiary D:

Dividends received		$ 0
Undistributed earnings		50
Gross up:		
Indirect credit (income tax) (50/50) X 50		50
Taxable income		$100
U.S. taxes	50	
Less tax credit	(50)	
No taxes due	$ 0	

(foreign and U.S. tax rates are the same)

2. How much credit for foreign taxes can be claimed this year? How much excess tax credit can be carried forward to future years?

There is a total tax credit of $157.15 million from a direct calculation ($68 + 39 + 0.15 + 50) plus another $0.60 million carry over credit from the other subsidiaries to Subsidiary C. The credit carry forward, or excess tax credit, is $27.9 million ($18 + 10.5 - 0.60).

3. If the taxes included as income taxes in the European subsidiaries above were mostly value added taxes, would you modify your computations?

Value added taxes are not considered income taxes by the United States. Therefore, the indirect credit for income tax will be lost in the above computations. In addition to value added taxes, excise, franchise, and property taxes do not qualify as a general rule.

4. What would be the considerations to change these operations from foreign subsidiaries to U.S. branches?

a. Foreign corporations lose the right of consolidation for tax purposes (except for some 100% owned Mexican and Canadian subsidiaries). As a consequence, taxes on dividends must be paid.

b. Branch form gives greater exposure of the U.S. parent's affairs to foreign officials.

c. Domestic form maximizes the tax deductibility of foreign operating losses. Losses can be spread over nine years.

d. Domestic form preserves the statutory depletion allowances and development costs available to taxpayer in the natural resource extraction business.

e. Domestic form gives some freedom from the Code's regulations against tax avoidance. Example: Section 367 requires an advance ruling from the Revenue Service in order to qualify a formation, division, or reorganization of a foreign corporation or liquidation of a foreign subsidiary for nonrecognition of gain.

f. Repatriation of earnings from a branch or U.S. subsidiary is often not subject to withholding taxes as are dividends.

g. Foreign firm makes possible deferment of U.S. tax payment until dividends are paid. This allows for planning of tax credits.

5. Unless a taxpayer can show that the loan was for a specific property, the *interest expense* must be allocated to various classes of gross income (assume U.S. and foreign). There are two methods of allocation: One method is based on *assets.* Here the interest expense is apportioned based on either the tax book value or the fair market value of the assets. Interest is apportioned to various operations in the same ratio that the assets in various operations bear to the total of all assets. Under the *gross income* method of allocating interest expense, the interest is apportioned on the basis of gross income from different operations (revenue minus operating expenses) if the allocation is at *least* 50% of the amount allocated to each source under the asset method. If the 50% test is *not* met, the 50% proportion is assigned to the category in question and the balance is assigned to the other category of operations. Thus, the rule is to allocate the

lower amount to foreign source income computed under the asset method or the gross income method, but at least 50% of the amount is allocated by the asset method.

Research and development expenditures are allocated to various product categories based on the Standard Industrial Classification Code. Then, a pro ration between domestic and foreign sales is made, unless the R&D is undertaken only for one government's legal requirements and the benefits of the R&D do not accrue to other operations (e.g., animal tests for the U.S. Food and Drug Administration in order to sell a drug in the U.S.). *Within* each product classification, the R&D is allocated either by a sales method or a gross income method. Under the *sales method,* the manager first may allocate 30% of the R&D expense to the area where at least 30% of the R&D was performed (assume the U.S.). The balance is allocated on the proportion of gross sales from each source to total sales. The 30% *exclusive apportionment* may be increased if the taxpayer can show either limited application or long-delayed application of the product elsewhere.[1] Under the *gross income* method, the allocation is based on the ratio of a source's gross income to total gross income for the firm, as long as the allocation of R&D is not less than 50% of the amount allocated under the sales method. If it is, then the taxpayer may allocate 50% of the amount calculated under the sales method to the lower source and the balance to the other source. Problem: X, a domestic corporation, manufactures and distributes electric motors, a product within SIC Major Group 35. Y, its wholly owned foreign subsidiary, sells these motors abroad. During 1979 X had $200,000 in interest expense and spent $80,000 on research and development in the United States. Sales and gross income for the two firms are:

	X	*Y*	*Total*
Sales	$ 9,000,000	$4,000,000	$13,000,000
Gross Income	4,000,000	1,000,000*	5,000,000
Asset values average of beginning and ending book values (ignore market value)	30,000,000	8,000,000	38,000,000

*Includes a $450,000 dividend plus a gross up of $550,000 in foreign taxes on the local operation's $1,000,000 net income.

Assume a tax rate of 50% and a foreign tax credit as shown in Subsidiary A. What are the tax allocations for the firm for interest and R&D? What are the final tax payments of the firm? If no allocation were required, how would the tax payments appear? What excess tax credits exist under allocation and non-allocation?

[1] If the taxpayer can show that the R&D will not have benefit for many years outside the U.S., then the present value of that benefit using a 10% discount rate can be used in place of the exclusive apportionment figure as a U.S. expense.

Taxation References

Arthur Andersen and Company, *Tax and Trade Guides.* Separate booklets, New York, various dates.

Beardwood, Roger, "Sophistication Comes to the Tax Havens." *Fortune,* Feb. 1969, pp. 95–178.

Commerce Clearing House, *Common Market Reporter.* Two vols., loose-leaf, Chicago, Ill., various dates.

Commerce Clearing House, *World Tax Series.* Chicago, Ill., various issues.

Coopers and Lybrand, *International Tax Summaries.* Loose-leaf, New York, various dates.

Eiteman, David K., and Arthur I. Stonehill, *Multinational Business Finance.* Reading, Mass.: Addison-Wesley Publishing Co., 1973, Ch. 7.

Ernst and Ernst, *International Business Series–Tax Bulletin,* New York, April 5, 1977.

Harriss, C. Lowell, "Value-Added Taxation." *Columbia Journal of World Business,* July-Aug. 1971, pp. 78–86.

Haskins and Sells, *International Tax and Business Service.* Two vols., loose-leaf, New York.

Hickman, Frederick W., "Tax Climate Is Improving for Doing Business in Eastern Europe." *Journal of Taxation,* Feb. 1974, pp. 65–69.

Horst, Thomas, "American Taxation of Multinational Firms." *American Economic Review,* June 1977, pp. 376–389.

Howard, Fred, "Overview of International Taxation." *Columbia Journal of World Business,* Summer 1975, pp. 5–11.

Hufbauer, G. C. and D. Foster, "U.S. Taxation of the Undistributed Income of Controlled Foreign Corporations," Office of International Tax Affairs, Department of the Treasury, Washington, D.C., April 1976.

—— and J. R. Nunns, "Tax Payments and Tax Expenditures on International Investment and Employment." *Columbia Journal of World Business,* Summer 1975, pp. 12–20.

International Bureau of Fiscal Documentation, *Guides to European Taxation.* Three vols. loose-leaf; and *Supplementary Service to European Taxation.* Loose-leaf, Amsterdam, Holland.

Jenks, Thomas E., "Taxation of Foreign Income." *The George Washington Law Review,* Vol. 42, 1974, pp. 537–556.

Kalish, Richard H., "Tax Considerations in Organizing for Business Abroad." *Taxes,* Feb. 1966, pp. 71–86.

Krause, Lawrence, and Kenneth Dam, "Economic Effects of Taxing Foreign-Source Income." *Federal Tax Treatment of Foreign Income,* The Brookings Institution, Washington, D.C., 1964.

Lent, George E., "Adjusting Taxable Profits for Inflation: The Foreign Experience," in Henry J. Aaron, *Inflation and the Income Tax.* Washington, D.C.: The Brookings Institution, 1976, pp. 195–213.

McIntyre, Michael J., *United States Taxation of Foreign Income with Special Emphasis on Private Investments in Developing Countries.* International Law Program, Harvard Law School, Cambridge, Mass., 1975. This is a revision of Arie Kopelman, *United States Income Taxation of Private Investments in Developing Countries.* United Nations Secretariat, New York, 1970.

Musgrave, Peggy B., "Exchange Rate Aspects in the Taxation of Foreign Income." *National Tax Journal,* Vol. 28, 1975, pp. 404-413.

——, "International Tax Base Division and the Multinational Corporation." *Public Finance,* Volume 27, pp. 394-413.

——, "The OECD Model Tax Treaty: Problems and Prospects." *Columbia Journal of World Business,* Summer 1975, pp. 29-39.

Owens, Elisabeth A., *Bibliography on Taxation of Foreign Operations and Foreigners.* International Tax Program, Harvard Law School, Cambridge, Mass., 1968 (under revision).

Phatak, Arvind V., *Managing Multinational Corporations.* New York: Praeger Publishers, 1974, Ch. 4.

Polk, Raemon M., "Financial and Tax Aspects of Planning for Foreign Currency Exchange Rate Fluctuations." *Taxes,* March 1978, pp. 131-142.

Prentice-Hall, Inc., *Tax Ideas-Tax Transaction Guide.* Two vols. loose-leaf, Englewood Cliffs, N.J., various dates.

Price Waterhouse and Company, *Information Guide Series.* Separate booklets, New York, various dates.

Rhodes, John B., "U.S. New Business Activities Abroad." *Columbia Journal of World Business,* Summer 1974, pp. 99-105 (annual report of Booz, Allen, and Hamilton).

Rosenberg, Herbert C., and Stuart R. Singer, "Selecting an International Finance Subsidiary: A Review of Available Methods." *Journal of Taxation,* May 1969, pp. 296-298.

Sato, Mitsuo, and Richard M. Bird, "International Aspects of the Taxation of Corporations and Shareholders." *International Monetary Fund Staff Papers,* Washington, D.C., 1976.

Schmitz, Marvin N., "Taxation of Foreign Exchange Gains and Losses." *Management Accounting,* July 1976, pp. 49-51.

"Special Report: Section 482." *Journal of Taxation,* Feb. 1968, pp. 66-79. See articles by Harry K. Mansfield, Sheldon Cohen, and Stanley S. Surrey.

Stone, Lawrence M., "United States Tax Policy Toward Foreign Earnings of Multinational Corporations." *The George Washington Law Review,* Vol. 42, 1974, pp. 557-567.

U.S. Congress, Committee on Ways and Means, *General Panel Discussion on Taxation of Foreign Income.* Exchange of letters between Professor Peggy Musgrave and Professor Robert Stobaugh, Feb. 1973, pp. 1881-1886.

Weston, J. Fred, and Bart Sorge, *International Managerial Finance.* Homewood, Ill.: Richard D. Irwin, 1972, Ch. 7.

APPENDIX 2

Glossary and Present Value Tables[1]

GLOSSARY

Acceptance. See *banker's acceptance.*

Accommodating Accounts. In the balance of payments, those accounts that for analytical purposes can be considered triggered by the need to finance other transactions included in the balance of payments. Also called compensating or financing accounts.

Account Party. The party whose bank issues a letter of credit—usually the buyer.

Accounting Exposure. See *balance sheet exposure, transaction exchange gain or loss, and translation exchange gain or loss.*

Accrual System. Accounting system in which the returns and costs are reported when legally incurred rather than when the cash flow associated with the receipt or the payment materializes.

[1]Some of these legal definitions are based on citations of Robert N. Corley and William J. Robert, *Principles of Business Law,* 10th ed. (Englewood Cliffs, N.J.: Prentice-Hall, Inc., 1975).

Advising Bank. A correspondent of an issuing bank that notifies the beneficiary of a letter of credit without adding its own engagement to that of the issuing bank.

Agent. A person authorized to act for another (a principal). The term may apply to a person in the service of another, but in the strict sense an agent is one who stands in place of the principal. If A works for B as a secretary, he is a servant in the legal sense, but he may also be an agent. If A takes orders for B, he acts in place of B and is an agent.

Annuity. In law, a sum of money paid yearly to a person during his/her lifetime. It arises by a contract under which the recipient or another person deposits funds with the grantor. The grantor then returns a designated portion of the principal and interest in periodic payments upon the arrival of the beneficiary at a designated age. In general, an annuity is payment of a flat sum of money over a specific period of time.

Arbitrage. Transactions made to take advantage of temporary imperfections in the market. For example, if one could buy potatoes for 20¢/lb in one market and sell them for 25¢/lb in another, one could make a profit of 5¢/lb through arbitrage. An arbitrage transaction does not involve any risk. Because contracts are made, the returns derived from the transaction are known from the beginning, even though part of the transaction may take place in the future. Also see *space arbitrage* and *covered interest arbitrage.*

Ask Price. The price at which a trader giving a quote is willing to sell a given item. Also called offer price.

Assignment. The transfer of a right, usually arising from a contract. Such rights are called "choses in action." A sells and assigns his/her contract right to purchase B's Plymouth convertible to C. A is an assignor. C is an assignee. The transfer is an assignment.

Autonomous Accounts. In the balance of payments, those accounts that for analytical purposes can be considered motivated purely by economic considerations rather than by the need to finance international transactions.

Bailment. The delivery of personal property (as opposed to real property) to another for a special purpose. Such delivery is made under a contract, either expressed or implied, that the property shall be redelivered to the bailor or placed at his/her disposal upon the completion of the special purpose. A loans B his horse. A places a watch with B for repair. A places her furniture in B's warehouse. A places her securities in B's bank safety deposit vault. In each case A is a bailor and B is a bailee.

Balance in Invisibles. In the balance of payments, the balance of the service accounts.

Balance of Indebtedness. Financial statement prepared for a given country summarizing the levels of assets and liabilities that the country has vis-à-vis the rest of the world. Also known as the investment position of the country.

Balance of Payments. Financial statement prepared for a given country summarizing the flow of goods, services, and funds between the residents of the country and the residents of the rest of the world during a certain period of time. The balance of payments is prepared by using the concept of double-entry bookkeeping in which the total of debits equals the total of credits or the total sources of funds equal the total uses of funds.

Balance Sheet Exposure. Various forms of accounting exposure which differ as to which assets and liabilities are translated at historic rates (unexposed) and which accounts are translated at current rates (exposed). "Exposure" is the net balance sheet exposure of assets minus liabilities which are translated at current rates. See also *exposure to foreign exchange risk.*

Banker's Acceptance. When a draft has been accepted by a bank, and the bank guarantees that payment will be made at some date in the future, that certified draft is called a banker's acceptance. It may be traded freely among other parties, and the bank will pay the party that submits the draft to it at maturity.

Banking Day. That part of any day on which a bank is open to the public for carrying on substantially all of its banking functions. (Article 4 of the U.C.C.: Bank Deposits and Collections)

Basic Balance. In the balance of payments, the net balance of the flow in trade of goods and services, unilateral transfers, and long-term capital.

Bearer. The person in possession of an instrument, document of title, or security payable to bearer or indorsed in blank (with no name or order following the indorsement).

Beneficiary. The party in whose favor a letter of credit is issued—usually the seller.

Bid Price. The price at which a trader giving a quote is willing to purchase a given item.

Bill of Lading. A record of the shipment of goods from a transporter confirming the receipt of goods for shipment and means of transportation. The general term, bill of lading, is used for marine and surface transport. The term airbill is usually used for air shipments.

Blocked Funds. Funds which cannot be repatriated because the local monetary authorities forbid conversion into foreign exchange.

Bond. A promise under seal to pay money. The term is generally used to designate the promise made by a corporation, either public or private, to pay money to the bearer. Bonds also can be issued by governments. U.S. government bonds; Rock Island Railroad bonds.

Capital Account. In the balance of payments, the section that records the changes in financial assets and liabilities. The capital account is divided into two major sections: long-term flows and short-term flows.

Capital Structure. The combination of long-term debt and various types of equity in the financing of the firm.

Cash System. Accounting system in which only cash flows are reported, independent of when the obligations are contracted.

Cashier's Check. A bill of exchange drawn by the cashier of a bank, for the bank, upon the bank. The drawer bank cannot put a "stop order" against itself after the check is delivered or issued to the payee or holder.

Collateral. Security placed with a creditor to assure the performance of the obligator. If the obligation is satisfied, the collateral is returned by the creditor. A owes B $1,000. To secure the payment, A places with B a $5,000 certificate of stock in X Company. The $5,000 certificate is called collateral.

Collecting Bank. Any bank handling an item for collection except the payor bank. (Article 4 of the U.C.C.: Bank Deposits and Collections)

Commission. The sum of money, interest, brokerage, compensation, or allowance given to a factor or broker for carrying on the business of his/her principal.

Compensating Accounts. See *accommodating accounts.*

Condition. A clause in a contract that has the effect of investing or divesting the legal rights and duties of the parties to the contract.

Confirming Bank. A correspondent bank that adds its own engagement to that of the issuing bank in a letter of credit guaranteeing that the credit will be honored by the issuer or a third bank.

Consignee. A person to whom a shipper directs a carrier to deliver goods, generally the buyer.

Consignment. The delivery, sending, or transferring of property ("goods, wares, and merchandise") into the possession of another, usually for the purpose of sale. Consignment may be a bailment or an agency for sale.

Consortia Bank. A more or less permanent group of banks whose objective is to provide joint financing to customers.

Convertible Euro-bond. A Euro-bond that can be converted into equity of the issuing company under prescribed conditions.

Convertibility. In foreign exchange, the ability to convert one currency into another.

Correspondent Bank. A bank that in its own country handles the business of a foreign bank. There are also domestic correspondents in different areas of the same country.

Cost of Capital. In corporate finance, the weighted rate of return expected by various parties financing the firm. The return that bondholders expect is in the market interest rate on the debt. The return that equity holders expect is a function of dividends received and capital gains as the stock appreciates in value, adjusted for risk. The weights used to combine these rates of return are the proportions that each of these sources of funds contributes to the capitalization of the firm. The cost of capital traditionally is used as a hurdle rate that projects must yield as a minimum in order to be accepted by the firm.

Covenant. A promise in writing. It is often used as a substitute for the word contract. There are covenants (promises) in deeds, leases, mortgages, and other instruments under seal and in unsealed instruments such as insurance policies and conditional sale contracts.

Covered Interest Arbitrage. A process of borrowing a currency, converting it into another currency where it is invested, and selling this other currency for future delivery against the initial currency. The profits in this transaction are derived from discrepancies between interest differentials and the percentage discounts or premiums among the currencies involved in the transaction.

Covering. The generation of cash flows in a given currency in the money market or in the forward exchange market at predetermined rates with the purpose of matching the cash flows generated by operations in that currency. The purpose of covering is to make cash inflows equal cash outflows for the given currency for specified maturities. This produces a "square position." Covering usually refers to trade transactions that produce a payable or a receivable in foreign exchange to be liquidated at a future date. The covering transaction eliminates the risk of fluctuations in foreign exchange rates during the intervening period. Covering and hedging are terms often used interchangeably. See also *hedging.*

Credit Entry in Balance of Payments. The part of an international transaction that represents a source of funds or international purchasing power to the country reporting the balance of payments. A credit entry reflects a decrease in the holdings of foreign assets owned by local residents or an increase in the liabilities to foreigners owed by the residents of the reporting country.

Credit Tranche. The amount that a member country of the International Monetary Fund can borrow from the fund over the gold tranche.

Cross Rate. The calculation of a foreign exchange rate from two separate quotes that contain the same currency. For example, if one has the rate of French francs per U.S. dollar and the rate of deutsche marks per U.S. dollar, one can calculate the cross rate between French francs and deutsche marks.

Current Account. In the balance of payments, the section that records the trade in goods and services and the exchange of gifts among countries.

Customer. As used in letters of credit, a customer is a buyer or other person who causes credit to be issued. The term also refers to a bank which procures issuance or confirmation on behalf of that bank's customer.

Debit Entry in Balance of Payments. The part of an international transaction that represents a use of funds or international purchasing power to the country reporting the balance of payments. A debit entry reflects an increase in the holdings of foreign assets owned by local residents or a decrease in the liabilities owed to foreigners by the residents of the reporting country. Debit entries are usually preceded by minus signs in balance of payments tables.

Depository Bank. The first bank to which an item for collection is transferred, which may also be the payor bank.

Direct Investment. Purchase of a foreign financial asset in which substantial involvement in the management of the foreign operation is presumed. In practice, it is any equity holding that represents more than 10% ownership of the foreign firm.

Discount Rate. (1) In capital budgeting analysis, the rate which is applied to future cash flows to bring them to a present value. (2) In trade terms, the rate which is applied to a non-interest bearing note which can be translated into a rate for early payment of the note. Thus, a note payable at face in six months might sell for 2% less than its face amount, implying an annual rate of 4%. (3) In foreign exchange markets, the difference between the forward and the spot rate.

Document of Title. This term includes bill of lading, dock warrant, dock receipt, warehouse receipt, order for the delivery of goods, and any other document which in the regular course of business or financing is treated as adequate evidence that the person in possession of it is entitled to receive, hold, and dispose of the document and the goods it covers.

Documentary Draft. A draft the honor of which is conditioned upon the presentation of a document or documents. "Document" means any paper including document of title, security, invoice, certificate, notice of default, and the like. Also referred to as a documentary demand for payment.

Draft. An order to pay. A check is one form of a draft.

Drawee Bank. The bank upon which a draft is drawn. Also called paying bank.

Edge Act Corporations. Financial institutions incorporated in the United States under the Edge Act. Edge Act corporations are owned by commercial banks and restrict their income mostly to foreign sources. The major advantage a commercial bank achieves in establishing an Edge Act corporation is to be able to conduct abroad some activities which are forbidden to U.S. banks.

Efficient Market. A market in which equilibrium conditions prevail, in which there are sufficiently large number of buyers and sellers to prohibit any incentive for arbitrage transactions, and in which the trade-offs between return and risk are fully equilibrated.

Elasticity. Elasticity measures the degree of responsiveness in one variable to changes in another variable. For example, the price elasticity of exports might measure the degree of responsiveness in exports to changes in prices; the income elasticity of imports might measure the degree of responsiveness in imports to changes in income.

Euro-bond. Bond denominated in the borrower's currency but sold outside the country of the borrower, usually by an international syndicate.

Euro-currency. Monies traded outside the countries where they are the domestic currencies. For example, Euro-dollars are U.S. dollars traded outside the United States.

Exchange Rate. The price of one currency expressed in terms of another currency.

Exposure to Foreign Exchange Risk. The amount of a person's or business's holdings that is not denominated in the domestic currency and whose value will fluctuate if foreign exchange rates vary. Also see *balance sheet exposure.*

Financing Accounts. See *accommodating accounts.*

Fixed Currency. A currency whose official value relative to gold and other currencies is maintained by a central bank. The bank intervenes to buy and to sell the currency when it deviates from the official value.

Floating Currency. A currency whose exchange rate relative to those of other currencies is allowed to fluctuate more or less freely. "Dirty floating" occurs if the central bank intervenes to keep the currency from deviating outside the country's desired range.

Floating Lending Rate. A lending rate that is established at a fixed number of percentage points above a given rate, such as the London interbank offer rate (LIBOR), and which is renegotiated periodically, often every six months. Negotiation occurs throughout the life of the loan.

Floating Policy. An insurance policy that covers a class of goods located in a particular place that the insured had on hand at the time the policy was issued, but which—at the time of loss—may not be the identical items that were on hand at the time the policy was issued. A fire policy covering the inventory of a hardware store is an example.

Foreign Bond. Bond sold outside the country of the borrower but in the country of the currency in which the bond is denominated. The bond is underwritten by local institutions and is issued under the regulations prevalent in that country.

Foreign Exchange. Currency other than the one used internally in a given country.

Forward Rate. Foreign exchange rate for currency to be delivered at a future date.

Gold Tranche. The amount that each member country of the International Monetary Fund contributes in the form of gold as part of its membership quota in the Fund. This amount can be borrowed readily by the contributing country.

Guarantor. One who by contract undertakes "to answer for the debt, default, and miscarriage of another." In general, a guarantor undertakes to pay if the principal debtor does not.

Hedging. The generation of a position in a given currency in the money market or in the forward exchange market at predetermined rates with the purpose of matching the net position generated in that currency with the net exposure position of the business operations as evidenced by balance sheets. The purpose of hedging is to make the net position at a given date equal zero. The accounts included in the exposed balance sheet items are determined according to accounting rules. When balance sheet items are translated into specific cash flows in the future which the firm wishes to protect aganist fluctuations in exchange rates, the hedging transaction becomes a covering transaction. Covering and hedging are terms often used interchangeably. Also see *covering.*

Income Elasticity. See *elasticity.*

Indemnify. Literally, to save from harm. Thus, one person agrees to protect another against loss.

Indexing. In some nations the practice of adjusting mortgage or other debt issues by some measure of inflation to preserve the purchasing power of the debt in constant monetary units. In Brazil, indexing is applied to wages, business accounts, and all debt issues, a broader scope than that of most nations using indexing.

Indorsement. Writing one's name upon paper for the purpose of transferring the title. When a payee of a negotiable instrument writes his/her name on the back of the instrument, he/she is indorsing the instrument.

Inflation. The overall rate of increase in prices of a package of goods and services in a given country. This rate of increase may differ among different economic sectors.

Interest Equalization Tax (IET). Tax imposed on U.S. residents who purchased foreign securities between 1963 and the end of 1973.

Intermediary Bank. A bank to which an item is transferred in the course of collection other than the depository or payor bank. (Article 4 of the U.C.C.: Bank Deposits and Collections)

Issuing Bank. The bank that issues a letter of credit–usually the buyer's bank.

Leads and Lags. The practice of quickly moving funds into a given currency (lead) or delaying the movement of funds into a given currency (lag) with the objective of benefiting from expected changes in exchange rates.

Letter of Credit. An agreement sent from one party (usually a bank) to another concerning funds which will be made available upon completion of some business transactions. Usually, a buyer sends a letter of credit to the seller of goods when they are not known to each other. Upon certification of shipment of the goods in question and submission of a draft, the local bank will arrange for funds to be made available to the exporter. It is established and regulated within the scope of Article 5 of the U.C.C.: Letters of Credit.

Liability. In its broadest legal sense, the word means any obligation one may be under by some rule of law. It includes debt, duty, and responsibility.

Locking in a Rate. In a foreign exchange market, establishing the exchange rates at which inflows and outflows of a currency will take place at a given future time.

Long Position. Situation occurring when anticipated inflows of a currency exceed the anticipated outflows of that currency over a given period of time.

Marginal. Incremental unit. Units usually refer to costs or revenues.

Merger. Two corporations are merged when one corporation continues in existence and the other loses its identity by absorption. Merger must be distinguished from consolidation, by which both corporations are dissolved and a new one created to take over the assets of the dissolved corporations.

Multiplier. In monetary economics, the factor by which an initial deposit could grow through multiple loans after the initial monetary deposit. The multiplier is defined as the reciprocal of the reserve requirement adjusted for leakages in the system.

Mutuality. A word used to describe the fact that every contract must be binding on both parties. Each party to the contract must be bound to the other party to do something by virtue of the legal duty created.

Negligence. The failure to do that which an ordinary, reasonable, prudent person would do, or the doing of some act which an ordinary, prudent person would not do. Reference must always be made to the situation, the circumstances, and the knowledge of the parties.

Negotiating Bank. A bank chosen by the beneficiary when a letter of credit allows negotiation.

Net Effective Interest Rate or Yield. The yield in a given currency adjusted for changes in the exchange rates.

Net Exchange Position. A net asset or liability position in a given currency. This is the term commonly used by exchange traders. Also called a net long or short position.

Net Exposure Position. See *balance sheet exposure.*

Net Present Value. The value in current dollars when future receipts and outlays are discounted at some rate.

Nominal Interest Rate. The interest rate specified to be paid on the face amount borrowed. In a bond the nominal rate is the coupon rate. The actual amount of funds borrowed may be more or less than the face amount, thus changing the net yield of the funds involved. See also *yield.*

Numeraire. The standard which is used for measurement. In international corporate finance this refers to the currency chosen by the firm as reference against which all other currency cash flows are measured.

Obligee. A creditor or promisee.

Obligor. A debtor or promisor.

OFDI. Office of Foreign Direct Investment. Created to regulate the amount of foreign direct investment that U.S. companies could finance from funds generated in foreign operations or from the parent company. The regulations were established on a voluntary basis between 1965 and 1967 and made mandatory from 1968 until they were eliminated in 1973.

Offer Price. The price at which a trader giving a quote is willing to sell a given item. Also called ask price.

Outright Forward Rate. Forward exchange rate expressed in terms of the amount of one currency required to buy a unit of another currency.

Par Value. Under the Bretton Woods system, the value of a currency measured in terms of gold or the U.S. dollar, which was maintained at a fixed rate relative to gold.

Paying Bank. The bank on which a draft is drawn. Also called drawee bank.

Payor Bank. A bank by which an item is payable as drawn or accepted. (Article 4 of the U.C.C.: Bank Deposits and Collections)

Pledge. The deposit or placing of personal property as security for a debt or other obligation with a person called a pledgee. The pledgee has the implied power to sell the property if the debt is not paid. If the debt is paid, the right to possession returns to the pledgor.

Points. In foreign exchange markets, the amount of premium or discount in the forward price from the spot price. A point is a unit of a decimal, usually the fourth place to the right of the decimal point. Which decimal place is implied varies from currency to currency.

Portfolio Investment. Purchase of a foreign financial asset with the sole purpose of deriving the returns that the security provides without intervening in the management of the foreign operation.

Preferred Stock. Stock that entitles the holder to dividends from earnings before the owners of common stock can receive dividends.

Presenting Bank. Any bank presenting an item except a payor bank. (Article 4 of the U.C.C.: Bank Deposits and Collections)

Price Elasticity. See *elasticity.*

Rate of Return. In capital budgeting, that discount rate for which the cash inflows can be discounted to equal the discounted cash outflows; i.e., where the net present value is zero.

Reinsurance. Under a contract of reinsurance, one insurance company agrees to indemnify another insurance company in whole or in part against risks which the first company has assumed.

Remitting Bank. Any payor or intermediary bank remitting for an item. (Article 4 of the U.C.C.: Bank Deposits and Collections)

Reserve Accounts. In the balance of payments, the accounts reflecting the changes in the amount of resources that the government of the country has at its disposal to settle international payments. These resources are composed of gold and foreign currency which is fully convertible into other currencies, such as the U.S. dollar.

Revolver. A loan with floating rates where not only the rates but also the amounts (within the limits of a given line of credit) are renegotiated periodically.

Revolving Loan. See *revolver.*

Risk Analysis. Study of the various outcomes under different assumptions and under different probabilities that each of these outcomes will take place.

Safe Harbors. Rules set in legislation which, if met, guarantee special (favorable) treatment to the party. Thus, a taxpayer who meets certain requirements may have a lower tax rate even though other taxpayers might conceivably win the favorable treatment as well when they did not meet the same requirements. Safe harbors are sufficient, but not necessary, qualification.

Satisfaction. The release and discharge of a legal obligation. Satisfaction may be partial or full performance of the obligation. The word is used with accord, which means a promise to give a substituted performance for a contract obligation; satisfaction means the acceptance by the obligee of such performance.

SDRs. Special Drawing Rights. Money created by the International Monetary Fund with the approval of a large majority of member countries and distributed among all member countries. This paper money is used only in transactions among governments and between governments and the IMF.

Security. Security may be bonds, stocks, and other property placed by a debtor with a creditor, with power to sell if the debt is not paid. The plural of the term, "securities," is used broadly to mean tangible items such as promissory notes, bonds, stocks, and other vendible obligations.

Settle. To pay in cash, by a clearing house settlement, in a charge or credit, by remittance, or as otherwise instructed. A settlement may be either provisional or final. (Article 4 of the U.C.C.: Banks Deposits and Collections)

Short Position. Situation in which anticipated outflows of a currency exceed the anticipated inflows of that currency over a given period of time.

Simulation. Analytical technique in which outcomes are estimated under alternative sets of assumptions.

Space Arbitrage. The purchase of a currency in a given market accompanied by a sale of that currency in another market where it commands a higher price.

Speculative Transaction. A transaction in which the eventual net return or cost is not known in advance. In international finance, the major sources of speculative risk occur when the transaction produces a net asset or liability position in a given currency and when the cash inflows and outflows in a given currency are not matched according to maturity.

Spot Rate. Foreign exchange rate for currency delivered within two days.

Spread. The difference between the bid and ask prices in a price quote.

Square Position. Position when the cash inflows match the cash outflows in a given currency for a certain date or period of time.

Swap Position. Position when a given currency is simultaneously purchased and sold, but the maturity of each of the transactions is different.

Swap Rate. Forward exchange rates expressed in terms of premiums or discounts from the spot rate.

Tax Haven. A country that imposes little or no tax or withholding on the profits from transactions carried on from that country, especially on income from dividends and interest.

Terminal Rate of Return. Internal rate of return when the net cash flows produced by the project during its life are assumed to be reinvested at a predetermined rate of return.

Terms of Trade. The ratio of export prices to import prices. Export and import prices in this ratio are each aggregated and combined into a sum for which the total in a given year equals 1,000.

Transaction Exchange Gain or Loss. The increase (gain) or decrease (loss) in a cash flow because the cash flow was denominated in another currency and the exchange rate between the two currencies changed. In consolidating foreign operations, it usually relates to conversion of the income statement and certain cash remittances (e.g., dividend payments) to the parent where parities change between an accounting date and a payment date.

Translation Exchange Gain or Loss. The foreign exchange gain or loss associated with the conversion (for financial consolidation) of the balance sheet expressed in another currency into the numeraire currency. The gain or loss arises when the exchange rate between the two currencies fluctuates and exposed assets do not equal exposed liabilities.

Trust Receipt. A document establishing that the borrower holds certain goods in trust for the lender.

U.C.C. Uniform Commercial Code.

Unilateral Transfers. In the balance of payments, the accounts that measure gifts sent in and out of the reporting country.

Value Date. Date when funds are to be received or paid according to a contract.

Voluntary Credit Restraint Program. Program in existence between 1965 and the end of 1973 restricting the amount of credit that commercial banks and other financial institutions in the United States could extend to foreigners.

Withholding Tax. A tax collected by the source originating the income, in contrast to one paid by the recipient of the income after the funds are received. For example, a withholding tax on interest payments to foreigners means that the tax proceeds are deducted from the interest payment made to the lender and collected by the borrower on behalf of the government.

Yield. The amount of funds involved in interest payments as a percentage of the amount lent or borrowed; the present market price of a security in the currency of the instrument.

TABLE A Present Value of $1

Years Hence	1%	2%	4%	6%	8%	10%	12%	14%	15%	16%	18%	20%	22%	24%	25%	26%	28%	30%	35%	40%	45%	50%
1	0.990	0.980	0.962	0.943	0.926	0.909	0.893	0.877	0.870	0.862	0.847	0.833	0.820	0.806	0.800	0.794	0.781	0.769	0.741	0.714	0.690	0.667
2	0.980	0.961	0.925	0.890	0.857	0.826	0.797	0.769	0.756	0.743	0.718	0.694	0.672	0.650	0.640	0.630	0.610	0.592	0.549	0.510	0.476	0.444
3	0.971	0.942	0.889	0.840	0.794	0.751	0.712	0.675	0.658	0.641	0.609	0.579	0.551	0.524	0.512	0.500	0.477	0.455	0.406	0.364	0.328	0.296
4	0.961	0.924	0.855	0.792	0.735	0.683	0.636	0.592	0.572	0.552	0.516	0.482	0.451	0.423	0.410	0.397	0.373	0.350	0.301	0.260	0.226	0.198
5	0.951	0.906	0.822	0.747	0.681	0.621	0.567	0.519	0.497	0.476	0.437	0.402	0.370	0.341	0.328	0.315	0.291	0.269	0.223	0.186	0.156	0.132
6	0.942	0.888	0.790	0.705	0.630	0.564	0.507	0.456	0.432	0.410	0.370	0.335	0.303	0.275	0.262	0.250	0.227	0.207	0.165	0.133	0.108	0.088
7	0.933	0.871	0.760	0.665	0.583	0.513	0.452	0.400	0.376	0.354	0.314	0.279	0.249	0.222	0.210	0.198	0.178	0.159	0.122	0.095	0.074	0.059
8	0.923	0.853	0.731	0.627	0.540	0.467	0.404	0.351	0.327	0.305	0.266	0.233	0.204	0.179	0.168	0.157	0.139	0.123	0.091	0.068	0.051	0.039
9	0.914	0.837	0.703	0.592	0.500	0.424	0.361	0.308	0.284	0.263	0.225	0.194	0.167	0.144	0.134	0.125	0.108	0.094	0.067	0.048	0.035	0.026
10	0.905	0.820	0.676	0.558	0.463	0.386	0.322	0.270	0.247	0.227	0.191	0.162	0.137	0.116	0.107	0.099	0.085	0.073	0.050	0.035	0.024	0.017
11	0.896	0.804	0.650	0.527	0.429	0.350	0.287	0.237	0.215	0.195	0.162	0.135	0.112	0.094	0.086	0.079	0.066	0.056	0.037	0.025	0.017	0.012
12	0.887	0.788	0.625	0.497	0.397	0.319	0.257	0.208	0.187	0.168	0.137	0.112	0.092	0.076	0.069	0.062	0.052	0.043	0.027	0.018	0.012	0.008
13	0.879	0.773	0.601	0.469	0.368	0.290	0.229	0.182	0.163	0.145	0.116	0.093	0.075	0.061	0.055	0.050	0.040	0.033	0.020	0.013	0.008	0.005
14	0.870	0.758	0.577	0.442	0.340	0.263	0.205	0.160	0.141	0.125	0.099	0.078	0.062	0.049	0.044	0.039	0.032	0.025	0.015	0.009	0.006	0.003
15	0.861	0.743	0.055	0.417	0.315	0.239	0.183	0.140	0.123	0.108	0.084	0.065	0.051	0.040	0.035	0.031	0.025	0.020	0.011	0.006	0.004	0.002
16	0.853	0.728	0.534	0.394	0.292	0.218	0.163	0.123	0.107	0.093	0.071	0.054	0.042	0.032	0.028	0.025	0.019	0.015	0.008	0.005	0.003	0.002
17	0.844	0.714	0.513	0.371	0.270	0.198	0.146	0.108	0.093	0.080	0.060	0.045	0.034	0.026	0.023	0.020	0.015	0.012	0.006	0.003	0.002	0.001
18	0.836	0.700	0.494	0.350	0.250	0.180	0.130	0.095	0.081	0.069	0.051	0.038	0.028	0.021	0.018	0.016	0.012	0.009	0.005	0.002	0.001	0.001
19	0.828	0.686	0.475	0.331	0.232	0.164	0.116	0.083	0.070	0.060	0.043	0.031	0.023	0.017	0.014	0.012	0.009	0.007	0.003	0.002	0.001	0.001
20	0.820	0.673	0.456	0.312	0.215	0.149	0.104	0.073	0.061	0.051	0.037	0.026	0.019	0.014	0.012	0.010	0.007	0.005	0.002	0.001	0.001	
21	0.811	0.660	0.439	0.294	0.199	0.135	0.093	0.064	0.053	0.044	0.031	0.022	0.015	0.011	0.009	0.008	0.006	0.004	0.002	0.001		
22	0.803	0.647	0.422	0.278	0.184	0.123	0.083	0.056	0.046	0.038	0.026	0.018	0.013	0.009	0.007	0.006	0.004	0.003	0.001	0.001		
23	0.795	0.634	0.406	0.262	0.170	0.112	0.074	0.049	0.040	0.033	0.022	0.015	0.010	0.007	0.006	0.005	0.003	0.002	0.001			
24	0.788	0.622	0.390	0.247	0.158	0.102	0.066	0.043	0.035	0.028	0.019	0.013	0.008	0.006	0.005	0.004	0.003	0.002	0.001			
25	0.780	0.610	0.375	0.233	0.146	0.092	0.059	0.038	0.030	0.024	0.016	0.010	0.007	0.005	0.004	0.003	0.002	0.001	0.001			
26	0.772	0.598	0.361	0.220	0.135	0.084	0.053	0.033	0.026	0.021	0.014	0.009	0.006	0.004	0.003	0.002	0.002	0.001				
27	0.764	0.586	0.347	0.207	0.125	0.076	0.047	0.029	0.023	0.018	0.011	0.007	0.005	0.003	0.002	0.002	0.001	0.001				
28	0.757	0.574	0.333	0.196	0.116	0.069	0.042	0.026	0.020	0.016	0.010	0.006	0.004	0.002	0.002	0.002	0.001	0.001				
29	0.749	0.563	0.321	0.185	0.107	0.063	0.037	0.022	0.017	0.014	0.008	0.005	0.003	0.002	0.002	0.001	0.001	0.001				
30	0.742	0.552	0.308	0.174	0.099	0.057	0.033	0.020	0.015	0.012	0.007	0.004	0.003	0.002	0.001	0.001	0.001					
40	0.672	0.453	0.208	0.097	0.046	0.022	0.011	0.005	0.004	0.003	0.001	0.001										
50	0.608	0.372	0.141	0.054	0.021	0.009	0.003	0.001	0.001	0.001												

SOURCE: By permission from Robert N. Anthony, MANAGEMENT ACCOUNTING: TEXT AND CASES, rev. ed. Homewood, Ill.: Richard D. Irwin, Inc., Irwin, Inc. 1960.

TABLE B Present Value of $1 Received Annually for N Years

Years (N)	1%	2%	4%	6%	8%	10%	12%	14%	15%	16%	18%	20%	22%	24%	25%	26%	28%	30%	35%	40%	45%	50%
1	0.990	0.980	0.962	0.943	0.926	0.909	0.893	0.877	0.870	0.862	0.847	0.833	0.820	0.806	0.800	0.794	0.781	0.769	0.741	0.714	0.690	0.667
2	1.970	1.942	1.886	1.833	1.783	1.736	1.690	1.647	1.626	1.605	1.566	1.528	1.492	1.457	1.440	1.424	1.392	1.361	1.289	1.224	1.165	1.111
3	2.941	2.884	2.775	2.673	2.577	2.487	2.402	2.322	2.283	2.246	2.174	2.106	2.042	1.981	1.952	1.923	1.868	1.816	1.696	1.589	1.493	1.407
4	3.902	3.808	3.630	3.465	3.312	3.170	3.037	2.914	2.885	2.798	2.690	2.589	2.494	2.404	2.362	2.320	2.241	2.166	1.997	1.849	1.720	1.605
5	4.853	4.713	4.452	4.212	3.993	3.791	3.605	3.433	3.352	3.274	3.127	2.991	2.864	2.745	2.689	2.635	2.532	2.436	2.220	2.035	1.876	1.737
6	5.795	5.601	5.242	4.917	4.623	4.355	4.111	3.889	3.784	3.685	3.498	3.326	3.167	3.020	2.951	2.885	2.759	2.643	2.385	2.168	1.983	1.824
7	6.728	6.472	6.002	5.582	5.206	4.868	4.564	4.288	4.160	4.039	3.812	3.605	3.416	3.242	3.161	3.083	2.937	2.802	2.508	2.263	2.057	1.883
8	7.652	7.325	6.733	6.210	5.747	5.335	4.968	4.639	4.487	4.344	4.078	3.837	3.619	3.421	3.329	3.241	3.076	2.925	2.598	2.331	2.108	1.922
9	8.566	8.162	7.435	6.802	6.247	5.759	5.328	4.946	4.772	4.607	4.303	4.031	3.786	3.566	3.463	3.366	3.184	3.019	2.665	2.379	2.144	1.948
10	9.471	8.983	8.111	7.360	6.710	6.145	5.650	5.216	5.019	4,833	4.494	4.192	3.923	3.682	3.571	3.465	3.269	3.092	2.715	2.414	2.168	1.965
11	10.368	9.787	8.760	7.887	7.139	6.495	5.937	5.453	5.234	5.029	4.656	4.327	4.035	3.776	3.656	3.544	3.335	3.147	2.752	2.438	2.185	1.977
12	11.255	10.575	9.385	8.384	7.536	6.814	6.194	5.660	5.421	5.197	4.793	4.439	4.127	3.851	3.725	3.606	3.387	3.190	2.779	2.456	2.196	1.985
13	12,134	11.343	9.986	8.853	7.904	7.103	6.424	5.842	5.583	5.342	4.910	4.533	4.203	3.912	3.780	3.656	3.427	3.223	2.799	2.468	2.204	1.990
14	13.004	12.106	10.563	9.295	8.244	7.367	6.628	6.002	5.724	5.468	5.008	4.611	4.265	3.962	3.824	3.695	3.459	3.249	2.814	2.477	2.210	1.993
15	13.865	12.849	11.118	9.712	8.559	7.606	6.811	6.142	5.847	5.575	5.092	4.675	4.315	4.001	3.859	3.726	3.483	3.268	2.825	2.484	2.214	1.995
16	14.718	13.578	11.652	10.106	8.851	7.824	6.974	6.265	5.954	5.669	5.162	4.730	4.357	4.033	3.887	3.751	3.503	3.283	2.834	2.489	2.216	1.997
17	15.562	14.292	12.166	10.477	9.122	8.022	7.120	6.373	6.047	5.749	5.222	4.775	4.391	4.059	3.910	3.771	3.518	3.295	2.840	2.492	2.218	1.998
18	16.398	14.992	12.659	10.828	9.372	8.201	7.250	6.467	6.128	5.818	5.273	4.812	4.419	4.080	3.928	3.786	3.529	3.304	2.844	2.494	2.219	1.999
19	17.226	15.678	13.134	11.158	9.604	8.365	7.366	6.550	6.198	5.877	5.316	4.844	4.442	4.097	3.942	3.799	3.539	3.311	2.848	2.496	2.220	1.999
20	18.046	16.351	13.590	11.470	9.818	8.514	7.469	6.623	6.259	5.929	5.353	4.870	4.460	4.110	3.954	3.808	3.546	3.316	2.850	2.497	2.221	1.999
21	18.857	17.011	14.029	11.764	10.017	8.649	7.562	6.687	6.312	5.973	5.384	4.891	4.476	4.121	3.963	3.816	3.551	3.320	2.852	2.498	2.221	2.000
22	19.660	17.658	14.451	12.042	10.201	8.772	7.645	6.743	6.359	6.011	5.410	4.909	4.488	4.130	3.970	3.822	3.556	3.323	2.853	2.498	2.222	2.000
23	20.456	18.292	14.857	12.303	10.371	8.883	7.718	6.792	6.399	6.004	5.432	4.925	4.499	4.137	3.976	3.827	3.559	3.325	2.854	2.499	2.222	2.000
24	21.243	18.914	15.247	12.550	10.529	8.985	7.784	6.835	6.434	6.073	5.451	4.937	4.507	4.143	3.981	3.831	3.562	3.327	2.855	2.499	2.222	2.000
25	22.023	19.523	15.622	12.783	10.675	9.077	7.843	6.873	6.464	6.097	5.467	4.948	4.514	4.147	3.985	3.834	3.564	3.329	2.856	2.499	2.222	2.000
26	22.795	20.121	15.983	13.003	10.810	9.161	7.896	6.906	6.491	6.118	5.480	4.956	4.520	4.151	3.988	3.837	3.566	3.330	2.856	2.500	2.222	2.000
27	23.560	20.707	16.330	13.211	10.935	9.237	7.943	6.935	6.514	6.136	5.492	4.964	4.524	4.154	3.990	3.839	3.567	3.331	2.856	2.500	2.222	2.000
28	24.316	21.281	16.663	13.406	11.051	9.307	7.984	6.961	6.534	6.152	5.502	4.970	4.528	4.157	3.992	3.840	3.568	3.331	2.857	2.500	2.222	2.000
29	25.066	21.844	16.984	13.591	11.158	9.370	8.022	6.983	6.551	6.166	5.510	4.975	4.531	4.159	3.994	3.841	3.569	3.332	2.857	2.500	2.222	2.000
30	25.808	22.396	17.292	13.765	11.258	9.427	8.055	7.003	6.566	6.177	5.517	4.979	4.534	4.160	3.995	3.842	3.569	3.332	2.857	2.500	2.222	2.000
40	32.835	27.355	19.793	15.046	11.925	9.779	8.244	7.105	6.642	6.234	5.548	4.997	4.544	4.166	3.999	3.846	3.571	3.333	2.857	2.500	2.222	2.000
50	39.196	31.424	21.482	15.762	12.234	9.915	8.304	7.133	6.661	6.246	5.554	4.999	4.545	4.167	4.000	3.846	3.571	3.333	2.857	2.500	2.222	2.000

SOURCE: Same as Table A.

Index